# Understanding Canadian Public Administration

## An Introduction to Theory and Practice

### Fourth Edition

**Gregory J. Inwood**

Ryerson University

**Pearson Canada**
Toronto

# To Tish, Alison, and Matthew

**Library and Archives Canada Cataloguing in Publication**

Inwood, Gregory J.

    Understanding Canadian public administration: an introduction to theory and practice /
Gregory J. Inwood.—4th ed.

Includes bibliographical references.
ISBN 978-0-13-511997-6

    1. Public administration—Canada—Textbooks.   2. Canada—Politics and
government—Textbooks.  I. Title.

JL108.I58 2012          351.71         C2010-905920-4

ISBN 978-0-13-511997-6

Vice-President, Editorial Director: Gary Bennett
Editor-in-Chief: Ky Pruesse
Editor, Humanities and Social Sciences: Joel Gladstone
Executive Marketing Manager: Judith Allen
Supervising Developmental Editor: Madhu Ranadive
Developmental Editor: Rachel Stuckey
Project Manager: Richard di Santo
Production Editor: Rachel Stuckey
Copy Editor: Lisa LaFramboise
Proofreader: Julia Hubble
Compositor: MPS Limited, a Macmillan Company
Permissions Researcher: Christina Beamish
Art Director: Julia Hall
Interior Designer and Cover Designer: Anthony Leung
Cover Image: Veer Inc.

# Brief Contents

# Contents

# Preface

This fourth edition of *Understanding Canadian Public Administration: An Introduction to Theory and Practice* builds on the main purposes for which the original was conceived and executed. It addresses the need for an introductory text on the theory and practice of public administration in Canada. As with the first three editions, this edition provides an overview of the essential theoretical issues in the field and then uses that theoretical grounding to examine the actual practice of public administration. As an introduction, both in a historical context and in the contemporary context of rapid change, the goal of this work is to foster an understanding of the basic elements of public administration, leaving detailed analysis of specific sub-fields to more specialized sources. As such, this text is geared to undergraduate university and college students, as well as public servants, who require a clear and concise introduction to the topic. It is intended as the primary text for courses in public administration.

One of the striking features of public administration is that it is constantly in a state of flux. As this edition goes to press, sweeping reforms of the federal public service are ongoing. Legislation has been introduced over the past few years intended to modernize the public service, alter the relationship between the government and its unions, change the definition of merit, reform the process of hiring, firing, and managing federal public servants, adapt a new code of conduct and rules for ethical behaviour, introduce a new accountability framework for senior public servants, and make numerous other changes. What, if anything, will come of these reforms remains to be seen—there have been approximately 37 inquiries into the state of the public service in the past 40 years, after all. However, the fact that many of these reforms are being mandated in law will make a difference which students of public administration will be able to observe.

*Understanding Canadian Public Administration* begins with an introduction to the basic elements of public administration and explains the field in the context of democratic government. It also focuses on the impact of recent developments such as restructuring. In particular, it compares the roles of the private and public sectors and examines the impact that the latter has had on the former. The text examines theories of public administration, grouping them broadly into three categories: classic, structuralist, and humanist. It critically analyzes the impact of each category on public administration in Canada and concludes with an assessment of how recent theoretical innovations, such as the New Public Management, have reshaped our thinking.

The real world of government organizations is examined, allowing students to see how theoretical ideas are translated into practice in the Canadian government. Here, the student learns about the executive, legislative, and judicial branches of government, as well as the nature of bureaucratic organizations. The relationship between democracy and bureaucracy is a recurring theme, illustrated with real-life examples.

This introductory material sets the stage for an analysis of how public policy is actually set within the context of a federal state. Policy outcomes and processes are also considered in the context of the roles of key government players: the executive, legislative, and judicial branches of government, the bureaucracy, and the central agencies. Outside government, other actors are examined, such as political parties, interest groups and social movements, and the media. The text explains problem definition, agenda setting, formulation, implementation, and evaluation of public policy and examines the issue of choosing governing instruments. Specific key issues such as financial and personnel management are also considered.

*Understanding Canadian Public Administration* addresses the outstanding need and demand for an easily accessible introductory text in the field that is neither encyclopedic nor esoteric. It is meant to be a simple (though not simplistic) explanation of the basics of Canadian public administration. The narrative is in an interrogative style that can be easily understood by undergraduate students. In addition, the text provides real-life examples that are relevant to students' experiences and incorporates these examples into the analysis of public administration. In this way, the topic is brought to life and made immediately relevant. The text invites students to examine the issues of public administration from their own viewpoints, through their own experiences, by posing questions about day-to-day issues that they may not have realized relate to the way public administration affects them.

A variety of pedagogical features in *Understanding Canadian Public Administration* enhances the student's learning experience. These include sections, found at the beginning and end of each chapter, entitled *What You Will Learn* and *What You Have Learned*, which clarify learning objectives through brief introductory and concluding passages. There are lists of *Key Words and Concepts* (boldfaced within the text and defined in the glossary at the end of the text), and suggested lists for *Further Reading* and useful *Weblinks*. Each chapter also contains summary questions with which the instructor can test the students' understanding of the material or generate essay questions; students can use these questions to self-test their comprehension of the material. Sidebars complement the main text; these short asides illuminate issues with supplementary information that might otherwise interrupt the flow of the narrative. Occasional editorial cartoons highlight points in a humorous, but effective, manner.

This fourth edition features many updates on topical issues and new developments in the field of public administration. While retaining the intention of providing a solid grounding in the basics, this edition addresses issues and themes which have emerged since the first edition was published. In particular, the two chapters on public policy in previous editions have been consolidated into a single chapter. Sections have been added and/or updated on Aboriginal self-government, human resources, accountability, financial management, and other areas. Throughout the text, updated data, statistical information, and policy issues have been introduced as well.

*Understanding Canadian Public Administration* is divided into 11 chapters. Chapter 1 provides an overview of some central issues of public administration. It defines the field, examines what bureaucracy means, and compares the public sector with the private sector. As well, it introduces the central concept of the role of the state.

Chapter 2 explores the link between public administration and democracy by illuminating the meaning of concepts such as responsible and representative government.

Chapter 3 deals with organization theory and is divided into three broad sections. The first critically examines classic theories and theorists; the second assesses structuralist theories and theorists; and the third assesses humanist theories and theorists. In this chapter, students are introduced to Weber, Marx, Taylor, and many other key actors in the development of public administration as both theory and practice.

Chapter 4 applies organization theory to the Canadian experience. It explores the impact of various approaches to public administration on Canadian thinking and practice, and examines the most recent trends and developments affecting the organization of the Canadian government, including emerging post–New Public Management issues.

Chapter 5 turns to the "real world" of public administration by examining the actual organizations and machinery of governing in Canada. It does so within a framework of factors that influence the organizational structure of government.

Chapter 6 discusses the relationship between public administration and law—both constitutional and administrative.

In Chapter 7, the wide-ranging issue of public policy is explored. The term is defined and placed within the context of the policy cycle, which involves problem definition, agenda setting, formulation, implementation, and evaluation of public policy. Various theoretical perspectives on public policy decision making are also surveyed.

Public administration is nothing without the people who make up the public service, and so Chapter 8 has been reworked to focus more sharply on the key elements that shape the world of those who work in government administration. Merit and patronage, equity and collective bargaining, and recruitment and retention are all considered. So, too, are the many issues surrounding the recent restructuring of the public service.

This leads us to consider the role of management in public administration, which is the topic of Chapter 9. Specifically, management reform and management of financial resources are explored in the context of current reforms of the public service.

The ethical dilemmas confronting public administrators are many and are of a different nature than those facing private-sector administrators. Chapter 10 explains why this is so and explores various public administration issues related to ethics and morality.

Chapter 11 focuses on accountability, a fundamental issue of public administration given increasing prominence in the wake of various government and private-sector scandals. Chapter 11 assesses the ways in which accountability is maintained in the public sector by looking at issues such as ministerial and Cabinet responsibility. It also explores the structures of accountability while revealing the inherent tensions among democracy, bureaucracy, efficiency, and other important values within public administration.

No text on a topic as broad as public administration is going to cover every possible issue and development in the depth each deserves. No attempt has been made to do so in *Understanding Canadian Public Administration*; rather, an overview is provided, recognizing that the literature is both rich and deep, and that students with particular interests not explicitly covered here can pursue them through the Endnotes, Further Readings or Weblinks listed herein. As well, it should be admitted that the focus is unabashedly federal, which is not to suggest that provincial and municipal public administration are not worthy of attention. Certainly they are, but space and time are cruel masters for those writing about so complex a matter as the public administration of this country, necessitating a sharper focus than we might otherwise prefer.

## mysearchlab

**MySearchLab** offers extensive help to students with their writing and research projects and provides round-the-clock access to credible and reliable source material.

### Research

Content on MySearchLab includes immediate access to thousands of full-text articles from leading Canadian and international academic journals, and daily news feeds from The Associated Press. Articles contain the full downloadable text—including abstract and citation information—and can be cut, pasted, emailed, or saved for later use.

### Writing

MySearchLab also includes a step-by-step tutorial on writing a research paper. Included are sections on planning a research assignment, finding a topic, creating effective notes, and finding source material. Our exclusive online handbook provides grammar and usage support. Pearson SourceCheck™ offers an easy way to detect accidental plagiarism issues, and our exclusive tutorials teach how to avoid them in the future. And MySearchLab also contains AutoCite, which helps to correctly cite sources using MLA, APA, CMS, and CBE documentation styles for both endnotes and bibliographies.

To order this book with MySearchLab access at no extra charge, use ISBN 978-0-13-257212-5.

Take a tour at www.mysearchlab.com.

## CourseSmart for Instructors

CourseSmart goes beyond traditional expectations–providing instant, online access to the textbooks and course materials you need at a lower cost for students.

And even as students save money, you can save time and hassle with a digital eTextbook that allows you to search for the most relevant content at the very moment you need it. Whether it's evaluating textbooks or creating lecture notes to help students with difficult concepts, CourseSmart can make life a little easier. See how when you visit www.coursesmart.com/instructors.

## CourseSmart for Students

CourseSmart goes beyond traditional expectations–providing instant, online access to the textbooks and course materials you need at an average savings of 50%. With instant access from any computer and the ability to search your text, you'll find the content you need quickly, no matter where you are. And with online tools like highlighting and note-taking, you can save time and study efficiently. See all the benefits at www.coursesmart.com/students.

# Acknowledgments

It is extremely gratifying to be asked to produce a fourth edition of this book. Doing so simply reminds me that a text such as *Understanding Canadian Public Administration* is the product of the distillation of years of reading and thinking inspired by countless intellectual contributions from others too numerous to list. As such, my debts are many but must mainly go unnamed. Still, happily, there are those whose direct contribution to this text I can acknowledge. The reviews and comments supplied by Darryl Eisan (Dalhousie University), Ross Gibbons (University of Western Ontario), Thomas Klassen (York University), Donald J. Naulls (Saint Mary's University), and Shaun P. Young (York University) were helpful in the genesis of the text for this edition. My own public administration students at Ryerson University—many of them practising civil servants—have provided invaluable feedback as I field-tested my ideas on them. Many of my colleagues in the Department of Politics and Public Administration have provided unstinting support and encouragement for which I am very grateful. The team at Pearson Education Canada has been extraordinarily patient with me and understanding of the pressures on my time. I particularly want to thank Joel Gladstone and Rachel Stuckey.

All of the above made important contributions to the writing of this book. Of course, responsibility for whatever errors and defects which appear in the text is mine alone.

*Gregory J. Inwood*

*Department of Politics and Public Administration,*
*Ryerson University*

# Chapter ❶

# Introduction:
# *The* Nature *of* Public
# Administration

## WHAT YOU WILL LEARN

Your study of public administration will require you to canvass many issues from a variety of perspectives. You will find that the field's theory and practice range across a surprisingly broad spectrum. This first chapter introduces the topic by addressing some basic issues related to the nature of public administration in Canada. By the end of the chapter, you will be able to answer the following questions:

■ How has the field of public administration been defined?

■ What is the relationship between public administration and democratic government?

■ What are some of the common assumptions about bureaucratic organizations, and how do these assumptions influence the way we view public sector organization and management in Canada?

■ What are the major differences and similarities between public and private sector administration?

■ How can the growth and ongoing restructuring of the bureaucratic state be explained, and what are the implications for democracy?

In order to answer these questions, this chapter highlights five central issues:

## 1. *What Is Public Administration?*

This introductory section addresses the following questions: How do we define public administration? What key terms and concepts are used in its study and practice? You will become familiar with the basic language used in this area in order to lay the foundation for an understanding of later material.

### 2. ⌐ Public Administration and Democratic Government

The second section concerns the tensions between democratic representation and bureaucracy. You will consider the following questions: If elected politicians, acting as representatives of the people, are responsible for government policy, how do nonelected public servants influence policy? Is the will of the people realized through the institutions of public administration?

### 3. ⌐ Bureaucracy

This section focuses on the nature of bureaucracy by examining its parts: personnel, formal rules, policy instruments, conventions of behaviour, and institutions. Consider what happens when values like democracy and efficiency clash within the organizational structure of bureaucracy.

### 4. ⌐ Comparing Public and Private Sectors

This section compares the public and private sectors. You will note important differences: What are the mandates and goals of the public sector compared to the private sector? How do efficiency and service differ in each? What roles do professionalism and ethics play in one sector compared to the other?

### 5. ⌐ Restructuring the Public Sector and the Role of the State

The fifth section looks at the extent, significance, and consequences of government restructuring. This section asks the following: Why is organizational change taking place? What forms does it take? How has organizational change redefined the nature and scope of public administration?

These sections are followed by a comparison of Canadian and international perspectives on the top 10 issues vital to the study and practice of public administration.

## What Is Public Administration?

You have embarked on the study (and perhaps career) of **public administration**. When you excitedly told your family and friends, though, you were probably greeted with polite but quizzical looks. They may not have said it aloud, but many were probably thinking to themselves, "What the heck is that?" Perhaps you yourself are unsure of what direction your studies will take you. This is not unusual:

*To the practitioner seeking a bit of advice or the student trying to understand the operation of government, a journey into the literature of public administration can be a bewildering experience. The collective wisdom of public administration emerges from at least six separate fields and disciplines; bits of knowledge sought by one set of experts may be hidden behind another's disciplinary boundary; principles drawn from one field have a tendency to contradict lessons drawn from additional sources; no unifying theory exists to help guide the investigator. Experts frequently cannot agree on a definition of public administration. Some*

*view the subject broadly so as to include the entire process of running a modern govern-
ment, while others view it as narrowly confined to the administrative policies that
governments formulate, such as laws regulating the hiring and firing of personnel. The
field comes from so many places—and leads to so many subjects—that even people who
make a profession out of studying the subject have trouble keeping up with it all.*[1]

However, the depth and breadth of the field, though intimidating, are precisely
the features that make it such an interesting study as well as a challenging career.

While the systematic and organized academic study of public administration is
relatively young (dating from around 1900), the practice of public administration
is ancient. One account that discusses administrative practices throughout
recorded history shows that in ancient China and Egypt, there were incredible feats
of organization (the construction of the pyramids, for example) as well as massive
public bureaucracies, red tape, and corruption of the sort we often associate
with contemporary bureaucracy.[2] Many characteristics of present-day public
bureaucracy existed during the period of the Roman Empire. The Roman Catholic
Church kept many of the Roman administrative practices alive during the Dark
Ages, and the rise of the Enlightenment in seventeenth-century Western Europe, as
well as the emergence of the modern nation-state in Germany shortly thereafter,
contained the seeds of modern public administration. By the 1800s the characteristics of contemporary systems of bureaucracy were emerging in Europe, Great
Britain, the United States, and Canada. But what exactly is public administration?

Rather than get bogged down in a definitional quagmire, we will dispense with
the traditional list of definitions.[3] We will view public administration from two perspectives: it is a field of academic study derived from several disciplines, including
political science, business administration, sociology, psychology, law, and economics; and it is also a set of administrative practices and institutional arrangements
geared toward providing public services and regulations through the public
bureaucracy. Knowledge derived from the academic side of public administration
supports the practices of the field, while the practices continuously feed academic
study, requiring a constant reviewing and updating of findings in light of the
increasingly professionalized real world of government.[4]

Study and practice, then, are mutually reinforcing. Education for public administration careers can be eclectic, based as it is on several different disciplines. Professor of public administration Dwight Waldo draws an analogy between the study of
public administration and that of medicine: aspiring doctors must draw on a variety
of sciences to prepare for their careers;[5] similarly, practitioners of public administration educate themselves by drawing on a range of academic literatures.

Writings on public administration go back thousands of years. But the first
modern statement referring to public administration as a distinct professional field
came in an essay written in 1887 by Woodrow Wilson, later president of the United
States (see Box 1.1). Wilson argued that political scientists had ignored the fundamental question of how governments are administered. He advocated focusing on
personnel, organization, and management of the public sector in the interest of
greater efficiency and economy. These concerns animate the field to this day. Over-
laying these concerns are others about the democratic nature of governing.

---

**BOX 1.1 | Woodrow Wilson on "The Study of Administration"**

Woodrow Wilson (1856–1924) made an important contribution to the understanding of public administration in an essay he wrote in 1887 for the journal *Political Science Quarterly*. Wilson later became president of the United States, but at the time he was an instructor at a college for women. He wrote, "It is the object of administrative study to discover, first, what government can properly and successfully do, and secondly, how it can do these proper things with the utmost possible efficiency and at the least possible cost either of money or of energy." Wilson also said that an important distinction needed to be made between "politics" and "administration." This observation served as the underpinning for the important theory of the politics–administration dichotomy, discussed in Box 1.2 (p. 6).

**Source:** Woodrow Wilson, "The Study of Administration," in Jay M. Shafritz and Albert C. Hyde, eds., *Classics of Public Administration*, 3rd ed. (Pacific Grove, CA: Brooks Cole, 1992): 11–24.

---

While the Canadian political system is directly derived from the British model, the American influence on Canadian public administration is indisputable.[6] Indeed, although a 1914 study entitled *Canada and Its Provinces* addressed some aspects of public administration and bureaucracy in Canada, the first study looking at a particular problem in Canadian public administration was actually written in 1918 by two Americans![7] American writers were originally concerned with corruption and the party "bosses" who ruled local politics with iron fists. Thus, administrative reform became an early concern, as did the management of personnel and budgets, and finding the "one best way" of administratively organizing the workplace through the systematic adoption and application of scientific theory and rationalism.[8] As we will see later, assumptions made in these approaches came under attack by the middle part of the century, fuelling debates about the theory and practice of public administration that continue today.

These issues spilled over the border into Canada (as well as elsewhere in the world);[9] public administration was long regarded as the poor cousin to political science, with its teachers and students buried in the recesses of political science departments. For generations, R. MacGregor Dawson's book *The Government of Canada* (1947) served as the main (and only) text for students studying Canadian political science. Dawson also published the first two Canadian books on public administration: *The Principle of Official Independence* (1922) and *The Civil Service of Canada* (1929).[10] Universities began to offer degrees in public administration, starting with Dalhousie University in 1936 and Carleton College (now Carleton University) in 1946.[11] In 1957 the Institute of Public Administration of Canada (IPAC) was formed, and a year later the journal *Canadian Public Administration* was launched to disseminate the views and experiences of both practitioners and scholars. Then, in 1987, the Canadian Association of Programs in Public Administration (CAPPA) was launched. Debates about the purpose of the association, the institute, the journal, and indeed the field of Canadian public administration revealed a belief that educational training in public administration should not simply be restricted to learning the administrative techniques necessary to run a government department. Rather, the study of public administration should be tied to the broader social sciences to produce a well-rounded approach rooted in a wider conception of the management of the state.[12]

From the 1960s onward, efforts increased to position public administration as a more distinct field of study. Rapid growth in the size of the public service fuelled the need for highly trained professionals versed in the art of public administration. Today, there are several colleges and over 20 universities in Canada with programs in public administration. As you work your way through your undergraduate degree, you might keep in mind that an increasing number of universities—now over 20—also offer master's degrees in public administration.[13] These programs offer opportunities through political science or administrative studies faculties or through specialized schools of public administration. In addition, Carleton University and l'École Nationale d'Administration Publique offer doctorate programs in public administration, while Ryerson University offers a Public Policy and Administration field in its interdisciplinary PhD in Policy Studies.

There is no single model for the location of public administration programs within universities. About an equal number of programs are located in faculties of social science or in faculties of administrative and business studies (44 percent each). Only about 8 percent are located in separate schools of public administration and management, with the remainder scattered in a variety of other places.[14] This orphan-like characteristic of the discipline reflects its hybrid nature as the product of a variety of academic influences. A report on graduate studies in Canadian public administration concluded there is a "considerable degree of variety in our master's programs because of differing objectives, institutional emphasis, and opportunities for specialization or combined degrees."[15]

While in the 1990s, government downsizing and layoffs led to doubts about the viability of public administration as a career and a course of study,[16] recent trends indicate quite the opposite. Governments are hiring as aging baby boomers retire from the public service and the value of a strong, professional public service is recognized. Schools of public administration are experiencing increased interest. For example, the universities of Toronto, Ottawa, Ryerson, and York have all launched new degree programs in public administration and policy in the past few years in anticipation of a hiring boom in the public service.[17] Another sign of the discipline's health is the rapidly growing literature on Canadian public administration. This all bodes well for you, the student of public administration.

## Public Administration and Democratic Government

Since public administration is about the public provision of services and regulations, it is necessary to consider politics. Politics is about who gets what, when, and how; or how the state responds to the public's demands and wants. This response will be different from how the private sector marketplace answers this question through the law of supply and demand. State action involves myriad complex decisions and actions by various actors and institutions in what we call the public sector.

We will explore these issues in more detail in chapter 2, "Public Administration and Democracy." For now, we will consider that a handy but somewhat artificial division of labour exists in the practice of public administration between those who make the decisions and those who carry out the decision-makers' wishes. In a **democratic society** such as Canada, these roles fall into the hands of **elected representatives** (the decision-makers) and public servants or bureaucrats (who carry out the decision-makers' wishes). This neat little division of labour is referred to as the **politics–administration dichotomy** (see Box 1.2). In this sense, then, public administration is the process of public servants carrying out politicians' public decisions. There is a division or dichotomy between politics and administration.[18]

---

### BOX 1.2 | The Politics–Administration Dichotomy

The politics–administration dichotomy reflects the notion that "politics" is about deciding what government should do, while "administration" is about how to do it; thus, there should be clearly defined responsibilities that differentiate the roles of politicians and public servants. The concept manifests itself in the desire to find the "one best way" of administering public affairs and reflects the desire to achieve the ultimate in efficiency in the provision of public services and in the business of government by putting public administration on the most rational basis possible. This means, for example, hiring and promoting the best possible candidate for a job (the **merit principle**) rather than a minister's political supporter (patronage). Public servants' political neutrality is vital to the realization of the politics–administration dichotomy. Public servants should serve the government of the day, not the political party that happens to hold power.

---

In reality, of course, the politics–administration dichotomy is less straightforward than the theory implies. Not only do public servants respond to orders from politicians, but they also sometimes initiate action on their own. In other words, the traditional role of public servants, which is to implement policy on the instructions of their political bosses, is accompanied by the role they play in policy formulation. This is because public servants enjoy a fair amount of discretionary power. After all, no elected official who is given the job of heading up a large and complex government department or ministry can know absolutely everything that goes on within it. In aiding the elected representatives, public servants engage in policy formulation as well as implementation.

During the 1960s and 1970s, some theorists and practitioners suggested that public servants ought to have a more hands-on role in formulating and implementing policy. In the 1980s, 1990s, and early 2000s, however, the view emerged that the bureaucracy had usurped too much power, and many governments enacted reforms to restore the proper relationship between the two sets of actors. These views represent some of the many attempts to sort out the proper balance between the power of public servants and elected representatives in a democratic society.

# Bureaucracy

The public provision of services and regulations, and the state's answer to the political question of who gets what, when, and how, take place within a structure known generically as a **bureaucracy**. We have all encountered bureaucracy. When you renew your driver's licence, file your income tax, register in a program at a community centre, go to court, or apply for a passport or a parking permit, you are involved in a relationship with a bureaucracy whose job it is to satisfy your needs and wants as a *citizen*. Of course, bureaucracy is also the organizational form for the private sector. Think of dealing with a bank, cable company, or department store, for instance, as a *customer*.

The term *bureaucracy* comes from a combination of the French word *bureau*, which means "desk," and a Greek word meaning "rule." Given the remarkable accomplishments that have emerged from bureaucratic organizations in both the public and private sector through the ages, it is striking that the term carries such pejorative connotations. It is often negatively associated with red tape, inefficiency, rigid lines of control, corruption, petty officiousness, delay, and so on. But this is nothing new. Honoré de Balzac (1799–1850) said that "bureaucracy is a giant mechanism operated by pygmies." Czar Nicholas I (1796–1855) claimed that "I do not rule Russia: Ten thousand clerks do." Winston Churchill (1874–1965) once complained that "some civil servants are neither servants nor civil."

Bureaucracies are made up of a mixture of elements: personnel, formal rules, policy instruments, conventions of behaviour, and institutions, all of which importantly affect the provision of services for citizens in any political system. But in a democracy there are particular issues in terms of these components and how citizens hold governments accountable. In the following paragraphs each of these components of bureaucracy is considered in relation to democracy.

## Personnel

When you seek a government service you may meet a public servant face to face, but behind that person stands a veritable army of people, usually arranged in a hierarchical relationship characterized by a division of labour. The public service in Canada employs hundreds of thousands of people at all three levels of government (federal, provincial, and municipal). From firefighters to diplomats, from judges to environmental scientists, from presidents of Crown corporations to street sweepers—all serve in bureaucracies dedicated to providing services, enforcing regulations, and formulating, implementing, and evaluating policies for citizens. None of these people are elected, yet together they wield a tremendous amount of influence. This raises the issue of whom they are accountable to and how that accountability is realized. This is discussed next and in chapter 11.

## Formal Rules

Bureaucracy is notorious for its "red tape," but there must be clear rules to ensure that all services are provided equally to all citizens, and that all regulations are fairly enforced. This is due to the special requirement of **accountability** in public bureaucracies. After all, the money spent to support the services and regulations being provided is *your* money—i.e., taxpayers' money—and so must be accounted for. However, this buildup of formal rules sometimes comes at the expense of efficiency, which may conflict with the values of democracy (through accountability). This is an important ongoing public administration conundrum.

## Policy Instruments

Services are provided and regulations enforced by means of policy instruments. The government has at its disposal a vast array of tools to ensure that citizen needs and wants are satisfied.[19] These range from instruments that rely on voluntary compliance on the part of citizens all the way to tools that use coercion or even violence. Laws, regulations, Crown corporations, expenditures, and taxes are but a few examples of different types of policy or governing instruments (see chapter 7).

## Conventions of Behaviour

Bureaucracies often develop their own internal logic and way of doing things, emphasizing formal rules, hierarchies of power, and divisions of labour. In a perfect world, there would always be "one right way" of doing something. Bureaucracies often behave as though they live in such a world, when they develop conventions of behaviour about how to fulfill their mandates based on the "one right way." Bureaucracies must not appear to be arbitrary and unfair, but must treat each citizen equally. This is why elaborate conventions of behaviour exist in each particular administrative culture. Theorist B. Guy Peters points out that this administrative culture exists alongside the political culture and societal culture of a society. Together, these contribute to public administration, as Figure 1.1 shows.

## Institutions

This term refers to the complex of government ministries and departments, regulatory bodies, Crown corporations, special operating agencies, and other institutions responsible for translating the will of the people into action (see chapter 5). The democratization of modern society has resulted in ever more elaborate structures to ensure that all interests in society are accommodated within the institutions of the state. Ironically, as bureaucracy has increased in size, the level of responsiveness has sometimes declined due to the growth of red tape and bureaucratic procedure.

All five of these components of bureaucracy profoundly affect the type and quality of public administration we get. In a democratic society, we expect that each component will contribute to administration that is fair and equitable in its treatment of citizens. But in fulfilling this mandate, bureaucracies often appear to lack efficiency. Thus, there often is a real tension between the value of democracy and efficient provision of service.

To illustrate how this tension can play out, imagine a government focused solely on efficiency. Such a government might, for instance, cut back on the number of politicians and on personnel within the public service, reduce and eliminate

**FIGURE 1.1    Culture and Public Administration**

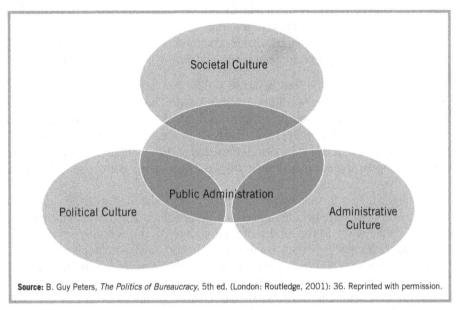

Societal Culture

Public Administration

Political Culture

Administrative Culture

**Source:** B. Guy Peters, *The Politics of Bureaucracy*, 5th ed. (London: Routledge, 2001): 36. Reprinted with permission.

regulations and red tape, streamline the delivery of services, or, in some cases, turn them over to the private sector and re-engineer the institutions of government to make them leaner. But democratic accountability could be trampled in the rush to create a more efficient public administration. Reducing the number of politicians may save money, but citizens will get less representation. Fewer elected officials also means centralizing power in the hands of the leader and cabinet, which may reduce the democratic quality of debate and discussion within government. Reduction of personnel, privatization, and deregulation all diminish the quality of democratic life, leaving ordinary citizens with fewer avenues through which to force the government to explain itself. This can also allow the private sector too much scope for action injurious to citizens, as happened with the global economic crisis in 2008–2009, or the disastrous oil spill in the Gulf of Mexico in 2010.

This debate about efficiency versus democracy is neither new nor particular to Canada. It is part of the larger ongoing debate in democracies about the values appropriate to the administration of the public will. An important part of that debate is the issue of what the role of government (that is, **the public sector**) ought to be. Are there some things the marketplace (that is, **the private sector**) can better attend to? These questions are considered in the next section.

## Comparing Public and Private Sectors

The question of the differences between public and private sectors goes back a long way in both the study and practice of the field:

*Since Woodrow Wilson wrote his classic essay exhorting reformers to help make the business of government "less unbusinesslike," the field of public administration has been seeking to differentiate itself from business administration. But comparisons between business and government are inevitable. In fact, they are important to understanding how management ideas from the private sector have been imposed on public administration and how this process affects what is actually done in public organizations. A key question is, how appropriate are these ideas, and how well has the transfer worked?[20]*

Since the 1990s, the line between public and private administration has become increasingly blurred. Public administration has been placed on a more businesslike footing and uses more business techniques, theories, and methods to run government. Furthermore, contracting out to the private sector has increased, and more and more services are being privatized outright. Public sector and private sector managers interact more frequently, and their career paths often cross over between the two sectors.

Today's students are sometimes surprised to learn that in Canada, the career of public servant was once held in high esteem as a noble calling in which individuals dedicated themselves to the service of their country.[21] This attitude changed. Private sector managers were seen as inherently superior and more intelligent, industrious, and efficient than their public sector counterparts, who were disdained as incompetent, lazy, and wasteful. This view is simplistic, patently unfair, and inaccurate. In any event, attitudes do seem to be changing again (see Box 1.3). Still, you may have heard the following popular refrain: "If only they would run the government like a business, then things would get done!" In fact, at least superficially, business and public administration are alike in that they perform many of the same basic functions. Both engage in the management of complex organizations of people through planning, organizing, staffing, and budgeting.

---

**BOX 1.3 | Bureaucrat Is Not a Dirty Word; Bureaucratic Ethics May Slowly Erode In the Face of Unrelenting Contempt**

*By Matt Young*

**"I** *want to be a bureaucrat."*

*When was the last time you heard someone say those words? Not too recently, I bet. Do you wonder why not? Let me tell you, because somehow, the proper name of this profession has been transformed into a dirty word, a barb to be slung about, a euphemism for waste, inefficiency, sloth, rote action, obstructionism and, perhaps worst of all, the complete absence of any sartorial acumen. Now do you see why so few people proclaim their bureaucratic aspirations?*

*On the cusp of graduating with a professional degree specializing in the bureaucratic arts and sciences, I have yet to enroll in Obfuscation 101, study Introduction to Time Mismanagement, or attend lectures on Advanced Fiscal Ineptitude. No, my classmates and I are eager, experienced, highly skilled, and committed to making a difference. Daily, we debate issues of public importance. We promptly complete our projects and assignments, and I'm quite certain I've even witnessed a number of innovative thoughts and approaches during my schooling.*

*When we talk of bureaucracy, we use a different vocabulary altogether. We discuss ideals such as the rule of law, justice, fairness, effectiveness, and service to the public interest above all else. We identify collective problems and strive to craft solutions for them. We assess models of public accountability. We measure the use of common resources to evaluate efficiency. We confront the reconciling of competing social demands. And we do all of this with gusto. . . .*

*We are the bureaucrats of tomorrow. We aspire not to profit nor to be recognized, but to make our communities, however large or small, better than before our arrival. And we're committed to doing that while upholding the rule of law, stewarding public resources, and treating everyone equally and with fairness. That's the credo of the bureaucrats I know.*

*So, what does it matter if we poke a little fun at government officials, if we disparage them for a laugh? It matters because it under-* *mines the sense of public duty, the ethic of public service that drives each of us into this profession. It belittles our commitment to an ideal and mocks our faith in our professional values. If this banter corrodes the bureaucratic ethos to the point that civil servants only half-heartedly engage in their responsibilities, we all suffer. The true cost will be measured by the degradation of our international development, law enforcement, environmental protection, health, and social service programs.*

*Nonetheless, I'm pleased to report that government institutions will be shortly infused with another eager cohort, a cohort that sees beyond the derision to the highest aspirations of our profession: integrity, commitment to the public interest, public service, and some of the best public programs in the world. This is our pledge, and your assurance, of the kind of Canada we want into the next generation.*

**Source:** Matt Young, "Bureaucrat Is Not a Dirty Word," *Globe and Mail* (May 3, 2005): A20. Copyright © Matt Young. Reprinted with permission.

However, there are underlying differences between business and government. As public administration theorist Wallace Sayre noted, "Business and public administration are alike only in all unimportant respects."[22] After all, we refer to the "business of business" but to the "art of government." We can distinguish between private and public administration by examining the mandate and goals, efficiency and service, and professionalism and ethics of both.

## Mandate and Goals

It may be easiest to grasp these differences by referring to what public administration is not. It is not the same as administration dedicated to the pursuit of private profit. Public administration is geared toward the provision of public services, not the "bottom line." This has important implications for the way bureaucracies function in the private and public sectors.

According to political scientist Graham Allison, the first difference between the public and private sectors is temporal.[23] Government managers tend to work with relatively short time frames dictated by the electoral cycle. A related difference is duration of service. Top-level public sector managers usually serve for a relatively short time before moving to another position, while, on average, private sector managers hold tenure for longer periods of time.

Third, goal measurement distinguishes the public from the private sector. The public sector manager often faces multiple or contradictory ends sought by governments. For example, the Ministry of Finance may want to reduce government spending, while another department may want to reduce child poverty, a goal that requires more money. Moreover, certain intangible goals unique to government are impossible to measure—for instance, whether an increased "quality of life" has been achieved through the implementation of family service policies. This contrasts with the relatively straightforward measurement of goals in the private sector: profits, market share, financial performance, and so on. Indeed, some would argue that public sector managers actually have to be more creative and imaginative than their private sector counterparts.

A fourth difference between the public and private sectors relates to human resource management. It is a much more complicated process to hire or fire someone in the public service. Consider the merit principle, that all Canadian citizens should have a reasonable opportunity for employment and promotion in the public sector based exclusively on fitness to do the job.[24] The strict application of this principle means that a detailed, time-consuming, and thorough process must be initiated to ensure that every hiring and firing in the public service is done fairly and equitably. In addition, provisions such as bilingualism and employment equity may mean that extra effort must be put into recruiting and training employees. These steps guide (some would say constrain) the public sector manager through a maze of regulations intended to ensure that human resource management is scrupulously fair and equitable. Overlying the process is the requirement that the public sector be representative of the population it serves (that is, all of Canada). The private sector manager has few such requirements.

Fifth, equity and efficiency concerns are different in the public and private sectors. Public sector managers emphasize equity among various constituents. The private sector, however, is more oriented toward efficiency and competitiveness.

Sixth, the public sector continues to be open to scrutiny by the attentive public and the media in a way that private business is not. Looking over the shoulder of every senior public sector manager is a reporter. Watching the actions of every government member are the opposition parties. The public scrutinizes the actions of every front-line clerk. Service to the public is the raison d'être of the public service, but along with this mandate comes a level of attention that simply is not present in the private sector. While recent corporate scandals, like those involving Hollinger, Bear Sterns, Lehman Brothers, Enron, WorldCom, and Bre-X, have drawn increased attention to private sector malfeasance, most corporate executives operate in relative obscurity; but the limelight frequently shines on public sector managers and especially on political leaders. Success seems to be downplayed, while errors are often magnified by a media looking for that juicy lead story for the news—a point made more than 50 years ago by Paul Appleby, journalist turned administrator turned academic, who said administrators live in a goldfish bowl, where "each employee hired, each one demoted, transferred, or discharged, every efficiency rating, every assignment of responsibility, each change in administrative structure, each conversation, each letter, has to be thought about in terms of possible public agitation, investigation, or judgment."[25] Today, the rise of social media like Facebook, Twitter, YouTube, blogs, and the internet in general have intensified this exposure.[26]

A seventh difference between public and private administration with regard to mandate and goals is the provision of what are called public goods. These are goods provided for the benefit of all members of society, such as national defence or roads and bridges. Sometimes these services are inherently unprofitable, but they must be provided nonetheless. So the state assumes responsibility for doing so. In any event, the value of the provision of some goods is often intangible. How, for instance, does one measure the efficient production of national defence?

An eighth factor is accountability. According to the Office of the Auditor General, the watchdog agency that conducts audits and examinations of government programs and departments,

*Parliament, the government and the public service are the guardians of public funds entrusted to them for delivering programs and services to benefit Canadians. An important part of the confidence that people have in our democratic institutions is their belief that public funds are spent wisely and effectively. There must be, and there must be seen to be, value from money spent, compliance with authority, and environmental stewardship. In a significant way, then, confidence in our national government depends upon clear and timely accountability by the government for its performance.*[27]

The public sector faces standards of accountability that are simply absent in the private sector. The public sector's actions must be available to public scrutiny, there must be a "paper trail" documenting every step, and its services must be transparent and above-board. Lines of authority and responsibility are complex. Public sector managers are scrutinized as well by legislatures and the courts. Parliament keeps an eye on the public service through a growing number of watchdog agencies, such as the Office of the Auditor General and the Canadian Human Rights Commission. Moreover, a whole body of administrative law has built up that is overseen by the courts, adjudicating disputes between the public service and the public (see chapter 6). Such scrutiny, both legislative and judicial, tends to constrain public sector managers, whereas their private sector equivalents enjoy more freedom from this kind of unrelenting attention. The private sector simply does not labour under these types of standards.

Finally, in the private sector, efficient operation leads to enhanced profitability. There is a clear and sobering focus on the "bottom line," which is often absent in the public sector. Thus, private businesses will shy away from operations that are inefficient and from which a profit cannot be derived. The private sector, in effect, receives its mandate from the marketplace through the law of supply and demand. Where do public sector managers get their mandate? From their political bosses, who, theoretically, are seeking to express the broadly understood will of the people. That popular will must be turned into action through legislative or regulatory means—that is, by the passing of laws and regulations—which may or may not result in profitable activities by government.

## Efficiency and Service

Notwithstanding the differences noted above, efficiency has become a dominant value of our time and there has been an increasing trend to impose it on the public sector.[28] Indeed, the "three Es" of *efficiency*, *economy*, and *effectiveness* are prominent in the minds of many public sector managers; a major aspect of holding public servants accountable has been to measure whether they have provided efficient, economical, and effective service. In response, a series of old and new government institutions have evolved. The Treasury Board of Canada Secretariat, one of the government's central agencies (see chapter 5), helps ensure that the public service as a whole is run efficiently and effectively; it has introduced numerous innovations like performance measurement systems to ensure that "the managers are being managed properly." Other government institutions, such as the Office of the Comptroller General and the Office of the Auditor General, assist public sector managers to perform their jobs more efficiently, economically, and effectively.

How does one "measure" success in the three Es? How, for instance, does a public sector manager—given the job of implementing programs to enhance the "quality of life" of citizens—determine success? How can increased national security be measured? How can you determine that preventive policies have been effective? Even defining the service provided can be a challenge. If the Ministry of Health has a mandate to secure the mental health of citizens, what is "mental health," and how can you determine whether it has been efficiently, economically, and effectively increased? Along with the three Es, government has the responsibility of providing services to citizens equitably and fairly. For instance, subsidizing air or rail links to remote communities may not be economical but may be undertaken in the interests of fairness. Thus, the three Es alone cannot be the guiding principle of public administration, as they are in the private sector. The public sector lacks the same motivation for efficiency as in the private sector: compete efficiently or perish. Indeed, governments often make decisions that are patently inefficient in a strict economic sense. For instance, it may not be efficient to decentralize a program by setting up regional offices across the country; but it may make good political sense to do so, as the government appears responsive to regional needs. Many government services are monopolistic; that is, they have no competition. For example, there is only one police force, and it does not need to be conscious of the efficient provision of services in the same way that a private corporation does. This does not mean that it should not be as efficient as possible, but the standard of efficiency is different from that of the private sector because there is no competition. In cases in which government activities do generate a profit against which efficiency can be measured, some people argue that those activities should be turned over to the private sector.

There are, however, different incentives for governments to provide services efficiently. While they do not compete in the free market to make a profit, government departments do compete with one another for public funds. This can be tough during periods of reduced government revenues and expenditures, which cause government institutions to impose more efficiency on their internal operations, reducing staff, introducing performance measurement, rationalizing program delivery, contracting out, and operating programs on a cost-recovery basis.

Another incentive in the public realm is that politicians must seek re-election. To achieve this, they must run an efficient government so that voters do not withdraw their support. But in reality, the public pays little attention to the nuts and bolts of effective public sector management unless a scandal is uncovered. Thus, this incentive for efficient management by politicians is a relatively weak one.

## Professionalism and Ethics

When Sir John A. Macdonald and the Fathers of Confederation founded Canada in 1867, there was little need for a large, sophisticated professional public service.[29] The activities of government were extremely limited, and governing could be accomplished with a ratio of about 100 public servants per politician. Today there are several thousand public servants per politician, since government has become involved in so many more aspects of life than was common in Macdonald's day.

But there is more to the differences than simply numbers of public servants. Back then, many bureaucrats owed their positions to **patronage**—the practice of rewarding loyal supporters, friends, and relatives with government positions. Today, however, most jobs in the public service are based on merit.

A patronage-based public service is by definition amateurish and unprofessional. Office-holders are not hired for *what* they know, but rather *who* they know. The result is a lack of skills and ability compounded by a high turnover rate, since every time a new government is elected, the old government's supporters are replaced by the new government's supporters. Thus, the capability of developing a professional, well-trained, and dedicated public service is undermined, and service to the public is compromised, since the best person for a job is not always hired.

Calls for reform of the patronage-based system started almost as soon as the new Dominion was created. In 1911, a group of Ontario businessmen made a proposal to the leader of the opposition, Robert Borden. The group promised support for Borden's Conservative Party if he promised to initiate a merit system of appointment to the public service. "Since they also wanted a stronger role for the federal government in promoting Canadian trade around the world," according to political scientist Reginald Whitaker, "they obviously saw a merit-based administration as the prerequisite to a more effective government that could act in their interests."[30]

Borden did win the subsequent election, and reforms were implemented after the First World War when the Civil Service Act, 1918 was passed. The Act called for the Civil Service Commission (later the Public Service Commission) to oversee all appointments to the public service, rather than leave them in the hands of politicians. Competitive exams were initiated as the basis of appointments, political activity by public servants was prohibited, the public service was reorganized, and a new job classification system was introduced. Many of these steps reflect the principles of the politics–administration dichotomy. In addition, special provisions were included in the reforms to favour returning war veterans, setting a precedent as an early form of affirmative action.

Over the long term, these changes fostered professionalism within the public service. Further reforms followed that reinforced competency and ability, particularly with regard to ongoing training and education, and issues like affirmative action programs related to language, gender, ethnicity, and disability (see chapter 8). As new technological, economic, and social developments shaped modern Canada, the government responded by continuously reforming the operation and organization of the public service. From the 1918 reforms to the Royal Commission on Government Organization (the Glassco Commission) in the 1960s to the Public Service Employment Act of 1967 to the Public Service Modernization Act in 2003 and beyond, successive governments have engaged in a never-ending process of maintaining and building the professionalism of the public service.

Related to professionalism is the issue of ethics, which raises particular concerns in the context of government bureaucracies. Governments are entrusted with a special responsibility to act in the best interests of society as a whole. Thus, government personnel are held up to the highest standards of ethical behaviour. But governments are composed of individuals, and individuals are susceptible to temptation. As two theorists of Canadian public administration put it, "Nothing is more dangerous than a public servant who is technically fit but ethically flabby."[31] To prevent individuals from succumbing to temptation, elaborate systems of checks and balances are built into government bureaucracy.

Ethics involves the study, implementation, and enforcement of activities designed to promote "proper" behaviour and to punish "improper" behaviour. Various formal methods of promoting ethics within government have emerged that can be applied both to politicians and public servants. In general, the stipulation is that public office is not to be used for private gain. Of course, the concern not to overstep the bounds of ethical behaviour sometimes means that high-ranking public servants must take extraordinary steps. "It's no wonder that to be a senior public servant these days is to live constantly on your guard," according to a former deputy minister in the Ontario government. "If someone sends you flowers for any reason, you immediately give them away. You politely decline an offer of free baseball tickets, no matter who is giving them to you and regardless of the fact that the person offering them has nothing to do with your job."[32]

To enforce ethical behaviour, a complex set of rules has been built up over the years that often results in delays in developing or implementing a policy. However, these rules also ensure that taxpayers know that decisions are being made on the merits of a particular issue and not because of the material self-interest of particular government officials. Because public servants are guardians of the public interest, ethical codes and rules ensure that there is some way of guarding the guardians. A series of scandals in Ottawa in the 1990s and early 2000s intensified interest in the issue of ethics and values in government, resulting in numerous reforms and initiatives (see chapter 10).

Comparing the issues of mandate and goals, efficiency and service, and professionalism and ethics between the private and public sectors reveals important distinctions. The issues are complex, yet we often hear rather simplistic and dogmatic calls for government to somehow achieve businesslike standards. These calls ignore the profound differences between public and private administration.

# Restructuring the Public Sector and the Role of the State

Many recent reforms to the public service reflect the conflict between the values of efficiency and democracy. But to place these developments in context requires an understanding of the evolution of the public sector in the longer term. This evolution can, for convenience's sake, be divided into three eras: the **minimalist state**, from roughly 1867 to the 1930s; the **Keynesian welfare state**, from the 1930s to the late 1970s; and the **neoconservative state**, from the late 1970s to the present.

## The Minimalist State

Confederation in 1867 was accomplished by a state with minimal responsibilities. The prevailing ideology was a laissez-faire attitude that suggested the role of the state be limited to national defence and the provision of infrastructure (roads, canals, railways) to help facilitate the expansion of business. There was little or no role for government in the provision of welfare and social services, which were regarded as private matters to be attended to by family or by religious or charitable organizations. Even the state's role in education was relatively limited by today's standards. Consequently, the public service was small.

This is not to suggest that it was nonexistent, of course. The early Canadian state played an important role in building the national economy, for instance, through the three planks of Sir John A. Macdonald's 1878 National Policy: a system of tariffs to protect infant Canadian industries from foreign (i.e., American) competition; an aggressive immigration policy to settle the great western prairies, which supplied raw materials and markets for central Canadian industry; and a transcontinental railway to assist in the creation of a national economy. From early on the Canadian state established a presence in the nation's economic life. But apart from the economy, the provision of law and order, national defence, the post office, and a handful of other areas, the role of the state was minimal.

## The Keynesian Welfare State

The middle part of the twentieth century saw the emergence of a much more activist, interventionist state in areas beyond economic matters. The horrors of the Great Depression starkly revealed that laissez-faire capitalism could not function unregulated, as hundreds of thousands of Canadians were thrown out of work without means of support. The strain this placed on private charities, religious agencies, and families proved unbearable. Gradually and reluctantly, the state began providing welfare and other social services previously regarded as private responsibilities.

But how could a society that had preached self-reliance now justify allowing government to accept responsibility for private concerns? The theoretical underpinning for this new view was provided by the British economist John Maynard Keynes, who argued that in bad economic times the government could prime the pump of economic growth by investing and spending. Spending on infrastructure as well as on social programs was thus justified.

The result was the Keynesian welfare state. In Canada, it included a commitment to full employment and the construction of the social safety net (welfare, unemployment insurance, pensions, family allowance, Medicare), which began in the 1940s. The acceptance of Keynesianism implied that the government would provide more and more services, which in turn spurred growth in the public sector. A large, sophisticated, well-trained public service emerged first at the federal level, and later at the provincial and municipal levels. Because the provinces have constitutional responsibility for most social policy issues, overall provincial government growth eventually outstripped that of the federal government.

## The Neoconservative State

Recently, we entered an era that in many ways reflected the attitudes and ideologies that rationalized the original minimalist state. Globalization prompted questions about the apparent inability of the Keynesian welfare state to perform as theory predicted.[33] Growing deficits, both real and exaggerated, informed the ideological framework within which the expanded interventionist role of the state was questioned. A concerted attack on the state by business and right-wing think tanks and the corporate-controlled media successfully conveyed the image of Canada on the edge of a precipice and convinced many that we could only pull back from disaster if we curtailed the state. From the 1970s onward, many governments began preaching fiscal responsibility above all else. This emphasis on efficiency, economy, and effectiveness usually translated into cutbacks in the public sector, coupled with reduced government spending on social policies.

A period of retrenchment of the public sector resulted. Privatization, contracting out of services, deregulation, firing of public servants, re-engineering, restructuring, and devolution became commonplace. Services were transferred to the private sector and to the newly emergent "third sector"—i.e., non-profit and voluntary organizations. The role of the family, religious agencies, and private charities re-emerged to fill the void left by the retreating neoconservative state.[34]

We can measure and compare the three eras by looking at how the expenditures and revenues of Canadian governments have changed over time. One common method for doing so is to note the percentage of Canada's gross domestic product (GDP) accounted for by government. GDP represents the total value of all goods and services produced in the country (see Figure 1.2).

In the fall of 2008, a cataclysmic global financial downturn caused another rethinking of the role of the state. Governments around the world—including the neoconservative Stephen Harper Conservatives in Canada—found themselves returning to Keynesian-style government stimulus spending to pull their

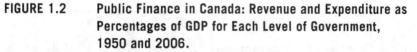

**FIGURE 1.2    Public Finance in Canada: Revenue and Expenditure as Percentages of GDP for Each Level of Government, 1950 and 2006.**

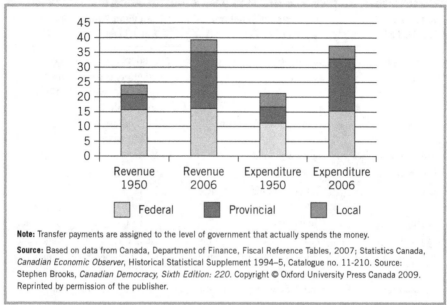

**Note:** Transfer payments are assigned to the level of government that actually spends the money.

**Source:** Based on data from Canada, Department of Finance, Fiscal Reference Tables, 2007; Statistics Canada, *Canadian Economic Observer*, Historical Statistical Supplement 1994–5, Catalogue no. 11-210. Source: Stephen Brooks, *Canadian Democracy, Sixth Edition: 220*. Copyright © Oxford University Press Canada 2009. Reprinted by permission of the publisher.

economies out of the most severe depression since the 1930s. Suddenly, the state was "in" again, having to come to the rescue of capitalism gone wild. One consequence was that government debt and deficits began to grow again, and new calls for cutting back the public service are being heard. How this new reality will play out will be determined over the next few years. In the meantime, the public sector has to once again recalibrate itself to deal with new, yet familiar, challenges.

As we proceed, ask yourself why the state was originally small in scope and what factors contributed to its growth. Can you think of an area of your own life in which the state does not have a role? These kinds of questions are central to public administration because they touch on the issue of what size, shape, and form the government ought to take. We will examine these questions in more detail in chapter 5, when we look at factors affecting the organization of government.

## WHAT YOU HAVE LEARNED

Several more issues surrounding public administration are addressed in the next chapters in this book. For now, to summarize what we have studied so far and signal what is to come, consider the differing perspectives on what constitutes the "top 10" concerns of public administration (see Box 1.4). Political scientist David Johnson's list and two other top-10 lists highlight some of the most important but very broad issues surrounding the practice and theory of public administration.

| BOX 1.4 | Top 10 Concerns of Canadian and International Public Administration |

| Johnson's Top 10 List | International Scholar's Top 10 List | Canadian Public Servants' Top 10 List |
|---|---|---|
| Political power | Regulation | Leadership development |
| Public policy | Health policy | Alignment between the needs of the organization and employee skills |
| Institutions | Organizational culture | Collaboration within the public sector |
| The public service | Environmental policy | Management accountability |
| Democracy | Democratic dialogue | Information sharing |
| Law | Public administration of quasi-public organizations | Ethics |
| Management | Governance | Work/life balance |
| Evaluation | Technology change and policy | Democracy/public engagement |
| Ethics | Municipal and urban public administration | Results-based management |
| Accountability | Performance and evaluation | Inter-jurisdictional relations |

**Sources:** David Johnson, "Public Administration's Top Ten List," in John James Guy, ed., *Expanding Our Political Horizons: Readings in Canadian Politics and Government* (Toronto: Harcourt Brace, 1997): 124–32; Michael McConkey with Patrice Dutil, *The Top Ten Topics in Public Administration Scholarship: An International Perspective* (Toronto: Institute of Public Administration of Canada, 2006).

It is interesting to compare Johnson's list to a recent survey of the top 10 topics in international public administration scholarship. Forty-eight scholarly journals from around the world were surveyed, and their contents from 2004 to 2006 were analyzed. Practitioners of Canadian public administration were also surveyed. As you can see, the study and practice of public administration are many and varied. The discrepancies in these lists reflect two things we noted earlier in this chapter—that public administration draws on a number of academic disciplines for its theoretical underpinnings (hence the variety of scholarly concerns), and that it covers a remarkably wide range of human activity and behaviour in the public realm.

## Key Words and Concepts

public administration (2)
democratic society (6)
elected representatives (6)
politics–administration dichotomy (6)
merit principle (6)
bureaucracy (7)

accountability (8)
private sector/public sector (9)
patronage (15)
minimalist state (17)
Keynesian welfare state (17)
neoconservative state (17)

## Review Questions

This chapter was divided into five substantive sections, each reflecting a key issue for public administration. You should be familiar with these issues, and be able to address the questions associated with each.

1. *What Is Public Administration?*
At this stage, you should ask yourself, Can I adequately define public administration as both an academic field and a practice? Can I explain the concept of bureaucracy?

2. *Public Administration and Democratic Government*
In considering the tensions between democracy and bureaucracy, ask yourself, What is the nature of the relationship between elected and nonelected officials, and why is this important in public administration? How do public servants influence governance? Is this problematic for democracy, or supportive of it? What is meant by the "politics–administration dichotomy"? Is it realistic or is its value simply theoretical?

3. *Bureaucracy*
Ask yourself, Can I explain the significance of personnel, formal rules, policy instruments, conventions of behaviour, and institutions for public administration? How can I describe the tension between the values of democracy and efficiency within government organizations? Which value should prevail?

4. *Comparing Public and Private Sectors*
In thinking about the public and private sectors, ask yourself, How do the mandates and goals of each differ? What set of characteristics set the two apart and how? Are the differences between public administration and private administration clear to me?

5. *Restructuring the Public Sector and the Role of the State*
Ask yourself, What major factors have influenced reforms to public administration over the years? List as many public services as you can. Select one and argue why it should, or should not, be turned over to the private sector. Do you know enough about the role of the state to be able to explain how and why the public sector has been undergoing a period of restructuring?

## Weblinks

Institute of Public Administration of Canada (IPAC)
**http://ipac.ca**

Canadian Association of Programs in Public Administration (CAPPA)
**www.cappa.ca**

Public Service Commission of Canada
**www.psc-cfp.gc.ca**

Canadian Political Science Association
**www.cpsa-acsp.ca**

Canada School of Public Service
**www.csps-efpc.gc.ca**

Treasury Board Secretariat Office of the Chief Human Resources Officer
**www.tbs-sct.gc.ca/chro-dprh**

United Nations Public Administration, Country Profiles
**www.unpan.org/DPADM/ProductsServices/ThematicPortals/
PublicAdministrationCountryProfiles/tabid/677/Default.aspx**

# Further Reading

### 1. What Is Public Administration?

Hodgetts, J.E. *The Canadian Public Service: A Physiology of Government, 1867–1970.* Toronto: University of Toronto Press, 1973.

White, Leonard D. "Introduction to the Study of Public Administration," in Jay M. Shafritz and Albert C. Hyde, eds., *Classics of Public Administration*, 3rd ed. Pacific Grove, CA: Brooks Cole, 1992: 57–65.

Wilson, Woodrow. "The Study of Administration," in Jay M. Shafritz and Albert C. Hyde, eds., *Classics of Public Administration*, 3rd ed. Pacific Grove, CA: Brooks Cole, 1992: 11–24.

### 2. Public Administration and Democratic Government

Aucoin, Peter, and Donald J. Savoie. "The Politics–Administration Dichotomy: Democracy versus Bureaucracy?" in O.P. Dwivedi, Tim A. Mau, and Byron Sheldrick, eds., *The Evolving Physiology of Government: Canadian Public Administration in Transition.* Ottawa: University of Ottawa Press, 2009: 97–117.

MacDonald, Flora. "Who Is on Top? The Minister or the Mandarins?" and Mitchell Sharp, "A Reply from a Former Minister and Mandarin," in Paul W. Fox and Graham White, eds., *Politics Canada*, 8th ed. Toronto: McGraw-Hill, 1995: 448–56.

Whitaker, Reginald. "Politics Versus Administration: Politicians and Bureaucrats," in Michael S. Whittington and Glen Williams, eds., *Canadian Politics in the 21st Century*, 7th ed. Toronto: Thomson Nelson, 2008: 54–77.

### 3. Bureaucracy

Beetham, David. *Bureaucracy.* 2nd ed. Minneapolis: University of Minnesota Press, 1996.

Breton, Albert, and Ronald Wintrobe. "Bureaucracy and State Intervention: Parkinson's Law?" in Barbara Wake Carroll, David Siege, and Mark Sproule-Jones, eds., *Classic Readings in Canadian Public Administration.* Toronto: Oxford University Press, 2005: 427–42.

Brooks, Stephen. "Bureaucracy," in James P. Bickerton and Alain-G. Gagnon, eds., *Canadian Politics*, 2nd ed. Peterborough: Broadview, 1994: 307–27.

Kernaghan, Kenneth, Brian Marson, and Sandford Borins. *The New Public Organization.* Toronto: Institute of Public Administration of Canada, 2000.

### 4. Comparing Public and Private Sectors

Allison, Graham T. "Public and Private Management: Are They Fundamentally Alike in All Unimportant Respects?" in Jay M. Shafritz and Albert C. Hyde, eds., *Classics of Public Administration*, 3rd ed. Pacific Grove, CA: Brooks Cole, 1992: 457–75.

Candler, Gaylord George. "The Comparative Evolution of Public Administration in Australia, Brazil and Canada," *Canadian Public Administration*, 49, 3 (2006): 334–49.

Siegel, David, and Ken Rasmussen, eds. *Professionalism and Public Service: Essays in Honour of Kenneth Kernaghan*. Toronto: University of Toronto Press and IPAC, 2008.

## 5. Restructuring the Public Sector and the Role of the State

Pal, Leslie A. "New Public Management in Canada: New Whine in Old Bottles?" in James P. Bickerton and Alain-G. Gagnon, eds., *Canadian Politics*, 4th ed. Peterborough: Broadview, 2004: 185–202.

Roberts, Alasdair. "A Fragile State: Federal Public Administration in the Twentieth Century," in Christopher Dunn, ed., *The Handbook of Canadian Public Administration*, 2nd ed. Toronto: Oxford University Press, 2010: 219–34.

## Endnotes

1. Howard E. McCurdy, *Public Administration: A Bibliographic Guide to the Literature* (New York: Marcel Dekker, 1986): iii.

2. See E.N. Gladden, *A History of Public Administration* (London: Frank Cass, 1972).

3. On various definitions of public administration, see David H. Rosenbloom, *Public Administration: Understanding Management, Politics and Law in the Public Sector*, 4th ed. (New York: McGraw-Hill, 1998): 4–5. For an early definition of the field, see Leonard D. White, *Introduction to the Study of Public Administration* (New York: Macmillan, 1926). See also Grover Starling, *Managing the Public Sector* (Homewood, IL: Dorsey, 1977): 1; and Frederick C. Mosher, "Public Administration," in Frederick S. Lane, ed., *Current Issues in Public Administration* (New York: St. Martin's, 1978): 4.

4. See Kenneth Kernaghan, "Speaking Truth to Academics: The Wisdom of the Practitioners," *Canadian Public Administration*, 52, 4 (2009): 503–23; and Iain Gow, "Evolution of Disciplinary Approaches and Paradigms in the Study of Public Administration in Canada," in O.P. Dwivedi, Tim Mau, and Byron Sheldrick, eds., *The Evolving Physiology of Government: Canadian Public Administration in Transition* (Ottawa: University of Ottawa Press, 2009): 2–39.

5. Dwight Waldo, "Education for Public Administration in the Seventies," in Frederick C. Mosher, ed., *American Public Administration* (Tuscaloosa: University of Alabama Press, 1975).

6. See O.P. Dwivedi and James Iain Gow, *From Bureaucracy to Public Management: The Administrative Culture of the Government of Canada* (Peterborough: Broadview, 1999): 55–56; and Keith Henderson, "American Perspectives on Canadian Public Administration," in O.P. Dwivedi, Tim Mau, and Byron Sheldrick, eds., *The Evolving Physiology of Government: Canadian Public Administration in Transition* (Ottawa: University of Ottawa Press, 2009): 272–91.

7. H.S. Villard and W.W. Willoughby, *The Canadian Budgetary System* (New York: Harper and Row, 1918).

8. Alasdair Roberts, *So-Called Experts: How American Consultants Remade the Canadian Civil Service, 1918–21* (Toronto: Institute of Public Administration of Canada, 1996).

9. A. Paul Pross and V. Seymour Wilson, "Graduate Education in Canadian Public Administration: Antecedents, Present Trends and Portents," *Canadian Public Administration*, 19, 4 (1976): 515–41.

10. Robert MacGregor Dawson, *The Principle of Official Independence with Particular Reference to the Political History of Canada* (London: P.S. King, 1922), *The Civil Service of Canada* (London: Humphrey Milford, 1929), *The Government of Canada* (Toronto: University of Toronto Press, 1947).

11. The first American university to offer a program in public administration was Syracuse University in 1924, followed by Princeton and the University of Southern California in 1929 and 1930. See Gaylord George Candler, "The Comparative Evolution of Public Administration in Australia, Brazil and Canada," *Canadian Public Administration*, 49, 3 (2006): 335.

12. J.E. Hodgetts, "The Intellectual Odyssey of Public Administration in English Canada," *Canadian Public Administration*, 40, 2 (1997): 171–85.

13. For a current list of graduate and undergraduate programs, see the CAPPA website, **www.cappa.ca**. See also Donald J. Savoie, "Studying Public Administration," *Canadian Public Administration*, 33, 3 (1990): 389–413; and Sanford F. Borins, "The Role of Universities in Public Administration Education," *Canadian Public Administration*, 33, 3 (1990): 348–65.

14. David A. Good, "2002 CAPPA/CCMD Survey of Schools and Programs of Public Administration and Public Policy: Report of the Findings," presentation to the University Seminar of the Canadian Centre for Management Development (Ottawa: April 2002).

15. See James Iain Gow and Sharon L. Sutherland, "Comparison of Canadian Master's Programs in Public Administration, Public Management and Public Policy," *Canadian Public Administration*, 47, 3 (2004): 404; and Fazley Siddiq and Lindsay Hardy, "A Survey on the Recruitment of Graduates of Master's Programs in Public Administration and Public Policy," report prepared for the 20th Annual University Seminar, Canada School of Public Service (Ottawa: May 2006).

16. See Jonathan Malloy, "The Next Generation? Recruitment and Renewal in the Federal Public Service," in G. Bruce Doern, ed., *How Ottawa Spends, 2004–2005: Mandate Change in the Paul Martin Era* (Montreal: McGill-Queen's University Press, 2004): 277–95.

17. Kathryn May, "Specialized Programs to Help Fill Thousands of Vacancies," *Ottawa Citizen* (November 6, 2006).

18. See Peter Aucoin and Donald J. Savoie, "The Politics–Administration Dichotomy: Democracy versus Bureaucracy?" in O.P. Dwivedi, Tim A. Mau, and Byron Sheldrick, eds., *The Evolving Physiology of Government: Canadian Public Administration in Transition* (Ottawa: University of Ottawa Press, 2009): 97–117.

19. See Leslie A. Pal, *Beyond Policy Analysis: Public Issue Management in Turbulent Times*, 4th ed. (Toronto: Nelson, 2010): chap. 4; and Pearl Eliadis, Margaret M. Hill, and Michael Howlett, eds., *Designing Government: From Instruments to Governance* (Montreal: McGill-Queen's University Press, 2005).

20. James L. Perry and Kenneth L. Kraemer, *Public Management: Public and Private Perspectives* (Palo Alto, CA: Mayfield, 1983): x, cited in Jay M. Shafritz and Albert C. Hyde, eds., *Classics of Public Administration*, 3rd ed. (Pacific Grove, CA: Brooks Cole, 1992:): 443.

21. See J.L. Granatstein, *The Ottawa Men: The Civil Service Mandarins 1935–1957* (Toronto: Oxford University Press, 1982). For a contemporary assessment by a former public servant, see Ruth Hubbard, *Profession: Public Servant* (Ottawa: Invenire, 2009).

22. Graham T. Allison, "Public and Private Management: Are They Fundamentally Alike in All Unimportant Respects?" in Jay M. Shafritz and Albert C. Hyde, eds., *Classics of Public Administration*, 3rd ed. (Pacific Grove, CA: Brooks Cole, 1992): 457–75.

23. Allison, "Public and Private Management" 462.

24. On the history of the merit principle, see Ken Rasmussen and Luc Juillet, "The Origins of Merit in Canada," in O.P. Dwivedi, Tim A. Mau, and Byron Sheldrick, eds., *The Evolving Physiology of Government: Canadian Public Administration in Transition* (Ottawa: University of Ottawa Press, 2009): 74–96; and Fred Ruemper, "Beyond Merit: The Representative Principle," in Randy Hoffman et al., *Public Administration: Canadian Materials*, 3rd ed. (Toronto: Captus, 1998): 252–71.

25. Paul Appleby, *Big Democracy* (New York: Alfred A. Knopff, 1945): 7, cited in Howard E. McCurdy, *Public Administration: A Synthesis* (Menlo Park, CA: Cummings, 1977): 107.

26. See Shannon Sampert and Linda Trimble, eds., *Mediating Canadian Politics* (Toronto: Pearson Canada, 2010).

27. See Canada, Office of the Auditor General of Canada, *Auditing for Parliament* (Ottawa: Minister of Public Works and Government Services Canada, 1997): 1.

28. See Janice Gross Stein, *The Cult of Efficiency* (Toronto: Anansi, 2001). For an early discussion, see A.W. Johnson, "Efficiency in Government and Business," in Barbara Wake Carroll, David Siegel, and Mark Sproule-Jones, eds., *Classic Readings in Canadian Public Administration* (Toronto: Oxford University Press, 2005), 299–312.

29. See Ralph Heintzman, "Introduction: Canada and Public Administration," in Jacques Bourgault, Maurice Demers, and Cynthia Williams, eds., *Public Administration and Public Management: Experiences in Canada* (Quebec: Les Publications du Quebec, 1997): 1–12.

30. Reginald Whitaker, "Politics Versus Administration: Politicians and Bureaucrats," in Michael Whittington and Glen Williams, eds., *Canadian Politics in the 21st Century*, 6th ed. (Toronto: Thomson Nelson, 2004): 59.

31. Kenneth Kernaghan and John W. Langford, *The Responsible Public Servant* (Halifax: Institute for Research on Public Policy: 1990): 3.

32. Elaine Todres, "The Ethical Dimension in Public Service," *Canadian Public Administration*, 34, 1 (1991): 14.

33. See Kenneth Kernaghan, "East Block and Westminster: Conventions, Values and Public Service," in Christopher Dunn, ed., *Handbook of Canadian Public Administration* (Toronto: Oxford University Press, 2002): 104–19.

34. See Timothy Lewis, *In the Long Run We're All Dead: The Canadian Turn to Fiscal Restraint* (Vancouver: UBC Press, 2003); and Stephen McBride and John Shields, *Dismantling a Nation: The Transition to Corporate Rule in Canada* (Halifax: Fernwood, 1997).

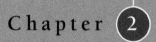

# Chapter 2

# Public Administration *and* Democracy

## WHAT YOU WILL LEARN

This chapter considers how democracy and power relate to the theory and practice of public administration in Canada. In order to examine Canadian public administration in any serious way, we must address the basics:

- What do we understand by the terms democracy and power?

- What is politics? What is the state? What is government? Are they the same thing? If not, how are they different, and how are they related? Why might we draw a distinction among them?

- How is power exercised in Canada? Who has it and who lacks it?

- What is the basis of power relations within society? Notions of equity? Equality? Freedom? Or is it simply that the person with the most toys gets to determine the rules of the game? In other words, what role do economic factors play in Canadian public administration?

Accountability is a prominent issue in any consideration of democracy and public administration, but is given fuller treatment in chapter 11, so it is raised here only in passing. This chapter is divided into five sections, each dealing with a particular but related aspect of democracy, political power, and public administration. It is prefaced with a brief section defining power and politics, followed by a consideration of the concept of democracy and a brief analysis of the concepts of state and government. Political culture and its interplay with the democratic context of public administration are then assessed by examining the Constitution and parliamentary and extra-parliamentary actors in public administration in Canada. We want to demystify Canadian public administration and its democratic context, to show that it has a very real and practical impact on our everyday lives. We will draw connections among what happens, how it happens, to whom it happens, and why it happens. By the end you will hopefully feel empowered toward the political system and prepared as a citizen to participate in and engage proactively with public administration, beyond simply casting a ballot once every few years or passively submitting to the bureaucratic machine as it steamrolls along. The chapter is divided in the following way:

1. *Power, Politics, and Public Administration*

This brief section sets the table for our discussions of democracy by asking simply: What is power? What is influence? Who has power and influence in Canadian society, and why? What is politics? What is the relationship between power and politics? This section also presents the debate about the public sector versus the private sector in a slightly different manner than in chapter 1, in light of democratic theory. We ask: How is it determined what is rightly in the public domain? What kind of struggle must be engaged to move issues from the private world to the public, or vice versa?

2. *What Is Democracy?*

This section asks: What is democratic theory? What does democracy mean to the theory and practice of public administration? What is the relationship of democracy to political power? This section assesses the concepts of direct democracy and representative democracy. How do these affect the way government is structured and run in Canada?

3. *State and Government*

These two terms are often used interchangeably. But they actually refer to two different things. We ask: What is the difference between state and government? Why is it important to have a conceptual difference between the two?

4. *Political Culture*

This section looks at several definitions and theories of this concept and asks: What are the major theoretical explanations for the quality and type of democratic life in Canada? Is there a single theory that explains how democratic Canada is (or is not)? What impact does this have on public administration in Canada?

5. *The Interplay of Democracy, Political Culture, and the Institutions of Public Administration*

Finally, this section resurrects the theme of democratic theory to introduce parliamentary and extra-parliamentary actors who influence and exercise power in the state and government in Canada. We ask: What is a constitution, and what impact does it have on the relations of power within Canadian public administration? What are those relations? Who are the actors? What are the key institutions, both parliamentary and extra-parliamentary, that affect public administration?

# Power, Politics, and Public Administration

Politics is fundamentally about **power**. This element always lurks beneath the surface of public administration, and in many cases is overt and plain to see. If you could imagine the origins of society, you might see where power comes from. You might see the interactions of individuals devolving into conflict or evolving into co-operation over the division of goods among them. There will virtually always be conflict or co-operation simply because there will never be enough goods for all those who want them, all the time. Therefore, some means must be devised to co-operatively divide goods and to prevent conflict from degenerating into violence. This is where the exercise of power comes into play. Someone must be designated (or must designate him- or herself) the arbiter over the division of the goods and have **authority** to exercise power and make decisions on behalf of the members of the society. This is the core of politics. Public administration, in turn, is the mechanism by which political decision making takes place.

Power is typically defined in public administration and politics as the ability to authorize, influence, or coerce behaviour. In other words, someone has power over you because they can direct or instruct you to do something (or refrain from doing something) by virtue of his or her 1) legal position of authority; 2) status or position; or 3) use of force.

Why people consent to alter their behaviour is a fascinating sociological question. The famous German sociologist Max Weber (see chapter 3) suggested that authority was derived from one of three sources of legitimacy. The first is **traditional legitimacy**, wherein rule is justified on the basis of long-established custom or habit. Because things have always been ordered in a certain way, the exercise of power is justified. The second is **charismatic legitimacy**. Under these circumstances, a leader is believed to be vested with exceptional personal qualities that make him or her uniquely suited to lead. In many cases, such leaders will claim to have been divinely chosen. Third, Weber refers to **legal-rational legitimacy**, in which a set of rationally created rules and legal statutes serve as the basis of power and sanctioned authority.[1]

Increasingly, modern states have moved to systems of legal-rational legitimacy, although there are many examples of the other two systems as well.[2] In modern states, the rise of mass literacy was accompanied by the rise of "public opinion," which increasingly could intelligently ask (and answer) the question, "Who ought to rule?" This also illustrates the diminishing role in many societies of religion, which often served as the rationale for charismatic and some traditional systems of legitimacy.

Moreover, a legal-rational system makes clear, "How will they rule?" For instance, leaders could justify their actions in traditional and charismatic systems simply by stating that this was what they had ordained. Under a legal-rational system, however, this arbitrariness is reduced by features such as rules of accountability and the **rule of law**, which is the principle that no one—not even a lawmaker—is above the law. In a democratic society, decisions about who holds power—and who can therefore legitimately authorize, influence, or coerce you into behaving in a certain way—are made through elected and nonelected institutions of public administration. These range from the prime minister, Cabinet, public service, and Parliament to the judiciary, police, and army—all of whom are given clearly prescribed roles.

Where do politics come into play? As political scientist Larry Johnston suggests, "The world we inhabit is political. We may choose to study politics or not, or having studied politics, decide that we will do so no more, but we *cannot choose to opt out of the political world*."[3] But it is not always perfectly obvious what we mean by *politics*. For some, it is simply the goings-on on Parliament Hill, far removed from real life, which intrude on us only when a scandal or particularly flashy issue emerges. Relatively few Canadians are passionately involved in this sphere. If you are a typical Canadian, you probably are not a member of a political party and you follow politics only casually, if at all. Indeed, fewer and fewer Canadians are even bothering with the most fundamental democratic political act—voting.

Still, politics is all around us, and failure to come to grips with this too often makes us citizen-victims, as other interests in society play the political game to their advantage. For the most basic fact about politics is that it arises out of scarcity: there are not enough resources for all people to satisfy all of their basic wants and needs all of the time. Limits on what is available, especially on what is desirable, such as wealth, mean that conflicting claims will be made as to who gets what. Competition over scarce resources is at the heart of politics. But if politics were just perpetual conflict, then presumably we would be in a state of perpetual war with each other. Politics, then, is about more than just conflict; it is also about how rival claims are settled through the resolution of conflict.

Moreover, it is obvious that conflict and competition are not the only forces driving humans. Co-operation is also important, indeed inevitable, to settle disputes over scarce resources. Hence we developed organizations, with divisions of labour and hierarchy, to realize societal goals through co-operation. Thus, in our understanding of power and politics, we might just as easily speak of co-operation as well as conflict and competition.

At the core of every definition of politics are notions about the exercise of power. One commonly cited definition is by American David Easton. His definition is somewhat general and abstract: *politics* is the authoritative allocation of values.[4] What this mouthful of terms means is really quite simple when you break it down. *Authoritative* refers to the idea that there must be a legitimate authority who can make decisions on behalf of society. Decisions about what? About what values will prevail. For instance, you may value freedom, but someone else may value security. So how do we decide whether society should invest in, say, human rights commissions to safeguard our freedoms or the armed forces to safeguard our security? We give the job to authorities, who then allocate values.

Another perhaps more straightforward definition by Harold Laswell is that politics is about "who gets what, when and how."[5] This is essentially another way of expressing what Easton said. But this definition's virtue—besides brevity—is its clarity and simplicity. Vladimir Lenin, the founder of the Soviet Union, said politics was "who does what to whom."[6] China's Communist leader, Mao Zedong, called politics "bloodless war."[7] Otto von Bismarck, the chancellor of Germany, called politics "the doctrine of the possible: the attainable."[8] Karl Marx argued that "political power, properly so called, is merely the organized power of one class for oppressing another."[9] Virtually all definitions of politics have this common underlying theme of power.

Today, we engage in conflict resolution and co-operative activities in all aspects of our lives: in familial settings, in the workplace, over grades in school, etc. But there are two things about politics that distinguish it from other forms of conflict resolution and co-operation: first, the nature of the issues is public, not private; second, we use public authority to settle them.

The issue of establishing which relations within society count as political (i.e., public), and which are private is often contentious. It was not until the twentieth century, for example, that relations between men and women were deemed political. But the women's movement raised our consciousness about the political factors underlying the subjugation of women. For instance, where public administration is concerned,[10] the very structures of bureaucracy have contributed to the oppression of women by men, according to feminist scholar Camilla Stivers.[11] Similarly, at one time relations between bosses and workers were considered to be a private affair in which public authorities had no business. That changed with the advent of a strong labour movement that politicized workplace relations and appealed to public authorities—the government—to do something about wage levels, unsafe working conditions, child labour, and so on.[12] In these views about women's roles and the conflict between capitalists and the working class, understanding manifestations of oppression is the key to the concept of power.

The boundary between political (or public) and private may not be distinct, but it is crucial for understanding politics. Much of political conflict occurs over where exactly this line should be drawn: what should be considered a matter for public life and decisions by the state, and what should remain private.

Only by clarifying the line between public and private can our democratic rights and responsibilities be discerned. Only those power relations in the public realm can legitimately be associated with the use of coercion or force. Only public authorities—the state—have the legitimate right to back up decisions with the full power of society, as the only entity that can claim to speak and act on behalf of the entire community. The state alone is responsible for some measure of social order, which is a necessary condition for all other societal activities. Without the state, there is no peaceful basis for reconciling conflicts in society.

## What Is Democracy?

What is democracy? Elections? Parliamentary government? Freedom? Democracy is what political scientists call a "contested concept," meaning that there is not always agreement on what the term means. If you sat down with a group of people—say, the other students in this course—and canvassed their views, you might find broad agreement on the outlines of democracy but differences on the details. It may be quite hard, in fact, for your group to reach a consensus.

We are interested here in noting where democracy intersects with public administration, and so will not digress too far into the definitional quagmire; but it is important to keep in mind that the values held by an individual or a society help determine what that individual or society means by *democracy*. In turn, these values are translated into political institutions and structures, roles, and actors that assume responsibility for enacting the public will; in other words, for governing.

Given the variety of nations with different governmental forms, politics, and policies, all of which call themselves "democratic," how can we be sure what the concept really entails? The word democracy comes from two Greek roots: *demos*, meaning "the people," and *kratos*, meaning "authority." In ancient Greek culture, democracy meant "government by the many." In some Greek city-states, all citizens participated in making laws (women and slaves were not considered citizens). Save for a few rare examples, such as some Swiss Cantons and the New England "town halls" of the seventeenth and eighteenth centuries, such systems, known as **direct democracy**, do not exist. In direct democracy, citizens exercise authority and power personally. Instead, most democracies, including Canada, now consist of a body of elected representatives that makes laws. This is **representative democracy**, in which citizens delegate others to exercise authority on their behalf. Let us briefly consider each model.

## Direct Democracy

The model of democracy that approaches most people's conception of "pure" democracy is one in which popular assemblies are constituted by the people to directly govern themselves. Strictly speaking, this ideal did not even prevail in the Athenian example, since elections were often carried out by lotteries rather than voting. The Athenians believed that elections could be manipulated by wealthy individuals (much like the impression that prevails today). Currently, few people expect democracy to be rule by the people as a whole, since societies have become so large and complex. Ironically, though, for the first time, we may have the technological capability to effect direct democracy with the internet and interactive telecommunications, although few concrete steps have yet been taken in this direction.[13]

There are, however, some mechanisms in Canada that approximate the direct democracy model. These include, for instance, *referenda*, in which citizens directly express their approval or disapproval of a particular issue via a simple vote. Two referenda, in 1980 and 1995, asked Québécois whether they would authorize their provincial government to negotiate sovereignty with the rest of Canada. Referenda were also held in British Columbia in 2005 and 2009, in Prince Edward Island in 2005, and in Ontario in 2007 asking citizens if they wanted to reform their electoral systems (all failed). Referenda results are generally binding on a government. Another form of direct vote is a *plebiscite*; in this case, the results are not binding on the government. Shades of direct democracy can also be seen in extending the election of governmental officials to include not just politicians, but also judges and other administrative officials. Other direct democracy mechanisms include recall, wherein voters can effectively "fire" their representative before an election by getting a certain number of voters to sign a petition to that effect. However, it is noteworthy that in jurisdictions that use these techniques there is often a low participation rate by citizens, and wealthy and powerful interests are often the only ones who can afford to spend money on campaigns that will influence citizens' choices.

## Representative Democracy

The Canadian form of government is, properly speaking, a representative democracy in which those elected to public office derive legitimacy to act authoritatively for others and are thus vested with power to make decisions having the force of law. This system allows a method of choosing representatives, monitoring their activities, and changing those responsible for governing through elections.

In a representative democracy, then, citizens are one step removed from the actual exercise of decision making. Almost all modern democracies are representative democracies, where government is carried out by an elected legislature. Citizens delegate law-making authority to their representatives, holding them responsible for their actions through various institutions of government (Parliament, for instance) and through periodic elections. Representative democracy can be summed up as a system in which "public policies are made, on a majority basis, by representatives subject to effective popular control at periodic elections which are conducted on the principle of political equality and under conditions of political freedom."[14]

## Political Democracy

We can usefully subdivide these conceptions about representative democracy into "political democracy" and "economic democracy." Direct democracy and representative democracy both have at their core some notion of equality. This implies, for example, that all citizens have equal rights; but in the real world, equality is elusive. Certain features of the Canadian system are associated with the idea of political democracy: majority rule; one person, one vote; competitive elections; and cabinet-parliamentary government. Theoretically, we might expect that, with all these principles and mechanisms, some measure of equality could be realized. In fact, a formal political type of equality does apply in that we all have rights to and access to these political mechanisms. Thus, oppressive government, in which equality is undermined or denied, should be virtually impossible.

Consider the following possibility, however: what if the majority of Canadians voted for a party that supported the suppression of French-language rights? Would that be democratic? The point is that the appearance of equality as vested in the mechanisms of democracy can be deceiving. What this hypothetical example points to is the imperfection of a democracy in which the simple principles, such as majority rule, can actually be used to achieve ends that seem antidemocratic, since there is nothing "democratic" about depriving citizens of their rights.

To avoid these consequences, we build protection against what may be called the "tyranny of the majority" into our institutions and processes. These might take the form of constitutional limits on the power of the state. For example, while a majority might vote to suppress French-language rights, no such law would stand up against the rights and freedoms protected in the Constitution.

As well, particular protection for groups and individuals in society may be entrenched in the formal and informal rules and procedures of politics. For example, the Canadian electoral system reinforces the power of the country's French-Canadian minority, most of whom live in Quebec and can therefore vote as a block to protect their own interests. Moreover, federalism and the division of powers in the Constitution mean that citizens aggrieved by one level of government can seek redress from the other.

Beyond formal and informal constitutional rules and procedures, the social and cultural values of a society also come into play. This is a point made by political scientists Gabriel Almond and Sidney Verba in their book, *The Civic Culture*.[15] A political culture that acknowledges and recognizes a multiplicity of group identities is likely to give rise to values such as tolerance. These group identities become important in protecting minority rights when individuals perceive, and society recognizes, that some members of society belong to discrete groups (religious, ethnic, linguistic, regional, occupational, and so on) in addition to sharing a common citizenship with everyone else. Under these circumstances, the likelihood of a democratic state being turned to oppressive ends is reduced, since everyone ultimately has a stake in the tolerance of society.

Can we say that political democracy ensures freedom and equality—two values of primary importance in contemporary Canadian society? If all the rules and procedures are followed, and if there are guarantees for minority rights against the tyranny of the majority derived from political culture, have we achieved some near-ideal form of representative democracy? To answer this question, we must look at democracy from yet another angle, and consider what may be called *economic democracy*.

## Economic Democracy

In Canada, we claim to have a democratic system because there is a fairly equal chance that all citizens can participate in the political system and because we as citizens can "throw the rascals out" if we disagree with the government of the day. But in the absence of economic and social equality, can we really claim to have a democratic society?

Look at it this way. Political democracy guarantees that there are institutions in place through which the will of the people can be realized. These include Parliament, and theoretically everyone has a chance to run for election, become a Member of Parliament, and exercise authority on behalf of the people. However, it is prohibitively expensive to run for Parliament. Increasingly, it seems this key symbol of Canadian democracy is becoming the preserve of the wealthy. Certainly, lower-income Canadians are grossly under-represented in the halls of power. The same holds true for the senior levels of the public service. Senior public servants tend to be well educated and from middle- and upper-income families. They can afford the university education that prepares them for a position in the public service. The question that arises is whether they, along with their parliamentary masters, can adequately and fairly represent and understand the views and needs of those who are systematically excluded from positions of power. There is no easy answer to this question. Though we explore it in more detail in chapter 8, it is flagged here as a disputed element in any discussion of the quality of democracy in a society.

Socialists critique democracy by suggesting that it is unrealistic to expect ordinary citizens, who are overburdened with the concerns of making ends meet, to have the time, energy, and resources to engage the political system in a meaningful way. They argue that political equality without economic equality is a sham. Politics becomes the preserve of the idle rich, while the majority toil endlessly with little time or opportunity to substantively affect the political system. Marxists go a step further and argue that any system, democratic or not, that exists within the framework of capitalism is by its nature unequal. This is because capitalism divides society into classes, with the upper (capitalist) class exploiting the lower (working) class through their disproportionate ownership of property and the means of production. The minority, then, exploits the majority, and this makes a mockery of notions of political democracy. In this view, only when some form of economic democracy is realized through the overthrow of capitalism can there be true equality.

In short, political democracy lacks a commitment to economic or social equality. There are societies that devote a considerable amount of effort to ensuring the economic and social equality of their citizens but that lack many of the institutional features that we assume characterize democracy, such as free, fair, open elections. So does attaching greater importance to the social and economic equality of individuals than to rules and procedures make those societies any less democratic than our own?[16]

There is one more aspect to democracy related to the question of equality. That is, respect for rights and freedoms. But which rights and freedoms warrant protection in a democratic society, and which may be legitimately limited by government? These questions form the basis of a debate about democracy that has been ongoing since ancient Greek times. For example, some would argue that taxation is a restriction on the personal freedom of individuals to dispose of their income as they see fit. Others argue that taxation promotes freedom by paying for policies that provide opportunities that the disadvantaged would not otherwise enjoy, like an education. Even a value such as freedom of speech becomes controversial. Are limits on spending to advertise a political point of view during an election a legitimate limit on freedom of speech, since only the wealthy can afford to try to influence public opinion in this way?

Rights and freedoms are important, but almost everyone recognizes that no right is absolute and that certain kinds of limits on rights actually promote democracy. The struggle between expanding and limiting rights is sometimes seen as the struggle between the competing pulls of individual rights and group rights, or between the private and public realms. Society must constantly find the balance between these conflicting impulses if it is to be considered democratic: it expresses its findings through the mechanisms of public administration.

## State and Government

Most of us are familiar with the debate over how much the state should be involved in the economy: e.g., in public broadcasting through the CBC; in the provision of water or hydro through municipal utility companies; or in the selling of alcohol through provincial liquor boards. As we saw in chapter 1, there is a long history of state involvement in the economy in Canada, stretching back to the pre-Confederation era. Canadian society has evolved from one in which there was little need or desire for state involvement in the lives of its citizens, to one in which the state is intimately and intricately involved in our lives in countless ways.

The great, clamorous debate about the appropriate role of the state in society is largely organized around ideological world views, for what the state's role clearly reflects is the nature of power relations in society. It reflects in whose interests the power of the state has been exercised. Why did the welfare state develop? Was it simply because politicians in power felt generous? Why has that same welfare state come under attack? Who benefits and who loses in a strong state, as opposed to a laissez-faire system in which the state disengages itself from the economy and from social life? How do these interests affect public administration?

To sort out these issues we must ask the following: what exactly do we mean when we use the term *the state*? Some use it interchangeably with government, but, in fact, it means something somewhat different. For example, to argue that a government is corrupt or wasteful and that it should be turfed out is not the same as arguing for the overthrow of the state. It simply challenges the authority of the individuals who at a particular moment in time have their hands on the state's levers of power. Most political activity is aimed at influencing and changing the government, rather than at reforming the state.

Weber suggested that it is most useful to view the state not in terms of its ends but of its means. He quoted the Communist revolutionary Leon Trotsky, who said that "every state is founded on force," and went on to suggest that the elemental characteristic of any state is this feature of the legitimate use of violence and coercion. Weber wrote,

*A state is a human community that (successfully) claims the monopoly of the legitimate use of physical force within a given territory. Note that "territory" is one of the characteristics of the state. Specifically, at the present time, the right to use physical force is ascribed to other institutions or to individuals only to the extent to which the state permits it. The state is considered the sole source of the "right" to use violence. Hence, "politics" for us means striving to share power or striving to influence the distribution of power, whether among states or among groups within a state.*[17]

Marx claimed that society as a whole was splitting into two classes directly facing each other: bourgeoisie (the capitalist class) and proletariat (the working class). In a famous and often-quoted line from the *Communist Manifesto*, he claimed that "the executive of the modern State is but a committee for managing the common affairs of the whole bourgeoisie."[18] But if class differences were obliterated by a revolution in which private property was abolished, there would be no need for the state to continue since the bourgeoisie in whose interests it acted would no longer exist. Hence, Marx argued, the state would "wither away."

Political economist Ralph Miliband explained the importance of the state in this way:

*More than ever before men [sic] now live in the shadow of the state. What they want to achieve, individually or in groups, now mainly depends on the state's sanction and support.*

*But since that sanction and support are not bestowed indiscriminately, they must, ever more directly, seek to influence and shape the state's power and purpose, or try and appropriate it altogether. It is for the state's attention, or for its control, that men compete; and it is against the state that beat the waves of social conflict. It is to an ever greater degree the state which men encounter as they confront other men. This is why, as social beings, they are also political beings, whether they know it or not. It is possible not to be interested in what the state does; but it is not possible to be unaffected by it.*[19]

According to Brooks, the state has three main characteristics:[20]

1. territorial boundaries, beyond which the state has no legitimate authority;
2. a complex set of institutions that wield public authority;
3. power.

Asserting, as Weber did, that the state has a legitimate monopoly on the use of force to maintain order says nothing about in whose interests this power is exercised. Some have tried to incorporate this question into their understanding of the state. Marxists, for example, see the state as an instrument used by the ruling class to oppress and exploit the working class. Feminists view the state as a patriarchal institution designed and maintained to ensure the dominance of men over women in society.[21]

Later on, we will consider whose interests the state serves, but for now, we want to make sure that we understand the difference, and the relationship, between the state and government. The latter is a term usually reserved for those who have been elected to power. This is a more personal conception, usually associated with a particular group of people, often through the instrument of a political party. We speak, for example, of the "Harper government," but not of the "Harper state," even though the prime minister and the political party and the elections that he may contest are all part of the larger state structure. Governments come and go; but the rules, procedures, and institutions of the state are more enduring than is the government and its policies. You might think of the state as the forum within which government exists.

A state is also characterized by the feelings its citizens have about it. In developed democracies, such as Canada, the state elicits widespread public identification with its institutions and values. Normally, the people strongly identify with their state. When citizens accept that a government ought, or has the right, to make decisions for them, political scientists refer to the system as having *legitimacy*.

Legitimacy in this sense is closely linked to the concept of authority: the legitimate right to exercise power. Underlying the distinction between state and government is an important practical difference in the basis on which each compels the obedience of citizens within its jurisdiction. The willingness of citizens to obey the decisions of the government, even though they may strongly disagree with them (consider reactions to the 1991 introduction of the Goods and Services Tax), is fundamentally based on the view that the state's authority is legitimate; that is, the rules and institutions of the state that determine how governments are chosen are accepted by most people as reasonable. The legitimacy of the state is therefore based on the consent of those who are governed.

Government may be upheld by consent of the governed. Or it may be upheld by the use of force. Usually both come into play to a varying extent. The state's authority may be questioned from time to time, as when citizens stage a tax revolt or protest in the streets over some issue. Thus, the state's authority is sometimes questioned, and it may resort to the use of force, crushing civil disobedience to maintain its ability to govern. Of course, governments that rely on threats or violence to stay in power are usually unstable and undermine their own legitimacy, because consent by the governed is missing. How consent is manufactured is the topic of some debate. In some societies, such as Canada, it arises out of the combined ideological forces of the education system, the media, family, government, the workplace, and various other political, social, and economic institutions that influence the ideological outlook of citizens. In other societies, more overt and sometimes quite crude attempts are made to manufacture the consent of the people through propaganda, the stifling of opposition parties, or media censorship. This is frequently resorted to in totalitarian systems.

The ability of a state and its political institutions to govern a given population and territory rests on the state's legitimacy to exercise power. In the resolution of conflict, a government requires the consent necessary to authoritatively allocate values and resources. All states attempt to maintain political order and viability, to resolve societal conflicts without tearing the country apart, to defend the territory against external enemies, and to maintain essential services for its citizens. The manner in which these and other policy-making activities are performed, while a balance is maintained between power on the one hand and legitimacy on the other, is at the core of the study of politics and government as realized through public administration.

More specifically, the issue may also be cast in terms of the tensions between the institutional arms of the state—the bureaucracy—and the value of democracy.[22] How we reconcile the challenges of modern government, with its requirement of large, complex bureaucracies, with the imperatives of democracy is a difficult, ongoing issue. Bureaucracies are hierarchical institutions designed to execute complex tasks, but are often criticized for being "undemocratic" or even "anti-democratic." However, the requirements of efficiency, professionalism, and skills found in bureaucracies are necessary to the functioning of societies, including democratic ones. Further, serving democratic ends sometimes means taking actions that are inimical to the bureaucratic values of efficiency, effectiveness, and economy. These considerations are flagged here but are taken up in more detail in subsequent chapters.

## Political Culture

To fully understand the nature of political power and democracy, we must also look at the question of **political culture**, which, though an important concept for public administration, is not without some controversy as to its precise meaning and application.[23] For example, understanding political culture can help us understand why Western Canada feels alienated from the rest of Canada and what this means for public administration. Understanding political culture can also assist in understanding other issues: the impact of language; the relationship between Quebec and the rest of the country; the growing participation of women in politics, in the workplace, and in public life; and how multiculturalism has affected the governance of the country.

There is a vast literature dealing with political culture, and definitions of it abound. Most refer to the values, attitudes, and beliefs citizens possess in relation to political life in the society. Political culture was first introduced as a concept by Gabriel Almond in his 1956 essay, "Comparative Political Systems," where he claimed it was "the particular distribution of patterns of orientation toward political objects among the members of the nation."[24]

There are four broad areas we look at in the study of political culture. First, we can look at attitudes toward political symbols and institutions and ask, How strongly do you, as a citizen, feel about political symbols, such as the flag? Do you feel sheepish about singing the national anthem at sporting events, or do you belt it out with gusto? Are there historical heroes from Canada's past that you look back on with pride? Or villains? Do you believe political institutions, such as Parliament, the courts, and the public service, are effective? Can government be trusted? What kinds of duties and obligations are implied by the idea of "citizenship"? How do citizens view the Constitution?

Second, we can look at attitudes toward others in the political system. Do citizens have strong loyalties to particular groups or regions of the country? Are you a "Canadian" first and foremost, or are you an "Albertan" or a "Newfoundlander"? How tolerant are majorities toward minorities? Are you tolerant of those expressing alternative political viewpoints or who are critical of the status quo? What types of protest are acceptable? How important is freedom of speech?

Third, we can look at political knowledge, values, and evaluations. How much do you, as a citizen, know about politics, about the workings of institutions, policy making, and political leaders? What kinds of beliefs, values, and sentiments do citizens have? How widely are they shared? How should resources be distributed? How much support should be given to the poor or disadvantaged groups in society?

Finally, we can look at the acquisition and transmission of political beliefs. Where do your beliefs and expectations about political life come from? How are they learned? How effectively are they transmitted from one generation to the next? Are citizens' beliefs becoming more coherent, more ideological?

This long list of questions suggests that political culture, as a concept, covers an awful lot of ground. This is partly because political cultures are so dynamic: that is, they are constantly changing and evolving. Indeed, the broad configuration of political culture today may well be the result of events from the distant past. Conditions change over time, populations grow or shrink, and remote historical episodes that were at one time terribly important fade from our collective memories. But just because we don't consciously remember the events of our collective past does not mean that they don't continue to influence the way we view political life today and continue to affect public administration.

Much of political culture is oriented toward our *subjective* perspectives on political life (that is, how we *feel* things are, as opposed to how they actually are) and relates directly to our political behaviour (how we vote, the way parties work, the effectiveness of political institutions, the formation of policy, interest group behaviour, the workings of the Constitution, and so on). Public administration must respond to these subjective perspectives, which give rise to actions that can ripple through the entire socio-political and economic system, affecting it in large and small ways (see Box 2.1).

---

**BOX 2.1  Charlie Brown and Seniors' Pensions**

In the late 1980s, the government of Brian Mulroney attempted to save money by de-indexing seniors' old age pensions. There was an outcry from "grey power" groups across the country. Many seniors developed the subjective perception that their income was under threat. Whether this was the case was a matter of some dispute, but ultimately incidental. Once they felt threatened, they mobilized. A demonstration on Parliament Hill encapsulated the feelings and power behind this threat. Prime Minister Mulroney waded into the crowd, affecting his most statesman-like demeanour for the cameras, no doubt sensing a photo opportunity in the making. But he was confronted by a tiny octogenarian named Solange Denis, who loudly berated him for his government's stand. The sight of this ordinary Canadian standing up to the power of the prime minister created a striking image. She admonished him for messing around with seniors' pensions, loudly proclaiming, "You lied to us, Charlie Brown." The prime minister's blustering reply was lost in the face of this forthright challenge, which was repeated on the airwaves for days afterward. The government backed down from its plan to de-index pensions. Apparently attacking seniors' entitlements is outside the bounds of acceptable behaviour in Canadian political culture.

---

Isolating and analyzing the precise way that Canadians feel about political life is a difficult task. Canada shares with many other industrialized democracies certain political values rooted in the Western tradition and containing essentially liberal elements modified by conservative and socialist democratic practices that have evolved since the eighteenth century. Thus, Canadian political culture embraces such values as equality before the law, the right to hold private property, the right of free speech and assembly, the right to vote and run for office, and so on. But these values do not set us apart from numerous other political communities that also share the same general political culture—and these values have increasingly been overlain with new values brought by a range of immigrants contributing to the multicultural reality that is now Canada. To understand the uniqueness of Canadian political culture, we need to consider how geography, economics, culture, and politics historically combined to shape this country.

## Geography

First, the sheer geographic size of Canada has had an immense impact on its political development and the structure of political life. Canada is the second-largest country in the world (Russia is the largest); Canada occupies some 9.2 million square kilometres, it spans six time zones, and it sprawls across half of a continent. Distance, climate, and natural geographic barriers, such as the Canadian Shield, the St. Lawrence Seaway, the Prairies, the Rockies, and the tundra, have all had an impact on attempts to carve a political community out of this land mass.

## Demography

Relative to its land size, Canada's population is small. As well, the population is unevenly distributed. About 80 percent of all Canadians live within three hours of the U.S. border, and 60 percent reside in one of two provinces: Ontario or Quebec. The cultural distribution of the population is also uneven. Eighty percent of all francophones live in Quebec, and Canada's Native peoples form majorities in the sparsely inhabited Nunavut and Northwest Territories. The major urban centres, meanwhile, are by far the most multicultural parts of the country.

So the physical size and expanse of the country, and the size, makeup, and distribution of the population pose unique problems of communication, transportation, and governance in Canada. The decision to adopt a federal political framework—that is, a division of powers among regional and central governments—is an institutional response to those kinds of problems; federalism aims to make government less remote to a far-flung and diverse population, as well as representative of distinctive regions.

## Three Founding Cultures

The presence of a significant linguistic minority—francophones—concentrated in one part of the country is a significant factor in Canadian political culture. The debate in 2006 about Parliament designating Quebec as "a nation within Canada" revealed the extent to which this is still true. The French–English relationship is sometimes summed up by the term *dualism*, and was captured in Lord Durham's famous 1839 pronouncement that Canada was "two nations warring in the bosom of a single state." Add to this the presence of a civilization that predates European settlement by several thousand years—Native Canadians—and that has always played a significant but largely ignored role in political, economic, and cultural affairs, and you have a unique mixture that defines Canadian political culture.

## Continentalism

The relationship between Canada and the United States as co-tenants on one continent, who share what was once referred to as "the longest undefended border in the world," is basic to the essence of both countries; but it is perhaps more significant to Canada because of the immense imbalance in power between the two countries, which has resulted in an ongoing challenge to Canadians to find and define their "national identity." Canadians may not be good at articulating what they *are*, but at least most can agree that what they are *not* is American. But Canada's ongoing struggle to maintain itself as a distinct political culture has been seriously compromised by the penetration of U.S. economic and cultural influences. The continuous fight against absorption into the U.S. empire is a particularly important theme in the study of Canadian political culture, as was the struggle to emerge from the shadows of Great Britain in an earlier age. Indeed, this process has been called "the evolution of Canada from colony to nation to colony."[25]

## Interpretations of Canadian Political Culture

There is widespread agreement that factors such as geography, demography, the presence of three founding cultures, and proximity to the U.S. all contributed to Canadian political culture. But how? These different elements must have created immense barriers to the creation of a single, united, and focused political culture, and this fact has given rise to several different interpretations of how Canadian political culture got its unique colouration. We will look briefly at the contributions of four important theorists: Louis Hartz, Seymour Martin Lipset, John Porter, and Harold Adams Innis.[26]

One very influential interpretation has been that offered by the U.S. sociologist Louis Hartz in his book *The Founding of New Societies*.[27] There are three main points in Hartz's thesis: the nature of the founding "fragment"; the point of departure of the emigrants; and the point of congealment in the new society. Hartz argued that "new" societies, such as Canada, Australia, and the United States, were profoundly shaped by the values carried to those societies by early settlers and immigrants (he tended to ignore the presence of Natives in his study). He argued that one had to look at the specific segment of the culture that the settlers came from in order to understand the political culture they established in the new land.

A second, complementary explanation of Canadian political culture is offered by the American sociologist Seymour Martin Lipset in his book *Continental Divide*.[28] He emphasizes the importance of "formative events," historical episodes such as the British conquest of Quebec, which has forever since shaped Québécois views about their position in Canadian society. Other formative events include the American Revolution, which resulted in the displacement of tens of thousands of Americans loyal to Britain. These United Empire Loyalists fled to Canada, carrying with them conservative, elitist, loyalist world views. In addition, the rebellions of 1837 and 1838 in Upper and Lower Canada, and the Riel rebellions of 1870 and 1885, are all examples of the kind of nation-shaping events to which Lipset is referring.

A third interpretation focuses on the central role that elites play in Canadian society. John Porter's important book *The Vertical Mosaic* is a study of how power is organized and exercised in Canadian society.[29] It provides a provocative analysis of the ways in which Canadian elites exercise far more influence over the state and Canadian society than is typical in other advanced industrial states. These elites, he contends, are crucial "gatekeepers," who exercise control over the economy, the public service, elected officials, the media, and intellectual and religious life. All societies have elites, but Porter argues that Canadian elites are particularly powerful because they are a small, closed group with overlapping membership in different sectors of Canadian society. Moreover, because such small groups exercise influence over all these domains, they have been able to deflect attention away from class division in Canadian society and toward ethnic, religious, and regional divisions.

Harold Adams Innis has been one of the most influential interpreters of Canadian society, spawning a whole subdiscipline called the *staples approach* within the academic discipline of Canadian political economy.[30] He contended that an understanding of the broad economic forces, and particularly the importance of such primary resources as fish, fur, lumber, minerals, and wheat, is germane to understanding Canadian political culture. These primary resources, or "staples," formed the core of the Canadian export economy from the outset, and that economy in turn has shaped the political and cultural outlines of Canadian society. A country such as Canada, which is overly dependent on the whims of the international marketplace into which it seeks to export its goods, has little control over its economy. Demand is dictated by economic forces beyond its boundaries. Thus, Innis maintained, Canadians have developed conservative, cautious, and even pessimistic or fatalistic attitudes, largely because they are not able to control their own economic destinies. This cautiousness is not just limited to economic matters, though; it filters through to the way Canadians think about their society and about political life, and helps to explain why Canadians hold such cautious views about social and political change.

These four interpretations of Canadian political culture do not necessarily contradict one another. In fact, in many ways they are complementary, though each scholar emphasizes different areas. However you want to explain the making of Canadian political culture, a long-range, historical perspective on Canadian society is useful—indeed necessary. When we turn to more recent developments, however, we seem as far as ever from a single, harmonious, unified national culture. We are bedevilled by ongoing debates about Native rights, what constitutes a "nation," the limits of multiculturalism, same-sex marriage, and so on. This suggests that, in fact, there are deep fractures or divisions in Canadian society. One way to look at these fractures is in terms of different political cultures within society, in conflict with one another.

Why is Canada so politically fragmented? At least part of the answer can be found when we look more closely at three key dynamics of Canadian society: Quebec nationalism and relations between the English and French in this country; the ongoing vitality of regionalism; and the pull of continentalism.

When the English General Wolfe defeated his French counterpart, Marquis de Montcalm, on the Plains of Abraham at Quebec City on September 13, 1759, the immediate problem facing the French was how to sustain a viable francophone culture under British rule. The solution presented itself in the form of the Quebec Act of 1774, whereby the French were permitted to retain their religion and legal traditions—their culture—in return for not supporting the Americans in their revolution against the English.[31] These rights remain intact, are at the root of Canada's linguistic duality, and are the chief instruments of the survival of Canada's francophone community. Those rights, along with the expanding shield of the provincial government, have formed the historical basis of Quebec's political self-definition as a "nation" and, by extension, the moral claim to national self-determination (see Box 2.2).

---

**BOX 2.2** | **The Government Recognizes Quebec as a Nation**

On November 27, 2006, the House of Commons passed the following motion, introduced by Prime Minister Stephen Harper: "That this House recognizes that the Québécois form a nation within a united Canada." The motion passed by a vote of 266 to 16 with all Conservatives, most Liberals, the NDP, and the Bloc Québécois voting in favour.

---

Describing Canada as "two nations within a single state" focuses attention on the historic role that anglophone–francophone relations and conflicts have played in the evolution of Canadian political culture. Language, however, is but one aspect of political culture, and it is clear that other relevant regional divisions also shape the collective lives of Canadians in significant ways. In fact, some observers have gone so far as to suggest that Canadian politics is the politics of regions.

Evidence of the political importance of regions is all around us. Imagine, for instance, that you are the prime minister and you want to form a Cabinet composed of the best and the brightest of your Members of Parliament. But there is a long-standing tradition of taking regional representatives into the federal Cabinet: for example, by making sure the minister of Fisheries is from the Atlantic region or British Columbia, that the minister of Agriculture is from the Prairies, that the minister of Finance is from Toronto or Montreal, and so on. Think about the way debates about the distribution of economic resources take place: why does Ontario want lower oil prices while the Western provinces want higher ones? Think of the regional orientation of the party system. We have had up to five political parties represented in the House of Commons at any one time. There were four parties in the 2004, 2006, and 2008 elections, but none had enough support country-wide to form a majority. Indeed, one of those parties, the Bloc Québécois, does not even try to run candidates in all parts of the country. In these and a thousand other ways, regionalism intrudes on Canadian political life and must be accommodated within the workings of public administration.

Regionalism is partly a function of patterns of immigration and settlement. Different groups of people have settled in different parts of the country at various times in our history, reinforcing the regional nature of the political culture. But immigration and settlement are also a function of economics. Regional differences in economic activity have contributed to the development of regional political cultures. Innis was among the earliest proponents of this view. In the industrialized heartland of Quebec and Ontario, the occupational mix of working populations is quite different from that found in the Prairies, the Atlantic provinces, or British Columbia, all of which rely heavily on resource-based economic activities or staples. Economies that over-rely on staples are subject to the fluctuations of world demand for their products, a factor over which they have no control. The regional economies fluctuate in terms of prosperity at different rates and times depending on the particular economic base of the region. Thus, while some regions enjoy prosperity, others falter, and the uneven performance of different segments of the Canadian economy aggravates regional political differences.

What is the importance of the regional dynamic of political culture for the political community as a whole? One thing it does is frustrate the development of a strong national political community. First, there is the bare fact of electoral arithmetic: about 60 percent of Canada's population lives in only two of the provinces, which means that the votes in that region carry enormous electoral weight; they can make or break nationally elected governments. This can only contribute to a feeling of alienation and powerlessness among Canadians in regions other than Quebec and Ontario, who have few reasons to believe that their influence will be felt nationally.

Second, it has been argued that Canada's particular style of a federal parliamentary institution tends to aggravate rather than moderate regional divisions. The fact that Canada's Senate is an appointed body, in the first place, decreases the legitimacy of the institution. And the fact that the appointment process is highly politicized—that is, often based on political patronage rather than on merit—is another blow to the Senate's legitimacy. The Senate's seeming ineffectuality in the main task for which it was created, representing regional interests, also decreases respect for the institution and creates the feeling among regional populations that they are without an effective champion in Ottawa's halls of power.

**Party discipline** is a third institutional practice that frustrates balanced regional representation and hence the development of a national political community. In the British parliamentary tradition that Canada follows, party discipline is central to the workings of **responsible government**, which is government in which the prime minister and Cabinet are accountable to, and can be removed by a majority of, the legislature. While MPs from various regions may try to influence their colleagues on the merits of a certain course of action for their region, they have few real opportunities to place the interests of their region over those of the party, due to party discipline.

However, there is another contextual dynamic at work: namely, Canada's continental location, which also obscures the evolution of a strong and easily identifiable political culture. The United States dominates the North American continent in a multiplicity of ways: its population size, the power of its economy, the vitality of its cultural institutions, and so on. Most recently, questions related to the security of the continent in the wake of September 11, 2001, have brought to the fore issues of identity and sovereignty.

The extent of Canada's economic ties to the United States is astonishing. Canada and the United States have the largest single trading relationship in the entire world. Since the Second World War, U.S. direct and indirect investment in Canada has grown to account for more than 75 percent of all foreign investment in the country. Furthermore, U.S. control over a variety of key industrial sectors, such as fuels, rubber, chemicals, transportation, and others, is remarkably high. U.S. enterprises account for more than 60 percent of the Canadian manufacturing sector, for example. Virtually no other free and sovereign country in the world has permitted this kind of foreign economic domination of its domestic economy. Our ambivalence as a nation about these issues is apparent through the lens of public administration. Free trade with the United States was a central issue in the 1911 election, in the late 1940s, and in the 1980s and 1990s. In the past 25 years, we have seen the Canadian government create an agency to *monitor and limit* foreign direct investment in Canada (the Foreign Investment Review Agency), then replace it with an agency that *facilitates and welcomes* it (Investment Canada).[32]

This U.S. penetration of Canada is, of course, a mixed blessing. Undoubtedly, Canada enjoys a high standard of living partly because of high levels of American investment; but at the same time, the levels and types of U.S. investment in Canada have limited the abilities of the Canadian government to exercise complete control over domestic economic policy making. Indeed, it has been suggested that with the progressive integration of Canada into the U.S. economy, Canada has become little more than a branch plant of the United States.[33] The **Free Trade Agreement (FTA)** and its successor, the **North American Free Trade Agreement (NAFTA)**, according to this view, simply provide the institutional mechanism to continue this process. Some also argue that the continentalization of the economy both undermines Canadian political sovereignty and erodes the distinctiveness of Canada's social and cultural fabric. Consequently, some have called NAFTA Canada's "real constitution."[34]

Economics have had a major effect on the continentalization of Canada, but it is difficult to precisely measure the extent to which they have consequences for political and cultural life in Canada. Supporters of the FTA and NAFTA argue that these are merely economic agreements with no impact on politics or culture. They are simply tools to enhance the nation's economic well-being and strength. Nor is it possible to measure the extent to which Canadians have absorbed American values. But certainly economic ties, proximity, population distribution, and the fact that a majority of Canadians share a language with Americans means that U.S. cultural values are easily transmitted to Canadians.

What else shows the distinctiveness of Canadian political culture?[35] Researchers have noted the apparent absence of a strong or consistent relationship between class and vote in Canada. In other words, Canadians do not tend to support political parties that appeal to them on the basis of which class they belong to. A second significant finding is the apparent weakness of left–right orientations within the population. In other words, Canadians do not generally think of themselves in ideological terms in relation to the political system—although this may be changing.

Until recently, a common observation was that one thing that Canada shares with other nations is a citizenry that demonstrates a great deal of political trust, which is reflected in a fairly high regard for those who govern; but this, too, seems to be changing. It has been noted that Canadians were more likely to defer to authority figures than were citizens of the U.S. and publics in other industrial countries, but that recently there has been a "decline in deference" among Canadians.[36] Canadians and Americans are also quite different in their attitude toward the role of government in society and the economy: Canadians have a much more positive view of the state.

Despite the linguistic and regional differences that raise substantial obstacles to developing an easily identifiable national political identity, and despite the powerful pull of continental forces, there are distinctive, discernible political values that together delineate Canadian political culture. But what is the relationship of political culture to the other topics raised in this chapter, such as democracy and power? This is the concern of the next section.

# The Interplay of Democracy, Political Culture, and the Institutions of Public Administration

While chapter 5 looks at some of the key actors and institutions of public administration, a brief introduction is included here in the context of our discussion of democracy. Specifically, we are interested in how the interplay of democracy and political culture produces certain types of institutions, and in turn how those institutions contribute to democracy and political culture. Rather than viewing the relationship as one-way and linear, then, we will look at the interplay between these things as circular and mutually reinforcing.

## The Canadian Constitution

The Constitution, both the written document and the unwritten set of conventions that accompany it, is the guidepost of society. It is the supreme law of the land, embodying the fundamental beliefs and values of a society, such as democracy and freedom. Any constitution typically does three things: it orders the relationship between the state and its citizens; it orders the relationships among citizens; and, in a federal system such as Canada's, it orders the relationships among the different levels of government. It is within the parameters set by the Constitution that public administration takes place.

The Canadian Constitution has evolved to reflect changing conditions in Canadian society. For example, the British North America Act, 1867, set out a division of powers between the federal government and the provinces that reflected the roles of the state in the latter half of the nineteenth century, and it sketched out the responsibilities of some of the government's major institutions. It is perhaps a testament to the flexibility of the original constitutional agreement that it has been formally amended only 18 times. Strikingly, most constitutional change has occurred outside the written Constitution, through alterations to the informal traditions and customs known as *constitutional conventions*, as well as to the common law. For example, the prime minister is clearly the most powerful figure in government, yet nowhere are the duties and responsibilities of this post spelled out in the BNA Act. They have evolved largely through habit and tradition, rather than in formal written constitutional rules.

The most significant amendment to the Constitution came in 1982, when it was patriated (that is, brought home from Great Britain, where it had resided as an ordinary statute of the British Parliament), and a **Charter of Rights and Freedoms** was added to it. The addition of the Charter most obviously signalled changing attitudes in the Canadian political culture about democracy, the role of the state, and the relationship of citizens to government.[37] The Charter has spawned a whole new set of issues for public administration, including, for example, whether the judges who interpret the legality of legislation through the Charter are, in fact, usurping Parliament's traditional role.[38] This alleged "politicization" of the judges resurfaced as a controversial topic in 2007 when Prime Minister Harper changed the process of judicial appointments, apparently to ensure that individuals with more socially conservative views could be appointed to the judiciary.[39] Citizens have embraced the Charter to protect their basic freedoms (of conscience and religion, association, and peaceful assembly), as well as basic legal rights (such as the right to be secure against unreasonable search and seizure; and the right to life, liberty, and the security of the person). In addition, the Charter guarantees equal protection and equal benefit of the law without discrimination based on race, national or ethnic origin, colour, religion, sex, age, or mental or physical disability. All these and other rights specified in the Charter are only subject to such reasonable limits by law as can be demonstrably justified in a free and democratic society. The catalogue of rights and freedoms strongly reflects the prevailing political culture, and their protection has had a profound effect on the practice of public administration, in that government institutions and public servants have had to conform in policy and behaviour to the Charter.

## The North American Free Trade Agreement

The great debate that raged in Canada around the 1988 election concerning free trade was deeply resonant of the political culture of the country and touches on all aspects of public administration. Essentially, the nationalists who opposed the signing of a free trade agreement with the United States argued that Canada's national identity was at risk if it submitted to the lure of the U.S. empire. They argued that as Canada integrated itself economically with the United States, it would only be a matter of time before Canada was culturally and politically integrated as well. Continentalists scoffed at these charges, arguing that the Free Trade Agreement was nothing more than an economic arrangement that would bring enhanced economic wealth and opportunity to Canada. It had nothing to do with sovereignty, or political or national identity.[40] The continentalists prevailed, and the FTA was signed into law in 1989. It was extended to Mexico in 1990 and rechristened NAFTA. Its provisions created a tariff-free border among Canada, the United States, and Mexico, and improved market access in areas such as services, agriculture, and resources. But NAFTA does much more than this. It entrenches a supranational dispute resolution process that requires the Canadian government to sacrifice decision-making powers over the economy to a commission. Canada also cannot act unilaterally in certain policy initiatives; instead, it must give advance notice of its intentions to its partners. Moreover, Canada cannot apply traditional trade remedies in the event of a dispute with the United States or Mexico. Thus, some have argued that NAFTA is a new pillar in the constitution of the country that constrains the state from taking certain policy actions. Moreover, in political culture terms, the free trade debate has become a flash point for those who argue for the supremacy of the free market versus those who argue for a positive, interventionist state—all of which has a direct impact on public administration.[41]

## Federalism

The Canadian Constitution divides jurisdiction between a federal government and provincial governments (municipal governments fall under the jurisdiction of the provinces). Why don't we have a unitary system with just one government? The Fathers of Confederation struck a bargain in 1867, in which the rights of linguistic and religious minorities would be protected. The only practical way they could do that was to create two levels of government and divide jurisdiction between the two. The federal government was given the majority of powers to construct and maintain the national economy, while the provinces were given powers to safeguard local social and cultural issues.

Clearly, the decision to divide powers in this way reflects the political culture of the country at the time; it has also had a lasting effect on public administration. One inescapable issue that continuously resurfaces is the French presence in Canada. At the same time, though, we must consider the other regions of Canada that are acknowledged through the Constitution and federal system. Ultimately, federalism is based on the desire to balance regional interests with a sense of national unity. Concretely, it tries to do this through sections 91, 92, and 95 of the Constitution Act, 1867. Section 91 lists powers that are the exclusive preserve of the federal government; section 92 lists provincial powers; and section 95 indicates that agriculture and immigration are areas of shared jurisdiction, but that in the event of a dispute, federal law prevails.

Conflict between the two levels over this division of powers is endemic in Canadian federalism. The resolution of disputes can occur in one of two main ways. The two levels of government can sit down at the bargaining table and talk through their problems, a process that necessarily gives a prominent role to provincial premiers as the spokespersons for regional interests. A whole machinery of intergovernmental relations has arisen around this development, including ministries in each government responsible for relations with the other level of government, and permanent intergovernmental secretariats to coordinate relations between Ottawa and the provinces.[42] This process has come to be known as *executive federalism*, since it is the executive of each level of government (the prime minister, premiers, and Cabinet ministers, and their senior advisors) who take the lead role.[43] The second major form of dispute resolution is the courts. The role of the judiciary in federalism has been vital. In a long series of judgments since Confederation, the judges have interpreted the division of powers between the two levels of government whenever governments could not settle their differences at the bargaining table (see chapter 6). In some instances, the judges have tended to rule in favour of the provinces, shifting the pendulum of power toward a decentralized form of federalism. In other instances, they have upheld Ottawa's position, contributing toward a centralized federal system. In any event, the role of the judiciary has been key to shaping the federal system.[44]

## The Parliamentary Actors

One of the elemental questions of public administration is, Who decides? Who decides, for example, that tuition is going to be increased? Did you? Who decides that we should purchase sophisticated helicopters for the Canadian navy at a cost of some $5 billion? Did you? Who decided that we should forgo a national, universally accessible day-care system? Did you? Who decided that we should enter into a free trade agreement with the U.S. and extend it to Mexico? Did you? Who decided that the community-based policing model is the preferable approach to dealing with modern crime problems? Did you?

Perhaps the facile answer is that our elected politicians decide these things; but a sophisticated analysis reveals that the waters of public administration run much deeper than this. There is a whole legion of players, some known to us, but most not, that makes these decisions. Who are these people? How public is the process of public administration? Do we as ordinary citizens have access to the decision-making process in any meaningful way? Do we even understand the stages of the decision-making process? We will begin with the *parliamentary actors* within government that influence public administration. They include the executive (which includes the public service), legislative, and judicial branches of government. We will then look at the *extra-parliamentary actors*: that is, the individuals, groups, and organizations that influence public administration from outside government. These include political parties, interest groups, social movements, and the media.

**The Executive** What is the **executive** branch of government? It is first the Crown, represented in Canada by the Governor General, whose role has evolved into a purely symbolic one. The prime minister and the Cabinet compose the politically significant parts of the executive branch. Together, they direct and control the public service, which is also part of the executive. (These relationships are presented in more detail in chapter 5). The prime minister and the Cabinet are the key decision-makers. Together they initiate policy and legislation, and have their hands on the purse strings of government. Cabinet is organized into committees, and its overall work is coordinated by powerful bodies called central agencies.

Of course, the prime minister and Cabinet do not act alone or in isolation. They are supported and assisted by a veritable army of public servants, whose job it is to proffer advice and carry out the decisions of their political masters. This largely faceless, nameless cast of thousands is headed by senior officials who not only administer on behalf of their political masters, but also influence the policy process with their advice and actions. Among the important issues this raises is this: to whom are they accountable? We need to understand how an appointed authority, such as the public service, can be held accountable and is reconcilable to a system of responsible government. This raises all sorts of thorny questions. For example, if there is a major screw-up or scandal in the government, as with the infamous Sponsorship Program scandal, who would you hold responsible? Is it the minister who heads the department? Or is it the public servant who gave bad advice? Furthermore, how responsive is this massive bureaucratic machine to individual citizens and interest groups? Is it just the wealthy and powerful who have the wherewithal to gain access to the corridors of power? What about ordinary citizens, who may lack the financial resources, organizational skills, or sophisticated knowledge and understanding of how government works? These questions have important implications for public administration and democracy.

**The Legislature** We also must consider the role of the **legislature** in the Canadian political system. After all, is this not what democracy is all about? We elect representatives to take our concerns to Parliament, where free and open debate about the merits of different positions takes place, and decisions are taken and passed into law on the basis of what is good for Canadians. This is typical of what many Canadians think the legislature is and what it does.

The Canadian Parliament is based on the British model. It consists of two parts: the elected House of Commons, and the appointed Senate. Given that the Senate is appointed, it generally lacks legitimacy in the eyes of most Canadians. Its members are appointed by the prime minister, usually as a reward for faithful service; it is thus a major vestige of patronage. The Senate was originally meant to fulfill two roles: a forum for regional interests, and a voice to protect minority rights. As to the second function, the requirement that a citizen own property before being considered for membership in the Senate ensured that it became a preserve of the well-off, but as Sir John A. Macdonald noted, the Senate should protect minorities—and the rich are always a minority. Macdonald also saw the Senate as a forum for "sober second thought." This attitude reflects the elitist political culture that is cautious and conservative and wary of the democratizing influences of the House of Commons. As for defending regional interests, the Senate has failed miserably in this regard. Since, proportionately, Ontario and Quebec have the most seats in the Senate, central Canadian interests have tended to prevail there—hence the calls emanating particularly from Western Canada to reform the Senate on the lines of a triple-E model: elected, equal, and effective. In addition, recent attempts at reform by the Harper government have included limiting senator's terms of office, which currently run from appointment to age 75.

The House of Commons is where most of the action is. Democratically elected in one of 308 geographically defined constituencies, each Member of Parliament (MP) is charged with holding the government to account. He or she does this by supporting or opposing the party that has the majority of seats. This is the essence of responsible government. The party with the most seats, whose leader is the prime minister, is primarily responsible for initiating policy, especially through the powers of taxing and spending. That party only retains power so long as it retains the support of the majority in the House. This would appear to give ordinary MPs a tremendous amount of leverage and power, but the practice of party discipline constrains them. This is the convention whereby MPs vote in the House according to the wishes of their leaders. In this way, some stability is achieved in government, and the business of passing laws is facilitated. But this also means that in many circumstances ordinary MPs are caught between a rock and a hard place: that is, they are forced to support their leader even when their constituents demand they act otherwise. Failure to subscribe to the rules of party discipline can mean a short and inglorious parliamentary career: rogue MPs are denied promotion to Cabinet minister or any of the other perks and privileges that the prime minister dishes out to ensure loyalty. The dominance of the executive branch over the legislative branch is firmly entrenched.[45]

This is not to suggest that Parliament is completely toothless and ineffectual. Legislators do play an important role in holding the executive accountable through mechanisms such as question period in the House of Commons, through various legislative committees that investigate government policies, and through the actions of the opposition parties in mobilizing public opinion. In addition, the power of the legislature is elevated under conditions of minority government when prime ministers have to pay more attention to the desires of MPs in order to ensure the government is not defeated prematurely.[46] But, overall, it is best to regard Parliament as a *law-passing* body rather than as a *law-making* body, whose role is secondary to that of the executive.

Can Parliament control the prime minister and Cabinet, or keep the public service accountable for its actions? Should the Senate be reformed, or should we just abolish it and put it out of its misery? Does Parliament respond to the needs of ordinary citizens? Where party discipline is concerned, should MPs be allowed to vote according to their conscience—assuming they have one? Should they be allowed more free votes in the House of Commons? Or does this pose a threat to the underpinnings of responsible government? All these questions animate public administration where these parliamentary actors are concerned.

**The Judiciary** The courts and the judges constitute the third branch of government in Canada: the **judiciary**. Judges are appointed rather than elected. The top court is the Supreme Court of Canada, which became so only in 1949. Prior to this, the **Judicial Committee of the Privy Council**, a British body of law lords, was the final court of appeal for Canadian judicial cases.

The judicial branch of government is important to public administration in two ways. First, it is responsible for interpreting constitutional law.[47] The judges are asked to make judgments on two broad types of issues. The first involves the division of powers in the Constitution. They are asked to determine whether a law passed by one level of government is within its jurisdiction as spelled out in the Constitution. If it infringes on the jurisdiction of the other level of government, the courts rule that it is ultra vires and, therefore, illegal. If it does not infringe on the other level of government, the courts rule that it is intra vires, or legal. As well, since the introduction of the Charter of Rights and Freedoms in 1982, the courts have been asked to rule on the constitutionality of laws related to human rights.

The second way that the judicial branch is important to public administration is through its responsibility for the area of administrative law.[48] This means that the judges are required to ensure that public servants do not overstep the law in fulfilling their duties and obligations, that regulations are followed according to the rules and procedures set out in legislation, that citizen rights are not abridged or denied in the process of carrying out the instructions of government, and that penalties are levied for violations of administrative procedure and process.

## The Extra-Parliamentary Actors

**Political Parties** The traditional view of political parties in Canada is that they play an important role in recruiting political leaders, and that they aggregate and articulate disparate interests, which are then mobilized for electoral purposes.[49] In Canada, the political party system has evolved from two dominant parties (the Liberals and the Progressive Conservatives) to three (with the addition of the

New Democratic Party) to a multiparty system with as many as five parties holding seats in Parliament at any one time. Parties are a particularly important reflection of the political culture. For example, the Liberals and Conservatives—the only two parties to form the government at the federal level—have usually been viewed as "brokerage parties" engaged in the task of downplaying divisions within Canadian society and forging the broadest possible coalition of voters to win power. This typically means pitching their appeal to the region with the most votes: central Canada. They are often regarded as subsuming principles to the pursuit of power, which has resulted in a range of "protest parties" emerging. These include the NDP and its predecessor, the Co-operative Commonwealth Federation (CCF), as well as the Social Credit Party, the Progressives, and several others. Regionalism is mirrored in the party system, as we can see from the rise of the Western-based Reform Party (which became the Canadian Alliance, which then merged with the Progressive Conservative Party to become the Conservative Party), and the Bloc Québécois, exclusively rooted in Quebec.

Elections and political parties are, of course, central to our general understanding of democracy in Canada. But think about parties in political culture terms. They reflect a political culture in which class issues are subordinated to issues of language and region (and earlier in our history, religion). Moreover, low participation by Canadians in the party system reflects our tendency to defer to elites. We lack the kind of mass populism that characterizes party systems in some other countries. Parties generate policy ideas, but these are rarely acted on unless they have the support of the leadership of the parties. In other words, they do not tend to reflect "grassroots" democracy. Still, parties are the key organizational variable in the House of Commons, as we saw earlier in the section on party discipline.

**Interest Groups** Interest groups are organizations of like-minded individuals that attempt to further their common interests by affecting public policy. Increasingly, they seem to dominate the policy-making process in Canada.[50] They arise as a result of citizens banding together to promote their own interests, but they often end up in conflict with other groups doing the same thing. All these competing groups try to get the attention of bureaucratic and political decision-makers. Almost every imaginable interest in Canadian society is represented by organized groups; you yourself are probably a member of several such groups at any one time. Besides the major business and labour groups, there are hundreds of organizations representing women, students, environmentalists, seniors, Aboriginals, farmers, musicians and artists, religions, and so on. The term *social movement* is generally applied to those groups with a social policy orientation, an increasing number of which have appeared in the political system in the past 30 years.

Clearly, though, not all interest groups are equal in their influence. As a result, it is perhaps overstating the case to say that the system of interest groups represents the pinnacle of democracy in large, complex modern societies, since everyone can be represented. Some groups are well-funded, institutionalized, and have the resources to pursue their interests effectively. Others, though, are just the opposite. They lack financial resources, knowledge of who the key decision-makers are, and how to get to them. This is not to say that they are totally ineffective, but clearly the odds of success are improved if you have the wherewithal to play the game well. Typically, business groups have the resources at their disposal to target decision-makers and public opinion at the same time; thus the ideological dominance of business values is reinforced through the interest group system. Athough business interests do not "win" on every issue they try to influence, clearly their position is predominant in the constellation of interest groups trying to influence public administration.

It is perhaps axiomatic that a society that values free association should feature interest-group politics. Interest groups provide important services to their members, but are also oriented toward influencing policy-making by advocating change or mobilizing to prevent change unfavourable to their interests. Interest groups also provide expert knowledge and information to policy-makers and often support governments sympathetic to their aims. They target Cabinet ministers and senior public servants as well as ordinary MPs. They use techniques such as personal lobbying, public information campaigns, the media, protests, and other tactics to get their messages across. Recent concerns over undue influence have prompted legislative reform to control the activities of interest groups, by requiring lobbyists to register themselves with the government and prohibiting public servants who quit their jobs from immediately turning around and lobbying their old departments.

**The Media** Finally, we need to consider the role of the media and its influence on public administration.[51] Again, political culture reveals that Canada is a society that values freedom of speech and a free press as a cornerstone of democracy. Hence the media plays an important role as a purveyor of information as well as of political attitudes and values. The media is constantly engaged in a process of defining what is political and of setting political discourse—that is, the way we talk about politics.

The media plays an extremely important role in matters such as selecting and evaluating political leaders. As well, the media plays a key role in the communication functions of government. It should be noted, however, that the media carries its own set of biases, contrary to the widely held view that the media is objective. This means that what the media chooses not to report can be every bit as important as what it chooses to report. In this way the media helps set the agenda for public discussion and debate, legitimizing certain actors and institutions and conferring or withholding status.

In the context of a nation that sits next door to the most powerful media empire on earth, a whole other set of issues becomes important, such as the Americanization of Canada and the national identity question. The decision to have a public broadcasting network, the CBC, was in part a reaction to this reality. Moreover, the regulatory regime that has been developed in Canada concerning the media is complex and contains many contentious issues. Should the CBC be privatized? Do we need Canadian content regulations as stipulated by the Canadian Radio-television and Telecommunications Commission (CRTC)? Should Canadian magazines be protected from U.S. competition? Should the reporting of poll results be restricted during elections? Should the internet and new social media be regulated and if so, how? All these questions, and many others, imply that the role, function, and place of the media are issues of ongoing concern for public administration.

## WHAT YOU HAVE LEARNED

We began this chapter with some basic concepts: *power, politics, democracy, state,* and *government*. Each term, while susceptible to a variety of interpretations, plays an important part in the world of Canadian public administration. We then examined some related questions to demystify Canadian public administration and its democratic context. It is important to draw connections between *what* happens, *how* it happens, *to* whom it happens, and *why* it happens. This helps us understand how power is exercised in Canada, who has it, and who lacks it. Furthermore, by introducing the topic of political culture and its interplay with democracy and public administration, we can begin to see the basis of power relations within society and the importance of values, such as equality and freedom.

This chapter considered how the concept of democracy relates to the theory and practice of public administration in Canada. Finally, the context of public administration was assessed by examining the issues of the constitution, NAFTA, federalism, and the key parliamentary and extra-parliamentary actors who play a role in public administration in Canada.

### Key Words and Concepts

| | |
|---|---|
| power (28) | responsible government (44) |
| authority (28) | FTA (45) |
| traditional legitimacy (28) | NAFTA (45) |
| charismatic legitimacy (28) | Charter of Rights and Freedoms (46) |
| legal-rational legitimacy (28) | executive (49) |
| rule of law (28) | legislature (50) |
| direct democracy (31) | judiciary (51) |
| representative democracy (31) | Judicial Committee of the Privy |
| political culture (37) | Council (51) |
| party discipline (44) | interest groups (52) |

### Review Questions

The chapter was divided into five sections. You should now be able to address the following set of questions:

*1. Power, Politics, and Public Administration*
You should now know something about democracy, power, and politics. Ask yourself: What is the relationship between power and politics? How are issues moved from the private to the public realm?

2. *What Is Democracy?*
After reading this section, ask yourself: What is the importance of democratic theory in public administration? What kinds of democracy are there, and which pertain most to Canadian public administration?

3. *State and Government*
Ask yourself: What is the difference between state and government, and how is each important to public administration?

4. *Political Culture*
In explaining the nature of democracy and governance, ask yourself: What is political culture? What theories help us understand it? And how does it influence public administration? What is the relationship of political culture to democracy and to the institutions of governing in Canada?

5. *The Interplay of Democracy, Political Culture, and the Institutions of Public Administration*
Ask yourself, how do both parliamentary and extra-parliamentary actors influence and exercise power in the state and government in Canada? What impact does the Canadian constitution have on the relations of power within Canadian public administration?

## Weblinks

Canadian Political Science Association
**www.cpsa-acsp.ca**

Mapleleafweb
**www.mapleleafweb.com**

Democracy Watch
**www.dwatch.ca**

Elections Canada
**www.elections.ca**

Parliament of Canada
**www.parl.gc.ca**

Supreme Court of Canada
**www.scc-csc.gc.ca**

## Further Reading

1. *Power, Politics, and Public Administration*
Almond, Gabriel. *Comparative Politics: A Theoretical Framework*. New York: HarperCollins, 1993.
Brodie, Janine. "Power and Politics," in Janine Brodie and Sandra Rein, eds., *Critical Concepts: An Introduction to Politics*, 3rd ed. Toronto: Pearson Prentice Hall, 2005: 2–20.
Easton, David. *A Framework for Political Analysis*. Englewood Cliffs, NJ: Prentice Hall, 1965.

## 2. What Is Democracy?

Dahl, Robert. *Democracy and Its Critics*. New Haven: Yale University Press, 1989.

Schmitter, Philippe C., and Terry Lynn Karl. "What Democracy Is . . . And Is Not," in George A. MacLean and Brenda O'Neill, eds., *Ideas, Interests and Issues: Readings in Introductory Politics*. Toronto: Pearson Prentice Hall, 2006: 166–76.

## 3. State and Government

Clement, Wallace, ed. *Understanding Canada: Building on the New Canadian Political Economy*. Kingston: McGill–Queen's University Press, 1997.

Miliband, Ralph. *The State in Capitalist Society: The Analysis of the Western System of Power*. London: Quartet, 1973.

Panitch, Leo, ed. *The Canadian State: Political Economy and Political Power*. Toronto: University of Toronto Press, 1977.

## 4. Political Culture

Ball, Terence, Richard Dagger, William Christian, and Colin Campbell. *Political Ideologies and the Democratic Ideal*. Canadian ed. Toronto: Pearson, 2006.

Bell, David V.J. "Political Culture in Canada," in Michael S. Whittington and Glen Williams, eds., *Canadian Politics in the 21st Century*, 7th ed. Toronto: Thomson Nelson, 2008: 228–59.

Pye, Lucian W., and Sidney Verba, eds. *Political Culture and Political Development*. Princeton: Princeton University Press, 1965.

## 5. The Interplay of Democracy, Political Culture, and the Institutions of Public Administration

Bradford, Neil. *Commissioning Ideas: Canadian National Policy Innovation in Comparative Perspective*. Toronto: Oxford University Press, 1998.

Nevitte, Neil, and Mebs Kanji. "'New' Cleavages, Value Diversity, and Democratic Governance," in James Bickerton and Alain-G. Gagnon, eds., *Canadian Politics*, 4th ed. Peterborough: Broadview, 2004: 79–97.

Simeon, Richard, and David Elkins. "Regional Political Cultures in Canada." *Canadian Journal of Political Science*, 7, 3 (1974): 397–437.

# Endnotes

1. Max Weber, "Politics as a Vocation," in H.W. Gerth and C. Wright Mills, eds., *From Max Weber: Essays in Sociology*, (New York: Oxford University Press, 1958): 79.

2. For different systems of public administration, see United Nations, Public Administration Programme Public Administration Country Profiles, **www.unpan.org/ DPADM/ ProductsServices/ThematicPortals/ PublicAdministrationCountryProfiles/ tabid/677/Default.aspx**.

3. Larry Johnston, *Politics: An Introduction to the Modern Democratic State* (Peterborough: Broadview, 1997): 15; emphasis in the original.

4. David Easton, *Systems Analysis of Political Life* (New York: John Wiley, 1965): 21.

5. Harold D. Laswell, *Politics: Who Gets What, When and How* (New York: McGraw-Hill, 1936).

6. V.I. Lenin, "Left Wing Communism: An Infantile Disorder," in *Selected Works*, (New York: International Publishers, 1943).

7. See Mao Tse Tung, *The Political Thought of Mao Tse Tung*, ed. Stuart Schram (New York: Frederick A. Praeger, 1969): 287.

8. Cited in James John Guy, *People, Politics and Government: A Canadian Perspective*, 4th ed. (Scarborough: Prentice Hall, 1998): 2.

9. Karl Marx and Frederick Engels, "The Communist Manifesto," in Arthur P. Mendel, ed., *The Essential Works of Marxism* (New York: Bantam, 1961).

10. For an overview of the role of women in the public service, see Caroline Andrew, "Women and the Public Sector," in Christopher Dunn, ed., *The Handbook of Canadian Public Administration*, 2nd ed. (Toronto: Oxford University Press, 2010): 319–29.

11. Camilla Stivers, *Gender Images in Public Administration* (Newbury Park, CA: Sage, 1993): 4. See also Susan D. Phillips, "Discourse, Identity and Voice: Feminist Contributions to Policy Studies," in Laurent Dobuzinskis, Michael Howlett, and David Laycock, eds., *Policy Studies in Canada: The State of the Art* (Toronto: University of Toronto Press, 1996): 242–65.

12. See Leo Panitch and Donald Swartz, *From Consent to Coercion: The Assault on Trade Union Freedoms*, 3rd ed. (Toronto: Garamond, 2003).

13. See Darin Barney, *Communication Technology* (Vancouver: UBC Press, 2005); Ronald J. Diebert, "Civil Society Activism on the World Wide Web: The Case of the Anti-MAI Lobby," in David R. Cameron and Janice Gross Stein, eds., *Street Protests and Fantasy Parks: Globalization, Culture and the State* (Vancouver: UBC Press, 2002): 88–108; and Cynthia Alexander and Leslie Pal, eds., *Digital Democracy: Policy and Politics in the Wired World* (Toronto: Oxford University Press, 1998).

14. Henry B. Mayo, *An Introduction to Democratic Theory* (New York: Oxford University Press, 1960): 70.

15. Gabriel A. Almond and Sidney Verba, *The Civic Culture* (Princeton, NJ: Princeton University Press, 1963).

16. See C.B. Macpherson, *The Real World of Democracy* (Toronto: CBC Enterprises, 1965).

17. Max Weber, *From Max Weber: Essays in Sociology*, eds. H.H. Gerth and C. Wright Mills (New York: Oxford University Press, 1946): 78.

18. Karl Marx and Frederick Engels, "The Communist Manifesto," in Arthur P. Mendel, ed., *Essential Works of Marxism* (New York: Bantam, 1961): 15.

19. Ralph Miliband, *The State in Capitalist Society: The Analysis of the Western System of Power* (London: Quartet, 1969): 3.

20. Stephen Brooks, *Canadian Democracy: An Introduction*, 6th ed. (Toronto: Oxford University Press, 2009): 8–9.

21. Jill Vickers, *Reinventing Political Science: A Feminist Approach* (Halifax: Fernwood, 1997).

22. See Kenneth J. Meier and Laurence J. O'Toole, *Bureaucracy in a Democratic State* (Baltimore: Johns Hopkins Press, 2006).

23. See Stephen Brooks, "Canadian Political Culture," in James B. Bickerton and Alain-G.Gagnon, eds., *Canadian Politics*, 5th ed. (Toronto: University of Toronto Press, 2009): 45–70.

24. Gabriel Almond, "Comparative Political Systems," *World Politics*, 18 (1956): 396.

25. Harold Innis, *Essays in Canadian Economic History*, ed. Mary Q. Innis (Toronto: University of Toronto Press, 1956): 405.

26. For an overview, see David J. Bell, *The Roots of Disunity: A Study of Canadian Political Culture* (Toronto: Oxford University Press, 1992). See also Heather MacIvor, *Parameters of Power: Canada's Political Institutions* (Toronto: Thomson Nelson, 2006); and Nelson Wiseman, "Provincial Political Cultures," in Christopher Dunn, ed., *Provinces: Canadian Provincial Politics* (Peterborough: Broadview, 2006): 21–56.

27. Louis Hartz, *The Founding of New Societies: Studies in the History of the United States, Latin America, South Africa, Canada and Australia* (New York: Harcourt, Brace and World, 1964); see also Gad Horowitz, "Conservatism, Liberalism and Socialism in Canada: An Interpretation," *Canadian Journal of Economics and Political Science*, 32, 2 (1966): 143–77; and H.D. Forbes, "Hartz-Horowitz at Twenty: Nationalism, Toryism and Socialism in Canada and the United States," *Canadian Journal of Political Science*, 20, 2 (1987): 287–316.

28. Seymour Martin Lipset, *Continental Divide* (New York: Routledge, 1990).

29. John Porter, *The Vertical Mosaic: An Analysis of Social Class and Power in Canada* (Toronto: University of Toronto Press, 1965). See also Wallace Clement, *The Canadian Corporate Elite: An Analysis*

*of Economic Power* (Toronto: McClelland and Stewart, 1975).

30. Harold Adams Innis, *The Fur Trade in Canada: An Introduction to Canadian Economic History* (Toronto: University of Toronto Press, 1956).

31. See Bayard Reesor, *The Canadian Constitution in Historical Perspective* (Scarborough: Prentice Hall, 1992): 9.

32. See John McDougall, *Drifting Together: The Political Economy of Canada-US Integration* (Peterborough: Broadview, 2006); David M. Thomas and Barbara Boyle Torrey, eds., *Canada and the United States: Differences That Count,* 3rd ed. (Peterborough: Broadview, 2008).

33. Among the first statements of this position was Kari Levitt, *Silent Surrender: The Multinational Corporation in Canada* (Toronto: Macmillan, 1970).

34. See Stephen Clarkson, *Uncle Sam and US: Globalization, Neoconservatism and the Canadian State* (Toronto: University of Toronto Press, 2002).

35. See Michael Adams, *Sex in the Snow: Canadian Social Values at the End of the Millennium* (Toronto: Penguin, 1998). For an earlier look at this question, see Richard Simeon and David Elkins, *Small Worlds: Provinces and Parties in Canadian Political Life* (Toronto: Methuen, 1980).

36. See Neil Nevitte, *The Decline of Deference* (Peterborough: Broadview, 1996).

37. See Alan Cairns and Cynthia Williams, eds., *Constitutionalism, Citizenship and Society in Canada* (Toronto: University of Toronto Press, 1985).

38. See Raymond Bazowski, "The Judiciary and the Charter," in James B. Bickerton and Alain-G.Gagnon, eds., *Canadian Politics,* 5th ed. (Toronto: University of Toronto Press, 2009): 197–220.

39. Campbell Clark, "Harper Brushes Off Judicial Critics on Appointments," *Globe and Mail* (February 22, 2007): A5.

40. See Gregory J. Inwood, *Continentalizing Canada: The Politics and Legacy of the Macdonald Royal Commission* (Toronto: University of Toronto Press, 2005); and Jeffrey M. Ayres, *Defying Conventional Wisdom: Political Movements and Popular Contention Against North American Free Trade* (Toronto: University of Toronto Press, 1998). For arguments against free trade, see Duncan Cameron, ed., *The Free Trade Deal* (Toronto: Lorimer, 1988). For arguments in favour of free trade, see John Crispo, ed., *Free Trade: The Real Story* (Toronto: Gage, 1988). Both sides of the debate are discussed in Marc Gold and David Leyton-Brown, eds., *Trade-Offs on Free Trade* (Toronto: Carswell, 1988).

41. See Bruce Campbell and Ed Finn, eds., *Living with Uncle: Canada-US Relations in an Age of Empire* (Toronto: Lorimer, 2006).

42. See Gregory J. Inwood, Carolyn M. Johns, and Patricia L. O'Reilly, "Intergovernmental Officials in Canada," in J. Peter Meekison, Hamish Telford and Harvey Lazar, eds., *Canada: The State of the Federation 2002: Reconsidering the Institutions of Canadian Federalism* (Montreal: McGill-Queen's University Press, 2004): 249–84; and Carolyn M. Johns, Patricia L. O'Reilly, and Gregory J. Inwood, "Intergovernmental Innovation and the Administrative State in Canada," *Governance,* 19, 4 (2006): 627–49.

43. See D.V. Smiley, *The Federal Condition in Canada* (Toronto: McGraw-Hill Ryerson, 1987); and Richard Simeon, *Federal-Provincial Diplomacy: The Making of Recent Policy in Canada. With a New Preface and Postscript* (Toronto: University of Toronto Press, 2006).

44. See Peter H. Russell, *Constitutional Odyssey: Can Canadians Become a Sovereign People?* 3rd ed. (Toronto: University of Toronto Press, 2004).

45. See Donald J. Savoie, *Governing From the Centre: The Concentration of Power in Canadian Politics* (Toronto: University of Toronto Press, 1999); Donald J. Savoie, "Power at the Apex: Executive Dominance," in James B. Bickerton and Alain-G. Gagnon, eds., *Canadian Politics,* 5th ed. (Toronto: University of Toronto Press, 2009): 115–32; and Graham White, *Cabinets and First Ministers* (Vancouver: UBC Press, 2005).

46. Jennifer Smith, "Canada's Minority Parliament," in James B. Bickerton and Alain-G. Gagnon, eds., *Canadian Politics,*

5th ed. (Toronto: University of Toronto Press, 2009): 133–54.

47. See Peter H. Russell, *Leading Constitutional Decisions*, 4th ed. (Ottawa: Carleton University Press, 1987).

48. See Byron Sheldrick, "Administrative Law and Public Governance: An Overlooked Dimension of Governance," in O.P. Dwivedi, Tim A. Mau, and Byron Sheldrick, eds., *The Evolving Physiology of Government: Canadian Public Administration in Transition* (Ottawa: University of Ottawa Press, 2009): 358–79; Carl Baar and Ian Greene, "Judicial Administration," in Christopher Dunn, ed., *The Handbook of Canadian Public Administration*, 2nd ed. (Toronto: Oxford University Press, 2010): 131–45; Sara Blake, "An Introduction to Administrative Law in Canada," in Christopher Dunn, ed., *The Handbook of Canadian Public Administration* (Toronto: Oxford University Press, 2002): 466–79;

and David Phillip Jones and Anne S. de Villars, *Principles of Administrative Law*, 2nd ed. (Scarborough: Carswell, 1994).

49. See William Cross, ed., *Political Parties, Representation, and Electoral Democracy in Canada* (Toronto: Oxford University Press, 2002); Hugh G. Thorburn and Alan Whitehorn, eds., *Party Politics in Canada*, 8th ed. (Toronto: Prentice Hall, 2001).

50. See Lisa Young and Joanna Everitt, *Advocacy Groups* (Vancouver: UBC Press, 2004).

51. See Shannon Sampert and Linda Trimble, eds., *Mediating Canadian Politics* (Toronto: Pearson Canada, 2010); Paul Nesbitt-Larking, *Politics, Society and the Media: Canadian Perspectives* (Peterborough: Broadview, 2001); and Rand Dyck, *Canadian Politics: Critical Approaches*, 4th ed. (Toronto: Thompson Nelson, 2003).

# Chapter 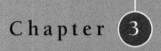 3

# Theories of Organization

## WHAT YOU WILL LEARN

In this chapter, we will focus on theoretical approaches to public administration by examining several schools of thought on bureaucratic organization. This chapter asks the following questions:

- What are the main concerns of organization theory?
- What are the origins of organization theory?
- What contesting values underlie the development of theories of public administration?
- What are the major classical theories of organization, and who were the major theorists?
- What debates have ensued over the nature and form of organization in both the private and the public sectors?
- What exactly are theoretical innovations meant to accomplish when translated into practice?

The discussion is organized around five central issues.

### 1. Perspectives on Bureaucratic Organization

This section provides a brief overview of how we can approach organizations from a theoretical perspective, and why we should do so to enhance our understanding of the development of bureaucracy and public administration over time. It notes the contribution of business management thinking and its uneasy marriage with public sector values and concerns.

## 2. The Classic Theorists

This section focuses mainly on the vital contributions of Karl Marx and Max Weber to our understanding of bureaucratic organizations. It outlines the contributions of these two great thinkers, and their influence on subsequent theorizing.

## 3. Structuralist Theories

This section looks at one of the two main schools of thought that have, historically, dominated the theories of organization literature—that is, the scientific management approach pioneered by F.W. Taylor.

## 4. Humanist Theories

Structuralist theories spawned a backlash in the form of *organizational humanism*. A variety of theorists are canvassed in this section, many associated with the famous Hawthorne experiments.

## 5. Other Theoretical Approaches

This section reveals a small sampling of some of the other significant approaches. After reading this chapter, you should have a firm grasp of the major theories of public administration and be familiar with the thinkers associated with each.

# Perspectives on Bureaucratic Organization

The literature on bureaucratic organization is rich and well developed. Indeed, there are a multiplicity of approaches to understanding the role and impacts of bureaucracies (both private and public sector).[1] You will recall from the first chapter that public bureaucracy is the organizing principle of government. Despite its pejorative reputation, it is nonetheless central to the study and practice of public administration. As American public administration scholar Robert Denhardt reminds us, "although we often think of the public bureaucracy as an impersonal mechanism, in fact, behind each of our encounters with public organizations lies a lengthy and complex chain of human events, understandings, and behaviours developed in the everyday lives of people just like us."[2]

Bureaucratic organizations are ubiquitous—that is, they exist everywhere, in all parts of our lives. When you registered in your program at university and signed up for your courses, you dealt with a bureaucratic organization. If you ran into difficulties, you might have cursed the "red tape" and bureaucratic mindset that held up the smooth processing of your registration. But chances are, you have spent little time thinking through the reasons for that red tape or the complexities of processing your application. What factors lay behind that red tape? Why is registration done the way it is done? How can the process be made more efficient? More fair? Cheaper? Quicker? More convenient? If you have ever pondered these questions (and who hasn't, while standing in line or waiting on the phone?), then you have confronted questions about the role of bureaucracy in our lives.

Most organization theory originated from studies about how to improve the management of private sector organizations, particularly large corporations. Hence, academically, organization theory is often associated with schools of business management. But issues that affect how businesses organize themselves are also of great concern to both practitioners and scholars in other disciplines, including public administration. In some cases, theories derived from business practices have been adapted to the public sector in an attempt to understand how government organizes itself. In other cases, the social sciences, and especially sociology, have developed their own unique explanations and analyses. In either case, when we talk about "organization theory," we are talking about our need to understand what people do, how things get done, and why we have organizations. A "theory" is simply a proposition or set of propositions which seek to explain or predict something—and, as psychologist Kurt Lewin once said, "There is nothing so practical as a good theory."

In the nineteenth and twentieth centuries, organizations became increasingly administered according to values of rationality, impersonality, and efficiency. If you designed an organization based on these values, what might it look like? In the public sector, other values come into play, such as democracy and fairness. Compare the design of an organization premised on rationality, impersonality, and efficiency to one based on democracy and fairness. Chances are, you would come up with two quite different animals. The problem has been how to marry these sets of values in organizations whose primary task is to serve the public interest through the formulation, implementation, and evaluation of government policies. So, in a sense, the development of the theory and practice of public administration has been the story of struggling to adapt and extend aspects of private sector management into the public sector, and blend those with theory and practice unique to the problems and opportunities of governing.

## The Classic Theorists

We begin with an overview of what might be called the "classic theorists" of bureaucracy and organizations—Karl Marx and Max Weber—as well as some other important contributors to the foundations of our thinking about organizations. The classic theorists pondered the effect on the power structure of society of the development of large-scale organizations. How does "big" government or "big" business influence a society's political life? Is bureaucracy simply an administrative apparatus designed to meet societal goals? Or does it actually come to shape those goals? Again, we find ourselves confronting the nature of the relationship between bureaucracy and democracy, first raised in chapter 1.

### Karl Marx

The first major figure in the classic school of thought is **Karl Marx** (1818–1883), for whom the concepts of **class conflict** and **alienation** were central to understanding bureaucracy. Marx was influenced in his ideas about bureaucracy by the German philosopher, G.W.F. Hegel. For Hegel, the bureaucracy represented a bridge between the state and civil society (the various interests in society outside the government itself). The state represented the overall general or common interest. The state bureaucracy, in Hegel's view, was the medium through which the transformation of the particular interest into the general interest could take place. For Hegel, the bureaucracy was in fact the "universal class" par excellence because it represented the generalized communal interest of all.

Marx rejected Hegel's characterization of the state bureaucracy. For Marx, bureaucracy was not some kind of ideal representation of the general will of society. It was more concrete than that: it was real people involved in a particular set of social relationships involving the exercise of power. Marx particularly disagreed with Hegel's conception of the bureaucracy as the "universal" element in society.

Such a notion was illusory, according to Marx, since the bureaucracy's interests were anything but universal. The bureaucracy was nothing more than a special interest in itself. It might hide behind the more dignified picture of a faithful servant of the general will and, therefore, appear somehow to be above personal interests, but reality was quite different. Whereas in society various interests struggled for possession of private property (the basis of wealth in capitalist societies), within the bureaucracy the struggle was over positions. In Marx's view, the desire to claw one's way up the bureaucratic career ladder in the quest for increased power, status, and prestige is what motivates bureaucrats.

Hegel had raised the question of how the people were to be safeguarded against abuse from bureaucratic authority. He answered by referring to **hierarchy**. The hierarchical structure of government meant that abuse by lower officials could be redressed by their superiors. Marx refuted this contention. He argued that hierarchy leads only to the punishment of officials who commit offences against the hierarchy itself; it protects the official when the hierarchy commits an offence against the people. Hierarchy, then, was far more likely to abuse citizens than were the petty actions of lower officials.

Marx's theory is distinctive because bureaucracy is not seen as merely an unfortunate tumour on the otherwise healthy body of the state but, rather, as inherent and inseparable from that body itself. In a capitalist society, Marx said, the role of the bureaucracy was to maintain the class distinctions and domination that sustained the rule of the business class. At the same time, the bureaucracy must mask this domination by presenting itself as representing the general interest. To maintain this facade, it must retain a certain degree of **autonomy** (freedom of action) from the ruling business class. Because of this autonomy, the bureaucracy occasionally acts in a way that may appear to counter the interests of the business class; but, overall, the bureaucracy will always act in the long-term interests of the capitalist class, since its main purpose is to sustain the power of the dominant class. Bureaucracy serves as an instrument of rule from above, institutionally detached from the mass of the people it is ostensibly designed to serve.

The concept of alienation is a major aspect of Marx's views; he saw bureaucracy as one of the primary institutions responsible for it. Bureaucracy is felt by most citizens as a distant, impersonal, and oppressive force—a perception promoted by bureaucrats themselves through the invention of special myths and symbols that make the bureaucracy a bewildering institution that compels compliance. More-over, alienation occurs not just between citizens and the bureaucracy, but also within the bureaucracy itself. The true nature of the bureaucracy is hidden from itself so that those occupying its posts view their jobs as essential rather than as oppressive or parasitic, as Marx would contend. This image is sustained within the bureaucracy by hierarchy, discipline, and authority, all of which promote alienation among bureaucrats themselves. For Marx, bureaucracy stifled its workers' initiative and imagination while reinforcing the fear of taking any responsibility and risk (see Box 3.1).

## BOX 3.1  Karl Marx on Bureaucracy

In his *Critique of Hegel's* Philosophy of Right (1843–44), Marx outlines the true character of bureaucracy and presents ideas that would be expanded upon later by the other great classic theorist, Max Weber. Marx wrote,

*Authority is . . . the principle of its knowledge . . . authority is its mentality. But inside the bureaucracy itself spiritualism becomes a crass materialism, faith in authority, mechanization of a fixed and formal behaviour, fixed principles, views, and traditions. As far as the individual bureaucrat is concerned, the state's ends*

*become his private ends, namely, chasing after higher posts and carving out a career. . . . The state continues to exist only as various bureau mentalities con-nected by relations of subordination and passive obedience.*

*The universal spirit of bureaucracy is secrecy, the mystery, which it secures internally by hierarchy, and against exter-nal groups by its character as a closed corporation.*

**Source:** Karl Marx, "Contribution to the Critique of Hegel's *Philosophy of Right*," in Robert C. Tucker, ed., *The Marx-Engels Reader*, 2nd ed. (New York: Norton, 1978): 25.

Marx did not initially consider that bureaucracy might, in fact, be a class unto itself. He was only concerned with disabusing Hegel's notion of the "universal class." But as he began to examine the historical role of bureaucracies, he con-cluded that during the transition from feudalism to capitalism (the transition from rule by the aristocracy to rule by the bourgeoisie), there was a contest for political power in which the state took a "relatively autonomous" position. He felt that the bureaucracy was able to stay above the fray, more or less, and gain an "abnormal" level of independence and political influence. The bureaucracy helped pave the way for capitalism, according to Marx, but once capitalism was established, the bureaucracy reverted to its previous role of supporting the ruling interests of soci-ety. As a result, Marx saw bureaucracy as a "parasitic" body that did not contribute to the productive forces of society but, rather, fed off the rest of society, its real task being to maintain the status quo.

Marx's hope for society was for the triumph of communism over capitalism. Under communism, exploitation of one class by another would end, and, therefore, there would no longer be any need for institutions that sustained that exploitation. As a result, the state would wither away along with the bureaucracy, and we would have a classless society. Beyond this, Marx said little about this new world.

To summarize **Marxist analysis** briefly, Marx argued the following:

- Capitalist society is marked by class conflict in which the capitalist (business class) oppresses and exploits the working class in the pursuit of profitability.

- The state (of which the bureaucracy is a key part) is "relatively autonomous" from the capitalist class but ultimately serves its long-term interests.

- The bureaucracy also has interests of its own, focused on its own survival and the career-building activities of its employees.

- Both society at large and bureaucrats suffer from alienation derived from the hierarchical nature of bureaucracy.

- Class struggle will result in revolution, leading to a classless society in which the state (and bureaucracy) will gradually wither away.

## The Neo-Marxists

Marx inspired a number of subsequent thinkers who have modified his original ideas, such that we can talk about a school of thought known as *neo-Marxism*. In general, these theorists consider the modern capitalist state to have two primary functions. One is to foster capital **accumulation**, meaning that the state passes policies that make it possible for capitalist enterprises to make profits. These might include low corporate tax rates, subsidies, grants, or other similar measures. The second is to ensure that the working class does not rise up and revolt against the dominant class. Thus, the state passes policies of **legitimation** to appease the working class without interfering with the accumulation of profits by capitalists. These may include social welfare policies, for instance. If these policies do not keep workers more or less quiescent, the state may also use coercion or even force to ensure that the working class complies with the needs of the capitalist class.

Neo-Marxists are divided over the precise nature of the state and its role in supporting capitalism. Some point to the close personal and professional relationships and networks between senior state officials and the corporate elite as evidence of common interests between the state and the bureaucracy. In a groundbreaking study, sociologist John Porter (although not a Marxist himself) documented the common social origins and ties between these groups in Canada as evidence that public policy naturally tends to favour the dominant classes.[3] Other neo-Marxists contend that bureaucracy serves the capitalist class not because of common social origins but because the state operates in a capitalist system and is thereby constrained by the structures of that system. Because of these "structural constraints," the interests of the state and the capitalist class coincide.

Neo-Marxists do agree, however, on the notion that the modern bureaucratic state is a threat to democracy. They contend that it has grown so powerful that it is no longer as responsible to elected legislatures as it should be, and that in any case, the bureaucracy is politicized in many countries, which enables the ruling party to appoint its own supporters to influential positions within the bureaucracy.

## Criticisms of Marxist Theory

One of the basic problems with Marx's analysis is that he himself did not elaborate on his ideas in this area, so they have been subject to a variety of interpretations (and misinterpretations). Neo-Marxists have been criticized for trying to have their cake and eat it, too. They claim that any state policy that assists capital is evidence of the state serving the capitalist class; but any policy that assists the working class is also interpreted as ultimately serving the interests of capital by legitimating the capitalist system. As well, neo-Marxists are criticized for arguing that the bureaucracy is merely a tool of the capitalist class, while at the same time arguing that the bureaucracy has become too powerful in its own right. In any case, there is no doubt that Marx and his followers have exerted a tremendous influence over the way we think about the role and nature of bureaucracy.

## Max Weber

Perhaps the greatest influence on our thinking about organizations is derived from the literature on the sociology of organization, and the dominant writer in this area remains **Max Weber**.

*Contemporary thinking . . . [about bureaucracy] begins with the work of the brilliant German sociologist Max Weber (1864–1920). His analysis of bureaucracy, first published in 1922 after his death, is still the most influential statement—the point of departure for all further analyses—on the subject. Drawing on studies of ancient bureaucracies in Egypt, Rome, China, and the Byzantine Empire, as well as on the more modern ones emerging in Europe during the 18th and 19th centuries, Weber used an "ideal-type" approach to extrapolate from the real world the central core of features characteristic of the most fully developed bureaucratic form of organization.*[4]

Weber argued that bureaucracy was essentially a system of administration carried out on a continuous basis by trained professionals, according to prescribed rules. He identified four main features common to modern systems of organization:

1. *hierarchy*, in which everyone has a clearly defined role within a division of labour and answers to a superior;
2. *continuity*, in the sense of full-time salaried occupations and career structures;
3. *impersonality*, in which work is based on prescribed rules and a written record; and
4. *expertise*, whereby personnel, selected on the basis of what they know rather than who they know (that is, on the basis of merit), are trained and control access to knowledge stored in files.[5]

## BOX 3.2 | Weber's Views on Organization

Weber's views on organization are summarized by Adie and Thomas:

*In bureaucracy there is a clearly defined layering of authority, a hierarchy, with each person under the control and supervision of a superior. Each person in the organization fills an office, or position, on the basis of free, contractual agreement, and following from a division of labour based on specialization of function, each person is appointed to a position on the basis of competence demonstrated to superiors. Each office has a specified sphere of competence, in that duties are specifically attached to it along with the necessary authority to carry them out. Each person obeys authority because that authority is attached to the position above his or her own.*

*Each person obeys another only because the other has the "legal" right to give orders. At the same time, no person is entitled to give orders to others unless his or her office clearly allows it, and the orders must pertain to the functions of that office. At all times, however, the individual is subject to strict and systematic supervision and discipline based on the principle of hierarchy. To avoid arbitrary, personalistic use of authority, it is clearly stated that the individual is always free to resign but that the employing authority can end a subordinate's appointment only under certain circumstances, e.g. dereliction of duty.*

**Source:** Robert F. Adie and Paul G. Thomas, *Canadian Public Administration: Problematical Perspectives,* 2nd ed. (Scarborough: Prentice-Hall, 1987): 17–18. Reprinted with permission by Pearson Education Canada Inc.

Weber felt that the closer an organization could be to this model, the more efficient it would be and the larger it would grow (see Box 3.2). Weber identified bureaucracy with efficiency since its central feature is rationality. Rationality is reflected in bureaucracy's complex division of labour, coupled with its impersonality and uniformity in the treatment of all citizens—all of which enhance its potential for efficiency. Weber felt that bureaucratic organization was becoming more prevalent in all political systems and in all organizations where complex and large-scale administrative tasks were undertaken, including businesses, trade unions, political parties, etc. Weber saw bureaucracy as central to modernization. Its source of power was the monopolization of knowledge and organization, and the concentration of this power was within the political domain.

Weber regarded the growth of the modern organization and the bureaucratic form it took as the single most important phenomenon of the modern world. That growth was the result of the superiority of bureaucratic forms of organization based on rationality and efficiency. Because individuals working within such an organization develop skills through training and experience, they develop into a body of professionals and experts. Because their positions are determined by their skills, and not by inheritance or purchase, as was once common, there is an ineluctable logic in the expansion, development, and evolution of bureaucracy as the dominant organizational form in modern society.

Weber saw bureaucratization as a rational, systematic, logical, and scientific approach to organization. He argued that, historically, people and societies were guided in their actions and behaviours by tradition, habit, instincts, and passions. In the sixteenth and seventeenth centuries, the ideas of the Enlightenment elevated reason and rationality, and largely replaced those earlier guides to action. Consider the concept of *authority*, for instance, and the decisions in society about who has the right to wield it. Weber argued that in the past, authority could be attributed to tradition (e.g., you are the king because your father was the king, as was his father, etc.) or to the charisma of an individual leader (e.g., you are able to secure compliance to your authority by the force of your personality). The increasing rationalization of modern life undermined these grounds for authority. An ideally rational organization in the Weberian sense was an organization performing its tasks with maximum efficiency. But bestowing authority on an individual for reasons of tradition or charisma was not logical in that it did not guarantee that the best person for the job would exercise authority. Efficiency could actually be impeded. An ideal type of organization would be perfectly rational, since rationality enhanced efficiency, whereas tradition and charisma did not, according to Weber.

Weber also noted that the nature of bureaucratic organizations had a profound effect on people as individuals. Bureaucracy's tendency toward impersonality, which is realized through the application of impersonal rules (i.e., rules that apply to all, regardless of station in life), depersonalizes individuals. The idea that bureaucrats advance through the strict application of rules contributes to that spirit of impersonality, since it promotes the pursuit of personal career goals through rigid application of formulistic rules. In some cases, following these rules supersedes other considerations due to the bureaucrat's desire for advancement and security. We will examine these kinds of pathologies in more detail later on.

## Criticisms of the Weberian Model

We know that organizations do not always work the way Weber prescribed. There is a disconnect between his model and the real world, and therein lies a problem with organization theory in general. It seeks to describe and explain *what is,* but often falls short. For example, we know that many organizations that display Weber's characteristics of an ideal bureaucracy (i.e., they are hierarchical, have continuity, are impersonal, and are staffed by experts) are, in fact, inefficient! Moreover, some are downright dysfunctional. For instance, hierarchy can generate a lack of initiative and individual responsibility; continuity can lead to ennui and apathy in the delivery of services; impersonality can foster indifference and insensitivity; expertise can result in inflexibility, hidebound tradition, and arrogance.

Moreover, while the impersonality of bureaucratic rules and authority is consistent with the democratic ideal of the equality of everyone before the law, in some cases it actually impedes values such as democracy and equality. The education level required to hold a position of authority in a government bureaucracy prevents many individuals from disadvantaged circumstances from becoming rule-makers themselves. While impersonal rules may protect individuals from arbitrary treatment at the hands of officials, they may also be used to frustrate popular demands for social justice. For instance, in the past, the hiring criteria of your local fire department might have required potential employees be a certain height and weight. Ostensibly, these objective criteria are deemed necessary due to the physical requirements of fighting fires. But what if they inadvertently discriminate against a whole group of people who do not meet those qualifications? For instance, women and some visible minorities tend to be shorter and of slighter stature than the white male average against which the standards were set. As a result, demands for equality of opportunity in employment run up against allegedly impersonal and objective rules and regulations. The result, systemic discrimination, is neither foreseen nor desired by the rule-makers but is, nonetheless, a reality.

Some argue that bureaucracy has significantly contributed to the destruction of privileges based on heredity (due to the merit principle) and made the organization of large-scale industry and commerce possible. However, right-wing critics of the Weberian view argue that increasing government bureaucracy, marked by greater regulation and intervention in the economy, has hindered capitalist development and the risk-taking initiative and entrepreneurial spirit of capitalism.

Leftist critics focus on a different problem. They suggest that Weber's model assumes a view about human nature that is contestable: Weber sees humans as constantly striving for power and self-gain and in need of discipline and control. Workers in the bureaucratic machine are subsumed under the organization, rather than possessing some sense of individuality. Thus, "the impact of bureaucracy on the individual is the extreme limitation of our personal freedom and spontaneity, and an increasing incapacity to understand our own activities in relation to the whole organization. We become cogs in a machine."[6]

From this perspective, bureaucracy has profoundly negative implications for democracy. Democracy requires participation by citizens who have a strong sense of self and belonging and who feel able to participate in decision making, but bureaucratic forms of organization stress obedience to authority and the sublimation of the self to the greater interests of the organization. These points are important to keep in mind when we look at some later theorists who argue that managers in bureaucracies would be more successful in attaining their goals if they permitted more democratic forms of decision making and participation to take place within organizations.

Weber's work on bureaucracy was premised on the notion of an *ideal-type;* that is, a model of the perfect bureaucratic machine. In his view, the closer you come to approximating the ideal-type, the closer you come to creating the most perfectly efficient type of organization. But the work of subsequent social scientists, who observed how bureaucratic organizations actually functioned in the real world, gave rise to some trenchant critiques of Weber's views. Some concluded that there was more to bureaucracy than the rules and structures of Weber's ideal model: informal patterns of behaviour co-existed with the formal rules, which, when they functioned in harmony, could produce greater efficiency and effectiveness. But when they were in conflict, efficiency and effectiveness were impeded.

The work of several theorists who followed Weber modified his views about bureaucracy. For instance, they took Weber's notion that politicians were at the top of the hierarchical ladder, giving orders to faithful public servants, and examined real-life cases where it appeared that the bureaucrats were actually following their own agendas. These new theorists noted that the politician was often at a distinct disadvantage in that he was a generalist with a lack of specific technical knowledge of how government departments functioned or how policy was made and implemented. The public servants, however, were often technical experts with many long years of experience. Picture yourself in the following situation:

You are the newly elected Member of Parliament for your riding, and the prime minister calls to tell you that she wants you to be the minister of the Environment in her Cabinet. You may not be an expert in environmental issues, but even if you are, the first day you walk into your office, you are met by the deputy minister and other senior bureaucratic officials, who have spent years developing policy in this area. Moreover, they have all developed an intimate knowledge of how government works. You, as the rookie, will have to be an awfully quick study to get up to speed, but in the meantime you may find yourself at the mercy of the "experts" who are supposedly also your "servants."

While Weber acknowledged that tensions could develop between politicians and their bureaucrats, it took the work of other theorists to document how this could affect the running of governmental bureaucracies. For instance, S.M. Lipset, in his book *Agrarian Socialism,* used a case study that showed that the political values and ideologies of public servants could directly influence and even override the express wishes of their political masters.[7] Lipset studied the 1944 government formed in Saskatchewan by the Co-operative Commonwealth Federation (CCF), the forerunner of the New Democratic Party (NDP), and its difficulties in initiating its socialist platform. Many of the top public servants in the province were opposed to socialism and were successful in having the CCF's reforms modified or even thwarted altogether, often by arguing that the reforms were "administratively unfeasible," although this was not necessarily the case. While they did not have it all their own way, some senior public servants boasted of "running my department completely" and of "stopping the harebrained radical schemes" of the CCF.

Lipset's study clearly outlined how the values and ideological predispositions of top public servants could have an important impact on the formal orders passed down from their political superiors. His study also revealed that the bureaucracy was not simply a passive tool but could itself develop informal values and even policy goals.

Another feature not accounted for by Weber is bureaucracy's pathological or distorted character. An example from popular culture is presented in the novel *One Flew over the Cuckoo's Nest,* by Ken Kesey, which was made into a movie starring Jack Nicholson.[8] In the story, a nurse in a mental hospital runs a ward in an authoritarian manner, following the organization's rules and regulations with no flexibility or allowance for individual circumstance or personality. The inmates passively accept the nurse's orders but are never "cured." When a new patient arrives (played by Nicholson in the movie), he challenges the nurse's authority and her insistence that "therapy" consists of routine schedules and rigid rules of behaviour. He organizes poker and basketball games, and tries to have the nurse rearrange the patients' schedule so they can watch the World Series. The nurse refuses, but with every refusal to indulge the patients in new activities outside the rigidly defined rules of the institution, the new patient introduces ever more radical and risky activities, culminating in a daylong fishing trip outside the institution and a wild party with alcohol and prostitutes. This is too much for the nurse to bear, even though the patients display a marked improvement in their conditions. She orders the disruptive new patient to the surgical wing of the hospital, where he is lobotomized—the thinking part of his brain removed.

This is a highly dramatic and fictional account of how a bureaucracy with the best of intentions can display pathological behaviour that actually impedes the bureaucracy's goals. The rules of the organization came to take precedence over the very objectives the rules were intended to realize. When the new patient defied the established routine and rules, the nurse used those same rules to beat him down, even though his unorthodox solutions to the patients' mental disorders were having positive effects.

Sociologist Robert K. Merton studied such dysfunctions in bureaucracies. In an important article, entitled "Bureaucratic Structure and Personality," he argued that certain aspects of bureaucratic procedure may, in fact, be dysfunctional to the organization and actually discourage behaviour that might otherwise be beneficial to the organization's goals.[9] He suggested that when an official is trained to comply with a set of rules and regulations, any situation that arises that is not covered by those rules may lead to inflexibility and timidity. The bureaucrat is not taught to be innovative or creative. He may actually be afraid to deviate from the rules, even in the face of absurd outcomes, because of fear of jeopardizing chances for promotion. This is sometimes referred to as *trained incapacity,* referring to the state of affairs in which one's learned abilities function as inadequacies or blind spots. The analogy is sometimes used of chickens trained to interpret the sound of a bell as a signal for food. That same bell may also be used to summon the trained chickens to the slaughterhouse!

Merton also notes that the devotion to rules often becomes an end in itself for officials. The bureaucrat loses sight of the goals of the organization and, instead, becomes bound up in red tape, trying to ensure that the rules are followed without deviation. Merton characterizes this kind of behaviour as *goal displacement,* an example of which is clearly present in *One Flew over the Cuckoo's Nest.* It is worth remembering that Weber's model of bureaucracy stressed the importance of impersonally applying prescribed rules and regulations to maximize efficiency. In many cases, bureaucrats are trained to be skeptical of complaints, since they are led to believe that universal impersonal application of rules is for the good of the organization. In time, bureaucrats come to identify the disciplined application of rules with their own self-interest and desire for promotion and status.

This notion of the substitution of self-interest for organizational interest is crucial. It means that bureaucrats will come to interpret any challenge to the existing rules as a threat to their own security. To protect themselves, they will apply the rules even more rigidly, since this is the only procedure they know that will bring the praise of their superiors. In time, they will cease to question whether the rules are relevant to the organization's objectives. For example, there's a story that in 1803, the British government created a post that required a civil servant to stand on the cliffs of Dover with a spyglass and ring a bell if he saw Napoleon coming. And legend has it that the position was not abolished until 1945!

Merton also focused on the impersonality of bureaucratic procedures and the problems this raised. He noted, in particular, the cold impersonal treatment jobless individuals met when applying for benefits from employment offices. The bureaucrats interpreted their own behaviour as "businesslike." They had little time for pleasantries since they were so rushed and overworked, so they went about applying the rigid rules of the application process with little regard to the feelings of their clients, who were often emotionally distressed due to their unemployment. The clients interpreted the clerks' behaviour as arrogance, and felt that they were being looked down upon. Many complaints from the public resulted, but no action was taken in response by the bureaucrats, who had been trained to impersonally apply a set of predetermined rules in a prescribed manner.[10] Two other post-Weberians, Victor Thompson (*Modern Organizations*) and Alvin Gouldner (*Patterns of Industrial Behaviour*), approached these issues from another angle.[11] They focused on the behaviour of clients on the receiving end of the bureaucracy. They argued that clients are notoriously insensitive to the needs of bureaucrats, and that clients tend to act like children when they encounter big organizations. Clients seem to want instant gratification and fulfillment of their needs, irrespective of how difficult or complicated it is for the bureaucrat to fulfill those needs. Thompson and Gouldner argued that clients tend to view bureaucratic organizations in personal terms, as either a friend or an enemy. All attempts by bureaucrats to evaluate clients are perceived as intrusions upon their personal lives. While clients are willing to accept the services provided by bureaucracies, they resent having to give anything in return. Moreover, while clients realize that they depend on large institutions for a variety of services, they feel powerless in their presence, which fosters feelings of alienation and anger. Such responses, Thompson insisted, were nothing more than the dysfunctional persistence of childish patterns of behaviour.

Thompson and Gouldner had come across the role of *passion* in human affairs as it related to large organizations. Bureaucracies require that people be patient, accept impersonal treatment, submit to evaluation, and place obligation above rights—in short, that they substitute self-discipline for passion. In the era of large bureaucracies, passion is a human attribute that is out of place, since bureaucracy draws its morality from the old Protestant work ethic, with its commitment to self-discipline and rationalism.

Weber's ideas were reassessed from another perspective, as well. His work was the basis of what other theorists called the *politics–administration dichotomy*. You will recall from chapter 1 that this was a view first articulated by Woodrow Wilson, who developed the notion that politics and administration are separate things. Frank J. Goodnow addressed this in his book, *Politics and Administration,* published in 1900.[12] Goodnow took the view that public administration, as practised under the party "boss system" in the United States, was in many ways corrupt and thereby inefficient since leaders typically apportioned jobs to their supporters, family, and friends rather than to the best-qualified candidates for a position. An ardent reformer, Goodnow argued for the separation of politics and administration. But although this "principle" of public administration prevailed for many years, it also increasingly came under attack. Indeed, few would admit the theory has much utility today. It is factually inaccurate in that politics and administration are inextricably linked in countless large and small ways, even if we do not want them to be. Nonetheless, as a "principle" it remains desirable in guiding public administration in areas such as appointments to the public service (where merit has replaced patronage).

But Herbert Simon, the first of only two non-economists ever to win the Nobel Prize in economics, postulated that the "principles of public administration" were really nothing more than "proverbs of administration."[13] As a result, these principles were often contradictory, inconsistent, inapplicable, and confusing. In short, public administration was anything but scientific, notwithstanding the claims of a couple of generations of theorists. For example, Simon noted that proverbs often come in mutually contradictory pairs ("look before you leap" is countered by "he who hesitates is lost"). Similarly, in administration, apparently contradictory principles seem to be at work. The Peter Principle states that individuals reach (and surpass) their level of competence in an organization, while the Great Shelf Principle suggests that individuals are generally shelved somewhere in the organization long before they have realized their potential. More directly, Simon cited the example of the span of control in organizations. **Span of control** refers to the structure of the hierarchy within an organization. Around 1750 BC, the Egyptians assigned 10 workers to each supervisor while building the pyramids in what may be the first recorded application of the concept of span of control. Traditional literature had argued that efficiency was maximized with a narrow span of control; that is, each manager "controls" only a limited number of subordinates. The theory was that too many subordinates resulted in poor communications within the organization and progressively looser and less effective control. But Simon pointed out that the literature also argued that, for an organization to maximize effective communications, there should be as few hierarchical levels as possible. These are two mutually contradictory principles, making it impossible for managers to "do the right thing" as far as the structure of their organization is concerned. The two span of control systems are represented in Figure 3.1.

As you have seen, Weber's basic model contained vitally important insights, but it has not gone unchallenged. The fact that he really only considered the formal structure of bureaucracy, with its official rules and procedures and authorized structure of hierarchy, meant that he ignored the unofficial practices that also contribute to the functioning of organizations. Various **bureaucratic pathologies** impede the achievement of maximum efficiency and rationality as espoused in the Weberian model. Many of these new insights found expression through the theorists we will now turn to in the structuralist and humanist schools of thought.

**FIGURE 3.1**     **Span of Control**

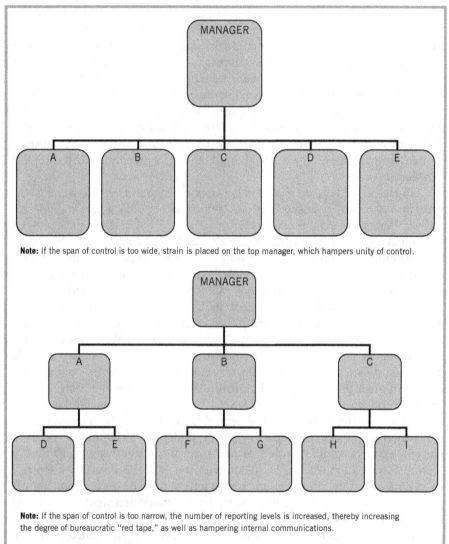

**Note:** If the span of control is too wide, strain is placed on the top manager, which hampers unity of control.

**Note:** If the span of control is too narrow, the number of reporting levels is increased, thereby increasing the degree of bureaucratic "red tape," as well as hampering internal communications.

## Structuralist Theories

Generally speaking, **structuralist theories** view workers in administrative organizations as little more than interchangeable parts—cogs in a machine lubricated by money. In this view, the goal of organization theory is to devise structures within which work can be rationalized so as to maximize the organization's efficiency. Little regard is paid to the needs or desires of the individual workers, who are expected to subsume their interests to the administrative machine. These theories rely on a particular view of human nature that suggests that individuals are motivated by material gain (wages, career advancement, etc.) and that workers require a strict regime of rules and regulations, determined and clearly spelled out by management, in order to function at maximum efficiency.

## Scientific Management

A profoundly important evolution in thinking about public administration came about as a result of new demands from business managers arising at the turn of the twentieth century, as a consequence of industrial capitalism. The term **scientific management** characterized this school of thought. Increasing industrialization and technological change in the workplace in the late 1800s created a great deal of disorganization in industry. Major adjustment problems were encountered in the transition from small-scale, craft-based production to large-scale, industrial factory-based production, where the work of employees was increasingly deskilled (for example, on the newly invented assembly line). The growing classes of capitalist owners and workers had to adapt to new forms of workplace organization to remain competitive, if large-scale efficiency was going to be achieved.

The growth of business operations increasingly separated owners from the daily routine of workers. Thus, a more rationalized form of organization and control was needed to maximize productivity and profit. The pioneers in this reorganizational challenge were mechanical engineers, who were strategically located in the production process because of their central position in organizing factory production on a daily basis. Cost accountants also became key players, due to their focus on measuring and controlling costs. These people and the theorists who supported their work tackled the question of organizations and administration from the point of view of what can be called the *managerial* tradition. Scientific management's origins and ideas were clearly directed at and for management, in contrast, as we will see, to the humanist theories of bureaucracy.

The father of scientific management was Frederick Winslow Taylor (1856–1915) (see Box 3.3). He was not so much interested in the organizational problems of society's power structure as he was in the practical problem of efficiency. Taylor's main unit of analysis was not society as a whole or bureaucracy as such, but the individual worker in the bureaucratic/organizational setting (i.e., the workplace). Taylor began to develop his system in the 1880s while employed as a pattern maker and machinist at the Midvale Steel Company in Philadelphia. At the time, work in factories was still not particularly "routinized" or "rationalized." The skilled craft worker still predominated, and workers were largely left on their own to perform their duties; the pace of the work was not yet set by the machines; and the individual worker placed his own "stamp" on the product—i.e., work was individualized. Foremen were also generally left to set their own standards and to regulate work breaks, etc. The tyranny of the clock had not yet been imposed.

Taylor regarded such practices as haphazard and inefficient. The Midvale plant was run on a piecework basis: machines ran around the clock, and labourers were paid on the basis of how many pieces they produced. Taylor observed this process and determined that workers could triple their productivity (and their wages) simply by reorganizing the flow of work. He attempted to regulate the

**BOX 3.3 Frederick Winslow Taylor: The Father of Scientific Management**

**A**lthough Taylor is regarded as the father of scientific management, the term actually originated elsewhere:

*Strangely enough, while Taylor's 1911 book Principles of Scientific Management is the work for which he is best known, the credit for coining the term scientific management belongs not to Taylor but to an associate of his, Louis D. Brandeis (1856–1941). Brandeis, who would later become a Supreme Court justice, needed a catchy phrase to describe the new style management techniques of Taylor and his disciples when he was to present arguments before the Interstate Commerce Commission that railroad rate increases should be denied. Brandeis dramatically argued that the railroads could save "a million dollars a day" by applying scientific management methods. The highly publicized hearings beginning in 1910 caused a considerable sensation and vastly expanded Taylor's reputation. Ironically, Taylor was initially opposed to the phrase, thinking that it sounded too academic. But he quickly learned to embrace it. So did the rest of the country. In the first half of the century, scientific management was gospel and Frederick W. Taylor was its prophet.*

**Source:** Jay M. Shafritz, Albert C. Hyde, and Sandra J. Parkes, eds., *Classics of Public Administration*, 5th ed. (Belmont, CA: Thomson Wadsworth, 2004): 4.

work routine and speed up its pace. Rather than allow individual workers to set the pace and to carry out their own tasks, Taylor set a time for how long any particular job should take, and outlined in a strict way the manner in which the job should be done. The workers reacted unfavourably to Taylor's attempted reorganization. They called him a "piecework hog" for working so hard; he was the kind of guy you love to hate in the workplace—the keener who volunteered to work on Sundays, and who rose every day at 5:00 a.m. to walk the two miles to work, never leaving before 5:00 p.m. He was born into an upper-class Philadelphia family and studied law at Harvard for a while but quit, complaining that he was going blind from all the reading. He signed up with the Midvale plant and engaged his fascination with time management and scientific solutions to workplace problems. (He applied this thinking to his personal life, too. Plagued by nightmares, he noticed that he always woke up on his back. He concluded that if he did not sleep on his back, he would not have nightmares. He rigged up an elaborate harness of leather straps and wooden prods that he wore while sleeping. If he rolled onto his back, he would be prodded awake. Thus he applied a scientific solution to his problem.)

In the workplace, Taylor sought to scientifically discover the shortest time possible for performing any particular task, and his tool was the stopwatch. Standing behind each worker, Taylor would record the time it took to perform even the most elementary motions: finding a steel rod, setting it on a lathe, picking up a tool, and so on. By studying a large number of workers, he felt he could identify the shortest possible time for performing each individual motion. By combining the best times, discarding useless motions, and adding gaps for unavoidable delays or rest breaks, Taylor could establish a pattern of work that was invariably shorter than the workers' informal pace. These experiments became known as the infamous **time and motion studies**.

When Taylor asked for help from management to implement his system, the workers responded by running their machines so fast and hard that pieces fell off! Taylor responded by fining them. Ultimately, he convinced management to use the penultimate weapon against the workers: cut the piecework rate in half so that the workers would have to speed up their production to survive financially. Taylor's battles with the Midvale workers were to last three years (see Box 3.4). Before leaving Midvale, Taylor astonished the plant engineers by revealing that he had conducted upward of 50 000 experiments on these problems, which he published in the book *On the Art of Cutting Metal.*

---

### BOX 3.4 | Taylor's View of Workers

Taylor based part of his work on the division of labour in the workplace on a view of workers that is repulsive by today's standards. Consider the following quotation from *The Principles of Scientific Management*:

*Now one of the very first requirements for a man who is fit to handle pig iron as a regular occupation is that he shall be so stupid and so phlegmatic that he more nearly resembles in his mental make-up the ox than any other*

*type. . . . Therefore the workman who is best suited to handling pig iron is unable to understand the real science of doing this class of work. He is so stupid that the word "percentage" has no meaning to him, and he must consequently be trained by a man more intelligent than himself into the habit of working in accordance with the laws of this science before he can be successful.*

**Source:** F.W. Taylor, *The Principles of Scientific Management* (New York: Harper and Brothers, 1911): 59.

---

He then began to look beyond time and motion studies to determine that workers were also using improper tools and defective equipment. He contended that there was "one best way" of performing any task, and his work resulted in a complete reorganization of the firm—planning, engineering, purchasing, and inventory control were all centralized, as was maintenance and cost accounting; assembly line techniques were introduced as well. Management's job, Taylor argued, was to "discover" this "one best way" by applying scientific principles to work procedures. The workers should not be left to solve the problems of production themselves; this was management's role. The worker should simply be told how to carry out the "one best way." What this implied was a radical separation of planning and performing, of thinking and doing.

While his theories were initially developed for the private sector, Taylor also attempted to introduce his system into public administration, beginning in 1906 in government-run arsenals and navy yards. The most famous incident took place at Watertown Arsenal near Boston. The arsenal was run by rule of thumb: the workers would receive an order for a set number of gun carriages and fill it by milling assorted parts found in the yard according to designs someone sketched in chalk on the factory floor. Taylor contended this was not the "one best way" of doing the job, and he argued that the selection of workers must be based on scientific criteria—i.e., some workers were better suited for some jobs than others, and the best person for each job must be determined and chosen. When the workers at Watertown heard that Taylor was coming, they went on strike, and the army was sent in to guard the arsenal with fixed bayonets. Later, a special congressional committee was formed that summoned Taylor to explain his system. So contentious was Taylor's time and motion system that the U.S. Congress passed a law banning stopwatches in government-run factories—a law that remained in place for 40 years—because of the unpopularity of Taylor and his ideas among working class voters.

Two more theorists in the scientific management tradition argued that there are universal principles of administration that should govern arrangements for human organizations. Luther Gulick and Lyndall Urwick produced an important collection of papers on the state of the art of organization theory, entitled "Papers on the Science of Administration."[14] The French theorist Henri Fayol had documented the five functions common to all managers in all organizations as: planning, organizing, commanding, coordinating, and controlling.[15] Gulick expanded on this approach in a famous acronym, **POSDCORB**, which stands for Planning, Organizing, Staffing, Directing, Coordinating, Reporting, and Budgeting. By subdividing all the tasks of an organization along these lines, efficiency could be maximized. This was Gulick's attempt to define the "one best way" for organization management by focusing on the top of the hierarchical pyramid in organizations. He was concerned with developing scientific principles and practices that management should systematically employ.

It is the underlying assumption of worker–management co-operation behind Taylorism and scientific management that was problematic. In the absence of this co-operation, all other principles of his approach were useless. Taylor saw scientific management as a solution to both productivity problems and class conflicts, which he viewed as wasteful. Once natural laws governing production were scientifically established, there would be no need for bargaining or conflict between labour and management, because one could not bargain with scientific fact. Thus, Taylor was hostile to trade unions, feeling that they generated conflict and were against the real best interests of the workers. He preferred to deal with workers as individuals rather than in groups (unions) because he felt that workers in groups exerted social pressure on individuals to conform to unscientific, more comfortable production norms (i.e., to "slack off"). Taylor wished to prevent such groups from developing, by making it in the workers' economic interest to co-operate with scientific management techniques.

The underlying premise of scientific management in terms of the relationship of workers to the industrial environment was explained by Taylor in analogies between people and machines. First, in terms of production, people were considered to be like machines (the mechanomorphic world image) whose specifications and performance could be scientifically measured and rated, and whose efficiency could be improved through mechanical adjustments, such as reducing superfluous motions. Second, Taylor argued that the factory structure should be considered a complex productive mechanism—a combination of machines and workers involved in the process of transforming raw material in the cheapest possible manner. Rationalization was the key, defined as producing a product in the most efficient manner. Goals were to be set and achieved by using workers and machines as standardized, interchangeable parts to be manipulated with the aim of maximizing productivity at minimum cost.

Mechanization of industry in the late 1800s and early 1900s had resulted in unprecedented productivity growth, particularly in America, but it also resulted in human organizational problems. The solution, according to scientific management, was to treat humans as machines. In terms of efficiency, this was a solution that resulted in amazing gains in productivity. Scientific management represents not just a theory of organization, but one of motivation and human behaviour. It characterizes the individual as driven by fear of hunger and deprivation, and by a desire for profit. These characteristics were manipulable, according to scientific management, in a manner compatible with efficiency, so long as it was possible to view humans as mere machines.

Taylor saw the **division of labour** as a basic principle controlled by a hierarchical pyramid of authority driven by efficiency. The emphasis on managerial control attracted American capitalists engaged in a bitter struggle with labour over the control of the modern industrial workplace. But once Taylorist measures were implemented in workplaces, they did not have all the desired effects of transferring decision-making authority to management and producing the most efficient and profitable operation. Henry Ford's adoption of scientific management in his assembly line, for instance, did not result in workers' quiet acquiescence to the highly regulated and automated routine of the production line. Instead, workers unionized and adapted their own defensive techniques to counter management's attempts to gain total control over the labour process. Their responses culminated in the sit-down strikes of the 1930s, the wildcat strikes of the 1940s, and labour militancy in the 1960s and 1970s. These struggles showed the alienating power of Taylor's approach and demonstrated that scientific management rationality did not necessarily result in the most efficient, effective production process. Instead, it often resulted in worker resistance or even sabotage of the production process. The often inhumane working conditions fostered by Taylor's techniques impeded efficiency, ironically destroying the very "rationality" of the system. Nonetheless, Taylorism attracted a diverse range of supporters. Besides American capitalists and industrialists, scientific management was an important plank in the ideology of Italian Fascists in the 1930s. It was also picked up by the left; Lenin, the father of the Communist revolution in Russia, was an enthusiastic admirer of Taylor, as were several U.S. socialist parties. The attraction can be explained by remembering that there was widespread admiration at the time for "scientific" advancement, which often overcame more ideological concerns about the welfare of workers.

### Criticisms of Scientific Management

Scientific management techniques caught on across the United States and the industrialized world; but critiques of scientific management also emerged and sometimes found expression in popular culture. Charlie Chaplin's *Modern Times* and Fritz Lang's *Metropolis*, for instance, were trenchant and biting commentaries on the dehumanizing tendencies of this approach to workplace organization. By now, some of the weaknesses of the scientific management school should be apparent to you. For instance, by focusing on the individual worker as the main unit of analysis, it fails to see the worker as a member of a broader social group. There is no recognition that the worker is socially influenced in his or her behaviour and attitudes by colleagues and by the social structure and culture of the group.

Moreover, Taylorism represents a theory of organization based on a particular model of human behaviour: a machine model. This was an engineer's perspective, which saw human relations in mechanistic terms. The organization member was seen as an instrument of production like any other tool, to be manipulated and used. Taylor assumed that the individual feelings of workers were more or less irrelevant to the problems of productivity. In this sense, Taylor's conception of the worker is very similar to Weber's view of the ideal bureaucrat: both are devoid of personal feelings, ambitions, and independent actions that might jeopardize the systems Taylor and Weber constructed. Thus, there is no consideration of the individual's feelings, attitudes, and private goals. In short, Taylor (like Weber) neglected the psychological and sociological variables of organizational behaviour.

Thus, the same types of criticisms levelled against Weber by the post-Weberians apply in some instances to Taylor. Taylor, for instance, looked at the problem of morale and productivity exclusively in terms of economic reward and punishment; the primary motivation of workers is assumed to be economic. But this is obviously an oversimplified view of human nature; clearly other, non-economic motivations also guide worker behaviour (e.g., alienation). Furthermore, Taylor's pro-management perspective led him to mistakenly believe that the interests of management and labour were reconcilable and could exist in harmony through scientific management. But this is naive; as long as there are bosses and workers and a prevailing capitalist economy wherein a dollar that goes to profit cannot also go to wages, tensions and hostilities will persist.

Over the years, a growing chorus of criticisms of Taylorism led to a contrary school of thought, which we can classify as the humanist or human relations approach to organization theory.

## Humanist Theories

Popular culture can often be seen as a barometer of society's attitudes; hence the alienating hyper-rationalism of industrial capitalism became the subject matter for numerous critical films and novels, from Charlie Chaplin's *Modern Times*, to Arthur Miller's *Death of Salesman*, to George Orwell's *1984*. Similarly, in the realm of management and public administration, **humanist theories** developed to critique the dehumanizing structuralist approach. Humanist theorists argued that maximizing efficiency required paying attention to the workers as individuals with identifiable needs beyond mere material rewards. It was the job of managers, according to this school of thought, to be sensitive to those needs in order to maximize efficiency, since a happy and contented worker who feels a part of the decision-making process is more likely to produce efficiently than one who is disgruntled and must be coerced by restrictive institutional structures and rules.

## The Human Relations Approach

As we saw above, one of Taylorism's main concerns was the scientific selection of workers on the basis of their aptitude for a position. Given such an orientation, it was only a matter of time before the industrial psychologist would join the engineer and accountant to discover the most efficient conditions for work. The turn toward the industrial psychologist was largely prompted by workers' hostile reactions to scientific management's attempts to implement its mechanistic principles in the working environment. Industrial psychologists went beyond scientific management, taking into account more than the mere physical elements of the human in relation to work suitability. They attempted to modify scientific management's "machine model" of organizational behaviour, and were concerned with the following: how to devise tests to select the best person for a job; how to discover whether that person was working at full efficiency or not; how work conditions, such as lighting, humidity, and temperature, affect productivity; how the effects of boredom, brought on by doing repetitive tasks, impeded productivity, and so on. This approach, then, began to emphasize the human element in the work enterprise—hence the name *human relations approach*.

This approach was more than simply an altruistic response to structuralism. Serious labour disruption brought about by the introduction of scientific management erupted in every advanced industrial nation by the early 1900s. The mobilization of organized labour into unions and the sometimes violent strikes around this process prompted some theorists to wonder how workers themselves felt about the organization of work, if only to keep the wheels of industry turning.

One important theorist who anticipated the shift in attitudes and approaches was Mary Parker Follett, who wrote a groundbreaking reflection in 1926, called "The Giving of Orders," several years before the humanist tradition really took hold.[16] She argued for an approach that today we would identify as "participatory management" (discussed in chapter 4), in which leadership and decision making was not a linear process from the top down but rather a kind of continuous feedback loop. When a manager made a decision, his or her subordinates responded to and reacted to that decision, and their response fed back up to management, according to Parker Follett. Thus, she was questioning the command-and-control structure so lionized by scientific management and suggesting that both the *formal* power of management and the *informal* power of employees affected the organization's functions and success.

To gain insight into workers' feelings and opinions, theorists began to use techniques such as questionnaires, surveys, and workplace observations. They wished to tap into the influence of the "human factor." This new approach was reflected in a slogan adopted by much of the American business community in the 1930s: "The human element is the most important element in business." This gave recognition to problems inherent in scientific management.

The receptiveness of some business people to such studies provided industrial psychologists with a real working environment in which to apply academic theories. The worksite became their "laboratory" for studying human behaviour in an organizational (primarily industrial) setting. Among the most famous of these experiments were the **Hawthorne experiments**. In 1924, the American National Academy of Sciences sent a team of researchers to the Western Electric Company's Hawthorne Works near Chicago to study the effects of illumination on worker efficiency. Taylor had pointed to the need for well-placed work breaks that would give workers relief from the strains of their job and thereby improve efficiency. The researchers in the Hawthorne study were keenly aware of the studies of fatigue and monotony that had attempted to reduce these phenomena, and consequently cut down on the problems of absenteeism and turnover, and to increase overall worker productivity. Researchers believed that an improved physical work environment would result in increased worker productivity.

The Hawthorne Works employed about 29 000 men and women. It was a massive industrial complex producing telephone equipment. The researchers initially conducted their lighting tests on various broad groups of workers throughout the plant, but the results were inconclusive, so they decided to focus on a narrower, more controlled group of workers who wound small induction coils onto wooden spools. The researchers improved the lighting in the room and found that worker productivity went up. But some researchers were not convinced of the certainty of the results; they argued that if productivity was tied to illumination, then a *decrease* in lighting would result in a *decrease* in productivity. So the scientists then tested this proposition; they replaced the higher intensity light bulbs with lower ones, and what happened surprised them: productivity slowly but steadily increased! The scientists kept lowering the light level, and productivity continued to slowly rise. Finally, the experimenters replaced the electric lights with three-foot candles; at this point the workers complained—noting that they were hardly able to see what they were doing—and the production rate decreased.

The researchers attempted to check their unusual findings by establishing a control group in another area of the plant. Here the level of lighting was never altered in the work room, yet the productivity of the workers in this control group continued to increase! This baffled the scientists. So they began a second series of experiments in 1927, in which they recruited five women who built telephone relays and segregated them from the other employees in a special room where the scientists could control temperature and humidity and their hours of work. The objective was to test the role of fatigue and monotony on productivity. The scientists experimented with longer rests and shorter workdays. In their conversations with the women, they discovered that the women frequently had no time to have breakfast, so the scientists provided them with sandwiches, coffee, and soup. Productivity went up. Moreover, productivity steadily went up until the rumour spread through the plant that the Hawthorne executives were about to dismiss the research team because of the effects of the experiments on other workers in the plant. At this point the workers in the experiment began producing an extraordinarily large number of telephone relays. At about the same time, scientists decided to observe the effects of increasing the women's fatigue by restoring the old 48-hour workweek. Productivity continued to climb! They eliminated the lunch break. Absenteeism went down! They cut down the rest breaks. There were still no signs of fatigue! No matter how the researchers tinkered with the rest periods or the workweek, they could not get the women to slow down.

What they finally figured out after about five years of study was that the workers were actually responding to the *researchers*, not to the conditions imposed on them or to the manipulation of their work environment. In the beginning, the women had responded to the novelty of having the researchers there; they felt it meant that management was worried about productivity. Then the women began to respond to the style of supervision. Given greater freedom, said the researchers, less strict supervision, and the opportunity to vary from a fixed pace without reprimand by a gang boss, worker morale increased, as did productivity.

The researchers felt they needed to know more about the effects of supervision, so they interviewed 20 000 workers but got so many different responses that they decided to conduct another experiment. This time the researchers would not supervise the workers directly but would watch them from a distance. The most important of these experiments began in 1931 in the bank wiring room where workers produced telephone switchboards. At the time, management was trying to improve worker productivity through a combination of wage incentives and low-key supervision. By industrial standards of the time, Hawthorne was a good place to work (given the Great Depression of the 1930s, just having *anywhere* to work was a good thing), but the employees were naturally concerned about losing their jobs. As a result, they artificially depressed their own productivity so that each worker wired no more than two banks a day. Any worker, of his or her own initiative, could have made more money by working harder. But the employees attacked those who did and berated those who worked too slowly. Thus, two banks a day was considered by all to be a fair day's work.

This phenomenon finally revealed the source of the researchers' confusion over their findings: the **informal group**. The researchers concluded that this was the dominant factor in employee productivity. The most powerful motivators on the job were the social norms and values of the group and the ability of supervisors to act as leaders in modifying those norms and values. Workers might acquire their sentiments on the basis of individual experience, but on the job they acted as members of groups.

Elton Mayo, one of the key researchers from the Harvard Business School at Hawthorne, is considered to be the father of the human relations approach in the same way that Taylor was the father of scientific management.[17] Mayo observed that human collaboration in work has always depended upon the evolution of a nonlogical social code that regulates the relations between persons and their attitudes to one another. Insisting on a merely economic logic of production interferes with the development of such a code and, consequently, gives rise in the group to a sense of human defeat. The human relations school came to the conclusion that economic incentives, rest breaks, free breakfasts, and improved physical working conditions could never be as powerful as the "social controls" exercised by the group in the workplace. In other words, the key finding of the decade-long study was one that we might assume is rather obvious today: workers are more responsive to peer pressure than to management controls. Mayo wrote, "the working group as a whole actually determined the output of individual workers by reference to a standard, predetermined but never clearly stated, that represented the group conception (rather than management's) of a fair day's work. This standard was rarely, if ever, in accord with the standards of the efficiency engineers."[18]

Despite the findings of the human relations school, however, the approach did not really begin to catch on until the publication of a book in 1938 called *The Functions of the Executive* by Chester Barnard, a career executive and president of the New Jersey Telephone Company.[19] Barnard was closely associated with the experimenters from the Harvard Business School who conducted the Hawthorne experiments. Barnard argued that organizations by their very nature were co-operative, rather than mechanical, in nature. They were held together by good communications and the continuing desire of individuals within an organization to see it thrive. Members of an organization make contributions to it but only when they receive adequate inducements to do so. There must, therefore, be a balance, and it was the task of the executive to maintain the dynamic equilibrium between the needs of the organization and the needs of the employees. Inducements include not only money but loyalty, good working conditions, and pride. Barnard gave credence to such ideas as upward communications and authority from below, rather than just hierarchical structuring. He recognized the existence of natural informal groupings in the work setting—giving support to the growing human relations school by pointing out that one cannot understand how an organization works simply by studying its organization chart, its charter, or its rules and regulations. You cannot really understand how the government of Canada works, for instance, by simply reading the Constitution. " 'Learning the organization ropes' in most organizations," he claimed, "is chiefly learning who's who, what's what, why's why, of its informal society."[20]

Two other Hawthorne experimenters from 1927–1932, F.J. Roethlisberger and William Dickson, published *Management and the Worker*—the first empirical study to test for the relationship between productivity and social relations.[21] This book, containing the definitive account of the Hawthorne studies, investigated the importance of informal groups and looked into the effects of psychological manipulation of workers and resulting productivity. Roethlisberger and Dickson tended to confirm empirically some of Barnard's earlier intuitive assertions concerning the efficient functioning of organization and the existence of informal groups.

This work and Elton Mayo's contributions are key to understanding the significant findings of this school of thought. Mayo developed a general philosophy concerning problems brought about by industrial civilization. He said these problems stemmed largely from the social disorganization generated by industrialization (i.e., the weakening of the family and other traditional groups that the individual had been associated with, such as the church and community). He said this resulted in the atomization (isolation) of the individual, leading to loneliness and anxiety and a sense of defeat called *anomie* (a term coined by the French sociologist Emile Durkheim), not unlike the phenomenon of alienation described by Marx. This created a social vacuum whereby a person might be in a crowd (in the workplace or community) but still feel alone, and feel no real sense of identity with her social surroundings. Mayo contrasted this with the past social cohesion rooted in the neighbourhood, centred around small towns and villages. He hoped, through the human relations approach, to recreate the communal village of rural times within the work group of a modern factory. For Mayo, this required a new society within the workplace to replace the decaying family and social institutions of the past. It would be in this workplace that individuals would find emotional security and social satisfaction as a result of the harmony of both the formal and informal organizations. Such individual worker satisfaction, Mayo argued, rested on open communications between the ranks, participation in decision making by workers, job security, and a spirit of democracy wherein the administrator became concerned not just with the work, but with the workers.

Its most optimistic adherents felt that the application of human relations to the work setting would bring an end to industrial strife and establish a new industrial order based on co-operation and harmony. This was the philosophy that guided Mayo's work and the early stages of the human relations approach. The key question in this approach became, How do you marry harmony and efficiency?

Mayo's philosophy, plus the research findings from Hawthorne, outlined the basic principles of human relations, which can be summarized in the following five points:

1. *Social Norms.* The level of organizational effectiveness is determined by social norms. The early experiments on illumination and fatigue demonstrated that the physiological capability of the worker was not the crucial factor in productivity; neither were the principles of administration, such as the division of work. Neither factor was as important as the social norms. To put it another way, the amount of work carried out by a worker is not determined by physical capacity but rather by his or her social capacity.

2. *The Group.* Group standards strongly influence the behaviour of individuals in organizations. The bank wiring room experiment showed how the group could enforce a standard level of productivity on all members. The group also provided a shield against executive reprisals. In both ways the group acted as a restraint on management power.

3. *Rewards and Sanctions.* Social rewards and sanctions are the strongest motivators on the job. The Hawthorne workers responded to the respect, affection, and appeals to group loyalty provided by their fellow workers. Management's system of economic incentives was, by contrast, less powerful.

4. *Supervision.* The most effective system of supervision is created when managers consult the group and its informal leaders in order to win acceptance of organizational objectives. Human relations specialists would advise managers to a) be human; b) be good listeners; c) not be "bosses"; and d) give the impression that the workers are making the decisions. They believe that effective communication, supplemented by a willingness to allow workers to participate in decision making, is the key to effective supervision.

5. *Democratic Administration.* Workers will achieve their highest level of effectiveness when they are allowed to manage their own affairs with no boss looking over their shoulder. Re-analysis of the Hawthorne experiments revealed that improvements in productivity in the relay assembly room followed the researchers' decision to allow the women to become a collegial,

self-managing group. This point relates to the issue of specialization: democratic administration implies that specialization is by no means the most efficient form of division of labour.

Psychologist Abraham Maslow took the Hawthorne findings a step further. The experiments had challenged the scientific management view that workers were essentially economic animals motivated simply by financial incentives. Maslow argued that the notion of monetary incentives for workers was too simplistic. He argued that people were motivated by a **hierarchy of human needs**, of which there were five categories, ranging from physiological needs to self-actualization. People are motivated to satisfy the first categories, the most basic physiological ones, and only once those have been satisfied do they move up to the next level (see Box 3.5). Once they have satisfied the lower needs, these cease to be motivators

---

**BOX 3.5  Maslow's Hierarchy of Human Needs**

1. *Physiological:* Food, shelter, clothing, sex, sleep

2. *Safety:* Security, stability, freedom from fear

3. *Belongingness and Love:* Friend-ship, love, membership in some community

4. *Esteem:* Achievement, competence, independence, prestige, status

5. *Self-Actualization:* Self-fulfillment, attaining ultimate goals in life

Source: Maslow, A.H. *Motivation and Personality*, 2nd ed. (New York: Harper and Row, 1970).

Maslow's hierarchy can be further subdivided into higher and lower level needs, as depicted here:

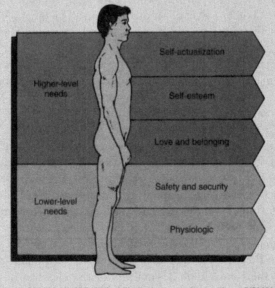

Source: Fotosearch, NU220002 LifeART Medical Illustrations, **www.fotosearch.com/LIF140/nu220002/**.

of human behaviour; but higher needs cannot be satisfied until lower ones are met.[22] Contrary to the scientific management literature, Maslow contended that there was no "one best way" to motivate employees: management had to be sensitive to the idea that workers have a variety of needs and motivations.

Thus, the human relations school no longer saw the worker as an isolated physical being but considered her a group member whose behaviour was greatly controlled by group norms and values, and motivated by a complex hierarchy of needs and desires. The lesson, then, was that management must *not* try to destroy the informal organization on the worksite but, rather, take it into consideration and use supervisors trained in human relations to harmonize the informal norms and values with the goals of the formal organization. Ultimately, the human relations skills of the organization's leadership set the tone of human relations. The good leader was one who was considerate of the workers' positions and problems.

## Criticisms of the Human Relations School

From a historical perspective, the Hawthorne study went in a new direction—it recognized that human beings are a complex and influential factor in organizational performance. Humans are not machines, and scientific management's "one best way" had to be tempered to recognize the effect of group behaviour. Many have taken the human relations movement as a counterbalance to Taylor and scientific management, and it is true that human relations certainly filled a blind spot in the earlier school of thought. However, in reality, the distinction between the two is more academic than practical. What managers in the real world tended to do was graft the principles of human relations onto the more formal principles of scientific management, seeking to maximize production as efficiently as possible behind a humane facade. The Hawthorne experiments were no less interested in improving efficiency than was Taylor; they shared the common desire to find principles that would aid managers in running a more efficient shop. The "iron fist" had been replaced by the "velvet glove," but the hand still belonged, ultimately, to management.

Criticisms of human relations theory are often centred on its neglect of organizational conflict in favour of a one-sided emphasis on harmony and on the fact that, notwithstanding their apparent concern with workers' needs and motivations, human relations theorists ultimately display pro-management values. For instance, one of the Hawthorne experiments involved 300 workers who were given the job of wandering around the factory floor, listening to the complaints of other employees. But management never intended to do anything about the complaints; it simply wanted to create the impression that it actually cared about the workers. In any event, these theorists' preaching about the virtues of internal democracy and worker participation in decision making were, when viewed against reality, certainly utopian. Advising that workers be given active participation in the workings of the firm immediately gives rise to a dilemma—either they construct a pseudo-democracy where employees are given the opportunity to participate only in decisions that do not hurt management, or they propose real, meaningful participation, which in the end means that management must voluntarily cede part of its power and prerogatives over employees. However, managers would be unwilling to sacrifice their own power for such an altruistic purpose. Real participation on a large scale would imply sacrificing the predominant position of management—an unlikely development in a capitalist enterprise. To put it another way, human relations theorists wanted to revolutionize the organization without a revolution, without touching its societal foundations.

This sort of critique found another form of expression in the work of Swiss sociologist Robert Michels, who documented the fundamentally antidemocratic tendencies of modern bureaucracies.[23] He posited the "iron law of oligarchy," in which he claimed all large organizations—political parties, corporations, religious bodies, government bureaucracies, etc.—ultimately fall under the sway of oligarchies—that is, small groups of ruling elites. Thus, a concentration of power at the top is inevitable, in Michels's view.

Other critics, such as the sociologists Clark Kerr and Abraham Siegel, challenged the notion that industrial co-operation rested primarily on the skills and understanding of industrial leaders.[24] They pointed to areas of work activity where industrial conflict was persistent and other areas where conflict was rare. Kerr and Siegel asked if differences in workplace harmony could really be accounted for in terms of the leadership skills (the human relation skills) of management. Was it that some industries adopted a human relations approach and others did not? Or were the roots of these differences in workplace conflict to be found elsewhere? Kerr and Siegel pointed to the powerful influence that job structure had on human relations on the job. For instance, resource industries are notoriously strike-ridden because of structural factors—the jobs are dangerous, such industries are boom-and-bust, employment is often centred in small, highly class-polarized towns, and so on. All of these factors contribute to the conflict-prone nature of the industry, notwithstanding the best efforts and theories of the human relations model. In some industries, the issue of technological change is vital. For the textile industry, the lack of conflict can be explained by the large numbers of unorganized marginal workers—mainly women and immigrants—who are less likely to strike. The reason for differing job structures in various working environments also has much to do with the nature of the work, and in most cases little to do with the orientation of management, whether trained in human relations or not.

Furthermore, human relations theorists have given little consideration to the effect that the worker's experience outside the organization has on work behaviour. It makes little sense, in this view, to talk about basic needs of all workers. If such needs exist, they are conditioned by the individual's place in the social structure or class structure outside work (e.g., white-collar versus blue-collar individuals). Thus, the human relations school is limited by its failure to look beyond the factory gates for explanations of the behaviour of humans in organizations.

Another criticism is that human relations is management-centred. Human relations theorists were as preoccupied with efficiency as were scientific management theorists. The human relations specialists simply emphasized different principles; they were concerned with informal groups and improved communications, and thought that executives should be benevolent toward employees because this would make workers happy and thereby raise productivity. Critics found this view superficial and irrelevant to workers' real needs. For instance, Mayo and other human relations theorists felt that unions and collective bargaining emphasized the divisions between workers and management, preventing effective communication and increasing the kind of conflict that bred anomie. That there was a natural community of interests between worker and management was not substantiated by human relations specialists, according to the critics. In addition, the point that financial incentives were not all that important in motivating workers was challenged; after all, wages and benefits are usually at the heart of collective bargaining disputes. These criticisms undermined the human relations approach to a certain extent, although this approach continues to have an influential legacy in both private and public organizations.

## Other Theoretical Approaches

Our survey of organization theory, although covering a lot of ground, cannot of course be comprehensive. To round out this overview, though, we will finish with a brief sample of other modern theoretical approaches.

One important attempt to develop a more sophisticated understanding of management styles utilizing both the structuralist and humanist frameworks is found in the work of Douglas McGregor, an American management scholar, who crafted what he called the "**Theory X and Theory Y**" explanations of organizational behaviour. In an article entitled "The Human Side of Enterprise," McGregor constructed a two-part typology, contrasting structuralist and humanist approaches (see Box 3.6).

Among the post–Second World War developments in organization theory, **systems theory** established itself as important. We might credit the origins of systems theory to the great English poet John Donne (1572–1631), who famously wrote that "No man is an Island, entire of itself;/ every man is a piece of the Continent,/ a part of the main." In this eloquent statement of our interconnectedness, Donne was laying the groundwork for modern social science. He also wrote "Any man's death diminishes me because/ I am involved in mankind; And therefore/ never send to know for whom the bell tolls;/ it tolls for thee," suggesting the extent to which we are collectively invested in a human social system.[25]

Systems theory explains organizations as *open systems* and methodologically studies those systems through the application of computers, statistical analysis, information systems, and quantitative measurement. These techniques attracted the attention of theorists who expressed a confidence in the same kind of rationality espoused generations earlier by structuralist theorists. The central work in this area was by Daniel Katz and Robert Khan, who wrote *The Social Psychology of Organizations* in 1966.[26] This was followed in 1967 by the publication of *Organizations in Action* by James D. Thompson.[27]

Systems theory sees organizations as made up of complex and dynamic interconnected elements: e.g., inputs, processes, outputs, and a feedback loop, whereby outputs re-enter the system as new inputs. This approach relied on the metaphor of

## Box 3.6 Theory X and Theory Y

| Theory X | Theory Y |
|---|---|
| Management is responsible for organizing the elements of productive enterprise—money, materials, equipment, people—in the interest of economic ends. | Management is responsible for organizing the elements of productive enterprise—money, materials, equipment, people—in the interest of economic ends. |
| With respect to people, this is a process of directing their efforts, motivating them, controlling their actions, modifying their behaviour to fit the needs of the organization. | People are *not* by nature passive or resistant to organizational needs. They have become so as a result of experience in organizations. |
| Without the active intervention by management, people would be passive—even resistant—to organizational needs. They must, therefore, be persuaded, rewarded, punished, controlled—their activities must be directed. This is management's task. We often sum it up by saying that management consists of getting things done through other people. | The motivation, the potential for development, the capacity for assuming responsibility, the readiness to direct behaviour toward organizational goals are all present in people. Management does not put them there. It is a responsibility of management to make it possible for people to recognize and develop these human characteristics for themselves. |
| The average man is by nature indolent—he works as little as possible. | The essential task of management is to arrange organizational conditions and methods of operation so that people can achieve their own goals *best* by directing *their* own efforts toward organizational objectives. |
| He lacks ambition, dislikes responsibility, and prefers to be led. | |
| He is inherently self-centred and indifferent to organizational needs. | |
| He is by nature resistant to change. | |
| He is gullible, not very bright, the ready dupe of the charlatan and the demagogue. | |

**Source:** Douglas Murray McGregor, "The Human Side of Enterprise," in J. Steven Ott, Sandra J. Parkes, and Richard B. Simpson, eds., *Classic Readings in Organizational Behavior*, 3rd ed. (Toronto: Nelson Thomson, 2003): 163–68.

the organization as an organism. To survive, any organism must seek inputs from its environment (food, for instance, or material for shelter), which it then converts into outputs (energy or housing). Those outputs in turn feed back to the organism, helping it in its ongoing quest for more inputs. In organizational terms—say, in a corporation—a business needs labour, capital, knowledge, and technology (inputs), which are converted into finished products for sale (outputs), which generate cash to purchase more inputs (feedback). There are elements in this process that are knowable and understandable, but there are also others whose presence and impact are hard to discern. Thus, when a manager makes a decision, she sets in motion unanticipated consequences due to the dynamic, multidimensional, and interconnected nature of the organization as a whole. Systems theorists sought to study this by focusing on decision-making processes, the flow of information through the system, and the measure and degree of controls present in it. They noted the ability of an organization to adapt in order to keep functioning, mainly by storing more inputs than it immediately needs to survive so that it can draw on them in hard times or crises.

The adaptability of an organization gained attention through theorists' work in the field of *cybernetics*, a term derived from the Greek word for "steersman"; as applied to organizations it means "the multidisciplinary study of the structures and functions of control and information processing systems in animals and machines. The basic concept behind cybernetics is self-regulation—through biological, social, or technological systems that can identify problems, do something about them, and then receive feedback to adjust themselves automatically."[28]

But another stream of thought within systems theory, known as **contingency theory**, suggests that there are no absolutes or universal rules that apply to all organizations in all circumstances: "the effectiveness of an organizational action (for example, a decision) is viewed as dependent upon the relationship between the element in question and all other aspects of the system—at the particular moment."[29] Those elements most importantly include the environment of the organization, its technology, and its size. Thus, all the actors with which the organization may interact—clients, customers, competitors, suppliers, regulators, etc.—as well as its technological systems and capabilities, and its size (i.e., small, and relatively intimate contact between the top, middle, and bottom layers; or large and dispersed), are all contingent factors affecting success and failure. Everything depends on (is contingent upon) the situation at hand. This view places a large emphasis on an organization's ability to develop rapid and accurate information systems to successfully adapt.

Systems theory ran into criticisms by the 1970s, however. In particular, human relations theorists argued that the systems theory model paid inadequate attention to issues such as the negative role of computers and information technology in dominating human organizations, the impact of centralized decision making, and the freedom of individuals within organizations to escape the tyranny of technological imperatives. Methodological problems arose as well. Faith in computer analysis, econometric modelling, and statistical analysis often proved misplaced when analyses of organizations revealed outcomes different from those predicted by the model. In Canada, cybernetics and systems theory received the imprimatur of Prime Minister Trudeau and his government, which attempted to initiate reforms built on the inherent rationalism of the approach.[30] But repeated frustrations led to its virtual abandonment by the 1980s. The standard diagrammatic depiction of systems theory as applied to the Canadian government is captured in Figure 3.2, which shows a model of the political system that contains the essential elements of inputs, process, and outputs feeding back into the inputs.

One of the offsprings of systems theory and contingency theory is *population ecology theory*. Theorists working in this area view organizations as organisms with a life cycle of birth, growth, and death. They also note the diversity of organizational types that exist. In these regards they owe an intellectual debt of gratitude to Darwinism, since much of their approach can be likened to evolution theory. Competition for scarce resources among populations, the need to reproduce, and survival of the fittest are all concepts borrowed from the natural sciences and applied

**FIGURE 3.2      A Model of the Political System**

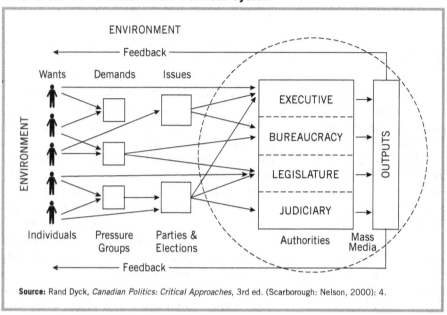

**Source:** Rand Dyck, *Canadian Politics: Critical Approaches*, 3rd ed. (Scarborough: Nelson, 2000): 4.

to organizations. Population ecology theory also pays attention to the different environments within which organizations exist, and attempts to understand the impact of environment on organizational form and durability. The theory also argues that a process of natural selection is at work among organizations. Those that adapt, thrive; those that remain static, die. At a more subtle level, this theory suggests that decision making by managers does not in itself lead to adaptation. Instead, the environment itself selects organizational forms (consistent with the process of natural selection in the animal world).[31]

As with the other theoretical models outlined above, population ecology has had its share of critics, who began with questioning the applicability of models from the natural sciences to organization theory. Critics also pointed out the methodological difficulties inherent in tracing causal factors for the success and failure of organizations, which do not lend themselves to easy identification or measurement. Still, the population ecology approach added to the diversity of organization theory and offers yet another way of thinking about how organizations function.

In the 1990s, the concept of "the learning organization" evolved from earlier systems theory. In this approach, the world and organizations within it are seen as related, interlinked forces wherein participation is fostered. The organization facilitates learning by all of its members and continuously transforms itself in a well-thought-out manner. The book *The Fifth Discipline*, by Peter Senge, set out the notion of achieving the learning organization in a manner reminiscent of Maslow's concept of self-actualization. Senge argued that "five disciplines" together permit the emergence of learning organizations: 1) personal mastery, wherein each individual in the organization is committed to a process of learning; 2) mental models, wherein the assumptions held by individuals are continuously challenged through an open culture promoting inquiry and trust; 3) shared vision, which promotes a common identity wherein people learn because they want to, not because they have to; 4) team learning, which is the accumulation of individual learning in the organization; and 5) systems thinking, the integrative process that brings together the other four disciplines into a coherent body of theory and practice.[32]

Yet another theoretical approach is encapsulated in the idea of "complex adaptive systems." This suggests that organizations are systems that must be capable of rapidly responding to changing circumstances in the context of nonlinear relationships between variables. Put another way, this means that given the increasing complexity and uncertainty in the world, even a small change in one part of a system can have far-reaching ramifications for an organization, which must be flexible and nimble enough to respond to that change. This approach is derived from the "butterfly effect" based on chaos theory, where it is hypothesized that the flap of a butterfly's wing in one part of the world could trigger a tornado in another part. Complex adaptive theory tries to prepare an organization to be ready and be able to anticipate any of a number of scenarios which might result from any of a number of changing variables.

Given the diversity of approaches outlined (and again, this is not a comprehensive overview), students of public administration may be forgiven for feeling a little overwhelmed. One way of sorting through the morass of approaches is provided by management professor Gareth Morgan. He developed a typology of different "images" of organizations—a classification system of several different metaphors that can be used to describe the attributes of organizations. He suggests we can classify organizations as, among other things, machines, organisms, brains, cultures, and instruments of domination.[33] If you give some consideration to the theories and theorists studied here, you should be able to make some sense of them in terms of this template. For instance, it is clear that some theorists, like Weber and Taylor, undertake their study of organizations while regarding them as machines, as we noted. The work of the human relations school can be seen to privilege the view of organizations as organisms, as can systems, contingency, and population ecology theories. Proponents of cybernetics and similar models see organizations as brains. Marx and (to some extent) Weber view organizations as instruments of domination. In short, a rich and varied set of perspectives has been brought to bear on our understanding of organizations.

But what about Canadian public administration more specifically? How have these varied approaches affected the organization of the public sector in Canada? This is the concern of the next chapter.

## WHAT YOU HAVE LEARNED

This chapter has focused on organization theory and public administration. As such, it has sought to elucidate the ideas behind that ubiquitous presence of contemporary life—the modern organization. It is important, in studying public administration, to understand the theoretical premises upon which organizations are constructed. It is also important to appreciate that organization theory crosses from the private to the public sector and back again. This makes for some difficulty in drawing conclusions since, as you saw in chapter 1, the public and private sectors are two quite different beasts. Nonetheless, theoreticians tell us that the study of one aids us in the understanding of the other. Hence, this examination of the theoretical literature reveals the interrelationship between the dominant ideas that animate our understanding of both sectors.

But another point about organization theory needs to be emphasized. It should be obvious to you by now that no one theory explains all there is to know about organizations. You should, therefore, be considering the utility of particular theories by subjecting them to a series of questions:

- What aspects of organizational reality does a given theory purport to explain? Is it concerned with the methods managers use to maximize efficiency, or with the well-being of workers and their role in decision making?

- What level of analysis is the theory aimed at? Individuals within organizations? Parts of organizations? The whole organization? The society within which the organization is located? Or some combination of all of these?

- What conception of human nature underlies the theory? We saw that Taylor assumed people were lazy and indolent unless motivated by personal monetary gain. But Maslow felt that humans were motivated by a much more complex set of factors. What does this tell us about the way each theorist viewed human nature?

- Does the theory appear to make sense of what actually goes on in the real world of organizations? Does it explain only the workings of private sector organizations, or is it applicable to the public sector as well?

- Does the theory make sense in light of your own knowledge and experience?

This is not a comprehensive list of questions, but it should give you some idea of the nature and utility of the theoretical aspects of public administration as it has been affected by organization theory.

## Key Words and Concepts

| | |
|---|---|
| Karl Marx (62) | scientific management (75) |
| class conflict (62) | time and motion studies (77) |
| alienation (62) | POSDCORB (78) |
| hierarchy (63) | division of labour (79) |
| autonomy (63) | humanist theories (80) |
| Marxist analysis (65) | Hawthorne experiments (82) |
| accumulation (65) | informal group (83) |
| legitimation (65) | hierarchy of human needs (86) |
| Max Weber (66) | theory X and theory Y (89) |
| span of control (73) | systems theory (89) |
| bureaucratic pathologies (73) | contingency theory (91) |
| structuralist theories (74) | |

## Review Questions

This chapter was divided into five sections, each of which addressed key issues regarding theoretical approaches to understanding organizations within public administration. You should now be able to answer the questions associated with each.

### 1.  Perspectives on Bureaucratic Organization

The development of bureaucratic organizations is central to public administration. This section noted the contribution of business management thinking and its uneasy marriage with public sector values and concerns, asking the following questions: What are the main concerns of organization theory? What are the origins of organization theory? What contesting values underlie the development of theories of public administration?

### 2.  The Classic Theorists

Karl Marx and Max Weber are two thinkers whose contributions to understanding organizations and bureaucracy, though widely divergent, are the basis for much subsequent theorizing. The section examined the strengths and weaknesses of their ideas and asked, What impact have the classic theories and theorists had on public administration? What are the strengths and weaknesses of their respective theories?

### 3.  Structuralist Theories

The scientific management approach, pioneered by F.W. Taylor, arose in response to the need to improve the efficiency of large-scale modern organizations, as well as the conditions of those who worked in these structures. What types of debates have ensued over the nature and form of organization in both the private and the public sectors? What exactly were these theoretical innovations meant to accomplish when translated into practice?

### 4.  Humanist Theories

This school of thought arose in response to the dehumanizing and alienating aspects of structuralist approaches to organizational management; but it also was ultimately concerned with improving the efficiency of organizations, though with a "human" face. This section asked, How did the human relations approach originate? How did it differ from structuralism, and what impact did it have? Finally, we examined the various critiques of this approach.

### 5.  Other Theoretical Approaches

This section looks at a handful of other theoretical approaches arising out of the work of earlier schools of thought. It asks, What other theoretical approaches have emerged? How have they drawn upon theories that went before and/or innovated new approaches to understanding public administration?

## Weblinks

Marx/Engels Archive
**www.marxists.org**

Max Weber
**www.faculty.rsu.edu/~felwell/Theorists/Weber/Whome.htm**

Dead Sociologists Society
**http://media.pfeiffer.edu/lridener/dss/DEADSOC.HTML**

F.W. Taylor
**www.stevens.edu/library/collections/fwtaylor.html**

## Further Readings

### 1. Perspectives on Bureaucratic Organization

Beetham, David. *Bureaucracy*. 2nd ed. Minneapolis: University of Minnesota Press, 1996.

Denhardt, Robert B. *Theories of Public Organization*. 5th ed. Belmont, CA: Thomson Wadsworth, 2008.

### 2. The Classic Theorists

Marx, Karl. "Contribution to the Critique of Hegel's *Philosophy of Right*," in Robert C. Tucker, ed., *The Marx-Engels Reader*. 2nd ed. New York: Norton, 1978.

Merton, Robert K. "Bureaucratic Structure and Personality," in Jay M. Shafritz, J. Steven Ott and Yong Suk Jang, eds., *Classics of Organization Theory*, 7th ed. Boston: Wadsworth Centage Learning, 2011: 107–15.

Weber, Max. "Bureaucracy," in Jay M. Shafritz, J. Steven Ott, and Yong Suk Jang, eds., *Classics of Organization Theory*, 7th ed. Boston: Wadsworth Centage Learning, 2011: 77–82.

### 3. Structuralist Theories

Barnard, Chester. "Informal Organizations and Their Relation to Formal Organization," in Jay M. Shafritz and Albert C. Hyde, eds., *Classics of Public Administration*, 3rd ed. Pacific Grove, CA: Brooks/Cole, 1992: 96–100.

Gulick, Luther. "Notes on the Theory of Organization," in Jay M. Shafritz, J. Steven Ott, and Yong Suk Jang, eds., *Classics of Organization Theory*, 7th ed. Boston: Wadsworth Centage Learning, 2011: 83–91.

Simon, Herbert. "The Proverbs of Administration," in Jay M. Shafritz and Albert C. Hyde, eds., *Classics of Public Administration*, 3rd ed. Pacific Grove, CA: Brooks/Cole, 1992: 150–65.

Taylor, Frederick W. "The Principles of Scientific Management," in Jay M. Shafritz, J. Steven Ott and Yong Suk Jang, eds., *Classics of Organization Theory*, 7th ed. Boston: Wadsworth Centage Learning, 2011: 65–76.

### 4. Humanist Theories

Follett, Mary Parker. "The Giving of Orders," in J. Steven Ott, Sandra J. Parkes, and Richard B. Simpson, eds., *Classic Readings in Organizational Behavior*, 3rd ed. Toronto: Nelson Thomson, 2003: 42–47.

Maslow, A.H. "A Theory of Human Motivation," in Jay M. Shafritz, J. Steven Ott, and Yong Suk Jang, eds., *Classics of Organization Theory*, 7th ed. Boston: Wadsworth Centage Learning, 2011: 171–82.

Mayo, Elton. *The Human Problems of an Industrial Civilization*. New York: Viking, 1960.

### 5. Other Theoretical Perspectives

Mills, Albert J., Tony Simmons, and Jean Helms Mills. *Reading Organization Theory: A Critical Approach to the Study of Organizational Behaviour and Structure*. 3rd ed. Toronto: Garamond, 2005.

# Endnotes

1. See Jay M. Shafritz, J. Steven Ott, and Yong Suk Jang, eds., *Classics of Organization Theory*, 7th ed. (Boston: Wadsworth Cengage Learning, 2011).

2. Robert B. Denhardt, *Theories of Public Organization*, 5th ed. (Belmont, CA: Thomson Wadsworth, 2008): 1.

3. John Porter, *The Vertical Mosaic: An Analysis of Social Class and Power in Canada* (Toronto: University of Toronto Press, 1965).

4. Jay M. Shafritz, Albert C. Hyde, and Sandra J. Parkes, eds., *Classics of Public Administration*, 5th ed. (Belmont, CA: Thomson Wadsworth, 2004): 6.

5. See H.H. Gerth and C. Wright Mills, eds., *From Max Weber: Essays in Sociology* (New York: Oxford University Press, 1946): 196–244.

6. Robert F. Adie and Paul G. Thomas, *Canadian Public Administration: Problematical Perspectives*, 2nd ed. (Scarborough: Prentice-Hall, 1987): 18.

7. S.M. Lipset, *Agrarian Socialism*, (Berkeley: University of California Press, 1950). For an insider's views on the CCF experience, see A.W. Johnson, *Dream No Little Dreams: A Biography of the Douglas Government, 1944–1961* (Toronto: University of Toronto Press, 2004).

8. This example is cited in Howard E. McCurdy, *Public Administration: A Synthesis* (Menlo Park, CA: Cummings, 1977).

9. Robert K. Merton, *Social Theory and Social Structure* (New York: Free Press, 1957).

10. Merton's observations on the cold, impersonal characteristic of welfare officers were first made in 1940. The persistence of these attitudes over time is striking. See "The Dark Side," *St. John's Evening Telegram*, 1973, cited in Albert J. Mills and Tony Simmons, *Reading Organization Theory: A Critical Approach* (Toronto: Garamond, 1999): 41–42.

11. Alvin Gouldner, *Patterns of Industrial Bureaucracy* (New York: Free Press, 1954), and Victor A. Thompson, *Modern Organization* (New York: Knopf, 1961).

12. Frank J. Goodnow, *Politics and Administration: A Study in Government* (New York: Russell and Russell, 1900).

13. See Herbert A. Simon, "The Proverbs of Administration," in Shafritz, Hyde and Parkes, eds., *Classics of Public Administration* 5th ed. (Belmont, CA: Thomson Wadsworth, 2004): 136–49; and Herbert A. Simon, *Administrative Behaviour* (New York: Free Press, 1954).

14. Luther Gulick and L. Urwick, eds., *Papers on the Science of Administration* (New York: Augustus M. Kelly, 1937).

15. Henri Fayol, *General and Industrial Management*, trans. C. Storrs (London: Pitman, 1971).

16. Mary Parker Follett, "The Giving of Orders," in J. Steven Ott, Sandra J. Parkes, and Richard B. Simpson, eds., *Classic Readings in Organizational Behavior*, 3rd ed. (Toronto: Nelson Thomson, 2003): 42–47.

17. Elton Mayo, *The Human Problems of an Industrial Civilization* (New York: Viking, 1960). The first five chapters provide short summaries of some of the Hawthorne experiments.

18 Mayo, *The Human Problems of an Industrial Civilization*, 79.

19. Chester Barnard, **The Functions of the Executive** (Cambridge: Harvard University Press, 1938).

20. Chester Barnard, "Informal Organizations and Their Relation to Formal Organization," cited in J.M. Shafritz, A.C. Hyde, and S.J. Parkes, eds., *Classics of Public Administration*, 5th ed. (Belmont, CA: Thomson Wadsworth, 2004): 107.

21. F.J. Roethlisberger and William J. Dickson, *Management and the Worker* (Cambridge: Harvard University Press, 1939).

22. A.H. Maslow, "A Theory of Human Motivation," in J.M. Shafritz, A.C. Hyde, and S.J. Parkes, eds., *Classics of Public Administration*, 5th ed. (Belmont, CA: Thomson Wadsworth, 2004): 123–30.

23. Robert Michels, *Political Parties: a Sociological Study of the Oligarchical Tendencies of Modern Democracy*, trans. Edan and Cedar Paul (New York: Collier, 1962).

24. See Clark Kerr et al., *Industrialism and Industrial Man: The Problems of Labour and Management in Economic Growth*, 2nd ed. (Harmondsworth, UK: Penguin, 1973); Albert J. Mills, Tony Simmons, and Jean

Helms Mills, *Reading Organization Theory: A Critical Approach to the Study of Organizational Behaviour and Structure*, 3rd ed. (Toronto: Garamond, 2005).

25. See Jay M. Shafritz, Karen S. Layne, and Christopher P. Borick, eds., *Classics of Public Policy* (New York: Pearson Longman, 2005): 3.

26. Daniel Katz and Robert Khan, *The Social Psychology of Organizations* (New York: Wiley, 1966).

27. James D. Thompson, *Organization in Action* (New York: McGraw-Hill, 1967).

28. Shafritz, Ott, and Jang, eds., *Classics of Organization Theory*, 402.

29. Jay M. Shafritz and J. Steven Ott, eds., *Classics of Organization Theory*, 4th ed. (Fort Worth: Harcourt Brace, 1996): 258.

30. See Peter Aucoin, "Organizational Change in the Machinery of Canadian Government: From Rational Management to Brokerage Politics," *Canadian Journal of Political Science*, 29, 1 (1986): 3–27.

31. See Michael Hannan and John Freeman, "The Population Ecology of Organizations," *American Journal of Sociology*, 82 (1977): 929–64.

32. Peter M. Senge, *The Fifth Discipline* (New York: Doubleday, 1994).

33. Gareth Morgan, *Images of Organization*, 2nd ed. (Thousand Oaks, CA: Sage, 1997). Morgan also uses the metaphors of organizations as political systems, psychic prisons, and unfolding logics of change.

# Chapter  4

# Organization Theory *and* Canadian Public Administration

## WHAT YOU WILL LEARN

One notable characteristic of the theorists surveyed thus far is that few are Canadian. The United States and Europe (especially Britain and Germany) have proven most influential in the spread of ideas about public administration. We will now assess, in turn, the impact of each of the major schools of thought on Canadian public administration. By the end of the chapter, you will be able to answer the following questions:

■ How influential have Marx, Weber, and the other theorists been in the Canadian context?

■ In what ways have Canadian thinkers adopted their ideas or developed their own counterpoints to those ideas?

■ Are there concrete instances of the impact of their thinking on the form and structure of the public sector?

■ How effective have applications of participatory management and other contemporary theories been in Canada?

■ What is the New Public Management, and how has it influenced thinking about recent reforms in Canadian public administration?

This chapter looks at these issues in two sections.

### 1. — *The Impact of Organization Theory*

The practice of public administration in Canada is informed by the large international body of theoretical literature, going right back to the origins of the field. But exactly how inspirational have the classic, structuralist, humanist, and other thinkers been? Their influence has sometimes been subtle. But there are also ways in which the work of particular individuals and schools of thought have shaped both the practice and theory of Canadian public administration.

## 2. — *Contemporary Developments*

This section considers the most recent developments in the theory and practice of public administration in Canada in light of the perspectives sketched out in chapter 3. The dynamism of the field should be evident to you as the ongoing evolution of theoretical approaches is canvassed.

# The Impact of Organization Theory

Among the classic thinkers, Marx's critique of bureaucracy has shed light on how the power structures in society affect democracy and governing. For instance, his assertion that class is the most important division in society has important implications for who occupies decision-making posts in the political and bureaucratic realm. Some research in Canada points to a dominant **elite** representing, directly or indirectly, the capitalist class, whose dominance is reinforced through a network of social, economic, and political ties. They hang out at the same exclusive clubs; send their children to the same private schools; sit on the same boards of directors of major corporations; are wealthy and well educated; and are generally an ethnically and religiously homogeneous group, historically tending to be white, Anglo-Saxon, male Protestants (if they are English) or Catholics (if they are French).[1]

This elite dominates the top positions in government (senior public servants and politicians), who generally act in the best interests of their own class. Many prime ministers and Cabinet ministers were first corporate lawyers, business persons, and directors of important corporations.[2] Many members of the Canadian Senate sit on the boards of major corporations or have close connections to the corporate elite.[3] Moreover, there is a good deal of mobility among corporate, political, and bureaucratic careers.

Marxist theory suggests that the organizations of the state are designed to perpetuate this class's power and influence. On one level, the bureaucracy is a cold, uninviting, and alienating place that is difficult to penetrate and understand. This tends to thwart ordinary citizens, most of the time, in questioning the government's actions and also permits those in control of the bureaucracy's complicated mechanisms to use them for their own ends. But the state is not solely organized for the purpose of the elite. This is too simplistic an assertion. Rather, the state is set up so that most of the time it acts in the long-term interests of the capitalist class. There are many debates among Marxist scholars about exactly how this process works, as well as criticisms of the theory by non-Marxists.

As for Weber, there is no doubt that his theories have been profoundly influential in Canadian public administration. For instance, the 1918 reforms to the public service (see chapter 1) very strongly reflect a Weberian sensibility. Those reforms introduced the concept of merit into the public service and entrenched hierarchy, a job classification system, professionalism, and competitive exams. The intent—true to Weber's ideas—was to put the Canadian public service on a more rational basis and operate according to prescribed rules and regulations.

Taylor's scientific management approach has also been influential. Taylor's major contribution was, first, the principle that work ought to be divided up so as to take maximum advantage of employees' skills. The assembly line is the most obvious application of this principle in the private sector. In the public sector, elaborate job classification schemes have existed at least since the 1918 Civil Service Act. The second principle is that of **homogeneity**, also called **unity of direction**, which asserts that similar activities ought to be grouped together in the same unit under a single supervisor and a single plan. In public administration, then, those things related to health are organized under one department, to education under another, etc. Moreover, within departments, there is a further division of labour, with scientists grouped in one unit, policy analysts in another, clerical staff in yet another, and so on, for purposes of job function, promotion, and wages.

Furthermore, scientific management attempted to replace imprecise job criteria based on workers' personal characteristics (i.e., patronage) with the specification of job duties and requirements (i.e., merit). Public service recruits were expected to display only those "scientific qualities" that made them fit for the job. This was reflected in the Civil Service Reform Act of 1918, which was bent on eliminating all irrelevant considerations in the hiring of government workers. Thus, in Canadian public administration, the impact of scientific management was felt fairly early and was reflected in the concerns about efficiency and economy within the public service, giving rise to the reforms of 1918.

The reforms created a Civil Service Commission responsible, in part, for choosing government personnel based on scientific principles, and an elaborate classification scheme for government workers. What resulted was a system of scientific management that could satisfy the demand for the elimination of patronage and for more efficient administration in government. Analysis of the component elements of jobs was inspired by the example of scientific management; once these were analyzed, examinations could be devised to determine which candidates were best qualified to fill specific positions. The development of new methods of uniform cost accounting necessitated a uniform job terminology, which would allow the legislature to more efficiently control the finances of the public service.

Having said this, we must note that the many units of organization within the complex machinery of government are structured in a variety of ways. Some are close to the models set out by Weber or Taylor. The Canadian army, for example, or the fire and police services come closest to Weber's model. Still others reflect scientific management. For instance, in the Canada Revenue Agency, large numbers of employees work in data-processing centres that are much like large factories, and there is strong pressure on employees to conform to the organization's rules and regulations to maximize the efficient processing of tax returns and other financial information. This type of organization is rigidly structured, with rules emanating from the top downward, and little attempt is made to seek employee input into management decisions. But not all government departments are best run in this way. For example, in some departments, the workplaces are scattered throughout the country in small, regional offices, with a good deal of local control and initiative. Control is decentralized, and reporting systems are less hierarchical. Input from below is encouraged because front-line employees often have a better idea of what works than their seniors in distant Ottawa do.[4] So these organizations reflect some aspects of the human relations approach.

The point here is to ask yourself, Does any one model explain all there is to know and understand, given the complexity of modern government in Canada? Is there homogeneity in organizational types across government departments? Within departments? Are there some government organizations that display two or more of the models under consideration simultaneously?

Overall, the human relations school has been least influential in Canadian public administration. You will recall that human relations theorists argued that organizations would produce the best work environments when they implemented non-routinized tasks, recognized the goals of their employees, decentralized decision making, and worked against a hierarchical decision-making structure. In Canada, there seems to be little overt evidence that public administration was profoundly influenced by human relations; government in this country has been characterized by rigid hierarchies, inflexible job classification structures, and elements more reminiscent of Weber and of scientific management.

One exception in Canada is that decentralization became a major theme in government. In 1965, the Royal Commission on Government Organization (the Glassco Commission), pushed decentralization with the catchphrase "let the managers manage." Decentralization was aimed at securing employees' participation and commitment, and was seen as a tool for reducing delays and red tape in decision making. Politicians saw decentralization as aiding certain political objectives, and this was probably a greater motivation for its implementation than was human relations theory per se. The human relations school did sensitize the government and public to its uses in curbing excess bureaucracy. Decentralization also aided in introducing freedom of information legislation and creating specialized government offices motivated to improve democracy within bureaucracies. However, 30 years after Glassco, another review of public administration practices titled part of its report "Let the Managers Manage." Have we really gotten anywhere?

## Contemporary Developments

Most recently, organization theory evolved further into a set of concepts that can loosely be referred to as **participatory management**. The general goal was to go beyond the platitudes of human relations theorists and implement genuine worker participation in decision making in the workplace. Participatory management was premised on the view that there is an innate tension in the work organization and that this is natural and unavoidable; however, such tension can be controlled and directed. Many different approaches exist under the broad heading of participatory management, including Management by Objectives (MBO), Organization

Development (OD), and Total Quality Management (TQM). Alongside participatory management, New Public Management (NPM) has emerged. NPM incorporates private sector principles and techniques in a much more deliberate and systematic manner than in the past. We will look briefly at some trends in participatory management before turning our attention finally to NPM.

## Participatory Management

**Management by Objectives (MBO)** is derived from a theory by Peter Drucker, founder of MBO, that stood Weber's basic argument on its head.[5] MBO is centred on the notion that specialization and hierarchy can be overemphasized at the expense of the organization's overall efficiency. If you subdivide an organization into numerous specialized agencies, each with its own functions, the actions of one agency may conflict with the goals of another. For instance, the human resources department may require savings to be realized by eliminating employees to reduce payroll costs; but other departments may already be stretched to the limit in terms of personnel. Thus, if human resources does its job well, other parts of the organization may suffer. The problem, according to Drucker, is the inability of the organization's specialized parts to focus on the overall goals of the whole. The solution is MBO. While there is little agreement over the precise means of implementing MBO, several steps can be identified:

1. Consultation between top managers and their immediate subordinates to determine the organization's broad goals.
2. Preparation of a statement by top management of the overall results expected in the upcoming year.
3. Meeting between top managers and their subordinates to parcel out the responsibility for these results to individual organizational units. This task is subdivided by focusing on a) routine objectives, b) problem-solving objectives, and c) innovative objectives.
4. Repetition of the process of parceling out the responsibilities (outlined in step 3) throughout the organization.
5. Management review of this plan for consistency and to ensure that the desired goals are met.
6. Year-end comprehensive review.[6]

Some critics claim that MBO is a system that only pretends to offer greater participation in decision making, but that it ultimately leaves control in the hands of senior management. Any participation in decision making that does take place is not really meaningful. Another problem is that establishing clear and measurable objectives is often difficult to do, especially in public administration (see chapter 1). Still, MBO was used in many organizations with varying degrees of success.

**Organization Development (OD)** is traceable ultimately to the Hawthorne studies but more directly to sensitivity training, a movement that started in the 1940s. American psychologist Kurt Lewin and his associates began conducting training workshops to improve racial relations and community leadership in a Connecticut town.[7] Originally aimed at individual development and growth, the workshops gradually expanded their focus to group organizational dynamics. In these groups, organization members learned to communicate their feelings and develop strategies around increasing organizational effectiveness through interpersonal communications. Gradually, the methodology expanded to include various methods, such as employee surveys and other feedback techniques, in order to develop an action research model of organizational change (see Box 4.1).

---

**BOX 4.1** | **Organization Development Action Research**

According to Shafritz, Russell, and Borick,

*The action research model is a process for identifying needs for organizational improvement through the use of external consultation but also through fostering psychological ownership of problems and solutions by organizational members. Briefly, action research involves the following:*

1. *Collecting organizational diagnostic data (ascertaining the problem), usually either through written questionnaires or interviews.*

2. *Systematically feeding back information to the organization members who provided input.*

3. *Discussing what the information means to members and its implications for the organization in order to be certain if the "diagnosis" is accurate and to generate psychological ownership of the need for actions to improve the situation.*

4. *Jointly developing an improvement plan, using both the consultant's knowledge and skills and members' insider perspective.*

5. *Repeating all of the preceding as needed.*

**Source:** See Jay M. Shafritz, E.W. Russell, and Christopher P. Borick, *Introducing Public Administration*, 5th ed. (New York: Pearson Longman, 2007): 271.

---

OD begins with the premise that organizations become rigid and inflexible over time; responding to change becomes difficult, if not impossible. The purpose of OD is to identify rigidities and prepare the organization to be flexible enough to adjust to changes in the broader environment before crisis or collapse occurs. Lewin's prescription saw development as a process of unfreezing, change, and refreezing. OD requires recognizing a culture or history within every organization that is often an impediment to positive reform, and then developing strategies to overcome that culture or history. Dysfunctional organizational behaviour is identified, and the organization is encouraged to "unlearn" that behaviour. For instance, objections to new innovations are often framed this way: "We tried something like that before, and it didn't work." This reflects the organization's historical memory but ignores the fact that circumstances may have changed, making reform more applicable. Once this is recognized, the reforms needed are identified and implemented. Finally, new behaviours are instituted to prevent the organization from slipping back into its old dysfunctional ways.

**Total Quality Management (TQM)** is an approach to participatory management that began to emerge in the 1980s, partly as an outgrowth of OD and partly as a response to Japanese management techniques. It is associated with the work of W. Edwards Deming, who taught his techniques to Japanese business leaders, especially in the automobile industry, after the Second World War.[8] In particular, the auto industry in Japan embraced TQM. In the American model, production focused on maximizing output and then employing a separate quality control group to detect and repair problems after the fact. The Japanese approach was to make each employee responsible for the quality of his segment of the work. Thus, while it might take longer to build a car, the overall quality was better, resulting in cost savings for the organization in the longer term, since repair and recalls were fewer. The guiding principle of TQM is "Get it right the first time." Therefore, quality control is no longer considered a discrete function of part of the organization but rather an integral part of what the entire organization does.

In Canadian public administration, these ideas were instituted starting in the mid-1970s, with varying degrees of success. For instance, the federal Department of Energy, Mines, and Resources; the Office of the Auditor General; and the Department of Industry, Science, and Technology all adopted TQM. Committee structures were put in place, composed of both management and elected worker representatives. Most of these experiments failed, due primarily to the imbalance of power between management and workers, which was reinforced by the public service's rigid job classification system.

Attempts to institute participatory management in the Canadian public service have run into some serious roadblocks. The entrenched hierarchical system reflective of Weberian and Taylorist models has proven remarkably resistant to change. Even with the best of intentions, efforts to increase the participation of workers in decision-making structures have frequently floundered on the rocks of rigid job classification systems, rules, regulations, and hierarchy.

Approaches like OD encounter a set of problems unique to public administration: top management is fragmented.[9] It consists of both political and administrative executives, not to mention legislative oversight bodies and outside actors like the media and the public, who may all influence key decision-makers directly and indirectly. Entrenched interests may resist the type of change required of OD, while

internal competition, turf wars, and petty jealousies may intrude across levels of leadership rooted in political and administrative differences.

Another school of thought emerging in the 1960s and 1970s in American public administration asserted the "end of bureaucracy," predicting that the Weberian model would be gradually supplanted by "more democratic, more flexible, though more complex, forms of large-scale organizations," which American administrative historian Dwight Waldo termed "postbureaucratic."[10] Rather than being assessed according to rank and status, employees would be evaluated more flexibly according to competence; organizational charts would give way to project groups. Hierarchical lines of authority would shift to more democratic and participatory models. Presaging NPM, a call emerged for the "reinvention of government." A more strategic orientation geared to the deployment of increasingly scarce resources caused officials and theorists to look to changing expectations and values as well as new structures and processes within government. Adaptivity was welcomed, even at the cost of morale and actual positions. Flattening of hierarchies, teamwork, processes of continuous learning, and a leadership style that excelled at articulating a vision rather than just giving orders was called for. The clearest expression of these new approaches in the federal government was found in a wide-scale review of the federal public service called *Public Service 2000* (see chapter 9), whose recommendations included "improved 'service to the public' . . . and an environment where 'public servants will be empowered and encouraged to decide themselves how best to use the resources made available to them in order to get the job done in the most efficient manner.'"[11] Some of the purported changes to Canadian public administration in recent years are shown in Table 4.1. Shields and Evans contrast traditional bureaucratic structures with the main features of newer models.[12] Following trends in private sector management toward "virtual" forms of corporate organization, the view emerged that large, hierarchically and vertically integrated corporations and organizations were too slow and cumbersome in responding to customer demands under the enhanced competition brought on by globalization. Attempts were made to flatten the organizational pyramid, create relatively autonomous operating units, and maximize the use of modern technologies to complete projects through teams that would come together for a project, disband upon completion, and reform with other personnel for subsequent tasks.

In the public sector, this model was emulated under the rubric of "flexible government." Presuming that traditional bureaucracies were rigid and unresponsive, advocates of flexible government called for an end to the permanence inherent in lifelong employment and careers in the public sector and for breaking down permanent structures and replacing them with more fluid virtual organizations. Concretely, this meant public sector downsizing, contingent public sector employment, contracting out, privatization, alternative service delivery, and deregulation. The reality, of course, was that these types of change were problematic and controversial, and encountered considerable resistance.[13] Nonetheless, they presaged another major development in administrative theorizing and reform: NPM.

**TABLE 4.1    Traditional Bureaucratic Organizations**

| Traditional Bureaucratic Organizations | The New Public Sector Organization |
|---|---|
| A.  Hierarchy and Central Command | Flattened and Decentralized Organization and Decision Making |
| B.  Rule-Governed and Upward Accountability | Results-Centred<br>• achievement of goals rather than process is what counts |
| C.  Static/Status Quo<br>• all change initiated and driven from above<br>• emphasis given to continuity over continuous change | Change-Driven High Performance Organizations<br>• risk-taking, continuous improvement and innovation are encouraged from all levels of the organization |
| D.  Standardized Citizen's Right to Public Services<br>• emphasis on universal legal rights to services | Client-Focused<br>• emphasis upon individual customer satisfaction and service to selective client groups<br>• clients as taxpayers |
| E.  Tayloristic-Style Operating Structure | Empowering Employees<br>• use of new human resource strategies such as Total Quality Management |
| F   Process-Driven Organization<br>• static tasks, hierarchical institution, rigidly specified job categories | The Learning Organization<br>• workforce is multiskilled<br>• a learning and adapting environment |
| G.  Fordist Production System<br>• workforce based upon economies of scale, i.e., large workforce involved in all aspects of production and service delivery | The Flexible Workplace<br>• "just-in-time" lean production<br>• extensive use of part-time and contract workers<br>• contracting out of tasks<br>• alternative service delivery |

**Source:** John Shields and B. Mitchell Evans, *Shrinking the State: Globalization and Public Administration "Reform"* (Halifax: Fernwood, 1998): 44. Reprinted with permission of Fernwood Publishing Co. Ltd.

## Critical and Feminist Theory

You may have noticed that in the various theoretical models, there is a strange silence on certain issues, particularly gender and race/ethnicity. Until the past 30 years, scholars of public administration and organization theory seemed to assume away any ascriptive or socio-economic characteristics or differences among the individuals who populated organizations. Mainstream textbooks were largely silent on these issues. Mills, Simmons, and Mills report that a study of 107 textbooks widely used in Canada and the United States in courses on management, organization theory, and organizational behaviour between 1959 and 1995 showed that, prior to the mid-1980s, 21 texts (81 percent) said nothing about race and ethnicity while the remaining five (19 percent) made only passing references to it. Since 1985, they go on to report, 27 texts (45 percent) had nothing to say about race, 30 (50 percent) mentioned it in passing, and only three (5 percent) addressed it in depth. Where gender was concerned, 30 texts (34 percent), including nine that were published in the 1990s, had nothing to say. All but a handful of the rest of the texts barely scratched the surface of the topic. Another study of texts published between 1960 and 2000 found very little acknowledgement in management textbooks of the growing influence of feminist scholarship.[14]

If you think back to the major theorists discussed in chapter 3, you probably noticed that all of them are men except for Mary Parker Follett. You may also have noticed that many of them, like Weber, Taylor, and the structuralists, privileged the idea of rationality—a masculine trait—and did not even consider the possibility of other ways of acting and knowing, such as intuition, emotionality, or non-rationality. You might have noticed as well that in the Hawthorne experiments, one group of subjects was exclusively male, while the other was female, yet no comment was made in the studies about the effect of gender on the experiments. Nor was it acknowledged that the experimenters were all male and that this may have prejudiced the findings in certain ways. Similarly, no account was taken of workers' and experimenters' differing ethnicity, race, or class positions and how that might have conditioned the subjects' responses or the experiment design. In these and countless other examples, organizational theory has been myopic.

Feminist scholarship has revealed the poverty of marginalizing differentiated groups. While feminist theory gave rise to a large body of literature critiquing the liberal state for its emphasis on individualism and a strict demarcation between private and public sectors, little of this theorizing was applied to public administration: "Feminist theories offered new theories of power, of virtue, of the nature of organizations, and of leadership and professionalism and brought to light fundamental ways in which women have shaped society and politics. Yet few if any of these ideas have made their way into conversations in public administration."[15]

One argument is that the genders operate in different ways in organizations. Women's growing participation in the workplace made this fact increasingly plain and caused feminist scholars to rethink organizational dynamics. This is particularly germane to public administration since the majority of public sector workers in Canada and many other countries are now women (although they are under-represented in the executive and the technical categories, and over-represented in the administrative support category, a fact we explore in more detail in chapter 8). In addition, women have entered schools of public administration and related disciplines in increasing numbers in recent years. It is estimated that in the United States, three out of four public administration graduate students are women[16] (see Box 4.2). Yet relatively little reflection about these trends has made its way into the scholarship until fairly recently.

Early feminists in Canada focused on the structures of inequality in public bureaucracies, pointing out, for instance, the "ghettoization" of women in so-called "pink collar" positions and women's relative absence from the upper echelons of power.[17] Others focused on women's lack of representation in political positions of

---

### BOX 4.2 A Woman's Place in Public Administration

The experience described here, although that of an American woman, is not unique and likely reflects many Canadian women's experiences as well:

*In 1981 I enrolled at Virginia Tech's Center for Public Administration and Policy. Launched on my doctoral studies, I occasionally grumbled to myself about the absence of discussion about women's issues, the all-male faculty, the fact that we never seemed to read anything by a woman (except for good old Mary Parker Follett), the articles that used he and his for the whole human race. I kept these complaints to myself, however; I wanted to be seen as a good student. I guess I hoped that my professors wouldn't notice— or at least attach any significance to the fact—that I was a woman.*

*Then came lengthy conversations with . . . other women students. I began to see both the absence of women from the course material and my own distance from women's concerns as moral issues. My intellectual curiosity was also aroused; I began to do some reading in feminist theory and decided I would do a paper on "something to do with women and public administration"— something that would explore the ways in which a feminist perspective might change thinking in the field. To prepare myself, I went back through Public Administration Review, intending to build on what had already been written. I was shocked (a sign of my naïveté) to find that in the past decade, there had been almost nothing written from a feminist viewpoint. . . . It seemed impossible (at the time), but despite what I knew was an outpouring of feminist work in political theory, organizational sociology, and even economics, public administration theory appeared to be innocent of a feminist theoretical perspective.*

**Source:** Camilla Stivers, *Gender Images in Public Administration: Legitimacy and the Administrative State* (Newbury Park, CA: Sage, 1993): vii.

power.[18] Later feminists began to argue that the predominance of male scholarship in organization theory has meant that organizations have mainly been seen from male perspectives. Gendered processes reinforce and perpetuate the maleness of organizations, including gendered divisions that produce gender patterning of jobs, masculine-rooted organizational symbols and images, and male-based values, such as dominance and subordination, characterizing interactions in the workplace.[19] A considerable body of research has also emerged that shows that women have different management styles than men: for instance, they act more co-operatively and share leadership more, and are less likely to fall back on the "command-and-control" Weberian models preferred by men. Women privilege different values than men, such as trust, openness, and acceptance, and they are less aggressive than men. Another approach argues that the state, rather than being inherently patriarchal, should be viewed as being constituted by individual institutions that vary in their makeup, some of which are "culturally marked as masculine," since the state is not a monolith that always acts to oppress or exclude women.[20]

These various theoretical approaches are increasingly important given both women's growing participation in organizations traditionally the purview of men and women's interest in broadening the scope of organizational theory. As American feminist scholar Camilla Stivers asserts, as long as administration is seen as genderless, women will continue to face the unpalatable choice of either adopting a masculine administrative identity or accepting marginalization in the hierarchy.[21] To assess the significance of feminist arguments about the role of women in organizations, you might ask yourself, What difference would it make if women were in charge of all major government organizations and if all the leading scholars in the field were women? (See Figure 4.1.)

## New Public Management

Much contemporary organization theory centres on **New Public Management (NPM)**. NPM found its origin in the approach to governing pioneered by Britain's former prime minister Margaret Thatcher and later followed by former American president Ronald Reagan and former Canadian prime minister Brian Mulroney.[22] NPM has been motivated by three things:

■ the debt and deficit problems of governments that resulted in a search for more economical ways of governing;

■ a growing alienation from politics and politicians among ordinary citizens, a rise in apathy, distrust of governments, and a decline in public confidence in public policies and services provided by governments; and

■ globalization and the emergence of a new economic order in which the traditional nation-state has declined in significance in comparison to transnational corporations and other global actors.

NPM theory's basic response to these developments was to argue for a rolling back of the state and its withdrawal from a number of areas. Changes in public administration focused on **privatization**, **deregulation**, **contracting out** of public

**FIGURE 4.1     Power in the Institutions of the Canadian State**

♀ = Majority Female
♂ = Majority Male

**Judicial Branch:**
Courts ♂

**Executive Branch:**
Cabinet ♂
Prime Minister ♂

**Legislative Branch:**
Senate ♂
House of Commons ♂

**Public Service:**
Executive ♂
Clerical ♀
Military ♂
Police ♂

**Crown Corporations:**
The Bank of Canada ♂
CBC ♂

**Source:** Adapted from Jill Vickers, *Reinventing Political Science* (Halifax: Fernwood, 1997): 10. Reprinted with permission of Fernwood Publishing Co. Ltd.

services, decentralization, **downsizing**, expenditure reduction initiatives (including layoffs of public servants, wage freezes, and rollbacks), **user fees**, commercialization of public enterprises, and similar measures. It also required the adoption and embrace of a new organizational culture by public servants.

According to political scientist Peter Aucoin, NPM requires state administrators to accommodate themselves to certain assumptions: public servants have gained too much power over politicians in recent years; the organizational mechanisms of government have become too complex and now actually impede political leadership in exercising authority and managing government; and management in government has become too concerned with rigid adherence to rules and procedures and too prone to bureaucratic pathologies.[23] Thus, criticisms of government bureaucracy emerged that focused on *re-engineering* the whole apparatus and role of government. More precisely, such criticisms prompted a search for management techniques that put the operation of government on a more businesslike footing.

The intellectual roots of NPM can be found in theorists' attempts to go beyond structuralist and humanist approaches, particularly to private sector management. An early source was Thomas Peters and Robert Waterman's *In Search of Excellence*, published in 1982.[24] The authors studied a number of well-run American corporations, looking for a formula in large organizations that suggested the necessary qualities for success. They argued for de-emphasizing Weberian rationality and focusing more closely on the messy human side of organizational life, as well as paying sharper attention to customers' needs. While their book was not without its critics, it was nonetheless widely read in business circles and, eventually, in the public sector, too.

Among the most influential proponents of NPM were David Osborne and Ted Gaebler, who argued that "governments must steer, not row." Their 1992 book, *Reinventing Government,* outlined 10 principles on the assumption that while government is necessary, it does not necessarily have to act like government but could be much more businesslike in its operations. They argued the following:

*Most entrepreneurial governments promote competition between service providers. They empower citizens by pushing control out of the bureaucracy, into the community. They measure the performance of their agencies, focusing not on inputs but on outcomes. They are driven by their goals—their missions—not by their rules and regulations. They redefine their clients as customers and offer them choices—between schools, between training programs, between housing options. They prevent problems before they emerge, rather than simply offering services afterward. They put their energies into earning money, not simply spending it. They decentralize authority, embracing participatory management. They prefer market mechanisms to bureaucratic mechanisms. And they focus not simply on providing public services, but on catalyzing all sectors—public, private, and voluntary—into action to solve their community's problems.* [25]

One theorist suggests that NPM arose in part as critique of bureaucracy. British public management professor Christopher Pollitt puts it this way:

*Bureaucracy is pictured as ruling the pre-NPM earth like a dinosaur. Like a dinosaur, it was too big, too slow-moving, too insensitive, insufficiently adaptable, and seriously underpowered as far as brains were concerned. Messages took too long to get all the way down the hierarchy from the tiny little head to the cumbersome feet and claws, and, by the same token, information travelled up from the ground level to the brain at an agonizingly slow pace. The large size demanded a huge and continuous supply of resources. . . . So bureaucracy was cast as the enemy of freedom, creativity and efficiency.* [26]

Of course, this characterization is problematic for a number of reasons. For instance, it assumes that "bureaucracy" is one big, undifferentiated whole. It is not. It is made up of countless components, some of which may fit the above description under certain circumstances but most of which are highly effective and efficient in the execution of their duties. Put another way, the critique ignores entirely the positive features of public service by painting a simplistic picture of some kind of singular "creature" when, in fact, we are talking about a diverse array of animals with a rich variety of organizational forms and structures.

NPM is largely driven by the same values that underlie those of the private sector: the **three Es** of *efficiency, effectiveness,* and *economy.* These are placed within the framework of "quality service" to citizens, who are referred to as "customers" or "clients." A much greater level of attention is paid to the relationship between expenditures and revenues, even at the cost of sacrificing long-established and cherished government policies and programs as administrators are confronted with "clients" demanding improved services at less cost. As Aucoin notes, "Concerns for economy and efficiency have thus been given a new priority in public management. Enhancing cost-consciousness, doing more with less and achieving value for money became the objectives of this finance-centred perspective on public management reform."[27] Organizations were effectively "debureaucratized." Donald Savoie suggests that "the philosophy [of NPM] is rooted in the conviction that private sector management is superior to public administration. The solution, therefore, is to transfer government activities to the private sector through privatization and contracting out." But, as he goes on to suggest, it is hardly practical to transfer *all* government activities to the private sector, so "the next best solution is to transfer business management practices to government operations." [28]

Political scientist Alan Tupper cites a trenchant critique of the NPM idea of treating citizens as clients or customers. He argues that "new public management debases Canadian democracy in deep but subtle ways. It denigrates democratic citizenship by portraying citizens as customers of government." He goes on to suggest that "new public management's stress on private sector management theories, market tests, and partnerships transforms government from a unique institution into a commonplace fixture that can be managed by the same principles as a grocery store."[29]

In any event, a literature on public administration has emerged that suggests that NPM was never very thoroughly applied in the Canadian context or, more precisely, that the Canadian variant of NPM that evolved was softer than the model imposed on Britain, New Zealand, Australia, and other places.[30] Some theorists argue that in many countries, NPM reforms are being reversed, and that we are already moving beyond NPM.[31] For now, it is suffice to note that the impact of NPM is apparent in a series of reforms instituted by the federal government, such as Program Review, PS2000, and the Public Service Modernization Act (see chapter 9), which called for improved service to the public, support for innovation, better human resource management practices, and new forms of accountability focused on results and performance.

A variety of impediments frustrated the wholesale application of NPM, not the least of which was lack of political will, with the result that Canadian reforms paled in comparison to those in other countries.[32] Nonetheless, the introduction of reforms to improve client satisfaction with government services proliferated (e.g., the 1995 Quality Service Initiative), as did new innovations deemed "alternative service delivery" mechanisms. What emerged was "an increasing number of instruments, ranging from traditional ones such as departments, Crown corporations, and mixed enterprises to newer ones such as special operating agencies, privatized public organizations, single-window service-delivery units, and partnerships," which, according to some theorists of public administration, are derived from NPM but move beyond it to the post-bureaucratic model.[33]

Critics of NPM point out that wholesale reform has been taking place without public consultation or popular approval. Others suggest that NPM represents yet another fad in a long line of changing tastes. Moreover, the critics contend, proponents of NPM have forgotten Wallace Sayre's law that public and private administration are fundamentally alike in all unimportant respects. Aucoin argues that

it is increasingly acknowledged that public service reform cannot be based on a paradigm that assumes that public administration is essentially the same as private administration. The public policy dimension is unique to public management as governance. Citizen-centred service requires attention to critical issues of law, rights, and due process not present in the marketplace of private service delivery. And managing the public service entails managing in a context of constraints and motivations that are distinct to the public sector. To the degree that privatization and contracting out cannot be extended to all functions of government, public administration, even in a highly devolved management regime, remains subject to political and administrative dynamics that require their own distinctive modes of reform and renewal.[34]

Responding to the shortcomings of NPM, American public administration theorists Janet and Robert Denhardt argue for a new framework for the reaffirmation of democratic values, citizenship, and service in the public interest organized around a core of seven principles:

1. Serve citizens, not customers.
2. Seek the public interest.
3. Value citizenship and public service above entrepreneurialism.
4. Think strategically, act democratically.
5. Recognize that accountability isn't simple.
6. Serve, rather than steer.
7. Value people, not just productivity.[35]

They also argue that "government should not be run like a business; it should be run like a democracy."[36]

As you can see, the development of organization theory has proceeded through several different stages, each having an impact on the public administration of Canada. You may be forgiven if the array of theories seems a little daunting. Imagine for a moment that you are a public sector manager having to implement some version of one of them! The complexities of doing so show that there is sometimes a gap between theory and practice, a point illustrated by two former public servants in an article that argued that there is often a distinction between the "surreal" world of theory and the "real" world of practice.[37] Theorist Iain Gow has noted that while "public administration in Canada is necessarily rooted in practical considerations," academic theorizing can nonetheless offer some assistance in analyzing, critically commenting upon and advising public servants in their work.[38] To put these theoretical concerns into more focus, we turn in the next chapter to that "real" world of organizations, looking at the actual machinery of government to see more concretely the impact of theory on practice.

## WHAT YOU HAVE LEARNED

This chapter has illuminated some of the ways in which various theoretical approaches to the concept of organization have influenced Canadian public administration. It observed that Canadian ideas have been heavily influenced by foreign ones in this area, particularly American, British, and German. The classic thinkers have been influential, though sometimes in subtle ways. The basic Weberian-type model has largely prevailed in the structure and organization of Canadian public administration, while structuralist and humanist theories have waxed and waned over time; and various alternative theoretical approaches arising out of these schools have also left their mark on Canadian public administration.

## *Key Words and Concepts*

| | |
|---|---|
| elite (100) | New Public Management (NPM) (110) |
| homogeneity (101) | privatization (110) |
| unity of direction (101) | deregulation (110) |
| participatory management (102) | contracting out ( 110) |
| Management by Objectives | downsizing ( 111) |
| (MBO) (103) | user fees ( 111) |
| Organization Development (OD) (103) | three Es (efficiency, effectiveness, and |
| Total Quality Management (TQM) (105) | economy) ( 112) |

## *Review Questions*

This chapter was divided into two sections addressing the impact of organization theory on Canadian public administration. You should now be able to answer the questions associated with each.

### 1. *The Impact of Organization Theory*

Sometimes it is hard to see the relevance of theoretical arguments to the real world. To discern which approaches have been most influential in shaping the organization of the Canadian government, this section explored the ways in which theory has been concretely applied in the Canadian experience. We asked the following questions: What theories have had the most influence on the development of Canadian public administration? How have contending schools of thought affected the actual organization and functioning of the Canadian public sector?

### 2. *Contemporary Developments*

The most recent developments in the theory of organizations were examined in this section. In trying to wed the theoretical with the concrete, we asked, How have recent theoretical developments affected organizations in the public sector in practice? After reading this chapter and the previous one, you should have a firm grasp of the major contending theories of public administration, the thinkers associated with each, and the impact of organizational life on the government and on us as individuals.

## Weblinks

Government of Canada
**www.canada.gc.ca**

Canada Gazette
**www.canadagazette.gc.ca**

Canada Public Service Agency
**www.psagency-agencefp.gc.ca**

## Further Reading

### 1. The Impact of Organization Theory

Johnson, David. *Thinking Government: Public Sector Management in Canada*, 2nd ed. Peterborough: Broadview, 2006: chaps. 5, 10.

Mills, Albert J., Tony Simmons, and Jean Helms Mills. *Reading Organization Theory: A Critical Approach to the Study of Organizational Behaviour and Structure.* 3rd ed. Aurora: Garamond, 2005.

Mintzberg, Henry, and Jacques Bourgault. *Managing Publicly.* Toronto: Institute of Public Administration of Canada, 2000.

Sossin, Lorne. "Democratic Administration," in Christopher Dunn, ed., *The Handbook of Canadian Public Administration*, 2nd ed. Toronto: Oxford University Press, 2010: 268–86.

### 2. Contemporary Developments

Borins, Sandford. "The New Public Management Is Here to Stay." *Canadian Public Administration*, 38, 1 (1995): 122–32.

Dwivedi, O.P., Tim A. Mau, and Byron Sheldrick, eds. *The Evolving Physiology of Government: Canadian Public Administration in Transition.* Ottawa: University of Ottawa Press, 2009.

Hood, Christopher. "A Public Management for All Seasons." *Public Administration*, 69, 1 (1991): 3–19.

Lindquist, Evert. "Public Administration Research and Organization Theory: Recovering Alternative Perspectives on Public Service Institutions," in Christopher Dunn, ed., *The Handbook of Canadain Public Administration*, 2nd ed. Toronto: Oxford University Press, 2010: 149–66.

Savoie, Donald. "What Is Wrong with the New Public Management?" *Canadian Public Administration*, 38, 1 (1995): 112–21.

Shields, John, and B. Mitchell Evans. *Shrinking the State: Globalization and Public Administration "Reform."* Halifax: Fernwood, 1998.

Tupper, Allan. "New Public Management and Canadian Politics," in Janine Brodie and Linda Trimble, eds., *Reinventing Canada: Politics of the 21st Century.* Toronto: Prentice Hall, 2003: 231–42.

## Endnotes

1.  The groundbreaking study in this regard was John Porter's *The Vertical Mosaic: An Analysis of Social Class and Power in Canada* (Toronto: University of Toronto Press, 1965). See also Dennis Olsen, *The State Elite* (Toronto: McClelland and Stewart, 1980); Wallace Clement, *The Canadian Corporate Elite: An Analysis of Economic Power* (Toronto: McClelland and Stewart, 1975); and Wallace Clement, *Class, Power and Property: Essays on Canadian Society* (Toronto: Methuen, 1983).

2.  See, for example, Gregory J. Inwood, *Continentalizing Canada: The Politics and Legacy of the Macdonald Royal Commission* (Toronto: University of Toronto Press, 2006): chapter 10.

3. An early analysis of the class ties between the Senate and business is Colin Campbell's *The Canadian Senate: A Lobby Within* (Toronto: Macmillan, 1978). For a class analysis of the role of front-line public servants, see Greg McElligott, *Beyond Public Service: State Workers, Public Policy and the Prospects for Democratic Administration* (Toronto: University of Toronto Press and IPAC, 2001).

4. For an analysis of different styles of organization within Canadian departments and agencies, see Henry Mintzberg and Jacques Bourgault, eds., *Managing Publicly* (Toronto: Institute of Public Administration of Canada, 2000).

5. Peter F. Drucker, *The Practice of Management* (New York: Harper and Row, 1954).

6. Drucker, *The Practice of Management*; adapted from Kenneth Kernaghan and David Siegel, *Public Administration in Canada* (Scarborough: ITP Nelson, 1995): 71. Repr. by permission of ITP Nelson.

7. See Jay M. Shafritz, E.W. Russell, and Christopher P. Borick, *Introducing Public Administration*, 5th ed. (New York: Pearson Longman, 2007): 270–71.

8. See W. Edwards Deming, *Quality, Productivity and Competitive Position* (Cambridge: MIT Centre for Advanced Engineering Study, 1982).

9. See Shafritz, Russell, and Borick, *Introducing Public Administration,*270; and Christopher Pollitt, "New Forms of Public Service: Issues in Contemporary Organizational Design," in Thomas J. Courchene and Donald J. Savoie, eds., *The Art of the State: Governance in a World Without Frontiers* (Montreal: Institute for Research on Public Policy, 2003): 209–35.

10. Cited in Shafritz, Russell, and Borick, *Introducing Public Administration,* 289.

11. Canada, *Public Service 2000: The Renewal of the Public Service of Canada* (Ottawa: Supply and Services, 1990): 46, cited in Laurent Dobuzinskis, "Public Administration," in Michael Howlett and David Laycock, eds., *Puzzles of Power: An Introduction to Political Science*, 2nd ed. (Toronto: Oxford University Press, 1998): 159. For an analysis from the perspective of the culture and values of public administration, see O.P. Dwivedi and James Iain Gow, *From Bureaucracy to Public Management: The Administrative Culture of the Government of Canada* (Peterborough: Broadview, 1999).

12. John Shields and B. Mitchell Evans, *Shrinking the State: Globalization and Public Administration "Reform"* (Halifax: Fernwood, 1998): 44.

13. See Donald J. Savoie, "Fifteen Years of Reform: What Have We Learned?" in B. Guy Peters and Donald J. Savoie, eds. *Taking Stock: Assessing Public Sector Reforms* (Montreal: McGill-Queen's University Press, 1998): 394–414.

14. Albert J. Mills, Tony Simmons, and Jean Helms Mills, *Reading Organization Theory: A Critical Approach to the Study of Organizational Behaviour and Structure*, 3rd ed. (Aurora: Garamond, 2005), 39 n1.

15. Camilla Stivers, *Gender Images in Public Administration: Legitimacy and the Administrative State* (Newbury Park, CA: Sage, 1993): 3. See also Roberta Hamilton, *Gendering the Vertical Mosaic: Feminist Perspectives on Canadian Society,* (Toronto: Copp Clark, 1996); and Joan Acker, "Gendering Organizational Theory," in Jay M. Shafritz, J. Steven Ott, and Yong Suk Jang, eds., *Classics of Organization Theory*, 7th ed. (Boston: Wadsworth Cengage Learning, 2011): 480–88.

16. Stivers, *Gender Images.*

17. On the history of women in the Canadian public service, see Nicole Morgan, *The Equality Game: Women in the Federal Public Service, 1908–1987* (Ottawa: Canadian Advisory Council on the Status of Women, 1988); and Caroline Andrew, "Women and the Public Sector," in Christopher Dunn, ed., *The Handbook of Canadian Public Administration*, 2nd ed. (Toronto: Oxford University Press, 2010): 319–29.

18. See Sylvia Bashevkin, ed., *Opening Doors Wider: Women's Political Engagement in Canada* (Vancouver: UBC Press, 2009).

19. Shafritz, Russell, and Borick, *Introducing Public Administration*, 295.

20. Louise A. Chappell, *Gendering Government: Feminist Engagement with the State in Australia and Canada* (Vancouver: UBC Press, 2003): 11. See also Susan B. Boyd, ed., *Challenging the Public/Private Divide: Feminism, Law and Public Policy* (Toronto: University of Toronto Press, 1997).

21. Stivers, *Gender Images*.

22. Peter Aucoin, "New Public Management and New Public Governance: Finding the Balance," in David Siegel and Ken Rasmussen, eds., *Professionalism and Public Service: Essays in Honour of Kenneth Kernaghan* (Toronto: University of Toronto Press and IPAC, 2008): 16–33.

23. Peter Aucoin, *The New Public Management: Canada in Comparative Perspective* (Montreal: Institute for Research on Public Policy, 1995): 3–4.

24. Thomas Peters and Robert Waterman, *In Search of Excellence: Lessons from America's Best-Run Companies* (New York: Harper and Row, 1982).

25. David Osborne and Ted Gaebler, *Reinventing Government: How the Entrepreneurial Spirit is Transforming the Public Sector* (New York: Penguin, 1993): 19–20.

26. Christopher Pollitt, *The Essential Public Manager* (Philadelphia: Open University Press, 2003): 32–33.

27. Aucoin, *The New Public Management*, 9.

28. Donald Savoie, "What Is Wrong with the New Public Management?" *Canadian Public Administration*, 38, 1 (1995): 113.

29. Alan Tupper, "New Public Management and Canadian Politics," in Janine Brodie and Linda Trimble, eds., *Reinventing Canada: Politics of the 21st Century* (Toronto: Prentice Hall, 2003): 239–40.

30. Aucoin, "New Public Management and New Public Governance."

31. Peter Aucoin, "Beyond the 'New' in Public Management Reform in Canada: Catching the Next Wave?" in Christopher Dunn, ed., *The Handbook of Canadian Public Administration* (Toronto: Oxford University Press, 2002): 50; and Leslie A. Pal, *Beyond Policy Analysis: Public Issue Management in Turbulent Times*, 4th ed. (Toronto: Nelson, 2010): 227.

32. See Aucoin, "Beyond the 'New' in Public Management Reform in Canada," 36–52; and Kenneth Kernaghan, Brian Marson, and Sandford Borins, *The New Public Organization* (Toronto: Institute of Public Administration of Canada, 2000).

33. See Donald J. Savoie, *Thatcher, Reagan and Mulroney: In Search of a New Bureaucracy* (Toronto: University of Toronto Press, 1994); and Aucoin, *The New Public Management*.

34. Aucoin, "Beyond the 'New' in Public Management Reform in Canada," 50.

35. Janet V. Denhardt and Robert B. Denhardt, *The New Public Service: Serving, Not Steering*, expanded ed. (Armonk, NY: M.E. Sharpe, 2007): 42–43.

36. Denhardt and Denhardt, *The New Public Service*, 3.

37. Ian D. Clark and Harry Swain, "Distinguishing the Real from the Surreal in Management Reform: Suggestions for Beleaguered Administrators in the Government of Canada," *Canadian Public Administration*, 48, 4 (2005): 453–76.

38. Iain Gow, "Evolution of Disciplinary Approaches and Paradigms in the Study of Public Administration in Canada," in O.P. Dwivedi, Tim A. Mau, and Byron Sheldrick, eds., *The Evolving Physiology of Government: Canadian Public Administration in Transition* (Ottawa: University of Ottawa Press, 2009): 3.

# Chapter (5)

# Public Administration and Institutions: *The* Real World *of* Organizations and *the* Machinery *of* Government

## WHAT YOU WILL LEARN

In this chapter, we will consider the place at which public administration theory and public administration practice in Canada intersect. To this end, we will look closely at the following questions:

- What contextual factors shape the structure and organization of public administration in Canada?
- What are the key relationships within those structures?
- What are the key institutions within which those relationships play themselves out, and why does structure matter in the provision of programs and services for Canadians?

Chapter 5 is divided into the following sections:

### 1. ⌐ *Factors Influencing Organizational Structure*

Here we look at the basic framework of the Canadian political system and ask, How have capitalist democracy, federalism, and cabinet-parliamentary government influenced the organization of the Canadian government? How have the very outlines of the state influenced public administration?

### 2. ⌐ *Political–Administrative Relationships*

Chapter 1 introduced you to the relationship between public administration and democratic government. This section elaborates on this relationship by focusing on the roles of politicians and public servants in more detail, and asks, Who is in control of the machinery and actions of the state?

### 3. — Departmental Organizations

Why do governments grow and shrink over time? Why do some prime ministers prefer large Cabinets with many departments, while others opt for more stripped-down models? This section introduces you to the actual organizational units of the Canadian government, both traditional and new. In so doing, we will explain why, organizationally speaking, the government looks the way it does.

### 4. — Regulatory Agencies

What role do regulatory bodies play in public administration? In an era of deregulation and downsizing, we have been rethinking the areas that government should be regulating. Why is this?

### 5. — Crown Corporations

The role of Crown corporations in Canada has been important. But recently, the wisdom of using public ownership (i.e., the use of Crown corporations) to achieve policy goals has been questioned. What explains their use over time in Canada, and why are Crown corporations as policy instruments being re-evaluated?

After reading this chapter, you should be able to explain the relationship between politicians and public servants, and the main factors influencing the organization of the public sector, including departments, regulatory agencies, Crown corporations, and alternative service delivery mechanisms, while keeping in mind the organizational theories studied earlier.

# Factors Influencing Organizational Structure

Before we dive into the nature of political and administrative relationships, we must be clear about some fundamentals. The first point is that public administration in Canada takes place within a capitalist democracy. Second, Canada has a federal system. Third, within that federal system, we have a cabinet-parliamentary government. What exactly do these terms mean? It is worth spending a moment clarifying them, since these systems are the framework for Canadian public administration. Then, we will look more closely at the organization of government within this framework.

## Capitalist Democracy

The first point about factors shaping the organization of government is that governing in Canada takes place within the context of capitalist democracy.[1] This is a political-economic system whose broad rules impose themselves on the scope of action of governments in obvious and subtle ways. At the most basic level, it combines capitalist relations of production with democratic electoral institutions that shape public administration; ultimately, organizational life must conform to this system.

You might look at it this way. At the root of capitalist economic systems is the right to private property. To defend that right, state structures are created that act in the interests of those who hold property. If we define *property* here to mean the "means of production" (i.e., capital, machines, factories, land, natural resources, information systems, etc.), then in a capitalist system, state structures act in the interests of the capitalists. In other words, business interests (capital) must be defended through the structures of the state. At the same time, in a democratic society, the will of the majority must prevail. Since the majority of Canadians are not capitalists (ownership of the means of production in Canada is concentrated in few hands), the state must also respond to the democratically expressed will of ordinary citizens. Geoffrey Hale, an expert on business–government relations, says, "the frequent dependence of politicians and governments on businesses, large and small, for economic development, job creation, and political support has made the mobilization of this support a major element of democratic political life since the late-eighteenth and early-nineteenth centuries."[2] Political scientist Neil Bradford asserts,

*This combination of capitalism and democracy must reasonably be seen to set broad and general parameters on policy-making. Elected officials clearly rely heavily on private investors to sustain growth, employment, revenue, and so forth. Given the value voters placed on these outputs, this dependence on "business confidence" reduces the political incentive for certain kinds of policy innovation, for example, those that directly challenge the existing property system.*[3]

The organization of government thus must meet the needs of property-holding capitalists by creating the conditions for profitability, to ensure that business confidence is maintained. But this must be balanced against the interests of others in the system, whose interests may be in direct contrast to the capitalists.

For instance, it may enhance profitability for a corporation to simply dump its waste in a nearby river; but that action certainly is not in the interests of the communities situated along the river. The citizens may mobilize and demand that the government do something about industrial pollution, and, hence, a ministry of the environment is created. The corporation may resist attempts by the new ministry to impose restrictions on polluting by threatening to move its plant to some other jurisdiction that has fewer environmental laws. Less drastically, it may look to other parts of the state structure for assistance. There may be, for instance, a ministry of industry that provides subsidies for the purchase of pollution-control equipment for corporations; or the ministry of finance may provide tax breaks to corporations that promise to meet certain environmental goals. Whatever the case, the organization of the state flows in a very direct way from the interaction and tension between capitalism and democracy.

## Federalism

A federal system of government is one in which the constitutional authority to make laws is divided between a national government and regional governments. Neither the national government acting alone nor the regional governments acting together have the authority to alter the power of the other level of government. They are coordinate and equal in their own constitutional spheres. Where there is a dispute, the governments negotiate or resort to the courts to adjudicate between them. According to K.C. Wheare, a British authority on federalism,

*federal government exists . . . when the powers of government for a community are divided substantially according to the principle that there is a single independent authority for the whole area in respect of some matters and that there are independent regional authorities for other matters, each set of authorities being co-ordinate with and not subordinate to the others within its own prescribed sphere.*[4]

What does this mean in the Canadian context? It means simply that we have a national government and 10 provincial governments (as well as 3 territories, but these are under federal jurisdiction and are not constitutionally a third level of government). Beyond this obvious point, though, lies a range of complex issues that affect public administration in myriad ways.

In the Canadian federal system, power is divided through the Constitution. Section 91 lists most of the federal government's powers, and section 92 lists most of the provincial governments' powers. Therefore, the organization of both levels of government is shaped by each level's respective constitutional responsibilities and the resulting relationship between the two levels of government. For example, section 91.7 confers the power to enact laws in the area of "Militia, Military and Naval Service, and Defence" exclusively to the federal government. Therefore, it would make little sense, and indeed would be in violation of the Constitution, for a province to have a department to create programs in this area.

Complicating this, though, is the ambiguous language of much of the Constitution combined with the overlapping nature of many issues confronting modern governments. Thus, both levels of government set up administrative organizations (e.g., departments, regulatory bodies, Crown corporations) in the same areas of jurisdiction. For instance, even though the Constitution stipulates that health care is a provincial responsibility, there are both federal and provincial ministries of health. Although this may appear to contradict the constitutional division of powers, it in fact reflects the flexibility of the federal system. In this case, while the federal government lacks jurisdictional authority over the delivery of health care, it both administers the Canada Health Act and provides fiscal resources to support this expensive policy area. In federalism, it is said that the golden rule always prevails: i.e., he who has the gold makes the rules. In constitutional terms, this is because the national government has what is called the "**spending power**." Although not listed anywhere in the formal written Constitution, the spending power is the convention that if the federal government has money to spend, it has the authority to do so even in an area of provincial jurisdiction.[5]

An important irony shapes the Canadian federal system. In 1867, the Fathers of Confederation gave most powers over issues such as education, health, and social policy to the provinces. In the context of the times, these were relatively unimportant areas in which governments were only minimally involved, as we noted in chapter 1 when we discussed the minimalist state. Furthermore, the

Fathers of Confederation gave most of the powers to raise and spend money to the federal level of government, in the interests of creating a national economic and social union. The result is that the provinces are constitutionally responsible for the most expensive policy areas, but they lack the fiscal capacity to pay for them. The federal government, however, has tremendous fiscal resources but lacks constitutional jurisdiction in the most expensive policy areas. This has recently led to the charge that a "fiscal imbalance" exists in Canadian federalism, fuelling considerable controversy over management of the federation's fiscal affairs.[6]

The ongoing search for ways around this basic dilemma is at the root of organizational reform for both levels of government. An elaborate network of intergovernmental institutions has emerged,[7] where senior public servants and ministers from both levels of government regularly meet to discuss the federation's administration. So entrenched is this network that political scientist Richard Simeon refers to it as a system of "federal–provincial diplomacy."[8] In fact, by the 1960s, meetings of federal and provincial ministers and their expert advisers became so numerous that they were supplanting legislatures as the primary arena of Canadian policy making.[9] Then, over the succeeding 50 years, intergovernmental relations intensified as the provinces in particular built up their capacity to engage the already well-endowed federal government. This gave rise to an increasing number and type of administrative institutions—central agencies, line departments, secretariats, conferences, partnerships, accords and agreements, and so on, as well as a large informal network of intergovernmental specialist officials.[10] So, ultimately, Canadian public administration is profoundly affected by our federal system of government.

## Cabinet-Parliamentary Government

The third major part of the framework of Canadian public administration is cabinet-parliamentary government. To place this in context, look at Figure 5.1, which outlines the three major *branches* of the Canadian government.

The **executive branch** consists of the monarch, the Governor General, and the Cabinet (which includes the prime minister). The public service is considered a part of the executive as well, in that it administers the programs devised by the executive and tenders advice on the formulation of those programs. The **legislative branch** consists of Parliament, which in turn is divided into an elected lower chamber called the House of Commons and an appointed upper chamber called the Senate. Finally, the **judicial branch** consists of the Supreme Court and all the courts and judges below it in the federal and provincial court systems.

There are two main features of cabinet-parliamentary government. The first is the relationship between the branches of government. The second, related feature is that the Constitution tells us that certain offices are conferred with tremendous powers, but practice reveals that they do not actually exercise those powers. In effect, to understand the relationship between the branches of government, you need to understand the "myth and reality" of cabinet-parliamentary government. Another way to conceive of this is to compare the "formal" and "political" powers of each branch of government.

**FIGURE 5.1 Basic Institutions of Canadian Government**

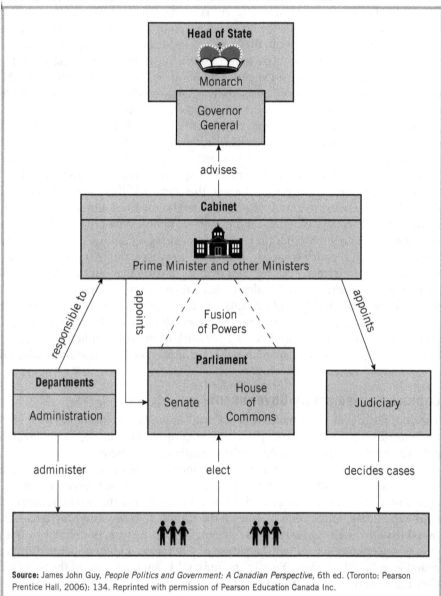

**Source:** James John Guy, *People Politics and Government: A Canadian Perspective*, 6th ed. (Toronto: Pearson Prentice Hall, 2006): 134. Reprinted with permission of Pearson Education Canada Inc.

To begin with, the "myth" asserts that tremendous powers are accorded by the Constitution to the monarch as the formal head of state. In Canada, the monarch is represented by the Governor General (and Lieutenant-Governor at the provincial level), who has the power on behalf of the monarch to decide which political party will form the government, when Parliament will be dissolved, and when a new election will be called, and the right to confer royal assent upon all legislation. In reality, these powers are almost completely symbolic. Because of the historical evolution of democratic government, the role and position of the nonelected monarch and Governor General have become essentially ceremonial.

So, in reality, who gets to exercise the formidable powers cited in the Constitution as the prerogative of the monarch? The answer: another part of the executive branch of government, the **Privy Council**, which is an advisory body. This is a term with which you might not be familiar, since it is hardly ever used anymore. Strictly speaking, it consists of all current and former ministers of the Crown; more commonly it is known nowadays as the **Cabinet**. Only current members of the Cabinet exercise the powers spelled out in the Constitution. They are chosen by the prime minister, who heads the Cabinet, and are usually government members of the House of Commons. Indeed, so much power has come to be vested in the prime minister and the Cabinet that it is common to refer to the Canadian system as executive-dominated.[11]

Why does the Constitution tell us that power is held in one place, while in reality it is exercised somewhere else? Partly because of **constitutional convention**. This is the idea of habit or tradition: that is, when things have been done a certain way for a long period of time, it becomes a convention. Conventions can be every bit as important as the actual written Constitution. The other reason is the doctrine of **responsible government**. This is the principle that the government (as represented by the Cabinet) must explain itself and be accountable to the elected representatives of the people (as represented by the House of Commons). For this to take place, there must be some mechanism by which power can be removed from the government by the people's representatives. In order to govern, the prime minister and Cabinet must have the *confidence* of the elected House of Commons. If a government loses that confidence (i.e., loses the support of the majority of members of the House), it loses the right to govern and can, therefore, be removed from power. The doctrine of responsible government has evolved to ensure that those who actually hold and exercise power (in the Cabinet) can be held accountable (by Parliament).

The other important issue is where the Cabinet comes from. Since its members are also members of the Parliament, we talk about a *fusion of powers* in the Canadian system. This differs from the American system, for instance, where there is a *separation of powers*. In the United States, the president (the executive branch) is not a member of Congress (the legislative branch), nor does he require the support of a majority of its members to retain power. This is a crucial difference. The fusion of powers in the Canadian system facilitates accountability, in that the prime minister and Cabinet must participate every day in question period and other activities of the House of Commons, explaining their policies and actions (or inaction) on a daily basis to their opponents and to the country as a whole. This is the heart of responsible cabinet-parliamentary government.

You should be able to infer that the second branch of government—the legislative branch—plays a significant role in the theory of responsible government, holding the executive to account. Some people mistake this power for the power to make laws. The truth about the legislative branch is that it is a law-*passing*, rather than a law-*making*, body. The main decisions about what laws the government seeks to introduce are made in Cabinet, and indeed in almost all cases it is Cabinet ministers who introduce legislation into Parliament for debate and approval. Ordinary Members of Parliament in the governing party who are not in the Cabinet (called *backbenchers*) and opposition party members of Parliament have a circumscribed role in law-making. This is because of the doctrine of *party discipline*, which suggests party members always vote according to the instructions of their leaders. This is necessary to ensure that Cabinet can have its legislative desires realized, since the government, to pass laws, must have the support of the majority in the House of Commons. In times of **minority government**, of course, the power of the legislature vis-à-vis the executive is enhanced, since the executive must be more responsive as it cannot command a majority in the House without attracting the support of at least some of the opposition party members.

The third branch of Canadian government is the judicial branch, which, unlike in some other countries, is composed of appointed rather than elected officials. The judges and courts are called upon to act as arbiters in the event of disputes between the other branches of government, between the two levels of government, and between citizens and government. Where constitutional law is concerned, the judicial branch mediates two types of disputes. The first are disputes related to the division of powers in the Constitution. If one or the other level of government passes a law that infringes on the jurisdiction of the other, a court action can be initiated to see if the law is intra vires (constitutional) or ultra vires (unconstitutional). The other type of constitutional law the judicial branch deals with relates to the relationship of government and citizens. When citizens feel their rights have been infringed or denied, they may appeal to the courts to rule whether a government's actions or law has violated the Canadian Charter of Rights and Freedoms. The Charter, added to the Constitution in 1982, provides a list of rights that governments may not infringe when they pass laws, "subject only to such reasonable limits prescribed by law as can be demonstrably justified in a free and democratic society."

The judicial branch is also concerned with administrative law, making sure that the administrative processes, rules, and regulations of policy are followed. The courts ensure that the administrators do not transgress the law in carrying out their duties and that penalties are assigned if they do. The courts are the principle agency through which controls over the administrative process are exercised.[12] The courts may examine three aspects of the administrative process. First, they may consider the validity of the way in which power was delegated to an administrative unit by the legislature. Here, the courts are looking to make sure that the delegation of power does not violate the principles of law, including the Constitution, and that there has not been an inappropriate or excessive delegation of power. Second, the courts may look into the rule-making process to ensure that the administrative body has not exceeded the powers granted to it in the making of rules and procedures. Finally, the courts may investigate whether the administrative body has applied the rules with which it is empowered in a fair and consistent manner to individual citizens.

The hallmark of the relationship between the judicial branch and the two other branches is that the judicial branch is regarded as independent of the control of the two other branches, far removed from the taint of political interference or partisanship. The principle of noninterference in judicial affairs is reflected in the fact that individual judges have complete liberty to hear and decide any cases that come before them. How do we know how important this principle is? On a number of occasions Cabinet ministers have been forced to resign their positions because of the reality, or even the perception, that they have interfered with a member of the judiciary.

In summary, you should now have a basic understanding of the importance of capitalist democracy, federalism, and cabinet-parliamentary government to public administration in Canada. To illustrate their importance, try to conceive of a Canada in which business interests and property rights are not pre-eminent in influencing public policy. For instance, what would the organization of public administration look like if the state, rather than private interests, owned everything? Or consider what Canada would look like with a unitary system of government. What would be different if there were no provincial governments? What if there were no division of powers between two levels of government in the Constitution? Now think about a government without a cabinet-parliamentary form. Imagine, for instance, that power had not devolved through historical practice and convention into the hands of the Cabinet, held accountable by the elected representatives of the people, but had instead been retained in the hands of the monarch. How different would the provision of services and the formulation, implementation, and evaluation of public policy be?

Now imagine that it is July 1, 1867. Prime Minister Sir John A. Macdonald invites you into his office to tell you that you are to organize the government of the new Dominion of Canada. What would that government look like, organizationally? How many and which ministries and departments would be needed to serve the needs of Canadians in the mid-to-late 1800s? What would the composition of Macdonald's new government be?

Flash ahead to the year 2020. The new prime minister has invited you into her office with the same assignment Macdonald gave you. Would the government you now design look the same as the earlier one? What would be different? Why? What factors did you take into account as you thought about how government would be designed in each of the two eras?

Let's suppose that the first principle you settled on was that the organization of government should allow for the most efficient provision of services possible. Presumably, you would opt for a streamlined model of government, with as few departments as possible. This requires you to think very precisely about what exactly government should do—i.e., what activities it should engage in and what services it should provide. You might start, for instance, by noting the obvious ones: you need structures that serve the interests of the main actors in a capitalist democracy, that respond to the opportunities and constraints of a federal system, and that respond to the rules and processes of cabinet-parliamentary government.

You must ask what government is to be responsible for. The safety and defence of the nation might be a starting point. Therefore, you would want to create an army and a department of defence to run it. Governments are also responsible for dealing with foreign countries, so you would need a department of foreign affairs.

Beyond these two duties, what else does government need to do? Communications and transportation are important services, and therefore you might consider creating a post office and a department of transportation. There ought to be a department responsible for coordinating the government's spending and revenues, so a finance ministry seems like a logical choice.

We could continue adding to this list in a number of other areas, too. But keep in mind that each time you add a department, agency, board commission, or other government body, you increase the complexity of governing, thereby potentially decreasing its efficiency.

Where do you draw the line? What interests in society need to be served? When considering a country like Canada, there are certain obvious features that need to be taken into consideration: regionalism, class, language, gender, ethnicity, economic factors (business, labour, popular sector), geography, climate, and so on. At some point, you will also need to think about how to coordinate the various organizations within the government to ensure that there is no overlap of duties and that money is being raised and spent in the most propitious manner. So you need to construct some "watchdog" organizations, adding another layer of complexity to your design.

While speculating in this manner is an interesting intellectual exercise, the fact is that capitalist democracy, federalism, and cabinet-parliamentary government prevail in the real world of Canadian public administration. In some ways, the basic conundrum of making a society run smoothly can be expressed this way: the pursuit of common goals requires organization. Within the bounds of capitalist democracy, federalism, and cabinet-parliamentary government, we have a variety of structures and organizations designed to facilitate the public's business.

To illustrate, let us now focus on the actual organizational features of the federal government. Over 3 million Canadians currently work in the public sector (federal, provincial, territorial, and municipal). This should give you some sense of its complexity and size. For now, we will focus only on the organization of the federal government. The structure of the federal government is divided into three broad components: departments, regulatory agencies, and Crown corporations. These are the main organizing structures, but they exist alongside a large number of other bodies as well. Before considering each component specifically, we will provide a brief overview of the political–administrative relationships that oversee this impressive machinery.

## Political–Administrative Relationships

Let us return here to a concept we introduced in chapter 1: the politics–administration dichotomy.[13] According to this principle, in the organization of government there is a division between the elected officials and the appointed ones. The elected officials (the politicians) are the key decision-makers because, as the theory of representative government tells us, they represent the people. The appointed officials—the public servants—are there to take orders, administer programs, and assist the politicians in formulating, implementing, and evaluating the government's policies.

But, as we also noted in chapter 1, this relationship does not always work the way the theory suggests. At various times in history, the alarm has been raised that the public interest has been sacrificed to the self-interest of public servants and their organizations. The fear of "rule by officials" is often cited in connection with bureaucracies that appear to be too powerful, which raises questions about the goals and values that public servants may have. After all, the traditional view is that public servants are concerned with the means by which government accomplishes its goals—not the ends that society aims for. In recent years, though, there has been a growing recognition that the values public servants have as individuals should be expressly acknowledged, and that those values should guide them in their actions. This brings us back to the age-old problem: How can public servants, who are not elected, be held accountable? What if public servants, guided by their own personal value systems, take actions that contradict official rules or procedures? These concerns were prominent amongst many of the organizational theorists we examined in chapter 4, from Marxists to proponents of New Public Management (NPM).

Imagine yourself in this position: you are a front-line worker in a government employment office. The rules say that each applicant for a job must be treated in exactly the same manner. Over time, you have gotten to know the case of one hard-luck individual who has just about used up his employment insurance benefits, hasn't yet qualified for provincial social assistance, has a young family, and is about to lose his apartment. His search for a job has been futile. One day, you are contacted by an employer who needs someone immediately. Your hard-luck case meets all the qualifications, but the rules say that you must post the job so that everyone has a fair chance to apply, and that you can send the employer a maximum of only three applicants. Your hard-luck case has just been in to see you before you learned of this new job. What do you do if your value system says that this person should be given first crack at the job, but the rules say that the job must be processed in the usual manner, even if it means the individual concerned will have virtually no opportunity to apply?

If you follow your own value system, you contribute to the concern that powerful bureaucracies acting in their own interests can actually undermine democracy, since you are accountable to no one, in this example, but your own conscience. But if you follow the prescribed rules, an individual may suffer dire consequences.

Think about it this way: governments are involved in making countless choices about what policies to enact. This necessarily involves making compromises between competing groups and individuals in societies, since not everyone is going to get all of what they want all of the time. Theoretically, the people's representatives make the choices about whose interests are to be satisfied, since they have the legitimacy to exert authority in democratic societies. If the people do not like their representatives' decisions, they can replace those representatives in the next election. Elections, therefore, are the mechanisms by which citizens hold governments accountable for their actions (or inactions). But what if the function of compromising is tainted by the fact that those responsible for enacting the compromises bring their own narrow self-interest to the process? What if, instead of faithfully serving the government of the day, the public service really serves only its own interests? Clearly, the democratic process would be undermined.

This underlying tension between bureaucracy and democracy is a recurrent theme in public administration, which is wrestled with by theorists and practitioners alike. There are no easy answers to the dilemmas raised by these tensions.

# Departmental Organizations

Governing Canada is a complex job. It follows, therefore, that the organizations that are responsible for that governing are complex as well. We can summarize them in a small number of organizational forms. Federal organizations are grouped into schedules under legislation called the Financial Administration Act (FAA). They include:

- departments (FAA, Schedule I);
- statutory and other agencies (FAA, Schedule I.1);
- agents of Parliament (FAA, Schedule I.1);
- departmental corporations (FAA, Schedule II);
- service agencies (FAA, Schedule II); and
- parent Crown corporations (FAA, Schedule III, although nine additional parent Crown corporations are not listed under Schedule III, and each has its own constituent legislation).

Two secondary institutional forms are not listed in the FAA:

- special operating agencies found within a department or agency; and
- subsidiaries of Crown corporations.

There are also other types of corporate entities, not part of government, in which the federal government has an interest:

- mixed enterprises;
- joint enterprises;
- international organizations;
- shared-governance corporations; and
- corporations under the terms of the Bankruptcy and Insolvency Act.[14]

We will not canvass all these organizations, but will highlight those that have traditionally been most important, beginning with departments, as well as those that have emerged recently as significant bodies.

About half the employees who work in the federal public service work directly or indirectly in **departments** (also referred to as **ministries**). These are **statutory bodies**: that is, they are created by law passed by Parliament. The head of each department is the **minister**, who is appointed by the prime minister. The prime minister and the other ministers together constitute the Cabinet and are responsible individually for their departments and collectively for the actions of the government as a whole.

The convention exists that the prime minister will always select Cabinet ministers from individuals who sit in Parliament. This means that both senators and Members of the House of Commons are eligible to become ministers; in reality, the prime minister virtually always limits his or her selection of ministers to those who are elected to the House of Commons because senators are appointed (by the prime minister) and, therefore, have less legitimacy as representatives of the people. Prime Minister Harper ran into a storm of protest in 2006 when he violated these conventions. Harper selected his friend and supporter, Michael Fortier, who had neither run in the election nor held a Senate seat, to sit in Cabinet. Fortier had been a Conservative Party candidate in previous elections, had run for the leadership of the party, and was co-chair of Harper's successful 2004 leadership campaign and co-chair of the Conservatives' election campaigns in 2004 and 2006. Harper got Fortier into the Cabinet by instantly appointing him to the Senate, arguing that he needed some representation from the Montreal area (which the Canadian people, in exercising their political wisdom, had declined to give him in the election). Fortier then pledged to run for a seat in the House of Commons. He resigned his Senate seat and ran in a Montreal riding in 2008, but he lost the race and returned to private life.

The talent on which the prime minister can draw ultimately depends on the composition of the House of Commons. There is usually a strong correlation between the distribution of Cabinet seats and provincial population. Moreover, certain regional, linguistic, and other constraints limit the prime minister's choices. For instance, a French-Canadian prime minister will usually select an English Canadian to be deputy prime minister. A Western Canadian is usually made minister of agriculture, while a Maritimer or British Columbian is usually made minister of fisheries.

There has been a gradual growth in the number of departments (and hence of Cabinet ministers) over time until recently in Canada (see Table 5.1). Sir John A. Macdonald got by in 1867 with 13 ministers, but since the 1970s the wholesale growth in government responsibilities has necessitated ever larger Cabinets. Brian Mulroney felt compelled to appoint 40 Cabinet members in 1984! Pierre Trudeau's largest Cabinet had 37 members, 9 more than his predecessor, Lester Pearson. Joe Clark, who followed Trudeau, reduced the Cabinet to 29 members, the same number used by John Turner. Kim Campbell continued the trend toward a reduced Cabinet with just 24 ministers, and was followed by Jean Chrétien, who had 23 ministries (although he also maintained a large number of "Secretaries of State," which are like junior ministers). Paul Martin had a large ministry, with close to 40 ministers, while Stephen Harper appointed 27 ministers in 2006.[15]

The number and types of departments (and hence Cabinet ministers) is entirely at the discretion of the prime minister. This considerable power is exercised through the Public Service Rearrangement and Transfer of Duties Act, which reads, "The Governor in Council may (a) transfer any powers, duties or functions or the control or supervision of any portion of the federal public

**TABLE 5.1    Government Departments, 1867 and 2010**

| Government Departments in 1867 | Government Departments and Central Agencies in 2010 |
|---|---|
| Agriculture | **Line Departments:** |
| Customs | Agriculture and Agri-Food |
| Finance | Canadian Heritage |
| Inland Revenue | Citizenship and Immigration |
| Justice | Environment |
| Marine and Fisheries | Fisheries and Oceans |
| Militia and Defence | Foreign Affairs and International Trade |
| Post Office | Health |
| Privy Council Office | Human Resources and Skills Development |
| Receiver General | Indian Affairs and Northern Development |
| Secretary of State | Industry |
| Secretary of State for Provinces | Justice |
| | National Defence |
| | Natural Resources |
| | Public Safety and Emergency Preparedness |
| | Public Works and Government Services |
| | Transport, Infrastructure and Communities |
| | Veterans Affairs |
| | Western Economic Diversification |
| | |
| | **Central Agencies:** |
| | Department of Finance |
| | Office of the Prime Minister |
| | Privy Council Office |
| | Treasury Board Secretariat |

**Source:** Adapted from Canada, Treasury Board of Canada Secretariat, *Annual Report to Parliament: Crown Corporations and Other Corporate Interests of Canada, 2008*, **www.tbs-sct.gc.ca/reports-rapports/cc-se/2008/cc-se03-eng.asp#Toc220113622.**

administration from one minister to another, or from one department in, or portion of, the federal public administration to another; or (*b*) amalgamate and combine any two or more departments under one minister and under one deputy minister"[16] (see Box 5.1).

The federal government, under the Financial Administration Act and the Public Service Employment Act, defines departments and the other parts of government in terms of statutory lines of control and accountability, according to financial and personnel criteria. More broadly, political scientist J.E. Hodgetts defines a department as an administrative unit consisting of one or more organizational components under the direct management and control of a minister of the

## BOX 5.1 | What's in a Name?

As political scientists Jackson and Jackson point out, the names of departments reflect the predominant values and biases of the government of the day. Consider the evolution of the department responsible for immigration:

1867–1892:   Canadian Immigration and Quarantine Services
1892–1917:   Immigration Branch, Department of the Interior
1917–1936:   Department of Immigration and Colonization
1936–1950:   Immigration Branch, Department of Mines and Resources
1950–1966:   Department of Citizenship and Immigration
1966–1977:   Department of Manpower and Immigration
1977–1993:   Canada Employment and Immigration Commission
1993:        Immigration divided between Department of Public Security and the Department of Human Resources
1993–2010:   Department of Citizenship and Immigration

**Source:** Adapted from Robert J. Jackson and Doreen Jackson, *Politics in Canada: Culture, Institutions, Behaviour and Public Policy* (Toronto: Pearson Prentice Hall, 2006): 353.

Crown.[17] Departments provide services and administer programs either for the public or for other parts of the government. Personnel are mainly drawn from the Public Service Commission, which establishes merit-based hiring criteria and administers the hiring and firing process. Funding for each department comes from an annual appropriation act passed by Parliament as part of the government's overall budget.

How do you distinguish the different types of departments? One common typology of departments divides them into three broad types of organizations.[18] First, and most commonly, there are the *vertical constituency* departments. Their primary function is to provide services directly to the public (e.g., Health or Industry), or some particular segment or group thereof (e.g., Indian Affairs and Northern Development). They are described as *vertical* departments because they represent direct links between citizens and the government.

The second type of department is the *horizontal administrative coordinative* type, whose main role is to provide services to other departments. For instance, the Department of Public Works and Government Services provides and coordinates a range of services, such as printing and purchasing, and real estate and office space, for other departments.

The third type is the *horizontal policy coordinative* type, whose responsibilities include developing the broad policy framework within which other government functions are carried out, and coordinating policies and programs across government. The Department of Finance is among the most important in this regard, along with other "central agencies" (described below), including the Department of Foreign

Affairs and Justice. Each provides coordination and policy advice to other departments regarding external relations and legal issues, respectively. Although usually small in size and budget, these are generally the key actors in the overall coordination of government policy. They can intervene in the affairs of other departments, for instance, for this purpose.

Not all departments are alike in organization or function, but we can generalize about the structure of departments to some extent. They are hierarchical bodies, with the minister, as the political head, at the apex. Below the minister is the administrative head of the department, the deputy minister (discussed in more detail below). Below that are a number of assistant deputy ministers, directors, managers, and so on. The problem with this type of structure lies in knowing how many subdivisions or units optimize efficiency in decision making and democracy (in terms of accountability). While increased bureaucratization of government functions has been the response to the increased complexity of governing modern society, at some point bureaucracy becomes dysfunctional, as we saw in chapter 3.

Just as too many departments can make Cabinet decision making too unwieldy, too many internal subdivisions within departments can hamper their effective operation. This is part of the span of control problem, which, as we noted in chapter 3, refers to the number of subordinates that report to one supervisor. Ideally, a balance must be reached between too narrow and too broad a span of control. In a narrow span of control, there are too many supervisors and the number of reporting levels is increased, thereby increasing the degree of red tape and impeding internal communications. In a broad span of control, however, there are too few supervisors, placing strain on top management. Luther Gulick was among the first to think systematically about this problem: "Just as the hand of man can span only a limited number of notes on the piano, so the mind and will of man can span but a limited number of immediate managerial contacts. . . . The limit of control is partly a matter of the limits of time and of energy. As a result, the executive of any enterprise can personally direct only a few persons. He must depend upon these to direct others, and upon them in turn to direct still others, until the last man in the organization is reached"[19] (see Figure 5.2.).

There is no sure way of knowing what constitutes an acceptable span of control, since any of a number of factors can come into play in the functioning of an organization. For instance, the number and type of tasks to be performed, the competence of individuals, the quality and amount of assistance available to the manager, and the geographical and physical setting (whether, for example, a department must have a number of regional offices, or can be centralized in Ottawa) can all be factors influencing the organizational design of departments.

These points can be illustrated by looking at the organizational chart of a typical federal government department. Figure 5.2 shows the organizational structure of the Department of Justice. Notice the hierarchical arrangement of offices, beginning with the minister, where ultimate authority rests. Below the minister are

**FIGURE 5.2    Department of Justice, 2010**

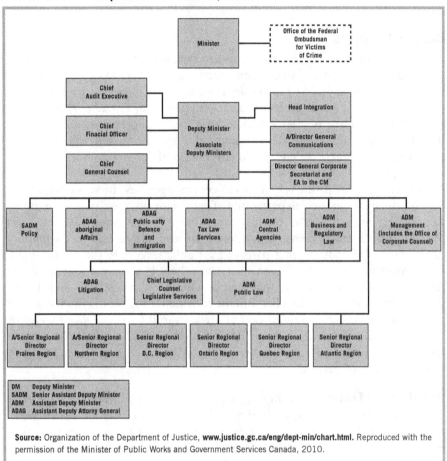

Source: Organization of the Department of Justice, **www.justice.gc.ca/eng/dept-min/chart.html.** Reproduced with the permission of the Minister of Public Works and Government Services Canada, 2010.

the senior deputy ministers, assistant deputy ministers, assistant deputy attorney general and other top management. As you study this organization chart, ask yourself: what type of span of control is evident here?

A generic model of the general categories of offices in federal government departments would look like this: the deputy minister (DM) sits at the administrative apex of a pyramidal hierarchy, with two or more assistant deputy ministers (ADMs) heading branches or bureaus of the department and reporting directly to the DM. Below the ADMs are directorates or branches, each headed by a director-general or director. These directorates are in turn subdivided into divisions headed by directors or divisional chiefs, which are also subdivided into sections, regions, districts, and areas. In general, this structure is used at both the federal and provincial levels, although different titles are sometimes used for roughly the same position in the hierarchy.

## Central Agencies

Another way of thinking about government departments is to divide them into two categories in terms of their main functions. In this typology, some departments are simply referred to as *line departments*: these have direct responsibility for the delivery of goods and services to the people of Canada. These departments tend to consist of a large number of subunits and employ a large staff to deal with the public. The Department of Agriculture and Agri-Food, for instance, is a line department employing thousands of civil servants in a wide range of jobs.

Other departments are referred to as **central agencies**; these are responsible for coordinating the line departments. Their main purpose is to support the decision-making activities of Cabinet, which they do in a variety of ways.[20] For instance, they supply Cabinet with information and advice, and they communicate Cabinet decisions to other parts of the public service, to the public, and to other governments. Central agencies ensure there is some consistency across departments—in other words, that there is *horizontal coordination*—and that the departments' overall spending fits with the revenue-raising capacity of the government as a whole. There are four central agencies in the federal government: the Finance Department; the Treasury Board Secretariat (TBS); the Privy Council Office (PCO); and the Prime Minister's Office (PMO). Let us consider briefly the role of each central agency.

**Department of Finance**  In many respects, this is the most powerful actor in the federal government. It plays a leading role in making economic policy, which contributes to its informal reputation as the centre of key economic decision making. Preparation and delivery of the government's revenue and expenditure budgets rest with this department, as does jurisdiction over taxation and trade and tariff policy. Moreover, the Department of Finance manages federal borrowing on financial markets and administers major federal transfers to provinces and territories. It also develops regulatory policy for the financial sector and represents Canada within international financial institutions. It provides the government with analysis and advice on the broad economic and financial affairs of the country.

To fulfill its mandate, the Department of Finance monitors and researches the performance of the Canadian economy in all important aspects, from output and growth to employment and income to price stability and monetary policy to the impact of globalization, and so on. In addition, this department is in constant communication with the other departments of government to coordinate initiatives that have an impact on the economy. Created in 1867 to replace the old office of Inspector General, the Department of Finance employed 38 officials. It grew as large as 6000, but currently it employs just over 700. It is generally conceded that the best and the brightest in the public service aspire to work in this powerful central agency. Concerns expressed by the Department of Finance about the economic health of the country usually become the concerns of other departments as well. In other words, Finance often sets the tone for the rest of government in terms of whether new policies and programs can be launched, or whether there will be cutbacks and restraint. Initiatives from other departments in government generally require the support of Finance if they are to go ahead, since Finance controls the purse strings.

**Treasury Board Secretariat**  The Treasury Board Secretariat (TBS) is the administrative arm of the Treasury Board, which is the only Cabinet committee that has a statutory basis. The TBS supports the Treasury Board by providing advice on policies, directives, regulations, and program expenditure proposals regarding the management of the government's financial, human, and material resources (e.g., lands and buildings). The TBS also supports the Treasury Board in its role as the general manager and employer of the public service. It is "management" where employee relations are concerned within government; this agency assumes the interest of employer in collective bargaining and personnel issues. In 2003, the Canada Public Service Agency was created to assume some aspects of the TBS's human resources management functions, and in 2009 the Office of the Chief Human Resources Officer was created, and absorbed the Canada Public Service Agency along with responsibility for pensions and benefits, labour relations, and compensation issues (see chapter 9). TBS is also the key actor in administrative policy within the government, overseeing departmental audits, and ensuring that accounting practices and standards are uniformly adhered to across the government.

TBS is also responsible for evaluating policy and particular programs. TBS assists the Cabinet by providing information about expenditures and the financial and personnel resources required by each department. As well, TBS prepares the main estimates for the government, which are the detailed spending plans that the government introduces each year in the House of Commons.

**The Privy Council Office**  As an organizational body, the Cabinet requires support to function on an ongoing, day-to-day basis.[21] This support primarily comes from the Privy Council Office (PCO), which acts essentially as the Cabinet's secretariat.

The PCO reports directly to the prime minister and is headed by the Clerk of the Privy Council and Secretary to the Cabinet, which is the highest position in the public service (see Box 5.2).[22] The Clerk and the PCO are intimately involved in the sensitive process of Cabinet decision making, and particularly in strategic planning and policy formulation. The PCO is both the Cabinet secretariat and the prime minister's source of public service advice across the entire spectrum of policy questions and operational issues that confront the government. This includes matters relating to the management of federal–provincial relations and constitutional issues.

## BOX 5.2  Clerk of the Privy Council and Secretary to the Cabinet

This is the most senior public servant in the government. In his or her role supporting the prime minister, the clerk has three primary responsibilities:

- As the prime minister's deputy minister, the clerk provides advice and support to the prime minister on a full range of responsibilities as head of government, including management of the federation.
- As the secretary to the Cabinet, this individual provides support and advice to the ministry as a whole, and oversees the provision of policy and secretariat support to Cabinet and Cabinet committees.

- As the head of the Public Service, the clerk is responsible for the quality of expert, professional, and nonpartisan advice provided by the Public Service to the prime minister, the ministry, and all Canadians.

The PCO also provides support to the deputy prime minister, government leaders in the House of Commons and the Senate, the president of the Privy Council and minister of Intergovernmental Affairs, and the minister designated as the federal interlocutor for Metis and nonstatus Indians. Box 5.3 shows the responsibilities of the divisional units within the PCO, the secretariats.

**The Prime Minister's Office**  The Prime Minister's Office (PMO) stands apart from the other central agencies in that it is staffed by partisan supporters of the government in power rather than by nonpartisan public servants. This is the prime minister's personal staff. As such, the PMO deals with the prime minister's voluminous correspondence; speech writing; scheduling the prime minister's time and appearances; media relations; liaising with other ministers, the government caucus, and party; and providing advice on appointments and policy. The PMO is headed by a chief of staff, who has ongoing daily contact with the prime minister. The PMO drafts the annual Speech from the Throne, which is the statement of the government's legislative and policy intentions for the coming year.

To a large extent, the success or failure of any prime minister rides on the quality of advice he or she gets from the PMO. Not surprisingly, the style of the prime minister is reflected in the role and functioning of the PMO. Pierre Trudeau was the first prime minister to really expand the PMO, which previously had been a relatively small organization. Today it is an extremely influential body. Some academic observers have maintained that under Jean Chrétien and especially Stephen Harper there has been an unhealthy concentration of power in the PMO. Not surprisingly, at least one former occupant of an influential position therein claims this is not true, arguing that government is too complex to be dominated by one agency.[23]

---

**BOX 5.3 | About PCO Secretariats**

Secretariats are the basic building blocks of the Privy Council Office (PCO). Although each secretariat plays a distinct role within the PCO, many share common functions.

Some secretariats support the Cabinet and committees of Cabinet and keep track of developments within specific policy sectors. Others provide advice on appointments, mandates, and government organization, legislation and counsel issues, security and intelligence, communications issues, and other direct concerns of the prime minister.

Key roles include the following:

**Supporting Cabinet Committees**

■ Assisting the Cabinet and its committees in preparing for and conducting meetings

■ Transmitting decisions and documents to departments

**Managing the Flow of Cabinet Business**

■ Helping ensure the Cabinet decision-making process functions smoothly according to the standards, design, and instructions of the prime minister

■ Managing changes in committee structure and the use of ad hoc committees (to focus on special policy areas and problems)

**Facilitating Policy Development**

■ Working with departments to prepare ministerial proposals for Cabinet

■ Ensuring complementarity between new proposals, existing policies, and government objectives

■ Arranging for follow-up measures for implementation

**Source:** Canada, Privy Council Office, *PCO Secretariats*, www.pco-bcp.gc.ca/index.asp?lang=eng&page= secretariats.

---

Taken together, these four central agencies play a vital series of coordinating and supportive roles for the government; they are powerful and important actors in the overall structure. An understanding of their place in the organization of the Canadian government is vital to understanding public administration.

## Agents of Parliament

In the constellation of bodies that make up the machinery of government, there is always the question of accountability. Recently, there has been an increasing trend toward empowering Parliament to better hold the government to account in the face of the growing concentration of power in the hands of the prime minister, his courtiers, and the bureaucracy in general—hence the evolution of bodies called **agents of parliament**. This is a unique group of independent statutory officers who scrutinize the activity of government and report directly to Parliament rather than to government or an individual minister. As a result, they exist to assist with Parliament's oversight role. These agents typically produce

**TABLE 5.2     Agents of Parliament**

| Name of Institution | Portfolio |
| --- | --- |
| Office of the Auditor General | Finance |
| Office of the Chief Electoral Officer | Privy Council |
| Office of the Commissioner of Official Languages | Privy Council |
| Office of the Information Commissioner | Justice |
| Office of the Privacy Commissioner | Justice |
| Office of the Public Sector Integrity Commissioner | Treasury Board |

**Source:** Treasury Board of Canada Secretariat, *Annual Report to Parliament: Crown Corporations and Other Corporate Interests of Canada, 2008*, **www.tbs-sct.gc.ca/reports-rapports/cc-se/2008/cc-se03-eng.asp#Toc220113622**.

reports to Parliament to account for their own activities, and their heads are typically appointed through special resolutions of the House of Commons and the Senate. To maintain their independence, they are said to exist at arm's length from the executive branch of government. The degree of influence exercised by the executive is therefore minimal, at least in theory. However, Stephen Harper has demonstrated that a determined prime minister can retain considerable distance from the influence of these bodies. Examples of agents of Parliament include the Office of the Conflict of Interest and Ethics Commissioner, the Public Service Commission, and the Canadian Human Rights Commission. Others are shown in Table 5.2.

## Government Agencies and Alternative Service Delivery

Apart from the traditional structures reviewed above, governments have been resorting to a variety of new innovations to provide services to Canadians.[24] About 400 government agencies now populate the landscape of Canadian public administration, many of which provide so-called "alternative service delivery" (ASD) arrangements in a number of packages: bodies created by restructuring existing institutions within government; bodies partnering with actors in other departments within government, with other governments, or with those outside government altogether; and structures entirely external to government. According to the Treasury Board Secretariat, "While departments continue to play an important role in service delivery, a growing need for flexibility, interdependence and innovation has produced an increasing diversity of organizational forms and service delivery arrangements to provide more responsive service to Canadians."[25] Some of these government agencies have a separate or distinct identity and are not listed in the FAA as separate legal entities, but are still considered part of the host department. Statutory and other agencies listed in Schedule I.1 of the FAA are similar to departments in that they are usually financed through parliamentary appropriations, but they often serve an operational purpose, such as an administrative, supervisory, advisory, regulatory, or adjudicative function.[26] Many are not directly responsible to a minister but usually report to Parliament through a minister. The amount of scrutiny and the means to hold them accountable varies across agencies, but generally is looser and more flexible than with departments. Agencies usually have a board of directors at their head rather than a deputy minister; thus different forms of management structures distinguish them from departments as well.

The motivations behind the proliferation of these agencies and ASD are varied. They include the desire to offer a more "citizen-centred" approach to service provision,[27] in response to the growing disillusionment with government evident in the broader society. They also are a result of the drive toward "less government," which has been predominant in recent years, and they are seen as potential cost-saving innovations. In addition, rigidities in existing institutions have increasingly been seen as impediments to service delivery, and more flexible alternatives to departments might address this problem. There is also the desire to break down the "silo mentality," in which government departments exist in isolation from each other, resulting in duplication of activities and frustration for citizens trying to find information across departments that never speak to or interact with one another. This desire is directly related to the trend toward "horizontality" in management, wherein attempts are made to cut across traditional boundaries (be they departmental, programmatic, issue-based, etc.) to more fully integrate and rationalize service delivery. ASD promotes horizontality by requiring different institutional actors to learn to work together in new ways. Finally, ASD mechanisms are often designed to accommodate the growing desire for greater citizen participation in governance. They provide interested actors with the "hands-on" opportunity to shape, create, and implement programs in ways traditional structures cannot or will not.

The scope of ASD is impressive.[28] It can include special operating agencies, service agencies, and Crown corporations, a variety of partnership arrangements, and the devolution of programs and services to other governments. It sometimes involves the commercialization of services, such that they are run in a more "businesslike" fashion than government is thought able to achieve. This might take the form of innovations such as employee takeovers, contracting out, and the application of user fees. In addition, outright privatization of government services is an option. In short, a plethora of new institutions have arisen alongside the traditional line department and central agency model.[29]

However, the trend toward ASD has not been problem-free. One important and difficult issue is that of accountability. While lines of responsibility are clear and unambiguous within traditional bodies such as departments, they are less so under ASD. In response to this issue, the government of Canada introduced a new policy on April 1, 2007, setting out in greater detail and with more precision the accountability relationships of ASD mechanisms.[30]

## Ministerial Responsibility

Whether we are talking about line department, central agency, or ASD, the ultimate responsibility for what government does or does not do rests with the political head of the institution, namely the minister. As a member of Cabinet, the minister is responsible for all the official acts of the public servants under his or her supervision. This is known as the doctrine of **ministerial responsibility**, an extremely important concept in understanding how government is held accountable to the people. This is particularly significant when you remember that a department can employ thousands of people and spend millions of dollars of taxpayers' money. Reinforcing this principle is another:

**collective ministerial responsibility**.[31] This is the convention whereby ministers must always show solidarity with their colleagues in Cabinet. Once a decision has been taken in a Cabinet meeting, the whole Cabinet supports it publicly. These concepts are discussed in detail in chapter 11.

But how can an individual minister heading up a department employing thousands of people and spending millions of dollars really be held responsible for everything that goes on in that department? Realistically and logistically, it is impossible for a given minister to know the intimate details of the thousands of decisions taken every year within his or her department, let alone those taken by the government as a whole. Still, there is the expectation that the principle of ministerial responsibility will be observed. In this way, a link is established that sees the public service connected to the political realm through the minister. Political scientists Jackson and Jackson put it this way:

*The Prime Minister appoints members of the Cabinet to assume responsibility for particular ministries or portfolios, and their associated departments, commissions, boards and corporations. Ministers are constitutionally responsible for all of the operations of their departments. Thus, legally, it is ministers who are assigned the powers and duties to be exercised by their departments. Departmental officials, on the other hand, are given scant attention in the law and are responsible exclusively to their ministers, not to Parliament. They are supposed to be non-partisan, objective and anonymous—shielded from the glare of public attention and from the partisan political arena of Parliament by their minister—in order to safeguard their neutrality and ensure their ability to serve faithfully whichever government is in power. In the event of a serious error in the formulation or administration of policy within a department, convention dictates that the minister, rather than officials, be held responsible to Parliament; and if the minister cannot account for the failures to the satisfaction of Parliament, then convention dictates that the minister should resign.*[32]

There are, however, limits to the application of this doctrine. As a consequence of these limits as well as the outbreak of the "sponsorship scandal," the federal government sought to institute a vastly reformed accountability regime in 2006. Accountability became one of the Conservative government's five policy priorities, and the Federal Accountability Act was passed. We assess these developments more fully in chapter 11.

## The Deputy Minister

While the minister is the *political* head of a department, the *administrative* head is the **deputy minister (DM)**. This is the senior-most public servant, an extremely powerful and influential post in the workings of government.[33] DMs receive their positions "at the pleasure of the prime minister," which is to say that it is the prime minister who hires and fires them. (Most other personnel in departments are recruited through the Public Service Commission, which is like a giant human relations department for the government; see chapter 8)

What exactly is the relationship between a minister and his or her top bureaucratic advisor—the deputy minister? This is an important question. The popular

British sitcom *Yes, Prime Minister* portrays a series of often hilarious episodes in which the senior advisor to the prime minister is engaged in a constant game of trying to control and shape the prime minister's decisions. The series portrays the clash between the "political will and the administrative won't." Interestingly, the writers for the series report that they had secret sources within the public service and were inspired from real-life examples within the British government.

In the real world of governing, there are several factors that may make it diffi-cult for a minister to resist the influence of his or her DM or other senior advisors. The experience of Flora MacDonald, former secretary of state for External Affairs in the Joe Clark government, points to this. A minister is typically pulled in several different directions at once. There are Cabinet responsibilities, party duties, attendance in the House of Commons, press conferences, constituency work, foreign travel, political brushfires, and countless other distractions. Invariably, most ministers have little time to effectively concentrate on their departments' day-to-day administrative needs. This must be left to the deputy minister and other senior staff. But MacDonald claimed that her senior staff went beyond simply tendering advice on the administration of the department she headed. MacDonald claimed that her senior advisors engaged in a concerted effort to impose their own agendas on both the running of the department and the development of policy. She felt that as a rookie Cabinet minister, she was at the mercy of the more experienced public servants.[34]

Another view is provided by Mitchell Sharp, who was a public servant early in his career and later became a Cabinet minister. He argued that top civil servants are powerful individuals in the machinery of government. After all, they hold their positions because they have demonstrated a high level of skill and ability in administrative matters. Weak ministers may be susceptible to manipulation by crafty civil servants, but Sharp also argues that most of the time this is not the case. A government, he argues, cannot be run by amateurs, and so a trained and professional civil service is vital; but ministers must be able to determine what constitutes good advice from their advisors. Moreover, Sharp felt that a first-class nonpartisan civil service dedicated to the public interest was a hallmark of parliamentary government that enabled elected "amateurs" to make the political decisions needed to govern effectively.[35]

Another issue concerns the longevity of ministers. Most serve for relatively short periods of time before being shuffled to another position in the Cabinet (or removed from Cabinet altogether). To ensure continuity in departments, DMs are not appointed by the ministers they serve. Rather, the prime minister appoints them, according to an 1896 order-in-council.[36] DMs thereby have some measure of security, knowing that they will not lose their jobs if ministers change. This security is reinforced by the nonpartisanship of DMs. They are not members or supporters of any political party but, rather, serve the government of the day no matter who is in power. Thus, when the government changes hands, the senior public servants retain their jobs, ensuring a measure of stability and continuity in the administra-tion of government. Admittedly, though, this places the DM in a somewhat awk-ward position, sandwiched between the nonpolitical public service and the political minister.

## BOX 5.4 | Deputy Ministers in an International Perspective

Canada has a long-standing tradition of apolitical senior public servants. How does this compare with other countries? According to political scientist Jacques Bourgault,

In the last few years, it seems that Canada has become quite a unique case, some would say anachronistic, due to the apolitical character of its senior officials. The United States have a spoils system for Deputy Secretaries positions (and the six levels immediately below . . . ). France uses a system of internal lists of public servants for the positions of chiefs of staff, Secretaries General and several Director General positions. . . . Socialist States insist on the necessary politicization of the administration provided by the Marxist-Leninist

doctrine, because of the role of the State in the class struggle.

Only countries that use the Whitehall model (Westminster political system) practice a certain separation between administration and politics. New public management, implemented in Australia, New Zealand and Great Britain, recommends a greater dependency of the administration on political leaders, in the name of greater democracy and efficiency. This manifests itself by a more political selection of incumbents, the contracturalization of hiring, and performance contracts with large financial bonuses. None of this seems to have really disrupted the Canadian practice.

**Source:** *Profile of Deputy Ministers in the Government of Canada*, page 16, BOURGAULT, Jacques, 2005. Reproduced with the permission of the Canada School of Public Service, [2007] and with the permission of the Minister of Public Works and Government Services Canada, 2010.

Apart from the appointment question, there are other questions surrounding the DM. What, exactly, are the DM's role and duties? What is the relationship of the DM to other actors in the political–administrative structure?[37] It is the primary duty of the DM to create the conditions under which the minister and prime minister can provide the best possible government. To this end, the DM plays a vital role in both formulating and implementing policy. There are several important conventions that guide the DM in his or her role: neutrality, anonymity, the politics–administration dichotomy, and loyalty. Let us consider each in turn.

The convention of *neutrality* suggests that the DM is nonpartisan, as we noted above. The DM should be politically neutral in serving the minister, but this convention is often difficult to maintain. Political pressures swirl around the DM constantly. Political interaction occurs in almost all facets of the DM's job, from dealing with Parliament and Cabinet to meeting with interest groups and citizens, all of whom have some vested stake in policy matters. Moreover, while remaining officially nonpartisan, the DM must be sensitive to political developments, trends, and issues. This is an extraordinarily difficult balancing act.

The second convention is that of *anonymity*. Can you name a Cabinet minister? Most people can. Can you name a deputy minister? Most of us would be hard-pressed to identify a single one at either level of government. Since it is the minister who is formally responsible for the actions of the government, it is the minister who must accept praise or blame for those policies. The DM toils anonymously in the shadows for two reasons. First, the DM is not elected by anyone and, therefore, is not directly accountable to anyone other than the minister and the prime minister. Second, the DM must be free to provide frank and impartial advice in a private and confidential manner. In return, the DM is shielded from public attack by the minister, who rightly accepts public responsibility for the department's actions.

This is part of the doctrine of ministerial responsibility. Having said this, it should be noted that this doctrine of anonymity has been eroding in recent years. Senior public servants have been singled out and asked to appear in public before Parliamentary committees in a number of high-profile scandals.[38] But overall, to retain anonymity the DM must renounce any desire for public recognition of his or her efforts or personal identification with the government's policies.

The third convention relates to the *politics–administration dichotomy*. It is the minister's duty to direct the public service and the DM's to see to it that directions are executed faithfully. In reality, as we discussed in chapter 1, this is an artificial division of duties. The senior civil service is very much involved in both administration and policy formulation. Interestingly enough, though, the same cannot be said of the minister, who is so consumed by other duties that he or she is rarely concerned with the department's administration.

Ironically, while the precepts of the politics–administration dichotomy are supposed to be followed, it is also expected that the DM will regularly provide policy advice to the minister. What does this policy advisory role cover? It entails initiating policy suggestions without seeking to usurp the minister's decision-making role. In other words, the DM should be able to say, "The government ought to adopt policy X for all these reasons." The minister ultimately says "yes" or "no" to this suggestion. Some have criticized this as providing the DM with "power without responsibility." Others have said that it is quite the opposite: "responsibility without power." Whichever view is correct, there is a fine line that DMs ought not to cross between simply providing advice and making decisions.

Finally, there is the convention of *loyalty*. The DM must in all circumstances remain loyal to the minister in providing the best possible government; but the DM's loyalties conflict, making this a complicated problem. DMs have a loyalty to Parliament as well as to the policies their departments implement. The DM also has a loyalty to the profession of public servant. These various pressures may compel the DM to speak out against certain policies as a matter of conscience. But the DM's position compels the DM to remain silent.

The relationship of the DM to his or her staff is also an important consideration. As the head of the administration, the DM must set the example for the other public servants, instill a sense of public service, an understanding of the power of bureaucracy, and a respect for what is most important in every department, program, and policy: the rights of the citizen. The DM also has a responsibility to keep abreast of public reaction to government policies, and to have a staff that can evaluate when policies are working properly or not. Thus, the DM must keep in close touch with his or her subordinates and be sensitive to their views.

The DM must also develop a good working relationship with the interest groups and citizens most directly affected by the policies of the government in a given area. The DM actively seeks out public opinion on these issues to represent the most current views of the public to the minister in the development of policy. At the same time, the DM must be careful not to become captive to any one group or interest. To avoid this pitfall, good DMs constantly seek countervailing sources of information and advice: they talk not only to the proponents of a particular policy, but also to opponents, and they seek independent advice on various issues, often from disinterested parties, such as academics. To effectively do their jobs, DMs canvass a range of views to get the best possible advice to tender to the minister.

A major job of the DM is to implant in the ministry an understanding of broader social and economic trends, and to effectively evaluate those trends in relation to the department's responsibilities and programs. This means that besides administering the day-to-day minutiae, the DM must also be able to see the big picture of governing. The DM is responsible for understanding the long-term impacts of social and economic change, and anticipating when and where those changes will affect his or her department. This contrasts with the short-term view typical of the minister, whose main concern is the next election just over the horizon. The juxtaposition of these two views often creates tensions between the DM and minister that a skilful and sensitive DM must nonetheless work around.

The DM has some particular administrative responsibilities in the area of personnel and finance. He or she must deal with matters of personnel, such as changes in the collective agreement, employment equity, bilingualism in the public service, and so on. As well, the DM is responsible for the overall preparation of departmental expenditure budgets. In all these duties, the DM must be responsible to other actors in government besides the minister, such as the Public Service Commission, and especially to central agencies like the Treasury Board Secretariat, the Ministry of Finance, and the Privy Council Office.

In 2007, the responsibilities of deputy ministers were further modified. In a controversial move (discussed in chapter 11), new accounting officer provisions of the Financial Administration Act (FAA) designated deputy ministers and deputy heads of designated government entities as the accounting officers for their organizations. This means that they now have a legal obligation to appear before committees of the Senate and House of Commons and answer questions on the management responsibilities set out in the FAA. While the framework of ministerial responsibility and accountability to Parliament still prevails, this new designation creates new legal obligations for deputy ministers, the consequences of which are not yet fully known. Ministers, and ministers alone, remain accountable to Parliament for all actions of the executive, including management, but the accounting officer is legally obliged to appear before the Senate and the House of Commons. While he or she is to do so in support of the minister's accountability, it is not hard to imagine situations in which the deputy minister is made to accept responsibility that rightly belongs to the minister.[39]

Clearly, the role of the DM is a demanding and complex one that requires an incredible amount of administrative management ability combined with a remarkable degree of political sophistication. The DM must constantly satisfy, at the same time, the demands of both the bureaucratic constituency and his or her political master. It is a remarkably sensitive balancing act, but one that must be maintained for a department to be successful in fulfilling its mandate.

## Political Staff

Yet another trend in recent years has been the growth in the number and influence of what are called "political staff" in ministers' offices. Unlike regular public servants, these are politically partisan advisors associated with the governing party who are brought into a minister's office to supply overtly political strategic advice. They are referred to as "exempt staff" because they are not subject to the same regulatory regime as regular public servants, such as the Public Service Employment Act (see chapter 8). Among the implications of this is that political staff are not subject to hiring guidelines based on merit. They are patronage appointments made on the basis of the view that ministers need countervailing sources of influence which can bring partisan political considerations into their deliberations over a given course of action. As we noted above in the section on central agencies, the Office of the Prime Minister is the most prominent example of a partisan body. Some observers have suggested that in an age where more and more power has been concentrated in the hands of the prime minister, his or her political staff have become even more important in some ways than Cabinet ministers in guiding government policy.

Another perspective suggests that one consequence of the growth in influence of political staff has been to essentially strengthen the hand of ministers in relations with the public service. As we noted above, politicians are often amateurs when it comes to running government, compared to senior public servants. Having political staff on hand to proffer advice can be helpful to balance relations between the politicians and the administrators. While not really authorized to "direct" public servants (that is the job of the minister, after all), political staff do sometimes act in ways that suggest they have such a right. Aucoin and Savoie conclude,

*Political staff have power, of course, only to the extent that ministers, and especially the prime minister, allow it. Today, prime ministers, especially those keen on personal command and control, want their political staff to exercise power on their behalf, since this augments the prime minister's power, extending it as deep into the public service as political staffers have the time and required expertise to go. In the extreme, senior public servants are likely to be willing spectators, if not altogether squeezed out of the action.*[40]

An advantage of using political staff is that they can do work that public servants ought not to get involved with—namely work related to the government's strategic political agenda. Nonetheless, the emergence of political staff in recent years as an important force in public administration is controversial given its apparent "politicization" of the public service.

# Regulatory Agencies

Besides *making* policy, government is also in the business of *enforcing* policy. Enforcement can take many forms, the most common of which is regulation. According to the Economic Council of Canada, regulation is "the imposition of constraints, backed by government authority, that are intended to modify economic behaviour of individuals in the private sector significantly."[41] Regulation is intended to ensure that private sector actors conform with the desires of government by modifying their behaviour through a number of possible mechanisms. For instance, the government may decide that promoting Canadian culture is a worthwhile goal and may, as a result, craft regulations to ensure that broadcasters include a certain percentage of Canadian content on the airwaves. The Canadian Radio-television and Telecommunications Commission (CRTC) does exactly this.

Among their varied functions, **regulatory agencies** can influence private sector behaviour with respect to prices, conditions, and quality of service; contents of goods for sale; methods of production; and so on. Many regulatory agencies also have investigative powers and can undertake research and can launch inquiries. Some regulatory bodies are imbued with quasi-judicial power. This means they can "judge specific cases involving the granting, denial, or removal of licences, the approval of rates or fares and the censuring of failure to comply with terms of licences."[42] The senior levels of regulatory bodies are staffed by government appointees, usually for five- or ten-year terms. These are often patronage appointments, used by the prime minister to reward loyal supporters. In general, these appointees enjoy an arm's-length relationship with the department that oversees their activities, thus creating a climate of independence from direct political interference. With some exceptions, their members are not appointed by the Public Service Commission, nor are they employees of the Treasury Board. Accountability is maintained in that regulatory bodies must submit their budgets to the Treasury Board for review and present annual reports through the responsible minister to the House of Commons.

Regulation takes place in a range of areas. Besides radio, television, and telecommunications, cited above, the government also regulates matters as varied as nuclear energy (Canadian Nuclear Safety Commission), labour relations (Canadian Industrial Relations Board), old age pensions (Canadian Pension Commission), and many others. Regulatory agencies receive their powers—which are often considerable—and their mandates through legislation. While some regulations are actually laws that require enforcement by the police and judicial system, most are simply administrative directives managed on an ongoing basis by a specialized government body.

Political scientists Howlett and Ramesh point out that the nature of regulations varies, depending on whether they are economic or social:

*Economic regulations have been the traditional form of regulation and their purpose has been to control specific aspects of the market economy, such as the prices and the volumes of production, or return on investment, or the entry into or exit of firms from an industry. A good example of this type of regulation is that carried out by the various kinds of marketing boards, regulatory bodies that are particularly prominent in the agricultural sector. The intent of such boards is to restrict the supply of agricultural output to keep farm commodity prices at or above a certain threshold of income deemed acceptable for farmers. Their objective is to correct perceived imbalances or inequities in economic relationships that may emerge as a result of the operation of market forces.*

*Social regulations are of more recent origin and refer to controls in matters of health, safety, and societal behaviour such as civil rights and discrimination of various sorts. They have more to do with our physical and moral well-being than with our pocketbooks, though the costs to business of certain regulatory measures, such as environmental protection, often are passed on to the consumer. Examples of social regulation include rules regarding liquor consumption and sales, gambling, consumer product safety, occupational hazards, water-related hazards, air and noise pollution, discrimination on the basis of religion, race, gender, or ethnicity, and pornography.*[43]

Sometimes the lines between issues of an economic or social nature are blurred because, while the origins of the problem may be economic, the effects are social. However, social regulations tend to address broader questions than economic ones, which are typically targeted very directly at a specific firm or sector. A further complication in a federal system, of course, is that both economic and social issues sometimes cut across lines of jurisdiction; determining which level of government should create and administer regulations can be tricky, as shown in the recent case of the attempt to develop a national securities commission to regulate the trade of stocks, bonds, and other financial instruments.

In some cases, regulations place directed constraints on behaviour, leaving little or no discretion to the body concerned in implementing the regulations. In other cases, the government allows private actors to self-regulate, sometimes through the adoption of voluntary codes of conduct.[44] This is the case, for instance, with the medical and legal professions, which are given substantial power to regulate their members and their activities. These powers are limited only where they contradict the broad guidelines provided in the government regulations. The government will often choose this option because it may be the least expensive form of regulation, reducing administration costs by passing them on to the profession concerned. In addition, it allows those with the most intimate knowledge of the activity being regulated to administer the rules. Governments have neither the time nor the inclination to enter the labyrinthine worlds of doctors and lawyers, and so are content to allow these (and other) groups to regulate themselves.

Why do governments use regulation rather than other administrative or organizational forms? First, regulation is justified on the grounds of "public interest." This means that government intervention in the market is sometimes needed to correct market failures: that is, situations in which private sector actors cannot or will not act as effective regulatory instruments themselves. The most obvious case of market failure is monopoly, where firms may earn excessive profits by exploiting consumers by charging excessive rates for their services, or by engaging in discriminatory behaviour toward certain customers. This argument has been under fire, though, on the basis that the public interest is not always served by regulation in these circumstances.

Instead, the regulator becomes "captured" by the interests that it was supposed to be regulating. As a result, the very public purposes of the regulatory agency are undermined and the private corporate interest is promoted at public expense.

Another motivation for regulation is to protect individual firms from competition. Such was the case, for instance, when Air Canada was created. Another reason is to create a policy tool that can engage in some planning for a specific sector of the economy. This may be most obvious in the telecommunications sector, where ongoing planning under the auspices of the CRTC has been used to moderate the impact of new television technologies, from antennae to cable to satellites to digital communications.

An important recent development concerning regulation, however, is the trend toward deregulation.[45] According to political economists Shields and Evans, "deregulation may entail the complete or partial withdrawal of the state from a specific activity, such as enforcement of labour standards or occupational health and safety, through privatizing the enforcement function, shifting towards a compliance framework based on workplace or sectoral self-regulation, or both."[46] Deregulation is an important component of the New Public Management, discussed in chapter 4.

As early as 1978, Prime Minister Trudeau and some of the premiers embraced deregulation, though in only a lukewarm manner. Since then, the Mulroney, Chrétien, Martin, and Harper governments have made it central to administrative reform for their governments, as have several provincial governments. Federally, the government has deregulated the oil and gas industry, foreign investment, financial services, transportation, and other areas. Indeed, various governments proceeded with deregulation in a pronounced manner by reorganizing government structures, sometimes even designating a specific minister responsible for deregulation.[47]

Sociologist Gary Teeple argues that there are several reasons for the accelerating pace of deregulation.[48] He suggests that there is usually a strong relationship between the development and application of new technology and the use of regulation. When new technology comes on line, a number of consequences are discernable: increased competition between producers with the same technology; competition between producers with different technology; monopolies in which only one or a small number of firms have access to the new technology for a period of time; damage to humans or the natural environment. In all of these situations, regulation can be justified, according to Teeple. Thus, he argues, the growth of government regulation corresponds more or less to the rate of technological growth in society. Since the Second World War, technological growth has proceeded at a pace unprecedented in human history and, not surprisingly, so too has the growth in regulatory bodies and agencies; but "with the present stage of permanent technological revolution beginning in the 1970s, the imposition of government regulations can no longer keep up with industrial innovation and its implications for society and nature."[49] Thus, regulation has come under attack as a hindrance to innovation and development.

Teeple further argues that the original rationale for much regulation was to prevent or control monopolies and other market failures. Increasingly, however, the economy is made up of global monopolies, oligopolies, and cartels. The rationale for seeking to control competition among national corporations is being swept aside. In any event, global corporations can move their operations to countries with minimal regulations as a means of lowering the costs of doing business. The mere threat of this action by a major employer in Canada is often enough to send government officials scurrying to find ways to repeal or tone down the regulatory framework. Moreover, the construction of global trade regimes and international free-trade areas often means that one country has to modify its regulations to match those of its partners. In Canada's case, there is pressure to lessen regulations to the lowest common denominator of its NAFTA partners. Since both the United States and (especially) Mexico have much less government intervention than Canada does, this implies reducing the regulatory role of the Canadian state to match that of the other two parties.

Teeple goes on to argue, though, that the impact of deregulation is frequently negative. For instance, deregulation actually reduces competition in some cases. It sometimes even opens the doors to illicit financial activities, since the watchdog role of regulatory bodies is relaxed. The global financial crash in 2008–2009, for instance, which saw the spectacular demise of large financial institutions, the "bailout" of banks by several governments, the collapse of real estate markets, and the decline of the stock market, was often cited as a result of widespread deregulation of international banking, securities, real estate, and related industries. Canada, in comparison to many other jurisdictions, was regarded as retaining a stronger regulatory regime and therefore did not suffer as much as other economies. Nonetheless, deregulation has recently been embraced by governments of many different ideological stripes in Canada.

Recently, governments have moved toward a program of regulatory reform, according to economist John Strick, in which they

*"regulate smarter" through greater efficiency, greater accountability, and increased sensitivity to those affected by regulation. Regulatory procedures were streamlined to reduce bureaucratic red tape and delays. Regulations were relaxed and modified in areas where it was deemed they impeded efficiency in the marketplace. A form of regulating the regulators was introduced through the application of cost-benefit analysis to new regulatory proposals in recognition of the potential high costs to the economy of regulation.[50]*

On March 24, 2005, the president of the Treasury Board announced Smart Regulation and launched a new website dedicated to regulatory renewal. The government said,

*Smart Regulation is aimed at improving the Government of Canada's regulatory system so that it can keep pace with today's realities and our evolving needs. This means building a regulatory system that is more effective in safeguarding the health and safety of all Canadians, ensuring a clean and sustainable environment, and creating the conditions for an innovative and competitive economy. In meeting these goals, Smart Regulation recognizes the interdependence of social, environmental, and economic objectives. It strives for a better coordinated system that remains forward-thinking, progressive and accountable to the citizens it serves.*

*Smart Regulation is based on public desire for high standards and transparency in regulation, combined with the advice provided by the Organisation for Economic Co-operation and Development (OECD), and the recommendations of both the Auditor General and the External Advisory Committee on Smart Regulation (EACSR), which released its report, Smart Regulation: A Regulatory Strategy for Canada, on September 23, 2004.*[51]

On April 1, 2007, the *Cabinet Directive on Streamlining Regulation* came into effect, further refining the regulatory regime of the federal government.[52]

A moment's reflection about your own daily routine will reveal that government is intimately involved in almost every aspect of your life—and regulations are a prominent part of that involvement. Bleary-eyed, you wake up to the sound of your alarm clock-radio, the electronic parts of which are regulated by safety standards set by the government. The DJ screams at you to rise and shine, as he plays the latest Canadian hit song, as required by government regulations covering Canadian content on the airways. You stumble into the bathroom, flip on the light, and turn on the water, both of which are supplied by public utilities heavily regulated with regard to delivery, service, and maintenance. You fumble for the toothpaste, whose ingredients are carefully regulated to ensure that they do not include anything harmful. As you head out for your morning walk with the dog, you put its leash on, mindful of municipal regulations (which also require that you suffer the indignity of having to "stoop and scoop"). If you drive to school, you are travelling in an invention that is among the most regulated technologies ever developed, from the additives in the fuel that propels it, to its safety systems, to the speed at which it can travel, and so on. If you take public transit, another legion of regulations governs everything from smoking to number of passengers to hours of operation. The list goes on and on. In short, the world of regulation has truly penetrated every aspect of our lives. Former prime minister Pierre Trudeau once said that the state had no place in the bedrooms of the nation. He might have reconsidered that observation in light of the pervasive growth of the state's regulatory powers.

# Crown Corporations

Another important organizational unit of government is the **Crown corporation**, which includes a variety of nondepartmental organizations involved in regulating the private sector through public ownership. There are about 400 such federal corporations in Canada, usually headed by boards of directors, whose members are usually appointed by the prime minister. These are typically patronage appointments. The legal definition of Crown corporations revolves around the issue of government ownership. Government doesn't have to own 100 percent of an enterprise for that enterprise to be publicly owned; a minority holding of less than 50 percent of the shares of a corporation qualifies as public ownership. However, the legislation covering Crown corporations refers only to enterprises that are 100-percent government owned.

A general definition supplied by Adie and Thomas suggests that "a Crown corporation could be described as an institution with a corporate form brought into existence by government action to serve a public function."[53] Crown corporations are a sort of blend between the private and public sectors. They function in most cases as private corporations but exist under conditions of greater accountability to government than private corporations. They enjoy a higher level of autonomy from Parliament than do departments, although they are ultimately responsible to Parliament through a designated minister. For instance, one of the most prominent Crown corporations is the Canadian Broadcasting Corporation (CBC), which reports to Parliament through the Canadian Heritage minister. Crown corporations are not subject to direct ministerial control, however. As a result, they have more autonomy with regard to personnel, finance, and service provision than do regular departments.

Crown corporations are also called government business enterprises (GBEs), Crown agencies, or public enterprises. According to Hale, their role

*has changed significantly in recent years with the maturing of the Canadian economy and changes in the political and management philosophies of many Canadian governments. These changes variously described as "the new governance" or "new public management," have blurred many traditional distinctions between government and business. In so doing, the range of policy tools or instruments available to governments for the delivery of public services and the delivery of public policy goals has been greatly expanded.*[54]

Crown corporations can act as *alternatives* to private sector businesses that fail or refuse to provide certain services; act in *competition* with them; act in *co-operation* or *partnership* with them; or *complement* or *supplement* them in the marketplace. They generally have the following characteristics:

■ They are legal entities engaged in the sale of goods and/or services to citizens, businesses, or other governments (domestic or foreign).

■ They are hybrid creatures with varying degrees of operational autonomy from governments.

■ They typically serve some public policy goal or, more generally, the "public interest."

■ They usually have a commercial orientation requiring more attention to customer service and operational efficiency than most traditional government departments.

■ They may have legal or regulatory privileges unavailable to private sector actors.[55]

Why would governments create Crown corporations in the first place? Why not simply rely on the traditional structures of government—that is, on departments? These questions are central to any explanation of the role of government ownership in Canada. We will consider several related explanations: nation building, resistance to the pull of continentalism, regional economic development, other economic rationales, ideology, and efficiency.

Crown corporations have historically been used in Canada as nation-building tools in the promotion of transportation, communication, and resource development, and to make Canada competitive with its neighbour to the south. For instance, pre-Confederation governments were heavily involved in developing infrastructure, such as canals and roads—a practice that continued after 1867 in other areas, such as airports. The Canadian National Railway, created in 1917, and Air Canada (Trans-Canada Air Lines), created in 1936, were needed to unite the country through transportation links from sea to sea. Petro-Canada was created in 1976 to give the Canadian government a "window" into the oil and gas industry, which was mainly foreign (i.e., U.S.) owned and controlled. The CBC was created in 1936 to protect and promote Canadian culture and cultural industries. At the provincial level, countless Crown corporations have been created over the years to pursue the goals of economic development and diversification. Ontario Hydro, for example, was created in 1906 by taking over the many private utility companies in the province so as to provide cheap and reliable sources of electric power to the province's manufacturers. By the 1970s and 1980s, every province in the country had established some sort of provincial development corporation to attract investment and jobs. So nation and province building have been important factors in explaining the proliferation of Crown corporations at both levels of government in Canada.

Sir John A. Macdonald once said in defence of government involvement in the economy that without it Canada would become "a bundle of sticks . . . without binding cord, [which would] fall, helpless, powerless, and aimless, into the hands of the neighbouring republic."[56] Later in the 1930s, an early advocate for a national public broadcasting system, Graham Spry, argued that the choice for Canadians was either "the state or the United States."[57] These arguments reflect what economist Hugh G.J. Aitken termed the practice of "defensive expansionism."[58] This is the notion that Canadian governments adopt an active role in the economy in order to resist or prevent continentalism—the economic, cultural, and, ultimately, political domination of Canada by the United States. In this view, Crown corporations are viewed as policy tools that permit Canadian governments to resist the overwhelming influence of the world's most powerful nation.

The third common explanation for the use of Crown corporations also has economic roots. This is the view that these policy tools promote regional economic development. Canada is regionally divided in a number of ways. Uneven economic development means that some regions are poorer and less economically diversified than other regions. At various times in Canadian history, governments have attempted to overcome this problem by targeting economic development at particular areas to stimulate the economies of these regions. For example, the Cape Breton Development Corporation was established by the federal government in 1967 to take over some failing coal mines that the private sector was about to abandon. The Maritime provinces have been particular targets of federal intervention in the form of Crown corporations, but such corporations have also been used in other depressed regions from time to time. In many of these situations, the government steps into an area where the private sector has failed or refuses to go. The bottom line of the private sector is profits, but governments must also take into consideration the health and welfare of communities, the costs of unemployment insurance and welfare, the possibility of mass migrations of people out of depressed regions into other parts of Canada, and so on. These are considerations that corporate offi-cials do not need to worry about.

Regional economic development is also fostered when governments create Crown corporations in industries that tend to have wide fluctuations in prices and incomes from year to year. For instance, the Canadian Wheat Board was estab-lished to add some stability to the price of wheat by regulating supply and demand, and ensuring that farmers would get a fair price year in and year out, notwithstand-ing fluctuations in the world price for their products. Finally, some Crown corpo-rations are used in order to provide low-interest loans and risk capital to private sector corporations to promote economic activity in particular regions. All these measures are intended to ensure that some healthy level of economic activity exists in all the regions of Canada.

Another economic argument for Crown corporations says that, in some cir-cumstances, particular industries may lend themselves to a natural monopoly. For instance, until recent technological change altered the landscape, it was often argued that the provision of services such as transit, sewage, telephone, hydro, or natural gas were most efficiently and effectively provided by one big company in each field. Whether the one company was to be public or private was a matter of some debate, but in many instances there was a proper and defensible role for the state, as the monopoly provider of a given service, to ensure that customers were not gouged by high prices, poor service, or discriminatory practices.

Besides the economic arguments, there are also ideological ones. Some com-mentators have focused on the differences between Canadian political culture and U.S. political culture, arguing that Canada has a stronger sense of the collective or community, and is more willing to use the state to defend that sense of community than are the Americans, where a more "rugged individualism" prevails. This mani-fests itself in a more pluralistic set of political ideologies than is found in the United States. There is a specific content to the ideologies of socialism, liberalism, and con-servatism in Canada. Each has important consequences for the choice and imple-mentation of economic development strategies by the Canadian state,[59] and will be considered in turn:

- Socialism is associated with the idea that society should be organized on the basis of co-operation rather than competition and that the collective is of paramount importance in securing the liberty of the individual, whose self-worth is recognized in the idea that all in society are equal. In this view, the state is seen as an active agent of intervention in the marketplace, up to and including nationalization of industry.

- Liberalism asserts that the individual is the single most important element in a society, a notion derived from political philosophers, such as Thomas Hobbes and John Locke, who essentially saw the community as an atomistic collection of individuals who best further societal living by pursuing their self-interests in healthy competition with others. The liberal, like the social-ist, believes in equality. But unlike the socialist, the liberal asserts that equal-ity of opportunity is sufficient for the pursuit of personal fulfillment, while the socialist asserts that equality of condition is necessary. Freedom of the individual from state interference is of primary importance for liberals, and shapes their view of economic development, which is that the market should operate unencumbered by state intervention.

■ In conservatism, the organic community is most important, and notions of social equality give way to deference to authority and tradition that guide societal relations. This view asserts that society is naturally hierarchically organized, and is evidenced in the Canadian tradition by such well-known features of Canadian history and development as the absence of a lawless, egalitarian, American-style frontier, by a preference for Britain rather than the United States as a social model, and generally by a weaker emphasis on social equality than is found in either socialism or liberalism. A particular trait of Canadian conservatism is the willingness of the political and business elites to use the power of the state for developing and controlling the economy, especially where staples (i.e., natural resource) development is concerned. This partly explains why it was Conservative governments in Canada that created Crown corporations, such as the CBC, Air Canada, Ontario Hydro, and others.

The presence of conservatism and socialism alongside liberalism permits a greater diversity of views about the role of the state to exist in Canada than does the more monolithic ideology of liberalism that dominates in the United States— hence the more common use of public ownership in Canada than in the United States.[60]

Indeed, almost all aspects of social and economic life in Canada are represented in the proliferation of Crown corporations at both the federal and provincial levels. Their use as policy tools has some advantages over the use of regular departments in providing services for citizens. For instance, as alluded to above, Crown corporations are one step removed from direct political control. This immunizes Crown corporations from compromising positions—for example, where the provision of a good or service may appear as a political favour from a minister to a supporter or friend (e.g., in the awarding of a contract).

In addition, there is often an advantage of efficiency in Crown corporations that is absent in departments. Departments can be weighed down with processes, procedures, rules, and regulations that impede the speedy and efficient achievement of a particular goal. Departments may also be less efficient due to contradictory, competing, or multiple goals. Budgeting and personnel policy may be more streamlined in Crown corporations than in government departments. For instance, labour relations in many Crown corporations come under the Labour Code instead of the more onerous legislation that governs personnel in departments. This allows for greater flexibility in a number of areas, such as setting wages and salaries. Finally, Crown corporations may be preferable to departments under certain circumstances for the simple reason that departments have enough on their plates already, making it preferable to "farm out" tasks and work to another government body.

Recently, Crown corporations have been under sustained attack by the right wing in Canada as costly, bloated, unresponsive, and unaccountable creatures that compete unfairly in the marketplace against private sector corporations. What began in the 1970s and 1980s as a call for increased accountability and control over Crown corporations has evolved into a call for their dismantling. Canadian neoconservatives have argued fairly successfully that many such corporations have outlived their usefulness and, more important, that they are inappropriate as a policy instrument, draining away taxpayer money and doing a job poorly that could be better done by the private sector. Thus, there has been a trend lately toward privatization of Crown corporations—that is, selling them to the private sector.

Advocates of privatization argue that the original public policy purposes of Crown corporations no longer apply, or that the public policy goals involved could be pursued more efficiently through private sector ownership. This has been the fate of Air Canada and Petro-Canada at the federal level (see Box 5.5). At the

## BOX 5.5 | Federal Crown Corporations and Privatizations

| Select Crown Corporations 2010 | Select Privatizations |
| --- | --- |
| Canada Post Corporation | Canada Communications Group |
| Canadian Broadcasting Corporation | Canadian Arsenals |
| Atomic Energy of Canada | Canadian National Railway |
| VIA Rail Canada Inc. | CN Subsidiaries: CN Hotels; CNCP |
| National Film Board of Canada | Telecommunications (CN half); |
| National Gallery of Canada | Northwestel Inc.; Terra Nova |
| National Arts Centre Corporation | Communications |
| National Capital Commission | Air Canada |
| Canada Mortgage and Housing Corporation | Eldorado Nuclear Limited |
| | Fishery Products International |
| Marine Atlantic Inc. | Teleglobe Canada Inc. |
| Bank of Canada | Telesat Canada |
| Royal Canadian Mint | Northern Canada Power Commission |
| Business Development | Northern Transportation Company Ltd. |
| | de Havilland Aircraft of Canada Inc. |
| Export Development Corporation | Canadair |
| St. Lawrence Seaway Authority | Petro-Canada |
| Canadian Wheat Board | Canada Development Corporation |
| Farm Credit Canada | Nanisivik Mines Ltd. |
| Atlantic Canada Opportunities Agency | Pêcheries Canada |
| | Route Canada |
| | Terra Nova Telecommunications |
| | Co-Enerco Resources Ltd. |
| | Nordion International |
| | NAV Canada |
| | National Sea Products |
| | Theatronics International |

**Sources:** Adapted from Alasdair Roberts, "A Fragile State: Federal Public Administration in the Twentieth Century," in Christopher Dunn, ed., *The Handbook of Public Administration* (Toronto: Oxford University Press, 2002): 29; and David Johnson, *Thinking Government: Public Sector Management in Canada*, 2nd ed. (Peterborough: Broadview, 2006): 172.

provincial level, the Liquor Control Board in Alberta and parts of Ontario Hydro in Ontario have been privatized. Many governments in Canada have established units within departments to look at which Crown corporations can be turned over to the private sector.

Those who oppose privatization argue that it is premised on shaky economic and ideological grounds. There is a good deal of skepticism that the free market can perform as well as its proponents claim. Certainly, there are underlying questions about whether nation building or resistance to continentalism can be realized without public ownership. There is also the lingering issue of whether the public interest is best served under conditions of free markets or under some mix of private and public ownership. Moreover, if privatization proceeds, who exactly is able to afford to buy the assets that the government puts up for sale? Generally, it is those corporate actors who are already powerful who will buy these public corporations. Therefore, it is argued that privatization simply contributes to an undesirable concentration of wealth and power in fewer hands. The ongoing discussion in Canadian society about the usefulness of these policy instruments is part of the larger ideological debate about the proper role of government in general.

## WHAT YOU HAVE LEARNED

The three categories of departments, regulatory bodies, and Crown corporations do not encompass all organizational units within the federal public service. As we noted, several new mechanisms have emerged. Other offices and institutions also exist—for example, agents of Parliament like the Office of the Auditor General and the Commissioner of Official Languages. These are independent of Cabinet and report directly to Parliament. But the majority of organizational units do fall within the ambit of departments, regulatory bodies, and Crown corporations. Let us summarize this part by returning to some general observations about public service and how these units fit in the overall bureaucratic scheme of things.

You will recall that the term *bureaucracy* refers to a kind of organization with particular structural characteristics. As Weber pointed out, bureaucracies are characterized by a well-developed division of labour, within which officials perform certain clearly defined roles by following prescribed rules and regulations. Moreover, those roles are defined by the office held, not by the individual occupying the role. This ensures that there is some continuity in the functions and structures of government. Detailed written records of all the actions taken by public servants are also a feature of this system, which allows a body of precedents to build up to guide future actions. The fact that office holding is a full-time occupation also contributes to continuity. Finally, the organizational structure is characterized by hierarchy. Decision making flows downward from above in a rigidly defined structure in which each level of the bureaucracy is responsible to the level above.

Adopting this type of bureaucratic organization has its benefits. It allows a kind of equality of treatment of all citizens by "routinizing" the decision-making process, which in turn allows maximum impartiality in dealing with citizens. It

also allows predictability, and thus fairness, in that the application of the law by bureaucratic officials must be the same for everyone. Clearly, however, these strengths are also weaknesses. Citizens with special circumstances may not fit into the routinized bureaucratic process. For example, certain university students applying for financial assistance may find they are unfairly disadvantaged by a bureaucratic interpretation of what constitutes an asset, which is appropriate in most cases but not in their own. You have no doubt encountered a situation in which you pleaded for treatment appropriate to your own circumstances, only to be told by some bureaucratic official, "If we change the rules for you, we'll have to change them for everyone."

Notwithstanding these limitations, bureaucracy is the worst system we have—except for all the others (to paraphrase Winston Churchill on democracy). The organization of the Canadian bureaucratic system into departments, regulatory bodies, and Crown corporations both reflects the major characteristics of bureaucracy and represents our best attempts to construct a complex organizational structure that responds to the needs of citizens and can balance the tensions between democracy and efficiency within the framework of bureaucracy. The fact that new agencies and alternative service delivery mechanisms have evolved, but have not supplanted traditional mechanisms, speaks to both the strengths and weaknesses of those traditional mechanisms.

## Key Words and Concepts

spending power (122)

executive branch (123)

legislative branch (123)

judicial branch (123)

Privy Council (125)

Cabinet (125)

constitutional convention (125)

responsible government (125)

minority government (126)

departments (130)

ministries (130)

statutory bodies (130)

minister (130)

central agencies (136)

agents of parliament (139)

alternative service delivery (140)

ministerial responsibility (141)

collective ministerial responsibility (142)

deputy minister (DM) (142)

regulatory agencies (148)

Crown corporation (152)

## Review Questions

This chapter was divided into five sections, each reflecting a key issue for public administration. You should now be familiar with these issues and be able to answer questions associated with each.

### 1. Factors Influencing Organizational Structure

Among the many factors influencing Canadian public administration, we isolated three for particular attention. How in your view would the structure of government differ if one or more of capitalist democracy, federalism, and/or cabinet-parliamentary government were absent from the Canadian setting? Can you explain the significance of each in terms of how they influence the very outlines of the state itself and have influenced public administration?

### 2. Political–Administrative Relationships

We returned here to some issues surrounding the relationship between public administration and democratic government. You may have some assumptions about who controls government, and how. Did this section confirm those assumptions or challenge them? How? Can you explain the relationship between politicians and public servants, and explain who is actually in control of the machinery and actions of the state?

### 3. Departmental Organizations

The main organizational units of the Canadian government are dynamic; growing and shrinking over time, rising and falling in influence and importance. Why do some prime ministers prefer large Cabinets with many departments, while others opt for more stripped-down models? How does the traditional departmental model stack up against alternative service delivery agencies? Why have these newer bodies emerged?

### 4. Regulatory Agencies

The presence of government in our lives is evident in examining the nature of regulatory bodies. Can you think of an area of life that government does not regulate? These most common of organizational forms of government, although increasingly under attack, sometimes seem ubiquitous. What role do regulatory bodies play in public administration? In an era of deregulation, why have we been rethinking the areas of life that government should be regulating?

### 5. Crown Corporations

Can you claim to have an understanding of the historical place of public ownership in Canadian public administration? Why has the role of Crown corporations as a policy tool recently been questioned?

## Weblinks

The Prime Minister of Canada
**www.pm.gc.ca**

The Privy Council
**www.pco-bcp.gc.ca**

Treasury Board
**www.tbs-sct.gc.ca**

Department of Finance
**www.fin.gc.ca**

Parliament of Canada
**www.parl.gc.ca**

Federal Government Departments and Agencies
**http://canada.gc.ca/depts/major/depind-eng.html**

Public Service Commission of Canada
**www.psc-cfp.gc.ca**

Supreme Court of Canada
**www.scc-csc.gc.ca**

Government of Canada Intergovernmental Affairs
**www.pco-bcp.gc.ca/aia**

Institute of Intergovernmental Relations
**www.queensu.ca/iigr**

Centre for Constitutional Studies
**www.law.ualberta.ca/centres/ccs**

Forum of Federations
**http://forumfed.org**

## Further Reading

### 1. Factors Influencing Organizational Structure

Johnson, David. *Thinking Government: Public Sector Management in Canada.* 2nd ed. Peterborough: Broadview, 2006.

Molot, Henry L. "The Public Service of Canada," in Christopher Dunn, ed., *The Handbook of Canadian Public Administration*, 2nd ed. Toronto: Oxford University Press, 2010: 55–74.

Peters, B. Guy, and Donald J. Savoie, eds. *Governance in the Twenty-First Century: Revitalizing the Public Service*. Montreal: McGill-Queen's University Press, 2000.

## 2.  Political–Administrative Relationships

Bourgault, Jacques. "The Role of Deputy Ministers in Canadian Government," in Christopher Dunn, ed., *The Handbook of Canadian Public Administration*, 2nd ed. Toronto: Oxford University Press, 2010: 504–20.

Dutil, Patrice, ed. *Searching for Leadership: Secretaries to Cabinet in Canada*. Toronto: University of Toronto Press and IPAC, 2008.

Dwivedi, O.P., and James Iain Gow. *From Bureaucracy to Public Management: The Administrative Culture of the Government of Canada*. Peterborough: Broadview, 1999.

Franks, C.E.S. "The Respective Accountability and Responsibilities of Ministers and Public Servants: A Study of the British Accounting Officer System and Its Relevance for Canada," in Donald Savoie, ed., *Restoring Accountability: Research Studies*, vol. 3, *Commission of Inquiry into the Sponsorship Program and Advertising Activities*. Ottawa: Public Works and Government Services Canada, 2006: 157–230.

Savoie, Donald J. "The Public Service Has a Personality." *Canadian Public Administration*, 49, 3 (2006): 261–81.

## 3.  Departmental Organizations

Aucoin, Peter. "The Staffing and Evaluation of Canadian Deputy Ministers in Comparative Westminster Perspective: A Proposal for Reform," in Donald Savoie, ed., *Restoring Accountability: Research Studies*, vol. 3, *Commission of Inquiry into the Sponsorship Program and Advertising Activities*. Ottawa: Public Works and Government Services Canada, 2006: 297–336.

Campbell, Colin, and George J. Szablowski. "What Central Agencies May and Ought to Do: Structure of Authority," in Barbara Wake Carroll, David Siegel, and Mark Sproule-Jones, eds., *Classic Readings in Canadian Public Administration*. Toronto: Oxford University Press, 2005: 53–79.

Hodgetts, J.E. "Structural Heretics: The Non-Departmental Forms," in Barbara Wake Carroll, David Siegel, and Mark Sproule-Jones, eds., *Classic Readings in Canadian Public Administration*. Toronto: Oxford University Press, 2005: 87–102.

Hurley, James Ross. "Responsibility, Accountability and the Role of Deputy Ministers in the Government of Canada," in Donald Savoie, ed., *Restoring Accountability: Research Studies*, vol. 3, *Commission of Inquiry into the Sponsorship Program and Advertising Activities*. Ottawa: Public Works and Government Services Canada, 2006: 115–56.

Savoie, Donald J. "Power at the Apex: Executive Dominance," in James Bickerton and Alain-G. Gagnon, eds., *Canadian Politics*, 4th ed. Peterborough: Broadview, 2004: 145–62.

Sutherland, S.L. "The Role of the Clerk of the Privy Council," in Donald Savoie, ed., *Restoring Accountability: Research Studies*, vol. 3, *Commission of Inquiry into the Sponsorship Program and Advertising Activities*. Ottawa: Public Works and Government Services Canada, 2006: 21–114.

Tardi, Gregory. "Departments and Other Institutions of Government," in Christopher Dunn, ed., *The Handbook of Canadian Public Administration*, 2nd ed. Toronto: Oxford University Press, 2010: 25–52.

Winfield, Mark. "Alternative Service Delivery in the Natural Resources Sector: An Examination of Ontario's Forestry Compliance Self-Inspection System." *Canadian Public Administration*, 48, 4 (2005): 552–74.

## 4.  Regulatory Agencies

Bird, Malcolm, and Christopher Stoney. "Government Approaches to the Regulation of 'Sin'," in G. Bruce Doern, ed., *How Ottawa Spends 2006–2007: In From the Cold: The Tory Rise and the Liberal Demise*. Montreal: McGill-Queen's University Press, 2006: 247–65.

Doern, G. Bruce. "Regulatory Processes and Regulatory Agencies," in Barbara Wake Carroll, David Siegel, and Mark Sproule-Jones, eds., *Classic Readings in Canadian Public Administration*. Toronto: Oxford University Press, 2005: 103–23.

Doern, G. Bruce, and Robert Johnson, eds. *Rules, Rules, Rules, Rules: Multilevel Regulatory Governance*. Toronto: University of Toronto Press, 2006.

Stemshorn, Barry, and Robert W. Slater. "Potential for a Regulatory Breakthrough? Regulatory Governance and Human Resource Initiatives," in Allan M. Maslove, ed., *How Ottawa Spends 2008–2009: A More Orderly Federalism?* Montreal: McGill-Queen's University Press, 2008: 59–81.

### 5. Crown Corporations

Ashley, C.A., and G.H. Smails. "From Canadian Crown Corporations," in Barbara Wake Carroll, David Siegel, and Mark Sproule-Jones, eds., *Classic Readings in Canadian Public Administration.* Toronto: Oxford University Press, 2005: 124–43.

Canada. Treasury Board Secretariat. *Canada's Crown Corporations: Meeting the Expectations of Citizens.* Ottawa: Treasury Board Secretariat, 2005.

## Endnotes

1. Neil Bradford, *Commissioning Ideas: Canadian National Policy Innovation in Comparative Perspective* (Toronto: Oxford University Press, 1998): 15.

2. Geoffrey Hale, *Uneasy Partnership: The Politics of Business and Government in Canada* (Peterborough: Broadview, 2006): 3.

3. Bradford, *Commissioning Ideas*, 15–16.

4. For a discussion of Wheare's views and other definitions of federalism, see Garth Stevenson, *Unfulfilled Union: Canadian Federalism and National Unity*, 4th ed. (Montreal: McGill-Queen's University Press, 2004): chap. 1. For an overview of the evolution of federalism, see Gregory J. Inwood, "Federalism, Democracy and the (Anti-)Social Union," in Mike Burke, Colin Mooers, and John Shields, eds., *Restructuring and Resistance: Canadian Public Policy in an Age of Global Capitalism* (Halifax: Fernwood, 2000): 124–44; and Richard Simeon, "Federalism and Intergovernmental Relations," in Christopher Dunn, ed., *The Handbook of Canadian Public Administration*, 2nd ed. (Toronto: Oxford University Press, 2010): 401–21.

5. See Christopher Dunn, "The Federal Spending Power," in Christopher Dunn, ed., *The Handbook of Canadian Public Administration*, 2nd ed. (Toronto: Oxford University Press, 2010): 422–44.

6. Both federal and provincial governments launched investigations into the fiscal imbalance in 2006. For the provincial view, see the Council of the Federation, Advisory Panel on Fiscal Imbalance, *Reconciling the Irreconcilable: Addressing Canada's Fiscal Imbalance* (Ottawa: Council of the Federation, 2006). For the federal view see the Expert Panel on Equalization and Territorial Formula Financing, *Achieving a National Purpose: Putting Equalization Back on Track* (Ottawa: Department of Finance, 2006).

7. See Gregory J. Inwood, Carolyn M. Johns, and Patricia L. O'Reilly, "Intergovernmental Officials in Canada," in J. Peter Meekison, Hamish Telford, and Harvey Lazar, eds., *Canada: The State of the Federation 2002: Reconsidering the Institutions of Canadian Federalism* (Montreal: McGill-Queen's University Press, 2004): 249–84.

8. See Richard Simeon, *Federal-Provincial Diplomacy: The Making of Recent Policy in Canada* (Toronto: University of Toronto Press, 2006).

9. Peter H. Russell, *Constitutional Odyssey: Can Canadians Become a Sovereign People?* 3rd ed. (Toronto: University of Toronto Press, 2004): 81. See also Herman Bakvis and Grace Skogstad, "Canadian Federalism: Performance, Effectiveness, and Legitimacy," in Herman Bakvis and Grace Skogstad, eds., *Canadian Federalism: Performance, Effectiveness, and Legitimacy*, 2nd ed. (Toronto: Oxford University Press, 2008): 3–22.

10. See Carolyn M. Johns, Patricia L. O'Reilly, and Gregory J. Inwood, "Formal and Informal Dimensions of Intergovernmental Administrative Relations in Canada," *Canadian Public Administration*, 50, 1 (2007); and Carolyn Johns, Patricia L. O'Reilly, and Gregory J. Inwood, "Intergovernmental Innovation and the Administrative State in Canada," *Governance*, 19, 4 (2006), 627–49.

11. See Donald Savoie, *Governing from the Centre: The Concentration of Power in Canadian Politics* (Toronto: University of Toronto Press, 1999); and Graham White, *Cabinets and First Ministers* (Vancouver: UBC Press, 2005).

12. Victor S. MacKinon, "Introduction to the Legal Environment: Theories and Principles," in Randy Hoffman et al., *Public Administration: Canadian Materials*, 3rd ed. (Toronto: Captus, 1998): 199.

13. Peter Aucoin and Donald J. Savoie, "The Politics–Administration Dichotomy," in O.P. Dwivedi, Tim A. Mau, and Byron Sheldrick, eds., *The Evolving Physiology of Government: Canadian Public Administration in Transition* (Ottawa: University of Ottawa Press, 2009): 97–117.

14. Canada, Treasury Board of Canada Secretariat, *Annual Report to Parliament: Crown Corporations and Other Corporate Interests of Canada, 2008*, **www.tbs-sct.gc.ca/reports-rapports/cc-se/2008/cc-se03-eng.asp#Toc220113622.**

15. For an analysis of recent changes to cabinet structures, see Evert Lindquist, Ian Clark and James Mitchell, "Reshaping Ottawa's Centre of Government: Martin's Reforms in Historical Perspective," in G. Bruce Doern, ed. *How Ottawa Spends, 2004–2005* (Montreal: McGill-Queen's University Press, 2004): 317–47.

16. Canada, Department of Justice, The Public Service Rearrangement and Transfer of Duties Act, **http://laws.justice.gc.ca/en/showdoc/cs/P-34/.**

17. J.E. Hodgetts, *The Canadian Public Service: A Physiology of Government 1867–70* (Toronto: University of Toronto Press, 1973): 89.

18. Robert J. Jackson and Doreen Jackson, *Politics in Canada: Culture, Institutions, Behaviour and Public Policy*, 3rd ed. (Scarborough: Prentice Hall, 1994): 376–77.

19. Luther Gulick, "Notes on the Theory of Organization," in Jay M. Shafritz and Albert C. Hyde, eds., *Classics of Public Administration*, 5th ed. (Belmont, CA: Thomson Wadsworth, 2004): 93.

20. See Canada, Privy Council Office, "Decision-Making Processes and Central Agencies in Canada: Federal, Provincial and Territorial Practices" (Ottawa: Privy Council Office, 1998).

21. See Canada, Privy Council Office, "The Role and Structure of the Privy Council Office" (Ottawa: Privy Council Office, 2010).

22. See Patrice Dutil, ed., *Searching for Leadership: Secretaries to Cabinet in Canada* (Toronto: University of Toronto Press and IPAC, 2008).

23. See Savoie, *Governing from the Centre*; and Eddie Goldenberg, *The Way It Works: Inside Ottawa* (Toronto: McClelland and Stewart, 2006).

24. See Canada, Treasury Board of Canada Secretariat, "Policy on Alternative Service Delivery," April 1, 2002: 1–2.

25. Canada, Treasury Board Secretariat, "Policy on Alternative Service Delivery," 2.

26. Canada, Treasury Board of Canada Secretariat, *Annual Report to Parliament: Crown Corporations and Other Corporate Interests of Canada, 2008*.

27. See Kenneth Kernaghan, "Putting Citizens First: Service Delivery and Integrated Public Governance," in O. P. Dwivedi, Tim A. Mau, and Byron Sheldrick, eds., *The Evolving Physiology of Government: Canadian Public Administration in Transition*, (Ottawa: University of Ottawa Press, 2009): 249–69; and Brian Marson, "Citizen-Centered Service in Canada: From Research to Results," in David Siegel and Ken Rasmussen, eds., *Professionalism and Public Service: Essays in Honour of Kenneth Kernaghan* (Toronto: University of Toronto Press and IPAC, 2008): 236–62.

28. See David Zussman, "Alternative Service Delivery in Canada," in Christopher Dunn, ed., *The Handbook of Canadian Public Administration*, 2nd ed. (Toronto: Oxford University Press, 2010): 250–67.

29. See John C. Strick, *The Public Sector in Canada: Programs, Finance and Policy*, (Toronto: Thompson, 1999): chap. 6.

30. See Canada, Treasury Board of Canada Secretariat, "Policy on Reporting of Federal Institutions and Corporate Interests to Treasury Board Secretariat," May 16, 2008, **www.tbs-sct.gc.ca/pol/doc-eng.aspx?id=12622.**

31. See David E. Smith, "Clarifying the Doctrine of Ministerial Responsibility as

It Applies to the Government and Parliament of Canada," in Donald Savoie, ed., *Restoring Accountability: Research Studies*, vol. 3, *Commission of Inquiry into the Sponsorship Program and Advertising Activities* (Ottawa: Public Works and Government Services Canada, 2006): 101–43.

32. See Robert J. Jackson and Doreen Jackson, *Politics in Canada: Culture, Institutions, Behaviour and Public Policy*, 7th ed. (Toronto: Pearson Prentice Hall, 2009): 363.

33. See Bryan Evans, Janet Lum, and John Shields, "Profiling of the Public Service Elite: A Demographic and Career Trajectory of Deputy and Assistant Deputy Ministers in Canada," *Canadian Public Administration*, 50, 4 (2007): 609–34.

34. Flora MacDonald, "Who Is on Top? The Minister or the Mandarins?" in Paul Fox and Graham White, eds., *Politics: Canada*, 8th ed. (Toronto: McGraw-Hill, 1995): 488–552.

35. Mitchell Sharp, "A Reply from a Former Minister and Mandarin," in Paul Fox and Graham White, eds., *Politics: Canada*, 8th ed. (Toronto: McGraw-Hill, 1995): 453–56.

36. Jacques Bourgault, *Profile of Deputy Ministers in the Government of Canada* (Ottawa: Canada School of Public Service, 2005): 15. See also Jacques Bourgault, "The Role of Deputy Ministers in Canadian Government," in Christopher Dunn, ed., *The Handbook of Canadian Public Administration*, 2nd ed. (Toronto: Oxford University Press, 2010): 504–20.

37. See David A. Good, "An Ideal Model in a Practical World: The Continuous Revisiting of Political Neutrality and Ministerial Responsibility," in David Siegel and Ken Rasmussen, eds., *Professionalism and Public Service: Essays in Honour of Kenneth Kernaghan* (Toronto: University of Toronto Press and IPAC, 2008): 63–83; Nicholas d'Ombrain, "Ministerial Responsibility and the Machinery of Government," *Canadian Public Administration*, 50, 2 (2007): 195–218; and Gordon F. Osbaldeston, *Keeping Deputy Ministers Accountable* (Toronto: McGraw-Hill Ryerson, 1989).

38. See, for example, Sharon L. Sutherland, "The Al-Mashat Affair: Administrative Accountability in Parliamentary Institutions," *Canadian Public Administration*, 34, 4 (1991): 573–603.

39. Canada, Privy Council Office, "Accounting Officers: Guidance on Roles, Responsibilities and Appearances before Parliamentary Committees, 2007," March 14, 2007, **www.pco-bcp.gc.ca/index.asp?lang=eng&page=information&sub=publications&doc=ao-adc/2007/ao-adc-eng.htm**. For critiques of the accounting officer model, see Peter Aucoin and Mark D. Jarvis, *Modernizing Government Accountability: A Framework for Reform* (Ottawa: Canada School of Public Service, 2005): 78–81; Alan Gilmore, "The Canadian Accounting Officer: Has It Strengthened Parliament's Ability to Hold the Government to Account?" in Christopher Dunn, ed., *The Handbook of Canadian Public Administration*, 2nd ed. (Toronto: Oxford University Press, 2010): 75–84; and C.E.S. Franks, "Not Anonymous Anymore: Ministerial Responsibility and the British Accounting Officers," *Canadian Public Administration*, 40, 4 (1997): 626–52.

40. Peter Aucoin and Donald J. Savoie, "The Politics–Administration Dichotomy," in O.P. Dwivedi, Tim A. Mau, and Byron Sheldrick, eds., *The Evolving Physiology of Government: Canadian Public Administration in Transition* (Ottawa: University of Ottawa Press, 2009): 112

41. Economic Council of Canada, "Interim Report: Responsible Regulations," cited in Jackson and Jackson, *Politics in Canada*, 341.

42. Richard Schultz, "Regulatory Agencies," in M.S. Whittington and G. Williams, eds., *Canadian Politics in the 1980s*, 2nd ed. (Toronto: Methuen, 1984): 438.

43. Michael Howlett and M. Ramesh, *Studying Public Policy: Policy Cycles and Policy Subsystems*, 3rd ed. (Toronto: Oxford University Press, 2009): 119–20.

44. See John C. Strick, "Regulation and Deregulation," in Christopher Dunn, ed. *The Handbook of Canadian Public Administration* (Toronto: Oxford University Press, 2002): 263–78.

45. See Strick, "Regulation and Deregulation," 276.

46. John Shields and B. Mitchell Evans, *Shrinking the State: Globalization and*

*Public Administration "Reform"* (Halifax: Fernwood, 1998): 69–70.

47. Richard J. Schultz, "Regulating Conservatively: The Mulroney Record, 1984–1988," in Andrew B. Gollner and Daniel Salée, eds., *Canada under Mulroney: An End of Term Report* (Montreal: Véhicule, 1988): 198.

48. Gary Teeple, *Globalization and the Decline of Social Reform: Into the Twenty-First Century* (Toronto: Garamond, 2000): 92–94.

49. Teeple, *Globalization and the Decline of Social Reform*, 93.

50. Strick, "Regulation and Deregulation," 277.

51. Canada, Treasury Board Secretariat of Canada, "Government of Canada Reports Progress on Regulatory Review," **www.tbs-sct.gc.ca/media/nr-cp/2005/1028_e.asp#BG**. Reproduced with permission of the Minister of Public Works and Government Services, 2010.

52. See Canada, Government of Canada, Cabinet Cabinet Directive on Streamlining Regulation, **www.tbs-sct.gc.ca/ri-qr/directive/directive00-eng.asp**.

53. Robert F. Adie and Paul G. Thomas, *Canadian Public Administration: Problematical Perspectives*, 2nd ed. (Scarborough: Prentice Hall, 1987): 377. On the role of Crown corporations in particular sectors, see Matthew J. Bellamy, *Profiting the Crown: Canada's Polymer Corporation 1942–1990* (Montreal: McGill-Queen's University Press, 2005); and Vanda Rideout, *Continentalizing Canadian Telecommunications: The Politics of Regulatory Reform* (Montreal: McGill-Queen's University Press, 2003).

54. Geoffrey Hale, *Uneasy Partnership: The Politics of Business and Government in Canada* (Peterborough: Broadview, 2006): 271.

55. Hale, *Uneasy Partnership*, 271.

56. Cited in Adie and Thomas, *Canadian Public Administration*, 387.

57. Cited in Ted Magder, "Taking Culture Seriously: A Political Economy of Communications," in Wallace Clement and Glen Williams, eds., *The New Canadian Political Economy* (Montreal: McGill-Queen's University Press, 1989): 288.

58. H.G.J. Aitken, "Defensive Expansion: The State and Economic Growth in Canada," in W.T. Easterbrook and M.H. Watkins, eds., *Approaches to Canadian Economic History* (Toronto: McClelland and Stewart, 1967): 183–221.

59. See Nelson Wiseman and David Whorley, "Lessons on the Centrality of Politics from Canadian Crown Enterprise," in Christopher Dunn, ed., *The Handbook of Canadian Public Administration* (Toronto: Oxford University Press, 2002): 383–84.

60. See William Christian and Colin Campbell, *Political Parties and Ideologies in Canada*, 2nd ed. (Toronto: McGraw-Hill Ryerson, 1983): 25–26; and Terrence Bell, Richard Dagger, William Christian, and Colin Campbell, *Political Ideologies and the Democratic Ideal*, Can. ed. (Toronto: Pearson Longman, 2006).

# Chapter  6

# Public Administration, *the* Constitution, *and* Law

## WHAT YOU WILL LEARN

Clearly, public administration is intimately connected to the law, particularly constitutional law and administrative law. In this chapter, we will frame our discussion of public administration and the law by first looking at the following issues:

- What is a constitution, and what does it do?
- What is the relationship between the Constitution and state institutions?
- How do elements of political culture relate to the law, and how does the British North America Act, 1867 (BNA Act) reflect the nature of Canadian society at Confederation, compared to how the Constitution Act of 1982 reflects the changed nature of Canadian society?
- How does the Constitution deal with the question of rights and freedoms in the Canadian Charter of Rights and Freedoms?
- How has the Canadian Constitution evolved and changed, or, alternatively, why it has changed so little in over 140 years?
- What is the definition, nature, and scope of administrative law?

This chapter is divided into the following sections:

### 1. The Law, the Courts, and the Administration of Justice

This section asks you to consider political culture and the rule of law in Canada. It asks: What is the rule of law? What are common law and civil law? What is the structure of the court system in Canada? How is justice administered in Canada?

## 2. What Is a Constitution?

While constitutions are fundamental to every society, they vary widely in their utility and application. This section asks: What is a constitution? What three main functions do constitutions serve? What are the component parts of the Canadian Constitution? How did the Canadian constitutional order come about?

## 3. Constitutional Law

This section addresses constitutional law in terms of conflict over the division of powers in the Constitution. It asks: How are disputes resolved before the courts when federal and provincial governments cannot agree on the jurisdiction of a law? What powers in the Constitution have proven the most contentious, and how have disputes over them been resolved? What role have the courts played in the resolution of conflict? What has been the legacy of judicial review of constitutional law? How has the constitutional issue of Aboriginal self-government become prominent?

## 4. Administrative Law

The last section in this chapter examines administrative law. It asks: What is administrative law? What is the power of discretion held by public servants? What happens when a dispute arises over the exercise of legal powers by an administrative agency? What is the relationship between constitutional and administrative law? What is the role of judicial review in administrative law?

# The Law, the Courts, and the Administration of Justice

Institutions for the administration of justice are a feature common to virtually all societies. The Egyptian kings were perhaps the first to delegate the administration of justice to judges, starting around 2900 BC; the Code of Babylonia and Code of Hammurabi emerged a little later in ancient Mesopotamia; and courts were common to Hebrew, Hindu, Arab, Chinese, Greek, Roman, Aztec, and other societies.[1] The direct historical trajectory of Canada's legal traditions can be found in the legal systems developed first by Aboriginal societies, and in the legal systems imported from Europe by settlers, mainly from Great Britain and France.

Canadians have a reputation as a peace-loving, orderly, cautious people. Our Constitution, it is said, reflects this in that its most memorable phrase is "peace, order, and good government." Compare this to the U.S. Constitution's declaration of "life, liberty, and the pursuit of happiness," or the French constitution's affirmation to "liberty, equality, fraternity." These phrases speak volumes about the political cultures of the three countries. Canada is said to be a nation that sent its police force into the wilderness to precede settlement and establish loyalty to the Crown, and hence the patterns of deference to authority were sown early on.

The early establishment of this firm belief in the law was fundamental to the evolution of the Canadian society. Moreover, we embraced the **rule of law**, which is the principle that both the rulers and ruled are answerable to the law, and both are prohibited from interfering with the independence of the courts, which uphold the rule of law through their positions as independent arbiters of societal disputes. This cornerstone of the Canadian constitutional order is evidenced daily by our obvious respect as a society for duly constituted authority.

The function of law is essentially to regulate human behaviour.[2] To be effective, the law must be knowable—that is, people must be made aware of the standards of behaviour they are expected to uphold. It must also be predictable—it cannot be arbitrary in its application. The law in Canada is based largely on statutes passed by the legislatures of the federal and provincial governments, and on the English **common law** tradition. This is a system of law wherein judges dispense justice on the basis of past custom and on the precedents built up over the years in prior legal findings. The cumulative body of law dating from the thirteenth century in England serves as the basis of common law.

Canada also has a system of **civil law**, most particularly in Quebec. This is based on Roman law, when the Emperor Justinian ordered the consolidation of all laws. Napoleon ordered the codification of French law on this model of Roman law, and the Napoleonic Code represented an authoritative written record of all laws. Judges in a civil law system are more constrained in making judgments than in common law. The civil code in Quebec, a legacy of the early relationship between French and English after the Conquest in 1759, is a key aspect of the distinctive political culture of the province. The Quebec Act of 1774 made Canada a "bijural" country. This awkward phrase simply means we have two types of law: common law, which is applied outside Quebec in matters of private law; and the Civil Code, which is applied to private law matters inside Quebec. Common law is used, though, for public law both inside and outside Quebec.[3]

Even though we continue to speak of a bijural system of law, we cannot forget the contribution of Aboriginal law. According to the federal Department of Justice,

*Aboriginal peoples in Canada have also contributed to our legal system. Aboriginal rights and treaty rights are recognized and protected under the Constitution. Aboriginal rights are those related to the historical occupancy and use of the land by Aboriginal peoples; treaty rights are those set out in treaties entered into by the Crown and a particular group of Aboriginal people. Reserves, for example, are the responsibility of the federal government.*

*Aboriginal customs and traditions have also contributed to new ways of dealing with people, such as healing and sentencing circles, community justice and restorative justice.*[4]

Interest in Aboriginal law has grown lately, particularly since Aboriginal rights were recognized and affirmed in the Charter of Rights and Freedoms in 1982, the Royal Commission on Aboriginal Peoples (RCAP), the British Columbia treaty process, and numerous land claim settlement processes. Aboriginal law is still a rapidly evolving legal area, and although the Supreme Court of Canada has delivered a number of ground-breaking decisions regarding Aboriginal legal issues, it has not yet authoritatively determined the content of Aboriginal law.[5]

Because Canada adopted a federal system in 1867, the courts are federal (see Figure 6.1). There are separate federal and provincial courts in Canada, although in some circumstances cases from provincial courts can be appealed to the Supreme

**FIGURE 6.1    Section 92, 96, and 101 Courts**

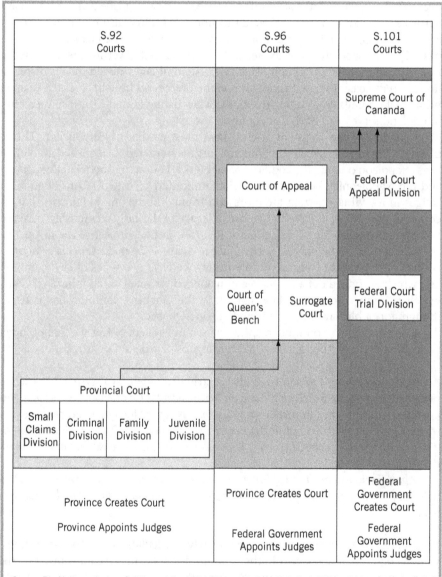

**Source:** F.L. Morton, ed., *Law, Politics and the Judicial Process in Canada,* 3rd ed. (Calgary: University of Calgary Press, 2002): 111.

Court of Canada; thus, a degree of horizontal integration exists. Several parts of the Constitution relate to the courts. For instance, Section 92 authorizes the creation of courts by the provinces, which also appoint the judges. Section 96 authorizes the creation of courts by the provinces, but in this case judges are appointed by the federal government. Section 101 authorizes the creation of courts by the federal government, which also appoints the judges. Together these bodies constitute a rather elaborate federal judicial system, at the apex of which stands the Supreme Court.[6] It was established in 1875 but did not become the final court of appeal until 1949. All types of law cases (common, civil, criminal, statutory, administrative, constitutional, federal, provincial) can be appealed to and be heard in the Supreme Court. It consists of nine learned and senior justices appointed by the prime minister. Three judges from Quebec hear civil law cases.

The federal nature of our court system has resulted in a sometimes bewildering array of interrelated courts. The basic structure is derived from the English system, but of course England was a unitary country, not a federal one. So we adapted, but we did not do what the United States (a federal country) did. The U.S. court system has two parallel, independent sets of courts: state supreme courts and courts of appeal for matters falling within state jurisdiction, and federal district courts and courts of appeal for matters of federal jurisdiction. Instead, Canada replicated England's basic structure of inferior and superior trial courts and two appeal courts appended to a federal structure. As a consequence, there are three important and distinctive features of the Canadian court system, according to law professors Fitzgerald and Wright:

*First, most matters arising under federal or provincial law are dealt with by courts that are administered by the provinces. These courts have remained largely as they had been when the province entered Confederation. Unlike the United States, there is no distinction between the courts that try matters of federal law and those that try matters of provincial law. Second, the judges of these courts may be federally—or provincially—appointed. The seriousness of the matter determines whether a case goes to a superior court for trial before a federally appointed judge. Third, all appeals from provincially appointed courts, including matters of provincial law, are heard by federally appointed judges. However, superior and provincial appeal courts are administered by each province while the supreme court of Canada is administered by the federal government.[7]*

One other important court relates particularly to administrative law. In 1970, the Federal Court of Canada was created to replace the Exchequer Court, which had been responsible for hearing cases concerning federal taxes, patents, and copyrights. The Federal Court of Canada consists of a Trial Division and an Appeals Division, and its tasks were expanded to include federal administrative law cases concerning agencies, boards, commissions, and tribunals.

The labyrinth of courts and the very administration of justice itself, of course, require supportive bodies and agencies to facilitate the formulation and implementation of law. Hence, on May 22, 1869, Prime Minister John A. Macdonald established a federal Department of Justice headed by an attorney general to do just that.[8] The mission of the current Department of Justice is shown in Box 6.1.

## BOX 6.1   The Mission of the Department of Justice

The mission of the Department of Justice is to:

- support the Minister of Justice in working to ensure that Canada is a just and law-abiding society with an accessible, efficient, and fair system of justice;

- provide high-quality legal services and counsel to the government and to client departments and agencies; and

- promote respect for rights and freedoms, the law, and the Constitution.

**Source:** "Canada's Department of Justice—Our Mis sion", **www.justice.gc.ca/en/dept/pub/about/**, Department of Justice Canada 2007. Reproduced with the permission of the Minister of Public Works and Government Services Canada, 2010. .

The Department of Justice is headed by a politician chosen by the prime minister to play a dual role as both minister of Justice and, by law, the attorney general.[9] The minister is concerned with the administration of justice in areas like criminal law, family law, human rights, and Aboriginal justice, but as attorney general, he or she must also act as the chief law officer of the Crown with responsibility for conducting all litigation for the federal government. This is a position that has its roots in an ancient practice of the sovereign appointing lawyers to represent the Crown in various courts. The department itself not only develops policy and drafts and reforms laws, but also acts as the government's legal adviser. As such, it prosecutes cases under federal law and represents the Government of Canada in court. A related but separate ministerial position is that of solicitor general, which came into being in fifteenth-century England as a deputy of the attorney general. Today, reflecting the times we live in, the federal solicitor general is called the Minister of Public Safety, and is responsible for overseeing the Royal Canadian Mounted Police, the Canadian Security Intelligence Service, Border Services, Emergency Management, Correctional Service Canada, and the National Parole Board. Some provinces, though not all, also have solicitors general.[10]

Supporting the minister of Justice is a deputy minister, who also performs dual roles. He or she manages the administration of the Department of Justice and advises the minister regularly on matters affecting the department. But the deputy minister of Justice is also the deputy attorney general, too. As with most other departments, a pyramidal hierarchy describes the organization of the department, with a team of assistant deputy ministers, directors, and so on below the deputy minister. Not surprisingly, over half of the department personnel are lawyers.

Although it is not a large department, Justice is very important. Some typologies of departments put it in the category of central agency (see chapter 5) since its influence is so widely felt. Legal advisers from the department can be found in over 40 other government agencies' legal units, and Justice Department personnel play a key role in drafting, reforming, and interpreting legislation, including that from other departments. For instance, one of the key responsibilities of the department since 1982 is ensuring that new legislation is consistent with the Charter of Rights and Freedoms. In addition, there are some 17 regional offices across Canada that provide legal advice to federal departments and agencies outside Ottawa. Thus Justice officials have their legal fingers in virtually everyone's pies.

According to the Justice Department, its administrative responsibilities for law making involve these steps:

*Once Cabinet has decided what new laws should be introduced during a session of Parliament, work begins on preparing bills (drafts of proposed laws). When the subject in question is the responsibility of a department other than Justice, specialists in that department work with Justice lawyers, who provide the legal expertise to draft the bill. Justice is consulted in the early stages of the work and continues to be involved through each step, from obtaining Cabinet approval to drafting—and redrafting—the bill until it is enacted by Parliament. At that point, it becomes part of the law of the land, and is referred to as an "act" (also known as a "statute").*[11]

Of course, we have focused on the federal Department of Justice here, but there are similar bodies in all the provinces that perform roughly the same set of tasks and have the same sets of administrative roles and responsibilities as their federal counterpart. One further element of confusion for the layperson, though, is the bewildering array of names of the courts in the provinces and territories (see Table 6.1). Some use American terminology, while others use British. This fact is derived from the constitutional provision in Section 92(14), which gives the provinces power over the administration of justice. Thus, each province is responsible for designing its own court system. In practice, however, the administration of justice is roughly similar across the country.

The law, the courts, and the administration of justice only exist within the framework of the Constitution. The Constitution encapsulates the rule of law, even though it is nowhere explicitly mentioned in the written documents of the Constitution. And it orders the positions and the roles of the courts and the supporting administrative institutions and actors—not always explicitly but certainly implicitly. We now turn to the Constitution before returning in more detail to constitutional and administrative law.

## What Is a Constitution?

Constitutions are fundamental to the existence of virtually every organized society on earth.[12] They come in every size, description, length, and style. Some contain rules of behaviour and guidelines that are rigorously adhered to even though they are nowhere written down. Others are not worth the paper they are written on. The simple fact that a nation has a constitution is no guarantee that it is necessarily a "democratic" society, that its constitution is observed, or even that the rights of citizens enshrined in the constitution will be protected. In fact, in several countries a form of state terrorism is conducted against citizens, often depriving them of liberty and life, even while the constitutions of those countries

**TABLE 6.1    Canadian Provincial and Territorial Trial Courts**

| Province | Superior Court | Other Section 96 Courts | Provincial Court |
|---|---|---|---|
| BC | Supreme Court | NA | Provincial Court |
| AB | Court of Queen's Bench | Surrogate Court | Provincial Court |
| SK | Court of Queen's Bench Unified Family Court | Surrogate Court | Provincial Court |
| MB | Court of Queen's Bench *Trial Division *Family Division | NA | Provincial Court |
| ON | Superior Court | Unified Family Court | Ontario Court of Justice |
| QC | La Cour Supérieure | NA | Cour du Québec *chambre civile *chambre criminelle et pénale *chambre de la jeunesse *chambre administrative *Cours municipales |
| NB | Court of Queen's Bench *Trial Division *Family Division | NA | Provincial Court |
| NS | Supreme Court | Supreme Court (Family Division) | Provincial Court |
| PEI | Supreme Court (Trial Division) | NA | Provincial Court |
| NF | Supreme Court (Trial Division) | Unified Family Court | Provincial Court |
| YT | Supreme Court | NA | Territorial Court |
| NWT | Supreme Court | NA | Territorial Court |
| NU | Nunavut Court of Justice | NA | NA |

NA = Not applicable.
**Source:** Carl Baar, "Court Systems in the Provinces," in Christopher Dunn, ed., *Provinces: Canadian Provincial Politics*, 2nd ed. (Peterborough: Broadview, 2006): 287.

contain ringing declarations of the rights of their citizens. A constitution, then, is no guarantee in and of itself that rights will be protected or that states will stay within the rules of the game.

But without a constitution, the concept of rights, as well as the appropriate limits on the actions of the state, would not even exist. A constitution is the fundamental law of a political system. All other laws are supposed to follow from, and be subordinate to, the laws of the constitution. A constitution provides a set of rules for the peaceful and civilized resolution of conflicts over scarce resources. Without it, there is no way of predicting either the powers of government or the rights of citizens. As political scientist J.R. Mallory put it, "the essence of a constitutional order is that it provides effective means of preventing abuses of power, and ensures that those in authority cannot take away the ultimate right of the governed to remove them or reject their policies."[13] Imagine a hockey game without a rule book. You can still play, but the game becomes largely meaningless unless there is some order imposed on the conduct of the participants. Otherwise, the strongest, biggest, meanest players would impose their version of the game on the rest. Now imagine a society in which there is no constitution—a society in a "state of nature," in which chaos and anarchy prevail; a society in which no individual can feel secure in the possession of her property or life; a society in which life was, as seventeenth-century political philosopher Thomas Hobbes put it, "solitary, poor, nasty, brutish, and short." This insecurity can be remedied only when people agree to binding and authoritative rules: hence, the development and evolution of constitutions.

All constitutions are meant to do three things. First, constitutions define the relationship between citizens and the state. They empower the state to regulate citizens' behaviour by passing laws on behalf of the community; and generally they delineate the boundaries of the state's powers by identifying both individual and collective rights that the state is not allowed to violate. For example, the constitution prohibits the state from censoring the free expression of ideas and, therefore, protects the individual right to freedom of speech. However, it also allows the state to place limits on those individual rights in the interests of the greater community through anti-hate laws, libel and slander laws, and so on.

Second, constitutions define the responsibilities and relationships of the different parts of the state. As you now know, there are three main parts of the state: a) the executive, which makes and implements the law; b) the legislature, which passes the law; and c) the judiciary, which interprets the law. Since each of these elements is complex, we need to understand the roles of each and how they relate to one another. A constitution provides us with this information. Two political scientists put it this way:

*In modern times, political power is understood to consist of three distinct types: Legislative power is the power to make law or policy. For instance, a political community might use its legislative power to pass a law stipulating that no one may drive an automobile when their blood has an alcohol content above .08%. Executive power is the power to "execute" or administer that law or policy. This would include the power to establish and maintain a police force to catch drunk drivers. Judicial power is the power to settle questions about specific violations of law (is there appropriate evidence to prove the driver's blood-alcohol level exceeded .08%?) and to choose a suitable punishment, from among those permitted in the relevant legislation, for those found guilty.*[14]

Third, constitutions in federal systems (like Canada) lay out the rules governing relations between the levels of government. This aspect of the Canadian Constitution has captured the attention of politicians and constitutional experts throughout our history, during which federal–provincial relations have played a prominent role.

If you were asked what the Canadian Constitution was composed of, what would you say? In essence, there are three basic elements:

1. written documents, such as the BNA Act, 1867, the Constitution Act, 1982, and the Charter of Rights and Freedoms;
2. the common law; and
3. constitutional conventions—that is, practices that emerge over time and that are generally accepted as binding rules of the political system.

Constitutional conventions are not written anywhere into the constitutional documents; they are simply traditional habits and practices. But they can be just as significant as the other parts of the Constitution. Conventions are rules of the Constitution that are not enforced by the law courts. They can be regarded as non-legal rules. An example would be the convention that the leader of the party that captures the most seats in the House of Commons is called on to form the government. Another convention stipulates that the Governor General will use his or her considerable powers only in accordance with the advice of the Cabinet or prime minister. For instance, the Queen, through the Governor General, enjoys the power of withholding royal assent from a bill that has been enacted by Parliament, but convention stipulates that royal assent is never withheld.

In Canada, the first two components of the Constitution—written documents and the common law—together make up the **constitutional law**. Conventions do not have the status of constitutional law. But this does not mean that constitutional law is more important. The major difference is that constitutional law is enforceable through the courts, whereas constitutional conventions are not.

In most countries, the bulk of the constitutional law is contained in a single constitutional document that came into being after independence, revolution, or war, and that was intended to symbolize and legitimize a new regime of law.[15] The Canadian case is somewhat different. Before we turn our attention to the actual constitutional documents, let us look briefly at the reasons for and effects of Confederation, which resulted in the constitutional order we now have.

## A History of Canada's Constitution

You are probably familiar with the less-than-stirring history of Canada's march from "colony to nation"[16] (and back to colony again, some would add). The outlines of the picture are clear: conservative, loyal Canada, rejecting the U.S. revolutionary experience, decides to take the slow, evolutionary path to nationhood. If nothing else, this picture seems to reflect Canadian political culture, rooted in the formative experiences of accommodation with French Canada rather than assimilation, and the loyalist influence on English Canada. Confederation reflected Canada's cautiousness and moderation, its preference for evolution over revolution, and its reluctance to break the imperial/colonial ties that bound it to Britain.

Thus, it is in British constitutional practices that we discover the essential foundations of Canada's constitutional order. Long before Confederation the colonists had adopted many of the practices of British constitutionalism: the Crown, Parliament, Cabinet, responsible government, an independent judiciary, and the rudiments of party politics. Much of this heritage took the form of constitutional conventions that had evolved over a much earlier period of political experimentation in Britain. It is to Britain that we must turn to find the legislation that created and expanded upon Canada's constitutional life, both pre- and post-Confederation.

The BNA Act, 1867, gave effect to Confederation following conferences in Charlottetown in 1864, Quebec City in 1864, and London, England, in 1867. It united the provinces of Canada, Nova Scotia, and New Brunswick into a single "Dominion" under the name of Canada. As well, the BNA Act established a bicameral national Parliament with representation by population in the elected, lower House of Commons, and representation by region in the appointed, upper house, the Senate. It established a common market and allocated important economic powers to the new federal Parliament for maintaining peace, order, and good government, and authority over trade and commerce, transportation and communication, banking, currency, customs and excise, and other forms of taxation. Criminal law also became a federal responsibility, as did marriage and divorce. The provincial legislatures were given other powers, notably over property and civil rights, municipal institutions, education, the administration of justice, the power of direct taxation, and matters of a purely local or private nature within the province. Nova Scotia and New Brunswick retained their existing legislatures and other institutions of government. The province of Canada was divided into two new provinces: Ontario (the old Canada West, formerly Upper Canada); and Quebec (the old Canada East, formerly Lower Canada). The Act also established a legislature and other institutions of government for each of Ontario and Quebec. Thus, the BNA Act established the rules of federalism, allocating governmental power between the central and provincial institutions of government.

The BNA Act did not follow the U.S. model of codifying all the new nation's constitutional rules, since, as the preamble to the Act stated, the new nation was to have "a constitution similar in principle to that of the United Kingdom," which was not a written constitution. Apart from the changes needed to establish the new federation, the British North Americans wanted the old rules to continue in both form and substance. After 1867, therefore, much of Canada's constitutional law continued to be found in sources outside the BNA Act, such as in conventions and in the common law.

As a result, the BNA Act, 1867 is silent on a number of issues you might suppose would be basic to the constitutional order. There is no general amending clause: the framers of the Constitution were content to let the amending power rest in the hands of the British Parliament. Consequently, the British Parliament enacted amendments to it right up until 1982, when the Constitution Act, 1982, finally supplied amending procedures that could be operated entirely within Canada.

The field of foreign relations is another notable gap in the BNA Act. It contains no express provision, for example, for a treaty-making power for the Canadian Parliament, except as it may relate to responsibilities as part of the British empire. Yet another gap in the BNA Act concerns the office of the Governor General. The Act vests executive authority for Canada in the Queen and confers several specific powers on a Governor General, but the Office of Governor General is nowhere created by the BNA Act, and no rules are provided for the appointment or tenure of that officer. The reason for this gap was the assumption that the office would be created and filled in the same way colonial governorships had always been created and filled: by the Queen, acting on the advice of the British colonial secretary. The Office of the Governor General has never been formalized in an amendment to the BNA Act. The office is still constituted by royal prerogative, and appointments are still made by the Queen, although, needless to say, she now acts on the advice of the Canadian prime minister.

It also never occurred to anyone to write the rules of responsible government into the BNA Act, and so there is no mention of the prime minister, or of the Cabinet, or of the dependence of the Cabinet on the support of a majority in the House of Commons. All these rather significant details were left in the form of unwritten conventions, as in the United Kingdom. Nor did the Canadians write into their BNA Act a new Supreme Court. Section 101 of the Act gave authority for such a court to be established, but it did not actually establish it, since we were accustomed to appealing our legal cases to the British Judicial Committee of the Privy Council (JCPC). The Supreme Court of Canada was finally established in 1875, but through an ordinary federal law or statute, and the right of appeal to the JCPC was retained until 1949, when our Supreme Court at last became "supreme."[17] Meanwhile, the existence, composition, and jurisdiction of the Supreme Court of Canada still depend upon that 1875 statute.

Finally, the BNA Act did not even include a bill of rights. The civil liberties of Canadians were instead left in the hands of our legislative bodies and in the rules of common law, as in Great Britain. In 1960, the Canadian government of John Diefenbaker enacted a Bill of Rights—not as an amendment to the Constitution but as a simple statute that applied only to the federal government. The Constitution Act, 1982 finally added to the Constitution the Canadian Charter of Rights and Freedoms, which is now entrenched (that is, alterable only by the process of constitutional amendment) and applies to provincial as well as federal laws. We will expand on the importance of the Charter later.

The BNA Act served as Canada's central written constitutional document for 115 years. Changes were made to it occasionally prior to 1982, but most were relatively minor. With the passage of time, however, the original document became deficient for modern Canada. Repeated efforts were made, dating from the 1930s, to correct the anomaly of British control over the amending of the Canadian Constitution, but in every case, Canadian provincial premiers and prime ministers failed to agree on any domestic **amending formula** until, in 1980, Prime Minister Pierre Trudeau forced the issue by deciding to attempt to do it unilaterally. That decision, after a long battle with the provinces for public support and in the courts, eventually led to renewed federal–provincial negotiations in the fall of 1981. A settlement was finally reached on November 5, 1981, despite the vigorous opposition of René Lévesque, then premier of Quebec.[18] In the past, when Quebec had alone dissented from proposed amendment procedures—as with the 1964 Fulton-Favreau formula and the 1971 Victoria Charter—the deals fell apart, implying that Quebec enjoyed a veto over constitutional change.[19] This time, in 1981, a Supreme Court judgment ruled that Trudeau simply needed the "substantial agreement" of the provinces—and not their unanimous consent—for his patriation plan. After obtaining the consent of all provinces but Quebec, a constitutional resolution was passed by the Canadian Parliament on December 8, 1981, and transmitted to Westminster for its approval on March 29, 1982. Proclamation of the Canada Act, 1982, and the Constitution Act, 1982, by Queen Elizabeth followed in Ottawa on April 17, 1982.[20]

The constitutional deal of 1982 essentially did three things:

1. It added a domestic amending formula requiring the consent of 7 of 10 provinces representing 50 percent of the population for most constitutional amendments.
2. It terminated the authority of the United Kingdom parliament over Canada.
3. It created and adopted the Charter of Rights and Freedoms.

But the struggle was a long and arduous one, and it left some Québécois with a sense of betrayal. Indeed, November 5, 1981, the date the deal was struck between the federal government and the nine English-speaking provinces, was referred to by some in Quebec as "the night of the long knives." The legitimacy of the 1982 deal, then, was diminished: Quebec still has not signed the Constitution Act, 1982.

Subsequent attempts by Prime Minister Brian Mulroney to bring Quebec back into the constitutional fold were stunning failures, and fed the momentum of separatist forces in the province.[21] The Meech Lake and Charlottetown Accords fanned the flames of Quebec nationalism and led to the second referendum in Quebec on sovereignty association in 1995. The result—the narrowest of victories by the federal government—prompted Prime Minister Jean Chrétien to introduce the "Clarity Bill" to test the constitutional validity of Quebec independence. In August 1998, Chrétien asked the Supreme Court of Canada to clarify whether Quebec enjoyed the legal right to unilaterally secede from Canada. The courts ruled that Quebec could not unilaterally secede but that the rest of Canada would be obliged to negotiate terms of secession if a *clear* majority of Quebecers voted to do so on the basis of a *clear* referendum question.[22] Subsequent to the "near-death" experience of the 1995 referendum and the failures of the Meech and Charlottetown accords, political leaders in Canada lost their taste for constitutional politics. They backed down from the high-stakes negotiations and bargaining and began to focus on non-constitutional approaches to running the federation.[23] Canadians everywhere breathed a huge sigh of relief!

An integral part of the 1982 Constitution Act was the inclusion of the **Charter of Rights and Freedoms**, which makes formal distinctions between different kinds of rights: 1) fundamental political freedoms; 2) democratic rights; 3) mobility rights; 4) legal rights; 5) equality rights; and 6) language rights. Most of these rights were part of Canada's Constitution before 1982; some can be found in the BNA Act, 1867; some are considered part of the common law. By specifically delineating these rights and including them in the Constitution, an important shift has occurred in the distribution of power in the Canadian constitutional system. Now, Canadian citizens are far more conscious of their common rights and the ways in which they can defend them. This has given rise to an increase in individual citizens becoming more "judicially conscious"—i.e., more willing to use the courts to defend their rights. It has also meant that interest groups have become more aware of this avenue of challenging governmental power. Court challenges to established authority have been on the rise, as Canadians got used to employing this new tool in the constitutional arsenal. The Court Challenges Program of Canada is an innovative national non-profit organization that was set up in 1994 to provide financial assistance for important court cases that advance language and equality rights guaranteed under Canada's Constitution. Thus, even the disadvantaged could take advantage of the Charter to press their views if they felt discriminated against. However, the program was cancelled in September 2006 by the government of Prime Minister Stephen Harper as a cost-saving measure.

The Charter also means that the judges and the judicial branch of government play an enhanced role in the Canadian political system and that old notions of parliamentary supremacy have had to be reassessed in light of a more activist judiciary.[24] Finally, it has meant that public servants have had to be more conscious in both the formulation of policy and the implementation of programs to ensure that citizens' Charter rights are not abridged or violated.

## Federalism and the Constitution

At this stage, it is useful for us to return to the issue of federalism and focus on how the Constitution defines the relationship between the different levels of government and on the judicial interpretation of the **division of powers**. Federalism depends on its articulation within the Constitution: that is to say, it is a legal term, based in the Constitution, which vests power in at least two levels of government by virtue of a country's basic constitutional law. In this theoretical model of perfect federalism, or classical federalism, there are "watertight compartments" of power.[25] Jurisdictional authority is clearly laid out, and neither level of government ever crosses the line. In Canada, the Fathers of Confederation consciously developed a system whereby the federal level of government has certain powers allowing it to intrude in provincial jurisdiction; thus, we have never had the "watertight compartments" of classical federalism. The federal government was clearly intended to be the more powerful of the two levels of government. Indeed, Sir John A. Macdonald prophesied a role of little significance for provincial governments; he saw them as glorified municipal councils.[26] Macdonald turned out to be a better prime minister than he was a prophet.

The key sections of the Canadian Constitution that deal with federalism are those laying out the division of powers: primarily sections 91 and 92, but also sections 93, 94, 95, 101, 117, and 132. Sections 91 and 92 are the most significant.

Each section lists powers held exclusively by the national and provincial govern-ments, but only a few subsections within sections 91 and 92 provide the basis for most of the power of the two levels of government, and most of the legal and polit-ical debate over jurisdiction.

Not surprisingly, the various players in the Confederation had differing con-ceptions of the new system. We noted that Macdonald wanted to create a strong central government and weak, insignificant provincial governments. Others felt differently. Oliver Mowat, who would go on to become the longest serving premier in Ontario history (1872–1896) and was a champion of provincial rights, resisted the establishment of too strong a central government.[27] In any event, the agree-ment gave the central government what were then considered to be the most important legislative powers and sources of public revenue. Ottawa was thus given authority over trade and commerce, shipping, fisheries, interprovincial transporta-tion, currency and banking, the postal service, and several other subjects largely related to managing the economy. Responsibility for immigration and agriculture was divided between the federal and provincial governments, but in the event of a conflict, Ottawa's legislation would prevail. The federal government was also assigned the job of building an intercolonial railway from Halifax to Montreal. When we consider that the two main functions of the state in the nineteenth cen-tury were military defence and economic growth, Ottawa certainly was assigned the major legislative powers of that era.

Customs and excise taxes were the most important sources of government rev-enue prior to Confederation, and these became the exclusive preserve of the federal government, which could raise money "by any Mode or System of Taxation," according to section 91(3) of the BNN Act. The provinces were limited to the less lucrative field of "direct taxation" through section 92(2), as well as royalties on provincially owned natural resources through section 109. Thus, provincial rev-enue sources were meagre compared to those available to the federal government. Recognizing this, the Confederation agreement also established the practice of transferring federal funds to the provinces. The economic dependence of the weaker provinces on federal funding began in 1867 and continues to this day.

In fact, there are sections of the BNA Act that appear to establish an almost colonial relationship between Ottawa and the provinces, by permitting the federal government to disallow laws passed by the provincial legislatures. In addition, the BNA Act gives provincial Lieutenant-Governors—appointees of Ottawa—the power to reserve approval of any act passed by a provincial legislature for up to one year after its passage. These powers of **reservation** (section 57) and **disallowance** (section 56) were widely used in the early years of Confederation and periodically in the first 40 years of the twentieth century. They clearly established the primacy of the federal government over the provincial governments. In most cases, the fed-eral government used these powers when a province challenged Ottawa's supremacy over economic matters. Section 92(10c) gives the federal government the authority to intervene in a provincial economy by declaring that the construc-tion of a "public work" (which could mean a road or bridge, or similar type of structure) is in the national interest. This power has been used more than 470 times since Confederation, although not since 1961. Finally, sections 93(3) and (4) give Ottawa the power to pass laws respecting education, an area of provincial jurisdiction. It may do so when education rights, held by denominational minorities when a province entered Confederation, are abrogated by provincial law. This power, however, has never been used.

Any reading of sections 91 and 92 must be undertaken cautiously, since conditions have changed considerably since they were first drafted. In 1867, the framers of Confederation did not have to wrestle with problems such as old age pensions, air transportation, broadcasting and telecommunications technology, nuclear energy, climate change, and so on. As a result, none of these are explicitly assigned to either Ottawa or the provinces. In addition, issues that were of minor significance in 1867 took on tremendous importance in the twentieth century, as the role of the state evolved over 150 years in ways unfathomable to the generation of the 1860s.

It is important to note that some powers are nowhere listed in the Constitution. The most important of these is the federal **spending power**, which is an implied power rather than a stated one. Ottawa spends billions of dollars every year on policies and programs that fall, strictly speaking, under provincial authority. As political scientist Keith Banting explains, "according to the federal view, the spending power allows the federal government to make payments to individuals, institutions, or governments for purposes on which Parliament does not necessarily have the power to regulate. That is, it claims the power to give money away, and attach conditions if it wishes, even if the purposes involved clearly fall within provincial jurisdiction, as specified by the BNA Act."[28] Ottawa's "right" to spend money in any way it sees fit has been upheld by the courts but provokes a good deal of controversy.[29] Nonetheless, that spending power has provided the constitutional basis for many major federal expenditures, which can cause friction between the two levels of government, as Ottawa wades into a field and distorts or usurps related provincial initiatives. In 1999, in the Social Union Framework Agreement (SUFA) that Ottawa signed with the territories and provinces (except Quebec), Ottawa agreed for the first time to certain limitations on the use of the spending power.[30] However, these limitations seem muted since, as we noted in chapter 5, a major dispute emerged between Ottawa and the provinces over the question of whether a "fiscal imbalance" exists in the federation.[31] Contention over the federal use of spending power is but one area of federal–provincial conflict, though. How are disputes resolved over the division of powers within federalism? In several ways, including going to court—an issue we will now look at.

## Constitutional Law

Constitutional law deals with the rules, practices, and institutions that constitute the state. Constitutional law issues occur when the courts are asked by an individual, group, corporation, or other government to declare a particular law unconstitutional. If the challenge succeeds, the law becomes null and void. One of the advantages of listing the division of powers in the Constitution is that it theoretically delineates what jurisdictional authority each level of government enjoys—or so we might think. In fact, the list of powers in sections 91 and 92 has often fuelled serious conflict between the two levels of government because items on the list are subject to a variety of interpretations. Powers such as "trade and commerce," "property and civil rights," and "direct taxation" may seem straightforward enough, but when important material interests are at stake for the constitutional experts, lawyers, judges, and citizens who launch constitutional challenges against federal or provincial law, words and phrases take on whole new meanings unintended by the Fathers of Confederation. Thus, the supposedly clear-cut list of powers becomes a source of endless haggling and interpretation, and, in fact, court interpretations over the division of powers have produced some unexpected results, effectively recasting Canadian federalism, for better or worse.

Let us begin by looking at the court's interpretation of perhaps the most sweeping power handed to the federal government. The preamble to section 91 authorizes the Parliament of Canada "to make Laws for the Peace, Order and Good Government of Canada, in relation to all Matters not coming within the Classes of Subjects by this Act assigned exclusively to the Legislatures of the Provinces," while section 91(2) authorizes the federal government to make laws for "The Regulation of Trade and Commerce."

## Peace, Order, and Good Government

At first blush, "Peace, Order and Good Government" (POGG) may appear to be a wide power under which a variety of laws could be justified. Over time, however, this power has been reduced to one available to the federal government only in times of emergency. The restrictions on the use of POGG began in 1896 with a ruling by the British Judicial Committee of the Privy Council (JCPC) in a case called *Local Prohibition*, concerning regulation of the lucrative sale of liquor. In an earlier case, *Russell v. The Queen* (1882), the JCPC held that the Canada Temperance Act, a federal law that established a local-option temperance scheme, was constitutional, since temperance did not fall under provincial jurisdiction. But later, in the *Local Prohibition* case, the provinces introduced their own local-option temperance schemes, and the JCPC ruled in their favour. To do so, it had to argue that the *Local Prohibition* case was upheld on the basis of the POGG power, even though this had not been articulated at the time of the case. In rationalizing this decision, the judges argued that the federal government could only use POGG if the issue at hand was one of "national dimensions": that is, if it was important nationally. Since, in the view of the judges, temperance was not an issue of national concern, the federal government was not justified in using POGG to launch its own temperance scheme. The judges in these cases left open the question of how to determine what constitutes "national dimensions."[32] Nonetheless, these cases represent the beginning of the winnowing away of the federal power of POGG.

The question of what, exactly, qualifies as "national dimensions" became moot in a sense, since three later cases determined that a new standard had to be met for the federal government to justify a law under POGG: i.e., national emergency. The JCPC considered a 1922 case involving to two federal laws, the *Board of Commerce Act, 1919* and the *Combines and Fair Prices Act, 1919,* which were intended to prevent the development of monopolies and the hoarding of essential goods (food, clothing, and fuel), and which required fair prices for those goods after the First World War.[33] The courts struck down the laws but said that they might have been justifiable laws under the conditions of a national emergency. In so saying, the courts specified that POGG should only be applied during times of war, or famine, or some similar emergency. So, with the *Board of Commerce* case, the courts actually made it harder for the federal government to employ this power than if they had simply argued that an issue had acquired "national dimensions," as in the earlier *Local Prohibition* case. The fact that an issue had acquired "national dimensions" would no longer be sufficient to justify such exceptional legislation.

Subsequent rulings on POGG also suggested that it was a power to be used only in wartime or similar exceptional circumstances. In *Fort Frances Pulp and Power Company v. the Manitoba Free Press*, 1923, for instance, the JCPC declared that war-related circumstances were sufficient to warrant legislating under POGG, and indicated that the courts would be out of line in questioning Parliament's authority to do so under the conditions of a war or war-related emergency.[34] In this case, the courts ruled that controlling the price and supply of newsprint would normally be a matter of provincial jurisdiction under section 92(13), "Property and Civil Rights in the Province"; but it was willing to concede that under wartime conditions, POGG could be used to "trump" provincial jurisdiction. Subsequent court rulings backed up this view.

In fact, in cases where the courts rejected the federal government's use of POGG as a valid basis for federal legislation, the legislation dealt with peacetime circumstances. The first of these was the decision in *Toronto Electric Commissioners v. Snider*, 1925, in which the JCPC struck down Canada's major industrial relations legislation. It argued that relations between employers and employees were a matter of civil rights in the province and, therefore, within provincial jurisdiction. The JCPC also struck down the peacetime use of POGG in three decisions in 1937 concerning the federal government's right to make laws regarding unemployment and social insurance, agricultural marketing boards, and labour relations.[35] The government of R.B. Bennett passed the laws as part of its New Deal legislation to mitigate the ravages of the Great Depression, but Bennett lost the 1935 election. His successor, William Lyon Mackenzie King, referred the legislation to the courts to test the laws' constitutionality. The Bennett government had attempted to justify the laws on the basis that the Depression of the 1930s was a national concern, and that it threatened the well-being of the country. In all three cases, the JCPC considered this argument inadequate.

In the 1970s, the federal government again tried to use POGG to justify legislation intended to deal with economic problems outside wartime. In a ruling on the constitutionality of Ottawa's Anti-Inflation Act, 1975, the federal government argued that growing inflation constituted an emergency, thereby justifying legislation that infringed on provincial jurisdiction. The judges agreed. This ruling made it easier for the federal government to use the POGG power by detaching it from the emergency doctrine. The court also declared that it was really up to Parliament, and not the courts, to determine when an emergency existed.[36]

The "Regulation of Trade and Commerce" power in section 91(2) also appears to be a broad source of authority for Ottawa, but it, too, has been interpreted narrowly by the courts, and limited largely to interprovincial and international trade. In contrast, the provincial power over "Property and Civil Rights in the Province" in section 92(13) has been interpreted more the way you might expect the trade and commerce power to have been interpreted. *Citizen's Insurance v. Parsons, 1881,* was the first major case to limit the trade and commerce power.[37] The JCPC ruled that a broad, literal interpretation of "trade and commerce" would unnecessarily restrict provincial rights under property and civil rights, and would bring all aspects of economic life under the authority of Ottawa. Never mind that this was the intention of the framers of Confederation! The JCPC limited Ottawa's powers over trade and commerce in this case by suggesting that the phrase "trade and commerce" meant the regulation of trade in matters of interprovincial concern, and the general regulation of trade affecting the whole country.

The legacy of the *Parsons* case has been problematic. For example, it is possible that some federal laws that regulate trade between provinces may also affect trade that occurs strictly within a province. Is such a law constitutional? Until the 1950s, the courts said "no." But over the years, a series of court decisions gradually loosened the restrictions placed on the trade and commerce power in the *Parsons* case.[38] Nonetheless, the overall effect of the *Parsons* case, and others like it, was to severely restrict the powers of the federal government.

## Federal–Provincial Bargaining

This brief overview of select examples of constitutional law judgments shows the impact of judicial review on federalism and, ultimately, on public administration in Canada. But the courts are only one avenue for addressing conflicts between Ottawa and the provinces, and their decisions do not always put an end to that conflict. Besides determining the constitutionality of law, the courts can also force the two levels of government back to the bargaining table.[39] For example, in *Employment and Social Service Act Reference,* 1937, the JCPC decision to strike down a federal law establishing a program to deal with national unemployment precipitated federal–provincial negotiations that led to a constitutional amendment giving the federal government power over unemployment insurance in 1940. In *Public Service Board v. Dionne,* 1978, the Supreme Court confirmed Ottawa's exclusive jurisdiction to regulate television broadcasting. Right after the decision, however, Ottawa indicated its willingness to negotiate with the provinces to share authority over this area. In *CIGOL v. Government of Saskatchewan,* 1978, a provincial tax on natural gas was found to be a direct tax and therefore outside provincial jurisdiction. Later, during the constitutional negotiations of 1981–1982, negotiations broadened the powers of the provinces in this area and permitted some form of resource taxation in section 92A of the Constitution Act, 1982, which had been ruled **ultra vires** in an earlier decision. In the *Patriation Reference,* 1981, the Supreme Court ruled that Ottawa's proposal to patriate the BNA Act and to change it in ways that affected provincial power was legal but that it was not constitutional in the conventional sense. This gave the federal government a legal victory but also suggested that the political consequences for proceeding were too high. The provinces and the federal government were forced back to the negotiating table.

More recently, the 1998 decision of the Supreme Court on the right of a province to unilaterally secede from Confederation illustrates the role of the courts in encouraging discussion and negotiations between the two levels of government. In this decision, the federal government asked the Supreme Court of Canada to rule on three questions:

1. Under the Constitution of Canada, can the National Assembly, legislature, or government of Quebec effect the secession of Quebec from Canada unilaterally?
2. Does international law give the National Assembly, legislature, or government of Quebec the right to effect the secession of Quebec from Canada unilaterally? In this regard, is there a right to self-determination under international law that would give the National Assembly, legislature, or government of Quebec the right to effect the secession of Quebec from Canada unilaterally?
3. In the event of a conflict between domestic and international law on the right of the National Assembly, legislature or government of Quebec to effect the secession of Quebec from Canada unilaterally, which would take precedence in Canada?[40]

The court response to this potentially explosive set of questions gave a little bit to both sides (the federal government and the separatist government of Quebec). It suggested that unilateral secession was illegal and unconstitutional but that if the citizens of Quebec voted to separate, the federal government would be bound to negotiate the terms of the secession. As with the 1981 *Patriation Reference,* the ball was thrown squarely back into the laps of the politicians. The federal Parliament, in 2000, then passed the Clarity Act, under which the right to determine whether a question on separation was clear as well as what constitutes a majority were reserved to Parliament itself. Not surprisingly, there were howls of outrage from Quebec separatists, who declaimed that this was an unacceptable intrusion on the province's right to determine its own future. However, the election in 2003 of a federalist Liberal government in Quebec, its re-election in 2007 (albeit with a minority government) coupled with the relegation of the Parti Québécois to third place in the Quebec National Assembly, and a third Liberal victory in 2008 seemed to mute the sovereignty debate in the province.

Constitutional law is not the only or always the best way to resolve conflicts between governments. Over the years, a system of intergovernmental bargaining and negotiation has developed, whereby governments discuss their differences in much the same way that countries carry out international negotiation: that is to say, at the highest political and bureaucratic levels.[41] At these meetings, each province puts its own regional concerns on the table, while the federal government brings national concerns to the discussion. Since each province comprises many different economic, social, and cultural interests, intergovernmental conflict is, to some extent, the clash of conflicting regional demands in Canada.[42] As well, the state— federal or provincial—has its own set of interests, whether it is to constantly expand in size and influence and power, or to seek jurisdictional control of a particular area.[43] Thus, intergovernmental relations are driven by both the demands of regional societies within Canada and by the demands of the states that represent those regions.

The provincial governments in Canada have a long history of trying to wrestle power and jurisdiction away from the federal government. Frequently, provincial governments are supported from within by powerful economic interests. We refer to this process as **province building**, when the political needs of governments are reinforced by the demands of provincially oriented economic interests. This is, in effect, the provincial counterpart to the nation building initiated by Sir John A. Macdonald. The term *province building* was originally applied to the efforts of then Ontario premier Oliver Mowat and then Quebec premier Honoré Mercier, who aggressively tried to expand the powers and rights of their provincial governments vis-à-vis the federal government in the late nineteenth century.

Divided jurisdiction has given rise to a sprawling and complicated network of political–administrative relations linking the two levels of government. There are two basic elements to this network of relations: the part we see, and the part we don't. The part we see involves meetings between the prime minister and the provincial and territorial premiers (First Ministers' Conferences). These meetings always generate a great deal of media interest, and at least part of the proceedings usually takes place before the cameras. Less publicized, but far more frequent, are the hundreds of meetings between federal and provincial Cabinet ministers and their bureaucratic advisors.[44] Some of these are established as regular annual (or more often than annual) meetings; others are called as a new issue or demand arises. A complex web of intergovernmental meetings and conferences is now a regular feature of Canadian federalism, which, as we noted earlier, in some ways reflects the way sovereign countries carry on international negotiations.[45]

The meetings and relations between the prime minister and premiers and between Cabinet ministers and between public servants from both levels of government have evolved into a formalized and regularized feature of Canadian federalism.[46] This feature is referred to as **executive federalism** because it involves meetings between the executives of both levels of government.[47] Executive federalism, by its nature, excludes the public, and it also excludes the elected members of the federal and provincial legislatures. Instead, negotiations and agreements are usually undertaken with little input from anyone but the federal and provincial executives. This, plus the fact that these negotiations are secret and private, often raises the charge that executive federalism is undemocratic because it undermines elected legislatures, whose role, if any, is simply to approve what the executives have come up with.[48] As well, there is usually no opportunity for public input or debate. Thus, decisions about important public issues, such as health care, education, taxation, and other matters of real concern to ordinary citizens, are removed from the public realm and discussed behind closed doors. Citizens, political parties, interest groups, and others are generally excluded from a process of decision making dominated by the prime minister, premiers, and Cabinet ministers and their advisors.[49]

In addition to these criticisms, executive federalism has been blamed for distorting the political agenda by reinforcing regional differences and obscuring the national interest. At the same time, executive federalism undervalues the importance of nonregional interests. It fuels government expansion because competitive relations between the two levels of government produce duplication of services. It also perpetuates intergovernmental conflict by, in effect, giving provincial premiers a stage from which to publicize and air their grievances. Still, in the absence of an alternative, executive federalism appears to be an enduring institution of contemporary Canadian politics.

As this overview suggests, constitutional law is multifaceted and complex. It ranges across a number of issues having to do with the relations between the branches of government (executive, legislative, and judicial), the state and citizens (the Charter of Rights and Freedoms, for instance), and the relations between the levels of government (the division of powers in the Constitution). There is, however, yet another constitutional issue we need to review before we conclude this chapter with a discussion of administrative law. This is the question of Aboriginal self-government.

## Aboriginal Self Government

One long-standing issue of tremendous importance for public administration in Canada is Aboriginal self-government. We will consider the constitutional dimension of this issue here, but first need to set the stage in order to explain its significance. Currently, about 4-5% of the Canadian population is Aboriginal.[50] This includes three constitutionally recognized but distinct groups—Status Indians, Inuit, and Métis. These groups are divided into approximately 600 nations. About 300 000 live on reserves, while over half of Status Indians live in urban centres, with the largest population in Toronto. Few would disagree that the life chances and general standard of living for Aboriginals is well below that of non-Aboriginal Canadians. For instance, Aboriginals in Canada have a higher than average unemployment rate, lower life expectancy, higher infant mortality rate, higher death rates (including a higher rate of death by violence), higher illness and accident rates, and a higher incarceration rate than the national average. In addition, Natives comprise about one-fifth of all murder victims, have a higher suicide rate, suffer from alcoholism at a higher rate, and live in over-crowded conditions at a higher rate than non-Natives.[51] We are concerned here with the dimensions of these issues that relate to placing Aboriginals on an equal constitutional and political footing with non-Natives and the other levels of government in Canada.

The main institutional response to the problems that beset Aboriginal communities is to seek self-government. The courts have not yet clarified whether there is an inherent Aboriginal right to self-government and indeed there is as yet no agreement on what precisely the term means. Some look to the municipal government model and suggest Aboriginal communities assume powers similar to those exercised by villages, towns, and municipalities while at the same time remaining subject to all federal and provincial laws. Some self-government agreements currently exist along these lines. For others, this is insufficient. Some see self-government as equivalent to a third order of government. Most Aboriginal leaders argue that they cannot accept any limitations on the inherent right to self government. They suggest that no Canadian government is in a position to grant a right that predates it and that has no source in any imperial, colonial, or dominion authority. They see the right to govern themselves as a pre-existing, continuing, natural right from the creator that cannot be given or taken away by any government. They base this view on the idea that they themselves never gave up the right to self-government and it has never been extinguished by any legislation because such power could not exist.[52] They point to colonial-era constitutional history to support this position. Indeed, the Royal Proclamation of 1763 clearly spoke of Indian peoples as nations and provided that settlers should not interfere with or disrupt the Aboriginal possession of any unceded land, prohibited colonial governments from allocating Aboriginal lands to newcomers, and ordered settlers not to trespass upon those lands unless they were made available for settlement by cessions or surrenders to the Crown through public meetings called for that purpose. The Proclamation read in part:

*And whereas it is just and reasonable, and essential to our interest and the security of our colonies, that the several nations or tribes of Indians, with whom we are connected, and who live under our protection, would not be molested or disturbed in the possession of such parts of our Dominion and territories as, not having been ceded to, or purchased by us, are reserved to them, or any of them, as their hunting grounds.*

These views have subsequently been supported by Supreme Court interpretations and international law, which affirm that Aboriginal rights may be extinguished only by treaty or conquest, or by an explicit act of Parliament.

Still, the inherent right to self-government is not defined in the Constitution, and disputes remain about the meaning of the term and how it can be realized in practice. Despite these differences, federal and some provincial governments have begun to negotiate agreements with First Nations peoples concerning how they will relate to other governments in Canada within the existing constitutional framework. That framework has evolved from the Royal Proclamation to today (see Box 6.2). The Indian Act of 1876 set the tone for a paternalistic relationship

---

**BOX 6.2  The Political–Legal History of Aboriginal Peoples**

- The Royal Proclamation, 1763
- The Indian Act, 1876
- The franchise, 1960
- The Hawthorn–Tremblay Report, 1964-1966
- The 1969 White Paper
- The 1982 Constitution Act
- The Charlottetown Accord, 1990
- Royal Commission on Aboriginal Peoples (RCAP), 1996
- The creation of Nunavut, 1999
- The federal government apology, 2008

between Ottawa and Aboriginals. It treated Aboriginals as "wards of the state" rather than as full citizens. Consequently, "in a little more than a century, Aboriginal peoples were deprived of their traditional means of livelihood, their cultures and languages were wiped out, and their communities became socially dysfunctional."[53] By mid-century, there was no Aboriginal policy as such and no constitutional category "Aboriginal." Two of the three sub-categories of Aboriginals, Inuit, and Métis received no particular treatment, while Indians with legal status, by contrast, were subjects of specific policy and an administrative regime in the Indian Act. The long-term goal of Indian policy was the eventual absorption of such Indians into the general population, or assimilation. In 1960 when the Conservative government of John Diefenbaker extended the franchise to Status Indians, partly in reaction to the general climate of the civil rights movement around the world, it assured that the extension of the franchise did not imply any erosion of traditional Status Indian rights. This was a two-edged sword: it reduced the marginalization of Indians as wards of the state, but it also implied a further integration into mainstream society.

Two subsequent policy actions by the federal government further defined the choices about the future relationship of Aboriginals. First, the Hawthorn–Tremblay inquiry, from 1964–1966, was commissioned to examine the status of Indians, and among other things, concluded that Indians could be considered "citizens-plus." This meant Indians have all the normal attributes of citizenship, but in addition should be beneficiaries of a "plus" category derived from being here first and having built rich, flourishing societies. The exact implications of the "plus" status were to be worked out in political agreements that accepted the fact that Indians were entitled to a positive special status. The report noted that historically, special status had been implicitly recognized in the Indian Act, but in a "negative" way. Thus Indians had been "citizens-minus," a fact that should be rectified.

The 1969 White Paper, released by the Trudeau government over the signature of then-minister of Indian and Northern Affairs Jean Chrétien, took a view diametrically opposed to that of Hawthorn–Tremblay.[54] Heavily influenced by Trudeau's liberal-individualist values and his fear that special status for Indians might fuel demands for special status among Québécois, the White Paper advocated an assimilationist strategy and philosophy. It argued that separate status contributed to economic backwardness and social and cultural isolation. The White Paper thus explicitly rejected Hawthorn–Tremblay's attempt to combine standard citizenship with benefits flowing from a unique legal status and instead reflected the ongoing goal of assimilating Indians into the broader Canadian community.

Status Indians vigorously opposed the White Paper recommendations, mobilized their communities against it, and, remarkably, despite having only rudimentary political organizations at the time, were able to defeat it. This represented the most important development in Aboriginal constitutional politics since the Indian Act as it effectively meant that the policy of assimilation was discredited. Moreover, the defeat stimulated Indian nationalism. It discredited the federal government Indian policy and made it clear that future policy reform would have to be a collaborative effort with Aboriginals themselves. The White Paper was a crucial event for Métis and Inuit as well, even though it did not formally deal with them, for if it had

BOX 6.3 | The Charter of Rights and Freedoms, 1982

Section 25 The guarantee in this Charter of certain rights and freedoms shall not be construed so as to abrogate or derogate from any Aboriginal, treaty or other rights or freedoms that pertain to the Aboriginal peoples of Canada, including:

(a) any rights or freedoms that have been recognized by the *Royal Proclamation of October 7, 1763*, and;

(c) any rights or freedoms that now exist by way of land claims agreements or may be so acquired.

Section 35 (1) The existing Aboriginal and treaty rights of the Aboriginal peoples of Canada are hereby recognized and affirmed; (2) this Act, "Aboriginal peoples of Canada" includes the Indian, Inuit and Métis peoples of Canada

**Source:** *Canadian Charter of Rights and Freedoms* Part I and Part II

been implemented, it would have made it impossible for Métis and Inuit to claim a distinct constitutional identity if Status Indians had lost theirs. Interestingly, a close friend and former key policy advisor to Prime Minister Stephen Harper, academic Tom Flanagan, resurrected the assimilationist position in 2000, arguing that distinct status for Aboriginals was unjust and doomed to fail.[55] This was met with a counter-position by another academic, Alan Cairns, who argued in favour of a "citizen's plus" approach to Aboriginal issues.[56] The debate continues.

The next major development was the patriation of the Constitution and the Charter of Rights and Freedoms in 1982 (see Box 6.3). Section 35(1) recognized and affirmed the "existing Aboriginal and treaty rights of the Aboriginal peoples of Canada" while Section 25 of the Charter protected "Aboriginal, treaty or other rights or freedoms that pertain to the Aboriginal peoples." The term "Aboriginal peoples of Canada" was new—it appeared in no previous constitutional documents—and was defined to include "the Indian, Inuit and Métis peoples of Canada." Constitutional recognition was a remarkable achievement for the Métis; it also added to the numbers and internal diversity of Aboriginal peoples. Furthermore, Section 37 obligated the federal government to convene a First Ministers Conference with the task of identifying and defining Aboriginal rights mentioned in the 1982 Act. As a result, four constitutional conferences were held on Aboriginal issues from 1983–1987. They failed to reach agreement on the main Aboriginal goal of self-government, but they did confirm that Aboriginals were not as other Canadians, and that they had a unique status that justified bargaining nation-to-nation within the system of executive federalism.

The high level of Aboriginal participation and activity around the 1982 agreement and the subsequent conferences were ultimately unfruitful, and successive governments moved on to other issues. For instance, the Mulroney government did not invite Aboriginals to the Meech Lake discussions to amend the Constitution in 1985; this accounted in part for the fierce opposition of Aboriginal groups to the Meech Lake Accord and their success in having it defeated. Indeed it was Aboriginal Elijah Harper, a Manitoba MPP, who blocked its passage in the Manitoba legislature. This contributed to the high level of prominence given Aboriginals in the next round of constitutional negotiations, the Charlottetown Accord of 1990.

The Charlottetown Accord proposed extensive changes to the relationship between Aboriginals and the other citizens and governments of Canada, including the following provisions:

1. A constitutionally entrenched third order of Aboriginal government based on the inherent right of self-government; thus Aboriginals would be removed from the jurisdiction of federal and provincial governments and assume jurisdiction over themselves
2. Separate Aboriginal representation in the House of Commons
3. Guaranteed Aboriginal representation in the Senate
4. A limited role in the preparation of lists of candidates for Supreme Court appointments; and possibly the creation of an Aboriginal Council of Elders that could make submissions to the Supreme Court on Aboriginal issues
5. Aboriginal consent for constitutional amendments directly referring to Aboriginal peoples
6. Participation in First Ministers Conferences that directly affected the Aboriginal peoples
7. Métis were to be brought under federal jurisdiction of s. 91(24), as they had long demanded
8. A commitment to negotiate with Métis over various issues related to self-government; the members of the Métis nation were to be defined, enumerated and registered as such
9. Aboriginal exemption from the Charter was further strengthened by ensuring that nothing in the Charter "abrogates or derogates from . . . in particular any rights or freedoms relating to the exercise or protection of their languages, cultures or traditions."
10. Aboriginal governments were specifically exempted from the Charter's democratic rights (including the right to vote and hold public office) to allow traditional practices of leadership selection that would otherwise violate the Charter
11. Four First Ministers Conferences were proposed on Aboriginal matters commencing in 1996 and following at two-year intervals
12. Aboriginal governments' authority and jurisdiction was described as being:

    A) to safeguard and develop their languages, cultures, economies, identities, institutions, and traditions; and
    B) to develop, maintain, and strengthen their relationship with their land, waters, and environment so as to determine and control their development as peoples according to their own values and priorities and ensure the integrity of their societies

This package represented an astonishing series of gains for Aboriginals, touching on virtually every major institution of the Canadian state. However, in the last days of bargaining over the Charlottetown Accord, a clause was added which said that Aboriginal laws or assertion of authority "may not be inconsistent with those laws which are essential to the preservation of peace, order and good government in Canada." In addition, Premier Robert Bourassa of Quebec attempted to protect Quebec's territorial integrity by adding the provision that the self-government clauses "should not create new Aboriginal rights to land." In the end, the Accord was rejected by both Aboriginals and non-Aboriginals, so the ongoing project of defining the place of Aboriginal communities in Canada remained unresolved.

When in doubt, Canadian governments frequently fall back on an institution outside the bounds of cabinet-parliamentary government, or the regular bureaucracy. They call a public inquiry. Such was Ottawa's response to the continuing conundrum around Aboriginal issues when, in 1996, it created the Royal Commission on Aboriginal Peoples (RCAP). The commission produced a staggering five-volume study with over 400 recommendations. Overall, it argued for a fundamental restructuring of the relationship between Aboriginals and non-Aboriginals, including a radical proposal for a third order of government. It called for an Aboriginal Parliament known as the House of the First Peoples, said all governments should recognize the inherent right of Aboriginal self-government as a treaty right affirmed in the Constitution, and called for an independent lands and treaties tribunal to decide on land claims. It also recommended that the Department of Indian and Northern Affairs be replaced by an Aboriginal Relations Department and an Indian and Inuit Services Department. As well, it said that governments should negotiate with Métis on self-government and provide them with an adequate land base, increase government funds for Aboriginals, and assure Aboriginal women full and equal participation in decision-making bodies.

The federal government's response to RCAP was to largely ignore it, to claim that the cost of the reforms ($30 billion) was too high, and to counter with a weaker conception of self-government. The federal government came to accept the recognition of the inherent right to self-government as already existing under Section 35 of the Charter, and in 1995, articulated five foundational principles to negotiating self-government:

1. Aboriginal peoples have the right to govern themselves, to decide on matters that affect their communities, and to exercise the responsibility that is required to achieve true self-government.
2. The federal government recognizes the inherent right to self-government as an existing Aboriginal right under Section 35 of the Charter.
3. Not all Aboriginal governments will be the same.
4. The costs of self-government will be shared among federal, provincial, territorial, and Aboriginal governments.
5. It is up to Aboriginals themselves to trigger the negotiating process.

Meanwhile, in 1999, the newly created Territory of Nunavut was brought into being by federal legislation. Constitutionally, it has the same status as Yukon and Northwest Territories, and is not technically Native self-government. However, approximately 85% of the population are Inuit, thereby guaranteeing that Aboriginal concerns predominate. The legislation resulted from an agreement between the Tungavik Federation of Nunavut, the federal government, and the government of the Northwest Territories, and represents an interesting new chapter in the continued evolution of the concept of self-government.

Part of the backdrop to Aboriginal constitutional issues is the social dislocation and disruption of traditional Aboriginal ways of life. Among the most egregious example is the policy of forcing Aboriginal children to attend government- or church-run "residential schools." A dark and shameful chapter of Canadian history unfolded until the 1970s as many Indian children were forced to leave their homes and communities to attend residential schools where they sometimes suffered emotional, psychological, physical, and sexual abuse. In 2008, the federal government issued a formal apology in the House of Commons to Aboriginal peoples for their treatment in the residential school system.

The evolution of issues related to Aboriginal self-government has also been played out extensively in the courts.[57] Issues have included the interpretation of the Royal Proclamation as to whether Indian sovereignty over their traditional lands exists and, if so, whether it is explicit or implicit; whether there is an inherent right of Aboriginal self-government; whether Aboriginals have unfettered legal title to lands they occupied before the Europeans arrived, or whether that right had been extinguished either via treaty or some other process; the definition of inherent Aboriginal rights, such as fishing, hunting, and trapping; whether compensation was due to Aboriginals forced off their traditional lands; whether treaties between the Crown and Aboriginal peoples should have the same status as international agreements between nations; whether treaties are similar to or different from legal contracts; and the admissibility of oral evidence alongside written evidence in court cases given the oral traditions of many Aboriginal societies. This partial list should give you an idea of the complexity involved.

Aboriginal politics are now a part of the Canadian political landscape. Aboriginals want the right to govern themselves in a manner consistent with their traditions, and to incorporate Aboriginal modes of political decision making into their own governments while retaining the rights and freedoms they possess as Canadians. They argue that the right to self-government is an existing right under section 35 of the Constitution Act, 1982; the problem is how to get the federal and provincial governments to recognize this right and to negotiate self-government. Currently the federal government, while it recognizes the inherent right to self-government, refuses to reopen any constitutional negotiations. As well, many provincial governments still refuse to recognize an inherent right at all and would not agree to recognize it constitutionally. Thus, the saga of Aboriginal constitutional politics continues to unfold.

## Administrative Law

**Administrative law** is related to constitutional law but is focused more exclusively on the relations between citizens and the administrative arm of government. If constitutional law looks at the *macro-legal* picture, administrative law looks at the *micro-legal* level. It is more concerned with the day-to-day legalities of how administration takes place.

| BOX 6.4 | Delegating Power |
| --- | --- |

According to Jones and de Villars, there are several reasons why Parliament delegates authority, including the following:

(a) The sheer magnitude of the business of government means that not everything can be dealt with by Parliament or a legislature.

(b) Much governmental activity is technical in nature, and only broad principles should be contained in legislation.

(c) Delegating power to an administrator allows greater flexibility in applying broad statutory provisions to changing circumstances.

(d) It may not be possible to devise a general rule to deal with all cases, which may be more conveniently determined in the discretion of a delegate.

(e) The need for rapid governmental action may require faster administrative response than can be accommodated by the necessity of legislative amendment.

(f) Innovation and experimentation in solving social problems may not be possible if legislation is required.

(g) Someone actually has to apply legislation, and that person has to have authority to do so.

(h) Emergencies may require broad delegation of powers with respect to a wide range of matters that would normally be dealt with by legislation.

**Source:** David P. Jones and Anne S. de Villars, *Principles of Administrative Law*, 5th ed. (Toronto: Carswell, 2004): 4–5. Reprinted by permission of Carswell, a division of Thomson Reuters Canada Limited. Footnotes omitted.

The most visible government institution of which most citizens are conscious is the department or ministry, but below this is a huge array of other bodies with lesser powers and narrower functions—"structural heretics," as Hodgetts described them.[58] These bodies are termed *agency*, *board*, *commission*, *tribunal*, *bureau*, or any of a number of other names. Indeed, there are a variety of names for administrative bodies and the same name may imply different functions in two different bodies. For instance, the National Energy Board makes licensing decisions; sets rates and conditions regarding energy matters; revokes, suspends or imposes conditions on licence holders; conducts research; and advises government on energy matters. Other boards might have a much more constrained and limited role (see Box 6.4).[59] This lack of uniformity in terms, coupled with the legalistic language typical of administrative law, makes it a challenging field, complicated and confusing to the outsider. Moreover, procedures are not uniform across different agencies and are a source of many problems in the administrative process. Personnel selection is uneven and often complicated by patronage appointments. Further, the process by which citizens launch grievances against administrative bodies is not coordinated. As administrative law expert Alan Leadbeater has noted,

*Independent administrative agencies at the federal level in Canada are not easily described or understood. They have a variety of powers and duties; their procedures*

*differ and are not always formalized; their members are appointed in a closed and informal selection process; there is no uniform right of appeal from their decisions and no single appeal body to deal with those appeals; finally, their success in performing delegated functions efficiently and effectively is not regularly or adequately evaluated.*[60]

Much of administrative law relates to both departments and less visible forums.

Lawyer Sara Blake draws our attention to the ubiquity of officials whose decision-making powers affect our lives: immigration officers, securities commissioners, building inspectors, parole boards, labour relations boards, professional colleges (for example, of physicians and surgeons), and so on. She reminds us,

*Much of our lives is governed by decisions made by administrative tribunals and government officials. Parliament and the provincial legislatures enact statutes that set out the framework of rules for a field of activity and then delegate the day-to-day decision-making power to tribunals and officials. These tribunals and officials then decide whether to admit an immigrant, whether to permit a person to trade in the stock market, whether to order an industry to clean up pollution, whether a person is eligible for Employment Insurance, whether to issue a building permit, whether to release a person from prison before the end of the sentence, the rights of employees, the licensing conditions imposed on a television broadcaster, professional discipline, and so on. . . . In Canada there are thousands of tribunals and officials who have statutory power to make decisions affecting our lives.*[61]

An enormous amount of what government does takes place in administrative bodies at the **discretion** of public servants. Discretion is simply the right to choose from a variety of options, since virtually no piece of legislation can be drafted so as to foresee every circumstance that might arise in the day-to-day application of its provisions. As a result, a great deal of power is left in the hands of public servants to determine how legislation is actually put into operation. What happens when these officials stray from the spirit, intent, or letter of the law that they are implementing? What recourse do citizens have when they feel wronged by the actions or inactions of officials? This is where administrative law comes into play.

The growth of public administration has been accompanied by a concern that arbitrariness and inconsistency might arise in the treatment of citizens by the growing legions of administrators. Personal liberty and control over one's own destiny seem increasingly under siege as a result of administrative mechanisms and measures that, while effective in achieving internal goals, may fail to take individuals' rights and freedoms into consideration. Moreover, the growth in administrative bodies has not always been well coordinated, either within the federal government or across federal–provincial boundaries. Finally, a key problem for the administrative machine has been developing norms and standards of behaviour that will guarantee effectiveness while simultaneously retaining a measure of discretion and flexibility for civil servants.[62] This is a circle not easily squared.

Administrative law is concerned with the manner in which government departments and regulatory agencies actually exercise the legal powers that they have been granted. When a dispute arises (for instance, if a citizen feels that a board is failing in its duties as prescribed by legislation), departments and regulatory agencies are obligated to abide by certain fundamental rules of administrative law enforced by the courts. Two theorists of administrative law explain,

*Administrative Law deals with the legal limitations on the actions of governmental officials, and on the remedies which are available to anyone affected by a transgression of these limits. The subject invariably involves the question of the lawful authority of an official to do a particular act which, in the absence of such authority, might well be illegal. . . . In our legal system, the mere fact that the government is the government does not give it any particular rights or powers. On the contrary, all governmental actions must be specially authorized by either legislation or the Royal Prerogative. This need for governmental officials to be able to point to the lawful authority permitting their actions makes Administrative Law a close cousin to Constitutional Law.*[63]

The modern state is characterized by a substantial delegation of authority and responsibility to various administrative bodies. One observer puts it this way:

*The fact of the matter is that while the legislators may give legal effect and governmental force to certain directions in policy or priorities in terms of programmes and activities, it is in the process of implementation, by way of delegated powers and authority, that policies become meaningful and make their impact on particular groups or the society as a whole. It is no secret that much of the legislation which is enacted by Parliament or the legislative authority (as much as 80–90%) originates within the Civil Service, and certainly the regulations made to give practical effect to enabling legislation are almost always subject to the decisive influence of civil servants.*[64]

Administrative law is intimately related to constitutional law, although it is a very young branch of the law overall. Constitutional law may be distinguished from administrative law "mainly by the fact that the former provides a skeleton of broad principles which the latter fleshes out."[65] Frank Scott, the great Canadian constitutional lawyer, once described constitutional law as "a law for the making of laws."[66] Administrative law is concerned with the administrative actions of officials whose powers are derived from laws enacted under the Constitution. A law found to be unconstitutional deprives the administrator of any right to exercise those powers; further, citizens may be adversely affected by the administrator's (illegal) actions and may seek remedies if those actions caused damages. Administrative law has been defined as the branch of law that "is concerned with the legal limits on the actions of government or its agencies and with the remedies that are available to persons who feel aggrieved by an improper, illegal, or unauthorized act by the government or one of its agencies."[67] Typically, a statute passed by the government contains only the bare bones of a law. It must then be fleshed out during the implementation stage by the public servants who actually put the law into operation. In so doing, many of their actions are left to discretion, and therein lies the need for

administrative law. In effect, there must be a check against the arbitrary and discretionary interpretation of the law by unelected officials whose job it is to implement
the wishes of the elected politicians, and through them, the people. These checks
are provided in administrative law by administrative tribunals and, ultimately, the
courts. The courts are the principal means by which controls over the administrative process are exercised through the power of judicial review.[68]

The courts play a role at several points in the review of administrative practice.
Initially they might examine the validity of power delegated to an administrative
body. They may investigate whether it is authorized by the principles of law,
including the Constitution, to be sure that there has not been an excessive or inappropriate delegation of power. The courts may look into the rule-making process:
that is, they may check to see if the regulatory body that has been given power is
exercising that power in its own rule making, or whether it has exceeded the grant
of power in constructing its own rules. Finally, the courts may investigate the propriety of the way in which the administrative body has exercised its adjudicative
power, which is the power to make decisions involving individual citizens.[69]

A whole series of legal principles, some of them centuries old, has infused the
development of administrative law. For instance, the principle of *audi alteram
partem* means that the individual must be given an opportunity to represent her
side of an issue in a formal hearing or by some other process. Moreover, citizens
generally have the following rights: representation by legal counsel, advance notice
of any proceedings and disclosure of evidence that the state may bring, and the
opportunity to cross-examine witnesses and to be heard by an impartial adjudica-
tor. Not every one of these principles is necessarily in effect in every single case of
administrative law, but over the years the courts have reinforced the importance of
these principles of natural justice to an ever-widening range of administrative individuals and organizations. This ensures that public servants who are challenged by
citizens cannot run roughshod over the rights of those citizens in their zeal in interpreting Parliament's will. Many of these legal principles are reflected in and reinforced
by various Charter rights, especially concerning due process.[70] Legal rights in
Sections 7–14 of the Charter are particularly relevant. For instance, Section 14 guarantees the right of a party or witness to an interpreter. The general right of protection
from being deprived of "life, liberty and security of the person . . . except in accordance with principles of fundamental justice" is also obviously highly pertinent to
administrative law.

These principles contribute to the elaborate decision-making process judges
engage in, in deciding to overturn or support a particular administrative action.
Judges must decide within the context of these principles whether an administrative action is based on an error of law, an error of fact, or inadequate evidence or
information. They must also determine when not to intervene in an issue, allowing
administrators to exercise their discretion in acting. In the event that judges do
decide a wrong is committed, they must next determine what the remedy is for the
aggrieved citizen. The courts have a number of options where remedies are concerned, ranging from simply quashing the administrative action or decision of the
agency concerned, to ordering the agency to take some action that it had failed to
take, to ordering the agency to compensate the citizen.

There are four main actors involved in administrative law. These are citizens, politicians, public servants, and judges. Each has a unique perspective on whether a law is working or has been administered properly. Somehow, at the intersection of these four groups of disparate perspectives, public policy must be made to work. It can be an imposing challenge.

If a given law is constitutionally valid, the next task is to determine the exact nature and scope of the powers delegated to officials. It is striking that most of the business of government is actually contained in delegated powers instead of in the actual laws passed by Parliament. Power can be delegated to a number of places (see Box 6.4). The legislation can say, for instance, that power is delegated to Cabinet, to a particular minister, to a particular public servant, to a judge, or even to a private citizen. In theory, there is no limit to the powers that Parliament can delegate because of the doctrine of parliamentary supremacy, which means that Parliament has the right to make or unmake any law whatsoever, and no other body has the right to "override or set aside the legislation of Parliament."[71] Therefore, an important aspect of administrative law involves how Parliament devises ways to supervise and control the delegation of powers to administrators.

What happens when the delegated authority oversteps the bounds of the instructions imparted to it by Parliament? The judges step in and ask the delegate to reveal what statutory authority permitted him or her to take action. If the delegate cannot demonstrate that his or her actions are justified under the relevant statute, then the delegate's actions are declared ultra vires by the court, and thereby beyond the delegate's jurisdiction to act. This can be a daunting process, since legislation is often vague and unclear. Therefore, the judges are asked, essentially, to determine precisely what the legislation was intended to do or allow. When a court finds an administrator's actions ultra vires, the next step is to find a legal remedy. This process of **judicial review** is generally limited to determining whether an administrator has acted strictly within the statutorily delegated powers. In other words, judicial review looks at whether the administrator has legal jurisdiction to act.

One important court case that illustrates the working of judicial review in relation to the question of jurisdiction involved the premier of Quebec in the 1950s. Then-premier Maurice Duplessis had ordered the revocation of a liquor licence belonging to a bar owner who had posted bail for some Jehovah's Witnesses[72] who had been arrested for distributing religious literature that attacked the Catholic Church. In predominantly Catholic Quebec, the actions of the Jehovah's Witnesses were seen by the premier as a provocation. However, in a court case entitled *Roncarelli v. Duplessis,* the courts ruled that there were jurisdictional errors in the administrative action of revoking Roncarelli's liquor licence. First, the legislature had not delegated power to the premier to revoke liquor licences but, rather, to a liquor licensing board. As well, revoking a licence because of posting bail for a group being prosecuted for their religious activity was an irrelevant and improper motive for the exercise of the power granted to the board. As a result, the board's actions (acting at the behest of the premier) were declared ultra vires; Roncarelli got to keep his licence and he was awarded damages.

Judicial review can occur for a number of reasons. If an action appears to be ultra vires, as the case above illustrates, it can be reviewed. Moreover, exercising

## BOX 6.5  Remedies

**W**hen a citizen feels aggrieved by the actions of an administrative official, he or she can apply for a *prerogative remedy:* a declaration, an injunction, damages, or a statutory appeal to a court or another administrative body. Each is explained briefly below:

**Certiorari:** an order from the superior court compelling an inferior tribunal or other statutory delegate to render up all records of its proceedings to permit the superior court to determine its lawfulness.

**Prohibition:** similar to *certiorari*, except that this order occurs before the conclusion of the proceedings by the inferior body, and prohibits it from proceeding in a manner that would take it outside its jurisdiction.

**Mandamus:** a command by the superior court compelling an inferior body to fulfill a delegated statutory duty.

**Habeas corpus:** a command that compels the respondent to bring the person of the application before the superior court in order to determine the lawfulness of the respondent's detention of the applicant.

**Quo warranto:** an order that requires the respondent to demonstrate by what authority he or she exercises the powers of a particular statutory office.

A declaration can be used to determine the lawfulness of an administrator's actions or the validity of the parent legislation. Claims for damages may be successful if the court finds that an illegal administrative action causes harm. Statutory appeal is sometimes expressly granted by the legislation setting up the administrative machinery in question.

**Source:** David P. Jones and Anne S. de Villars, *Principles of Administrative Law*, 5th ed. (Toronto: Carswell, 2004): 10–11. Adapted by permission of Carswell, a division of Thomson Reuters Canada Limited. Footnotes omitted.

discretion for an improper purpose, with malice, in bad faith, by reference to irrelevant considerations, or by not considering relevant matters, through procedural errors or through making an error in law, can all lead to judicial review. There are three central features of administrative law: the rule of law, which is the requirement that all government action must be expressly permitted by validly enacted laws; the denial of any special status to the government merely because it is the government; and the right of ordinary courts to determine such questions of legality.[73] If judicial review concludes that a delegated authority has overstepped the bounds of his or her authority, administrative law allows the application of one of several types of remedies (see Box 6.5); there are also nonjudicial remedies that can be sought. Parliamentarians are often alert to perceived abuses by administrative officials and, especially if they are from the opposition, are eager to point them out. The resulting embarrassment for the government may cause a review of administrative practices. In addition, the office of the ombuds is increasingly common. It is responsible for reviewing the propriety and fairness of government actions. Reporting directly to Parliament, the ombuds draws attention to administrative action in such a way that few public servants want to be highlighted in its reports. Finally, administrative practice is itself sometimes self-correcting: that is, administrators learn through trial and error or public criticism which practices are permissible, and then alter their behaviour and actions accordingly.

Judicial review can be entirely avoided if the legislation contains what are called *privative clauses*. These deprive the courts of any jurisdiction to review the actions of delegates. Thus, the legislation can expressly state that the administrator's actions shall not be reviewed in any court. The courts, naturally, do not appreciate being frozen out in this manner and have devised a number of imaginative rulings to allow them to review administrators' actions even when privative clauses have been in effect.

What of the individuals who occupy the offices of administrative tribunals, agencies, boards, and so on? They are unique in the pantheon of public servants for several reasons. They perform adjudicative duties in many cases but lack the job security and independence that judges enjoy. Appointments to administrative bodies "are usually for a relatively short fixed term, until a specific purpose is achieved, or 'at the pleasure' of the government that made the appointment."[74] In other words, a position could be terminated at any moment—say, when a government changes and the new regime wants to have people in place that reflect its ideological or policy predispositions. One of the notable features about administrative appointments of this sort is that they can be much more political in nature than strictly merit-based.[75] Balancing the tension between the administrative and the political is thus one of the key ongoing issues related to administrative bodies and law.

In summary, administrative law, closely related to constitutional law, deals with the legal remedies available to citizens aggrieved by administrative actions. Determining what Parliament means when it delegates powers and authority is a large measure of what administrative law is all about. Thus, administrative law deals with three broad areas of public administration: the ways in which power is transferred from Parliament to administrative agencies; how those agencies use that power; and how the actions taken by administrative agencies are reviewed by the courts.[76] Administrative power has grown tremendously in Canada in terms of powers delegated to the approximately 1500 federal, provincial, and territorial administrative bodies that currently exist, raising questions about power, control, and accountability in democratic society. As arcane as it may seem to the uninitiated, administrative law is fundamentally important. Those concerned with administrative law must wrestle with many important questions: How much power should be delegated to administrative agencies? How much administrative discretion is too much? What constitutes a fair hearing for those aggrieved by administrative behaviour? Is it reasonable to allow administrative agencies to make law, implement law, and determine the fairness of that same law? How can administrative abuses be effectively checked? What internal and external safeguards are needed to prevent abuse by administrators? When should the courts become involved in the review of agency decisions? How can Parliament control the many and diverse administrative agencies for which it is ultimately responsible? Fundamentally, administrative law is about the making of fair procedures in administrative agencies, but this is a complex and daunting task.

## WHAT YOU HAVE LEARNED

This chapter has shown that public administration is intimately connected to the law. While constitutional law deals with the rules, practices, and institutions that constitute the state and can be considered the macro-legal environment, administrative law is the micro-legal level, dealing with the discretionary actions of public servants in operationalizing the instructions of Parliament on a day-to-day basis.

Constitutional and administrative law issues reflect the broader political culture of the society. In Canada, our proclivity for constitutional wrangling, a trait almost unprecedented anywhere else in the world, seems to have abated for now, but the significance of the Constitution is as great as it ever was. The development of a complex web of administrative bodies and the judicial regime to ensure that administrators are observing the laws of the land is impressive, if somewhat arcane.

### Key Words and Concepts

rule of law (169)
common law (169)
civil law (169)
constitutional law (176)
amending formula (178)
Charter of Rights and Freedoms (179)
division of powers (180)
reservation (181)

disallowance (181)
spending power (182)
ultra vires (185)
province building (187)
executive federalism (187)
administrative law (194)
discretion (196)
judicial review (199)

### Review Questions

The four sections of this chapter each dealt with a specific set of issues related to public administration, the constitution, and the law. You should now be able to address the following questions:

*1.  The Law, the Courts, and the Administration of Justice*
The political culture of a society has an impact on the legal-constitutional regime, a point that should be evident from this section. How can you link the origins and application of the rule of law in Canada to its political culture? Why does Canada have both common law and civil law systems, and what do these terms mean? What is the structure of the court system, and what institutions are responsible for the administration of justice in Canada?

*2.  What Is a Constitution?*
Can you define the term *constitution* and explain its three main functions? What exactly is the Canadian Constitution, and how did it evolve? What primary roles does the constitution play in public administration?

## 3. *Constitutional Law*

The division of powers in the Constitution is often a source of conflict. Why? What different means exist to resolve those conflicts? What is the significance of the courts when federal and provincial governments cannot agree on the jurisdiction of a law? What powers in the Constitution are most contentious, and why? What is the significance of the Charter of Rights and Freedoms? What is judicial review, and what has been its legacy? How has the issue of Aboriginal self-government affected constitutional law and politics?

## 4. *Administrative Law*

What is the difference between constitutional law and administrative law? How are the two related? What happens when a dispute arises over the exercise of legal powers by an administrative agency? What powers can the courts exercise in disputes concerning administrative bodies? What recourse do citizens have when wronged by an administrative body?

## Weblinks

Canada in the Making: Primary and Secondary Sources in Government Documents
**www.canadiana.org/citm/primary/primary_e.html**

Canadian Bar Association
**www.cba.org**

Canada's Court System
**www.canada.justice.gc.ca/eng/dept-min/pub/ccs-ajc**

The Supreme Court of Canada
**www.scc-csc.gc.ca**

Judgments of the Supreme Court of Canada
**http://scc.lexum.umontreal.ca/en/index.html**

Assembly of First Nations
**www.afn.ca**

Indian and Northern Affairs Canada
**www.ainc-inac.gc.ca**

Department of Justice Canada
**www.canada.justice.gc.ca**

*Provincial Courts:*

British Columbia
**www.courts.gov.bc.ca**

Alberta
**www.albertacourts.ab.ca**

Saskatchewan
**www.sasklawcourts.ca**

Manitoba
**www.manitobacourts.mb.ca**

Ontario
**www.ontariocourts.on.ca**

Quebec
**www.justice.gouv.qc.ca**

New Brunswick
**www.gnb.ca/cour**

Nova Scotia
**www.courts.ns.ca**

Prince Edward Island
**www.gov.pe.ca/courts**

Newfoundland
**www.court.nl.ca**

# Further Reading

## 1. The Law, the Courts, and the Administration of Justice

Baar, Carl, and Ian Greene. "Judicial Administration," in Christopher Dunn, ed., *The Handbook of Canadian Public Administration*, 2nd ed. Toronto: Oxford University Press, 2010: 131–46.

Gall, Gerald. *The Canadian Legal System*. 5th ed. Toronto: Carswell, 2004.

Greene, Ian. *The Courts*. Vancouver: UBC Press, 2006.

Isaac, Thomas. *Aboriginal Law: Commentary, Cases and Materials*. Saskatoon: Purich, 2004.

McCormick, Peter. *Canada's Courts: A Social Scientist's Ground-Breaking Account of the Canadian Judicial System*. Toronto: James Lorimer, 1994.

McCormick, P., and I. Greene. *Judges and Judging: Inside the Canadian Judicial System*. Toronto: Lorimer, 1990.

Swainger, Jonathan. *The Canadian Department of Justice and the Completion of Confederation, 1867–78*. Vancouver: UBC Press, 2000.

Tardi, Gregory. *The Legal Framework of Government: A Canadian Guide*. Aurora: Canada Law, 1992.

## 2. What Is a Constitution?

Cheffins, R.I., and P.A. Johnson. *The Revised Canadian Constitution: Politics as Law*. Toronto: McGraw-Hill Ryerson, 1986.

Milne, David. *The New Canadian Constitution*. Toronto: Lorimer, 1982.

Morton, F.L. *Law, Politics and the Judicial Process in Canada*. 3rd ed. Calgary: University of Calgary Press, 2002.

Rocher, François, and Miriam Smith. "Four Dimensions of the Canadian Constitutional Debate," in François Rocher and Miriam Smith, eds, *New Trends in Canadian Federalism*, 2nd ed. Peterborough: Broadview, 2003: 21–44

Russell, Peter. *Constitutional Odyssey: Can Canadians Become a Sovereign People?* 3rd ed. Toronto: University of Toronto Press, 2004.

## 3. Constitutional Law

Belanger, Yale D. *Aboriginal Self-Government in Canada: Current Trends and Issues*. 3rd ed. Saskatoon: Purich, 2008.

Finkelstein, Neil R., and Brian MacLeod Rogers, eds. *Administrative Tribunals and the Charter.* Toronto: Carswell, 1990.

Heard, Andrew D. "The Charter in the Supreme Court of Canada: The Importance of Which Judges Hear an Appeal." *Canadian Journal of Political Science,* 24 (1991): 289–308.

Hogg, Peter W. *Constitutional Law of Canada.* 5th ed. Toronto: Carswell, 2010.

Mellon, Hugh, and Martin Westmacott, eds. *Political Dispute and Judicial Review: Assessing the Work of the Supreme Court of Canada.* Scarborough: Nelson, 2000.

## 4. Administrative Law

Blake, Sara. *Administrative Law in Canada.* 2nd ed. Toronto: Butterworths, 1997.

Brown, Donald J.M., and John M. Evans. *Judicial Review of Administrative Action in Canada.* Toronto: Canvasback, 1998.

Elliott, David W. *Administrative Law and Process.* 3rd ed. Toronto: Captus, 1999.

Macaulay, Robert W., and James L.H. Sprague. *Practice and Procedure Before Administrative Tribunals.* Toronto: Carswell, 2001.

Mullan, David J. *Administrative Law: Essentials of Canadian Law.* Toronto: Irwin Law, 2001.

Salembier, Paul. *Regulatory Law and Practice in Canada.* Markham, ON: Buttersworth, 2004.

Sheldrick, Byron. "Administrative Law and Public Governance: An Overlooked Dimension of Governance," in O.P. Dwivedi, Tim A. Mau, and Byron Sheldrick, eds., *The Evolving Physiology of Government: Canadian Public Administration in Transition.* Ottawa: University of Ottawa Press, 2009: 358–79.

Sossin, Lorne, and France Houle. "Tribunals and Guidelines: Exploring the Relationship between Fairness and Legitimacy in Administrative Decision-Making." *Canadian Public Administration,* 46, 3 (2006): 283–307.

Swaigen, John. *Administrative Law: Principles and Advocacy.* Toronto: Emond Montgomery, 2005.

## Endnotes

1. John James Guy, *People, Politics and Government: A Canadian Perspective,* 7th ed. (Toronto: Pearson, 2010): 226–27.

2. For a discussion of the legal system in Canada, see F.L. Morton, ed., *Law, Politics and the Judicial Process in Canada,* 3rd ed. (Calgary: University of Calgary Press, 2002).

3. Canada, Department of Justice, "Where Our Legal System Comes From" in *Canada's System of Justice,* July 31, 2009, **www.canada.justice.gc.ca/eng/dept-min/pub/just/03.html.**

4. Canada, Department of Justice, "Where Our Legal System Comes From."

5. Thomas Isaac, *Aboriginal Law: Commentary, Cases and Materials* (Saskatoon: Purich, 2004): 1. See also Jane Dickson-Gilmore and Carol La Prairie, *Will the Circle be Unbroken? Aboriginal Communities, Restorative Justice, and the Challenges of Conflict and Change* (Toronto: University of Toronto Press, 2005).

6. See Peter McCormick, *Canada's Courts: A Social Scientist's Ground-Breaking Account of the Canadian Judicial System* (Toronto: James Lorimer, 1994). For a history of the Supreme Court, see Peter H. Russell, *The Judiciary in Canada: The Third Branch of Government* (Toronto: McGraw-Hill Ryerson, 1987).

7. Patrick Fitzgerald and Barry Wright, *Looking at Law: Canada's Legal System,* 5th ed. (Toronto: Butterworth, 2000): 96–97.

8. For a history of the founding and early development of the Department of Justice, see Jonathan Swainger, *The Canadian Department of Justice and the Completion of Confederation, 1867–78* (Vancouver: UBC Press, 2000).

9. The following description of the Department of Justice is adapted from Canada, Department of Justice, "Canada's Department of Justice," July 19, 2010, **www.canada.justice.gc.ca/eng/dept-min/pub/about-aprop/.**

10. See Fitzgerald and Wright, *Looking at Law,* 114–15.

11. Canada, Department of Justice, "Canada's Department of Justice."

12. The following discussion draws from Stephen Brooks, *Canadian Democracy: An Introduction*, 6th ed. (Toronto: Oxford University Press, 2009): chap. 5.

13. J.R. Mallory, *The Structure of Canadian Government* (Toronto: Gage, 1971): 1.

14. Patrick Malcolmson and Richard Myers, *The Canadian Regime: An Introduction to Parliamentary Government in Canada*, 4th ed. (Toronto: University of Toronto Press, 2009): 13–14.

15. Peter Hogg, *Constitutional Law of Canada*, (Toronto: Carswell, 2002): 2.

16. See A.R.M. Lower, *From Colony to Nation* (Toronto: University of Toronto Press, 1946).

17. See Peter McCormick, *Supreme at Last: The Evolution of the Supreme Court of Canada* (Toronto: James Lorimer, 2000).

18. See Robert Sheppard and Michael Valpy, *The National Deal: The Fight for a Canadian Constitution* (Toronto: Fleet, 1982).

19. On the Fulton-Favreau formula, the Victoria Charter, and the ongoing search for an amending formula for the Canadian Constitution, see Garth Stevenson, *Unfulfilled Union: Canadian Federalism and National Unity*, 4th ed. (Montreal: McGill-Queen's University Press, 2004): chap. 10.

20. See Keith Banting and Richard Simeon, *And No One Cheered: Federalism, Democracy and the Constitution Act* (Toronto: Methuen, 1983).

21. See Andrew Cohen, *A Deal Undone: The Making and Breaking of the Meech Lake Accord* (Vancouver: Douglas and McIntyre, 1990); Patrick Monahan, *Meech Lake: The Inside Story* (Toronto: University of Toronto Press, 1991); Martin Westmacott, "The Charlottetown Accord: A Retrospective Overview," in Martin Westmacott and Hugh Mellon, eds., *Challenges to Canadian Federalism* (Scarborough: Prentice Hall, 1998): 100–11; and Robert M. Campbell and Leslie A. Pal, *The Real Worlds of Canadian Politics: Cases in Process and Policy*, 3rd ed. (Peterborough: Broadview, 1994): chap. 3.

22. See Jose Woehrling, "The Supreme Court's Ruling on Quebec's Secession: Legality and Legitimacy Reconciled by a Return to Constitutional First Principles," in Hugh Mellon and Martin Westmacott, eds., *Political Dispute and Judical Review: Assessing the Work of the Supreme Court of Canada* (Scarborough: Nelson, 2000): 83–101; and "Reference re the Secession of Quebec," in F.L. Morton, ed., *Law, Politics and the Judicial Process in Canada*, 3rd ed. (Calgary: University of Calgary Press, 2002): 56–85.

23. See Harvey Lazar, ed., *Canada: The State of the Federation 1997: Non-Constitutional Renewal* (Kingston: Institute of Inter-governmental Relations, 1998).

24. See Gerald Baier, "The Law of Federalism: Judicial Review and the Division of Powers," in François Rocher and Miriam Smith, eds., *New Trends in Canadian Federalism*, 2nd ed. (Peterborough: Broadview, 2003): 111–33; Michael Mandel, *The Charter of Rights and the Legalization of Politics in Canada* (Toronto: Thomson Educational, 1994); and Paul Howe and Peter H. Russell, eds., *Judicial Power and Canadian Democracy* (Montreal: McGill-Queen's University Press, 2001).

25. See Carolyn M. Johns, "Federalism and Intergovernmental Relations," in Joan Grace and Byron Sheldrick, eds., *Canadian Politics: Democracy and Dissent* (Toronto: Pearson Prentice Hall, 2006): 85–116; and Nathalie Des Rosiers, "Federalism and Judicial Review," in Martin Westmacott and Hugh Mellon, *Challenges to Canadian Federalism* (Scarborough: Prentice Hall, 1998): 66.

26. Macdonald's view of Confederation is discussed in J.R. Mallory, *The Structure of Canadian Government* (Toronto: Gage, 1971): 331–34. See also P.B. Waite, ed., *The Confederation Debates in the Province of Canada, 1865* (Toronto: McClelland and Stewart, 1963).

27. See John Ibbitson, *Loyal No More: Ontario's Struggle for a Separate Destiny* (Toronto: HarperCollins, 2001); and Donald Swainson, ed., *Oliver Mowat's Ontario* (Toronto: Macmillan, 1972).

28. Keith Banting, *The Welfare State and Canadian Federalism*, 2nd ed. (Kingston: McGill-Queen's University Press, 1987): 52. See also Christopher Dunn, "The Federal Spending Power," in C. Dunn, ed., *The Handbook of Canadian Public*

*Administration*, 2nd ed. (Toronto: Oxford University Press, 2010): 422–44.

29. See, for instance, David Kwavnick, *The Tremblay Report* (Toronto: McClelland and Stewart, 1973). See also Herman Bakvis, Gerald Baier, and Douglas Brown, *Contested Federalism: Certainty and Ambiguity in the Canadian Federation* (Toronto: Oxford University Press, 2009).

30. See Gregory J. Inwood, "Federalism, Globalization and the (Anti-)Social Union," in Mike Burke, Colin Mooers and John Shields, eds., *Restructuring and Resistance: Canadian Public Policy in an Age of Global Capitalism*, (Halifax: Fernwood, 2000): 124–44; Kathy O'Hara and Sarah Cox, *Securing the Social Union* (Ottawa: Canadian Policy Research Networks, 1998); and Alain-G. Gagnon and Hugh Segal, eds., *The Canadian Social Union Without Quebec: Eight Critical Analyses* (Montreal: Institute for Research on Public Policy, 2000).

31. For the provincial view, see the Council of the Federation, Advisory Panel on Fiscal Imbalance, *Reconciling the Irreconcilable: Addressing Canada's Fiscal Imbalance* (Ottawa: Council of the Federation, 2006), **www.councilofthefederation.ca/pdfs/Report_Fiscalim_Mar3106.pdf**. For the federal view, see the Expert Panel on Equalization and Territorial Formula Financing, *Achieving a National Purpose: Putting Equalization Back on Track* (Ottawa: Department of Finance, 2006), **www.eqtff-pfft.ca/english/index.asp**.

32. See Peter H. Russell, *Leading Constitutional Decisions*, 4th ed. (Ottawa: Carleton University Press, 1987): 54–63.

33. Russell, *Leading Constitutional Decisions*, 69–75.

34. Russell, *Leading Constitutional Decisions*, 77–81.

35. Russell, *Leading Constitutional Decisions*, 113–30.

36. See Peter H. Russell, "The Anti-Inflation Case: The Anatomy of a Constitutional Decision," *Canadian Public Administration*, 10, 4 (1977): 632–65.

37. Russell, *Leading Constitutional Decisions*, 33–40.

38. See Stephen Brooks, *Canadian Democracy: An Introduction*, 6th ed. (Toronto: Oxford University Press, 2009), 207.

39. See Brooks, *Canadian Democracy*, 208.

40. Canada, Supreme Court of Canada, "Reference Re Secession of Quebec," **http://scc.lexum.umontreal.ca/en/1998/1998scr2-217/1998scr2-217.html**. Accessed August 24, 2010.

41. On intergovernmental bargaining and negotiation concerning health care, for instance, see Patricia L. O'Reilly, "The Federal/Provincial/Territorial Health Conference System," in Duane Adams, ed., *Federalism, Democracy and Canadian Health Policy* (Montreal: McGill-Queens University Press, 2001): 107–30.

42. See Garth Stevenson, *Unfulfilled Union: Canadian Federalism and National Unity*, 4th ed. (Montreal: McGill-Queen's University Press, 2004): chap. 9

43. See Alan Cairns, "The Past and Future of the Canadian Administrative State," in Douglas E. Williams, ed., *Reconfigurations: Canadian Citizenship and Constitutional Change* (Toronto: McClelland and Stewart, 1995): 62–96.

44. See Carolyn M. Johns, Patricia L. O'Reilly, and Gregory J. Inwood, "Intergovernmental Innovation and the Administrative State in Canada," *Governance*, 19, 4 (2006): 627–49; and Carolyn M. Johns, Patricia L. O'Reilly, and Gregory J. Inwood, "Formal and Informal Dimensions of Intergovernmental Administrative Relations in Canada," *Canadian Public Administration*, 50, 1 (2007): 21–41.

45. The classic analysis of this phenomenon remains Richard Simeon, *Federal-Provincial Diplomacy: The Making of Recent Policy in Canada.*, (Toronto: University of Toronto Press, 2006). See also J. Peter Meekison, Hamish Telford and Harvey Lazar, eds. *Canada: The State of the Federation 2002. Reconsidering the Institutions of Canadian Federalism,* (Montreal: McGill-Queen's University Press, 2004).

46. See O'Reilly, "The Federal/Provincial/Territorial Health Conference System." On the roles and responsibilities of intergovernmental officials, see Gregory J. Inwood, Carolyn M. Johns and Patricia L. O'Reilly, "Intergovernmental Officials in Canada," in J. Peter Meekison, Hamish Telford, and Harvey Lazar, eds., *Canada: The State of the Federation 2002: Reconsidering the Institutions of Canadian*

*Federalism* (Montreal: McGill-Queen's University Press, 2004): 249–84.

47. On executive federalism, see J. Stefan Dupre, "Reflections on the Workability of Executive Federalism," in Richard Simeon, ed., *Intergovernmental Relations* (Toronto: University of Toronto Press, 1985): 1–32; Donald V. Smiley, "An Outsider's Observations of Federal–Provincial Relations Among Consenting Adults," in R.D. Olling and M.W. Westmacott, eds., *Perspectives on Canadian Federalism* (Scarborough: Prentice-Hall, 1988): 279–84; and Albert Breton, "Competition and Cooperation in the Canadian Federal System," in *Royal Commission on the Economic Union and Development Prospects for Canada, Report*, vol. 3 (Ottawa: Minister of Supply and Services, 1985): 486–526.

48. See Jennifer Smith, *Federalism* (Vancouver: UBC Press, 2004).

49. See Gregory J. Inwood, "Federalism, Globalization and the (Anti-)Social Union," in Mike Burke, Colin Mooers and John Shields, eds., *Restructuring and Resistance: Canadian Public Policy in an Age of Global Capitalism*, (Halifax: Fernwood, 2000): 124–44;

50. See Stephen Brooks, *Canadian Democracy: An Introduction*, 6th ed. (Toronto: Oxford University Press, 2009): 456–57

51. See Brooks, *Canadian Democracy*, 95.

52. See Michael S. Whittington, "Aboriginal Self-Government," in Michael S. Whittington and Glen Williams, eds., *Canadian Politics in the 21st Century*, 6th ed. (Toronto: Thomson Nelson, 2004).

53. See Whittington, "Aboriginal Self-Government," 115.

54. See Lydia Miljan, *Public Policy in Canada: An Introduction*, 5th ed. (Toronto: Oxford University Press, 2008): 261–65.

55. Thomas Flanagan, *First Nations? Second Thoughts* (Montreal: McGill-Queen's University Press, 2000).

56. Alan Cairns, *Citizens Plus: Aboriginal Peoples and the Canadian State* (Vancouver: UBC Press, 2000).

57. See Brooks, *Canadian Democracy*, 465–75.

58. J.E. Hodgetts, *The Canadian Public Service: A Physiology of Government 1867–1970* (Toronto: University of Toronto Press, 1971).

59. See Alan Leadbeater, *Council on Administration: Administrative Law Series Prepared for the Law Reform Commission of Canada* (Ottawa: Minister of Supply and Services, 1980): 3.

60. Leadbeater, *Council on Administration*, 1.

61. Sara Blake, "An Introduction to Administrative Law in Canada," in Christopher Dunn, ed., *The Handbook of Canadian Public Administration* (Toronto: Oxford University Press, 2002): 466.

62. See René Dussault and Louis Borgeat, *Administrative Law: A Treatise*, 2nd ed., vol. 1 (Toronto: Carswell, 1985): 4.

63. David P. Jones and Anne S. de Villars, *Principles of Administrative Law*, 4th ed (Toronto: Carswell, 2004): 3–4. The following discussion of administrative law is derived from their overview.

64. George E. Eaton, "Understanding Canadian Parliamentary Government," in Randy Hoffman et al., *Public Administration: Canadian Materials*, 3rd ed. (North York: Captus, 1988): 63.

65. Dussault and Borgeat, *Administrative Law*, 13. See also Margot Priest, "Structure and Accountability of Administrative Agencies," in *Administrative Law: Principles, Practice and Pluralism: Special Lectures of the Law Society of Upper Canada* (Toronto: Carswell, 1992): 63–78.

66. Cited in David Phillip Jones and Anne S. de Villars, *Principles of Administrative Law: Student Edition*, 2nd ed., (Toronto: Carswell, 1994): 4.

67. Donald J. Bourgeois, *Public Law in Canada* (Scarborough: Nelson, 1990): 195.

68. See Nathalie Des Rosiers, "Federalism and Judicial Review," in Martin Westmacott and Hugh Mellon, *Challenges to Canadian Federalism* (Scarborough: Prentice Hall, 1998): 63–75

69. Victor S. MacKinnon, "Introduction to the Legal Environment: Theories and Principles," in Randy Hoffman et al., *Public Administration: Canadian Materials*, 3rd ed. (North York: Captus, 1998): 199–200.

70. Paul Atkinson, *The Canadian Justice System: An Overview* (Markham, ON: Buttersworth, 2005): 93.

71. A.V. Dicey, *Introduction to the Study of the Law of the Constitution* (London: Macmillan, 1920): 40.

72. See Peter W. Hogg *Constitutional Law of Canada*. 5th ed. (Toronto: Carswell, 201: 668-69

73. Jones and de Villars, *Principles of Administrative Law*, 9.

74. Atkinson, *The Canadian Justice System*, 91.

75. See Lorne Sossin, "The Uneasy Relationship Between Independence and Appointments in Canadian Administrative Law," in Grant Huscroft and Michael Taggart, eds., *Inside and Outside Canadian Administrative Law: Essays in Honour of David Mullan* (Toronto: University of Toronto Press, 2006): 50–80.

76. See Kenneth F. Warren, *Administrative Law in the Political System*, abridged 3rd ed. (Upper Saddle River, NJ: Prentice Hall, 1997): 23.

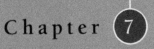

# Chapter 7

# Public Administration
# *and* Public Policy

## WHAT YOU WILL LEARN

The formulation, implementation, and evaluation of **public policy** are vitally important aspects of public administration. By the end of this chapter, you will be able to answer the following questions:

- What does public policy involve?
- What major theories of public policy decision making explain the way public officials make decisions on behalf of citizens?
- What is the policy cycle of problem definition and agenda-setting, formulation, implementation, and evaluation?

This chapter is divided into three sections highlighting these central issues:

### 1. *Defining Public Policy*

This brief introductory section will ask you to consider what public policy is. You will discover that a number of definitions exist.

### 2. *Models and Theories of Public Policy*

One way of understanding public policy is to construct theoretical explanations for how decision making takes place. Of these, there is no shortage. This section looks at a variety of models and theories of public policy, and asks, What factors influence policy-makers in the decision-making process? How can we theoretically explain the policy we get? How do we use theoretical models to explain *how* policy is made as well as *why* policy is made (or not made)?

## 3. ─ *The Policy Cycle*

One explanation of policy-making requires us to think of the process as part of a cyclical model of problem definition and agenda-setting, formulation, implementation, and evaluation. How problems reach the packed agendas of government policy-makers is an issue of great importance. This section asks, How are policy problems defined? Why do some problems receive attention from policy-makers, while others do not? What goes on in the formulation of public policy? Who is involved? What policy instruments are available for governments to use in realizing their goals? How do they choose among these instruments? A relatively new concern of governments has been how to evaluate whether their policies have been effective. How do public officials and others assess the quality, utility, and success of public policies?

# Defining Public Policy

Public policies in general cover a wide range of fields, and you can tell something about the interests of particular governments by the policies they emphasize.[1] One government may stress economic policy; another, social policy. Yet another might see foreign and defence policy as important, while others do not. Justice policy, language policy, multicultural policy, education policy, and environment policy are just some of the countless areas that public administration deals with. A particular prime minister may have a strong personal interest in an issue, as did former prime minister Pierre Trudeau on constitutional and national unity policy. Interest groups may be particularly effective in persuading the government to focus its energies on one area, as did the big business lobbies with the free trade issue. In other cases, public opinion may dictate that a government proceed with a certain policy only at its peril. Sometimes a crisis, such as September 11, 2001, mad cow disease, SARS (severe acute respiratory system), or the 2008–2009 global economic recession, will catapult an issue to the forefront. The mix of factors that determine which issues will be addressed as public policy is complex and changes over time, but whatever the public policy, it is the job of public administration to help formulate, implement, and evaluate it.

There is a large, well-developed, and growing literature in Canada on public policy.[2] It has been defined as "a set of interrelated decisions taken by a political actor or group of actors concerning the selection of goals and the means of achieving them."[3] American political scientist Thomas Dye said public policy is "whatever governments choose to do or not to do,"[4] pointing out that "policy" can be a case of either action or inaction. Thus, passing a law is an obvious, deliberate, and conscious policy act on the part of a government, but not passing a law may be a conscious decision as well. Canadian political scientist Les Pal also defines public policy as involving both action and inaction when he says it is "a course of action or inaction chosen by public authorities to address a given problem or interrelated set of problems."[5]

Consider, for instance, a law that the courts find violates the Constitution. Such a law is, therefore, of no force or effect. The government is then faced with a number of options. First, it can decide to redraft the law to bring it into conformity with the Constitution. It can override the court's decision by employing the Charter of Rights and Freedoms (in certain select areas). Or it can do nothing. All these responses are "public policy." A case in point occurred in January 1988, when the Supreme Court of Canada struck down the government's abortion law on the basis that it violated certain sections of the Constitution. The government of the day took stock of the judgment and decided to do nothing. That is, it declined to either overrule the court or redraft and reintroduce the law. Thus, there is currently no abortion law in Canada. Why did the government take this "inaction"? It simply weighed the political costs of taking sides in the controversial abortion debate in Canada and decided that inaction was, in fact, the most prudent action and perhaps even the most viable "policy."

In many ways, public policy involves conscious choices by governments that lead to action or inaction. These take many forms, such as passing a law or regulation, creating a Crown corporation, spending or raising money (i.e., taxing), holding a royal commission or inquiry, and so on. Public policy can be less obvious, however. Suppose the minister of Education came to your campus to speak on the future of post-secondary education. This may be considered part of the ongoing process of public policy making, in that the minister may use the speech to signal a new direction in government thinking, test the reaction of educators and students to existing government policy, defend the status quo, or float trial balloons. All of this activity is public policy.

Let us consider the question of how public policy is made by placing it in broader theoretical perspective. Several models of decision making have been developed to explain how we move from the mobilization of ideas to actual public policy. Imagine yourself, for example, as a key decision-maker in the government. How exactly do you arrive at decisions about which policies government ought to pursue? Do you try to anticipate the demands of the society you serve and initiate action accordingly? Do you wait until societal interests and actors demand action? Once you acknowledge that there are demands for government to respond to an issue, how do you then determine whether the best response is inaction, a new law or regulation, an inquiry, a treaty with a foreign country, education, or something else entirely? The huge array of policy choices demands some sort of decision-making process. This is where models can help us. Models sketch out the parameters of the decision-making process and explain why certain policy choices are made under certain circumstances.

The most basic model says that public policy making is a democratic process in which the will of the people is translated into policy through the work of competitive political parties and elected representatives, who play the crucial role in determining which issues will advance. However appealing it is to think that public policy is a reflection of the "will of the people," this view is simplistic, for it ignores a number of realities. For one, there is no unified, single "will" out there; rather, there is a multiplicity of voices all clamouring for attention. Moreover, this view ignores the fact that sometimes governments act in the absence of public demand. The decision-makers are not simply passive receptors of instructions from the people. They are active players themselves in the development of policy initiatives. Thus, we need more sophisticated theory than traditional democratic theory to explain public policy.

# Models and Theories of Public Policy

Social life is lived out in complex organizations and systems, so to understand policy we must put it in context. For this purpose, we will draw on the work of political scientist Patricia O'Reilly, situating the models and theories along a continuum from the individual to the collective, the simple to the complex, and the rational to the nonrational.[6]

Some policy analysts look more to simplistic or parsimonious models of policy making, while others readily accept and even embrace the idea that policy making is complex and cannot be made to fit into simplistic models. Some focus on the role of individual decision-makers, others on more collective or societal forces affecting decision making. More simplistic models or theories tend to assume that both policy actors and policy analysts are capable of a high degree of rationality that allows them to understand causal affects, such as "Gun registration will lower gun violence in the streets." More complex models or policy stories, however, assume that neither policy actors nor policy analysts are capable of much rationality, especially with regard to causation, leading to a long history of poor policy choices.

We will look first at the micro, individual level and second at the more macro, collective, or social level of some of the main models and theories used in policy analysis.

## The Level of the Individual

At the more micro, individual level, we will look at the rational-comprehensive, public choice, incremental, mixed-scanning, garbage can, and interpretive models and theories. Imagine the following scenario: You are a key decision-maker in the government, charged with the development of a policy on some important matter. You take as a given the following influences on your decision making: the environment that constrains you (i.e., demographic, geographic, urban-industrial, bilingual, multicultural, and other characteristics of Canada); the current distribution of power (both within the country as a whole and within the government); the predominant ideas and attitudes that Canadians hold; the institutional constraints; and the procedural rules of the game you are required to follow.[7] Beyond these factors, though, how do you actually make a policy decision? Consider the following options.

**The Rational-Comprehensive Theory** You wake up in the morning confident that for every policy problem confronting Canadians, there is a rational solution. You arrive at work and are met by a problem. You carefully draw up a list of goals, values, or objectives related to the problem and rank them according to their importance. You next carefully consider various alternatives for dealing with the problem, and examine them thoroughly. In so doing, you weigh the consequences of each alternative by considering the costs and benefits of each, and the advantages and disadvantages of each. Next you compare the alternatives to one another. Finally, you choose the alternative that will allow you to attain your goals, values, and objectives. Voila! You have created public policy through a rational decision-making process. At the end of the day you head home, confident that your rational application of problem-solving skills has saved the day for Canada!

This, in a nutshell, is the **rational-comprehensive model**.[8] This is a widely accepted approach rooted in a Weberian perspective that suggests that policy making is a rational, logical process of making decisions, which involves a number of discrete steps or stages. All the decision-maker has to do is follow the steps, and the result will be effective public policy. For every policy problem, a set of alternative solutions exist. One need only identify these, weigh the costs and benefits of each, and then choose the preferred course of action. The trend toward "evidence-based policy" is a current example of this approach, which has a good deal of appeal, but is not without significant criticisms.[9]

First, problems confronting decision-makers are not always well defined. For instance, when car drivers in major urban centres begin to complain about "squeegee kids," what exactly is the problem? Is it a traffic safety problem, or is it an issue of poverty and a lack of meaningful employment opportunities? Should we treat the symptom (squeegee kids) or the cause (youth alienation)? A second criticism focuses on the unrealistic scenario of unlimited time and resources. There is the assumption that the decision-maker can collect, relatively easily, whatever data is needed to make an informed decision and take the time to reflect on it carefully and thoughtfully. This is clearly not possible in the pressure cooker of the real world. Moreover, many of the "alternatives" proposed will be derived from value judgments on the part of those affected by the issue, and on the part of the decision-makers themselves. In other words, personal biases and interests impinge on the cold, rational calculations that the model calls for. Those interests can become entrenched if past policy decisions have tended to favour them. For instance, there may be broad agreement in society that health-care costs are escalating too rapidly; but health-care professions may be reluctant to accept any fiscal solution to the problem that erodes their privileged financial solution, such as reducing doctors' pay or deinstitutionalizing health care. The rational-comprehensive model has also been criticized for excluding different modes of rationality, based as it is on a narrow Western tradition rooted in ancient Greek and European civilizations. Non-Western cultures (e.g., Aboriginal cultures) may use decision-making processes that rely less on rationalistic traditions of the Western world but that are, nonetheless, every bit as valid.[10] One example is the way Aboriginal people are often portrayed by non-Aboriginal policy-makers. As one Aboriginal leader put it, "the most we can hope for is that we are paraphrased correctly."[11]

Notwithstanding criticisms of the rational-comprehensive model, it nonetheless has a good deal of appeal. In a perfect world, it would indeed be useful to follow the steps it outlines. In an imperfect world, though, perhaps the best we can hope for is to adhere to the main precepts of the model, while recognizing its shortcomings.

**The Public Choice (or Rational Choice) Model**  Another variant of the individual rational model that has gained considerable prominence, particularly in the United States, is that of **rational choice**, or as it is more commonly called in Canada, **public choice**. This theory is heavily influenced by classical liberal economic theory and derived from the view that individuals are rational, self-interested, utility-maximizing creatures. It argues that our pursuit of individual fulfillment is constrained only by a world in which scarcity is the prevailing condition. As noted earlier, there is not enough of everything for everybody at all times. Therefore, we make rational calculations based on self-interest as to how to get the things we want, need, and desire. But we are in a constant competition with other individuals engaged in the same basic process of fulfilling their desires.

Decision making about how to fulfill those desires in the political realm is no different from the process in the economic marketplace, according to this theory. Thus, you make decisions in the economic marketplace on the basis of a rational calculation of your self-interest (e.g., I am hungry. How much money do I have in my pocket? How much is that pizza compared to that submarine sandwich?). So, too, will you support political parties that promote policies most likely to maximize your individual well-being. Here, as policy-maker, you would wake up in the morning confident that every policy problem has a rational solution, but, rather than draw up a list of goals, values, or objectives related to a problem and rank them according to their importance, you would rank them according to your self-interest and choose the alternative that maximizes the attainment of your own goals, values, and objectives. This might mean enacting policies that will bring you the greatest chances for re-election if you are a politician, or that will expand your bureaucratic empire or secure your own position and promotion if you are a public servant. From this perspective, it is folly to talk about some vague "public interest" or "will of the people," since all are engaged in a competition to see their own particular and narrow self-interest prevail. (There are also some important collective elements to public choice theory, to which we will return below.)

The problems with the public choice approach are several-fold. First, the theory assumes a view of human nature that is by no means universally accepted. It assumes that people are always inward-looking, self-interested competitors, while making no allowance for other values, such as altruism and co-operation. Second, even if policy-makers *do* often act in self-interest, it is unlikely that anyone could be *this* rational, for the same reasons discussed above in relation to the rational-comprehensive model. Finally, public choice theory is often criticized for its lack of attention to context. Its proponents are accused of leaving out important elements, such as preference formation (i.e., how do preferences develop, and how do people choose between attractive options?), and the influences and barriers created by institutions, culture, and ideas. The model is also criticized for being unable to deal with change—even of individual interests and preferences. While the simplicity of both the rational-comprehensive and the public choice theory is attractive, it may also be misleading. What both gain in simplicity, they lose in truth.

**The Incremental Model**  Some theorists have turned to an analysis of decision making that is less dependent on full rationality. Returning to your role as decision-maker, suppose you recognize that, realistically, you can only work within a more constrained set of circumstances, considering only some of the policy alternatives and guessing at a limited number of potential consequences. You do not cast your net broadly in the search for solutions; instead, you begin by looking for solutions that require only minimal change from the status quo. In other words, you look for *incremental* change, rather than wholesale change. You engage in a process of give-and-take and mutual consent among interested parties to the issue. This approach allows you to avoid proposing radical change that might involve an all-or-nothing policy solution. Instead, you can offer pragmatic, moderate change to the status quo that does not upset entrenched interests.

Overall, the **incremental model** for understanding policy making has had many proponents. It is an approach with strong explanatory value, particularly as to why government appears to be such a lumbering beast. But this model, too, has been criticized. It has been suggested that incrementalism is really just a conservative approach to policy development, which, by its nature, favours the status quo and entrenched interests. Moreover, in crisis situations, incrementalism may actually be detrimental to finding solutions. Other critics argue that incrementalism's combination of both rationality and pragmatism (or what its leading proponent, the economist Charles Lindblom, termed "the science of muddling through")[12] is still assuming too much rationality or science. Critics emphasize the "muddling through" part of it and de-emphasize the "science" part. Some policy analysts argue there is likely a balance between rationality and incrementalism, sometimes called mixed scanning.

**The Mixed-Scanning Model**  **Mixed scanning** is a model developed by sociologist Amitai Etzioni, who tried to synthesize the most useful aspects of the rational-comprehensive model with those of the incremental model.[13] In this way, the difficulty of attending to every detail inherent in the rational-comprehensive model is overcome, and more profound change is possible than the incremental model allows. In mixed scanning, you explore the main alternatives to the existing policy (rather than all possible alternatives), and thereby avoid paralyzing details and minutiae. An overview of possible change is developed that avoids the conservatism of incrementalism and the unrealistic characteristics of rational-comprehensive approaches. Some applications of the mixed scanning model suggest that the type of decision-making process you employ may depend on your position within the organization's hierarchy. It may be that the lower-level functionaries will lean toward incremental means of decision making, lacking the authority and information for large-scale alterations to policy. The higher officials probably engage in a more comprehensive scanning of the alternatives, given that they have the "big picture" before them.

**The Garbage Can Model** Stronger critics argue that both incrementalism and mixed scanning models assume too much human capacity for rationality. The **garbage can model** of policy making is probably the most famous of the rebuttals to these rationality-based models. Some theorists have argued that the policy process functions more like a garbage can, in which sits a mix of policy problems and potential solutions.[14] However, this is no ordinary garbage can. Even for its proponents, to have left the garbage can contents in their naturally disordered state would have set the policy analysts on the uncomfortable path to (postmodern) anarchy; so, in their quest for order and causation, they have sought process within the garbage can. There they saw "streams," "channels," "communities," and "windows" through which policies flow, with some policies percolating to the top of the policy agenda and others not. Individuals enter and exit the decision arenas/ "garbage cans" such that the policy outcomes are the result of decision making within the garbage can. Because of this, policy "outcomes cannot ordinarily be predicted by rational analysis. . . . [so] official presentations of orderly policy with respect to a problem generally represent post-hoc rationalizatons of what has been decided largely on a non-rational basis."[15] That is, policy-makers make policy as best they can and then justify it.

The garbage can model, as you could probably guess by now, is criticized for being both too complex and irrational by the analysts we have already discussed, and too simple and rational by others, particularly those adhering to an interpretive approach.

**The Interpretive Framework** Critical thinkers employing an **interpretive framework** (and postmodern thinkers, below) argue that no decision-maker can ever be rational and comprehensive because organized life is socially constructed, and in social settings we can never know causation. We do not live in a laboratory, where variables can be controlled in order to understand their interactions. We cannot remove everything but mercury and fish from a lake to see if the fish die. We cannot know for sure that alternative *A* or *B* will cause *X*. To pretend that we can will lead us to poor policies. You, as the policy-maker, would be better off spending your work hours "de-constructing" the "story" behind each policy issue and learning to interpret the meaning behind the actions and intentions of the members of the policy community—including yours and your government's. This, it is argued, would help avoid the lack of understanding that led, for example, to the serious problems of the gun registry in Canada or to the "short" wars in foreign territories that continue for years. Some analysts argue that politics is all one big fight over preferred interpretations.[16] Was the war in Iraq a war against terror and for democracy or against difference and for oil? Was the policy decision to support the war based on fact or interpretation?

While many analysts would accept the argument that meanings are socially constructed, particularly in the macro approaches that follow, and that how we think about the world affects the world, the problem is that the interpretive approach is atheoretical. That is, it does not postulate hypotheses and laws (which is why we are not calling it a model or theory above), while much of political science has—in fancying itself a science—engaged in the pursuit of such hypotheses and laws. For example, if a policy-maker wants to eliminate Aboriginal child poverty, he or she would like to know what causes this poverty and might hypothesize that redistributing public funds to the "head of the Aboriginal household" would result in healthy, happy children who would grow up to be productive citizens. Unfortunately, many of these hypotheses may later prove to be most unscientifically wrong. Many of the more science-oriented analysts (the deductive types) do not seem to worry much about this problem of erroneous hypotheses; they simply continue to use them until bad policy decisions lead to the demise of the hypotheses. Others (inductive, empirical "behaviouralists") go back to the drawing board when the policy fails and try to measure the causes behind the real outcome (failure to eliminate Aboriginal child poverty),[17] leading to an adjustment to their original hypotheses. Interpretive analysts would say they would both be better off just dropping the hypotheses altogether and going into the Aboriginal community to ask its members what the most effective course of action might be. Some very famous American policy failures, such as the Vietnam war and the "war on poverty," were designed by white men in suits who had never lived in, and in most cases never even visited, Vietnam or American inner city ghettos, so it is little wonder their hypotheses about jungle warfare and inner-city poverty were off the mark.[18]

A primary objection to the interpretive method is that it does not lend itself well to comparative analysis. It goes in and teases out the meanings that shape politics, but it does so under specific conditions: for example, it might study a group of Aboriginal children in a particular location at a particular time. It tells "their story," not anyone else's. Good policy analysis, although more accurate, would take a very long time and cost a great deal of money. You as a policy-maker in the public service do not have enough resources for this, and your political boss wants a new policy for the next election. So you turn to hypotheses that, although relatively uninvestigated, at least sound right—such as "more money leads to more happiness."

## The Level of the Collective

Moving along our continuum from the more micro, or individually oriented, to the more macro, or collective-oriented, policy analyses, the latter also sit on a continuum from assumed rationality to nonrationality, and range from the more simplistic to the more complex. We will take an even quicker look at the pluralist model, structural analysis (that is, Marxist, feminist, and **cultural analysis**), neo-institutional and **ideational analysis**, and **post-positivist analysis**. These approaches all share a concern for the broader forces that shape decision making. Many of them are also referred to as "determinists," "structuralists," or "constructionists" because they see politics and policy as socially constructed.

**Pluralism** The **pluralist model** of policy analysis asserts that individuals in society join together to pursue common goals and form groups or organizations to influence policy-makers. These groups are many in number, and, indeed, you probably belong to several at one time. For instance, as a student, you belong to organized interests—such as your student council, or the Canadian Federation of Students—which attempt to influence government. You may also be working full-or part-time, in which case you may belong to a union that presents its views regarding policy to decision-makers. Your employer may belong to a business association as well. There are countless groups and associations that, when they turn their attention toward influencing government, are generally referred to as *interest groups*, *pressure groups*, or *advocacy coalitions*.[19]

Pluralism suggests that there is an ongoing competition among shifting groups in society, who all attempt to influence you, the policy-maker, to create public policy that favours their interests.[20] Individuals may band together with others on the basis of common religion, ethnicity, language, class, occupation, gender, region, ideology, or other factors. Sometimes alliances between groups with common interests will be constructed, occasionally under the banner of a political party. In this view, government is seen as a neutral arbiter or referee for groups with equal opportunity to influence it toward appropriately democratic public policy.

An essential component of this theory is that power is widely diffused in society. A concentration of power is avoided, and no one individual or group can monopolize public policy. As long as groups play by the rules of the game—that is, the broadly accepted societal political values and procedures—they all have a potentially equal influence on public policy making.

More sophisticated versions of the theory point out that the main competition between groups tends to occur at the elite level. The leadership of each interest or coalition of interests engages in bargaining and negotiation with the government. The reward for the interest group elite is policies that promote their interests, and the interests of their supporters. For the political elite, the competition is for votes—and the reward is re-election.[21]

As a description of politics, pluralism provides a powerful explanation for how state policy is made. But the early proponents of this view ignored the fact that, although people do band together into groups around common interests, these groups are patently unequal in resources. Some are wealthy, sophisticated, and powerful. Others are lacking fiscal and other resources, knowledge of the political system, and influence. It is obviously easier, for instance, for the big banks to organize and mobilize their resources to influence government decision-makers than it is for the poor to do so. In a famous formulation of this critique of pluralism, political theorist E.E. Schattschneider wrote, "[T]he flaw in the pluralist heaven is that the heavenly chorus sings with a strong upper-class accent."[22] Moreover, it is argued that some issues that might otherwise be placed on the public policy agenda are actually "organized out" of politics. You will recall that our definition of public policy indicated that it is both *decisions* and *non-decisions* by governments. Thus, powerful groups influence government not only *to do* things on their behalf but also *not to do* things, effectively preventing some issues from ever seeing the light of day.

Interestingly, this theory is not far removed from public choice theory, where individuals rather than groups seek to further their interests. However, public choice departs from the pluralist view that the state is somehow a neutral arbiter among the competing interests in society; in the public choice model, public servants and politicians engage in a complex process of negotiating and bargaining to maximize their own self-interests. Public choice theorists, unlike pluralists, admit that this can lead to poor policy. Or as Hay puts it, "Individual rationality translates into collective irrationality."[23] This is the case in the classic example of the "tragedy of the commons," where individual people, corporations, and states each choose quite rationally to pollute the environment—an irrational action for the collective.[24]

Like all of our approaches, pluralism has metamorphosed after years of critique. In its more sophisticated contemporary form, using the language of pressure groups, political/policy communities, and networks (discussed below), it now recognizes the *power* of entrenched interests and institutions—including those of the policy-maker. This has led to a greater emphasis in public policy on "who and what gets left out"—for example, in the non-decisions we saw earlier in our definition of public policy. Why, for instance, are street people virtually ignored in politics, until the Olympics come to town? This leads us to our next macro approach to policy analysis.

**Structural Analysis** The **structural** or deterministic group of analyses argue that power relations are already structured into our system in class, gender, race, culture, ethnicity, sexuality, disability, and any category that denotes social, political, and economic exclusion. These Marxists, feminists, and cultural analysts argue that policy analysis must start by recognizing this reality, which largely determines any policy outcome. Except for Marxism, which tends to be more the product of intellectuals than of the subjects of its concern—that is, the working class—much of this is often now called "identity politics" because these groups identify with their place in the political relations of power of their society; those who do not are often seen to be operating under a constructed false consciousness—that is, they do not know or are not conscious of their own best interests. In order to make a good policy, you the policy-maker would need to both cope with the complaints of the consciously excluded and see through the false consciousness of the unconsciously excluded—that is, you would have to believe that one group knows its own best interests and listen to that group; but not believe another group and instead decide for yourself what its best interests are on its behalf.

Critics, of course, say that the idea that someone else can decide your self-interest is false, unnecessarily patronizing, and endlessly open to abuse; plus, they criticize the "theories," especially Marxism, that treat this determinism as law. (Capitalism will *necessarily* exploit the working class, and so on.) The rebuttal to this rebuttal is that the new global world is looking more and more as Marx predicted—a world where the rich get richer and the working class get poorer, even if many of the losers in the system are accepting of their fate.

Other structural (now more often called constructivist) analysts who focus on the structured or socially constructed realities of specific groups, such as women, people of colour, Aboriginals, gays and lesbians, the disabled, and so on, are critiqued for their narrow focus. The world, it is argued, is not constructed solely around these groups, as it would seem when one reads these analyses. A broader analysis would take into account their conditions of oppression as well as other factors affecting public policy—that is, their concerns are legitimate and important, but they do not the entire analysis of public policy make.

**The Neo-Institutional Model** Another of the structurally oriented analyses, **institutionalism**, is now, like pluralism, in its "neo" or new stage—which really just means some of the key elements of the old model have been kept, but the model has been rather seriously revamped by its critics. Given that political analysis began as institutionalist analysis, focusing on bodies like Parliament, Cabinet, the Supreme Court, the bureaucracy, and so on, institutionalism has clearly had considerable influence on the "discipline" of political science. Like other structuralist or determinist theories, it has had to back off its bolder claim that institutions determine outcomes, because other analysts came in and provided evidence that *their* favoured analytical categories (for example, ideas and interest groups) had had just as much or more influence on outcome. For example, the Parliament of Canada did not decide as a singular rational institution to legalize gay marriage. The story behind this *institutional* decision is one where interests in a policy community of pressure groups, the media, judicial and government actors, electoral groups, and perhaps even a friend of the prime minister came together under an *ideational* climate of equality and rights discourse and succeeded in pressing the governing institutions into a policy outcome. **Neo-institutionalism** incorporates these forces—the role of other policy community actors and the role of ideas, especially—into its analysis.

Variants of the new institutionalism either lean toward greater simplicity, where the world is more rational (historical institutionalism/path dependency, where history has determined a path toward policy outcomes) or toward greater complexity, where the world is less rational (a more interpretive institutionalism, where the analyst has to look at each case to determine the mix of institutions, ideas, and interests that have helped construct particular policy outcomes). Outright critics, of course, reject neo-institutionalism and utilize either the previously discussed micro or macro approaches, or they move toward the truly anarchic analysis of postmodernism.

**The Postmodern Approach** As we saw earlier, the **postmodern approach** (this approach does not believe in theories, so we cannot refer to it as postmodern theory—although many textbooks do) rejects simplicity and rationalism. In the study of politics and public policy, this approach has been mostly shunned, but its influence is being felt in subtle ways. At a minimum the postmodern approach provides a check on rationalism, recognizing the randomness of life events and the importance of change as a variable in policy studies. At a maximum, however, there can only be discreet context-ridden studies, speaking only to their specific time and place. Pushed to the limit, a postmodern analysis is the "garbage can" without the processes (streams, windows, etc.). It is just a random set of events and actors, and therefore no policy *theory* will give us laws of human action in policy making. We need, this approach argues, to accept this and do the best we can in a world of imperfect knowledge. This approach makes a lot of people nervous and insecure. Its vehement critics sit on both ends of the political spectrum: on the right, where conservatives crave more law and order; and on the left, where radicals see the postmodern approach as politically disempowering. Increasingly, however, more moderate critical analysts are seeing this approach as an important check on human arrogance in a field such as policy studies, which has long failed to live up to the grand promises of its early days.[25]

While we have tried to present this complex and varied literature in simplified form, generally from the individual to the collective, from the simple to the complex, and from the rational to the nonrational, this is necessarily an oversimplification. Many of these models and theories overlap and steal ideas and techniques from each other: for example, there is now a "rational choice institutionalism" and a "rational choice behaviouralism" (not to mention a "neo-neo-synthesis," which we have spared you). What you might take from all of this is that policy-makers exist in a complex, changing world, which they are asked to hold steady and simplify in order to make policy decisions. This is no easy job.

## The Policy Cycle

We can think about policy making as a cyclical exercise involving several distinct but related stages: problem definition and agenda-setting, formulation, implementation, and evaluation. Figure 7.1 depicts the relationship of the parts of the **policy cycle**.[26] Each stage of the process is the responsibility of certain individuals and institutions. For instance, **problem definition and agenda setting** is a broad-based exercise involving many actors inside and outside government. The **formulation** stage is mainly the responsibility of the Cabinet. The Legislature has a limited role here, and public servants play an advisory role. **Implementation** is the responsibility of the public service: the Cabinet and Legislature oversee this stage to ensure that their orders are being followed faithfully. Finally, the **evaluation** stage is the responsibility of the public service, the judiciary, and

**FIGURE 7.1    The Policy Cycle**

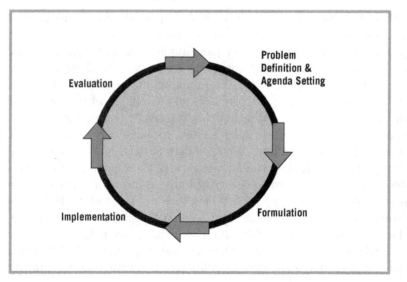

citizens. Public servants are constantly engaged in checking their own work, while citizens (often acting as interest groups or through the media) keep an eye on the government and its officials to help ensure that tax dollars are being spent wisely. In addition, the courts are ever-present to evaluate the constitutionality and legality of public policy.

In reality, the policy-making cycle is less clear-cut than Figure 7.1 depicts. In fact, the boundaries between the stages are rather indistinct, as are the roles assigned to key actors and institutions. The process, rather than unfolding sequentially, may occur simultaneously or in some other order. In any event, the different steps constantly influence one another. Table 7.1 elaborates on the model by showing what each stage means and who is primarily responsible for each stage, and provides examples based on government macro-economic policy choices. The next sections of this chapter deal with problem definition and agenda-setting, formulation, implementation, and evaluation of policy.

## Defining the Policy Problem and Setting the Agenda

How do we as a society decide what the most pressing policy problems are? So many issues confront government and society that there is no easy answer to this question. Why we pay attention to a particular issue and not another is an intriguing question related to an intriguing issue—problem definition. What are the elements of problem definition? How does the problem definition process shape and impact the rest of the policy process? An important part of understanding public policy lies in understanding how problems are defined in the first place, and how they end up on government agendas.

Sometimes problems emerge full-blown in front of us and cannot be avoided. If a pandemic strikes, like the H1N1 virus in 2009, the problem seems rather obvious as does the need to address it with public policy. Other issues are more ambiguous. This is important because how a problem is defined in the first place influences the policy response to it, as Box 7.1 shows. Who gets to define the problem—in other words, whose bias is most successfully mobilized—heavily determines the nature of the policy response, or even indeed whether there is to be a policy response or not (mobilization of bias is discussed below). Personal values and ideology may shape our perception of a problem. How an issue is "framed," then, is very important. A relatively new political creature that has emerged to help define policy problems is the so-called "spin-doctor" of the political system. These can be lobbyists engaged by an interest group to promote their point of view, or political staff or politicians who do the same thing. Their job is essentially to show the decision-makers that their suggested course of action is preferable because they have been able to define the problem in terms that lead ineluctably to their solutions. For instance, the Harper government promoted a tough "law and order" agenda by arguing that Canadian communities were increasingly unsafe and that only tougher sentencing and longer jail times would make the streets safe again. This reflected their ideological predispositions toward security and order, but did not reflect the facts of already decreased levels of crime. They nonetheless tried to frame or spin the issue to suit their definition of the problem.

**TABLE 7.1    The Policy Cycle**

| Policy Stages | What it Means | Who Does It | Examples |
|---|---|---|---|
| Problem Definition and Agenda-Setting | How problems are perceived and defined, command attention, and get onto the political agenda | Executive, legislative, and judicial branches of government; interest groups; political parties; media; citizens | The business class argued that the poor performance of the Canadian economy in the 1990s resulted from too much government intervention in the economy, resulting in large government debts and deficits. |
| Policy Formulation | The design and drafting of policy goals and strategies for achieving them, involving the use of policy analysis | Executive branch of government | The federal cabinet led by the prime minister and finance minister charted a course of severe cutbacks in government spending |
| Policy Implementation | Provision of institutional resources for putting policies and programs into effect within a bureaucracy | Public service | Transfer payments to the provinces and territories were drastically reduced, the public service was cut, and services to citizens were pared back in the 1995–1996 budget |
| Policy Evaluation | Measurement and assessment of policy and program effects, including success or failure of process, output, and outcome | Executive, legislative and judicial branches of government; interest groups; political parties; media; citizens | By the early 2000s, the deficit was eliminated and debt reduced, but health care, social services, and education programs were reduced, leading to new problem definition and agenda-setting exercises |

**Source:** Adapted from Michael E. Kraft and Scott R. Furlong, *Public Policy: Politics, Analysis and Alternatives* (Washington DC: CQ Press, 2007): 71.

## BOX 7.1    Problem Definition—The Case of Alcohol

How would you define the policy problems associated with alcohol consumption? Is it a commodity to be promoted to generate much needed government revenues? Is it a public health issue? Try to ascertain the key policy problem as you consider the following article:

*In 2005, Canadians downed the equivalent of 7.9 litres of pure alcohol for every drinker and teetotaller over age 15. And many of us drink often—consuming about 30 per cent more than the world average. The social cost of our new lifestyle is staggering: $14.6 billion in 2002, and no doubt more in the years since. The health care bill alone is $3.3 billion—higher than the price tag to treat cancer.*

*We spent 1.6 million days in the hospital because of illnesses and accidents caused by people under the influence of alcohol. For the first time, more people died from liver cirrhosis—regarded as a benchmark of a country's problem drinking—than on the roads in drunken car crashes. And the International Agency for Research on Cancer is about to announce a link between alcohol and two of the most commonly diagnosed cancers as well.*

*Yet government has treated alcohol like a gold mine, with policies that encourage us to drink and even handicap the struggle for sobriety once people become addicted.*

*Until now. Health Canada is set to unveil a proposed National Strategy on Alcohol that will include 41 recommendations drafted by experts in alcohol treatment, addiction research, provincial liquor monopolies—even distillers and breweries— to shift alcohol's innocent image as a benign indulgence and curb dangerous drinking.*

*"Alcohol has a huge toll on society, and that toll is slowly increasing," says Juergen Rehm, chair in addiction policy at the University of Toronto's faculty of medicine.*

*"It is always surprising why a society like Canada is willing to tolerate such a high cost. The majority of Canadians drink, and in their heads, 'The cost of alcohol is the alcoholics. It's not us.' And that's just wrong."*

*We suspected frat boys were prone to binge drinking. And this is backed by the Canadian Addiction Survey, a major study of drinking and drug habits. It found that young men, including teenagers below the legal drinking age, imbibe at least five drinks at a time—a level researchers deem hazardous.*

*A bigger surprise is what the survey reveals about the rest of us. In 2004, 79.3 per cent of Canadians confessed to drinking, which, contrary to our growing obsession with fitness and diet, is nearly a 10-per-cent jump from a decade ago. And these numbers tell only part of the story: The level of drinking professed in the survey accounts for just 32 per cent of the bottles actually sold in liquor stores, bars and restaurants. Whether we are deluded or deceptive, Canadians grossly underestimate the number of drinks we quaff.*

At the LCBO, business is certainly booming. Since the liquor monopoly began its renovations 11 years ago—geared to women, who drink less than men but shop more—it has handed over richer and richer dividends to the Ontario government. Last year, it reported sales of $3.68 billion and poured $1.5-billion in profits and taxes into provincial coffers. After slumping in the 1970s and 1980s due to growing awareness of health issues and the perils of impaired driving, alcohol sales have also staged a spectacular recovery in the rest of the country. Statistics Canada reports that we purchased $16.8-billion in wine, beer and spirits in 2005—and that excludes the market in home brew and make-your-own beer and wine (which accounts for an estimated 10 per cent of alcohol consumption). . . .

All of this imbibing would be good, clean fun were it not for the repercussions—that whopping $14.6-billion in deaths, disease, disability, hospital stays, missed days at work and police time in 2002 alone.

In fact, the tally from booze—cheerfully marketed and sold by government in almost every neighbourhood in Canada outside Alberta (where alcohol is sold in private liquor stores)—dwarfs the cost of illicit street drugs.

In the courts, more than 30 per cent of criminal offences have been linked to alcohol, with more federal inmates committing violent crimes addicted to alcohol than to drugs. On the roads, an average of four people a year are killed and about 200 injured in crashes sparked by impaired driving.

And it is not only the falling-down alcoholics who are ringing up most of the bills. Most of the damage—ranging from suicide to fetal alcohol syndrome to the incalculable social costs of broken marriages—is inflicted by people without an addiction tying one on. "Most of the harms are problems of intoxication," says Dr. Stockwell, who calculates that 73 per cent of alcohol purchased in Canada is consumed at levels above the albeit conservative Canadian guidelines for safe drinking. (No more than two drinks a day; nine a week for women, 14 for men.) "And a lot of those are just regular people in the population, not people in clinics. They're just occasional heavy drinkers. It's not just focused on a small number of alcoholics. It's spread right across the population."

This might account for the $3.3-billion medical bill for injuries and diseases such as liver cirrhosis resulting from drinking—which exceeded the $2.7-billion spent on treating cancer in 2002. And explain why, according to a major study on the cost of our drinking habit published last year, alcohol killed 8103 people in 2002—a 20 per cent jump in a decade. More than 1200 hard-core drinkers died from liver cirrhosis. Hundreds of others committed suicide, which is more often triggered by alcohol than by either depression or schizophrenia.

Researchers are discovering more and more evidence to implicate alcohol in our rising cancer rates too.

The World Health Organization has long ranked alcohol as one of the top 10 risk factors for disease on the planet, and its cancer research agency has included ethanol—the alcohol we drink—on a hotlist of the 100 nastiest, Class 1 carcinogens for two decades.

But now the International Agency for Research on Cancer is about to finger alcohol as a cause of even more types of cancer than previously understood. In coming days, the agency is set to announce that breast and colorectal cancers—two of the most common diagnosed worldwide—will officially join the list with mouth, larynx, throat, esophageal and liver cancers. The IARC scientists who reviewed the international research and made this call were stunned not only at how convincing alcohol's link to these two cancers was, but also by the low levels of drinking that raise risk.

"In our view, it's quite remarkable that alcohol consumption is related to female breast cancer," says Dr. Robert Baan, a senior scientist at the IARC's headquarters in Lyon, France. "The literature with breast cancer is with tens of thousands of patients. That's an enormously large study, and they have been able to establish with statistical confidence that already a very moderate consumption of alcohol increases the risk for breast cancer."

A casual drink or two a day, he says, raises a woman's risk of being diagnosed with breast cancer by 13 per cent.

"It's estimated that 2 billion people around the world are regular alcohol consumers, and there are 76 million people around the world who have a diagnosable disease or disorder connected to their habit,"

he says. "From a public health perspective, the global burden related to alcohol consumption in terms of morbidity and mortality is really considerable."

All of which raises a troubling paradox. When Ottawa and the provinces rake in liquor revenues—$7.68-billion in taxes and profits in 2004—it's a bonanza for our schools, our hospitals, and our highways. But if we are drinking ever more, with most alcohol being consumed at risky levels and more of us becoming sick and disabled, should our governments be feeding our habit?

At the LCBO, being socially responsible is part of the corporate mission statement. On every sleek advertisement is an admonition to "drink responsibly." And the retailer takes enormous pride in the 1.7 million people its trained staff challenged at the cash register last year for appearing intoxicated or below the provincial drinking age of 19. Still, addiction experts charge that the lure of lucrative profits and the nagging threat of widespread privatization of liquor stores have blinded governments and their alcohol empires to their original role of controlling—not promoting—the sale of booze.

"I see the LCBO as having a social role of trying to help minimize the risks of drinking," says Dr. Rehm. "And all those other activities which directly or indirectly promote the image of alcohol being a necessary part of our lifestyle and having no negative consequences is not helping the overall society and it's not helping to reduce the social costs associated with alcohol."

*Mind you, most of us are not exactly lobbying the government to restrict our access to booze. Who among us strolls along the aisles of abundance, with their promise of good cheer, and wishes there were less choice and higher prices? Consider a study on our perceptions of alcohol released by the Canadian Centre on Substance Abuse. It found that while the social and economic costs of drinking are more than double those of illicit drug use, only one in four Canadians rate alcohol abuse as a "serious problem" while close to half consider drugs as such. And the more people drink, the less apt they were to regard alcohol abuse as a pressing issue.*

*Or take smoking. "We almost religiously hunt smokers in the public and we glorify alcohol," observes Dr. Rehm, "even though on a world scale, alcohol and smoking have about the same net burden of disease."...*

*"Alcohol is the key to an awful lot," Dr. Stockwell says. "There's a lot of revenue in Canada. It's a huge industry with hundreds of thousands of people employed across the country—major manufacturers with lots of power and influence. And it's a commodity which most of us use and really value and enjoy.*

*"And so, if the government gets uppity and increases the price or restricts our access, we're not happy ... There have been general elections lost over government raising the tax on alcohol."*

**Source**: Margaret Philp, "Alcoholics Accelerated," *Globe and Mail* (March 24, 2007): F1. Reprinted with permission.

Once a problem is defined, it needs to get on the government's policy agenda. Some issues get onto the government's agenda automatically—for instance, passing an annual budget, approving funds for existing and new programs, and filling important positions like Supreme Court appointments. But it is unavoidably true that there are more issues to be dealt with than there is time on the political agenda. So what determines which optional items end up there? Policy scholar John Kingdon suggests problem, policy, and political "streams" flow through society, which, when they intersect, create opportunities taken advantage of by influential "policy entrepreneurs." These are leaders inside and outside government with a strong interest in a policy who exert their energies and skills to get an issue onto the government's agenda.[27] The problem stream is composed of the many and various sources of information available about an issue. This may be found in government reports, studies by think tanks, media reports, or other sources. Given the cacophony of noise emanating from various policy problems, sometimes a "focusing event" is necessary to propel an issue to the forefront of the government's agenda. Clearly a natural disaster like a flood or ice storm, or an act of terrorism like the September 11, 2001 attacks serve to focus policy-makers' attention and place issues squarely on their agenda. Sometimes serendipity intervenes. Newly elected Prime Minister Brian Mulroney was looking for a signature policy initiative when the report of a major royal commission landed on his desk.

He jumped on the commission's definition of what ailed the Canadian economy and proceeded to negotiate a free trade agreement with the United States even though free trade had been nowhere on previous governments' agendas for 50 years, and Mulroney himself had previously opposed such an initiative.[28]

The *policy stream* refers to the available policy options. Policy proposals can be numerous and originate in a number of places—from within or outside government. Ministers will make speeches floating trial balloons, departments will release studies, the media will publish exposés, academics will release learned studies, and so on. The ideas generated generally circulate among those most intimately involved with and concerned about a given policy problem. There are many interests and actors in the policy process. Analysts of public policy sometimes try to capture the full constellation of interests and actors—both governmental and nongovernmental—that might have a stake in an issue and therefore seek to influence public policy. As such, they talk about a **policy community** as constituting all the actors in the policy-making process that have an interest in a particular policy field. These actors can be either primary (lead actors) or secondary (actors with a tertiary interest, as with the "attentive public"). A policy community can be distinguished from a **policy network**, which includes only those like-minded actors that might collaborate with other like-minded groups to advance an issue (the term is also used to refer to the patterns of relations among members of a policy community).[29]

Since only the fittest ideas survive in the policy stream struggles to define problems and get them on the agenda, Kingdon compares this process to natural selection, "The generation of policy alternatives is best seen as a selection process, analogous to biological natural selection. In what we have called the policy primeval soup, many ideas float around, bumping into one another, encountering new ideas, and forming combinations and recombinations."[30]

Kingdon also refers to a "political stream" where political events have an impact on agenda setting. One of the most obvious is a change of government following an election. When Harper succeeded Chrétien, a number of policy initiatives near and dear to the Liberals were quickly dropped and replaced by those that the Conservatives thought were more important. When a government comes into power with a predisposition toward free markets rather than state intervention, policy agendas are affected. When the national mood favours lower taxes or greater accountability in government, policy agendas are affected. When powerful interest groups manage to insert their issues into the consciousness of decision-makers, the agenda can be affected. Kingdon explains, "In the political stream, participants build consensus by bargaining—trading provisions for support, adding elected officials to coalitions by giving them concessions that they demand, or compromising from ideal positions that will gain wider acceptance"[31]; hence the emergence of certain issues on the agenda.

The question of agenda-setting also raises issues about the nature of human knowledge and the social construction of that knowledge.[32] As we saw above, early scholars of public policy assumed a fair measure of rational decision-making in the process of defining policy problems and setting policy agendas. So-called "objective" analysis of issues would lead to "objective" prescriptions. It was generally thought that policy problems were matters for "experts" who had the technical capability to determine what issues were of real significance and therefore should be placed on the policy agenda. Later work, however, challenged this assumption and argued that problems were socially constructed phenomena requiring agreement over what constituted the reality of an issue and whether it required a solution. Therefore, even recognizing that a problem exists, much less that it should be on the agenda of governments, is a process of contestation between differing subjective interpretations of what belongs, for instance, in the private sphere and what belongs in the public sphere.

Clearly problem definition and agenda-setting are vitally important parts of the policy cycle. The determination of which issues "make it" and which do not sets the stage for all subsequent action (or inaction) on the part of public administrators. The way in which issues are recognized and propelled forward is an important determinant of what governments do and do not do in the various stages of public policy.

## Formulating Public Policy: How Are Decisions Made?

Policy formulation is the next step in the policy cycle. Simply put, policy formulation is "the development of proposed courses of action to help resolve a public problem."[33] The first order of decision making with regard to policy formulation is a choice—to do nothing, or to do something. Government may decide to do nothing for a number of reasons. Perhaps the issue is outside the government's jurisdiction (a sometimes handy excuse when one level of government does not want to wade into controversial issues). Sometimes it lacks the resources to tackle an issue. Sometimes it assumes that the parties directly affected can work out a self-regulated policy for their problem. If, however, the government decides to take action, it has at its disposal a huge array of options. Recall that in the policy stream, there is a constant flow of information that can be used to assess policy actions. The political, economic, administrative, and social costs of policy options need to be studied, along with the likely effectiveness of various options. The field of policy analysis makes a contribution here, as policy actors collect and compare data, information, and ideas that will likely contribute to salient policy choices. Failure to undertake solid policy analysis can be fatal to the prospects of a course of action.

The key decision-makers, where public policy formulation is concerned, are politicians and public servants. More specifically, the prime minister and Cabinet enjoy the ultimate decision-making authority. They are assisted by senior public servants but retain the final "yes" or "no" in determining the government's policy. Having said this, remember our discussion of the politics–administration dichotomy in chapter 1, where it was pointed out that this is the theory, but that sometimes practice is different given the high level of expertise and potential influence in the hands of public servants. Parliament plays the role of scrutinizing government and passing legislation, and the courts play the role of judging whether policy is "legal" or not. This oversimplifies the complex functions and activities of the executive, legislative, and judicial branches of government but, nonetheless, summarizes the main policy roles of each. However, interest groups also influence policy formulation. They often have a great deal of expertise and information related to particular issues and can serve a vital function in educating policy-makers. Policy-makers must also retain some detachment from interest groups since those groups represent vested interests, whereas the public servants are supposed to govern in the general interest. The issue of "capture" of public servants and politicians by interest groups is an ongoing concern.

Policy formulation can be conceptualized as occurring in phases.[34] In the appraisal phase, data and information are gathered and integrated. The dialogue phase involves discussion among interested actors—some with opposing viewpoints, some with coincident viewpoints. This may involve anything from broadly participatory public meetings to closed get-togethers with expert representatives within and outside government in dialogues that may be structured or informal. Then next phase is formulation per se, where public officials, having had a chance to consider appraisals of policy options and to hear the dialogue around various options, draft a proposed course of action. Not everyone will be happy with developments at this phase. Policy choices more often than not involve winners and losers, and the losers do not always go quietly into the night. Once recommendations have been made at the formulation phase, stakeholders will often renew their efforts during the consolidation phase. Feedback is provided here on the policy choice, which may cause decision-makers to go back to the appraisal and/or dialogue phases, or they may forge ahead with the choice they have articulated.

Canadian governments do more now than they have ever done. They pass more laws, create more regulations, spend and raise more money, and employ more people. As the scope of government activity has increased, the machinery of government and the decision-making process have become more complex. The question "How much government is too much?" is central to the issue of public policy formulation. Once we figure out the proper scope of government, then we can know what areas government ought to be acting in.[35] But how do we answer that question? Fundamentally, we must make value judgments to determine what areas of life government should be involved in. These value judgments are shaped and constrained by our socialization, which includes our family life, education, workplace experience, exposure to popular culture, and so on. Once we identify our core values as a society, we construct constitutional rules that influence the actions of government, and then the laws, regulations, Crown corporations, and so on, through which public policy is formulated.

Thus, much of public policy formulation comes down to value judgments about how to achieve societal and private goals within the confines of a broad set of "rules of the game." For example, as a society we may generally agree that the education of children is a predominant value. We long ago agreed as a society to permit the state to take on the major responsibility for this function. Put another way, we determined that the "private" issue of education, once achieved in the home, should completely become a "public" issue of state concern. Beyond this, however, we must also decide what specific policy should be formulated to realize this societal goal. Once decided, we must then figure out how to implement that policy.

## Implementing Public Policy: How Does Anything Get Done?

What exactly happens once a policy decision has been taken? First, the decision must be implemented. It is of little use for the government to decide on a course of action if there is no effective way of carrying out its intentions. Following this, the policy must be evaluated to see that it is successfully attaining the objectives that the government has set out.

In theory, the implementation stage of the policy process is dominated by public servants, who are mainly responsible for carrying out the will of the elected representatives who made the key decision to proceed with a particular policy. In an ideal policy-making world, politicians impart directions to public servants, who then faithfully carry them out. The Cabinet and legislature retain a role in this stage of the policy cycle by overseeing the actions of the public servants. Part of the implementation process involves deciding exactly which policy instrument will be used to realize the government's goals. A variety of options is available, and we will discuss the choice of governing instrument. First, though, we look at some problems associated with implementation.

When scholars initially turned their attention to the implementation process, they noticed that there was often a disturbing gap between the expectations of political actors who formulated policy, and the actions of bureaucratic actors who implemented it. For instance, if legislators passed a law to eliminate child poverty, why has poverty among children actually been increasing? If tough new environmental standards have been passed, why has pollution been getting worse? In these and countless other examples, there seems to be a disconnect between intention and action, leading to the conclusion that implementation of policy making deserves more thorough attention.[36]

In fact, the implementation of public policy is complicated by numerous factors.[37] Governments must often draft legislation in broad and general terms. Indeed, the objectives of policy are often unclear and may be expressed in fuzzy, multiple, or contradictory terms. It is then left up to the public servants to interpret the meaning of those terms and, ultimately, to provide the actual content of the policy in day-to-day implementation. What this implies is that public servants enjoy a generous amount of *discretion* in translating into action the legislative expectations of their political masters. In turn, narrow bureaucratic goals may displace those of the legislators. For instance, if legislation calls for reforming the delivery of certain social services, and if this threatens the positions of public servants in the department responsible, those reforms may be sabotaged in the implementation stage. Conversely, the reforms may be exaggerated if their impact is to expand a bureaucratic empire. This may then lead to conflict with other administrative agencies over the appropriate areas of involvement of the first agency, with the result that implementation is thwarted by bureaucratic in-fighting. A further layer of interference may occur when the central agencies (i.e., Finance Department, Treasury Board, the Privy Council Office, or the Prime Minister's Office) stick their noses into the process. Thus, in the implementation stage, the content of policy can be modified, elaborated, or even reversed.

Within the bureaucracy itself, then, there may be resistance to implementing policy. Old habits, ideas, and programs die hard. As a result, when a department is given instructions to draft the regulatory framework for enacting a new law, it may draft those regulations so as to minimize change to customary procedures. There may also be costs associated with change that are difficult to overcome. Prevailing values may be challenged, which is often compounded by ways that implementers' perspectives differ form those of the policy's formulators. The individuals enacting a program may decide, for whatever reason, that they will focus on the one or two objectives with which they are most comfortable—leaving the other objectives to fall by the wayside. The question of political feasibility also often gets in the way of implementation: whatever the merits of a policy, if it is too politically costly, politicians may resist implementing it.

Another actor is the front-line worker, who actually meets with the public and is responsible for delivering a policy, program, or service. These could include the people who issue your driver's licence, give you a parking ticket, pick up your garbage, collect your bus fare, and so on. Consider your teachers as front-line workers, for instance. Each is instructed to follow policy that is sent down from "on high" from the Ministry of Education, but despite the best intentions of legislators and public servants who dictate through policy that children are entitled to a "good education," they are not the ones responsible for delivering that policy to its ultimate users: children in the schools. It is the teacher—the front-line worker—who holds that responsibility. Thus, the front-line worker has a great deal of influence over the quality of the delivery of services and often has a direct influence on a given policy's success or failure.

Since Canada is a federal state, initiatives at one level of government can be affected by other levels. The federal government and the provinces are engaged in numerous shared-cost and joint federal–provincial programs; but disputes constantly arise as to how to implement these programs. For instance, under the Canada Health Act, the federal government articulated a set of five principles that guide the delivery of health services by the provinces. Health care is a provincial responsibility but since the federal government contributes the lion's share of funding, it feels that it is entitled to set some of the rules regarding implementation. This has caused a long series of disputes between the two levels of government over policy implementation.[38]

In addition, forces outside government influence the implementation stage. Policy decisions are often the result of compromise and negotiation between interests with conflicting views. A decision will spawn both proponents and opponents, winners and losers. In many cases, the losers will not simply give up and go away once a policy is announced. Rather, they will move from trying to influence the formulation stage to influencing the implementation stage. They may, for instance, carefully monitor implementation to ensure that whatever regulations and guidelines have been enacted adhere to the letter of the law. Or they may even take the extreme step of trying to impede the policy's implementation. Lobbying, protests, strikes, and court challenges are among the range of responses available to opponents of a policy.

Ever since the enactment of the Charter of Rights and Freedoms, implementing public policy has been subjected to heightened scrutiny. The courts have always been an avenue to check the constitutional legality of legislation but have done so primarily with regard to whether a law was within the jurisdiction of the level of government that passed it. With the advent of the Charter, however, the constitutional validity of laws can be challenged on the basis of whether they violate human rights. The range of policies subjected to Charter challenges has been incredibly broad, including abortion, fetal rights, mandatory retirement, strikes and secondary picketing, Sunday shopping, children's advertising, minority language education rights, French-only signs, official bilingualism, extradition, drunk driving, cruise missile testing, narcotics, Breathalyzer testing, refugees, assisted suicide, pornography, hate literature, political rights of public servants, constituency boundaries, dangerous offenders, sexual assault, battered women, prisoners' rights, prostitution, and other issues. Analysis of Charter cases in the first 10 years of the Charter's life reveals that legal rights, mainly dealing with the enforcement of criminal law, were the most common basis of Charter cases. The result, according to some analysts, is that the Charter has effectively created a "new constitutional code of conduct for Canadian police officers in dealing with suspects and accused persons, and in the process has pushed the Canadian criminal process away from the 'crime control' side of the ledger toward the 'due process' side of the ledger."[39] In other words, the legality of the implementation of policies has served as the most common form of Charter violation complaint.

It may appear from this brief survey of some of the factors affecting implementation that policy as articulated by formulators does not stand a chance of being enacted as planned. Yet a tremendous amount of progress is made, year after year,

by governments in enacting a panoply of policy. Success may depend on the means and resources available to government. That is, once we sort out the thorny problem of whether the government *ought* to be involved in a particular issue, we must also ask what *form* that involvement should take. Governments have a variety of tools at their disposal, and we refer to the selection of these tools as the "choice of **governing instruments**."

Unfortunately, the process of selecting appropriate instruments is rarely straightforward. It can be influenced by any of a number of factors, such as by the way things have been done in the past, by dominant ideas and ideologies, by the personal preferences of particular politicians or public servants, by the availability of resources, by the relative strengths of interest groups trying to influence the government, by the media, by public opinion, and so on. For example, taxation on personal and corporate income has become one of the chief policy instruments of modern governments. Yet now, most governments feel severely constrained since more personal taxation may invoke a defeat at the election polls or taxpayers' revolt, while more corporate taxation might provoke a "capital strike" by business.

Even knowing which policy instrument to use leaves unanswered the question of whether the government has the *policy capacity* to achieve its goals. Since the 1990s there has been a growing literature on policy capacity,[40] defined as "the institutional ability to conduct policy analysis and implement its results effectively and efficiently."[41] Governments have recently experienced a reduced capacity to develop policy, which may be attributed to factors such as cutbacks and restructuring exercises, in which policy analysts and policy shops in government were often the first things reduced or eliminated. At the same time, there has been increased focus on management as opposed to policy. However, as political scientist Leslie Pal reports, "policy is popular again."[42] Governments are realizing that to achieve their objectives, they must place a greater emphasis on developing strong policy capacity.

Part of the issue of determining the means by which policy is to be achieved is tied up with the notion of what goal is to be served. Justice? Efficiency? Equality? Security? What do we do when these goals clash? What standard do we use to measure the success or failure of a particular policy?[43] These are difficult questions. Consider, for instance, the great free-trade debate of the late 1980s. As the Canadian government sought an economic policy to ensure growth and prosperity, it was confronted by two value-based arguments. The pro-free-traders argued that the economic gains from free trade were unassailable and that the goal of economic efficiency should guide which policy instrument (free trade) ought to be adopted. The anti-free-traders, on the other hand, argued that intangible values, such as national identity and culture, would be threatened by free trade, and, therefore, they preferred the policy option of diversified trade and limited tariffs.[44]

Related to these value problems are those associated with cost. Policies, more often than not, have some kind of price tag attached. It is up to government to determine whether a particular price—financial and/or political—is worth paying for a given policy. First of all, there is the "dollars and cents" aspect to policy: the fiscal means must be present in order to embark on policy. But there is also the political question of whether a particular action (or inaction) will cost votes. The policy of regional economic development grants, for instance, may be popular in depressed regions of the country that require economic assistance to spur employment and growth; but that policy may be unpopular in the regions that have to help pay for the grants via transfer payments from the rich provinces to the poorer ones. All these issues influence the question of the "means" of public policy.

Politics is said to be about who gets what, when, and how. The making of public policy partly answers that question. When you get something in the form of government policy, someone else may be deprived of something since there are finite resources to spread around. For instance, you may desire a policy that calls for lower personal taxes. This may mean, however, that the quality of health care must diminish because there is now less money to spend on it or that tuition must go up since governments have less tax revenue to put into the post-secondary education system. Thus, the issue of who benefits and who pays is central to policy decisions. Given that resources are scarce and there is not enough of everything to go around for everyone at all times, governments must make difficult decisions about how to apportion the resources of society through the policies they enact.

How governments deal with this through public policy is related again to values. In Canada, one dominant value is that those least able to help themselves should be assisted by those who can. This has led to controversy over the role of government in redistributing wealth through taxation policy, social programs, regional economic development programs, and so on. Major government expenditures to the less well-off regions of Canada through policy tools—such as equalization programs, income transfers to individuals (e.g., Employment Insurance), and industrial assistance programs that subsidize businesses—are controversial, even if most Canadians subscribe to the principle that the better-off should help the less well-off. Thus, governments are constantly trying to strike a balance in devising policy that will help redistribute wealth but not infringe too much on the right to private property or on the workings of the free market.

One answer to the question of how resources are spent or apportioned by government comes from the observation that policy choices reflect the **mobilization of bias**. This means that any individual or group with a particular interest or concern (a "bias") can organize and mobilize itself to influence government to act in its favour. At first blush, this argument would tend to support the view that Canadian society is democratic, in that anyone can mobilize herself and influence government. Closer inspection, however, reveals that those with the fiscal and organizational means will tend to be more successful at getting the attention of government and are more likely to have their interests served by public policy than are the unorganized, the marginalized, and the less well-off. Thus, it is best to remember that the decision-making process, where public policy is concerned, is weighted in favour of certain actors in Canadian society, and that the question of how the scarce resources of society are divided up is never the result of an equal competition.

Finally, besides the material or financial costs of resources, we must also consider symbolic resources that governments spend and save. Perception is vitally important in politics and public administration—and perception is often shaped by symbols. The flag is a symbol of national unity that costs relatively little to disseminate but that can reap large rewards or cause deep division. Remember that the Sponsorship Program had, at its base, the simple initiative of "showing the flag" more in Quebec to enhance the federal government's profile in *la belle province*. Careless use of resources entirely displaced the intended symbolic message and replaced it with another, involving corruption, cronyism, and misappropriation of public funds by the Liberal Party. The ensuing scandal even partly caused the defeat of a government![45] The Charter of Rights and Freedoms, language laws, and multiculturalism are all powerful symbols as well, which can be invoked virtually without having to spend a cent. Thus, it is wise not to overlook the importance of symbols in calculating the resources available to governments in the making of public policy.

**Choice of Governing Instrument** As we noted above, one of the key steps in implementing any policy involves deciding on the means by which the policy will be enacted. One way of exploring this question is to look at governing instruments, defined as "the major ways in which governments seek to ensure compliance, support and implementation of public policy."[46] In other words, is it better to use the carrot, the stick, or the sermon?[47] Most studies of instrument choice trace their intellectual origins to the work of Theodore Lowi, who was among the first to categorize the types of instruments available to governments, as well as to differentiate them according to how coercive they were.[48] As well, a classic study of instrument choice was produced by the Economic Council of Canada over 25 years ago.[49] Recently, Canadian governments have shown an increased interest in issues of instrument choice and implementation.[50] We will look at various governing instruments in terms of their level of intrusiveness in the economy and in the lives of citizens. This expands upon the issues raised earlier regarding the scope of government, while also bringing to mind the related issues of means and resources.

Fundamentally, when government creates public policy, it is trying to get us to adjust our behaviour in some way. When it passes a law calling, for example, for a stop sign at the corner of Maple and Elm streets, this requires us to adjust our driving habits. When it provides tax breaks for purchasing Registered Retirement Savings Plans (RRSPs), this encourages us to adjust our savings and investment habits. When we fail to comply with the state in these matters, various penalties can be applied. Failure to stop at a stop sign might result in a ticket. Failure to purchase RRSPs might mean higher real tax rates and a diminished quality of life when we retire. In short, the state has at its disposal a range of policy instruments to influence our behaviour, backed up by a range of sanctions and coercive measures to ensure our compliance.

But what motivates policy-makers to select certain policy instruments and not others? For one answer, consider the role of the state in terms of the level of

intrusiveness of policy instruments, an approach outlined by political scientist
Nicolas Baxter-Moore. *Intrusiveness* means "the extent to which various instruments as means of government intervention intrude directly and publicly on
private decision making."[51] Baxter-Moore developed a scale of government
intrusiveness, in which he categorized the various instruments available
for government use (see Figure 7.2). The scale has the advantage of accounting for
both decisions and non-decisions of government and thus accords with our
definition of public policy. It ranges from minimum to maximum degrees of
intrusiveness.

The scale is divided first into non-decisions and decisions. Each of these categories is then subdivided into degrees of state intrusiveness, ranging from minimum to maximum. At the minimum end of the scale is the idea that conflict
between citizens is privatized. Indeed, government may concretely signal that it
refuses to get involved, as in instances where certain professions are given the
power to regulate themselves rather than have the government regulate them.
Medicine and law, for instance, are self-governing professions. There is no government public policy at this point, but moving across the scale we encounter our first
example of government intrusiveness. This takes the form of a *symbolic gesture or
response*, wherein, for instance, the prime minister makes a speech or establishes a
royal commission or task force to inquire into an issue without actually committing
the government to take a course of action. It also includes conferences, information, studies and research, the reorganization of government departments, and
other similar devices.

Privatization of conflict and symbolic responses both fall under the heading of
non-decisions. Other policy instruments fall under the heading of decisions, which
in turn is subdivided into incentives and directives. Incentives begin with exhortation, which means political and bureaucratic leaders attempt to secure the compliance of citizens without threats or inducements: the government uses persuasion to

**FIGURE 7.2    A Reconstruction of the Policy Instruments Continuum**

| | | | |
|---|---|---|---|
| **Non-Decisions** | | Privatization | Minimum |
| | | Symbolic Responses | |
| **Decisions** | Incentives (Indirect Public Intervention) | Exhortation | |
| | | Tax Expenditures | |
| | | Public Spending | **Degree of State Intrusiveness** |
| | Directives (Direct Public Intervention) | Regulation | |
| | | Taxation | |
| | | Public Ownership | |
| | | State of Emergency | Maximum |

**Source:** Adapted from Nicolas Baxter-Moore, "Policy Implementation and the Role of the State: A Revised
Approach to the Study of Policy Instruments," in Robert J. Jackson et al., *Contemporary Canadian Politics* (Scarborough: Prentice-Hall, 1987).

get us to buy into what it is trying to accomplish. Moving along the scale of intrusiveness, we next find tax expenditures, which permit individuals and corporations to retain money that would otherwise normally go to taxes. This policy instrument essentially entails the failure to do something (e.g., collect taxes) that might otherwise have been done.

Public spending is the next most intrusive category of public policy. It includes items such as subsidies, grants, and transfer payments, loans and loan guarantees, and some cases of joint public–private ownership, where the government is a minority shareholder. Exhortation, tax expenditures, and public spending are examples of incentives involving indirect public intervention. Directives are the final category, within which the government takes an increasingly intrusive role. Regulation is the first example of a directive but is somewhat less intrusive than taxation. Public ownership is more intrusive than either regulation or taxation. The most intrusive government public policy, however, is to declare a state of emergency. In this case, all normal civil liberties and government institutions are suspended, control is exercised autocratically, and state security forces (the army and police) are used to support the government's directives, using force if necessary.

Given this scale of intrusiveness and the range of policy choices available, how do decision-makers decide which policy to employ? Policy-makers are constrained in their choice of governing instruments by societal views regarding what the appropriate level of state involvement should be in the society. They are constrained by the appropriateness of various means at their disposal. (It would make little sense, for instance, to try to secure the compliance of citizens to obey traffic laws by imposing a state of emergency.) Finally, the resources need to be available to ensure that a policy goal is realistically achievable.[52] The creation of a national, universally accessible, federally funded daycare system seemed improbable in an age of spiraling debt and deficits. However, when we entered the post-deficit era, and resources became available, we saw this issue resurface on the public policy agenda.

**Recent Developments in Policy Implementation**  Implementation of policy has recently undergone important changes. As with other aspects of public administration, the trend toward transferring responsibilities to the private sector means that in some instances policy implementation is being taken over by nongovernmental actors. As we noted in chapter 4, the thinking among New Public Management (NPM) advocates is that government should "steer" rather than "row."[53] A major premise of this approach is that government should arrange for the provision of services, but not deliver (or implement) those services itself.

To put it another way, many policy decisions fall on the least intrusive end of the scale discussed above: namely, *privatization of conflict*, reflecting NPM approaches. Implementation has been affected by the recent increases in demands for greater privatization and deregulation, coupled with citizen participation and control, democracy, and responsiveness of government institutions.[54] The impact of NPM on policy implementation is summarized in Box 7.2.

Yet the outcomes of NPM policy innovations are sometimes not clear (as with other systems of management). For instance, restructuring of the health-care sector brought new efficiencies and cost savings in Ontario, but it also unexpectedly

BOX 7.2 **The Impact of the NPM on Policy Implementation**

1. NPM assumes traditional government structures are rule-bound, inflexible, and incapable of adapting quickly.

2. NPM questions government involvement in a variety of traditional policy fields.

3. Policy-makers increasingly look to nongovernmental actors to deliver policies (private sector corporations, community groups, nonprofit organizations, citizens, the family, etc.)

4. There is a new emphasis on outcomes of policy in terms of quality of service.

5. NPM looks to hybrid forms of policy delivery that have greater flexibility than traditional governmental forms, including contracting out, partnerships, and other forms of nongovernmental implementation of policy.

**Source:** Leslie A. Pal, *Beyond Policy Analysis: Public Issue Management in Turbulent Times*, 4th ed. (Toronto: Nelson, 2010): 216–17.

brought a 4000 percent increase in the incidence of certain bacterial infections in hospitals. Fewer staff, dealing with greater caseloads, had less time to wash their hands between treating patients, with the result that bacterial infections soared. Unforeseen consequences frequently seem to bedevil implementation, whatever form it takes.

All in all, the concept of implementation is a difficult one to analyze, much less execute. It involves so many factors and actors: Cabinet and legislature, courts, public servants, interest groups, and citizens. It entails an evolving process of bargaining, negotiation, incentives, decisions, log-rolling, discretion, and so on. It is also hard to say with authority where the formulation process ends and implementation begins, since the two are continuous and interrelated. Still, it is crucial to understanding the public policy aspects of public administration. In any event, once formulated and implemented, some mechanism must exist to ensure that the policy has achieved its objectives. The evaluation of policy is the next step in the policy cycle.

## Evaluating Public Policy: Was the Policy Any Good?

Evaluation is one area that distinguishes the public sector from the private sector. It is relatively straightforward to determine whether a widget company is making a profit. On the basis of this "bottom-line" standard, an evaluation can be made. But in the public sector, as we noted in chapter 1, this clear-cut bottom-line standard does not exist. Thus, evaluation can be more of a challenge in the public sector than in the private sector.

As noted above, evaluation is that part of the policy cycle that is mainly conducted by the public service and the attentive public. It is an ongoing process that can be conducted either formally and systematically, or informally and haphazardly. The former case might involve, for instance, a team of forensic accountants being contracted by a municipal government to determine if county finances are in order. The latter case might involve the complaint by a citizen that a parking meter is not functioning properly. In both cases, some form of evaluative exercise is going on that forces government officials to account for their action (or inaction). In short, public policy is being scrutinized and assessed.

It might seem surprising that the systematic evaluation of public policy is a young art. It is only in the past 20 or 30 years that theorists of public administration acknowledged how little was being done academically in this area. Furthermore, while we could argue that practitioners of public administration had always carried on some form of evaluation of public policy—however informal it might have been—the Canadian federal government only initiated ongoing, professional, and rigorous self-evaluation in the past few decades. According to political scientist Ray Rist,

*Policy evaluation began and rapidly expanded at a time in many western democratic societies when there were strong pressures to address the social problems of these same societies. The 20 years from 1960–1980 witnessed a dramatic increase in the use of the public sector to address social issues as far-ranging as drug abuse, education of poor children, crime, availability of affordable housing, environmental pollution and health care for the elderly, to name but a few. . . .*

*But while large sums of funds were to be spent, there was also the need to ensure that the funds were spent effectively. Stated differently, there was a need to ensure that the policies and programs delivered on what they had promised. Assessing the impacts and performances of the new initiatives fell to the emergent field of policy and program evaluation.*[55]

Initial attempts to make use of the burgeoning field of evaluation theory, though, faltered on the faulty premise of rationalism. Theorists and practitioners alike assumed that it was possible to make a factual, objective assessment of a policy based largely on quantitative methods derived from scientific inquiry. As Rist suggests, however, over time they realized that there was no simple linear relationship between evaluation and its use by policy-makers to produce sound policy.

As with the other parts of the policy cycle, it is possible to identify the key actors who should be involved in evaluation. These are the public servants and the public. However, the boundaries are blurred between the stages and who performs at each stage. The legislature has an important evaluative role through the mechanisms of the opposition parties, legislative committees, and question period in the House of Commons. The courts are frequently asked to judge whether public officials are implementing what the formulators have asked, in accordance with the Constitution and the rules and regulations set out in legislation.

Policy evaluation both *is* and *is not* a complicated affair. We constantly evaluate even the simplest of activities we are engaged in. However, it becomes much more complicated when the object of evaluation is a large, multifunctional, complex public organization. This is partly due to the shared nature of the responsibility for policy—cabinet, public servants, Parliament, and so on. Responsibility for evaluating a policy is often spread out among many disparate actors. In addition, the object of policy, usually citizens, is heterogeneous by definition, with a huge array of needs and demands. There is often a time lag between implementing a policy and the point at which we can determine whether it is working as intended or not. Even determining the criteria by which we decide it is working can be daunting, as we will see below. Perhaps the most significant difference between evaluation by individuals and evaluation in public organizations is the political context.

There is no consensus in the literature as to what, exactly, evaluation should entail. It is a multidisciplinary creature, drawing on political science, accounting, economics, education, industrial engineering, management sciences, medicine, psychology, sociology, statistics, mathematics, urban studies, and other areas. Evaluation should not be confused with policy analysis, which is embarked on before a policy is implemented. Rather, program evaluation is a retrospective consideration of how a policy has worked.

There are a number of problems associated with evaluation, which we review below. For now, though, think about your own experience as a student. First, it is natural that people are reluctant to have their work assessed, for fear of being criticized. So we approach evaluation with some reluctance. Still, you hand in your first-rate essay and patiently wait for that A+ you are sure it deserves. But your paper is now in the hands of someone who had no part in its creation, has a different perspective on what an essay ought to look like, and has high expectations about its content. After receiving your C, you wonder what planet your professor is from. In particular, you wonder what standards of evaluation were applied to your work. If you pursue the question, you will probably find that a set of "objective" criteria exists against which every essay was graded, including proper spelling, punctuation, and grammar; a coherent thesis and argument; a clear structure and organization; evidence of research and familiarity with the literature in your field of study; and original thinking. But how objective are these criteria, in reality? Your professor invariably has a strong background in certain areas but is not an expert in everything. What if she was not feeling well when she graded your paper, or was distracted by other work or family responsibilities? How do you know that she does not hold the opposite ideological position from your essay, and disagreed with your stance, no matter how eloquently put?

All these issues colour the evaluation of your work. Similarly, a host of problems interfere with the easy and objective evaluation of the work of the public service. The purpose of program evaluation is, in part, to ensure that government can be held accountable. In addition, it is expected to assist managers in making informed decisions about how to resource programs, determine a program's worth, and provide useful advice to Cabinet. Evaluation permits the government to anticipate future problems and plan ahead to avoid them. It also sometimes promotes experimentation and innovation. Finally, evaluation helps to legitimize government programs, since evidence is presented to citizens of their effectiveness and efficiency. Still, notwithstanding all these laudable goals and effects of evaluation, the practice is often regarded with suspicion and disdain by those being evaluated.

Evaluation can be usefully categorized into three types: administrative, judicial, and political evaluation.[56] **Administrative evaluation** generally involves examining the efficient delivery of government services, and determining whether the best value for money is being realized within the framework of democracy and justice. **Audits** of budgetary systems, personnel reviews, managerial performance reviews, and the like are typical of this type of evaluation, which is usually conducted within government by specialized agencies. Methodologically, administrative evaluation tends to be technical in nature and involves compiling and analyzing data on program costs and benefits.

**Judicial evaluation** is related to the practice of judicial review (see chapter 6). It is concerned with the legal issues arising out of administrative actions when government programs are implemented. Judicial evaluation is a facet of constitutional and administrative law, where the judges and the courts pass judgment on the behaviour and practices of the public service, either on their own or at the behest of a government, corporation, or citizen filing a case against a government agency.

**Political evaluation** is a vaguer concept, since it is an ongoing process that can occur formally or informally and lacks technical and methodological sophistication. This type of evaluation is less interested in objectively establishing the utility and value of a particular policy, and more interested in subjectively establishing a case for its demise and replacing it with a policy more favourable to the evaluator's interests. Perhaps the most visible manifestation of this type of evaluation occurs at election time when citizens are asked, in a sense, to evaluate their government's overall performance. This is evaluation as it is most broadly understood. Political evaluation also occurs, though, in royal commissions and task forces, parliamentary committees, central agencies, line departments, Cabinet, and through the actions of interest groups, protestors, lobbyists, the media, and so on. When you write a letter to the editor of your local newspaper or to a Member of Parliament to protest against some government program, you are engaging in an informal and uncoordinated form of government policy evaluation. In short, evaluation occurs anywhere that "politics" takes place. We will be concerned in this chapter with *administrative evaluation*.

**Problems of Evaluation** Program evaluation is fraught with difficulties. Program objectives are not always straightforward or clearly defined. Politicians and public servants are often reluctant to expressly state the goals of a particular program lest it offend those not served by it. They may want to avoid blame should something go wrong, so legislation objectives are sometimes vaguely worded. Politicians often derive their support from broad coalitions of interests in society; they frame legislation in terms that appeal to disparate groups so that each can interpret the intent of the legislation as serving their own goals.[57]

The root of the problem is that program objectives are not always easily measurable. If the government increases funding for scholarships for post-secondary students, and there is a decrease in student indebtedness, did the one cause the other? Perhaps more students found summer or part-time work; perhaps more well-off students entered the system; perhaps Kraft Dinner was on sale more often in the year under review! Where goals are measurable, things that are easily measured will attract the eye of those conducting evaluations. We desire rationality and clear causation, but this contorts the rationale of evaluation and may result in influencing the program to conform with that which is measurable (see Box 7.3). Political scientist Alan Maslove states,

*Indicators may emerge from the political-bureaucratic process which minimize problems or make them more amenable to solutions and which suit the emotional commitments and interests of the decision-makers and those who influence them. Indicators may be selected to promote the adoption of desired policies, to make these policies appear as successful as possible, and to direct public discussion in the desired directions.*[58]

Furthermore, establishing control groups to test whether a policy applied to one group but not to another is effective is next to impossible. Even establishing causality—that is, showing that program X caused a certain result—can be challenging because of the difficulty of isolating the impact of a particular program. Outside factors may intrude on the success or failure of a program. For instance, is a decline in drunk driving the result of increased educational campaigns,

---

**BOX 7.3 | How Bureaucrats Explain Negative Findings**

**A**ccording to political scientist Thomas Dye,

*Government administrators and program supporters are ingenious in devising reasons why negative findings about policy impacts should be rejected. Even in the face of clear evidence that their favourite programs are useless or even counterproductive, they will argue that:*

1. *The effects of the program are long range and cannot be measured at the present time.*

2. *The effects of the program are diffuse and general in nature, no single criterion or index adequately measures what is being accomplished.*

3. *The effects of the program are subtle and cannot be identified by crude measures or statistics.*

4. *Experimental research cannot be carried out effectively because to withhold services from some persons to observe the impact of such withholding would be unfair to them.*

5. *The fact that no difference was found between persons receiving the services and those not receiving them means that the program is not sufficiently intensive and indicates the need to spend more resources on the program.*

6. *The failure to identify any positive effects of a program is attributable to inadequacy or bias in the research itself, not in the program.*

**Source:** Thomas R. Dye, *Understanding Public Policy*, 9th ed. (Upper Saddle River, NJ: Prentice Hall, 1998): 349. Reprinted by permission of Pearson Education, Inc., Upper Saddle River, New Jersey.

increased police spot checks, or an aging population less inclined to consume alcohol? Another problem is that some programs themselves comprise several subprograms. Does the measurement of the success of the subprograms add up to the measurement of the success of the overall program? Or consider that the world of public policy is constantly changing. Programs may have a short shelf life, and there may simply not be enough data about a program to make a reasonable assessment of its utility.

In some cases, goals—for example, those regarding national security or sensitive financial information—cannot be stated publicly or explicitly. In other cases, new and innovative programs may defy easy assessment simply because they are in uncharted waters. Programs devised to promote racial tolerance or gender equality may fall into this category. More specifically, objectives for these types of programs may be deliberately left vague to permit flexibility in their implementation. And then, there are some things governments do not want to know. For instance, if a government is committed ideologically or politically to a course of action, it may not want to know that it will not work. The opponents of the Free Trade Agreement (FTA) and the North American Free Trade Agreement (NAFTA), for example, argued that trade deals were to blame when tens of thousands of workers were thrown out of work in the early 1990s; but the government insisted that it had conducted no evaluations of the impact of free trade, so it could not confirm that free trade was responsible for the recession that gripped the country.

Evaluation proposals must first scale the wall of skepticism that surrounds policy-makers, convincing them to commit sufficient resources to projects that might in the end criticize their work. They must then traverse the minefield of policy reversals, changes in funding and personnel, and changing priorities in public policy. In addition, mustering capable troops to conduct evaluations has been a problem given the lack of expertise in this relatively new field. Given the wide range of disciplines that evaluation draws on, findings may be contested by "experts" from disparate fields. In addition, the assumption that only the "experts" know best sometimes flies in the face of the real, lived experiences of people affected by government programs. For instance, scientists working for the Ministry of Fisheries may scientifically assess a fishery and determine that it should be closed to preserve the dwindling stock of fish. For the fishers who make their livelihood there, that recommendation is disastrous. Moreover, the fishers' evaluation of previous attempts by scientists to monitor the stock may have pointed out gross errors in their calculations. But because the fishers are not "experts," their concerns may be ignored.[59]

In addition, some programs serve several masters, and public service managers are accountable to more than one agency. This may result in the manager being pulled in several different directions at once, which may in turn detract from the overall quality of the program. Public servants are often reluctant to subject their work to critical examination. It is often said in this context that a dog will not fetch the stick with which it will be beaten. Public servants also resist evaluation because it is costly. In 2005, total expenditure by the federal government for evaluations was $54.8 million. However, this figure should be placed in perspective: it represents only 0.16 percent of departmental expenditures, and only 11 of 47 small agencies had evaluation budgets totalling $1 million—and 60 percent of that related to just two small agencies.[60] Public servants also perceive evaluation as time-consuming. Political scientist Timothy Plumptre rather pithily summarized the problems with evaluation when he compared it to chastity: "People support it in principle, but in practice they prefer if it is mandatory for others and optional for them. . . ."[61]

**Evaluation in Action** Notwithstanding these difficulties, today a culture of evaluation has gradually infused the public service, and evaluation is seen as an important aspect of accountability—almost all evaluations conducted by the public service are available for public scrutiny. The government uses a range of types of evaluations; methods as complex as econometric modelling and computer simulations exist alongside traditional interviewing of program beneficiaries and experts. Great care must be taken in determining what type of evaluation is suitable for a particular program. Indeed, many exercises have floundered on the rocks of inadequate consideration for "appropriate" evaluation. Hence, evaluation assessment studies are a part of the evaluation landscape.

An appropriate evaluation study of a program requires consideration of six factors.[62] First, the nature of the program to be evaluated must be considered. This includes a definition or description of what is to be evaluated; the length of time that a program has been running, since a program should be "field-tested" before attempts are made to evaluate; and the type of state intervention used in the program, whether it involves regulation, expenditure, taxation, or other policy instruments.

Second, the questions to be addressed by the evaluation must be carefully thought through. Evaluators need to consider whether their evaluation is dealing with the rationale of the program, its impacts and effects, its objective achievements, or alternatives to the program. Each of these will prompt a different set of questions.

Third, the client of the evaluation study must be clearly identified. Potential clients include Cabinet, the media, Parliament, program planners and managers, the public, researchers, and senior public servants. Consider again a program designed to ease student debt load. Cabinet might ask if the program is having a demonstrable effect on fiscal resources dedicated to student loans, and the political impact of garnering the electoral support of students. The students themselves might ask whether enough is being done to ease their debt load, and why the government is not doing more. The program manager might ask whether the program is being delivered effectively and efficiently, or whether a new computer system or other technology or redeployment of staff would help in the program's delivery.

The fourth component of an evaluation study relates to the actual technique used to conduct the evaluation. A range of methodologies is available to program evaluators, and great care must be taken to ensure the right type of evaluation is conducted. Decisions must be made about whether to employ quantitative or qualitative methods, analysis, description, surveys, polling, interviews, focus groups, or other tools. Questions must be asked about how rigorous and systematic the evaluation needs to be, or how casual and informal, and so on.

Fifth, every program evaluation study must carefully consider the resources and time available. Almost invariably, trade-offs must be made that may sometimes compromise the process. The short-term perspective of the governmental budget cycle means that long, languorous, time-consuming studies are a luxury. Moreover, clients often want results "yesterday." Evaluations that report to Parliament must subscribe to the parliamentary cycle and timelines. The costs involved must be justified. This can entail considerable effort that detracts from the actual evaluation.

Sixth, evaluation studies must be credible and have legitimacy in the eyes of clients as well as other observers. Credibility can be enhanced if the evaluator has an arm's-length relationship from the subject being evaluated, as well as from the client being served. This is where institutions such as the **Office of the Comptroller General** (OCG), the Office of the **Auditor General** (OAG), and the Treasury Board are useful. They establish criteria and guidelines for evaluation that help ensure the evaluation is objective. Ultimately, though, the test of credibility is in the hands of the public. If a program is perceived by citizens to be a boondoggle, all the evaluation studies in the world are unlikely to change their minds. In this regard, recent Access to Information legislation has given citizens (as well as public servants) improved tools with which to conduct their own evaluations of government programs.

**Contemporary Evaluation Practices**  The advent of contemporary management practices, including those inspired by the NPM, have invigorated the practice of evaluation even as it changed its character to more overtly focus on results.[63] It has been pointed out that "many governments are now engaged in what is commonly described as results-based management, involving the development of performance indicators and measures related to an organization's business objectives, measuring the outputs and outcomes of programs and services, and using these data to evaluate the performance of the organization and its employees."[64] Indeed, internationally there was an explosion of interest in new program evaluation techniques and development in the 1990s and early 2000s. The European Evaluation Society was formed in 1994, as was the United Kingdom Evaluation Society. As well, evaluation societies appeared in Australia in 1991, France in 1996, Germany, Italy, and Switzerland in 1997, Malaysia in 1999, and more recently in Russia, Belgium, Ethiopia, Finland, Ghana, Israel, and Kenya.[65] The Canadian government created the Centre for Excellence in Evaluation in 2001 as part of a capacity-building exercise to enable it to conduct better evaluations. However, overall "the extent that the Canadian federal government has influenced the development of the field of program evaluation and evaluation capacity in Canada is less clear and direct than in the United States and United Kingdom."[66]

In 2009, the Treasury Board updated its policy on evaluation, re-emphasizing the importance with which evaluation should be regarded by public service managers and focusing sharply on the practice of "managing for results."[67] According to the Treasury Board Secretariat, "The objective of this policy is to create a comprehensive and reliable base of evaluation evidence that is used to support policy and program improvement, expenditure management, Cabinet decision making, and public reporting."[68] A Centre of Excellence in Evaluation was created to assist in the implementation of the new policy.

By the start of the twenty-first century, the federal government had developed a sophisticated, though not problem-free, infrastructure for evaluating policy. All of the main departments and agencies had internal audit and evaluation sections, and they regularly published their findings of their audits and evaluations. The Centre of Excellence for Evaluation served as a focal point for leadership of the evaluation function, launching new initiatives and supporting capacity building and strengthening of the evaluation community. The OAG conducted performance audits of departments and agencies.[69]

In addition, the OCG was resurrected in 2003 by the Paul Martin government and charged with enhancing and strengthening comptrollership in all government departments. The government published two documents entitled *Responsible and Prudent Financial Management* and *Strengthening Public Sector Management*, which outlined a new expenditure management system and the place of evaluation therein.[70] Again, politics seemed to be a prime motivation as the government was feeling the pressure of the Sponsorship Program scandal (see chapter 11) and wanted to be seen enhancing accountability.

In 2006, with the arrival of a new government came a new approach to evaluation tied to a new emphasis on accountability, of which the Federal Accountability Act was the centrepiece. The budget speech of that year indicated that the government would review its expenditure management system and that every department would have to undertake a review of all federal grants and contributions at least once every five years.[71]

Evaluation issues continue to bedevil the government, particularly those problems associated with the concept of "measurement." Although the idiom "what gets measured gets managed" emerged to encapsulate the advantages of performance measurement, at least three main problems persisted, as Pollitt observes:

- *Conceptual problems (how far are the measures meaningful and understandable to the various social, political, and public service groups which are affected by them?)*

- *Motivational problems (mainly—though not entirely—small "p" problems of bureaucratic politics: who measures who, for what purposes and with what safeguards against distortion and misuse?)*

- *Technical problems (can everything important be measured, and measured reliably, at reasonable cost and without too much delay?)*[72]

One recent report on the views of deputy ministers toward evaluation identified a number of ongoing problems. For instance, there is a lack of resources and weak linkages with policy and the expenditure management system. In addition, for heads of evaluation, access to competent evaluators is a major problem. Despite the Treasury Board Secretariat's call for more evaluations on the effectiveness of horizontal initiatives and programs, lack of capacity and coordination of horizontal evaluations are a major obstacle.[73] Moreover, evaluation has not been well integrated with senior management decision making, there is a lack of feedback between evaluation findings and policy development, and the cutbacks of the 1990s continue to adversely affect the government's ability to conduct evaluation to the extent that many evaluation studies are still contracted out, limiting the development of in-house government experts.[74]

One recent approach to wrestle with these broad problems and further refine the system of evaluation has been to adopt value-for-money auditing, framed by two key questions:

1. *Relevance—Are we doing the right thing?*
   - *Program addresses a demonstrable need, is appropriate to the federal government, and is responsive to Canadians.*

2. *Performance—Are we achieving value?*
   - *Economy: Are tax-payer resources well utilized?*
   - *Efficiency: Are program outputs (services and products) achieved in an affordable manner?*
   - *Effectiveness: Extent to which program objectives have been achieved? That is, what results were produced? Are the costs of achieving program outcomes minimized?*[75]

As we can see, the contemporary face of evaluation is evolving, and there are continuous calls for a change of focus. But, according to one public servant, the real focus must always ultimately be on the public good,

*Part of the problem, in my view, is that evaluations have focused on the program manager as the primary client. Program managers are largely concerned with questions of efficiency and effectiveness that guide service delivery and program improvements. While critical to the conduct of an evaluation, focusing evaluation solely on the needs of this group reduces its utility to decision makers such as deputies, central agencies, Ministers, Parliament, and ultimately Canadians. The information demands of these stakeholders requires a focus on larger issues centred on the public good as opposed to program operations.*[76]

A similar concern was raised by Pollitt, who invoked Oscar Wilde's quip about "a man who knows the price of everything and the value of nothing" in warning about the real importance of evaluation. Pollitt wrote that "governments may end up knowing how much everything costs, how long everything takes, what percentage of errors are committed in processing various kinds of claims, how many output targets have been met and many other things, yet will remain ignorant of the values which different groups of citizens place upon different public services, and of the reasons why those values are held."[77]

This overview of recent developments in the world of the evaluation of public policy shows that interest in the process has waxed and waned over time. After an initial outburst of interest in the 1960s and 1970s, the place of evaluation in the realm of government activities declined in stature and status. Many of the difficulties associated with the practice asserted themselves, and no sustained effort was made to ensure that evaluation became a regular feature of government accountability. A renewed interest in evaluation arose in the 1990s and early 2000s, with the advent of new management philosophies and techniques. Evaluation is now linked to the overarching goals of fiscal prudence, quality of service, program review, management for results, performance measurement, and other related issues that have arisen in contemporary governance. Peter Aucoin summarizes the importance of this evolutionary process:

*The advent of Program Evaluation as a component of decision making in the Canadian government in the 1970s constituted a significant innovation that was internationally recognized. Although a great deal has changed over the past three decades, the current emphasis on Result-Based Management as well as Results-Based Reporting indicates the extent to which the pursuit of continuous improvement through the evaluation of performance continues to be front and centre on the governance and public management reform agenda.*[78]

So, the next time you feel aggrieved by a government action (or inaction), rest assured that it has probably undergone a process of evaluation that has concluded that—like cod liver oil—it is good for you.

Once evaluation has taken place, then what? Usually, evaluation will reveal one of three things. First, the policy is working just fine, and so needs no further refinement or change. Second, the policy is deficient in certain regards but on the whole is redeemable. Perhaps it only requires some tinkering. Third, the policy is an abject failure and should be entirely scrapped, and a new approach developed. Notice that in all three cases, information is being fed back into the policy cycle that will affect the other stages. If the first scenario prevails and the policy does not need any change, then formulators can go on to another issue and implementers can continue to do their job, secure in the knowledge that they are doing the right thing. If either scenario two or scenario three prevails, then policy-makers are confronted with a new set of challenges. Thus the process cranks (or creaks) back into gear, with either minor reform or wholesale change by the formulators and implementers. Such is the never-ending, dynamic, and evolving world of the policy cycle.

## WHAT YOU HAVE LEARNED

Public policy is an important aspect of public administration, albeit difficult to define. We may think of the public policy process as a cycle, involving the continuous interplay of problem definition and agenda-setting, formulation, implementation, and evaluation of various public policies. While the steps of the process can be conceptualized as discrete, in fact in the real world there is considerable overlap between them; each influences the other. You should now be able to answer the following questions: What is public policy? What theories of public policy decision making explain the way that public officials (both bureaucratic and political) make decisions on behalf of citizens?

## Key Words and Concepts

public policy (210)

rational-comprehensive model (214)

public choice or rational choice
   model (215)

incremental model (216)

mixed scanning (216)

garbage can model (217)

interpretive framework (217)

cultural analysis (218)

ideational analysis (218)

post-positivist analysis (218)

pluralist model (218)

structural analysis (220)

institutionalism (221)

neo-institutionalism (221)

postmodernist approach (221)

policy cycle (222)

problem definition and agenda
   setting (222)

policy formulation (222)

policy implementation (222)

policy evaluation (222)

policy community (229)

policy network (229)

governing instruments (235)

mobilization of bias (236)

administrative evaluation (243)

audits (243)

judicial evaluation (243

political evaluation (243)

Office of the Comptroller General (247)

Auditor General (247)

## Review Questions

This chapter was divided into three main sections, each dealing with the issue of policy making in public administration. These central issues were highlighted:

*1. Defining Public Policy*
This brief introductory section considered what "public policy" is and explained that, while a number of definitions exist, in this text we focus on the idea that public policy is "a set of interrelated decisions taken by a political actor or group of actors concerning the selection of goals and the means of achieving them." More simply, we quoted Thomas Dye's maxim that public policy is "whatever governments choose to do or not to do." Ask yourself, which definition best explains what public policy is?

*2. Models and Theories of Public Policy*
Governments do an awful lot of things—but ask yourself after reading this section, How do governments do what they do? What theoretical explanations illuminate the question of how policy is made (or not made)?

*3. The Policy Cycle*
This section dealt with the tools and means by which will is translated into action. It showed that policy is not self-executing but must be enacted to be effective, and then must also be evaluated. Ask yourself, How are decisions about the level of intrusiveness of government made? What are among the choices that policy-makers must consider when deciding on a policy? What policy instruments are available for policy-makers, and in what circumstances are they likely to be employed? What factors influence the choice of policy instruments? In the contemporary era, what is the capacity of the state to manage policy making? How

much is being left to the private sector and the voluntary sector? What is the impact of the NPM on public policy? Finally, what is the relationship between problem definition and agenda-setting, formulation, implementation, and evaluation? Who is responsible for each? Do these terms adequately sum up the policy process? Or is there more to it than this apparently simple illustration would imply?

## Weblinks

Canadian Parliamentary Channel (CPAC)
**www.cpac.ca**

Association for Public Policy Analysis and Management (APPAM)
**www.appam.org**

Canadian Centre for Policy Alternatives
**www.policyalternatives.ca**

Government of Canada Policy Research Initiative
**www.policyresearch.gc.ca**

Institute for Research on Public Policy
**www.irpp.org**

Canadian Public Policy
**http://economics.ca/cpp**

Policy.ca
**www.policy.ca**

Public Policy Forum
**www.ppforum.ca**

Canadian Evaluation Society
**www.evaluationcanada.ca**

Canadian Journal of Program Evaluation
**www.evaluationcanada.ca/site.cgi?s=4&ss=2&_lang=en**

Treasury Board of Canada Secretariat
**www.tbs-sct.gc.ca**

Centre of Excellence for Evaluation
**www.tbs-sct.gc.ca/eval/eval_e.asp**

Expenditure Management System of the Government of Canada
**www.tbs-sct.gc.ca/pubs_pol/opepubs/TB_H/EXMA_e.asp**

## Further Reading

### 1. Defining Public Policy

Anderson, James E. *Public Policy Making.* 3rd ed. New York: Holt, Rinehart and Winston, 1984.

Brooks, Stephen. "Policy Analysis in Canada," in Christopher Dunn, ed., *The Handbook of Canadian Public Administration.* Toronto: Oxford University Press, 2002: 192–203.

Burke, Mike, Colin Mooers, and John Shields, eds. *Restructuring and Resistance: Canadian Public Policy in an Age of Global Capitalism*. Halifax: Fernwood, 2000.

Pal, Leslie A. Beyond Policy Analysis: Public Issue Management in Turbulent Times. Fourth Edition. Toronto: Nelson, 2010.

Shafritz, Jay M., Karen S. Layne, and Christopher P. Borick, eds. *Classics of Public Policy*. New York: Pearson Longman, 2005.

Simeon, Richard. "Studying Public Policy." *Canadian Journal of Political Science*, 9, 4 (1976): 548–80.

## 2. Models and Theories of Public Policy

Dobuzinskis, Laurent, Michael Howlett, and David Laycock, eds. *Policy Analysis in Canada: The State of the Art*. Toronto: University of Toronto Press, 2007.

Lecours, André, ed. *New Institutionalism: Theory and Analysis*. Toronto: University of Toronto Press: 2005.

Orsini, Michael, and Miriam Smith, eds. *Critical Policy Studies*. Vancouver: UBC Press, 2007.

Painter, Martin, and Jon Pierre. *Challenges to State Policy Capacity: Global Trends and Comparative Perspectives*. New York: Palgrave Macmillan: 2005.

Prince, Michael. "The Return of Directed Incrementalism: Innovating Social Policy the Canadian Way," in G. Bruce Doern, ed., *How Ottawa Spends, 2002–2003: The Security Aftermath and National Priorities*. Toronto: Oxford University Press, 2002: 176–95.

Sabatier, Paul A., ed. *Theories of the Policy Process*. 2nd ed. Cambridge, MA: Westview, 2007.

## 3. The Policy Cycle

Braybrooke, David, and Charles E. Lindblom. *A Strategy of Decision*. New York: Free Press of Glencoe, 1963.

Carroll, Barbara Wake, and David I. Dewar. "Performance Management: Panacea or Fools' Gold?" in Christopher Dunn, ed., *The Handbook of Canadian Public Administration*. Toronto: Oxford University Press, 2002: 413–29.

Dobell, Rodney, and David Zussman. "An Evaluation System for Government: If Politics Is Theatre, then Evaluation Is (Mostly) Art," in Barbara Wake Carroll, David Siegel, and Mark Sproule Jones, eds., *Classic Readings in Canadian Public Administration*. Toronto: Oxford University Press, 2005: 353–74.

Doern, G. Bruce. *Progress and Constraints in Five Canadian Federal Agencies: The Road to Better Public Services*. Montreal: Institute for Research on Public Policy, 1994.

Eliadis, Pearl, Margaret M. Hill, and Michael Howlett, eds. *Designing Government: From Instruments to Governance*. Montreal: McGill-Queen's University Press, 2005.

Leclerc, G. "Institutionalizing Evaluation in Canada," in J. Mayne, J. Hudson, M.L. Bemelmans-Videc, and R. Conner, eds., *Advancing Public Policy Evaluation: Learning From International Experiences*. Amsterdam: North Holland, 1992: 49–58.

Muller-Clemm, W.J., and Maria Paulette Barnes. "A Historical Perspective on Federal Program Evaluation in Canada." *Canadian Journal of Program Evaluation*, 12, 1 (1997): 47–70.

Posavac, Emil J., and Raymond G. Carey. *Program Evaluation: Methods and Case Studies. Seventh Edition*. Upper Saddle River, NJ: Prentice Hall, 2007.

Rist, Ray C., ed. *Policy Evaluation: Linking Theory to Practice*. Aldershot, U.K.: Edward Elgar, 1995.

Weiss, Carol H. *Evaluation*. 2nd ed. Upper Saddle River, NJ: Prentice Hall, 1998.

Wholey, Joseph S., Harry P. Hatry, and Kathryn E. Newcomer, eds. *Handbook of Practical Program Evaluation*. San Francisco: Jossey-Bass, 1994.

Woodside, Kenneth. "The Political Economy of Policy Instruments: Tax Expenditures and Subsidies in Canada," in Barbara Wake Carroll, David Siegel, and Mark Sproule-Jones, eds., *Classic Readings in Canadian Public Administration*. Toronto: Oxford University Press, 2005: 496–516.

# Endnotes

1. See Lydia Miljan, *Public Policy in Canada: An Introduction*, 5th ed. (Toronto: Oxford, 2008): chapters 1–2.

2. See, for example, Laurent Dobuzinskis, Michael Howlett, and David Laycock, eds., *Policy Analysis in Canada: The State of the Art* (Toronto: University of Toronto Press, 2007); Michael Orsini and Miriam Smith, eds., *Critical Policy Studies* (Vancouver: UBC Press, 2007); André Lecours, ed., *New Institutionalism: Theory and Analysis* (Toronto: University of Toronto Press, 2005); Leslie A. Pal, *Beyond Policy Analysis: Public Issue Management in Turbulent Times*, 5th ed. (Toronto: Nelson, 2010); Robert M. Campbell, Leslie A. Pal, and Michael Howlett, *The Real Worlds of Canadian Politics: Cases in Process and Policy*, 4th ed. (Peterborough: Broadview, 2004); Michael Howlett, M. Ramesh, and Anthony Perl, *Studying Public Policy: Policy Cycles and Policy Subsystems*, 3rd ed. (Toronto: Oxford University Press, 2009); and Miljan, *Public Policy in Canada*.

3. W.I. Jenkins, *Policy Analysis* (London: Martin Robertson, 1978): 15, cited in G. Bruce Doern and Richard W. Phidd, *Canadian Public Policy: Ideas, Structure, Process* (Toronto: Methuen, 1983): 33–34.

4. Thomas R. Dye, *Understanding Public Policy*, 5th ed. (Englewood Cliffs, NJ: Prentice-Hall, 1992): 1.

5. Pal, *Beyond Policy Analysis*, 2.

6. I am indebted to Patricia O'Reilly for her lucid and comprehensive review of the current policy literature in a draft of her work on models and theories of public policy.

7. These factors are outlined in Richard Simeon, "Studying Public Policy," *Canadian Journal of Political Science*, 9, 4 (1976): 559–62.

8. Robert J. Jackson and Doreen Jackson, *Politics in Canada: Culture, Institutions, Behaviour and Public Policy*, 7th ed. (Toronto: Pearson Prentice Hall, 2009): 502 ff. See also James E. Anderson, *Public Policy Making*, 3rd ed. (New York: Holt, Rinehart and Winston, 1984): 8–10.

9. Michael Howlett, M. Ramesh, and Anthony Perl, *Studying Public Policy: Policy Cycles and Policy Subsystems*, 3rd ed. (Toronto: Oxford University Press, 2009): 181–82; See also Michael Howlett, "Policy Analytical Capacity and Evidence-Based Policy-Making: Lessons from Canada," *Canadian Public Administration*, 52, 2 (2009): 153–75

10. Pal, *Beyond Policy Analysis*, 20–21.

11. Ute Lischke and David T. McNab, eds. *Walking a Tightrope: Aboriginal People and their Representations* (Waterloo: Wilfrid Laurier University Press, 2005): 1. See also Frances Abele, "Between Respect and Control: Traditional Indigenous Knowledge in Canadian Public Policy," in Michael Orsini and Miriam Smith, eds., *Critical Policy Studies* (Vancouver: UBC Press, 2007): 233–56.

12. Charles E. Lindblom, "The Science of 'Muddling Through,'" *Public Administration Review*, 19, 2 (1959): 79–88.

13. Amitai Etzioni, "Mixed Scanning: A 'Third' Approach to Decision Making," *Public Administration Review*, 27, 5 (1967); and *Modern Organizations*, (Englewood Cliffs, NJ: Prentice-Hall, 1964).

14. See Michael D. Cohen, James G. March, and Johan P. Olsen, "A Garbage Can Model of Organizational Choice," *Administrative Science Quarterly*, 17 (1972): 1–25; and John W. Kingdon, *Agendas, Alternatives and Public Policies*, 2nd ed. (New York: Harper Collins, 1995).

15. G. David Garson, "'Garbage Can' Models: Multiple Stream Theory," 2008, North Carolina State University, **www2.chass.ncsu.edu/garson/pa765/garbagecan.htm**.

16. See Deborah Stone, "Policy Paradox: The Art of Political Decision Making," in Jay M. Shafritz, Karen S. Layne, and Christopher P. Borick, eds., *Classics of Public Policy* (New York: Pearson Longman, 2005): 62–71.

17. For further reading, see Colin Hay, *Political Analysis: A Critical Introduction* (Houndmills, U.K.: Palgrave, 2002); Paul A. Sabatier, *Theories of the Policy Process*, 2nd ed. (Cambridge, MA: Westview, 2007); and David Marsh and Gerry Stoker, eds., *Theory and Methods in Political Science*, 2nd ed. (Houndmills, U.K.: Palgrave, 2002).

18. See Peter deLeon, *Advice and Consent: The Development of the Policy Sciences*, (New York: Russell Sage Foundation, 1988).

19. See Miriam Smith, *A Civil Society? Collective Actors in Canadian Political Life* (Peterborough: Broadview, 2005); Lisa Young and Joanna Everitt, *Advocacy Groups* (Vancouver: UBC Press, 2004); Hugh G. Thorburn, "Interest Groups in the Canadian Federal System," in R.S. Blair and J.T. McLeod, eds., *The Canadian Political Tradition*, 2nd ed. (Scarborough: Nelson, 1993): 316–29; and Paul Pross, *Group Politics and Public Policy*, (Toronto: Oxford University Press, 1986).

20. The classic statement of pluralist theory is Robert A. Dahl, *Who Governs?* (New Haven: Yale University Press, 1961).

21. See Joseph Schumpeter, *Capitalism, Socialism, and Democracy* (New York: Harper, 1943).

22. E.E. Schattschneider, *The Semisovereign People: A Realist's View of Democracy in America* (Hinsdale: Dryden, 1975): 34.

23. Hay, *Political Analysis*, 10.

24. See Garrett Hardin, "The Tragedy of the Commons," in Morton E. Winston and Ralph D. Edelbach, eds., *Society, Ethics and Technology*, 3rd ed. (Toronto: Thomson Nelson, 2006).

25. See Hay, *Political Analysis*, chap. 7.

26. See Werner Jann and Kai Wegrich, "Theories of the Policy Cycle," in Frank Fischer, Gerald J. Miller, and Mara S. Sidney, eds., *Handbook of Public Policy Analysis: Theory, Politics and Methods* (Boca Raton: CRC Press, 2007): 43–62.

27. See John W. Kingdon, *Agendas, Alternatives and Public Policies*, 2nd ed. (New York: Harper Collins, 1995). 196–208

28. See Gregory J. Inwood, *Continentalizing Canada: The Politics and Legacy of the Macdonald Royal Commission* (Toronto: University of Toronto Press, 2005).

29. On policy communities and networks, see William D. Coleman and Grace Skogstad, "Policy Communities and Policy Networks," in William D. Coleman and Grace Skogstad, eds., *Organized Interests and Public Policies* (Toronto: Copp-Clark, 1990): 14–33; Michael M. Atkinson and William D. Coleman, *The State, Business and Industrial Change in Canada* (Toronto: University of Toronto Press, 1989); and

Evert A. Lindquist, "New Agendas for Research on Policy Communities: Policy Analysis, Administration and Governance," in Laurent Dobuzinskis, Michael Howlett, and David Laycock, eds., *Policy Studies in Canada: The State of the Art* (Toronto: University of Toronto Press, 1996): 219–41.

30. Kingdon, *Agendas, Alternatives and Public Policies*, 200.

31. Kingdon, *Agendas, Alternatives and Public Policies*, 199.

32. Michael Howlett, M. Ramesh, and Anthony Perl, *Studying Public Policy: Policy Cycles and Policy Subsystems*, 3rd ed. (Toronto: Oxford University Press, 2009): 93

33. Michael E. Kraft and Scott R. Furlong, *Public Policy: Politics, Analysis and Alternatives* (Washington DC: CQ Press, 2007): 78.

34. The following paragraph is based on Howlett, Ramesh and Perl, *Studying Public Policy*, 111–12.

35. See Simeon, Richard. "Studying Public Policy." *Canadian Journal of Political Science*, 9, 4 (1976)

36. Among the important first studies of implementation as a distinct part of the policy cycle is a study by public management theorists Jeffrey L. Pressman and Aaron Wildavsky, *Implementation*, 2nd ed., (Berkeley: University of California Press, 1979).

37. See Jeffrey D. Straussman, *Public Administration*, 2nd ed. (New York: Longman, 1990): 244–45.

38. See Duane Adams, ed., *Federalism, Democracy and Health Policy in Canada* (Montreal: McGill-Queen's University Press, 2001).

39. F.L. Morton, Peter H. Russell, and Troy Riddell, "The Supreme Court's First Decade of Charter Decisions: Judging the Judges, 1982–1992," in Paul Fox and Graham White, eds., *Politics: Canada*, 8th ed. (Toronto: McGraw-Hill, 1995): 80.

40. Canada, *Strengthening Our Policy Capacity: Report of the Task Force on Strengthening the Policy Capacity of the Federal Government* (Ottawa: Canadian Centre for Management Development, 1995); B. Guy Peters, *The Policy Capacity of Government* (Ottawa: Canadian Centre for Management Development, 1996); George Anderson,

"The New Focus on Policy Capacity in the Federal Government," *Canadian Public Administration*, 39, 4 (1996): 470–71; Canada, Policy Research Secretariat, "Policy Research in Canada: A Capacity for the Future," March 1999; Herman Bakvis, "Rebuilding Policy Capacity in the Era of the Fiscal Dividend: A Report from Canada," *Governance*, 13, 1 (2000): 71–103; Martin Painter and Jon Pierre, eds., *Challenges to State Policy Capacity: Global Trends and Comparative Perspectives* (New York: Palgrave Macmillan, 2005).

41. Pal, *Beyond Policy Analysis*, 37.

42. Pal, *Beyond Policy Analysis*, 26.

43. Miljan, *Public Policy in Canada*, 13.

44. Inwood, *Continentalizing Canada*.

45. Canada, Commission of Inquiry into the Sponsorship Program and Advertising Activities, *Who Is Responsible? Fact Finding Report* (Ottawa: Public Works and Government Services, 2005).

46. G. Bruce Doern and Richard W. Phidd, *Canadian Public Policy: Ideas, Structure, Process* (Toronto: Methuen, 1983): 110.

47. See Marie-Louise Bemelmans-Videc, Ray C. Rist, and Evert Vedung, *Carrots, Sticks and Sermons: Policy Instruments and Their Evaluation* (New Brunswick, NJ: Transaction Publishers, 1998).

48. Theodore Lowi, "Distribution, Regulation, Redistribution: The Functions of Government," in R.B. Ripley, ed., *Public Policies and Their Politics: Techniques of Government Control* (New York: W.W. Norton, 1966): 27–40.

49. See Michael J. Trebilcock, D. G. Hartle, R. S. Prichard, and D. N. Dewees, *The Choice of Governing Instrument*, (Ottawa: Economic Council of Canada, 1982); and "The Choice of Governing Instrument: A Retrospective," in Pearl Eliadis, Margaret M. Hill, and Michael Howlett, eds., *Designing Government: From Instruments to Governance* (Montreal: McGill-Queen's University Press, 2005): 51–73.

50. Michael Howlett, "Policy Instruments and Implementation Styles: The Evolution of Instrument Choice in Canadian Environmental Policy," in Debora L. VanNijnatten and Robert Boardman, eds., *Canadian Environmental Policy: Context and Cases* (Toronto: Oxford University Press, 2002): 25–45. See also Susan Delacourt

and Donald G. Lenihan, eds., *Collaborative Government: Is There a Canadian Way?* (Toronto: Institute of Public Administration of Canada, 2000).

51. See Nicolas Baxter-Moore, "Policy Implementation and the Role of the State: A Revised Approach to the Study of Policy Instruments," in Robert J. Jackson, Doreen Jackson, and Nicolas Baxter-Moore, eds., *Contemporary Canadian Politics: Reading and Notes* (Scarborough: Prentice Hall, 1987): 336–55. See also Rand Dyck, *Canadian Politics: Critical Approaches*, 5th ed. (Toronto: Thomson Nelson, 2008): 514–17; and Geoffrey Hale, *Uneasy Partnership: The Politics of Business and Government in Canada* (Peterborough: Broadview, 2006).

52. See Simeon, "Studying Public Policy."

53. David Osborne and Ted Gaebler, *Reinventing Government* (Reading, MA: Addison-Wesley, 1992): chap. 1.

54. See Pal, *Beyond Policy Analysis*, 216 ff.

55. Ray C. Rist, "Introduction," in Ray C. Rist, ed., *Policy Evaluation: Linking Theory to Practice* (Aldershot, U.K.: Edward Elgar: 1995): xv.

56. See Howlett, Ramesh, and Perl, *Studying Public Policy*, 178–96.

57. See, for example, James E. Anderson, *Public Policy Making* (New York: Holt, Rinehart and Winston, 1984): 139–43.

58. Alan M. Maslove, "Indicators and Policy Formation," *Canadian Public Administration*, 18, 3 (1975): 483.

59. See Susan McCorquodale, "Federal Spending on the Atlantic Fisheries," in Susan Phillips, ed., *How Ottawa Spends, 1995–1996: Mid-Life Crisis* (Ottawa: Carleton University Press, 1995): 364.

60. T.K. Gussman Associates, "Improving the Professionalism of Evaluation: Final Report," May 31, 2005, Treasury Board of Canada Secretariat, **www.tbs-sct.gc.ca/cee/prof-eval-eng.asp**.

61. Timothy Plumptre, *Beyond the Bottom Line: Management in Government* (Halifax: Institute for Research on Public Policy, 1988): 267.

62. See Canada, Treasury Board of Canada, "Guide for the Development of Results-Based Management and Accountability

Frameworks," August 2001, http://www.tbs-sct.gc.ca/cee/tools-outils/rmaf-cgrr/guide01-eng.asp.

63. See Christopher Pollitt, "Management Techniques for the Public Sector: Pulpit and Practice," in B. Guy Peters and Donald J. Savoie, eds., *Governance in a Changing Environment* (Kingston: McGill–Queen's University Press, 1995): 226–31.

64. Ken Kernaghan, Brian Marson, and Sandford Borins, *The New Public Organization* (Toronto: Institute of Public Administration of Canada, 2000): 273.

65. See Ian Greene, "Lessons Learned from Two Decades of Program Evaluation in Canada," August 2, 2005, York University, www.yorku.ca/igreene/progeval.html. See also Christopher Pollitt, "How Do We Know How Good Public Services Are," in B. Guy Peters and Donald J. Savoie, eds., *Governance in the Twenty-First Century: Revitalizing the Public Service* (Montreal: McGill-Queen's University Press, 2000): 119–52.

66. J. Bradley Cousins and Tim Aubry, *Roles for Government in Evaluation Quality Assurance: Discussion Paper* (Ottawa: Treasury Board of Canada, 2006), www.tbs-sct.gc.ca/cee/tools-outils/qae-aqe/rgeqa-rgaqe-eng.pdf.

67. Canada, Treasury Board of Canada Secretariat, "Policy on Evaluation," April 1, 2009, www.tbs-sct.gc.ca/pol/doc-eng.aspx?id=15024.

68. Canada, Treasury Board of Canada Secretariat, "Policy on Evaluation."

69. Danielle Labbé, "Valuing the Evaluation Function: Problems and Perspectives," June 1, 2006, Treasury Board of Canada Secretariat, www.tbs-sct.gc.ca/eval/ppt/jun06-001/vef-vfe_e.asp?printable=True.

70. See Evert Lindquist, Ian Clark, and James Mitchell, "Reshaping Ottawa's Centre of Government: Martin's Reforms in Historical Perspective," in G. Bruce Doern, ed., *How Ottawa Spends, 2004–2005: Mandate Change in the Paul Martin Era* (Montreal: McGill-Queen's University Press, 2004): 337.

71. Canada, Department of Finance, *The Budget Speech, 2006* (Ottawa: Department of Finance, 2006): 18.

72. Pollitt, "How Do We Know How Good Public Services Are?" 122. See also Barbara Wake Carroll and David I. Dewar, "Performance Management: Panacea or Fools' Gold?" in Christopher Dunn, ed., *The Handbook of Canadian Public Administration* (Toronto: Oxford University Press, 2002): 413–29.

73. Cousins and Aubry, *Roles for Government in Evaluation Quality Assurance.*"

74. Labbé, "Valuing the Evaluation Function."

75. Canada, Treasury Board of Canada Secretariat, "Modernizing Evaluation Tools: Value-for-Money Profile," November 2006, www.tbs-sct.gc.ca/eval/ppt/dec06-001/vfmp-por_e.asp?printable=True.

76. Terry Hunt, "The Role of Culture and the Future of the Evaluation Function: Considerations and Key Functions," *Canadian Journal of Program Evaluation*, 21, 3 (2006): 125.

77. Pollitt, "How Do We Know How Good Public Services Are?" 122.

78. Peter Aucoin, "Decision-Making in Government: The Role of Program Evaluation," March 29, 2005, Treasury Board of Canada Secretariat, www.tbs-sct.gc.ca/cee/tools-outils/aucoin-eng.asp.

Chapter **8**

# Public Administration *and the* Management *of* Human Resources

## WHAT YOU WILL LEARN

In chapter 1, we identified personnel as a key issue in the study and practice of public administration. Under the guidance of their political masters, public servants—the people who work in the central agencies, departments, regulatory bodies, Crown corporations, and other government institutions—are responsible for formulating, implementing, and evaluating public policies. To coordinate and manage the vast range of services government offers, a large, sophisticated merit-based public service has emerged, made up of professionals from many occupations, who offer an astonishing array of skills.[1]

The federal government is the largest enterprise in the country. It is more than four times larger than the next largest employer, with seven times more revenue than the next largest organization, with more than 1600 programs and 2000 points of service in Canada and overseas.[2] Because it is a *public* sector organization rather than a private sector one, the issues relating to the organization and structure of the federal workforce are of particular importance, including the following:

■ What and who constitutes the public service?

■ What has been the historical development of the public service?

■ What are the main organizational features of the public service?

■ What contemporary issues concern human resource management in the public sector?

We consider these issues in the following sections:

### 1. ⌐ A Brief History of the Public Service: Who Works There, Anyway?

This section provides a brief history of the public sector and introduces some of the basic issues therein. It asks, What issues have animated the evolution of the public service? How is the public service workforce organized, and who works there? Merit and patronage have been raised as important issues several times already in this book, but we take another look at them here. This section also asks, What steps have been taken to find a balance between patronage and merit?

### 2. ⌐ The Public Service Today: An Overview

In many respects, the public sector has pioneered progressive change in the workplace, but not without a struggle. This section asks, What factors affect its current composition? Why are region, language, equity, and unionization important? What are the most important equity issues? How has the public service changed to reflect the face of Canada? What is the importance of representativeness? How was the right to collective bargaining achieved in the public service? What political rights do public servants enjoy? What is the doctrine of political neutrality? What trends currently dominate in the relationship between public servants and the political system?

## A Brief History of the Public Service: Who Works There, Anyway?

A famous National Film Board documentary by the late, great Canadian film-maker Donald Brittain captured the disparaging attitude many people have toward the bureaucrat, whom Brittain characterized in this way:

*He is that most despised of human creatures. His activities have brought down upon his shoulders the scorn and outrage of history's multitude. He is homo bureaucratus; the bureaucrat. He is the paper-pusher of the world. . . . He has been compared to the cockroach. Like the cockroach, he appears to have no useful function. Like the cockroach, he has many enemies. Like the cockroach, he has survived all attempts at extinction.[3]*

This tongue-in-cheek characterization reflects popular attitudes. Compared to private sector organizations, the public service has made a very poor impression in the minds of many. Part of this perception depends on what citizens understand by *public service*. A 2007 poll revealed, when asked which professions Canadians trust most, six of the top eight are actually public servants (firefighters, nurses, teachers, doctors, police officers, and judges).[4] Senior public servants do not fare so well, it is true, coming in at 15th out of 23; and politicians rate ahead only of used car salespeople. But government, and indeed society, could scarcely function without the legions of public servants who every day protect us from danger, process our forms, regulate our behaviour, and punish our crimes and misdemeanours. Despite this, negative—if facile—attitudes about public servants persist.

Love it or hate it, the public service in Canada is always striving to improve itself. Indeed, reform of the public service reaches back to the earliest days of Confederation. Mind you, Canada is not alone in this regard. The United States, Britain, Finland, New Zealand, Australia, Sweden, Singapore, Malaysia, and countless other jurisdictions are responding to globalization, fiscal issues, and citizens' growing disillusionment with government by changing the way their public services do their jobs. But the history of public service reform in Canada includes a series of pitfalls whenever *reform* has been understood to mean "reduce." When Pierre Trudeau became prime minister in 1968, he promised to reduce the number of government employees by 25 000. Ten years later, their numbers had grown by 40 000. Brian Mulroney assumed office in 1984 with the promise that he would issue "pink slips and running shoes" to the public service. By the time he left in 1993, the public service had increased by over 13 000. The Chrétien government reversed this between 1993 and 1999, when there was a 23 percent reduction in the federal public service. By the end of 1999, public service employment had reached an historic low of 186 314.[5] But these reductions created serious workload issues, as we will see. In 1999 the first employment increase in seven years took place, and the public service grew by 2.6 percent, or 3800 employees. As of 2009, there were 274 000 federal public servants.[6]

To place this in some context, let us consider the history of the public service through the lens of patronage and merit. The origins of patronage in the Canadian public service reach back to the colonies of New France and British North America. The political culture of both was shaped by the fact that they were primarily military colonies: that is, hierarchically organized societies in which personal ambition was rewarded through service to the king, who held centralized political control and whose functionaries doled out patronage positions. Thus, the patterns of public service human resources management were established in colonial times when public servants received their posts for life. This generated stability for the governance of the colony and laid the basis for a "professional" career-based civil service, despite the presence of patronage politics. For instance,

*[I]mmediately prior to Confederation, out of nine deputy departmental heads in the Province of Canada, six had risen through the ranks by promotion, four had over twenty years' experience, and the most senior among them, the clerk of the Executive Council, could claim well over forty years' public service employment! The pattern was continued after 1867. At the time of the First World War, for example, the two dozen deputies at the federal level had an average of twenty years' experience.[7]*

So, while we generally assume that the major "human resources policy" of the early days of this country was essentially the widespread use of patronage to reward friends of the government, in fact, a "meritocracy" of sorts was evident quite early on at the upper reaches of the civil service:

*[P]atronage played an important role in nineteenth-century Canadian political culture because of its role as a vehicle for social promotion for the professional middle classes.*

*In a largely pre-industrial economy, the many employment possibilities offered by an expanding state—from customs inspectors and postal clerks to appointments to the judicial bench—were irresistibly attractive to the middle classes in search of security and prestige. The pursuit of such social rewards provided the foundation for political life in nineteenth-century Canada and gave rise to an intensely partisan political culture. . . . [Sir] John A. Macdonald used the patronage potential of an expanding state with mastery to build up his federal Conservative Party across the new federation and to dissolve, as far as possible, the forces of regionalism which threatened the stability of the new federal state. However, his success and example stimulated emulation and competition at the level of provincial governments, especially in Ontario, where long-serving Liberal Premier Oliver Mowat built up a smoothly functioning patronage machine based on an expanding and centralizing provincial state that eclipsed even Macdonald's federal Conservative machine for impartial and impersonal efficiency.[8]*

However, citizen outrage over the pettiness of patronage lower down in the public service, coupled with the example of merit systems in Great Britain and the United States, prompted reforms. Indeed, between 1867 and 1918, five federal royal commissions devoted at least part of their investigations to the evils of patronage.

Political scientist Laurent Dobuzinskis suggests that the move toward a meritocratic system of administration along Weberian lines began in Western Europe but had spread to North America by the 1880s.[9] By then, the need for professional administrators in both government and industry had become increasingly obvious; the drive for a merit-based professional civil service mixed with the scientific management approaches wafting up from the United States. The result was a sort of hybrid of British and American traditions.[10] The **Civil Service Acts of 1908 and 1918**, the creation of the **Civil Service Commission** in 1908, and the extension of its authority in the 1918 reforms marked the drive toward professionalization of the Canadian public service. These developments reinforced the independence of the public service from political interference—a factor that remains a cornerstone of the modern **Public Service Commission** today.

The reforms of 1918 were directly predicated, strangely enough, on a U.S. model not particularly suited to Canadian conditions. Political pressures surrounding the government of Sir Robert Borden during the First World War forced the prime minister to reform the civil service to end the squabbling between Conservatives and Liberals over patronage appointments. A U.S. consulting firm was hired to make recommendations for reform. The firm devised a blueprint for a complex, inflexible, and highly centralized human resources system designed for the conditions of corrupt machine politics in U.S. cities. This was Taylor's scientific management with a vengeance:

*. . . a mechanistic view of the world of work, of clear-cut and precise specialization of labour, one that assumed considerable organizational stability—so much stability that each step in the process of classifying and filling jobs should be done thoroughly even if it took many months, because each appointment was expected to last for years and years. This resulted in heavy, time-consuming processes and not a great deal of concern for human resource management. Employees were, in essence, seen as cogs in a large machine.[11]*

By the middle of the twentieth century, public servants were playing an active role in the emergence of the welfare state. They provided the technical, managerial, and professional capability to mobilize the resources of the Canadian government toward a massive shift in the traditional relationship between the state and society. These senior public servants played a vital role in shaping the managerial class and human resources policy and outlook of the Canadian public service. A new intellectual community, rooted mainly in the universities (especially the University of Toronto and Queen's University in Kingston), began to emerge, turning its attention to how the state could better manage the new issues of rapid industrialization and urbanization. Specifically, a cadre of individuals trained in the social sciences developed the conceit that they could make Canada a better country through improved human resource management and, ultimately—with a professional, skilled public service in place—in public policy making.[12] Individuals such as O.D. Skelton and Clifford Clark left Queen's University in the 1920s and 1930s to become deputy ministers (of External Affairs and Finance, respectively), attracting a new generation of like-minded university graduates, many of them economists, to form what historian J.L. Granatstein termed a new "mandarin" class of influential senior public managers.[13] Through the 1940s and 1950s, this small group played an influential role in professionalizing the public service. Recruitment to the upper ranks of the public service is noteworthy because of the way it reinforced the mandarins' position and power. For instance, over the past 50 years, nearly 95 percent of the deputy ministers (DMs) have come up from the ranks of assistant or associate deputy ministers. Even though the authority to appoint DMs is widely regarded as one of the more potent aspects of prime ministerial power, DMs are rarely, in fact, recruited directly by the prime minister. Instead, most are recommended and approved on the advice of the secretary to the Cabinet (who, you will recall, is the senior-most civil servant). This has led two observers to conclude that "the senior public service in Canada, then, has developed a pattern of internal recruitment, professionalism, and political neutrality, although some deputy ministers in later life have become Cabinet ministers or senators."[14] In the past, however, it also meant that the senior levels of the public service were remarkably homogeneous. As sociologist John Porter noted in *The Vertical Mosaic*, the senior public servants were part of an interconnected political, economic, social, and intellectual elite that shared certain characteristics: they tended to be white, Anglo-Saxon, Christian males who were well educated, moved in the same social circles, and acted as "gatekeepers" to keep out others who were not like themselves.[15] Perhaps more to the point, this group of managers seemed to regard human resources management as almost incidental to their work. They were greatly concerned with the broad picture of policy making and with macro-economic management of the country and related issues, but they paid little concrete attention to the day-to-day issues of employee satisfaction, morale, working conditions, or even the performance and competence of their underlings. It is not an exaggeration to suggest that despite its huge significance, human resources management has been a central concern of government for only the past 30 years.

However, the rapid changes brought about by immigration, as well as the changing role of women in Canadian society, made this "clubby" public service elite anachronistic. New attitudes crept into the thinking of public service managers, not the least of which was the notion that the entire public service, and most particularly its senior levels, should bear some resemblance to the society it serves—hence the more recent wholesale reform of human resource policies, such as affirmative action, employment equity, pay equity, and so on.

By the 1950s and 1960s, the state was assuming an ever-larger role in the management of the economy and the day-to-day lives of Canadians. The earlier metaphors derived from Weber's and Taylor's views of a mechanistic, rule-bound hierarchical organization were reinforced by increasingly rigid structures and processes and, simultaneously, challenged by new thinking about the roles of public servants. Two postwar developments, in particular, changed the nature and role of the public service in profound ways. The first was a rudimentary affirmative action plan to provide employment for Canadian soldiers returning from the Second World War (a similar, more modest effort had been initiated after the First World War, as well). Starting in 1940, over about 12 years, the public service tripled in size, absorbing surplus labour, and helping to prevent a return to the conditions of the Great Depression of the 1930s. However, this development, while impressive quantitatively, had relatively little qualitative effect. As Nicole Morgan, an authority on public service management, put it,

*[T]he first period of growth was unparalleled but had no effect on the traditional structure of the public service. In this instance, growth was carefully managed; it was concentrated in a few departments, distributed fairly evenly across the country, and made up of older men whose outlook had been shaped by the Hungry Thirties and the war. In a period of intensive growth, the civil service, as it was then called, was modelled on our military.*[16]

The postwar years saw a massive expansion of government at all levels, in response to the growth of society and technological change, but a lag in renewing human resources policy. Departments expanded and more employees were brought into the public service, but more important, qualitative changes to human resources policy were required. Moreover, a variety of new professional, technical, and managerial careers were needed in the public service. For example, the widespread introduction of computerized systems meant that positions for skilled computer technicians had to be created and categorized, and their pay levels and job descriptions had to be formalized. Given the rigid and bureaucratic nature of human resources management in this era, this was no easy task. It also had to be done for the countless other new positions created to keep pace with the broader changes in Canadian society. The depths of the difficulties in this era of rapid expansion were encapsulated in the Glassco Commission of 1961, and were expressed in the need to make the management of human resources (and indeed of government generally) more efficient, economical, and effective.[17]

Moreover, as the 1960s and 1970s unfolded, the issues of language training and bilingualism, unionization, affirmative action, and departmental reorganization converged. By this time, the literature of business management was replete with theories derived from the human relations school of organizational theory (see chapters 3 and 4). New management techniques were washing over the public service, and a new public service ethos was emerging that saw the public servant as an agent of change in the community, and not just a passive servant of the people, awaiting policy directives and instructions from Parliament. Participatory democracy became the watchword (although in practice it meant "you participate, we'll decide"), and the rapidly changing public sector scrambled to keep up.

Renewal of the public service became a pressing concern, and the strong expectation developed that new recruits to the upper levels would produce a more representative public service. Today, due to contemporary demographic patterns and the recent retirement of many senior managers, recruitment from outside the ranks of the public service is becoming more commonplace.[18] Since the broader society from which those recruits are coming has changed, it is axiomatic that the public service will continue to evolve into an institution far removed from the days of the old boys' network. Another striking development occurred when the first cohort of baby boomers began to graduate from the expanded university system in the 1960s and 1970s. From 1965 to 1975, the public service doubled in size. Many of these new, young employees began to see themselves not just as loyal servants but as agents of change. Morgan suggests that "although the second period of growth was less important in terms of numbers, it revolutionized both the structure and role of the public service."[19] These highly skilled and well-trained graduates, mainly from business schools, the social sciences, and economics, increasingly challenged civil servants' traditional views, pursuing organizational objectives and career goals that greatly transformed the public service. A new climate developed that encouraged policy experimentation and initiative. The technocratic expert who could provide sophisticated work based on the new sciences of cybernetics, computer modelling, systems theory, and other innovations came to be valued. The number of government departments, regulatory bodies, and Crown corporations mushroomed. New planning techniques were introduced, including financial management systems, such as Planning, Programming, Budgeting Systems (PPBS), and its successors. But this explosion of new systems left a troubling legacy. As Dobuzinskis reports,

*[T]raditional administrative tasks (e.g. personnel management) received relatively less attention; thus a gap was created between the macro-policy concerns of the upper echelons of the public service and the more strictly managerial concerns of middle-ranking officials. This gap was to become more and more pronounced, until it was finally acknowledged in the late 1980s. The same preoccupation with policy issues, as distinguished from the study of public administration, also gripped the academic community in the same period. (For instance, most graduate programs offering a Master's degree in public administration placed a greater emphasis on policy analysis than on organizational and managerial problems).[20]*

Even the merit system began to reveal itself as a barrier to sound management practices. By the 1980s, it was apparent that the rules governing recruitment and promotion had set up systemic barriers to certain socio-economic groups and that, consequently, the public service was still disproportionately staffed by white Anglo-phone males, especially at the upper levels. This failure of public service to be representative of society developed into a contentious issue.

Organizationally, the public service experienced growing pains in the postwar years, and a new legislative framework was put in place. The *Civil Service Act of 1961* was passed after it became apparent that the Civil Service Commission and the Treasury Board were stepping on each other's toes in terms of authority over government personnel. The Act gave the Treasury Board sole responsibility for determining pay levels and administrative organization. That was when the **Public Service Employment Act** (PSEA) established the Public Service Commission (PSC), and gave it responsibility for appointments to the public service and over-sight regarding the political activities of public servants. In addition, the **Public Service Staff Relations Act** (PSSRA) established the Public Service Staff Relations Board, which was given the responsibility to administer the Act and which con-firmed the role of the Treasury Board (TB) as the "employer" in collective bargain-ing and negotiating with public service employees. The **Financial Administration Act** (FAA) also gave Treasury Board human resources management authority for the public service. The independence of the Public Service Commission from inter-ference by government was maintained by having it report to Parliament rather than to Cabinet, although the three commissioners who head the Public Service Commission are appointed by the Cabinet for a set term of 10 years. A number of other Acts also came into force and gave more definition to the overall human resources framework: the Official Languages Act, the Employment Equity Act, the Canadian Charter of Rights and Freedoms, the Canadian Human Rights Act, the Privacy Act, and Part II of the Canada Labour Code.

As well, a variety of societal changes affected the public service in the postwar years. First, this was, in part, a response to the need to keep up with the rapid tech-nological changes of the twentieth century.[21] Second, the public service had to respond to the rise of new social movements in areas such as women's rights and gender equality, environmentalism, gay and lesbian rights, animal rights, seniors' rights, and the rising militancy of youth, "engaged in the politics of identity and . . . interested in the democratization of both everyday life and governance."[22] Finally, a fiscal crisis gripped the state from the 1970s, reshaping thinking about what the public service should be doing and what it should look like. Public sector man-agers were forced to shift their attention from designing grand systems for policy to the more prosaic details of managerial and administrative concerns. By the 1980s and 1990s, these factors seemed to overwhelm the public service and a malaise settled over it. When this was coupled with cutbacks and layoffs, it became apparent that renewal of the public service was an emerging issue.

Another factor profoundly affecting the public service was ideological in nature. The rise of neoconservatism, first in Great Britain under Margaret Thatcher, then in the United States under Ronald Reagan, and finally in Canada under Brian Mulroney, Jean Chrétien, Paul Martin, and Stephen Harper, brought increased disparagement of the public service. Many believed the state had become too large, complex, and unwieldy and a primary instrument of obstruction to the free operation of markets. Globalization reinforced these perspectives by raising the idea that states (that is, the public sector) interfere with the flow of goods and services in the global marketplace. The growing chorus of demands to reduce the size of government and put the art of governing on a more businesslike footing based on the theories of New Public Management (NPM) profoundly affected the public service's identity, role, composition, and morale.

Neoconservative arguments were challenged, however, by those who saw a legitimate role for government intervention in the economy. Jocelyne Bourgon, then clerk of the Privy Council and secretary to the Cabinet (the top civil servant in the public service) reminded Canadians that those reinventing government, while perhaps doing the inevitable, must not make government more businesslike, since the public and private sectors are inherently different. She also argued that the challenges of reinventing government were tremendously more complex than those in the private sector: "The management of change in the private sector may be a question of financial survival," she argued, "but for those of us in the public sector, it is about the future of the country, the national interest and the public good. We must guard against the simplistic notion that the public sector should be run like a private enterprise."[23] However, these arguments largely succumbed to the powerful juggernaut of the professional economists, business lobbies, and think tanks propounding the neoconservative doctrine.

As a result of the spread of neoconservatism and NPM, the public service has undergone a major self-examination over the past 25 years. In her *Report to the Prime Minister on the Public Service of Canada*, Jocelyne Bourgon described a "quiet crisis" in the Canadian public service. The years of downsizing and pay freezes, criticism and insufficient recruitment efforts made it difficult to retain, motivate, and attract people to the public service. This is related to another factor affecting the public service: demographic changes. The departure of experienced public servants who took early retirement buyouts or simply left in frustration, coupled with insufficient hiring of new young blood, means that the public service is bulging with middle-aged managers and workers. The historical memory, institutional experience, and knowledge of the "old-timers" were drained away. As well, there was an absence of the invigorating new ideas and perspectives that new recruits would normally bring to an organization. It was as if someone had cut off the head and feet of the organization and left the bloated body.

Thus, numerous reform exercises such as PS2000, La Relève, and the Public Service Modernization Act were launched (discussed in greater detail following), with mixed results. For instance, in 1992, as a result of PS2000, the Public Service Reform Act was passed, which helped lessen the bureaucratic red tape around hiring and firing. Perhaps more significantly, it also mandated employment equity programs. These reforms did, however, lead to some contention over the extent to which the merit principle was compromised for the goal of increased efficiency.

Moreover, a general rethinking of the place of the public service ensued. The key issues included merit, the ability to perform duties without political interference, **representativeness**, and access by all Canadians to employment opportunities within the public service.[24] Some important institutional changes were also made. For instance, in 1999–2000, two new federal agencies were created that significantly reduced the number of employees traditionally under the purview of the Treasury Board. First, Parks Canada was created in April 1999, resulting in the transfer of 3900 employees from the Ministry of Canadian Heritage. In November 1999, Revenue Canada became a separate agency known as the Canada Customs and Revenue Agency (now the Canada Revenue Agency), resulting in the transfer of about 40 000 employees. These innovations represented new ways to contain the growth of the public service and to reconfigure the universe of government human resources management since they fall outside the Public Service Staff Relations Act (the legislation that gives the Treasury Board the authority to act as the manager and employer of the federal public service).

Still, severe stresses and strains were produced by these various issues intersecting with one another. As a result, re-evaluation of human resources management has been a constant feature of the public service. Organizational confusion as to who should be doing what continuously challenges the regime of accountability. As well, in the 1990s, the PSEA and the PSSRA were reformed to better facilitate changing staffing and people management. Investment in leadership and management training was invigorated through the creation of an institution designed

*to inculcate corporate values and prepare senior managers to work in rapidly changing internal and external environments. The idea of a "university" for senior managers had been in circulation for over 20 years and, in 1988, the Canadian Centre for Management Development (CCMD) was established . . . its mandate included commissioning research from public servants and from academics on public management issues, and providing a forum for the exchange of ideas.*[25]

In 2003, its mandate was altered to provide training for public servants at all levels, and its name was changed to the Canada School for Public Service (CSPS). As mentioned earlier, an initiative called "La Relève" (see chapter 9), introduced new succession planning and corporate development programs.

Given the organization and structure of management where human resources is concerned, it is no wonder that specialized training, such as that being developed by the CSPS, is needed. Consider, for instance, the complexity of the organizational duties and roles of the main bodies responsible for human resources management. Figure 8.1 depicts the responsibilities of the main actors in contemporary human resource management.

Clearly, many changes have occurred in the public service in Canada since 1867. Originally a relatively small, patronage-based haven for friends of the governing party, it has evolved into a huge, complex, merit-based professional institution composed of legions of highly skilled and technically gifted people. It has changed in other important ways, too. For instance, it has become more representative. Once the preserve of white, Anglophone, middle- and upper-class males, the public service has recently taken proactive and progressive steps to become a more inclusive equal opportunity employer. To ensure that the public service reflects the regional, multicultural, linguistic, and gender makeup of Canada, procedures such as affirmative action, employment equity, and pay equity programs have been introduced to encourage and promote the employment of women, visible

**FIGURE 8.1    Responsibilities in Human Resources Management in the Federal Public Service**

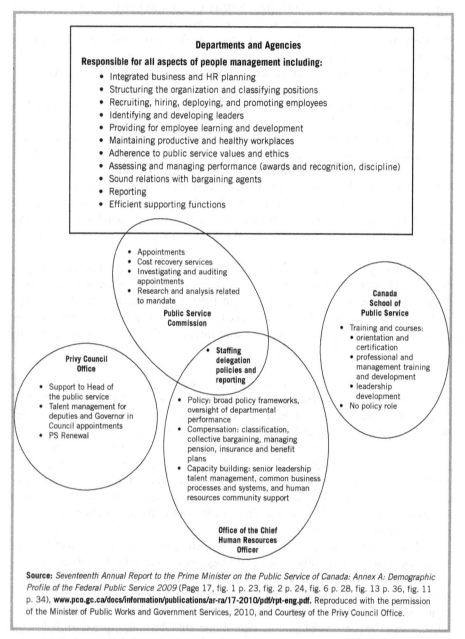

**Departments and Agencies**

**Responsible for all aspects of people management including:**

- Integrated business and HR planning
- Structuring the organization and classifying positions
- Recruiting, hiring, deploying, and promoting employees
- Identifying and developing leaders
- Providing for employee learning and development
- Maintaining productive and healthy workplaces
- Adherence to public service values and ethics
- Assessing and managing performance (awards and recognition, discipline)
- Sound relations with bargaining agents
- Reporting
- Efficient supporting functions

**Public Service Commission**
- Appointments
- Cost recovery services
- Investigating and auditing appointments
- Research and analysis related to mandate

**Privy Council Office**
- Support to Head of the public service
- Talent management for deputies and Governor in Council appointments
- PS Renewal

**Staffing delegation policies and reporting**

**Office of the Chief Human Resources Officer**
- Policy: broad policy frameworks, oversight of departmental performance
- Compensation: classification, collective bargaining, managing pension, insurance and benefit plans
- Capacity building: senior leadership talent management, common business processes and systems, and human resources community support

**Canada School of Public Service**
- Training and courses:
  - orientation and certification
  - professional and management training and development
  - leadership development
- No policy role

**Source:** *Seventeenth Annual Report to the Prime Minister on the Public Service of Canada: Annex A: Demographic Profile of the Federal Public Service 2009* (Page 17, fig. 1 p. 23, fig. 2 p. 24, fig. 6 p. 28, fig. 13 p. 36, fig. 11 p. 34), www.pco.gc.ca/docs/information/publications/ar-ra/17-2010/pdf/rpt-eng.pdf. Reproduced with the permission of the Minister of Public Works and Government Services, 2010, and Courtesy of the Privy Council Office.

minorities, the disabled, and Aboriginals. Moreover, since the Second World War, the public sector has been the fastest-unionizing sector of the Canadian economy. This development—the culmination of a long struggle—has given workers in the public service collective agreements and expanded their political rights, which were once severely circumscribed.

Each of these developments has contributed significantly to Canadians' enjoying a very high standard of living in a country with a well-developed and sophisticated provision of public services. Indeed, Canada has always ranked extremely high in the United Nations Human Development Index, a scale devised to measure purchasing power, life expectancy, literacy, and educational attainment: ranging from first (in 1996) to fourth (in 2009).[26] At the same time, each of the developments cited above has also been marked by controversy, reflecting disputes over what the public service (that is, the state) should or should not do.

# The Public Service Today: An Overview

Attitudes about the public service in Canada are currently changing. Recognizing some of the damage that has been done to a once-great institution, the government is making an effort to restore a sense of pride and worth to a public service career. In his 2007 *Annual Report to the Prime Minister*, then-clerk of the Privy Council Kevin Lynch said that "many would say that the Public Service seems to have been renewing itself for much of the past 20 years. Is this process never going to end? Why is it is necessary to put people and institutions through still more change and, some would say, upheaval, when there are so many other things to be done by government in the service of Canadians?" In answering his own question, the clerk went on to suggest,

*The answer, to put it simply, is: if the Public Service, as a core national institution, does not renew itself for future as well as for current service to the government and people of Canada, it risks becoming less relevant, less useful and less respected as the years go by. If we do not commit ourselves to a continuing process of renewal, the Public Service will not remain a creative national institution, central to the governance and development of our country.[27]*

Even if you have never worked in the public sector, chances are that you know someone who has or does. When you account for federal, provincial, and local governments, the public sector in Canada employs about one in four Canadians. By comparison, before Confederation the public service employed about 2700 people, and by 1896 it had grown to about 10 000.[28] In 1993, 196 674 people were employed under the authority of the federal Public Service Commission alone. By 1999, however, this number fell to 142 906.[29] But if the transitions involving Parks Canada and the Canada Customs and Revenue Agency are taken out of the equation, the public service actually began to grow again in 2000. The rest of the federal workforce is under the jurisdiction of the Armed Forces, RCMP, Crown corporations, agencies, and other bodies that together make up the broader public service. When you take into consideration employment at the federal, provincial, territorial, and local government levels, the size of the public service fell to a low in the late 1990s, followed by considerable rebuilding (see Figure 8.2).

**FIGURE 8.2**   **Number of Employees, Government Sector, Canada, 1991–2005**

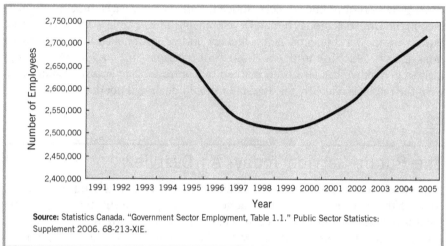

Source: Statistics Canada. "Government Sector Employment, Table 1.1." Public Sector Statistics: Supplement 2006. 68-213-XIE.

According to the 2006 Census, federal, provincial and territorial, and local governments as well as government business enterprise employment reached an annual average of 3.1 million employees, with about 2.9 million of these employees working in the federal, provincial and territorial, and local governments.[30] This contrasts with 1999, when government employment fell to just over 2.5 million. The breakdown of employment by level of government shows that in 2006, the provinces and territories accounted for 51.0 percent of total government employment, or nearly 1.5 million. The federal government accounted for 13.6 percent, or 393 000 employees, and local governments accounted for 35.4 percent, or slightly over 1 million employees. The relative sizes of the three levels of government have remained relatively stable over the years. Overall, however, government employment has risen moderately. For instance, between 2003 and 2006, federal government employment rose 7.4 percent (just under 2.5 percent per year), or 27 000. Provincial and territorial government employment advanced 3.7 percent (just over 1.2 percent per year), or 52 000. Local governments saw an increase of 5.0 percent (nearly 1.7 percent per year), or 49 000. About half of employees at the provincial and territorial level of government worked in the health and social service sector; about one-quarter worked in ministries, departments, agencies, and similar institutions; and the rest worked in colleges and universities.[31]

It has recently been fashionable to complain that government has become too big. But comparing the growth of the federal government to the growth of the Canadian population, and the growth in government spending to the size of the economy overall, reveals a different interpretation. From 1983 to 2009, Canada's population grew by 31 percent (from 25.6 to 33.5 million), while the number of federal public servants increased by 9.2 percent (from 251 000 to 274 000). The public service, therefore, represents a lower proportion of the Canadian population today (0.82 percent) than it did in 1983 (1.0 percent). Figure 8.3 shows that real Gross Domestic Product (GDP) doubled and real federal program spending in

**FIGURE 8.3    Trends in the Economy, Population, Federal Program Spending, and the Size of the Federal Public Service, 1983–1984 to 2008–2009**

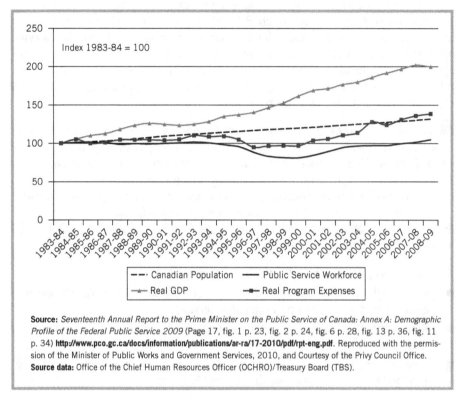

**Source:** *Seventeenth Annual Report to the Prime Minister on the Public Service of Canada: Annex A: Demographic Profile of the Federal Public Service 2009* (Page 17, fig. 1 p. 23, fig. 2 p. 24, fig. 6 p. 28, fig. 13 p. 36, fig. 11 p. 34) **http://www.pco.gc.ca/docs/information/publications/ar-ra/17-2010/pdf/rpt-eng.pdf**. Reproduced with the permission of the Minister of Public Works and Government Services, 2010, and Courtesy of the Privy Council Office. **Source data:** Office of the Chief Human Resources Officer (OCHRO)/Treasury Board (TBS).

constant dollars increased by 38.4 percent over 25 years. Whereas federal program spending as a proportion of GDP was 0.2 percent in 1983, it had decreased to 0.14 percent by 2009.[32]

The question of how to organize all those people who work in the public service is vital to the smooth functioning of government. Until recently, the federal public service was divided into six occupational categories: executive group (4898 employees); scientific and professional (27 350 employees); administrative and foreign service (90 284 employees); technical (17 422 employees); administrative support (26 849 employees); and operational (19 951 employees).[33] In 2005, a new classification standard was applied to the Foreign Service group and a new Border Services classification group was created. These categories help determine pay levels and occupations. According to the Treasury Board, the policy objective of the classification system is "to ensure that the relative value of all jobs in the Public Service is established in an equitable, consistent and effective manner and provides a basis for the compensation of public servants."[34] Within these six categories, virtually every profession and trade known to modern society is found, organized in a uniform manner that permits rational staffing and appointments consistent with the merit principle. No matter which department an employee works in, he receives the same remuneration as any other employee in that level and category. This job categorization creates a clear chain of command and responsibility; within each department a descending order of command is organized such that each employee is responsible to a superior.

Currently, job categorization is undergoing major reform. The Classification Modernization Program was launched in 2003 in concert with key management modernization priorities of the federal government, including the **Public Service Modernization Act** (PSMA). It was also aligned with the 2006 Federal Accountability Act and the clerk of the Privy Council's public service renewal initiatives, relating to recruitment, knowledge transfer, succession planning, learning and training, talent management, and retention.[35]

*Even earlier, in 2001, the government initiated a new approach to modernizing human resources management. The prime minister announced the formation of the Task Force on Modernizing Human Resources Management in the Public Service to recommend a modern institutional framework for managing human resources. The Task Force was guided by three principles: protecting the merit principle, delegating human resource management matters to the lowest possible managerial level, and ensuring that managers were accountable for results. The work of the Task Force resulted in the 2003 Public Service Modernization Act.[36]*

The purposes of the Act included the following:

- *increased flexibility in staffing and managing people with reinforced safeguards to sustain a merit-based, non-partisan public service;*
- *more constructive, co-operative labour-management relations to support a healthy, productive workplace;*
- *more coherent training and learning to help employees pursue professional development and meet the corporate needs of the public service;*
- *and clarified roles and strengthened accountability for the institutions and individuals responsible for managing the public service.[37]*

Following this, the government created the Public Service Human Resources Management Agency of Canada, reporting to the president of the Treasury Board. This agency changed its name to the more succinct Public Service Agency in 2007. There were now four agencies with some responsibility for human resources management in the federal government: the Treasury Board Secretariat, the Public Service Commission, the Public Service Agency, and the Canada School of Public Service.[38]

Also in 2003, the Treasury Board introduced the Management Accountability Framework (MAF), partly in response to the various accountability scandals that were rocking government at the time. The MAF set out the Treasury Board's expectations of senior public service managers for good management. Consisting of 10 key elements, the MAF is depicted and explained in Figure 8.4.[39]

Currently, the major issues confronting human resource managers in the public service are focused on the ongoing implementation of the Public Service Modernization Act, which shifts "responsibility for HR management away from central agencies into the hands of deputy heads and from HR professionals to line

## FIGURE 8.4    The Management Accountability Framework

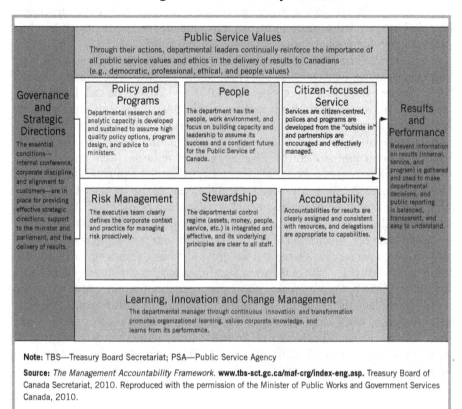

**Public Service Values**
Through their actions, departmental leaders continually reinforce the importance of all public service values and ethics in the delivery of results to Canadians (e.g., democratic, professional, ethical, and people values)

**Governance and Strategic Directions**
The essential conditions—internal conference, corporate discipline, and alignment to customers—are in place for providing effective strategic directions, support to the minister and parliament, and the delivery of results.

**Policy and Programs**
Departmental research and analytic capacity is developed and sustained to assume high quality policy options, program design, and advice to ministers.

**People**
The department has the people, work environment, and focus on building capacity and leadership to assume its success and a confident future for the Public Service of Canada.

**Citizen-focussed Service**
Services are citizen-centred, polices and programs are developed from the "outside in" and partnerships are encouraged and effectively managed.

**Results and Performance**
Relevent information on results (internal, service, and program) is gathered and used to make departmental decisions, and public reporting is balanced, transparent, and easy to understand.

**Risk Management**
The executive team clearly defines the corporate context and practice for managing risk proactively.

**Stewardship**
The departmental control regime (assets, money, people, service, etc.) is integrated and effective, and its underlying principles are clear to all staff.

**Accountability**
Accountabilities for results are clearly assigned and consistent with resources, and delegations are appropriate to capabilities.

**Learning, Innovation and Change Management**
The departmental manager through continuous innovation and transformation promotes organizational learning, values corporate knowledge, and learns from its performance.

**Note:** TBS—Treasury Board Secretariat; PSA—Public Service Agency

**Source:** *The Management Accountability Framework.* www.tbs-sct.gc.ca/maf-crg/index-eng.asp. Treasury Board of Canada Secretariat, 2010. Reproduced with the permission of the Minister of Public Works and Government Services Canada, 2010.

managers, thereby giving managers more authority and flexibility—but also more responsibility and accountability—to manage their people."[40] Other issues include: capacity building in human resources planning and accountability; embedding public service values and ethicsat all levels of the public service, including the implementation of legislation regarding the disclosure of wrongdoing; the modernization of the classification system;the re-engineering of corporate human resources processes and information systems; achieving targets and required cultural changes in the areas of official languages and employment equity; creating a more inclusive, representative, and accessible public service; the management and development of leadership; and implementing a new learning policy for employees.[41]

Perhaps the boldest reform was to the merit principle, which was explicitly defined in statute for the first time. This made a rather cumbersome and rule-bound system of appointments more flexible. The new PSEA redefined merit as appointments where the selected candidate meets "essential qualifications for the work to be performed, as established by the deputy head, including official language proficiency." As Juillet and Rasmussen conclude, "it would now no longer be necessary to show that the selected person was the best qualified candidate, but only that he or she possessed the necessary qualifications to perform the work."[42]

Managers could take into consideration a candidate's assets not deemed essential to the job and could consider a single person for a position rather than interview several. This implied a more limited application of the merit principle while increasing the discretionary power of managers in hiring.

In 2006, the prime minister created another task force to investigate the state of human resources management. The Prime Minister's Advisory Committee on the Public Service issued four reports between 2007 and 2010. The task force articulated concerns about recruitment and retention, policy and legislative barriers, development programs, human resources management policies and practices, and branding the public service.[43] Following recommendations by this committee, the prime minister announced further changes. Deputy ministers were given primary responsibility for human resource management in their departments, and in March 2009 the Canada Public Service Agency and the parts of the Treasury Board Secretariat that deal with pensions and benefits, labour relations, and compensation were consolidated into a new Office of the Chief Human Resources Officer.[44]

As you can see, the agenda of major issues confronting human resource managers in the public service is large and daunting. Consider demographic trends, for example (see Box 8.1). One of the most significant factors is a growing concentration of the 45–54 age group, which now constitutes about 50 percent of all federal employees. In fact, the age profile of the federal public service is reversed from that of 15 years ago, when employees aged 24–44 comprised 60 percent of the workforce, and fewer than 30 percent were over 45. Today more than 50 percent of all public servants are over 45. Currently, about 10 percent of public servants have 30-plus years of pensionable service, and about 8 percent are eligible to retire.

---

### BOX 8.1 | Demographic Profile of the Public Service of Canada

- 274 000 employees (251 000 in 1983)
- 55.1% women (42% in 1983)
- 42.6% of executives are women (less than 5% in 1983)
- 59.7% of employees in the regions and 40.3% in the National Capital Region
- 86.1% indeterminate employees; 9.2% term employees; 4.7% casuals and students
- 70.9% declare English their first official language; 29.1% declare French
- Average age: 43.9 years (39 in 1983)

- Average age of executives: 50.3 years (48.7 in 1983)
- Public Service represents 0.82% of the Canadian population (1% in 1983)

**Note:** The "Public Service" refers to the core public administration (departments and agencies for which the Treasury Board is the employer) and separate employers (principally the Canada Revenue Agency, Parks Canada, the Canadian Food Inspection Agency, and the National Research Council Canada).

**Source:** *Seventeenth Annual Report to the Prime Minister on the Public Service of Canada: Annex A: Demographic Profile of the Federal Public Service 2009* (Page 17, fig. 1 p. 23, fig. 2 p. 24, fig. 6 p. 28, fig. 13 p. 36, fig. 11 p. 34), **www.pco.gc.ca/docs/information/publications/ar-ra/17-2010/pdf/rpt-eng.pdf**. Reproduced with the permission of the Minister of Public Works and Government Services, 2010, and Courtesy of the Privy Council Office. **Source data:** Office of the Chief Human Resources Officer (OCHRO)/Treasury Board (TBS).

**FIGURE 8.5    Federal Public Service Population by Age Bands for 2004 and 2009**

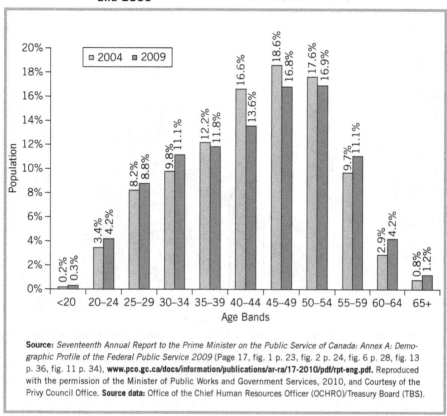

**Source:** *Seventeenth Annual Report to the Prime Minister on the Public Service of Canada: Annex A: Demographic Profile of the Federal Public Service 2009* (Page 17, fig. 1 p. 23, fig. 2 p. 24, fig. 6 p. 28, fig. 13 p. 36, fig. 11 p. 34), **www.pco.gc.ca/docs/information/publications/ar-ra/17-2010/pdf/rpt-eng.pdf.** Reproduced with the permission of the Minister of Public Works and Government Services, 2010, and Courtesy of the Privy Council Office. **Source data:** Office of the Chief Human Resources Officer (OCHRO)/Treasury Board (TBS).

Where retirements are concerned, the Clerk of the Privy Council reported in 2010 that the public service retirement rate declined slightly in 2008–2009 (by 0.1 percent), after steadily increasing by 0.9 percent between 2004–2005 and 2007–2008, and that "Projections for the next several years call for a slight increase followed by a level retirement rate, assuming a stable employee population."[45]

Figure 8.5 compares the public service age distribution of 2004 to that of 2009. It shows a general shift toward an aging workforce. The share of employees aged 35–54 dropped by 5.9 percentage points to 59.1 percent; that of employees aged 55 and older increased by 3.1 percentage points to 16.5 percent and is expected to almost double over the next decade, imposing an increased strain in terms of sick leave and higher health-care costs. Public sector pensions are also a major source of concern. Because of recent recruitment efforts, the number of public servants aged 34 and under increased by 2.8 percentage points to 24.4 percent. The average age of public servants has recently begun to decrease, from 44.3 years in 2007 to 43.9 in 2009, a fact that bodes well for public administration students if this trend holds.

But the numbers are particularly acute in the executive category of the federal public service. For example, about 75 percent are between the ages of 45 and 59, with an average age of 50, and about 18 percent of those are currently eligible to

**FIGURE 8.6    Federal Public Service Executive Population Distribution
by Age Bands for 2004 and 2009**

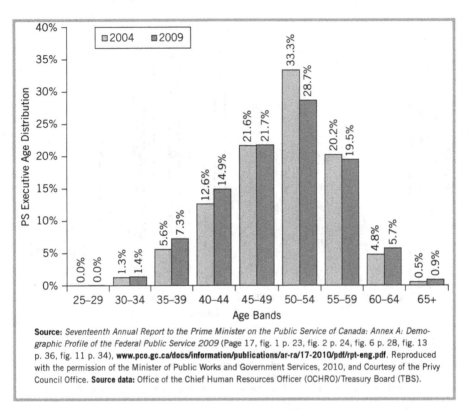

**Source:** *Seventeenth Annual Report to the Prime Minister on the Public Service of Canada: Annex A: Demographic Profile of the Federal Public Service 2009* (Page 17, fig. 1 p. 23, fig. 2 p. 24, fig. 6 p. 28, fig. 13 p. 36, fig. 11 p. 34), **www.pco.gc.ca/docs/information/publications/ar-ra/17-2010/pdf/rpt-eng.pdf**. Reproduced with the permission of the Minister of Public Works and Government Services, 2010, and Courtesy of the Privy Council Office. **Source data:** Office of the Chief Human Resources Officer (OCHRO)/Treasury Board (TBS).

retire. Since 2000, the number of executives under the age of 45 has increased about 48 percent, from 618 to 917. Figure 8.6 compares the age distribution of executives in 2004 and 2009. The proportion of executives under 50 years of age increased from 41.1 percent in 2004 to 45.3 percent in 2009; the proportion over 50 decreased from 58.8 percent to 54.8 percent. The average age of executives decreased slightly over this period, from 50.6 years in 2004 to 50.3 years in 2009. Clearly, demographic trends pose a serious challenge here.

The good news is that governments at all levels are thinking seriously about recruitment. So, suppose you decide on a career in the federal public service—how do you get in? First, the Public Service Commission sponsors various recruitment programs for students and others. The Post-Secondary Recruitment Program (PSR) seeks post-secondary graduates who have the qualifications needed to fill entry-level positions. Jobs are advertised by means of recruitment campaigns, which generally begin in the fall and winter. In addition, there is a general inventory open year-round to university students of all fields of study. There are also targeted recruitment campaigns aimed at attracting the "best and the brightest" among university graduates to the public service. Typically, you will have to write an entrance exam to determine whether you are a qualified candidate. Once you secure a position, there are competitions for promotions and an appeal process to ensure that every employee has a fair chance to advance. In some cases, new job openings will be deemed "open," meaning that individuals from outside the public service can apply. In other circumstances, the candidate search will be "closed," meaning that it is limited to those who already work within the public service.[46]

The merit of your application to the public service is a key factor in whether you are hired, of course. But the government is also committed to employment equity:

*The Government of Canada is committed to a public service that reflects the rich diversity of the Canadian society it serves. Canada is becoming more diverse and the fabric of Canadian society is changing. This is creating a need for policies, programs, and services that address these changes. As our labour market evolves, the talents required for a dynamic and innovative public service will be increasingly found by attracting the best talent from employment equity groups.*[47]

Therefore, analyzing employment in the public service is not simply a matter of "How many?" Looking at a variety of factors, such as region, language, equity, and unionization, will give us a more nuanced picture, but first we will consider the extent to which the public service is, or ought to be, representative of the society it serves.

## The Theory of Representativeness

The Public Service Employment Act, as amended in 1992, forbids discrimination in hiring or promotion on the basis of race, national or ethnic origin, colour, religion, age, sex, marital status, disability, or conviction for an offence for which a pardon has been granted. Since the 1992 reforms, the Public Service Commission's staffing decisions are still guided by the merit principle, but it has also initiated employment equity plans for historically under-represented groups: women, Aboriginal peoples, persons with disabilities, and visible minorities. The broad goal has been to make the public service more representative of the society it serves. Social changes have seen more women enter the paid workforce, and immigration has brought about demographic change. The difficult question is how to adapt the public service to these changes so that it reflects the broader Canadian society.[48]

Essentially, the theory behind representativeness is that if the public service reflects the population, it will make decisions in the best interests of those it serves and ensure that the values of both are commensurate. Of course, there is no guarantee that the values of an individual public servant will be the same as those of the group she comes from, since socialization is a complex thing. Thus, critics of the theory of representativeness suggest that you cannot guarantee a responsive public service simply by creating one composed of individuals whose numbers are in proportion to the size of their group in society. The public service has its own institutional values and interests that often supersede those of individuals, no matter how those individuals were previously socialized. The other side of this coin, though, is that there is no guarantee that a responsive public service need be representative. There are countless examples in Canadian history of the elite, exclusive upper echelons of the public service enacting policy that benefits groups different from those who hold offices of power.

In any event, the theoretical arguments about representativeness seem moot in light of real-life experience. A regime of representativeness is under construction in Canada, and has been for more than 40 years. Proactive steps have been taken in a number of areas to promote regional and linguistic representativeness. Moreover, various equity initiatives concerning women, visible minorities, Aboriginals, and the disabled have been enacted (see Table 8.1). We will now consider each in turn, bearing in mind that despite these recent efforts, the Canadian public service is still not a "microcosm" of the society it serves, and the further up the hierarchy you go, the truer this is.

## Region

It may not seem obvious at first, but where public servants work is an important consideration. The assumption that the "government" is in Ottawa is a mistaken one. Consider the following:

- *In 2006, 42 percent of federal public servants worked in the National Capital Region (Ottawa-Gatineau).*
- *About 13 percent work in Ontario; 12 percent in Quebec outside the National Capital Region (roughly equal to their proportion of the overall population when you factor in employees in the National Capital Region).*
- *About 11 percent work in the Atlantic provinces (slightly more than their proportion of the overall population).*
- *About 12 percent work in the prairies; 10 percent in British Columbia or the Territories (slightly less than their proportion of the overall population).*
- *About 1 percent work outside Canada in our embassies and trade missions.*[49]

The proportion of public servants found in each region of the country has both symbolic and pragmatic importance. First, there has been a deliberate effort to decentralize the functions of government away from Ottawa to help combat alienation from the nation's capital, by putting the face of the government in the very communities that it serves. In other words, establishing field offices across the country lets Canadians see their tax dollars at work, and personalizes the distant and aloof structures of power found in Ottawa. Second, and more pragmatically, locating government offices outside Ottawa creates jobs in regions that might lack other employment opportunities. Nothing puts a smile on the face of a Cabinet minister like the prospect of opening a federal facility in his or her riding!

## Language

Linguistic considerations have always played a prominent role in the development of the public service. In the era of patronage, French Canadians could always count on receiving appointments from the handful of French-Canadian Cabinet ministers. When patronage was eliminated as the basis of hiring, there was no mechanism to ensure that the proportion of French-speaking civil servants matched the proportion of the French-speaking population in Canada. As a result, the use and importance of French within the halls of power diminished over time. Political scientist J.E. Hodgetts reported that between 1918 and 1945,

**TABLE 8.1** Representation of Federal Public Service Employees by Designated Group and Occupational Category as of March 31, 2008

| Occupation Category | All Employees # | Women # | Women % | Aboriginal Peoples # | Aboriginal Peoples % | Persons with Disabilities # | Persons with Disabilities % | Members of Visible Minorities # | Members of Visible Minorities % |
|---|---|---|---|---|---|---|---|---|---|
| Executive | 4898 | 2042 | 41.7 | 165 | 3.4 | 278 | 5.7 | 326 | 6.7 |
| Scientific and Professional | 27 350 | 12 385 | 45.3 | 697 | 2.5 | 1094 | 4.0 | 3 662 | 13.4 |
| Administrative and Foreign Service | 90 284 | 55 832 | 61.8 | 4121 | 4.6 | 5554 | 6.2 | 8 533 | 9.5 |
| Technical | 17 422 | 5663 | 32.5 | 612 | 3.5 | 896 | 5.1 | 1 106 | 6.3 |
| Administrative Support | 26 849 | 21 719 | 80.9 | 1395 | 5.2 | 2093 | 7.8 | 2 730 | 10.2 |
| Operational | 19 951 | 3948 | 19.8 | 1200 | 6.0 | 1086 | 5.4 | 850 | 4.3 |
| Total | 186 754 | 101 589 | 54.4 | 8190 | 4.4 | 11 001 | 5.9 | 17 207 | 9.2 |

**Source:** Human Resources and Social Development Canada. *2005 Employment Equity Annual Report*, Appendix C, Figure 4. Reprinted with the permission of Her Majesty the Queen in Right of Canada 2007.

for instance, the number of French-speaking civil servants dropped by more than 10 percent.[50] At the senior levels of the public service, the numbers were particularly dismal. Former prime minister Pierre Trudeau recalled arriving in Ottawa in the late 1950s to work as a public servant in the Privy Council Office, and being astonished to discover that if he wanted to write a memo to another French-Canadian civil servant, he had to do so in English!

Political scientists Robert and Doreen Jackson explain the under-representation of French-Canadians in the civil service this way:

*Many factors combined during these years to reduce levels of francophone recruitment in the federal bureaucracy. The public service became less attractive for French-Canadians because no provisions were made to ensure service to French-Canadians. Nor were francophones' bilingual skills included in an assessment of their qualifications. Francophones were also hindered by the merit system's examinations and interviews, which reflected the patterns of thought and cultural styles of English-speaking Canada. The competitions also emphasized the technical and commercial skills taught in the English educational system, placing French-Canadians, with their classical education, at a disadvantage.[51]*

Incidents like the one experienced by Trudeau in an ostensibly bilingual country and federal public service prompted him to pass the Official Languages Act in 1969 to rectify this type of discrimination. Trudeau embarked upon an ambitious exercise to make "French power" a reality in Ottawa, and to make the federal government truly bilingual.

Much of the groundwork for this process was laid by the Royal Commission on Bilingualism and Biculturalism, which reported between 1967 and 1970.[52] The Royal Commission recommended the Public Service Commission be made responsible for language training, instructing it to walk a tightrope between, on the one hand, promoting the use of French in the federal public service and recruiting more bilingual workers, and, on the other hand, ensuring that the merit principle was respected. Progress has been slow, especially in the upper ranks, but today the percentage of French Canadians in each of the occupational categories of the public service matches or exceeds the percentage of French Canadians overall (about 24 percent). The Office of the Commissioner of Official Languages is the body responsible for monitoring and reporting on the implementation of the Official Languages Act, and it does so annually with its report to Parliament.[53] According to the Clerk of the Privy Council, "English is identified as the first official language (OL) of 70.9% of public servants, while 29.1% identify French as their first official language . . . this proportion has remained relatively stable since 1983, when the figures were 72.7% and 27.3%."[54]

## Equity

**Employment equity**—a term coined by Judge Rosalie Abella in her groundbreaking Royal Commission Report on Equality in Employment—came into widespread use in the 1980s and is similar in meaning to **affirmative action**.[55] The Public Service Commission defines *employment equity* as "employment practices designed to ensure that the regular staffing process is free of attitudinal and systemic barriers in order that the Public Service reflects all groups present in the Canadian labour force, and designed to ensure that corrective measures are applied to erase any historical disadvantage experienced by certain designated groups."[56] Judge Abella intended it to help eliminate discrimination in the workplace, which, she noted, had affected various groups in Canadian society. "One hundred years ago, the role for women was almost exclusively domestic," she wrote. "Fifty years ago some visible minorities were disenfranchised; 25 years ago, native people lacked a policy voice; and 10 years ago, disabled persons were routinely kept dependent. Today, none of these exclusionary assumptions is acceptable."[57]

The Clerk of the Privy Council reported in 2010 that "In general, the representation levels of the four designated employment equity groups within the public service have risen modestly in recent years (with a slight decline for persons with disabilities in 2009). Employment levels in 2009 for women, Aboriginal peoples, and persons with disabilities exceeded their workforce availability. However, the representation of visible minorities was 1.9 percent below their availability."[58]

Let's consider the position of women.[59] In 1983, the majority of public service employees were men (58.2 percent), but women gained ground over the past decade. By 2009, 55.1 percent of public servants were women (see Figure 8.7). While the representation of women in 2009 was 10.2 percent higher than that of men, it was also 2.3 percent above the workforce availability of women.

**FIGURE 8.7    Proportion of Men and Women in the Public Service— Selected Years, 1983–2009**

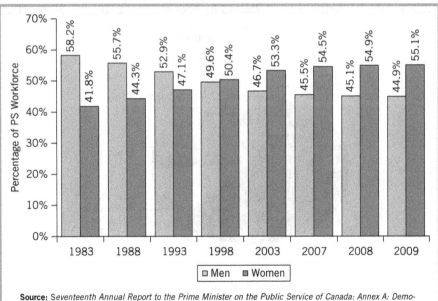

Source: *Seventeenth Annual Report to the Prime Minister on the Public Service of Canada: Annex A: Demographic Profile of the Federal Public Service 2009* (Page 17, fig. 1 p. 23, fig. 2 p. 24, fig. 6 p. 28, fig. 13 p. 36, fig. 11 p. 34), **www.pco.gc.ca/docs/information/publications/ar-ra/17-2010/pdf/rpt-eng.pdf.** Reproduced with the permission of the Minister of Public Works and Government Services, 2010, and Courtesy of the Privy Council Office. **Source data:** Office of the Chief Human Resources Officer (OCHRO)/Treasury Board (TBS).

In 1967, women made up only 27 percent of the employees in the public service, compared to 55 percent today. However, women have historically been heavily "ghettoized" in "pink-collar" occupations. For instance, 83 percent worked in "office and administrative support" positions in 1967, compared to about 30 percent today. Whereas only 12 percent of those working in program administration 30 years ago were women, today 47 percent are women. While gains in women's representation overall are impressive, there are several occupational groups where women have made virtually no progress. Consider, for instance, that women constitute only about 9 percent of engineers and land surveyors, 6 percent of electronics experts, 3 percent of firefighters, and 5 percent of general labour and trades, and it is evident that progress is uneven across the public service.

At the executive level of the public service, for example, fewer than 1 percent of senior officers were women in 1967, whereas today 42 percent are women, revealing progress but continued under-representation overall. The first and so far only woman to be appointed to the position of the top public servant—the clerk of the Privy Council—was Jocelyne Bourgon, who served in that role from 1994 to 1999, and in 2010, 11 of 28 deputy ministers were women. Overall, the percentage of female public servants who work in the executive, scientific, and professional, or administrative and foreign service categories has been rising since the 1980s, while women hold a proportionately smaller number of administrative support jobs than in the past (see Figure 8.8). Moreover, women constitute the greatest numbers of all persons hired into the scientific and professional category (54.8 percent). Women are also being promoted at a greater rate than men, receiving approximately 6 out of 10

**FIGURE 8.8    Distribution of Women by Occupational Category, 2008–2009**

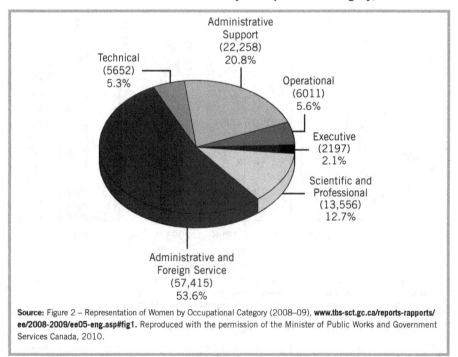

Administrative
Support
(22,258)
20.8%

Technical
(5652)
5.3%

Operational
(6011)
5.6%

Executive
(2197)
2.1%

Scientific and
Professional
(13,556)
12.7%

Administrative and
Foreign Service
(57,415)
53.6%

promotions. Interestingly, though, 4 in 10 women continue to enter the public service through the administrative support category.

However, a more focused assessment reveals some lingering problems.[60] For instance, female employees constitute 60 percent of hiring in term and casual positions. While the overall number of women in the executive category has increased, most are concentrated in the lower reaches of that group. A spate of retirements means that up to 70 percent of the executive category could leave in the next few years, although political scientist Jonathan Malloy argues that we are witnessing "evolutionary" rather than "revolutionary" demographic shifts in the public service—that is, the retirements are not happening all at once.[61] Since most potential retirees are men, and more men than women overall are leaving the public service, this could open the doors for women in senior management positions. However, under conditions of downsizing and budget cutbacks, most federal departments reduced external recruitment and demand for management trainees. Moreover, downsizing means more work for fewer people. Since women are disproportionately responsible for "home work" and child rearing, they are at a distinct disadvantage in a work climate where expectations are that more time will be spent at the office.

Attitudes toward women working in the public service have been slow to change. Hiring, promotion, sick leave, and handling of absenteeism have all been implemented differently for women than for men. Consider that until 1955, there was a prohibition against married women even being employed in the public service! This reflected the view that men were the natural breadwinners and that women belonged in the home. Before 1969, it was permissible for hiring requests going to the Public Service Commission to specify either male or female, and, more recently, it was considered normal to ask female employees about plans to marry and have children, when assessing their qualifications. Camilla Stivers, a professor of public administration, argues that both the study and the practice of public administration are structurally male. She claims that the "images of expertise, leadership, and virtue that mark defences of administrative power contain dilemmas of gender. They not only have masculine features, but help to keep in place or bestow political and economic privilege on the bearers of culturally masculine qualities at the expense of those who display culturally feminine ones."[62]

Some argue that differences between the way men and women relate to their work environment mean that traditional "male" approaches are still overused in the public service; fostering a "competitive" management style reflects a male way of thinking. As Martha Hynna, a management consultant and former senior public service mandarin, explains, "[T]he contrasting 'integrative' style of management, which values team-building, participation, responsiveness, and the ability to integrate various points of view, more closely reflects the way in which many women have been socialized and behave in a work environment." She further suggests that "there are important differences in the way men and women communicate. These differences can lead to misinterpretation and misunderstanding, and, in a culture where 'toughness' is valued, this can sometimes result in men underestimating the competence and effectiveness of women."[63]

While the Public Service Commission lauds the goal of developing a truly representative workforce, it admits that results are mixed in relation not only to

**FIGURE 8.9     Representation of Aboriginal Peoples, 1999–2009**

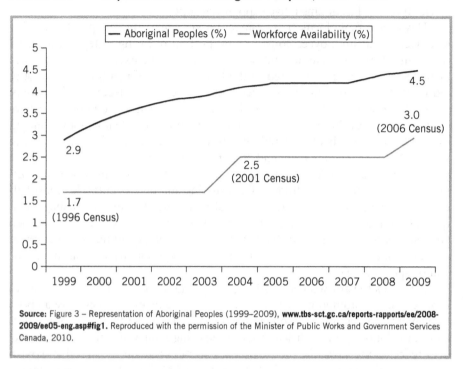

Source: Figure 3 – Representation of Aboriginal Peoples (1999–2009), **www.tbs-sct.gc.ca/reports-rapports/ee/2008-2009/ee05-eng.asp#fig1**. Reproduced with the permission of the Minister of Public Works and Government Services Canada, 2010.

women but also to Aboriginals, persons with disabilities, and members of visible minorities. According to the Treasury Board, more than 4 percent of public service employees are Aboriginal, higher than their workforce availability of 3 percent. Aboriginal peoples make up 3 percent of all public service executives—double the proportion of five years ago (see Figures 8.9 and 8.10). Figure 8.9 illustrates the upward trend in both the representation of Aboriginal peoples in the core public administration and their workforce availability from 1999 to 2009 based on the 1996, 2001, and 2006 census. The percentage of Aboriginal peoples working in the core public administration increased from 2.9 percent in 1999 to 4.5 percent in 2009. The workforce availability of Aboriginal peoples was 1.7 percent in 1996, increasing to 2.5 percent in 2001 and then 3.0 percent in 2006. From 1999 to 2009, then, the representation of Aboriginal peoples in the core public administration has always exceeded their workforce availability.

Figure 8.10 reveals the distribution of all Aboriginal peoples working in the core public administration by occupational category. As of March 31, 2009, the total population of Aboriginal peoples in the core public administration was 8892. There were 186 Aboriginals working in the executive category (2.1 percent of the total population of Aboriginal peoples in the core public administration); 766 (8.6 percent) in the scientific and professional category; 4395 (49.4 percent) in the administrative and foreign service category; 658 (7.4 percent) in the technical services category; 1502 (16.9 percent) in the administrative support category; and 1385 (or 15.6 percent) in the operational category.

**FIGURE 8.10   Distribution of Aboriginal Peoples by Occupational Categories, 2008–2009**

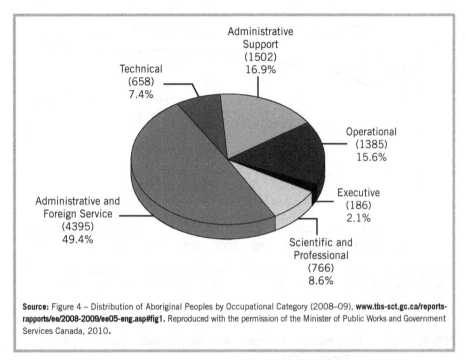

Source: Figure 4 – Distribution of Aboriginal Peoples by Occupational Category (2008–09), **www.tbs-sct.gc.ca/reports-rapports/ee/2008-2009/ee05-eng.asp#fig1**. Reproduced with the permission of the Minister of Public Works and Government Services Canada, 2010.

In general, however, Aboriginals (including Status and non-Status Indians, Metis, and Inuit) face an appalling number of barriers to representation in the public service. Isolated culturally, they lack role models in the upper ranks. As well, poor educational opportunities make entry to and advancement in the public service prohibitively difficult. The public service's traditional emphasis on formal educational qualifications over life experience has discriminated against Aboriginals. Some Aboriginals do not recognize Ottawa as their legitimate government, which dissuades them from entering the federal public service. To overcome these barriers, the federal government has instituted programs and strategies (used earlier in its history to promote French Canadians and women), including aggressive recruitment campaigns and training assistance.

Some progress has been made in the area of persons with disabilities (see Figures 8.11 and 8.12). Nearly 4 percent of federal public service employees are persons with disabilities. The percentage of persons with disabilities increased from 4.6 percent in 1999 to 5.9 percent in 2009. The workforce availability of persons with disabilities was 4.8 percent in 1996, decreasing to 3.6 percent in 2001 and then increasing to 4.0 percent in 2006. In 1999 and 2000, the representation of persons with disabilities was below their workforce availability; however, from 2001 onward, the representation of persons with disabilities has exceeded their workforce availability.

**FIGURE 8.11    Representation of Persons with Disabilities, 1999–2009**

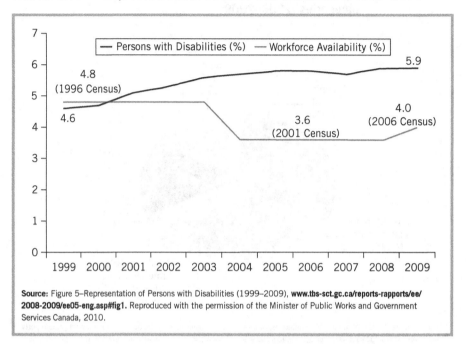

Source: Figure 5–Representation of Persons with Disabilities (1999–2009), **www.tbs-sct.gc.ca/reports-rapports/ee/ 2008-2009/ee05-eng.asp#fig1.** Reproduced with the permission of the Minister of Public Works and Government Services Canada, 2010.

**FIGURE 8.12    Distribution of Persons with Disabilities by Occupational Category, 2008–2009**

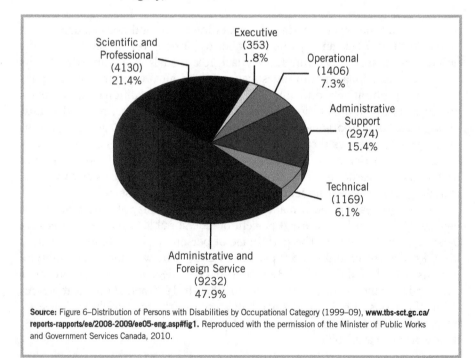

Source: Figure 6–Distribution of Persons with Disabilities by Occupational Category (1999–09), **www.tbs-sct.gc.ca/ reports-rapports/ee/2008-2009/ee05-eng.asp#fig1.** Reproduced with the permission of the Minister of Public Works and Government Services Canada, 2010.

**FIGURE 8.13    Representation of Persons in a Visible Minority Group, 1999–2009**

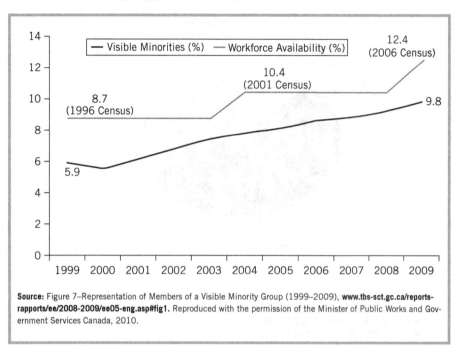

Source: Figure 7–Representation of Members of a Visible Minority Group (1999–2009), **www.tbs-sct.gc.ca/reports-rapports/ee/2008-2009/ee05-eng.asp#fig1.** Reproduced with the permission of the Minister of Public Works and Government Services Canada, 2010.

Figure 8.12 illustrates the distribution of persons with disabilities working in the core public administration by occupational category. As of March 31, 2009, the total population of persons with disabilities was 11 468. The number working in the executive category was 315 (2.7 percent); in the scientific and professional category it was 1182 (10.3 percent); in the administrative and foreign service category it was 5692 (49.6 percent); in the technical services category it was 930 (8.1 percent); in the administrative support category it was 2089 (18.2 percent); and in the operational category it was 1260 (or 11.0 percent).

Figure 8.13 illustrates the upward trend in both the representation of members of a visible minority group in the core public administration and their workforce availability from 1999 to 2009 based on the 1996, 2001, and 2006 census. The percentage of members of a visible minority group working in the core public administration increased from 5.9 per cent in 1999 to 9.8 percent in 2009. The workforce availability of members of a visible minority group was 8.7 percent in 1996, increasing to 10.4 percent in 2001 and then 12.4 percent in 2006. From 1999 to 2009, the representation of members of a visible minority group in the core public administration has remained below their workforce availability.

Figure 8.14 shows the distribution of all members of a visible minority group working in the core public administration by occupational category. As of 2009, the total population of members of a visible minority group in the core public administration was 19 264. Breaking down these numbers, we find 353 (1.8 percent) in the

**FIGURE 8.14**  **Distribution of Persons in a Visible Minority Group by Occupational Category, 2008–2009**

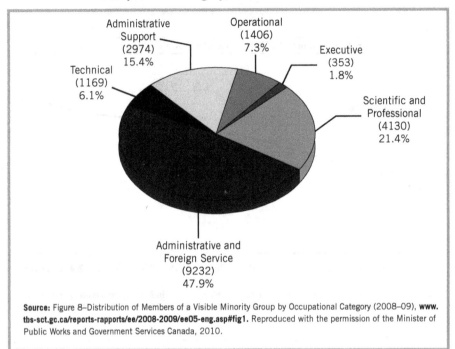

Source: Figure 8–Distribution of Members of a Visible Minority Group by Occupational Category (2008–09), **www. tbs-sct.gc.ca/reports-rapports/ee/2008-2009/ee05-eng.asp#fig1**. Reproduced with the permission of the Minister of Public Works and Government Services Canada, 2010.

executive category; 4130 (21.4 percent) in the scientific and professional category; 9232 (47.9 percent) in the administrative and foreign service; 1196 (6.1 percent) in the technical services category; 2974 (15.4 percent) in the administrative support category; and 1406 (7.3 percent) in the operational category.

The diversity of the executive category among the employment equity groups of the federal public service is somewhat different than that of the public service overall. Figure 8.15 shows representation levels of executives for the four employment equity groups, comparing 2000 to 2009.

Perusal of these tables reveals the relatively low numbers of members of the designated employment equity groups in the executive cohort. The representation of women in the executive ranks increased steadily to 43 percent of executives in 2009. This is a rise of nearly 15 percentage points since 2000, and a full percentage point higher than in 2008. However, the figure was below the workforce availability of 44.9 percent. Representation of the other three employment equity groups also increased at the executive level from 2000 to 2009. It rose from 1.9 percent to 3.6 percent for Aboriginal persons, from 2.9 percent to 6.2 percent for persons with disabilities, and from 3.1 percent to 6.9 percent for visible minority employees; but only persons with disabilities exceeded workforce availability.

The 1995 Employment Equity Act and other progressive changes to the public service have brought a variety of challenges, including that of "managing diversity."[64] For example, there is the difficulty of promoting changes in organizational values and ensuring that managers are sensitive to cultural and other differences. In addition, there is the view that many equity initiatives constitute reverse discrimination.

**FIGURE 8.15    Representation of Equity Groups among Executive in 2000 and 2009, with Estimated Workforce Availability Based on the 2006 Census**

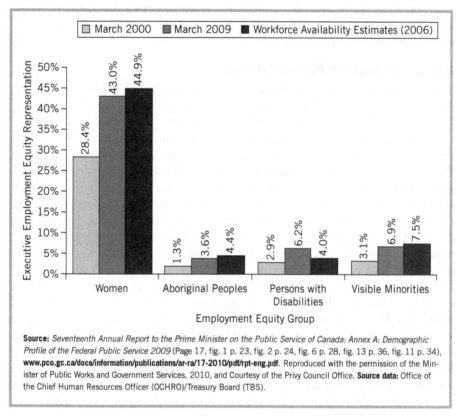

Source: *Seventeenth Annual Report to the Prime Minister on the Public Service of Canada: Annex A: Demographic Profile of the Federal Public Service 2009* (Page 17, fig. 1 p. 23, fig. 2 p. 24, fig. 6 p. 28, fig. 13 p. 36, fig. 11 p. 34), **www.pco.gc.ca/docs/information/publications/ar-ra/17-2010/pdf/rpt-eng.pdf**. Reproduced with the permission of the Minister of Public Works and Government Services, 2010, and Courtesy of the Privy Council Office. **Source data:** Office of the Chief Human Resources Officer (OCHRO)/Treasury Board (TBS).

Moreover, in times of fiscal conservatism, the view is put forward that equity is not "affordable," as the opponents of **pay equity** argued, which involves determining equal pay for work of equal value.

Constitutional and administrative law heavily influence the equity regime in Canada. For instance, the provinces and federal government have enacted human rights codes, the first of which was created by the CCF government of Saskatchewan more than 40 years ago. These codes prohibit discrimination in employment against women, visible minorities, and other designated groups. Section 15 of the 1982 Charter of Rights and Freedoms guarantees "equal protection and equal benefit of the law without discrimination," but importantly, it goes on to suggest that this guarantee "does not preclude any law, program or activity that has as its object the amelioration of conditions of disadvantaged individuals or groups, including those that are disadvantaged because of race, national or ethnic origin, colour, religion, sex, age or mental or physical disability." In addition, the Canadian Human Rights Act, passed in 1977, established the Canadian Human Rights Commission to investigate complaints about discrimination by federal departments, Crown corporations, and business under federal jurisdiction. A variety of other federal and provincial legislation reinforces the equity regime.

Women, Aboriginals, visible minorities, and persons with disabilities all face a variety of barriers, both inside the public service and in the broader society, which make the achievement of representativeness an ongoing challenge. Overall, despite some progress in this area, as the title of a recent report by the Standing Senate Committee on Human Rights suggested, the federal public service is "not there yet" where employment equity is concerned.[65]

## Unionization of the Public Service

The struggle by Canadian public servants to unionize was a long and arduous one, "described as an evolution from 'collective *begging* to collective *bargaining*.'"[66] Prior to 1872, trade unions were illegal in Canada. After that, public service unionization was put off by the convenient fiction that the rights of government workers could be restricted because of the principle of the supremacy of Parliament. Even when federal civil servants finally won the right to **collective bargaining** in 1967, the government imposed restrictions on their rights well beyond those imposed on private sector workers. "Vital issues, including pensions, job classifications, technological change, staffing, and use of part-time or casual labour, were wholly or partly excluded from the scope of bargaining," according to political economists Leo Panitch and Donald Swartz. "Serious consideration was given to denying federal workers the right to strike as well, but in the end, the right to strike was granted, largely because the postal employees, particularly in British Columbia and Quebec, waged a number of what, in effect, were recognition strikes in the mid-1960s."[67] Public sector employees make up slightly more than half of all union members; in fact, the two largest unions in Canada are public sector unions—the Canadian Union of Public Employees (CUPE) with about 10 percent of total union membership, and the National Union of Public and General Employees (NUPGE) with about 7.8 percent.[68] The unique nature of public sector bargaining gives rise to a number of issues absent in the private sector. As one observer states, in the public service,

*collective bargaining, which is generally an exercise in economic power, becomes an exercise in political power. Public opinion and the prospects of re-election substitute for profit maximization in the employer's calculus. A related issue is whether government policy should be decided at the bargaining table, instead of the appropriate legislature.*[69]

Prior to the era of collective bargaining, the federal government established a National Joint Council of the Public Service, made up of representatives of staff associations and managers representing the government.[70] This was intended as a mechanism through which employees could be consulted regarding matters such as conditions of employment. It proved unsatisfactory, however, and by the late 1950s and 1960s, public servants were increasingly agitating for full unionization. In 1961, a new Civil Service Act gave employees the right to be consulted on pay determination, a major point of contention that was not covered under the National Joint Council. Even this advance proved difficult to realize, due to the complex way in which consultations were structured. Still, the 1961 reforms meant that, henceforth, public servants would be paid as a matter of right rather than as a matter of privilege of the Crown, as was previously the case.

The three main political parties campaigned in the 1963 election with a promise, if elected, to introduce collective bargaining in the public service. Legislation followed in 1967, when the Public Service Staff Relations Act was passed, giving employee organizations the right to negotiate directly with the government as trade unions, with the right to compulsory arbitration conciliation and the right to strike. The Act is administered by the Public Service Staff Relations Board.

In fact, the legal framework for unionization of the public service is found in three statutes. First, the Financial Administration Act was amended to make the Treasury Board the "employer" for purposes of collective bargaining. As well, it assumed responsibilities for staff requirements, pay, job classification, and training policy from the Civil Service Commission. Second, the Public Service Employment Act was passed, replacing the Civil Service Commission with the Public Service Commission. It became the central staffing agency of the government. Finally, the Public Service Staff Relations Act was passed to provide the "machinery" of collective bargaining. For example, the authority to certify bargaining units and administer dispute resolution was handed to the Public Service Staff Relations Board. Following several years in the 1990s of disputatious labour–management conflict, a Treasury Board Advisory Committee on Labour Management Relations in the Federal Public Service (the Fryer Committee) was struck and reported in 2000 and 2001.[71] This contributed, in 2003, to a new Public Service Employment Act and Public Service Labour Relations Act passed as part of the Public Service Modernization Act to improve collective bargaining, offer greater opportunities for mediation, and resolve conflict in a more flexible manner. Implemented in stages, it came into force in 2005 with the goals of modernizing staffing in the public service by

- *clarifying responsibilities and eliminating inefficiencies in the system, while retaining the core values of merit, non-partisanship, excellence, representativeness, and the ability to serve the public with integrity and in their official language of choice;*

- *giving a new meaning to merit that moves away from the rules-based concept of "best-qualified" to a values-based approach that allows managers to hire qualified and competent individuals more quickly; and*

- *creating new mechanisms for staffing recourse, including the replacement of appeal boards by the Public Service Staffing Tribunal (PSST).*[72]

Despite advances for public sector workers, certain public servants are denied the right to strike, since they are considered to provide "essential services" for public safety or security. There are also restrictions on what the government deems "negotiable": job security, classification, and other issues have been excluded in the past from the set of issues that public servants can bargain over with their employer. As well, several classes of employees are specifically excluded from the legislation governing collective bargaining. Governments have shown a willingness to suspend collective bargaining and restrict salary increases through legislation, as the Mulroney and Chrétien governments did between 1992 and 1996 in an effort to address the deficit at the time.[73] Still, the introduction of collective bargaining in the federal public service in 1967 significantly altered relations between the government, as employer, and its employees, and continues to evolve.[74]

## Public Servants and Politics

The political rights of public servants are also protected by the Public Service Commission, as is the responsibility to see to it that public servants can "speak truth to power" without fear of reprisal. The fact that Cabinet ministers cannot recruit, assign, transfer, promote, or make any other decision regarding the career of a public servant serves to maintain the integrity and nonpartisanship of the public service and keep it free from undue political interference.

Ultimately, politicians must be able to trust that their public servants will not engage in partisan politics, but will serve them loyally:

*[T]here is nothing more important to the effectiveness of the Public Service than that Ministers of successive Governments have confidence in the loyalty of Public Servants. Those who advise them . . . must be without partisan associations. . . . These conditions form the basis of careers in the Public Service, enabling Public Servants to carry out their essential duty of serving successive Governments of different political parties without any legitimate questioning of their loyalty and commitment.*[75]

Indeed, when reforms to the civil service were enacted in 1918, serious penalties were imposed on any public servant engaging in political activities. The zeal with which reformers sought to eradicate patronage meant that, though they could still vote, public servants suffered the curtailment of virtually all other political rights that we, as citizens, take for granted.

This continued until 1967, when the Public Service Employment Act loosened the constraints on the political rights of public servants. It allowed public servants below the rank of deputy minister to run for election under certain circumstances, and to attend political meetings and donate funds to candidates or parties. They still could not work for or against a candidate or political party, however. In 1991, the Supreme Court struck down the sections of the Public Service Employment Act containing these remaining prohibitions, on the grounds that they violated public servants' political rights. As lawyer Michael Mandel reports, "[T]he Supreme Court held that the limits on federal civil servants' partisan political activity were too broad in that they included every employee without any distinctions for type of job and type of political activity."[76] As a result, today's federal public servants, with the exception of deputy ministers, are free to participate fully in the political system. Current Public Service Employment Act regulations state that public servants who seek to be nominated as candidates and to stand for election in the House of Commons, or any other legislature in Canada, must apply to the commission for a leave of absence without pay.

There are some particular principles that set the parameters of the relationship between the public service and the political system.[77] Prominent among them is the doctrine of **political neutrality**.[78] In short, this convention states that public servants must consistently act in ways that assure their political impartiality. They are not members of the governing party, nor are they party activists who happen to be working within the government. Instead, they occupy a special position of trust through which they are expected to serve the government of the day faithfully, no matter which party is in power.

The doctrine of political neutrality is made up of several elements. First is the politics–administration dichotomy, which, you will recall from chapter 1, states that policy and administration are separate activities. Politicians make policy; public servants administer it. Second is the merit principle, which, in this setting, implies that positions are awarded not on the basis of political affiliation but according to the person's skills and qualifications. Third, and related, is the notion that public servants do not engage in partisan political activities. To do so would compromise their positions as neutral advisors to the government. Fourth, although public servants have their own personal views of the quality of the government's policy and administration, it is not their place to express those views publicly. Fifth, in return for honest and straightforward advice to their political masters, public servants' anonymity is guaranteed. Thus, politicians accept public responsibility for the government's action or inaction; they take the blame when things go wrong and the praise when things go right. The public servant, however, toils anonymously in the background. Finally, public servants enjoy tenure in their positions as long as they perform their jobs satisfactorily. In return, they are expected to offer loyal service and to execute the government's decisions, irrespective of their personal opinions.

Overall, striking a balance between the need for political neutrality and the political rights of public servants is a challenging task. But recent developments, both federally and provincially, suggest a trend toward broadening public servants' political rights. The extent to which this trend may compromise the quality of advice and service provided to politicians is yet to be seen, but indications are that erring on the side of democratic freedom has not diminished the public service's professionalism or effectiveness. There is, however, a marked trend toward eroding the doctrine of neutrality because of increased pressures on public servants.[79] For instance, strengthened access-to-information legislation has created a "chill" among public servants who are more and more reluctant to commit their ideas to paper for fear they will appear on the front pages of the newspapers. Related to this, it has caused public servants to be more reluctant to "speak truth to power." As well, public servants are being called out into the limelight more often, before parliamentary committees, for instance, to explain their political masters' decisions. Finally, concentration of power in the executive has resulted in a disproportionate amount of influence over the public service by the prime minister and political staff. Consequently, public servants are more "politicized"—that is, they have become conditioned to offer advice that fits the political agenda of the government of the day rather than the best possible neutral advice designed for the problem at hand. These ongoing developments mean that there is never a shortage of contentious issues for students of public administration when it comes to the management of human resources.

## BOX 8.2 | How Government Works—A Cynic's View

Once upon a time the government had a vast scrap yard in the middle of nowhere.

Parliament said, "The public interest must be protected. Someone may steal from it at night." So they created a night watchman position and a person was hired for the job.

Then the Privy Council Office said, "How does the watchman do his job without instruction?" So they created a planning committee to seek input from affected ministries and hired three people, one person to write the instructions, one person to do time studies, and one person to liaise with the committee.

Then the Public Service Commission said there should be open and fair merit-based competitions for the position. So they hired two people, one to develop the guidelines for the competition and one to oversee the administration of the hiring process.

Then Treasury Board Secretariat said, "How will we know the night watchman is doing the tasks correctly?" So they created a Quality Control department and hired two people. One to do the studies and one to write the reports.

Then the Chief Human Resources Officer said, "How are these people going to get paid?" So they created the following positions—a time keeper, and a payroll officer—then hired two people.

Then the Auditor General said, "Who will be accountable for all of these people?" So they created an accountability unit and hired three people, an Administrative Officer, Assistant Administrative Officer, and a Legal Secretary.

Then the Finance Department said, "We have had this position in operation for one year and we are $18,000 over budget, we must cutback overall cost." So they laid off the night watchman.

**Source:** Adapted from *Basic Jokes*, The Night Watchman, **www.basicjokes.com/dtitles.php?id=819**.

## WHAT YOU HAVE LEARNED

Can the public service move forward in the area of human resources management under the current stresses and strains that it faces? In the early years, issues such as patronage versus merit, the growth of government, the return of war veterans, the arrival of new university graduates, and bilingualism challenged the public service. Later, issues such as shrinking government, affirmative action, employment equity and pay equity, as well as the need to do more with less in an era hostile to the very institution of the public service lowered morale and brought other new problems. Currently, retention, recruitment, and succession planning are among the most significant challenges. In sum, the public service has had to change constantly. What, then, are the expectations that Canadians currently hold of their public service? According to the Public Service Commission,

*Canadians want some things to change, but they wish that basic Public Service values be protected. The Public Service Commission plays a key role in addressing this requirement. Its role is to meet the dual challenge of preserving the values of merit-based, non-partisan and representative staffing that are the cornerstone of our staffing process, while helping create for managers and public servants the conditions for creativity and innovation that will need to be the hallmarks of the Public Service of the future.*[80]

The extent to which the challenges of the current era have been met is a matter of some dispute. Certainly the auditor general has been critical, calling human resource management "a major weakness" of government.[81] The jury is still out on the reforms of the early twenty-first century, though. The next chapter focuses on the management of the public service, including fiscal management, to place the issues raised in chapter 8 in a broader context.

## Key Words and Concepts

Civil Service Act, 1908 (261)
Civil Service Act, 1918 (261)
Civil Service Commission (261)
Public Service Commission (261)
Public Service Employment Act (265)
Public Service Staff Relations Act (265)
Financial Administration Act (265)
representativeness (266)

Public Service Modernization Act (272)
employment equity (280)
affirmative action (280)
pay equity (289)
collective bargaining (290)
political neutrality (292)

## Review Questions

*1. A Brief History of the Public Service: Who Works There, Anyway?*
This section provided an overview of the composition of the public sector workforce and introduced some of the basic issues that have confronted the public service over time. It focused on merit and patronage, and the tension between these. Ask yourself, What is the public service? What historical developments shaped the public service? What issues have recently emerged, and how are they being addressed? How can the merit principle be reconciled with new developments?

*2. The Public Service Today: An Overview*
The public sector's response to the questions raised in the first section is evident in the many progressive changes it has pioneered in the workplace. This section addressed some of those changes, as well as those produced by attaining collective bargaining rights by public servants. Answer these questions: How large is the public service? How have equity issues come to the forefront within the public

service? How has the public service changed recently? What is the significance of representativeness? How has unionization of the public service affected the union movement in Canada, the political rights of workers in the public service, and their relationship to the government?

Public servants clearly have a special relationship to the political system. Historically, their political rights were severely circumscribed. More recently, there has been a trend toward loosening the strictures against political activity. But the notion that public servants' political rights are different from those of ordinary citizens has been difficult to overcome, running headlong, as it does, into principles such as the doctrine of political neutrality. As a result, ask yourself, What grounds existed to limit the political rights of public servants, and how has this changed? What is the doctrine of political neutrality? How has it affected the work that public servants do? What is the relationship between public servants and the political system?

## Weblinks

Public Service Commission of Canada—Career Recruitment
**www.jobs.gc.ca**

Public Service Commission—Post-secondary Recruitment
**http://jobs-emplois.gc.ca/psr-rp/index-eng.htm**

Canadian Union of Public Employees
**www.cupe.ca**

Public Service Alliance of Canada
**www.psac.com**

Official Languages Act
**http://laws.justice.gc.ca/en/O-3.01/index.html**

Public Service Modernization Act
**http://laws.justice.gc.ca/en/p-33.4**

Employment Equity Act
**http://laws.justice.gc.ca/en/E-5.401/index.html**

Canada School of Public Service
**www.csps-efpc.gc.ca**

Treasury Board of Canada Secretariat
**www.tbs-sct.gc.ca**

## Further Reading

1.  *A Brief History of the Public Service: Who Works There, Anyway?*

Brock, Kathy, Matthew Burbidge, and John Nator. "A Resilient State: The Federal Public Service, Challenges, Paradoxes and a New Vision for the Twenty-First Century," in Christopher Dunn, ed., *The Handbook of Canadian Public Administration*, 2nd ed. Toronto: Oxford University Press, 2010: 235–49.

Dwivedi, O.P., Tim Mau, and Byron Sheldrick, eds. *The Evolving Physiology of Government: Canadian Public Administration in Transition.* Ottawa: University of Ottawa Press, 2009.

Johnson, A.W. *Dream No Little Dreams: A Biography of the Douglas Government of Saskatchewan 1944–1961.* Toronto: University of Toronto Press, 2004.

Juillet, Luc, and Ken Rasmussen. *Defending a Contested Ideal: Merit and the PSC of Canada, 1908–2008.* Ottawa: University of Ottawa Press, 2008.

Lindquist, Evert. *A Critical Moment: Capturing and Conveying the Evolution of the Canadian Public Service.* Ottawa: Canada School of Public Service, 2006.

## 2. The Public Service Today: An Overview

Dwivedi O.P., and John Halligan, "The Canadian Public Service: Balancing Values and Management," in John Halligan, ed., *Civil Service Systems in Anglo-American Countries.* Cheltenham, U.K.: Edward Elgar, 2003: 148–73.

Hubbard, Ruth. *Profession: Public Servant.* Ottawa: Invenire, 2009.

Malloy, Jonathan. "The Next Generation? Recruitment and Renewal in the Federal Public Service," in G. Bruce Doern, ed., *How Ottawa Spends, 2004–2005: Mandate Change in the Paul Martin Era.* Montreal: McGill-Queen's University Press, 2004: 277–95.

Siegel, David, and Ken Rasmussen, eds. *Professionalism and Public Service: Essays in Honour of Kenneth Kernaghan.* Toronto: University of Toronto Press and IPAC, 2008.

Swimmer, Gene, ed. *Public-Sector Labour Relations in an Era of Restraint and Restructuring.* Toronto: Oxford University Press, 2001.

Wernick, Michael. *French to Follow? Revitalizing the Official Languages in the Workplace.* Ottawa: Canadian Centre for Management Development, 2003.

# Endnotes

1. See Reginald Whitaker, "Politics Versus Administration: Politicians and Bureaucrats," in Michael Whittington and Glenn Williams, eds., *Canadian Politics in the 21st Century,* 7th ed. (Toronto: Thomson Nelson, 2008): chap. 3.

2. Canada, Treasury Board Secretariat, *Strengthening Public Sector Management: An Overview of the Government Action Plan and Key Initiatives* (Ottawa: President of the Treasury Board, 2004): 2.

3. Donald Brittain, *Paperland: The Bureaucrat Observed* (Ottawa: National Film Board of Canada, 1979).

4. Leger Marketing, *Profession Barometer 2007,* www.legermarketing. com/eng/.

5. This number refers to all federal public service employees working in departments and agencies listed under Schedule 1, Part 1 of the Public Service Staff Relations Act. See Canada, Treasury Board of Canada Secretariat, *Employment Statistics for the Federal Public Service April 1, 1999–March 31, 2000* (Ottawa: Treasury Board Secretariat, 2000): 2, http://dsp-psd.pwgsc.gc.ca/Collection/BT22-63-2000E.pdf.

6. Canada, Privy Council Office,*Seventeenth Annual Report to the Prime Minister on the Public Service of Canada* (Ottawa: Queen's Printer, 2010), www.pco-bcp.gc.ca/docs/information/publications/ar-ra/17-2010/pdf/rpt-eng.pdf.

7. Ralph Heintzman, "Introduction: Canada and Public Administration," in Jacques Bourgault, Maurice Demers, and Cynthia Williams, eds., *Public Administration and Public Management: Experiences in Canada* (Sainte-Foy: Les Publications du Quebec, 1997): 5.

8. Heintzman, "Introduction." On the role of patronage in pre-Confederation Ontario, see S.J.R. Noel, *Patrons, Clients, Brokers: Ontario Society and Politics, 1791–1896,* (Toronto: University of Toronto Press, 1990).

9. Laurent Dobuzinskis, "Public Administration," in Michael Howlett and David Laycock, eds., *Puzzles of Power: An Introduction to Political Science,* 2nd ed. (Toronto: Oxford University Press, 1998):

156. The following paragraphs are derived from Dobuzinskis's overview of the development of the public service. See also Ken Rasmussen and Luc Juillet, "The Origins of Merit in Canada," in O.P. Dwivedi, Tim A. Mau, and Byron Sheldrick, eds., *The Evolving Physiology of Government: Canadian Public Administration in Transition* (Ottawa: University of Ottawa Press, 2009): 74–96.; and Alasdair Roberts, "A Fragile State: Federal Public Administration in the Twentieth Century," in Christopher Dunn, ed., *The Handbook of Canadian Public Administration*, 2nd ed.(Toronto: Oxford University Press, 2010): 219–34.

10. See O.P. Dwivedi and John Halligan, "The Canadian Public Service: Balancing Values and Management," in John Halligan, ed. *Civil Service Systems in Anglo-American Countries* (Cheltenham, U.K.: Edward Elgar, 2003): 148–73; and Keith Henderson, "American Perspectives on Canadian Public Administration," in O.P. Dwivedi, Tim A. Mau, and Byron Sheldrick, eds., *The Evolving Physiology of Government: Canadian Public Administration in Transition* (Ottawa: University of Ottawa Press, 2009): 272–91.

11. John Edwards cited in Alasdair Roberts, *So-Called Experts: How American Consultants Remade the Canadian Civil Service, 1918–21* (Toronto: Institute of Public Administration of Canada, 1996): 3–4.

12. See Doug Owram, *The Government Generation: Canadian Intellectuals and the State 1900–1945* (Toronto: University of Toronto Press, 1986).

13. J.L. Granatstein, *The Ottawa Men: The Civil Service Mandarins, 1835–1957* (Toronto: University of Toronto Press, 1998).

14. Jacques Bourgault and Barbara Wake Carroll, "The Canadian Senior Public Service: The Last Vestiges of the Whitehall Model?" in Jacques Bourgault, Maurice Demers, and Cynthia Williams, eds., *Public Administration and Public Management: Experiences in Canada* (Sainte-Foy, QC: Les Publications du Quebec, 1997): 98.

15. John Porter, *The Vertical Mosaic: An Analysis of Social Class and Power in Canada* (Toronto: University of Toronto Press, 1965).

16. See Nicole Morgan, *Implosion: An Analysis of the Growth of the Federal Public Service in Canada 1945–1985* (Montreal: Institute for Research on Public Policy, 1986): xvi–xvii.

17. See Canada, Royal Commission on Government Organization, *Report,* 5 vols. (Ottawa: Queen's Printer, 1962–1963).

18. See Arthur Kroeger and Jeff Heynen, *Making Transitions Work: Integrating External Executives into the Federal Public Service* (Ottawa: Canadian Centre for Management Development, 2003).

19. Morgan, *Implosion,* xvii.

20. Dobuzinskis, "Public Administration," 157.

21. See Gary Teeple, *Globalization and the Decline of Social Reform: Into the Twenty-First Century* (Toronto: Garamond, 2000).

22. See Susan D. Phillips, "A More Democratic Canada . . . ?" in Susan D. Phillips, ed. *How Canada Spends: A More Democratic Canada? 1993–1994* (Ottawa: Carleton University Press, 1993): 6–7.

23. Canada, Public Service Commission, "Change and Management in the Public Service; Talking Points for Mme. Jocelyne Bourgon, Clerk of the Privy Council and Secretary to the Cabinet to the Association of Professional Executives of the Public Service of Canada," May 11, 1994, 3, Public Service Commission of Canada, **www.pco-bcp.gc.ca/ClerkSP/Manageme.htm**. See also Isabella Bakker, "The Politics of Scarcity: Deficits and the Debt" in Michael S. Whittington and Glen Williams, eds., *Canadian Politics in the 1990s,* 4th ed. (Scarborough: Nelson, 1995): 55–79.

24. Canada, "Values of the *Public Service Employment Act,*" March 14, 2008, Public Service Commission, **www.psc-cfp.gc.ca/centres/val-psea-lefp-eng.htm**.

25. Ian D. Clark, "Restraint, Renewal, and the Treasury Board Secretariat," *Canadian Public Administration,* 37, 2 (1994): 216.

26. United Nations, *Human Development Report, 2009: Overcoming Barriers; Human Mobility and Development* (New York: United Nations Development Programme, 2009), http://hdr.undp.org/en/statistics/.

27. Canada, Privy Council Office, *Fourteenth Annual Report to the Prime Minister on the Public Service of Canada* (Ottawa: Privy Council Office, 2007): 2. See also Evert

Lindquist, *A Critical Moment: Capturing and Conveying the Evolution of the Canadian Public Service* (Ottawa: Canada School of Public Service, 2006), **http://dsp-psd.pwgsc.gc.ca/collection_2008/csps-efpc/SC103-25-2006E.pdf**.

28. Heintzman, "Introduction," 5.

29. Canada, Treasury Board of Canada Secretariat, *Employment Statistics for the Federal Public Service, April 1, 1999–March 31, 2000*, 2.

30. Canada, Statistics Canada, "Public Sector Employment," *The Daily* (May 30, 2007), **www.statcan.ca/Daily/English/070530/d070530c.htm**.

31. Canada, Statistics Canada, "Public Sector Employment." According to Statistics Canada, for the purposes of the census, "the public sector includes all economic entities controlled by government. It is comprised of four major components: federal government (ministries, departments, agencies and non-autonomous funds, and autonomous funds and organizations); provincial and territorial government (ministries, departments, agencies and non-autonomous funds, autonomous funds and organizations, universities and colleges, and health and social service institutions); local government (municipalities and non-autonomous funds, autonomous funds and organizations, and school boards); and government business enterprises (at the federal, provincial/territorial and local levels)."

32. Canada, Privy Council Office, *Seventeenth Annual Report to the Prime Minister on the Public Service of Canada*.

33. Canada, Human Resources and Social Development Canada, *Employment Equity Act: Annual Report 2008*, June 11, 2009, Department of Labour, **www.rhdcc-hrsdc.gc.ca/eng/labour/publications/equality/annual_reports/2008/page30.shtml**.

34. Canada, Treasury Board of Canada Secretariat. *Employment Statistics for the Federal Public Service, April 1, 1999–March 31, 2000*, 1.

35. See Canada, Public Service Agency, *Modernizing the Classification System: Annual Report 2005–06* (Ottawa: Public Service Agency, 2005); and Canada, Public Service Human Resources Management Agency, *2006–2007 Estimates: Report on Progress*, (Ottawa: Public Service Human Resources Management Agency, 2007).

36. Canada, Treasury Board Secretariat, *Public Service Modernization Act: Backgrounder*, February 6, 2003.

37. Canada, Treasury Board Secretariat, *Public Service Modernization Act: Backgrounder*.

38. Canada. Treasury Board Secretariat. *Public Service Modernization Act: Backgrounder.*

39. See Evert Lindquist, "How Ottawa Assesses Department/Agency Performance: Treasury Board's Management Accountability Framework," in Allan M. Maslowe, ed., *How Ottawa Spends, 2009-2010: Economic Upheaval and Political Dysfunction* (Montreal: McGill-Queen's University Press, 2009): 47–88.

40. Canada, Public Service Human Resources Management Agency, *2006–07 Estimates: Report on Plans and Priorities* (Ottawa: Public Service Human Resources Agency, 2007), 8 **www.tbs-sct.gc.ca/rpp/2006-2007/PSHRMAC-AGRHFPC/pshrmac-agrhfpc-eng.pdf**.

41. Canada, Public Service Human Resources Management Agency, *2006–07 Estimates: Report on Plans and Priorities*, 8.

42. Luc Juillet and Ken Rasmussen, *Defending a Contested Ideal: Merit and the PSC of Canada 1908-2008* (Ottawa: University of Ottawa Press, 2008): 213.

43. Canada, Privy Council Office, *Fourteenth Annual Report to the Prime Minister on the Public Service of Canada.*

44. Canada, Privy Council Office, *Sixteenth Annual Report to the Prime Minister on the Public Service of Canada* (Ottawa: Queen's Printer, 2009), **www.pco-bcp.gc.ca/docs/information/publications/ar-ra/16-2009/pdf/rpt-eng.pdf**.

45. Canada, Privy Council Office, *Seventeenth Annual Report to the Prime Minister on the Public Service of Canada.*

46. For a current listing of career opportunities in the public service, see the *Careers in the Federal Public Service* page at the Public Service Commission of Canada website at **jobs.gc.ca**.

47. Canada, Public Service Agency. *Employment Equity in the Federal Public*

Service 2004–05: Annual Report to Parliament (Ottawa: Public Service Human Resources Management Agency, 2006), http://dsp-psd.pwgsc.gc.ca/Collection/CP51-6-2005E.pdf.

48. For an early consideration of these issues, see V. Seymour Wilson and Willard A. Mullins, "Representative Bureaucracy: Linguistic/Ethnic Aspects in Canadian Public Policy," Canadian Public Administration, 21 (1978): 513–38.

49. Canada, Privy Council Office, Fourteenth Annual Report to the Prime Minister on the Public Service of Canada, 38.

50. J.E. Hodgetts, William McCloskey, Reginald Whitaker, and V. Seymour Wilson, The Biography of an Institution: The Civil Service Commission of Canada 1908–1967 (Montreal: McGill-Queen's University Press, 1972): 473.

51. Robert J. Jackson and Doreen Jackson, Politics in Canada: Culture, Institutions, Behaviour and Public Policy, 7th ed. (Toronto: Pearson Prentice Hall, 2009): 367.

52. Canada, Royal Commission on Bilingualism and Biculturalism, Report, 5 vols. (Ottawa: Queen's Printer, 1967–1970).

53. See, for example, Canada, Office of the Commissioner of Official Languages, Annual Report 2006–2007 (Ottawa: Public Works and Services Canada, 2007).

54. Canada, Privy Council Office, Seventeenth Annual Report to the Prime Minister on the Public Service of Canada, 22.

55. Rosalie Silberman Abella, Equality in Employment: A Royal Commission Report (Ottawa: Supply and Services Canada, 1984): 7.

56. Canada, Public Service Commission, Annual Report 1992 (Ottawa: Supply and Services, 1993): 46.

57. Abella, Equality in Employment, 1.

58. Canada, Privy Council Office, Seventeenth Annual Report to the Prime Minister on the Public Service of Canada, 20.

59. The following data concerning women, Aboriginals, persons with disabilities, and visible minorities are derived from Canada, Treasury Board Secretariat of Canada, Employment Equity in the Public Service, 2008–09: Annual Report to Parliament www.tbs-sct.gc.ca/reports-rapports/ee/2008-2009/ee05-eng.asp#fig1; and Canada, Privy Council Office, Seventeenth Annual Report to the Prime Minister on the Public Service of Canada.

60. See Susan D. Phillips, Brian R. Little, and Laura A. Goodine, "Reconsidering Gender and Public Administration: Five Steps Beyond Conventional Research," Canadian Public Administration, 40, 4 (1994): 576. See also Sandra Burt and Sonya Lynn Hardman, "The Case of the Disappearing Targets: The Liberals and Gender Equality," in Leslie A. Pal, ed., How Ottawa Spends, 2001–2002: Power in Transition, (Toronto: Oxford University Press, 2001): 201–22.

61. Jonathan Malloy, "The Next Generation? Recruitment and Renewal in the Federal Public Service," in G. Bruce Doern, ed., How Ottawa Spends, 2004–2005: Mandate Change in the Paul Martin Era (Montreal: McGill-Queen's University Press, 2004): 283.

62. Camilla Stivers, Gender Images in Public Administration (Newbury Park, CA: Sage, 1993): 4.

63. Martha Hynna, "Women in the Public Service—A Thirty-Year Perspective," Canadian Public Administration, 40, 4 (1997): 618

64. See Kenneth Kernaghan and Mohamed Charih, "The Challenge of Change: Emerging Issues in Contemporary Public Administration," Canadian Public Administration, 40, 2 (1997): 227–28. For a more recent assessment, see Nan Weiner, "Workplace Equity: Human Rights, Employment and Pay Equity," in Christopher Dunn, ed., The Handbook of Canadian Public Administration, 2nd ed. (Toronto: Oxford University Press, 2010): 167–85.

65. Canada, Senate, Employment Equity in the Federal Public Service: Not There Yet; Preliminary Findings of the Senate Standing Committee on Human Rights (Ottawa: Senate Standing Committee on Human Rights, 2007).

66. Morley Gunderson and Robert Hebdon, "Collective Bargaining and Dispute Resolution in the Public Sector," in Christopher Dunn, ed., The Handbook of

*Canadian Public Administration*, 2nd ed. (Toronto: Oxford University Press, 2010): 187.

67. Leo Panitch and Donald Swartz, *From Consent to Coercion: The Assault on Trade Union Freedoms*, 3rd ed.(Aurora: Garamond, 2003): 18–19.

68. Gunderson and Hebdon, "Collective Bargaining and Dispute Resolution in the Public Sector," 200.

69. Gene Swimmer, "Critical Issues in Public Sector Industrial Relations," in Amarjit S. Sethi, ed., *Collective Bargaining in Canada* (Scarborough: Nelson, 1989): 401.

70. The following discussion is derived from P.K. Kuruvilla, "Collective Bargaining in the Canadian Public Service," in Kenneth Kernaghan, ed., *Public Administration in Canada: Selected Readings*, 5th ed. (Toronto: Methuen, 1985): 224–35.

71. Timothy J. Bartkiw and Gene Swimmer, "Federal Public Service Labour Relations: Business as Usual?" in G. Bruce Doern, ed., *How Ottawa Spends, 2007–2008: The Harper Conservatives—Climate of Change* (Montreal: McGill-Queen's University Press, 2007): 209.

72. Canada. Public Service Commission. *Legislation*, July 7, 2007, **www.psc-cfp. gc.ca/centres/legislation-eng.htm**.

73. Bartkiw and Swimmer, "Federal Public Service Labour Relations," 201.

74. See Gene Swimmer, ed., *Public Sector Labour Relations in an Era of Restraint and Restructuring* (Toronto: Oxford University Press, 2001); Gene Swimmer and Mark Thompson, eds., *Public Sector Collective Bargaining in Canada* (Kingston: IRC Press, 1995).

75. Canada, *Public Service 2000: The Renewal of the Public Service of Canada*, (Ottawa: Supply and Services, 1990): 63, 64.

76. Michael Mandel, *The Charter of Rights and the Legalization of Politics in Canada*

(Toronto: Thomson Educational, 1994): 294.

77. See Michael Cassidy, ed., *Democratic Rights and Electoral Reform in Canada* (Toronto: Dundurn, for the Royal Commission on Electoral Reform and Party Financing, 1991).

78. For an early statement of this doctrine, see Kenneth Kernaghan, "Politics, Policy and Public Servants: Political Neutrality Revised," *Canadian Public Administration*, 21 (1976): 432–56. See also Kenneth Kernaghan, "East Block and Westminster: Conventions, Values and Public Service," in Christopher Dunn, ed. *The Handbook of Canadian Public Administration*, 2nd ed.(Toronto: Oxford University Press, 2010): 289–304; and David A. Good, "An Ideal Model in a Practical World: The Continuous Revisiting of Political Neutrality and Ministerial Responsibility," in David Siegel and Ken Rasmussen, eds., *Professionalism and Public Service: Essays in Honour of Kenneth Kernaghan* (Toronto: University of Toronto Press and IPAC, 2008): 63–83.

79. See Peter Aucoin and Donald J. Savoie, "The Politics–Administration Dichotomy: Democracy Versus Bureaucracy?" in O.P. Dwivedi, Tim A. Mau, and Byron Sheldrick, eds., *The Evolving Physiology of Government: Canadian Public Administration in Transition* (Ottawa: University of Ottawa Press, 2009): 97–117; and Donald J. Savoie, *Breaking the Bargain: Public Servants, Ministers and Parliament* (Toronto: University of Toronto Press, 2003).

80. Canada, Public Service Commission, *The Road Ahead: Recruitment and Retention Challenges for the Public Service* (Ottawa: Public Service Commission, 2002): 26.

81. Canada, Office of the Auditor-General, *Public Service Management Reform: Progress, Setbacks and Challenges* (Ottawa: Minister of Public Works and Services, 2001).

# Public Administration, Management Reform, *and* Financial Management

## WHAT YOU WILL LEARN

Two central elements of public administration permit governments to do what they need to do. These are *money* and *personnel*. This chapter looks at the following:

- What are the pre-eminent issues in management reform in the public service?

- How does the management of financial resources involve making decisions about how to divide the government "pie"?

- How do governments try to answer the question of "who gets what, when, and how?"

- How have complex and elaborate systems of budget making and financial management evolved, and how are they subject to ongoing review and reform, audit and evaluation?

Chapter 8 showed that the management of human resources in the public sector is a complex affair. In this chapter, we examine some of the major reforms in the management of human resources affecting what the managers of the public service do and how they do it. We also note that even in times when government coffers are full, financial management is complicated, but in an era of diminishing revenues, it is hotly disputed. To resolve conflict over how financial resources are raised and spent, someone has to ensure that financial resources are being used wisely and that every dollar of taxpayers' money can be accounted for. This results in some of the most contentious political debate within government and society. In their attempts to create a transparent and fair system of budgeting, Canadian governments have experimented with a variety of systems but, so far, no one system has been able to satisfactorily address all the issues surrounding the administration and management of government finances.

This chapter examines issues related both to management reform and to financial management. In reality, the two are linked. The chapter is divided into the following sections:

1. *Restructuring the Public Service: The Management View*

Recent changes have altered the composition of the public service. Downsizing, re-engineering, pay freezes, cutbacks, layoffs, and firings were endemic throughout the 1990s and early 2000s. This section asks the following: What are the most important recent reforms to the management of the public service? How has restructuring affected the public service? What has it done to the morale of those remaining in the public service? How has it affected the delivery of services to the public? What are the implications of privatizing and contracting out? What does the future hold for those seeking a career in the Canadian public service?

2. *Financial Management*

The issues of power and politics raised in chapter 2 revolved around this question: Who gets what, when, and how? We return to this by examining that most fundamental of issues related to government—money. Some observers of public administration have indeed concluded that to get anything done, governments need three things: money, money, and money.[1] Canadian governments manage billions of dollars of taxpayers' money (that is, *your* money) every year. How is that money managed? What budgeting systems have been established to ensure that probity, honesty, economy, efficiency, and accountability are maintained? Who is ultimately responsible for the management of funds? What kinds of competition do departments engage in to ensure that they get their share of the loot? What is the budgetary cycle?

# Restructuring the Public Service: The Management View

The last two decades were difficult ones for the public service in Canada. Recognizing the debilitating trends of low morale, cutbacks, wage freezes, and the general disparagement aimed at public servants, managers have recently turned their attention to the vexing issue of how to rebuild a once-proud institution. As we noted in chapter 8, public service renewal has again moved to the forefront of the agenda of many Canadian governments. Before we explore the specifics of management reforms, we need to review the depth and breadth of change in the public service over the years.

Imagine that it is 1980 and that you're fresh out of university. You are attracted to the prospect of a career in the public service because you have always understood that serving your country in this way is a lofty and honourable ambition. Your instructors in public administration courses have regaled you with tales of the proud and powerful mandarinate that dominated the halls of bureaucratic power in the postwar years, reconstructing the country after the war, building the great edifice known as the "social welfare state," and contributing in no small way to the greatest era of sustained prosperity in the country's history. You are versed in the literature of Keynesian macro-economic management, as well as the latest systems approaches and modern social science management techniques. The world is your oyster, and you confidently accept your responsibility as a management trainee in an important federal department, content in the knowledge that your long and satisfying career will lead you, in no time, right to the deputy minister's office.

Now flash ahead to 2015. You have somehow survived the various purges that decimated the ranks of your colleagues in the 1990s and early 2000s. You are a few short years from retirement and are being pressured to leave early, even though it will adversely affect your pension and post-work lifestyle. The much-vaunted Keynesian management systems that you were taught were discredited by newfangled approaches known as monetarism and neoconservatism, theories whose underlying premises characterize you as useless parasite sucking the lifeblood out of the nation. Then you were told the state was back in vogue after the global economic meltdown of 2008–2009, which governments the world over had to resolve, and which partly resurrected the image of the public service. But successive prime ministers, from Trudeau to Harper, denigrated your work. The negative impression of the public service was adopted by the public and the media, who still regularly vilify you and your colleagues. You are held responsible for everything from the national debt to the lack of competitiveness of Canadian industry to the sorry state of the health care system to the rise in crime to the decline in morality, and on and on! Somewhere along the way, you found your march up the career ladder blocked by a huge cohort of your fellow public servants, all around your age and with the same ambitions. At some point, you realized that you had been "shelved."

What on earth happened in the intervening years?

Managing the public service has always been a challenging task. Notwithstanding the nostalgic recollections of the "glory years" after the Second World War, there have always been stresses and strains, conflicts and challenges for public service managers. But from the 1980s onward, the nature and set of issues and challenges seem to have both altered and intensified, and the management of the public service ran into serious—and heretofore largely unknown—difficulties. A variety of internal problems coincided with a change in societal views about the role and place of the public service. Just as the transition between the minimalist state and the Keynesian welfare state was difficult (the Great Depression of the 1930s), so, too, was the transformation from the Keynesian welfare state to the neoconservative state. (These terms, you will recall, were used in chapter 1.)

Government surpluses, deficits and debt, technological change, globalization, and the rise of new social movements and interest groups, coupled with a more assertive and skeptical citizenry, have created new problems for public service managers. These have been exacerbated by two issues. First, managers' ability to respond to the forces of change has been hampered by inadequate internal systems and processes for managing their departments. Second, widespread external criticism has emerged that the public service has grown out of control and is incapable of doing its job.

The notion that the public service had grown out of control has had a profound effect on the image of public service as a lofty and honourable calling, and has contributed to the strikingly low levels of morale therein. This impression was confirmed forcefully by the clerk of the Privy Council's warnings of a "quiet crisis" in the public service (see below). The overall result was confusion, insecurity, hopelessness, anger, and frustration among many public servants. The management of the public sector has been undergoing a virtually continuous process of reform, at least since former prime minister John Diefenbaker unleashed the Glassco Commission on the world of Canadian public administration in 1960, with its admonition to "let the managers manage." Al Johnson served in the government of Saskatchewan and federally at the senior-most level, and by his reckoning there have been reforms relating to the effective and efficient management of the public service about every two to five years since the Glassco Commission.[2] This is in itself a factor contributing to the ennui felt in this once-respected institution.

Reform is not a factor exclusive to the Canadian public sector, of course. Much has been written and noted about similar trends in countries such as New Zealand, Great Britain, and Australia.[3] Contemporary reforms include borrowing "best practices" from the private sector, focusing on "clients" (instead of serving "citizens"), forming strategic alliances with the private sector and other levels of government, relying increasingly on volunteer and nonprofit organizations for the delivery and development of services, and using new technologies to improve service delivery and communication with Canadians.

In Canada, the preoccupation with renewal has brought continual attitudinal, institutional, and structural changes[4] within a new paradigm—one in which government was made to run more like business, and in which public servants were therefore expected to become more and more entrepreneurial in their work. This renewal took place within a public service where managers were suffering "death by a thousand cuts." These "cuts" included a lack of vision and leadership among senior managers and political executives; a lack of autonomy among front-line managers; a rapid turnover of senior managers (deputy ministers rotate their positions on average every 22 months); a "vertical solitude" between senior and middle managers in which trust and respect is lacking; a stale organizational culture; severe financial cutbacks; and other related problems.[5] As well as PS2000 and La Relève, several other initiatives were launched with varying degrees of success, to address these serious problems.[6] We cannot review them all here, but will consider some of the more important ones of the past 20 years. The point here is to give you a picture of the ongoing upheaval that has beset the public service, and that has in some ways only sustained the problems that reforms were meant to address.

## PS2000

The current era of reform arguably has its roots as far back as the early 1960s with the Glassco Commission (the Royal Commission on Government Organization). It was also given impetus in the 1970s with the Lambert Commission (the Royal Commission on Financial Management) and the D'Avignon Report (the Special Committee on the Review of Personnel Management and the Merit Principle), and in 1980s with exercises like the **Productivity Improvement Program** started by the Trudeau government, and the **Ministerial Task Force on Program Review** and the **Increased Ministerial Authority and Accountability** exercise in the Mulroney years.[7] **PS2000** followed on the heels of these initiatives. Surveys of public sector managers in 1986 and 1988 by two Ottawa University professors revealed striking differences from the attitudes of private sector managers.[8] Low morale was endemic, and the further down the hierarchy, the lower it was. Thus, there was a disjunction between the attitudes of senior managers and their subordinates. Moreover, the scores obtained from rating various attitudes tended to be lower in the public service than in the private sector. The results of the surveys provided the impetus for PS2000, announced by the prime minister in December 1989. It was led by the clerk of the Privy Council, Paul Tellier, with the intent that the public service would engage in a thorough self-examination, and "heal itself."

Ten task forces were set up under the leadership of deputy ministers, who were charged with finding ways to simplify personnel policies, to loosen central agency controls and increase the managerial freedom of department managers, and to increase efficiency and program delivery.[9] Thousands of public servants and others outside government were consulted, and a White Paper was issued, summarizing the findings of the exercise:

*The white paper highlighted several challenges, including fast-paced economic and social changes, the growing complexity of policy issues, the need for a simpler and more transparent political process, the multiplication of controls, too many procedures hindering change, low morale among public servants, low public administration productivity, growing financial constraints, and the citizens' lack of confidence in the public service. These challenges begged for a more open relationship between Canadians and the public service, as well as for greater flexibility in government procedures. A change in bureaucratic culture was called for to pave the way to a culture based on consultation and service to the citizens.[10]*

PS2000 suggested that each department should produce that 1990s business-school contrivance, the *mission statement*. Managers would delineate specific service-oriented goals and embrace notions of participatory management. PS2000 called for department managers to consult broadly, not only with their own employees but also with citizens, to establish service standards and a more service-oriented culture. Organizational reform was achieved by flattening structures such that no more than three executive levels existed under each deputy minister. (Recall our discussion of span of control in chapter 3.) The goal here was to improve communication and to empower managers. Furthermore, it was suggested that the number of categories and levels within groups be reduced to simplify both personnel matters and decision-making procedures. Finally, the government decided to reinforce the importance of new organizational models of service delivery, called Special Operating Agencies (SOA), which had been introduced earlier by the Treasury Board.

Ian Clark called the budget reforms resulting from PS2000, which allowed managers more control over their funds, its most important recommendation.[11] But as another observer of this process concluded, "[E]mpowerment of public servants was the cornerstone of Public Service 2000."[12] Whether it worked or not is the subject of some dispute. The auditor general concluded in his 1993 report that while some progress had been made, there was still a feeling of skepticism among public service managers.[13] Political scientist Peter Aucoin echoed this sentiment in his assessment of PS2000.[14] Even the head of the public service at the time, Paul Tellier, whose job it was to develop and implement PS2000, described it as a failure. He claimed his plan was defeated by the "culture of caution" that permeated the public service, especially among managers.[15] In any event, many middle-level managers regarded it as fiat passed down from above: an executive-level exercise removed from the real day-to-day concerns of the middle-level manager. To them, it lacked legitimacy. By the end of 1993, PS2000 had faded from view, supplanted by other, newer reform attempts.

## Program Review

When the Liberals came to power on the heels of the demise of PS2000, a major restructuring of government had already begun. Chrétien's predecessor, Conservative prime minister Kim Campbell, had reduced the number of government ministries from 32 to 23. This necessitated building new management structures and consolidating the activities and operations of the old departments into the fewer new ones. Chrétien opted for a similar streamlined government, and created 24 ministries. He also dedicated his government to three main tasks: renewing federalism, reviewing all government programs, and reforming the public service. Significantly, he designated one of his Cabinet members as minister for Public Sector Renewal. Marcel Massé was given this job, and proceeded to implement the new goals of public service management.[16] Of these three goals, the one that most interests us here is the **Program Review** (mentioned in chapters 4 and 7).[17] The driving force behind this round of reforms was deficit reduction. During the 1993 election campaign, the Liberals had promised to reduce the deficit to 3 percent of gross domestic product (GDP) by 1997–1998. Beyond this, according to two observers of the public administration process, Program Review involved

*clarifying the core responsibilities of the federal government and rebalancing the division of labour among the different levels of government and the private and not-for-profit sectors in the Canadian governance system, and equipping the federal public service with the tools necessary to improve the efficiency of public sector management.[18]*

In spring 1994, all government departments and agencies were expected to reform their programs to fit newly announced expenditure targets. Six "tests" of Program Review were instituted, which all programs were to be measured against. These tests asked the following questions: Was there a public interest at stake? Was there a legitimate role for government in the issue? Was the federal government the right level of government jurisdictionally? Could the activities of the program be transferred to the private or voluntary sector? How could efficiency be improved? And was the program in question affordable?[19] In his February 1995 budget, then–Finance minister Paul Martin called for reductions in program spending of $29 billion over a three-year period, as well as the elimination of 45 000 civil servant jobs (14 percent of the entire public service). Transfer payments to the provinces for health, welfare, and post-secondary education were unilaterally reduced by $4.5 billion, although the provinces were given greater flexibility in how they were to spend whatever sums they did receive. Expenditure reductions varied across departments and agencies, with some having to cut as little as 5 percent from their budgets, and others having to cut as much as 60 percent. Only the Department of Indian Affairs and Northern Development was spared. The most deeply affected departments were Transport, Industry, and Natural Resources.[20] A Program Review Secretariat was created within the Privy Council Office to oversee these developments.

According to two analysts of Program Review, the exercise did not meet its expectations. "Our general diagnosis is that it has not been as effective as it might have been," they suggest. "It has undoubtedly triggered some expenditure reductions, and these are likely to continue." However, it did not fundamentally reform the governance of the system, which was a basic goal of Program Review.[21] Part of the problem lay in the fact that, like PS2000, the Program Review was conducted largely by "insiders." It was also a top-down process, for the most part. It should be obvious why it was difficult to get middle-level public servants to embrace reform that was not based on consultation, especially when it might have adversely affected the very programs that they administered. Moreover, those people outside government who would be most affected by the program cutbacks resulting from expenditure cutbacks were not consulted either. In the end, the results of Program Review were assessed by a senior public servant as falling far short of its ambitious goals:

*From my perspective, the Federal Program Review, while producing dramatic results in terms of dollars or job cuts, was primarily a scramble for cash, and did not represent a "re-design" or "re-invention" of government as had been claimed by some. Federal Departments cut what could be cut, and little real attention was paid to the six starting criteria. There was little or no attempt made to examine the structure and process of government on a horizontal basis, to lessen the pressures which require departments to incur such enormous overhead costs (e.g., the massive impact of bloated Central Agencies and their multiple controls and demands on departments, the costs of the unwieldy, obsolete and ineffective personnel system—which every critic since Glassco has vainly tried to reform—and the unwieldy centralized and control-oriented financial and administrative systems).[22]*

Yet another round of reforms ultimately failed to achieve the fundamental reorientation of the public service called for by the various crises confronting it. These reforms may even have worsened the situation, as morale among public servants plummeted and the malaise noted earlier deepened with each brilliant new scheme launched.

## La Relève and the Leadership Network

The battering of public service morale led, to the declaration of a "quiet crisis" by the clerk of the Privy Council, who launched **La Relève** as a means of plumbing the depths of public servant dissatisfaction and of finding solutions to renew the institution. The "quiet crisis" resulted from a number of factors: "the loss of talent through many years of downsizing; a demographic skew after years of limited recruitment; constant criticism of the public sector which seriously affected morale; many years of pay freezes; and increasing interest by the private sector in acquiring the skills possessed by public servants."[23] The term *La Relève* itself is an acronym for Leadership, Action, Renewal, Energy, Learning, Expertise, Values, and Excellence. Beginning in January 1997, more than 15 000 public servants from all departments and regions were consulted about their perceptions of working in the public service. Conferences were staged across the country, and parliamentarians were briefed on the La Relève Task Force findings, as were interested academics, professional associations, the provincial governments, foreign countries, and the media. The La Relève Task Force identified the key challenges confronting the modern public service as globalization, new information technologies, and changing attitudes toward traditional hierarchical institutions. It urged a more responsible and participatory role for managers at all levels, and a "democratization" of the decision-making process, which emphasized leadership across the public service.

One result of La Relève was the targeting of demographics, representativeness, and recruitment as three important contemporary challenges to the public service.[24] Student work programs and co-operative education programs were instituted to address the demographic reality of a civil service in need of new blood. Departments and agencies made a concerted effort to renew the public service workforce through recruitment, training, and development initiatives. As well, the high level of departures by senior managers inspired an effort to renew the leadership cadre of the civil service. As we noted in chapter 8, campaigns to recruit university graduates and professionals with specialized skills were developed, along with ones to better train public servants and increase their mobility within the organization. This approach involved investing in experienced public servants and recruiting new ones. Career management planning, advisory services, and support for continuous learning were implemented across the public service. Then, in 1998, La Relève evolved into the Leadership Network, which was established as an agency reporting to the Cabinet secretary and focusing on effective management training and education for assistant deputy ministers. The Leadership Network was eventually placed under the umbrella of the Canada Public Service Human Resources Management Agency (later changed to the Canada Public Service Agency, in 2003, and then the Office of the Chief Human Resources Officer in

2009), where it evolved into a variety of leadership development programs. While there is still a long way to go, Box 9.1 reveals that some career public servants do retain a latent and powerful sense of pride.

---

## BOX 9.1    At Your Service with Pride

The following article was written by a career public servant, Bob Chartier of Saskatoon, who works in the Department of Indian and Northern Affairs:

*I am a public servant. In the 30 years of my career, there have been more times than I would care to admit when I was not very comfortable saying that out loud, much less in print. However, like everyone lately, my world has been rocked. The embassy bombings, the bombing of the federal building in Oklahoma City and the Sept. 11 images of public servants—police officers and firefighters—running towards the horror instead of away from it will stay with us forever. I have had to recognize that many terrorists target governments and, as we know, public servants are the front line of governance.*

*For years, public servants struggled with a "poor cousin" image in the workplace. It was insinuated that the brightest and the best would always go into the private sector. The rest of us, for many different reasons, made the decision to spend our lives teaching your kids, hooking up your intravenous, protecting your border, checking the maintenance record on the aircraft taking you to Cancun and responding to 911 calls.*

*Oh, we heard your snickers over the years.*

*We have heard your comments about road crews leaning on their shovels, striking nurses, mindless clerks processing paper, lazy teachers and cops in doughnut shops. And this was the tame stuff. I believe it's time to rethink our views on public service. First of all, understand that we do the things that no one else really wants to do and that there is no real money in it. Try to buy police services from a street vendor. What price would the market pay to find an illegal immigrant? Ask a major private-sector company to write a new fair-trade policy. Try to shop around for a good deal on a passport.*

*The private-enterprise capitalist system is fine by me. It is adept at doing those things it is supposed to do, but it can't do it all. When it comes to writing good policy on parole violations, we don't freelance the contract; we ask a public servant with a weighty academic background, a wealth of experience and an ear to the street to compose it. When we need protection, high standards in our goods, food and water, we again look to the public servant. Whoa, let's stop right there. On that water thing. You're right. We have Walkerton and North Battleford to consider. I grew up in North Battleford and, as a working government guy, I was appalled that, for decades, city workers there drew drinking water a kilometre downstream from* the spot they dumped the sewage. Let's be honest. Public servants make mistakes. Big ones, little ones and some really stupid ones. But so does the private sector. Our trouble, as public servants, is that our mistakes can cause a lot more grief.

It is true, we are notorious for our red tape, our obsession with paper and our slowness. But we are working really hard. We can and will be just as fast, as effective and as quality-minded as the private sector, even more. We have many masters, however, and sometimes when we try to cut the red tape we get beat up for what is then called a lack of accountability. It's always hard for us to know whom we really serve—politicians or citizens. But I believe we can serve both and do it with accountability and effectiveness.

So what have we got here? Well, we have jobs that have no market value. We are under constant public scrutiny. We get paid what citizens, not the market, think we are worth and we provide always essential but often hidden services. And most of us really like our work. We love your kids, we fell for you in the intensive-care unit, we want to find the bad guys and we are driven to develop policy that reflects Canadian values.

Public servants may now feel even more like a target for evil, but they will go to work every day. They will be here for us, the first to run into the trouble and to lead in the rebuilding. The war on terrorism will not be fought in the market, it will be defended at the border, in policy making decisions on privacy and in the day by day readiness of emergency workers. And that is why I serve the public, with pride.

**Source:** Bob Chartier, "At Your Service with Pride," *Maclean's* (January 14, 2002): 9. Copyright © Bob Chartier. Reprinted with permission.

## The Public Service Modernization Act and Beyond

As we noted in chapter 8, in 2001 the government promised in its Speech from the Throne yet another set of reforms. It created a Task Force on Modernizing Human Resources Management, which recommended a modern framework for human resources management. The task force assessed reforms in other countries, such as Australia, the U.K., and New Zealand. Legislation to modernize the public service was subsequently introduced in 2003. The **Public Service Modernization Act** (PMSA) created a new Public Service Employment Act and a new Public Service Labour Relations Act, as well as amending other pieces of legislation. According to two theorists of public administration, the PSMA aims to provide

(a) increased flexibility in staffing and managing people with safeguards to continue a merit-oriented, and politically neutral public service; (b) cooperative labour-management relations; (c) a coherent training and learning programme to meet the professional development and corporate needs of the government; and (d) a clear role and strengthened accountability for the government institutions and individuals responsible for managing the public service.[25]

In addition, a number of other reports and initiatives came together in the early twenty-first century to continue with the reform agenda in public administration. The auditor general's report of 2000 found a lack of coordination in government appointment practices, while the report of 2003 exposed the issues that ultimately led to the sponsorship and advertising contracts inquiry known as the Gomery Commission (see chapter 11). The House of Commons Standing Committee on Public Accounts report in December 2001 expressed concern about the management of human resources in the public service. The annual reports of the Public Service Commission as well as the clerk of the Privy Council repeatedly spoke to the need for increased flexibility in managing human resources as well as simplifying processes therein. In the *2008–2009 Public Service Renewal Action Plan*, for instance, the government identified a dozen commitments to advance the four priority areas the clerk identified in his *Fifteenth Annual Report to the Prime Minister on the Public Service of Canada*: planning, recruitment, employee development and enabling infrastructure (later changed to renewing the workplace).[26]

In 2010, the clerk of the Privy Council summarized the challenges recently faced by the federal government, and lauded the public service for its quick and versatile responses. He wrote, "From our experience in the implementation of the Economic Action Plan, we have seen how it is possible to simplify decision making and speed the flow of information to ministers and Canadians without undermining either due process or the quality of decisions. In the process, we have become much better at what we term responsive and responsible risk management."[27] He went on to cite the government's handling of the 2009 H1N1 pandemic, the 2010 earthquake in Haiti, and the staging of the 2010 Vancouver Olympic and Paralympic Winter Games as examples of how the community of public service professionals could respond and react to pressing needs and occasions. In addition, the clerk cited the 2009–2010 Public Service Renewal Action Plan as achieving the following:

- *In the area of recruitment, departments and agencies are taking a more strategic and coordinated approach, building on their integrated business and human resources plans. They are also taking advantage of the redesigned jobs portal.*
- *Employee development and training programs have been established in almost every department and agency, and learning plans are becoming a regular and meaningful feature of the workplace.*
- *More rigorous performance management is now embedded at senior levels in departments and agencies. Talent management is in place for all executives, and we are moving toward implementation for some non-executive levels.*
- *We have earned dividends on our investment in leadership development, through initiatives such as the Advanced Leadership Program. We see a new generation of leaders emerging to take on senior positions across the Public Service.*[28]

Despite these optimistic assessments, reform continues apace. The Office of the Chief Human Resources Officer, for instance, undertook its own review in 2010–2011.

In order to reduce the web of rules and to assist deputy heads in taking greater responsibility for people management within their organization, the Office of the Chief Human Resources Officer launched a People Management Policy Review Project. This involves a review of all human resources mandatory policy instruments to ensure they are relevant and provide deputy heads with the flexibility to manage people in a way that suits their organization's culture and operational needs.[29] Box 9.2 summarizes the main actors and their responsibilities in human resources management.

---

### BOX 9.2   Main Human Resources Responsibilities

- **Privy Council Office:** The Privy Council Office is responsible for the selection, management, and development of deputy heads, the most senior leaders in the Public Service, and it supports the clerk as head of the Public Service. It provides advice on the government's structure and organization; fosters a high-performing and accountable public service; and ensures the submission of an annual report on the public service to the prime minister.

- **Canada Public Service Agency:** As the focal point for people management in the core public administration, the agency is responsible for leadership and service in human resources planning, accountability, modernization, employment equity, values and ethics, and official languages. It is also responsible for classification policy, the federal learning policy, and management of development programs.

- **Treasury Board of Canada Secretariat:** Among its many responsibilities, TBS manages pensions, health and dental care, labour relations, compensation, pay administration, occupational health and safety, pay equity, consultations with bargaining agents, collective bargaining, and setting terms and conditions of employment for unrepresented and excluded employees.

- **Canada School of Public Service:** CSPS is responsible for supporting training and professional development, including training associated with leadership development and language training, for public servants. It also provides information to the agency on the compliance of departments and agencies with the required training elements specified in the *Policy on Learning, Training and Development.*

- **Public Service Commission:** The Public Service Commission is an independent agency reporting to Parliament, whose mandate is to safeguard the integrity of the public service staffing system and the political neutrality of the public service. It sets policy on recruitment and appointments within the public service in accordance with the PSEA. It conducts investigations and audits regarding appointments and investigates any allegations of improper political activity by public servants.

- Line departments and agencies: Departments and agencies deliver public programs and services to Canadians. Under the PSMA, primary

responsibility for human resources management has shifted from central agencies and the Public Service Commission to deputy heads in departments and agencies, and from human resources professionals to line managers.

This survey of management reforms may leave you with the impression that reform of public service is a Sisyphean task. You will recall that Sisyphus was condemned by the Greek gods to endlessly roll a boulder up a hill, only to see it roll back down each time he got near the peak, and to repeat this throughout eternity. However, the early results of initiatives in the past decade suggest that a corner may have been turned, and that the public service is emerging from its darker days when the fallback reform position was to cut spending. What is less clear is whether this corner has been turned as a result of fiscal realities, or because of crises, or because of reduced public tolerance for mismanagement, or for some combination of these and other reasons. For now, it may be worth noting that in the absence of robust financial resources, public sector renewal appears to be a self-defeating exercise, since it mainly requires self-inflicted denigration of the institution in the face of hostile external attacks. For the brief period of balanced budgets and surpluses, the rationale for public sector reform as fiscal constraint was removed, and the future of the public service looked brighter than it had for a long time; but after the global economic crisis of 2008–2009, we returned to a position of significant deficits and debts. Whether meaningful reform can be sustained, or whether matters will return to a slash and cut mentality remains to be seen. We turn now to a consideration of financial management for a broader perspective on these issues.

# Financial Management

Financial management of an enterprise that generates and spends billions of dollars of taxpayers' money is no small task. The complexities of budgeting have spawned an extensive literature dedicated to developing the best possible system for the management of the public's fiscal resources. We will consider these developments briefly in historical perspective before turning to the nuts and bolts of public sector financial management, as it is currently practised. Keep in mind, though, that financial management is mainly about "who gets what" from government and society.

## The State and Economy

The rise of a new class of "mandarins" in the postwar years (as noted in chapter 8) coincided with and made possible a huge expansion of the role of the state in Canada. While the state in Canada has always had some role in the economic life of the nation (see chapter 1), in the 1930s and 1940s the federal government shifted its attention from such things as tariffs and transportation—the pillars of Canada's "national policy" of the late nineteenth century—to new responsibilities. Monetary policy and the construction of a new welfare state on the basis of Keynesian theory emerged as what some observers called a "new national policy." The federal government consequently expanded its role into areas where it had previously feared to tread. The crises of the Great Depression in the 1930s and the Second World War in the 1940s accelerated this process, with profound consequences for the management of the federal public service:

*As a result, by 1945 the federal civil service had swollen to 115 000 employees, compared to the 10 000 estimated in 1896. The wages alone for these government employees represented a sum five times larger than the total government budget 50 years earlier. The total 1945 budget was $5.25 billion, compared to $36 million in 1896. The range of federal government activities had expanded to include such responsibilities as old-age pensions, unemployment insurance, family allowances, subsidized housing and other social policies, as well as a new conception of the federal government's role in economic management.* [30]

The implications for the financial management of the government's business were huge. The result has been a dramatic growth in government spending until recently. Donald Savoie sums up the trend in the following way: he points out that the total federal government budgetary spending in 1920–1921 was $476 million. This figure actually dropped in 1923–1924 to $352 million. But from then on it gradually climbed higher. In 1939, total expenditures were $533 million. By 1950–1951, they had risen to $2.4 billion; in 1960–1961, they reached $6.7 billion; in 1970–1971, they were $15.3 billion; in 1980–1981, $62 billion; in 1983–1984, $96.6 billion; and in 1987–1988, total government expenditures reached $122.5 billion.[31] Strikingly, after more than a decade of restructuring, total expenditures climbed to $175.2 billion by 2000–2001, in 2006–2007, they sat at $205 billion and by 2009–2010 had reached $247 billion.

These numbers are difficult to contemplate; they are abstractions that are hard to conceptualize. So look at them this way: the total value of the goods and services produced by a country is referred to as its gross domestic product (GDP). If we look at the percentage of GDP accounted for by government, we get another perspective on the growth of the state. In 1930–1931, federal government expenditures represented 6.8 percent of GDP. They represented 16 percent of GDP by 1940–1941, levelled off to 12.8 percent in 1950–1951, reached 17.6 percent in 1960–1961, 21 percent in 1976–1977, 23.6 percent in 1982–1983, and 23 percent in 1986–1987. In the 1990s and early 2000s expenditures hovered around 12–13 percent, which suggests that the federal government has always been and still is a key player in the economy (see Figures 9.1 and 9.2).

**FIGURE 9.1    Government Expenditures as a Percentage of GDP**

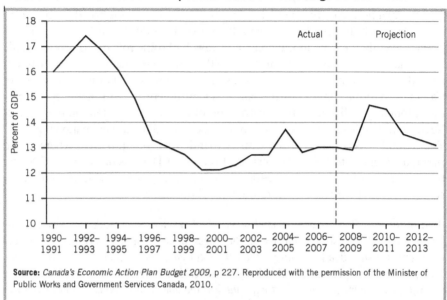

Source: *Canada's Economic Action Plan Budget 2009*, p 227. Reproduced with the permission of the Minister of Public Works and Government Services Canada, 2010.

**FIGURE 9.2    Government Revenues as a Percentage of GDP**

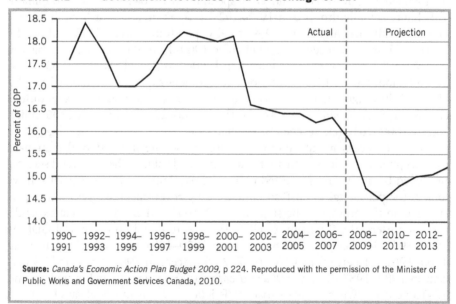

Source: *Canada's Economic Action Plan Budget 2009*, p 224. Reproduced with the permission of the Minister of Public Works and Government Services Canada, 2010.

The issue of raising and spending money can usefully be conceptualized by thinking about some government departments as "savers" or "guardians" and others as "spenders," engaged in both competitive and cooperative behaviour to determine the allocation of resources.[32] The distinction between the two can be expressed this way,

*Guardians oversee the budget as a whole to ensure that the total of all budget allocations does not lead to over-expenditure, unwanted deficits, or unsustainable debts. Spenders are preoccupied with providing programs and services of sufficient quantity and quality to meet the increasing demands of the citizens they serve. They are not concerned with the budget as a whole because they know the guardians are, and guardians do not develop and advocate expenditure programs because that is the job of spenders.[33]*

While this framework is common in academic analyses, changes to the way that governments budget since Program Review have led to the inclusion of other actors who can be thought of as "priority setters" and "financial watchdogs," according to David Good.[34] The key "savers" are the Department of Finance and the Treasury Board, and the Privy Council Office also plays an important part. The spenders are virtually all the other departments. The two types are engaged in a constant struggle. Each has its own set of clients, both within government and out in the broader society, pressuring government departments to take action—or not to take action; each has its champions and villains within Cabinet, Parliament, interest groups, the media, and the public. For example, the Ministry of Agriculture, a "spender" department, wants government to dedicate sufficient resources to agricultural interests in Canada in order to guarantee the ongoing viability and vitality of this sector of the economy. The ministry is pressured by the farming community; manufacturers of farm equipment; chemical, pesticide, and herbicide makers; rural Canadians; and others to make sure that agricultural ways of life are protected and promoted. The Finance Department is chief among the "saver" departments. It has ultimate responsibility for the government's overall fiscal health and keeps a firm hand on the purse strings. It is constantly pressured by "spender" departments, such as Agriculture, to reapportion the government pie, but it is simultaneously pressured by other actors, as well: the business community might be asking for tax breaks; organized interests and think tanks might be producing studies showing the importance of reducing the debt; the auditor general may be demanding an end to the government's profligate ways. The Finance Department bears the brunt of all these and countless other pressures in managing the government's financial resources.

For many years it seemed as though the "spenders" were winning the battle, if not the war.[35] But through the 1980s and 1990s, the "savers" launched a forceful counteroffensive, resulting in significant downsizing and a deliberate and concerted effort to wrestle the deficit and debt to the ground. Moreover, there was an increased emphasis on improving the various financial controls and reporting mechanisms used to oversee the entire government budgetary process. While the spenders re-emerged in the era of surpluses,[36] their influence waned again when the economic crisis of 2008–2009 resulted in a return to deficits for the Canadian government. Meanwhile, in the past 15 years key "priority-setters" emerged in the Privy Council Office and Prime Minister's Office, increasingly using the budgetary process as a communications tool to signal important political and policy messages to voters and citizens. According to Good, "In the face of continuous fiscal restraint and increasing demands for programs and services, the PMO and PCO are shaping the priorities of the minister of finance's budget."[37] The emergence of priority-setters was accompanied by the rise of financial watchdogs. While always a part of the process, "Now with the bite of their public reports and commentary sharpened by a highly attentive and probing media and a less deferential and more skeptical public, they have become more central to the action."[38] Watchdogs of importance are the Office of the Auditor-General, created in 1878 but recently increasingly influential (see chapter 11), and the newly created (2006) parliamentary budget officer (see Box 9.3), a position that has quickly asserted perhaps more independence than its creator, the Harper government, had intended.

To this complicated panoply of actors, G. Bruce Doern adds external "budget-watchers" that have emerged as increasingly important in the past 15 years. Doern argues,

*At present, there are simply more competitive multiple analytical sources of analysis, forecasting and commentary which are more active, public and aggressive in offering fiscal advice and in assessing fiscal performance. These include banks, financial rating agencies, international agencies such as the OECD and IMF, think tanks (with a range of political perspectives) and academic centres and teams . . . .[39]*

The key question, though, has always been how best to design and implement controls and mechanisms for financial management. This is a profoundly important issue because, as two observers put it, "the authorities granted to governments by legislatures to collect and expend public funds, and the obligations to report on the use of these funds, are at the heart of parliamentary governance

**BOX 9.3 | The Parliamentary Budget Officer**

In 2006, the position of parliamentary budget officer was created. The mandate of this new watchdog is as follows:

*The mandate of the Parliamentary Budget Officer is to provide independent analysis to Parliament on the state of the nation's finances, the government's estimates and trends in the Canadian economy; and upon request from a committee or parliamentarian, to estimate the financial cost of any proposal for matters over which Parliament has jurisdiction.*

**Source:** Canada, Library of Parliament, "PBO at a Glance," http://www2.parl.gc.ca/Sites/PBO-DPB/AtAGlance.aspx?Language=E.

and democracy."[40] This assertion is supported by the dramatic events of late 2008, as depicted in Box 9.4

Budgeting involves many actors and institutions, making it a highly complex exercise. Parliament, Cabinet, departments, central agencies, and the auditor general are key players within government. The media and interest groups have historically been keen observers of the process, often acting as watchdogs to uncover government malfeasance, while ordinary citizens are increasingly being consulted

---

### BOX 9.4  The 2008 Budget Debacle and Constitutional Crisis

**H**ow important are budgets? The 2008 budget provided a dramatic example of the extent to which the life of a government can be dependent on budgetary politics. In its budget update in late 2008, just six weeks after the October election, the Harper government gratuitously included measures in the budget so offensive to the opposition parties that they threatened to bring the government down unless the measures were removed. The opposition parties could defeat the government by voting a motion of *non-confidence*. If passed, the government would lose the constitutional right to govern as it would lose the support of the majority of the Members of Parliament (a non-confidence vote on a matter of money results in the fall of a government; see chapter 11). The Conservatives had 143 seats. The Liberals with 77 seats, New Democratic Party with 37 seats, and the Bloc Quebecois with 49 seats, together constituted a majority of seats in the House (there were also 2 independents), and informed Governor-General

Michaëlle Jean that they were prepared to govern together in a coalition and that she should give them the opportunity to do so. Because Harper only had a minority government, the situation was dire. To avoid a showdown with the opposition and rather than face certain defeat in the House over the budget, Harper advised the Governor-General instead to prorogue Parliament. Prorogation is a step a Prime Minister can take which basically terminates a session of Parliament. There was considerable debate amongst constitutional experts and ordinary Canadians as to whether the Governor General should accept the advice of the prime minister, or give the opposition coalition the opportunity to govern. But on December 4, 2008, after meeting with Harper for more than two hours behind closed doors, the Governor General granted the request to prorogue Parliament until January 26, 2009. The Conservatives then introduced a revised budget which the Liberal Party found palatable enough to support.

on the budget-making exercise that dominates the life of governments—an exercise that was once closed, secretive, and exclusive to a handful of mandarins and the finance minister.

The most recent important reforms to the budgeting process can be summed up in three initiatives: the Expenditure Management System (EMS); departmental business plans; and improved reporting to Parliament. At the root of the system we are about to explore is one fundamental principle, which we briefly looked at in earlier chapters: responsible government. At the end of the day, the government is held responsible by Parliament for its actions to the citizens of the country. In particular, the government is held responsible for its handling of the taxpayers' money, and it can only hold power as long as it demonstrates that it has acted reasonably and responsibly in managing those monies.

Consider the organizational features of government financial management that underpin this theory. At Confederation in 1867, the statutory basis of financial management was established in the BNA Act, section 102, which gives Parliament the right to control public money and calls for the creation of a single consolidated revenue fund to receive all money belonging to Canada. Authority to pay money out of the consolidated revenue fund is given to Parliament in section 106. Parliament is formally and constitutionally responsible for approving the raising and spending of public money. Donald Savoie explains the importance of this point:

*Several principles underpin Parliament's role in the budget process. The first is that the government—or the executive—can have no revenue which is not sanctioned by Parliament, and the second is that the government can make no expenditures except those approved by Parliament. In addition, Parliament does not grant a permanent right to spend, so that the government must submit a new budget every year. Thus funds allocated by Parliament but not spent must lapse. Detailed spending plans are submitted annually in the form of spending "estimates." The government must also account to Parliament for its management of public moneys, both revenues and expenditures.*[41]

Once again, though, we should note that there is a disjuncture between theory and practice. In the real world of Canadian politics, control over the public purse is in the hands of the executive (that is, the Cabinet). Because of the practice of party discipline, the executive receives support for its budgetary plans virtually automatically. So, in reality, the role played by Parliament is more one of "watchdog," "legitimating" the government's financial plans, rather than setting them. In times of minority government, Parliament's role may be enhanced since the executive often must bargain with one or more of the opposition parties to support the budget. In return, those parties may be able to negotiate out of the budget those items they find most objectionable, as in 2008, or have included items close to their own hearts, as did the NDP under Jack Layton in the 2005 Liberal budget.

Canadians are apprised of the state of their finances through four major reports that are made annually to Parliament. First, the most visible and politically significant of these reports is the budget by the minister of Finance, "which includes a comprehensive financial statement, including a forecast of financial requirements for government operations for the forthcoming year, and the ways and means proposed by the government to achieve its multiple objectives."[42] The budget speech delivered by the minister of Finance each year has been described as "the focal point of the federal government's efforts to define and mobilize public support for its fiscal and economic agenda. As such, it is an opportunity for the federal government to define its priorities, exercise leadership, and obtain legal and political support for its policies, through both the formal processes of Parliament and direct appeals for public support."[43] Second, the government annually provides estimates to inform Parliament of its spending plans for the coming year. The estimates provide the basis for the legislation that Parliament passes to authorize government spending. Third, every month in the *Canada Gazette,* a "Statement of Financial Operations" is published. This provides detailed information on financial transactions for the previous month, as well as a running total for the year. Finally, the government's annual audited financial statements are found in the Public Accounts of Canada, presented to Parliament by the president of the Treasury Board on behalf of the government, although they are prepared under the direction of the Treasury Board president and the minister of Finance by the receiver general of Canada. The reports are also presented to the auditor general, who reviews them and presents to Parliament his or her independent assessment of the management of Canada's finances. In turn, the auditor general's report becomes part of the Public Accounts of Canada. These are reviewed by a parliamentary committee called the Standing Committee on Public Accounts, which also reports to Parliament.

This brief sketch only scratches the surface of the process, which, as you can see, is complex and involves many important actors. Before taking a more in-depth look at the process in the context of the annual budgetary timetable, it will be useful to review the major trends in reporting and control of the public purse. Here we expand on systems that have come and gone over the years in Ottawa.[44]

## Managing Government Fiscal Resources

As with many recent reform developments, our discussion of financial control systems begins with the Glassco Commission, which set the stage for reform of financial management systems and improved reporting to Parliament; it continues to influence developments in this area to this day. Prior to Glassco, there was an emphasis on accountability in terms of ensuring accuracy and probity in raising and spending money. This is still true. However, less attention used to be paid to the budget as a tool of effective management, planning, and evaluation, and the budget was not considered a tool of macro-economic management of the Canadian economy until after the rise of Keynesianism. Typically, control of the budget was in the hands of the Department of Finance. Other departments would negotiate with Finance over the increased dollars they would receive to run their programs after accounting for inflation or the establishment of new programs. The process was incremental, with a little bit added each year, and with little attention paid to the cumulative impact of the many decisions that went into the annual budget.

The key problem that Glassco identified in financial management was the practice of setting departmental (and hence governmental) budgets by approving transactions before they occurred. This meant that individual managers would offer their best "guesstimate" of how much money they would need to offer services and run programs for the upcoming fiscal year. This technique, besides not being particularly systematic, had the effect of putting upward pressure on the government's overall expenditures. Few managers would admit to needing fewer resources than in previous years, since this might imply that their program or service was of diminishing importance, and therefore disposable. Moreover, this system monopolized power over the government's overall financial resources, and managers had little opportunity to see the "big picture" of governmental budgeting.

In this context, Glassco's rallying cry to "let the managers manage" meant increasing managers' authority as well as their responsibility and accountability. The Glassco Commission suggested introducing methods by which the value and efficiency of expenditures could be measured, and a five-year budgetary planning cycle. Shortly thereafter, in 1966, the Treasury Board was separated from the Department of Finance. It was given its own minister and department, and took over managing the government's expenditure budget, personnel, and administrative policy.

By the 1970s, economic growth had slowed. The new challenge was to figure out how to do more with less: that is, how to provide the same or even higher levels of service with less and less funding. Flattened tax revenues, a decline in business confidence and investment, and new overseas competition in sectors of the economy that Canada had traditionally been strong in all combined to exert pressure on the state's ability to carry on "business as usual." As well, the tax burden had gradually shifted, so that corporations were now paying a smaller proportion of the overall burden while individuals were paying a greater one. The government's extensive use of tax breaks and tax expenditures began to catch up with it. The positivist, activist vision of the Canadian state eroded as taxpayers increasingly came to see many government programs as wasteful, although this did not necessarily stop them from demanding that services still be provided.

As a result, and following from Glassco, a veritable alphabet soup of decision-making systems was introduced into financial management. The thrust of these systems was to introduce rationality, planning, and advanced management techniques into the process. The first step along this path was to change the nature of expenditure requests by managers. In the past, such requests had been based on a rudimentary **line-item method of budgeting**, which simply involves listing the main objects of expenditure (e.g., How many paper clips does the department need? How much will be paid out in salaries? How much does it cost to rent office space?). Little or no attempt was made to evaluate the effectiveness of these expenditures. But henceforth, a manager would be expected to produce formal statements outlining his department's objectives, and how he planned to systematically evaluate the effectiveness of the programs the department administered. The **Planning, Programming, Budgeting System** (PPBS) was the first attempt to reorganize financial management in this way.[45]

PPBS was based on the budgeting techniques in vogue in the United States, and was adopted by the Treasury Board in 1969. It sought to provide a framework for budgeting that went beyond line-item budgeting to analyze new initiatives and develop longer-range plans to meet departmental and governmental objectives reflective of Management by Objective (MBO) approaches (see chapter 4). This became known as **program budgeting**. There would be ongoing assessments of the impact of programs and whether they met the government's stated goals and objectives in the most efficient way. Also, "an important objective was to improve policy analysis, program evaluation, and performance measurement throughout the public service in order to better hold department managers to account and to better inform decision making and resource allocation."[46] PPBS introduced the idea of the "A" budget, the "B" budget, and the "X" budget into each department. Managers would design the "A" budget to cover the costs of ongoing programs. The "B" budget was intended for new or expanded programs, and the "X" budget was meant to cover low-priority items that might be reduced or eliminated.

While the beauty of PPBS was its rational basis, its fatal flaw was the added bureaucracy required to administer it. Copious amounts of paperwork and reporting were necessary to keep it afloat, and gradually the Cabinet decision-making process it was supposed to support was swamped. Moreover, the introduction of PPBS coincided with a serious downturn in the Canadian economy, and the resulting mishmash of financial management resulted in the commissioning of yet another inquiry to sort out the mess. The Lambert Commission (the Royal Commission on Financial Management and Accountability) was struck in 1976 to investigate standards for financial management and accountability. Even before the commission reported, however, the government created the position of comptroller general to do just that. While most of the Lambert Commission's recommendations were initially ignored by the government, it did contribute to the general climate that suggested a need for improved financial management.

In fact, the next set of reforms actually resembled several of the suggestions put forth by Lambert. In 1979, the Conservative government of Joe Clark became concerned that "spenders" had overwhelmed "savers" in the government's budgetary processes, so it introduced a new system called the **Policy and Expenditure Management System** (PEMS).[47] While Clark's government lasted only nine months in office, his innovations were adopted by the successor Trudeau administration. The goal of PEMS was similar to those of many earlier reforms: it improved ministerial control over financial management in the area of priority setting and allowed ministers to more easily appraise both the medium- and long-term picture of policy development and financial management. Moreover, PEMS was meant to promote a more collegial decision-making process in Cabinet with respect to allocating fiscal resources across the government. An "envelope" system was introduced regarding expenditures, in which ministers were figuratively handed an envelope with a set amount of cash in it, and expected to make their department's spending fit the amount. Cabinet committees determined how much went into each departmental envelope.[48] To assist them in this work, departments were required to submit strategic overviews of their activities, as well as multi-year operational plans.

Through the 1980s, piecemeal changes were made to PEMS, including a shift away from the envelope system in favour of *reference levels* for departments, a more flexible way of apportioning resources. In addition, the delivery of the minister of Finance's annual budget was brought in line with the annual expenditure cycle (usually in February). Consultations with groups outside government became a regular feature of the budgetary process, in contrast to the highly secretive methods of the past. Once again, however, the excessive bureaucratic and administrative work required to keep PEMS alive proved daunting. Gradually, it too fell into disrepute, particularly as the problems of growing deficits and debt continued to bedevil the government, notwithstanding the introduction of these rational planning and financial management techniques.[49] As a result, PEMS gave way to EMS—the **Expenditure Management System**—in January 1995.

Under EMS, there was a heavy emphasis on "getting government right," which had become the buzz-phrase of the day. Where budgeting was concerned, this meant focusing on efficiency, and EMS introduced the practice of having departments produce annual **business plans**. These were documents based on a private sector model of reporting that would replace the multi-year operational plans introduced under PEMS. Business plans, delivered to the Treasury Board by each department in the fall of each year, were meant to show how departments planned to improve or restructure programs—increasingly referred to now as *lines of service*—over a three-year period. The business plans were also intended to signal ways in which departments could adjust their activities to promote efficiencies and improvements in services to clients, as well as measure performance.[50] The business planning process was introduced by the Treasury Board Secretariat as part of an initiative called "Managing for Results."

An increased emphasis was also placed on "results-based" reporting and evaluation. To place these developments in the context of the overall budget system, it is necessary to go back to the observation above, that Parliament alone can authorize the spending and raising of money, which it does in the Estimates. The Estimates are the means by which the government seeks Parliament's permission to access the Consolidated Revenue Fund. The Estimates comprise three parts: Part I summarizes the government's expenditure plans for the year, while Part II shows the amounts that the government requires for specific votes (that is, for each department or agency). Part III of the Estimates contains the most detailed information regarding each department's expenditure requirements. Part III was added to the Estimates in 1981, as a result of the reforms made during the PEMS era, and was influenced in its design and presentation by the Office of the Comptroller General. Unfortunately, the Estimates were often so convoluted and difficult to read that they were of little use as accountability mechanisms for Parliament. Thus, they have been simplified through the business plan format to make it easier for Parliament to hold the government accountable. Since 2005, the Estimates have also set out results, as well as simply reporting spending by departments. Concerted efforts have been made to improve the reporting functions of departments, and to improve performance measurement and evaluation, through EMS. Table 9.1 shows the objectives, inputs, and players in the EMS.

In her *2006 Annual Report*, the auditor general underscored the importance of EMS by saying,

*The EMS is at the heart of the operation of government. It touches everything the government does, since all government activities involve spending. A system that works well promotes efficient, responsive, and accountable government. Without a good system, nothing departments and agencies do individually will result in sound overall*

**TABLE 9.1    The Main Objectives, Inputs, and Players of the Expenditure Management System**

| Basic Objectives | Main Inputs | Key Players |
|---|---|---|
| Overall fiscal control | • Fiscal strategy<br>• Spending and revenue forecasts<br>• Budget preparation | • The Cabinet<br>• The Department of Finance |
| Efficient allocation of resources | • Priority setting<br>• Policy development<br>• New spending approvals<br>• Production of estimates | • The Cabinet<br>• The Privy Council Office<br>• The Department of Finance<br>• The Treasury Board and its Secretariat<br>• The departments |
| Operational efficiency | • Operational planning<br>• Financial management and controls<br>• Performance monitoring and measurement | • The Treasury Board and its Secretariat<br>• The departments |
| Parliamentary control | • Examination and approval of the Estimates<br>• Accounts and program performance | • The House of Commons<br>• Parliamentary committees<br>• The auditor general |

**Source:** *Report of the Auditor General of Canada: November 2006, Office of the Auditor General of Canada to the House of Commons: An Overview of the Federal Government's Expenditure Management System.* **www.oag-bvg.gc.ca/internet/English/att_20061100xe01_e_14485.html.** Reproduced with the permission of the Minister of Public Works and Government Services, 2010.

*management of government spending. An effective EMS is essential to getting the results the government wants and to being accountable to Canadians for what is done on their behalf.* [51]

Alas, as with all previous financial management systems, EMS, too, has spawned its own sets of problems. These were recognized when, in 2006, the government announced it was reviewing the EMS. The government is wrestling with the linkage (or lack thereof) between the stated goals of budgeting and service to citizens through improved management of their resources, as allocated through the budgetary process. In part, this concern is connected to the ongoing problem of declining citizen trust in government (as with the sponsorship program and other scandals) as much as to the need to improve on-the-ground service provision. Therefore, government is reviewing roles and responsibilities of key actors, including the central agencies and the managers of service delivery, in an attempt to close the gap between expectations and deliverables. So, for instance, the Treasury Board initiated a review of EMS, focusing on accountability and on its role as an oversight body aimed at cultivating management excellence. To this end, performance measurement is receiving intensified attention, including an annual assessment of the role of deputy ministers in the financial management pantheon. The Expenditure Management Information Project is a key part of this ongoing process.

In its 2006 and 2007 budgets, the government announced it would seek to strengthen the EMS, reallocate resources to new priorities, implement cyclical departmental and horizontal program reviews, and link planning and results management. The new EMS was to focus on four principles:

■  *Departments and agencies will manage their programs to clearly defined results, and assess their performance against those results.*

■  *The Treasury Board Secretariat will oversee the quality of these assessments and ensure that departments explicitly address risk as well as cost-effectiveness.*

■  *Building on these assessments, Cabinet will systematically review the funding and relevance of all program spending to ensure that spending is aligned with Canadians' priorities and effectively and efficiently delivers on the Government's responsibilities.*

■  *Cabinet will undertake a rigorous examination of all new spending proposals, taking explicit account of the funding, performance and resource requirements of existing programs in related areas.*[52]

Moreover, the Harper government announced in 2008 that the newest version of EMS would involve a review of all spending over a four-year cycle.[53] Despite these pronouncements, action on reforming EMS has been slow, perhaps reflecting the rapidly changed economic circumstances that emerged right after these reforms were announced.

When EMS was instituted, the government was fixated on eliminating the deficit, which leads to another set of concerns. In the words of the auditor general,

*The current Expenditure Management System was designed in the mid-1990s when, facing budget deficits, the government was trying to reduce its spending. Departments and agencies had to operate in a fiscal environment that restricted new funding as much as possible. However, a system suited to times of fiscal restraint is not necessarily the best one for periods of fiscal abundance—for example, a budget surplus. Changes in the scale and nature of government spending will call for corresponding changes in how spending is managed.*[54]

In other words, questions about value-for-money had been put on the back burner while questions about expenditure reduction held everyone's attention. But while officials busily examined their A-base budgets each year, looking for waste and duplication to eliminate, they neglected the quality of the implementation of programs and services. Cabinet committee activity reflected this as well. Ministers were so preoccupied with deficits that they paid little attention to results. Subsequently, when surpluses emerged, Cabinet was quite conditioned to simply seek to add new spending without really looking at existing programs in terms of value-for-money or results.

In short, the service delivery oversight role had been neglected. As this reality dawned, a new effort developed to improve oversight of service delivery. Service improvement initiatives were launched, and emphasis was placed on looking more critically at the so-called "back-office" functions of units within departments: that is, on budgets and personnel practices. In addition, attention began to be given over to examining the complex administrative systems that had been allowed to develop while everyone was fixated on deficits. For example, it was found that there were over 100 separate finance and human resources systems, which could be reduced to just 7 finance and 4 human resources systems. Despite these advances, however, the systems, though fewer in number, could not easily talk to one another. For instance, pay offices in different departments were, in some instances, using different software systems, so managers could not easily share data.

In addition, when EMS was examined closely, it became apparent that there needed to be an improved balance between following the rules and exercising discretion, and between oversight and flexibility. The federal government decided that the litmus test would be **risk management**. Senior public servants noticed that as a consequence of the various scandals rocking government, citizens had become quite risk-averse. So, too, had public servants. But heeding the growing number of rules designed to prevent abuse meant slowdowns and reductions in efficiency as well as muddled, overly bureaucratized accountability systems. Therefore, there had been a gradual loss of innovation, creativity, and imaginative initiatives on the part of the public service. The government sought to overcome these problems by encouraging a more risk-taking culture that empowered managers within a framework of carefully articulated values.[55] The Management Accountability Framework (discussed in chapter 8) was a part of this process. The "web of rules" that existed was reduced, and a rationale was constructed against which rules could be measured. For example, rules had to match the values of the public service, allow managers to manage risk to the operations of their departments, and promote consistent management across the whole of government. To accomplish these objectives, the oversight role had to be taken away from central agencies and returned to departments. For instance, the Treasury Board reduced its number of auditors from 900 to 400, as audit functions were decentralized and oversight of fiscal matters was allowed to take place within departments themselves. Meanwhile, the Treasury Board undertook to systematically review the over 180 sets of rules regarding oversight and accountability in an effort to reduce them to under 45. Deputy ministers were given more tools to manage oversight within their own departments, rather than having central agencies looking over their shoulders.

The grants and contributions program is a case in point. The rules regarding applications and reporting for federal grants had become so cumbersome that many small agencies and individuals simply could not cope with them administratively. It made little sense to offer funding for a social program if the agencies that could deliver the program were too intimidated by the mountain of forms and mid-term and annual reporting requirements of the application process. And those that could, often found their organizations bogged down in "administrivia" rather than program and service provision. As a consequence of this problem, the government set up a Blue Ribbon Panel, which reported on ways to streamline and improve the grants and contributions program.

Government also tackled the issue of risk management by devising a grid of low-, medium-, and high-risk activities to help determine those situations where central agency intervention was desirable. As a result, the "bottom line" has become the process of linking existing spending to new spending with an eye on outcomes and results in a culture of risk management and service to citizens.

Finally, the auditor general identified one other growing concern with EMS. While the Main Estimates support the government's annual request to Parliament for authorization to spend money, there are also what are called Supplementary Estimates, which are usually presented in the fall and again toward the end of the fiscal year. The issue is that since the late 1990s, the proportion of spending proposals made through these Supplementary Estimates, rather than through the Main Estimates, has increased significantly. Supplementary Estimates are necessary in certain circumstances, since the government cannot always forecast when it might need additional funds for some discrete, unforeseen circumstance; but the auditor general noted with concern "their routine use for spending that could be proposed in the Main Estimates. What is troubling about the increased reliance on Supplementary Estimates is that it limits parliamentarians' opportunity to examine the full range of proposed government spending." In addition, she said, "I am also concerned about the approval of Supplementary Estimates late in the fiscal year. Departments start to spend on programs and initiatives and charge the expenditures against the existing appropriations by 'cash managing' until the Supplementary Estimates are approved. This puts program spending at risk, because Parliament could reduce or reject the Supplementary Estimates. It also undermines parliamentary control of government spending because the money is spent before Parliament has examined and approved the spending proposal."[56] In other words, the very principle of responsible government was subtly being undermined by the increased tendency to resort to Supplementary Estimates.

Clearly, EMS—and the budgetary process in general—is a complex system that is a challenge to understand. Perhaps a look at the day-to-day process of budget making and the various roles of the key actors in that process will help clarify this most important aspect of public administration. To this end, we now turn to an examination of the budgetary cycle as it unfolds within the EMS framework.

## The Budgetary Cycle

The budget has been described as "a financial expression of the government's priorities, policies and plans."[57] Historically, the budget was released after the presentation of the Main Estimates, which were the documents that announced the government's detailed spending plans. The budget, therefore, focused on the measures needed to fund the government's plans, or the "ways and means," like taxes and other measures. But more recently the budget has evolved into the central tool for announcing new spending measures as well as tax measures. The budget itself has no legal authority, although measures announced in the budget may come into effect immediately, formally speaking, they must be presented to Parliament as legislative proposals before they can become law.

It may appear that the central focus of the budget process is on the minister of finance when he or she delivers the budget speech to the House of Commons. And this is undoubtedly a key moment in the life of the government. But it is important

**FIGURE 9.3    The Expenditure Management System**

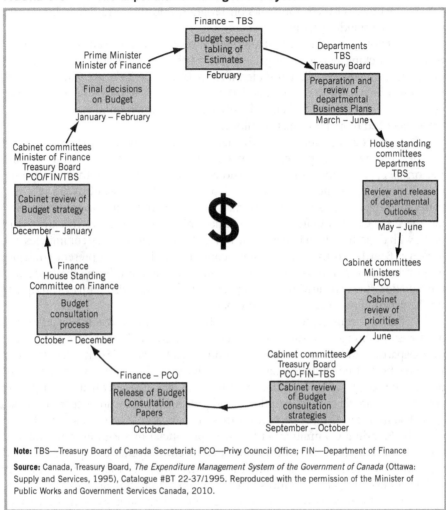

**Note:** TBS—Treasury Board of Canada Secretariat; PCO—Privy Council Office; FIN—Department of Finance

**Source:** Canada, Treasury Board, *The Expenditure Management System of the Government of Canada* (Ottawa: Supply and Services, 1995), Catalogue #BT 22-37/1995. Reproduced with the permission of the Minister of Public Works and Government Services Canada, 2010.

to understand that the budget, and financial management in general, go on throughout the year, as Figure 9.3 reveals. We outline the cycle and the key actors within EMS below.[58]

In the spring, from March to June, the Cabinet conducts strategy sessions that examine the results of the last budget, determining priorities largely on the basis of advice received from the Cabinet policy committees. Then, in the summer, Cabinet uses this information to guide the process of determining and defining reallocation and policy options for the consultation process that will take place in the fall.

The Cabinet policy committees oversee the design and implementation of new initiatives announced in the previous budget, and decide on new policy proposals in response to the strategic directions laid out by Cabinet. Meanwhile, departments and agencies prepare their multi-year business plans based on resources allocated in the previous budget. Their goal is to figure out how to match up their business plans and programs within available resources. At this time, departments also release documents called "Outlooks on Program Priorities and Expenditures" for review by the standing committees.

The Treasury Board reviews departmental business plans to ensure that departments are sticking to budget targets, and to assess the implications of these plans on the government overall. It also identifies areas where it feels intervention or support might be needed to ensure that departments adhere to their strategies and targets. The Treasury Board will also identify new reallocation options, while flagging areas that need more performance information.

Parliamentary committees use the departmental outlooks as the starting point for their reviews of the process. They look at expenditure trends, priorities, and performance, and report their conclusions to Parliament before the end of June.

During the summer, from June to September, while most of us are relaxing, various central agencies play an important part in the unfolding drama. In particular, the Privy Council Office, the Department of Finance, and the Treasury Board work with departments to integrate the advice from Cabinet policy committees, the Treasury Board, and the parliamentary committees. They then present strategies and options to the minister of finance for his consideration during the budgetary consultation stage. Meanwhile, the Department of Finance also prepares an update on the general fiscal and economic outlook.

In the fall, from September to December, Cabinet as a whole considers and approves the budget consultation strategies devised by the minister of Finance. The Department of Finance, assisted by other central agencies and departments, prepares budget consultation papers as the basis of discussions with Canadians about what ought to go into the upcoming budget. These consultation papers cover the economic and fiscal outlook, and prospective fiscal and expenditure targets. The minister of Finance releases these papers and then begins consultation with the Standing Committee on Finance, provincial finance ministers, interest groups, and the public. Work continues in the central agencies, departments, and Cabinet policy committees to refine their contributions to the budgetary process in light of evolving circumstances. The Standing Committee on Finance submits its report at this time as well, commenting on the fiscal strategy being drafted for the upcoming budget. Meanwhile, the minister of Finance busily tries to incorporate all these inputs into the development of the budget.

In the winter, Cabinet reviews the budget strategy by considering the government's fiscal targets, any new spending initiatives and reallocations, and any proposed reductions in spending. The Department of Finance puts the finishing touches on the budget, while the Treasury Board finalizes the Estimates. Finally, as the country breathlessly awaits, the minister of finance stands up in the House of Commons, sometime around the end of February, and delivers the budget, while the president of the Treasury Board tables the Estimates.

While this may appear to be the end of the story, it is in fact only the beginning . . . of the next round of budget preparation. For, upon delivery of the budget by the minister of Finance, the departments go back to the task of preparing their business plans all over again . . . and the cycle continues.

**FIGURE 9.4    Roles in the Expenditure Management System**

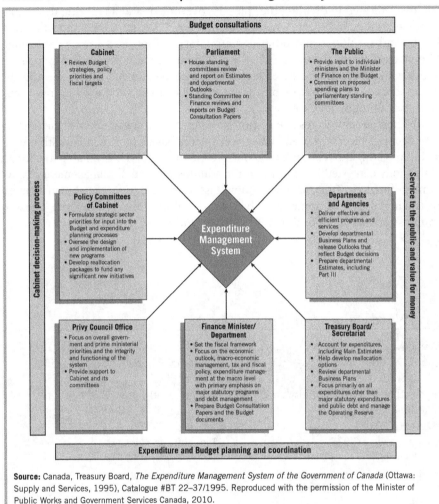

**Source:** Canada, Treasury Board, *The Expenditure Management System of the Government of Canada* (Ottawa: Supply and Services, 1995), Catalogue #BT 22–37/1995. Reproduced with the permission of the Minister of Public Works and Government Services Canada, 2010.

As should be obvious, EMS involves a veritable army of actors playing a variety of important roles (see Figure 9.4). It is a complex process whose importance cannot be underestimated, since, once again, it is in the budget that the age-old political question of "Who gets what, when, and how?" is answered.

## WHAT YOU HAVE LEARNED

When public sector managers use new human resource or financial management systems, they must ensure that the cure is not worse than the disease. Clearly, there has been a lot of experimentation in public sector management. The quantity and, more important, the quality of public services that Canadians have come to expect hang in the balance.[59] In this chapter, we addressed the complexity of managing the public service, and we considered what the managers of the public service do and how they do it, in the context of ongoing reform and in relation to money.

The management of financial resources involves elaborate decision making systems dedicated to dividing the "pie" of government and answering the fundamental question, "Who gets what, when, and how?" We noted the impact of both deficits and surpluses, and other contemporary stresses and strains confronted by managers in the public service. We also noted the increased emphasis on auditing and evaluation, as well as performance assessment, efficiency, and the importation of private sector business techniques to accompany the traditional concerns of probity and honesty.

In their attempt to resolve disputes and create a transparent and fair system of budgeting, successive Canadian governments have experimented with a variety of budgeting models. So far, no one system or model has been able to address all the hotly contested issues around the administration and management of government finances. This chapter examined issues related to financial management by tracing the development of budgetary reform inspired by the Glassco Commission and actualized by PPBS, PEMS, and EMS.

## Key Words and Concepts

Productivity Improvement Program (306)
Ministerial Task Force on Program Review (306)
Increased Ministerial Authority and Accountability (306)
PS2000 (306)
Program Review (307)
La Relève (309)
Public Service Modernization Act (311)

line-item method of budgeting (322)
Planning, Programming, Budgeting System (322)
program budgeting (323)
Policy and Expenditure Management System (323)
Expenditure Management System (324)
business plans (324)
risk management (327)

## Review Questions

*1. Restructuring the Public Service: The Management View*
The composition of the public service has undergone significant changes over time, as have approaches to managing, from an era in which downsizing, re-engineering, pay freezes, cutbacks, layoffs, and firings were endemic to the current era of reinvestment and growth. After reviewing the most recent trends in human resources management, ask yourself, Why has wholesale and ongoing reform of the public sector management been necessary? Has the public sector really turned the corner and overcome its past liabilities, or is it still mired in the same old problems? What are your future prospects should you decide on a career in the Canadian public service?

## 2. Financial Management

The fundamental questions of power politics raised in chapter 2 revolved around the question of "Who gets what, when, and how?" We returned here to this question by examining that most fundamental of issues related to government: money. Ask yourself, Does the complexity of managing the public's money pose special problems compared to managing money in the private sector? What is the "public interest" in relation to the management of money in the public sector? How do we know if the public's money is being well managed? Do the systems of budgetary management control and oversight give citizens the requisite "bang for the buck" they deserve?

## Weblinks

Department of Finance
**www.fin.gc.ca**

Canada School of Public Service
**www.csps-efpc.gc.ca**

Public Service Commission of Canada
**www.psc-cfp.gc.ca**

Treasury Board Secretariat of Canada
**www.tbs-sct.gc.ca**

Office of the Auditor General
**www.oag-bvg.gc.ca**

Office of the Chief Human Resources Officer
**www.tbs-sct.gc.ca/chro-dprh**

Parliamentary Budget Officer
**http://www2.parl.gc.ca/Sites/PBO-DPB**

## Further Reading

### 1. Restructuring the Public Service: The Management View

Albo, Gregory. "Democratic Citizenship and the Future of Public Management." In G. Albo, D. Langille, and L. Panitch, eds., *A Different Kind of State? Popular Power and Democratic Administration*. Toronto: Oxford University Press, 1993.

Campbell, Colin, and George Szablowski. *The Superbureaucrats: Structure and Behaviour in Central Agencies*. Toronto: Macmillan, 1979.

Canada. Public Service Commission. *One Hundred Years of History*. Ottawa: Public Service Commission of Canada, 2008, **www.psc-cfp.gc.ca/abt-aps/tpsc-hcfp/index-eng.htm**.

Good, David A. *The Politics of Public Management: The HRDC Audit of Grants and Contributions*. Toronto: University of Toronto Press, 2003.

Hodgetts, J.E., William McCloskey, Reginald Whitaker, and V. Seymour Wilson. *The Biography of an Institution: The Civil Service of Canada, 1908–1967*. Montreal: McGill-Queen's University Press, 1972.

Juillet, Luc, and Matthew S. Mingus. "Reconsidering the History of Administrative Reforms in Canada," in Jerri Killian and Niklas Eklund, eds., *Handbook of Administrative Reform: An International Perspective*. Boca Raton: CRC Press, 2008: 215–31.

Shields, John, and B. Mitchell Evans. *Shrinking the State: Globalization and Public Administration "Reform."* Halifax: Fernwood, 1998.

## 2. Financial Management

Good, David A. *The Politics of Public Money: Spenders, Guardians, Priority Setters, and Financial Watchdogs Inside the Canadian Government*. Toronto: University of Toronto Press and IPAC, 2007.

Hale, Geoffrey. *The Politics of Taxation in Canada*. Peterborough: Broadview, 2002.

Lewis, Timothy. *In the Long Run We're All Dead: The Canadian Turn to Fiscal Restraint*. Vancouver: UBC Press, 2003.

Lindquist, Evert. "How Ottawa Reviews Spending: Moving Beyond Adhocracy?" in G. Bruce Doern, ed., *How Ottawa Spends, 2006–2007: In from the Cold; The Tory Rise and the Liberal Demise*. Montreal: McGill-Queen's University Press, 2006: 185–207.

Strick, John C. *The Public Sector in Canada: Programs, Finance and Policy*. Toronto: Thompson Educational, 1999.

# Endnotes

1. Robert F. Adie and Paul G. Thomas, *Canadian Public Administration: Problematical Perspectives*, 2nd ed. (Scarborough: Prentice Hall, 1987): 252.

2. See A.W. Johnson, *Reflections on Administrative Reform in the Government of Canada, 1962–1991* (Ottawa: Office of the Auditor General of Canada, 1992).

3. See John Halligan, "A Comparative Perspective on Canadian Public Administration within an Anglophone Tradition," in O.P. Dwivedi, Tim Mau, and Byron Sheldrick, eds., *The Evolving Physiology of Government: Canadian Public Administration in Transition* (Ottawa: University of Ottawa Press, 2009): 292–311; John Halligan, ed., *Civil Service Systems in Anglo-American Countries* (Cheltenham, U.K.: Edward Elgar, 2003); and Peter Aucoin, *The New Public Management: Canada in Comparative Perspective* (Montreal: Institute for Research on Public Policy, 1995).

4. See Evert Lindquist, "Surveying the Public Administration Landscape: Frameworks, Narratives and Contours," in Christopher Dunn, ed., *The Handbook of Canadian Public Administration*, 2nd ed. (Toronto: Oxford University Press, 2010): 3–24.

5. Gilles Paquet and Robert Shepherd, "The Program Review Process: A Deconstruction," in Gene Swimmer, ed., *How Ottawa Spends 1996–1997: Life under the Knife*, (Ottawa: Carleton University Press, 1996): 42. The phrase "vertical solitude" is from David Zussman and Jak Jabes, *The Vertical Solitude: Managing in the Public Sector* (Halifax: Institute for Research on Public Policy, 1989)

6. For an overview, see Michel Paquin, "Administrative Modernization within the Canadian Government," in Jacques Bourgault, Maurice Demers, and Cynthia Williams, eds., *Public Administration and Public Management: Experiences in Canada* (Sainte-Foy, QC: Les Publications du Quebec, 1997): 144–54.

7. See David Johnson, *Thinking Government: Public Sector Management in Canada*, 2nd ed. (Peterborough: Broadview, 2006): 463ff.

8. Zussman and Jabes, *The Vertical Solitude*.

9. On the mandate of PS2000, see Government of Canada, *Public Service 2000: The Renewal of the Public Service of Canada* (Ottawa: Supply and Services Canada, 1990): 3–4; and P.M. Tellier, "Public Service 2000: The Renewal of the Public Service," *Canadian Public Administration*, 33, 2 (1990): 123–32.

10. Paquin, "Administrative Modernization Within the Canadian Government," 147.

11. Ian D. Clark, "Restraint, Renewal, and the Treasury Board Secretariat," *Canadian Public Administration*, 37, 2 (1994): 290–340.

12. Paquin, "Administrative Modernization Within the Canadian Government," 148.

13. Canada, Auditor General of Canada, *Auditor General's Report to the House of Commons* (Ottawa: Ministry of Supply and Services, 1993).

14. See Aucoin, *The New Public Management*

15. Sandro Contenta, "A New Attack on Red Tape," *Toronto Star* (March 12, 1994): B4.

16. See Marcel Massé, "Getting Government 'Right': The Challenges of Governing

Canada," in James John Guy, ed., *Expanding Our Political Horizons: Readings in Canadian Politics and Government* (Toronto: Harcourt, Brace, 1997): 8–14.

17. See Paquin, "Administrative Modernization within the Canadian Government," 152–53.

18. Gilles Paquet and Robert Shepherd, "The Program Review Process: A Deconstruction," in Gene Swimmer, ed., *How Ottawa Spends, 1996–1997: Life under the Knife,* (Ottawa: Carleton University Press, 1996): 39–40.

19. See Canada, Privy Council Office, *Getting Government Right: A Progress Report* (Ottawa: Minister of Supply and Services, 1996).

20. See Susan D. Phillips, "The Liberals' Mid-Life Crises: Aspirations versus Achievements," in Susan D. Phillips, ed., *How Ottawa Spends, 1995–1996: Mid-Life Crisis* (Ottawa: Carleton University Press, 1995): 15. See also David A. Good, *The Politics of Public Money: Spenders, Guardians, Priority Setters, and Financial Watchdogs Inside the Canadian Government* (Toronto: University of Toronto Press and IPAC, 2007): 266–72.

21. Paquet and Shepherd, "The Program Review Process," (1996): 40.

22. Cited in Paquet and Shepherd, "The Program Review Process," 51. For other assessments of PS2000, see John Holmes, *Public Service Management Reform: Progress, Setbacks and Challenges* (Ottawa: Office of the Auditor General of Canada, 2000); John Edwards, *Looking Back from 2000 at Public Service 2000* (Ottawa: Office of the Auditor General of Canada, 2000); Peter Aucoin, *Comparative Perspectives on Canadian Public Service Reform in the 1990s* (Ottawa: Office of the Auditor General of Canada, 2003); and Ian D. Clark, *Distant Reflections on Federal Public Service Reform in the 1990s,* (Ottawa: Office of the Auditor General of Canada, 2000).

23. Canada, *First Progress Report on La Relève: A Commitment to Action* (Ottawa: La Relève Task Force, 1998): 2. See also David Johnson and Andrew Molloy, "The Quiet Crisis and the Emergence of La Relève: A Study of Crisis Perception and Executive Leadership Within the Canadian Federal Public Service, 1997–2002," *Canadian Public Administration,* 52, 2 (2009): 203–23.

24. See David A. Good, *The Politics of Public Management: The HRDC Audit of Grants and Contributions* (Toronto: University of Toronto Press, 2003): 47.

25. O.P. Dwivedi and John Halligan, "The Canadian Public Service: Balancing Values and Management," in John Halligan, ed., *Civil Service Systems in Anglo-American Countries* (Cheltenham, U.K.: Edward Elgar, 2003): 168. See also Evert Lindquist, Ian Clark, and James Mitchell, "Reshaping Ottawa's Centre of Government: Martin's Reforms in Historical Perspective," in G. Bruce Doern, ed., *How Ottawa Spends, 2004–2005: Mandate Change in the Paul Martin Era* (Montreal: McGill-Queen's University Press, 2004): 317–47.

26. Canada, Treasury Board of Canada Secretariat, *Public Service Renewal,* January 13, 2009, **www.tbs-sct.gc.ca/chro-dprh/ren-eng.asp**. See also Canada, Privy Council Office, *2008–09 Public Service Renewal Action Plan,* **www.pco-bcp.gc.ca/docs/clerk-greffier/plan/2008-2009/docs/plan-eng.pdf** Accessed April 21, 2010.

27. Canada, Privy Council Office,*Seventeenth Annual Report to the Prime Minister on the Public Service of Canada* (Ottawa: Queen's Printer, 2010), 5, **www.pco-bcp.gc.ca/docs/information/publications/ar-ra/17-2010/pdf/rpt-eng.pdf**.

28. Canada, Privy Council Office, *Seventeenth Annual Report to the Prime Minister on the Public Service of Canada,* 9–10.

29. Canada, Office of the Chief Human Resources Officer, *People Management Policy Review Project,* March 23, 2010, Treasury Board of Canada Secretariat, **www.tbs-sct.gc.ca/chro-dprh/pmprp-epgp-eng.asp**.

30. Ralph Heintzman, "Introduction: Canada and Public Administration," in Jacques Bourgault, Maurice Demers, and Cynthia Williams, eds., *Public Administration and Public Management: Experiences in Canada,* (Sainte-Foy, QC: Les Publications du Quebec, 1997): 8.

31. Donald J. Savoie, *The Politics of Public Spending in Canada* (Toronto: University of Toronto Press, 1990): 4.

32. This characterization was first expressed in Aaron Wildavsky, *The Politics of the Budgetary Process* (Boston: Little-Brown, 1964). See also Savoie, *The Politics of Public Spending in Canada,* (1990).

33. Good, *The Politics of Public Money:* 23.

34. Good, *The Politics of Public Money.*

35. For an overview of 30 years of federal budgetary policies and developments, see G. Bruce Doern, "Evolving Budgetary Policies and Experiments: 1980 to 2009–2010," in Allan M. Maslowe, ed., *How Ottawa Spends, 2009–2010: Economic Upheaval and Political Dysfunction* (Montreal: McGill-Queen's University Press, 2009): 14–43.

36. See Michael J. Prince, "Budgetary Trilogies: The Phases of Budget Reform in Canada," in Christopher Dunn, ed., *The Handbook of Canadian Public Administration* (Toronto: Oxford Press, 2002).

37. Good, *The Politics of Public Money,* 34.

38. Good, *The Politics of Public Money,* 34.

39. Doern, "Evolving Budgetary Policies and Experiments," 36.

40. Pater Harder and Evert Lindquist, "Expenditure Management and Reporting in the Government of Canada: Recent Developments and Backgrounds," in Jacques Bourgault, Maurice Demers, and Cynthia Williams, eds., *Public Administration and Public Management: Experiences in Canada* (Sainte-Foy, QC: Les Publications du Quebec, 1997): 72. The following discussion is partly derived from this source.

41. Savoie, *The Politics of Public Spending in Canada,* 26.

42. Harder and Lindquist, "Expenditure Management and Reporting in the Government of Canada," 73.

43. Geoffrey Hale, *The Politics of Taxation in Canada* (Peterborough: Broadview, 2002): 120.

44. See Doern, "Evolving Budgetary Policies and Experiments," 14–43.

45. For an overview of PPBS, see Good, *The Politics of Public Money,* 251–55.

46. Harder and Lindquist, "Expenditure Management and Reporting in the Government of Canada," 76. See also O.P. Dwivedi and John Halligan, "The Canadian Public Service: Balancing Values and Management," in John Halligan, ed., *Civil Service Systems in Anglo-American Countries* (Cheltenham, U.K.: Edward Elgar, 2003): 148–73.

47. See Richard Van Loon, "The Policy and Expenditure Management System in the Federal Government: The First Three Years," *Canadian Public Administration,*26 (1983): 255–85; and Good, *The Politics of Public Money,* 255–61.

48. See Ian D. Clark, "Recent Changes in the Cabinet Decision Making System in Ottawa," *Canadian Public Administration,*28, 2 (1985): 185–201; and Doern, "Evolving Budgetary Policies and Experiments," 28–29.

49. See Peter Aucoin, "Organizational Change in the Machinery of Canadian Government: From Rational Management to Brokerage Politics," *Canadian Journal of Political Science,* 19, 1 (1986): 3–27.

50. See Evert A.Lindquist, "On the Cutting Edge: Program Review, Government Restructuring and the Treasury Board of Canada," in Gene Swimmer, ed., *How Ottawa Spends, 1996–1997: Life under the Knife,* (Ottawa: Carleton University Press, 1996): 205–52; Evert A. Lindquist, "Business Planning Comes to Ottawa: Critical Issues and Future Directions," in Peter Aucoin and Donald J. Savoie, eds., *Managing Strategic Change: Learning From Program Review* (Ottawa: Canadian Centre for Management Development, 1998); and Harder and Lindquist, "Expenditure Management and Reporting in the Government of Canada," 85–86.

51. Canada, Auditor General, *2006 November Report of the Auditor General,* November 28, 2006,www.oag-bvg.gc.ca/internet/English/parl_oag_200611_01_e_14969.html.

52. Canada, Department of Finance, "Chapter 5: A Stronger Canada Through a Stronger Economy," *Budget 2007: Aspire to a Stronger, Safer Better Canada,* March 19, 2007, www.budget.gc.ca/2007/plan/bpc5a-eng.html#spending.

53. Canada, Department of Finance,. *Budget in Brief 2008: Responsible Leadership* (Ottawa: Department of Finance, 2008): 6, www.budget.gc.ca/2008/pdf/brief-bref-eng.pdf.

54. Canada, Auditor General, *2006 November Report of the Auditor General.*

55. See Geneviève Lépine, *The Web of Rules: A Study of the Relationship Between Regulation of Public Servants and Past Public Service Reform Initiatives* (Ottawa: Public Policy Forum, 2007), **www.ppforum.ca/sites/default/files/web_of_rules_reportFN.pdf**. On risk management as applied in the British experience, see Bridget Hutter, "Risk Management and Governance," in Pearl Eliadis, Margaret M. Hill, and Michael Howlett, eds., *Designing Government: From Instruments to Governance*, (Montreal: McGill-Queen's University Press, 2005): 303–21.

56. Canada, Auditor General, *2006 November Report of the Auditor General.*

57. Canada, Auditor General, *2006 November Report of the Auditor General*. See also Andrew Graham, "Budgets, Budgeting, and Control in the Public Sector Context," in Christopher Dunn, ed., *The Handbook of Canadian Administration*, 2nd ed. (Toronto: Oxford University Press, 2010): 482–503.

58. This description is derived from Canada, Treasury Board, *The Expenditure Management System of Canada* (Ottawa: Minister of Supply and Services Canada, 1995).

59. See Peter Aucoin, "The Politics and Management of Restraint Budgeting," in André Blais and Stéphane Dion, eds., *The Budget-Maximizing Bureaucrat: Appraisals and Evidence* (Pittsburgh: University of Pittsburgh Press, 1991): 119–41.

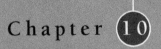

# Chapter 10

# Public Administration *and* Ethics

## WHAT YOU WILL LEARN

One of the distinguishing features of public administration is that, in the interests of accountability, public servants are subject to ethical guidelines that are often absent in the private sector. This chapter asks:

- How do we ensure the honesty and integrity of those dedicated to serving the public interest?
- What if the guidelines promoting ethical behaviour impede efficiency in providing services—which values should prevail?
- How is the behaviour of public servants shaped and constrained in the context of ethical dilemmas?
- What measures have been taken to ensure the highest standards of conduct by public servants?

This chapter is divided into the following two sections:

### 1. — *Ethical Dilemmas in the Public Service*

This section sketches out some of the broad controversies surrounding the ethical standards of behaviour in the public sector. It asks, What behaviours are acceptable within the public sector, and what are not? Are standards of behaviour in the public sector significantly different from those in the private sector? What is the "public interest"? What is the importance of discretion, partisanship, public comment, conflict of interest, lying to the public, and public versus private-sector ethics?

( 2. ⌐ *Codes of Conduct*

Powerful arguments have been put forth to suggest that ethical behaviour can only be maintained if public sector employees are subject to written codes of conduct that spell out both acceptable activities and penalties for failure to comply. Others have suggested that written codes are unsuitable and that education and role models are preferable means for ensuring ethical behaviour. This section asks, What are ethical codes of conduct? How do they work, and are they effective? Why is it felt that codes of conduct are required? What other mechanisms can be used to ensure that the highest ethical standards are upheld? What alternative means exist to ensure public servants' integrity?

## Ethical Dilemmas in the Public Service

The issue of **ethics** in the public service is relatively new as a subject of study in Canadian public administration. It has also recently spawned new practices, institutions, and behaviours. But questionable ethical behaviour has been a feature of Canadian political life since before Confederation. As two observers put it,

*Scandals and rumours of scandals have been an ever-present curse within the Canadian political system from well before Confederation. Canadian history is replete with "horror stories" involving the Château Clique and the Family Compact, the Grand Trunk and the CPR, the Ross rifle and liquor licensing. Of more recent vintage, allegations and verified incidents of unethical political party financing arrangements, as well as conflicts of interest involving government contracting, influence-peddling, favouritism and nepotism have attracted attention on the federal and provincial stages.[1]*

Moreover, the Civil Service reforms of 1918, while ushering in a meritocracy, said little or nothing about ethical behaviour. More recently, as noted elsewhere in this book, a spate of scandals in the 1990s and early 2000s have reminded us of the ongoing need to ensure the highest ethical conduct of officials is upheld.

One of the reasons ethics has garnered more attention of late is the changing nature of public administration, much of which we documented in earlier chapters. In the days when government was small, a coterie of mandarins controlled the public service and infused it with a set of shared values, attitudes, and beliefs. Ethical norms and standards were derived largely from these role models at the apex of the bureaucracy. But as government grew and became more complex and unwieldy, and as scores of new recruits brought their own ethical "baggage" with them, the shared values of an earlier era gave way to new ones. Control, formerly enforced by inculcating public servants with the same values as the mandarins, eroded. As the public service grew, the chains of command lengthened; and as they lengthened, they loosened, making room for new interpretations of what constituted ethical behaviour.

Related to these developments was an increase in opportunities for bureaucratic discretion, as well as a change in attitude about the appropriate role of public servants. More and more, public servants were seen as agents of change, rather than simply as passive servants of the public will, and the old distinctions between politics and administration were increasingly challenged. Moreover, as morale in the public sector plunged, the notion of a "career" public servant underwent a metamorphosis, so the core values that used to characterize the career also have undergone change. In addition, the new climate of evaluation emerging in Canadian public administration meant taking a closer look, not just at management, but at the ethical and moral behaviour of public servants, and ways to evaluate it. Freedom of information and privacy acts and commissioners proliferated, as did ombuds offices. The practices of auditors general and comptrollers provided the templates for considering ways in which the ethical behaviour of public servants could be measured, and calls for establishing **ethics commissioners** emerged and have been heeded in many jurisdictions.[2]

In 1996, a groundbreaking report entitled *A Strong Foundation* was published, which provided in-depth discussion of values and ethics in the federal public service.[3] Also known as the Tait Report, after its author John Tait, it called for government bodies to identify core corporate values and standards of ethical conduct. The Tait Report looked at core values in the public service, such as democratic values (respect for elected officials, accountability, nonpartisanship), professional values (innovation, resourcefulness), ethical values (probity, public interests), and people values (openness, fairness, courage). Following the Tait Report, in 1999 the clerk of the Privy Council named two senior public servants "co-champions" of a government-wide dialogue on ethics in the public service. They worked to impress upon the broader public service the centrality of values and ethics in the work of public servants and contributed to the development of a comprehensive framework for values and ethics in the public service. Also in 1999, the Office of Values and Ethics was created to undertake public service–wide initiatives to promote values and ethics. The office was also made responsible for the conflict of interest code for public servants and for developing an internal disclosure policy.[4] It was later incorporated into the Office of the Chief Human Resources Officer. In 2003 a Values and Ethics Code for the Public Service was instituted (see Box 10.1).

Recent changes rooted in neoconservative approaches and the New Public Management (NPM) have created a new orientation toward ethics. For instance, the trends toward "partnering" and contracting out, and toward merging public and private sector practices have meant that the value systems of the two are increasingly bumping up against one another, posing new challenges.

Ethical behaviour in the public service is particularly important because it contributes to the public's perception of our political institutions: it promotes trust and efficacy. Since public servants and politicians are the guardians of the public interest, there should be a special bond between the state and its citizens, expressed through citizens' belief that public officials can be depended upon to act in their best interests. Lately, though, public confidence in government has diminished. Canadians are reported to be more cynical and disrespectful of public institutions. Not all of this can be blamed on the unethical behaviour of public officials, but

## BOX 10.1 | Public Service Values

**P**ublic servants shall be guided in their work and their professional conduct by a balanced framework of public service values: democratic, professional, ethical and people values.

These families of values are not distinct but overlap. They are perspectives from which to observe the universe of Public Service values.

**Democratic Values:** *Helping Ministers, under law, to serve the public interest.*

■ Public servants shall give honest and impartial advice and make all information relevant to a decision available to Ministers.

■ Public servants shall loyally implement ministerial decisions, lawfully taken.

■ Public servants shall support both individual and collective ministerial accountability and provide Parliament and Canadians with information on the results of their work.

**Professional Values:** *Serving with competence, excellence, efficiency, objectivity and impartiality.*

■ Public servants must work within the laws of Canada and maintain the tradition of the political neutrality of the Public Service.

■ Public servants shall endeavour to ensure the proper, effective and efficient use of public money.

■ In the Public Service, how ends are achieved should be as important as the achievements themselves.

■ Public servants should constantly renew their commitment to serve Canadians by continually improving the quality of service, by adapting to changing needs through innovation, and by improving the efficiency and effectiveness of government programs and services offered in both official languages.

■ Public servants should also strive to ensure that the value of transparency in government is upheld while respecting their duties of confidentiality under the law.

**Ethical Values:** *Acting at all times in such a way as to uphold the public trust.*

■ Public servants shall perform their duties and arrange their private affairs so that public confidence and trust in the integrity, objectivity and impartiality of government are conserved and enhanced.

■ Public servants shall act at all times in a manner that will bear the closest public scrutiny; an obligation that is not fully discharged by simply acting within the law.

■ Public servants, in fulfilling their official duties and responsibilities, shall make decisions in the public interest.

■ If a conflict should arise between the private interests and the official duties of a public servant, the conflict shall be resolved in favour of the public interest.

**People Values:** *Demonstrating respect, fairness and courtesy in their dealings with both citizens and fellow public servants.*

■ Respect for human dignity and the value of every person should always inspire the exercise of authority and responsibility.

■ People values should reinforce the wider range of Public Service values. Those who are treated with fairness and civility will be motivated to display these values in their own conduct.

■ Public Service organizations should be led through participation, openness and communication and with respect for diversity and for the official languages of Canada.

■ Appointment decisions in the Public Service shall be based on merit.

■ Public Service values should play a key role in recruitment, evaluation and promotion.

**Source:** "People Values" from *Values and Ethics Code for the Public Service*, www.tbs-sct.gc.ca/pubs_pol/hrpubs/TB_851/vec-cve1-eng.asp#tphp. Reproduced with the permission of the Minister of Public Works and Government Services Canada, 2010.

much public perception is shaped by this factor. For example, the resignation of a half-dozen Cabinet ministers from the Mulroney government for a variety of offences, both real and perceived, and an unsavoury series of scandals in the Chrétien, Martin, and Harper governments contributed heavily to the growing public disgust with politicians. Changing attitudes toward authority seem to be a part of the contemporary political culture, and they influence the public's attitude regarding the ethical standards that should be applied to public servants and their political masters. According to political scientist Neil Nevitte, there has recently been a marked decline in the public confidence in government institutions. For example, in 1981, about 36.9 percent surveyed claimed to have "high" confidence in government institutions in Canada. By 1990, this number had dropped to 29.4 percent.[5] A long trend has revealed itself—most Canadians do not trust government, nor do they have great confidence in the democratic process:

■ In 1960, over 75 percent of citizens expressed their trust in the government of Canada "to do what is right"; in 2002, that figure had dropped to 27 percent;

■ Only 18 percent of Canadians say they trust politicians, and only 36 percent say they trust federal public servants;

■ 58 percent of Canadians say that "government does not care";

■ 77 percent of Canadians feel that elected officials have "lost touch";

■ 28 percent of citizens believe that "Government is crooked";

■ 46 percent of Canadians say that federal politicians are corrupt;

■ Only 20 percent believe they are honest;

■ 52 percent of the public say that ethical standards in the federal government have slipped badly in the last decade;

- Only 16 percent of Canadians believe that the public interest drives government decision-making;

- Canadians believe that the media (45 percent) and big business (38 percent) have too much influence over government decisions on public issues;

- on the other hand, 52 percent believe that average citizens have too little influence on public decisions.[6]

In 2004, the government began to construct a broader and deeper ethics regime, focusing on Parliament but with effects on the public service, too. A process for creating a code of conduct for Members of Parliament and a tougher code for Cabinet ministers was introduced. As well, an independent ethics commissioner for the House of Commons, Cabinet, and order-in-council appointees was established. An independent ethics officer for the Senate was created, as was a process for the Senate to create its own code of conduct. These steps followed similar ethics regimes created at the provincial level as early as 1988 (see Table 10.1).

The concept of the **public interest** (that is, the general well-being of society as a whole) underscores the expectation of ethical behaviour in the public service. One of the early considerations of this issue was undertaken by E. Pendleton Herring in his 1936 book, *Public Administration and the Public Interest.*[7] Herring was concerned with the tremendous growth in the scope of government activity and, in particular, with the growing bureaucratic discretion in decision making. He noted that laws and regulations were often vaguely worded, and that public servants were left to interpret what the politicians meant before implementing their instructions. This called into question who was really in charge—the public servants or the

**TABLE 10.1    Dates of Establishment of Offices of Independent Ethics Commissioners in Canada**

| | |
|---|---|
| Ontario | 1988 |
| British Columbia | 1990 |
| Nova Scotia | 1991 |
| Alberta | 1992 |
| Newfoundland and Labrador | 1993 |
| Saskatchewan | 1994 |
| Northwest Territories | 1998 |
| Prince Edward Island | 1999 |
| New Brunswick | 2000 |
| Nunavut | 2000 |
| Manitoba | 2002 |
| Yukon | 2002 |
| Quebec | 2002 |
| Ottawa—House of Commons | 2004 |
| Ottawa—Senate | 2005 |

**Source:** Ian Greene, "The Harper Impact on the Federal Ethics Regime," paper presented to the Annual Meeting of the Canadian Political Science Association, Saskatoon, June 1, 2007. **www.cpsa-acsp.ca/papers-2007/Greene.pdf**.

politicians? More to the point, the public servant might be required to make deter-
minations about what constitutes the public interest. According to Herring, the
most effective way this could be accomplished, while still remaining true to the
spirit and intent of the legislation, was for the public servant to establish a sound
working relationship with the societal interest affected by the legislation, and "bro-
ker" differences between competing groups. An added concern, Herring points
out, is that between the time a law is passed and the time an administrative agency
is responsible for its implementation, societal conditions that inspired the law may
have changed, and to implement the law as originally intended may actually run
counter to the public interest as newly expressed.

Unfortunately, Herring also argued, the concept of the public interest that
ought to guide public servants in these circumstances is an ambiguous one. It is
defined in part by the subjective perceptions of the public servant involved. Thus,
the ethical standards of these individuals must be beyond reproach. In any event,
we rely tremendously on their discretion in the administrative process. We elaborate on the issue of discretion below.

The notion of the public interest is perhaps the single most important concept
guiding the ethical dimension of administrative behaviour.[8] John Tait wrote,

*The ideal of service is one of the deepest sources of public service motivation. In the
heart of most public servants lies the conviction that service to the public, to the public
good, or to the public interest is what makes their profession like no other. It is why they
chose it, for the most part; and why they keep at it, with enthusiasm and conviction,
despite difficulties and frustrations along the way. Service to the public and to the public interest is the vision of the public service, and it is a creative, essential and compelling vision.[9]*

But developing a set of guidelines so that every decision can objectively be said to
serve the public interest is impossible. There are too many variables involved,
and the concept itself is too ambiguous. It changes over time and under different
circumstances. It often differs according to whether one is politician, public servant,
or citizen. This does not mean, though, that we should throw our hands up in
despair and declare that there is no ethical standard that can be used to determine
the public interest.

How, then, is a standard arrived at? One answer is for various groups in
society to mobilize themselves to influence government. Government, in turn,
acts as a neutral referee between these groups, determining whose interests are
met and whose are declined. In this scenario, the objective application of a set of
guidelines is all that government requires in order to determine as fairly and
honestly as possible who the winners and losers are. However, what this ignores
is that not all the groups involved have equal resources. Some are well-financed,
sophisticated organizations with access to the halls of power. Others are relatively penniless, with little knowledge of how government works, and are shut
out of the network. Under these circumstances, can we still say that the public
interest is being served if some are able to get their views across to government
and others aren't?

This raises ethical issues because the objects of attention of these groups are politicians and public servants. The question that arises is this: Can we be sure that ethical values of fairness and honesty are being followed in circumstances in which some citizens seem able to achieve privileged access to decision-makers and others cannot? What happens when decision-makers succumb to the blandishments of the well organized? Do they override the broader public interest? More directly, what if some material reward is offered by those interests—the promise of a job after leaving office, for instance, or cash or services? To consider the issue from a slightly different perspective, is the public servant who responds only to the voices he or she can hear doing a proper job? Or is the public servant who actively seeks out the marginalized, the dispossessed, and the unorganized—that is, all interests related to a particular issue—doing the ethical thing? Is it the job of the public servant to solicit the views of societal interests, or merely to respond to them? To simply respond is to leave some citizens out, but if the public servant solicits views, he or she must invariably do so on the basis of his or her personal value judgments about what groups should be heard. In other words, the public servant is injecting his or her own ethical and moral value system into the process of public administration. Is it ethical to sit back and accept that the public interest is defined somewhere else, knowing that some societal interest will not get a fair hearing? Is it ethical to step forward and try to shape the "public interest" by injecting your own views into the struggle, even though this would seem to run counter to the job of public servant? The resolution of these conflicts is rooted in the debate over how to ensure ethical standards of behaviour among public servants. There are no easy answers to these questions.

"Administrative ethics," according to one observer, "involves the application of moral principles to the conduct of officials in organizations."[10] As you will recall from our discussion of organizational theory in chapters 3 and 4, understanding the behaviour of individuals in organizations is a challenging and complex undertaking. Even assuming you can understand their motives, it is still not certain that all the members of an organization subscribe to the same general moral code. In other words, it is not always clear what rights and duties individuals respect when they engage in activity that affects the public interest. At the root of the problem is the fact that moral behaviour in organizations requires individuals to assume an objective and disengaged perspective; they must separate their own self-interest from the interest of those they are serving, and be as unbiased in the application of rules and procedures as is humanly possible. However, the complicating factor is that we are all humans and we all carry biases with us. Finding common moral ground with others in the organization is a challenge for two reasons. First, questions need to be answered about who *may judge*; second, questions need to be answered about who *is to be judged*. The former raises the notion that public servants are supposed to be neutral in fulfilling their duties: they should not be guided by their own morality or principles but by those of the organization. The latter suggests that responsibility for the organization's decisions should rest not with the individuals, but with the organization itself (through its senior officers).

In an ideal organizational world, public servants carry out their superiors' orders and implement the government's policies. In this scenario, they are ethically neutral vessels or instruments. They need not exercise independent moral judgment and are not expected to act on moral principles that they may themselves hold. Instead, they simply act on the principles contained in the orders they are given and the policies they are to implement. Simply put, "They serve the organization so that the organization may serve society." [11]

This is not to deny that individual public servants have moral and ethical belief systems of their own. Clearly, they do. But the theory described above suggests that, in effect, they park those belief systems at the door when they arrive at work. Their goal is to understand what policy their political masters intend and to faithfully enact it. If there is a conflict, they do not fall back on their own personal moral code but, rather, look to whatever legal or constitutional guidelines exist that might apply in the given case. This view sees administrators as instruments serving the organization's goals. If they find themselves in a position of unbearable moral or ethical conflict, they have the option to resign. Thus, it is argued, the organization is made capable of serving any social end, regardless of the personal views of those who hold office.

Is this a realistic view of the roles of individuals within organizations where ethical issues are concerned? It may seem as though it requires humans to become robotic automatons. This criticism is not far off the mark. Requiring people to suspend their own morality to serve the organization's greater ends seems like a hyper-Weberian recipe geared solely toward efficiency at the expense of other, more human values. And yet, consider an organization at the other end of the spectrum. Think of one in which all decisions and actions are subject to the moral and ethical belief systems of each and every individual concerned. Would anything get done? *Could* anything get done? Surely, paralysis of the organization would result. Ideally, then, a smoothly functioning and responsible organization must somehow strike a balance between the strictures of pure neutrality described above, and the chaos of moral relativism that would result if each individual in the organization were left to inject her own personal morality into every decision and action.

The dilemmas posed by trying to strike that balance are many and varied. To illustrate, we will now turn to some particular examples, including the following issues: discretion, partisanship, public comment, conflict of interest, lying to the public, and the ethics of the public versus private sector. [12] In each of the following scenarios, imagine that you are a public servant confronted with the ethical dilemma. How would you respond?

## Discretion

The first issue concerns **discretion**, which means simply the power of free decision of choice within certain legal bounds. It reflects our abilities to exercise judgment and discriminate between courses of action. Public servants exercise a certain amount of power. As a result, they are frequently placed in situations where their own personal judgment of the integrity of their actions comes into play. Thus, public servants enjoy a high level of discretion in their conduct.

For example, a directive may come down the chain of command from the minister, through the deputy minister, to the assistant deputy minister, and so on, down to you, working in the front lines of a government service-providing agency. By the time the directive gets to you, its instructions, while well intentioned, bear little relation to the issues you face on a day-to-day basis. They may even run counter in some ways to citizens' expectations about the type of service you provide. For example, suppose you issue support payments to social assistance recipients. The rules from on high dictate that recipients must produce proof of residence before you can give them a cheque. Now suppose a regular client comes in and tells you that he has been kicked out of his apartment but has a new place lined up for next week. Technically, without proof of residence, you cannot issue the cheque. But you have come to know this individual and some of the problems he is experiencing in trying to get his life in order. What do you do?

Your own personal sense of integrity and compassion suggest that issuing a cheque this once will not hurt anyone and will certainly benefit this individual, who faces the prospect of a few nights in a shelter. But your institutional training warns you that issuing the cheque is a breach of rules. Clearly, your own discretion comes into play in these circumstances.

Discretion in small cases may be acceptable, providing the law is not transgressed and no one is denied what they are entitled to from the government. But we enter a hazy area when discretion is applied too liberally or too frequently, so that the rules are made a mockery of, the law is broken, or citizens are denied their entitlements. When discretion is abused, we enter the realm of unethical conduct. Public servants enjoy a certain amount of discretion in fulfilling their duties, which means there is scope for misconduct—for instance, in handling confidential information. As with many of our examples, the issue often comes down to a question of whether the means justify the end. In other words, do public servants' discretionary acts justify the outcome?

## Partisanship

**Partisanship** is another pitfall for public servants. This refers to the notion that public servants should remain loyal to the government in the execution of their duties, and not to the political party that happens to hold power. In other words, they are to be politically neutral in discharging their duties. The "Statement of Principles" of the Institute of Public Administration of Canada puts it this way:

*Public employees should be sensitive to the political process and knowledgeable about the laws and traditions regarding political neutrality that are applicable to their spheres of employment.*

*It is the responsibility of public employees to provide forthright and objective advice to, and carry out the directions of, their political superiors.*

*Public employees have a duty to carry out government decisions loyally, irrespective of the party or persons in power and irrespective of their personal opinions.*[13]

But consider this example: what if you, as a public servant, are ordered to conceal information that might affect the outcome of an election? In this instance, you are pulled in two directions at once. On the one hand, you have a duty to follow the orders of your superiors; on the other hand, you have a responsibility to serve the public interest. You are trained to be nonpartisan, yet by taking no action, you are perhaps tilting the balance of an election toward one party over another.

This dilemma is related to several features of public administration discussed earlier. For instance, it reflects the associated problems of the politics–administration dichotomy: politicians make the rules and public servants implement them. It raises the question of merit and patronage. Presumably, in an era of widespread patronage appointments, nonpartisanship was largely irrelevant—indeed, even antithetical—to the workings of government; but in a merit-based era, the opposite is true. Finally, it raises the issue of loyalty. Public servants are required to serve the government loyally, irrespective of their personal feelings about policy. The reward for loyalty is tenure; public servants cannot be arbitrarily dismissed as long as they perform their jobs satisfactorily. But clearly, these principles are severely tested by the type of ethical issue alluded to above.

## Public Comment

The notion of **public comment** reflects the idea that public servants should remain anonymous and stay out of the public limelight. But the temptation to go public with information may be hard to resist, if not doing so conflicts with an individual's personal integrity. Consider this example: You receive confidential ministry documents that suggest a possible cover-up of government neglect regarding the discharge of toxic chemicals into the environment. Coincidentally, an old friend who works as a journalist calls you up and invites you for lunch. Do you reveal the information to her?

Here's another example: you are a senior public servant in possession of facts that reveal that the government's policy in a certain area is marginally damaging to some Canadians, although overall the policy benefits those it was intended to help. You are required to appear before a parliamentary committee to testify about certain aspects of the legislation; however, you are not questioned directly on the material in your possession. Do you nonetheless explicitly criticize your minister and department by revealing the information publicly? It is worth noting that a recent trend in Canadian public administration has seen senior public servants being called more and more often to explain their departments' actions. This would seem to undermine the principle of refraining from public comment. We explore this development in more detail in chapter 11, when we consider the changing nature of accountability.

## Conflict of Interest

**Conflicts of interest** can bedevil public servants in large and small ways. Is it a conflict of interest to accept a modest gift or a dinner from a corporation seeking a government contract? Should there be a "cooling-off period" after you, as a former high-level public servant, leave a post to work in the private sector, before you can turn around and begin to lobby your former department? What if you are pressured to award a contract to a particular firm, even though you know that firm did not present the best bid? What if you possess financial information concerning an upcoming budget and could profit from that information by playing the stock market? Should you tell your family or friends? Is it a conflict to "moonlight"—that is, to accept employment outside your regular public sector job?[14]

Conflict of interest is a common ethical dilemma in the public service. It arises when there is a possibility that public servants will materially benefit from activities related to their employment, or in situations where the objective performance of their job is interfered with. The Institute of Public Administration of Canada's "Statement of Principles" cites the following prohibitions concerning conflicts of interest:

*Public employees should not engage in any business or transaction or have any financial or other personal interest that is, or may appear to be, incompatible with the performance of their official duties.*

*Public employees should not, in the performance of their official duties, seek personal or private gain by granting preferential treatment to any persons.*

*Public employees should not solicit nor, unless duly authorized, accept transfers of economic value from persons with whom they have contact in their official capacity.*

*Public employees should not use, or permit the use of, government property of any kind for activities not associated with the performance of their official duties, unless they are authorized to do so.*

*Public employees should not seek or obtain personal or private gain from the use of information acquired during the course of their official duties which is not generally available to the public.[15]*

These are guidelines only, of course, but they indicate the scope of potential conflicts that the public servant is confronted with and that he must avoid. A complicating factor is that there are differences between real, apparent, and potential conflicts of interest, and appearances can be as important as reality. So conflict of interest is a slippery concept, but a significant one in the realm of public servants' ethical conduct.

## Lying for the Public Good

Other sorts of ethical dilemmas confront public servants. Are there ever circumstances in which public servants ought to lie to the public? The issue of **lying for the public good** has been considered since the earliest of times: "Plato, in *The Republic*, used the expression the 'noble lie' in presenting a fanciful story to persuade people to accept class distinctions and thereby safeguard social harmony; and Machiavelli's prince was most certainly encouraged to engage in deceit, if it was in his interest to do so."[16]

Imagine a case involving scientists in the Ministry of Agriculture allegedly being required to suppress information concerning the harmful effects on humans of drinking milk from cattle treated with a particular growth hormone. Allegations were made that senior public servants ordered a cover-up, and may have shredded sensitive documents that could have substantiated the claims of the scientists counselling caution. Millions of dollars in the Canadian agri-business sector were at stake, as was the livelihood of countless dairy farmers and their families. Is it possible that senior public servants, and perhaps even their political masters, were "captured" by the interests promoting the use of the hormone, prompting a web of deceit to descend over the issue? To put it more directly, if you were a public official in this case, would you withhold the truth about the harmful effects of the hormone if you knew so much was at stake? If there was 100 percent scientifically validated evidence that the hormone was harmful, probably not. But what if there was only a 50 percent chance? Or a 10 percent chance? Or a 1 percent chance?

It is conceivable that there are circumstances under which lying actually promotes the public good, and this fact complicates the search for ethical guidelines all the more. Consider the following three examples, for instance.[17] First, imagine that you are confronted with an overwhelming national crisis wherein harm can only be averted by deceit. Second, consider the opposite case, where the effect of the lie is so harmless that it hardly seems to matter. Third, consider a situation in which the release of vital information invades the privacy of individuals whom you are sworn to protect. Is lying justifiable in any of these cases?

It is probably safe to say that most people abide by a personal moral code that tells them that lying is wrong. Yet in the public service, are there situations in which lies are justifiable? Is it ethically and morally wrong, for instance, to withhold the truth about national security issues? Is it wrong to withhold potentially damaging information about a government policy? Should public servants be guided by the admonition, "Don't do or say anything you don't want to read about in the papers"? Again, there are no easy answers to these questions; they indicate the depth of the ethical dilemma confronting public servants.

## Public Sector Versus Private Sector Ethics

Should you implement policies with which you disagree, or from which you can visualize damage resulting? In other words, do public servants owe their primary allegiance to the public, to their political masters, or to their own personal moral code and conscience? Can the rules be bent for particular cases, or must they be rigidly adhered to in all cases? Is the measure of acceptable behaviour the consequences of actions taken, or is there some other higher moral standard? These are questions that are wrestled with daily in the public service.

If we search for answers to them by comparing practices in the public sector to those in the private sector, we may be frustrated by what we find. Some argue that, in their obligations to the public, public servants have an additional, more rigorous set of standards and constraints than those found in the private sector. The former chairman and chief executive officer of Imperial Oil argued that "there is an added ethical dimension expected of those in the public service" due to the fact that they must uphold the public trust.[18] Many acceptable practices in the private sector are either forbidden or frowned on in the public sector. These include accepting certain kinds of gifts, discussing certain kinds of appointments, promising or threatening government action under certain circumstances, receiving or holding large amounts of cash, withholding information contrary to the public's need to know, and leaking information that should be kept private.

These activities underline the differences between the private and public sector where ethical behaviour is concerned—differences further illustrated by the following:

*A democratic government is not a family business, dominated by its patriarch; nor is it a military battalion, or a political campaign headquarters. It is a producing organization which belongs to its members, and it is the only such organization whose members include all the citizens within its jurisdiction. Those who work for and are paid by the government are ultimately servants of the whole country, which owns and supports the government.*[19]

Moreover, there is a regime of constitutional and administrative law that informs the actions of public servants and that applies to their work in a more direct manner than in the private sector. As a result, it is generally recognized that citizens expect higher standards of ethical conduct from public servants than they do from business persons. In addition, when government functions are moved outside the traditional bureaucracy, concerns arise over

*the extent to which it is possible to infuse program delivery agencies (e.g., service agencies in Canada) with core public service values, especially if the organizations are headed by persons brought in from the private sector to manage them on a more "businesslike" basis. The creation of agencies at arm's-length from ministerial control raises concern as to ministers' responsibility for the agencies' decisions. Moreover, the appointment of business people to head public agencies and the increased mobility of employees between the public and private sectors threaten political neutrality by increasing the likelihood of partisanship and patronage.*[20]

Finally, the two have different motivations. As we noted in chapter 1, private sector activity is motivated by the bottom line, whereas the public sector has no such motivation. These qualitative differences should not be overlooked.

Now, however, we have entered an era in which governments are supposed to be run in a more businesslike fashion. Does this mean importing the private sector's ethics along with its management practices? The trend now is for governments to increasingly share responsibility with stakeholders, creating a new balance between the private and public worlds. As one observer puts it, "We are witnessing a shift from emphasis on the government as regulator to the government as co-regulator. Interdependency is what creates the new balance—and this has definite moral implications."[21] No longer will the government be the sole or most important watchdog of the public good under these conditions. But are private sector actors willing and able to assume this part of government's traditional role, along with the benefits accruing from these new partnerships? From an ethical point of view, is it appropriate to expect commercial associations, whose goal is profit maximization, to develop and implement policy, and to self-regulate? These questions have not yet been satisfactorily answered.

This is not a comprehensive list of all possible ethical dilemmas public servants face, but it should give you some sense of the complexity of the issues. There is, unfortunately, not always a straightforward "correct" answer to many of the situations cited above, which has led to the call for some sort of institutionalization of ethical conduct. It is argued that only by putting rules, regulations, and guidelines on paper for all to see and read can the proper ethical standards needed in the public sector be understood and upheld. As a result, arguments for standardized "codes of ethics" have become increasingly common. But as we will see, this solution is not without its detractors.

## Codes of Conduct

According to two professors of public administration, there are seven "commandments" to which the responsible public servant is expected to adhere:

*[A]ct in the public interest; be politically neutral; do not disclose confidential information; protect the privacy of citizens and employees; provide efficient, effective, and fair service to the public; avoid conflicts of interest; and be accountable.*[22]

To ensure that the public retains confidence in the administrative machinery of the government, issues must be managed sensitively. This explains the codes of conduct, regulations, guidelines, and laws that have evolved over the past few decades. A whole "ethics bureaucracy" has emerged. Interestingly, in an era of reform marked by a trend toward deregulation, some literature points to ethics regulations within government as a key area of growth: "Beginning with Prime Minister Pearson, successive political leaders have developed rules to guide the conduct of, at first, ministers, then bureaucrats, and now members of Parliament."[23] Indeed, it is highly ironic—and a topic worthy of further research—that as the era of managerialism proceeded with deregulation as one of its hallmarks, regulatory efforts and initiatives in the area of ethics, values, and accountability have mushroomed. Langford and Tupper go so far as to say,

*Ottawa's many ethics initiatives now constitute an "ethics program" or "business line"—a collection of interrelated activities directed toward a common goal. . . . The federal ethics program is a sprawling collection of laws, general statements of government intent, administrative regulations and processes. It engages numerous government agencies, tens of thousands of appointed and elected officials, lobbyists, political parties and, by implication, considerable time, effort and public expenditure.*[24]

The connection between years of downsizing and deregulation and the apparent rise in unethical behaviour has not been established empirically. But it is a noteworthy phenomenon that hyper-regulatory efforts in ethics, values, and accountability are occurring in step with the new managerialism's efforts to *reduce* government.

Clearly, some of the issues raised above defy easy resort to written or codified rules of conduct. Thus, the issue of codifying the ethical behaviour of public servants is contentious. Some believe that other means are needed to achieve the objectives intended by a code of conduct approach. This section will consider the pros and cons of codes of ethics, as well as two other techniques for reinforcing ethical behaviour: training and education, and role models.[25]

## Do Codes of Conduct Work?

According to one view, responsible behaviour by public servants should be measured against the expectation that ethical behaviour in government should reinforce the democratic process. It should be ensured that officials respect the rights of citizens and uphold values seen by the broader society as essential to democracy. But it is not always easy to ensure that officials in public service are sensitive to these values. Nor is it obvious that they are sufficiently self-questioning about the bigger ethical concerns in their daily decision making or execution of policies.[26]

Consequently, the drive toward codifying ethical behaviour has gained momentum. In the 1970s and 1980s, governments began to trip over themselves in issuing "codes of conduct" and "ethical guidelines to behaviour" and "conflict of interest regulations." A veritable explosion of interest developed in the issue of ethics. This was partly in response to major scandals, such as Watergate in the United States during the 1970s, when U.S. president Richard Nixon was forced to resign after having been charged with unethical and illegal behaviour. It was also a response to the increasing role of the media in uncovering government malfeasance.[27] While many of these codes of conduct related primarily to political actors, concern spread to the actions of public servants, too. The Canadian government jumped on the bandwagon and introduced a Conflict of Interest Code in 1985, after having staged a Task Force on Conflict of Interest the year before.[28]

In 1995, the clerk of the Privy Council formed a Task Force on Public Service Values and Ethics, composed of deputy ministers, to investigate contemporary issues and developments in this area.[29] As noted above, an Office of Values and Ethics was created in 1999. In 2003, the Office of Values and Ethics released a "Code of Conduct for Public Servants," which set out the expectations, rules, and behaviours expected of public officials; in 2010 this underwent a revision. Ongoing concerns about punitive action against public servants who disclose wrongdoing inspired the passage of the Public Servants Disclosure Protection Act in 2005 (it came into force in 2007). This legislation protects so-called "whistle-blowers," commits the government to adopting a Charter of Values of Public Service, requires the Treasury Board to establish a code of conduct applicable to the public sector, and requires heads of departments and agencies to establish codes consistent with the code.[30]

The media has played a prominent role in placing these ethical dilemmas before the public. It was a story in the *Globe and Mail*, for instance, that aroused suspicions about the federal Sponsorship Program. The media plays two roles simultaneously: as investigator, it uncovers malfeasance and brings it to light for the public; and as watchdog, it acts as a deterrent to public servants and politicians fearful of having their names splashed across the front pages of the newspaper. But as one award-winning analysis showed, the media can sometimes contribute to gross distortions of the level and amount of "corruption" perceived to exist.[31]

Ultimately, it would seem that the effectiveness of codes of conduct depends on ongoing scrutiny of public officials' activities by their colleagues, by other organizations, by the media, and by an attentive public. This, of course, depends on openness and accountability. But there is no sure-fire way of ensuring ethical behaviour that is consonant with the public interest. It ultimately depends on the individuals who aspire to public office and on the system of values that they have been socialized into. This, of course, creates a contemporary dilemma for governance, since public institutions are held in less regard than they once were. Thus, a vicious cycle has been created in which the low quality of public servants attracts the scorn of the public, which feeds the perception that the public service is no longer a higher calling, which means that "quality" people avoid making their careers there, which means that the scorn of the public is reinforced, and so on. Recently, schools of public administration and the public sector itself have sought to break the cycle by placing more emphasis on public service ethics.

Written codes of ethics are one way of achieving this. Another is better training, and yet another is providing role models in the upper ranks of the public service who subscribe to and demonstrate the highest standards of ethical conduct. According to one observer, interrelated objectives in seeking improved ethical standards in the public service include the following:

(1) *to promote public trust and confidence in the ethical performance of public servants;* (2) *to decrease and, if possible, to eliminate, unethical practices by discouraging and punishing them;* (3) *to legitimate the imposition of sanctions for unethical behaviour;*

*(4) to sensitize both current and aspiring public servants to the ethical and value dimensions of bureaucratic decisions; (5) to reduce uncertainty as to what constitutes ethical and unethical behaviour; (6) to develop skills in the analysis of ethical and value issues; (7) to assist public servants to resolve ethical and value dilemmas; and (8) to promote moral development.*[32]

Are written codes of conduct the best way to ensure ethical behaviour? Critics suggest that codes may not be as useful in promoting ethical behaviour as they seem.[33] First, the guidelines set out in codes are often difficult to apply in real-life situations. As the examples of ethical dilemmas above suggest, it is impossible to develop a single code to comprehensively account for every situation that might arise in the course of a public servant's job. As well, codes of ethics are often difficult to enforce—indeed, many codes contain no reference to enforcement. Third, given modern governments' complexity, is it reasonable to assume that a generalized code of ethics can be drafted that applies to all government departments, regulatory bodies, and agencies? Surely, the differences in organization and structure, policy focus, and activities mitigate against a sort of one-size-fits-all approach to codifying ethical behaviour. Fourth, codes of behaviour sometimes cast their nets so wide that innocents are caught up in them, as when public servants are required to disclose not only their own financial interests, but also those of immediate family members. Fifth, managing some ethical issues by referring to a code of ethics is inappropriate. For instance, no code can set out what level of risk to the public is acceptable in a given policy decision. The specificity of some ethical decisions belies the generality of codes of ethics. Finally, where widespread or systematic corruption commonly informs the actions and decisions of public servants, these will override the most elegantly and articulately formulated code.

Still, these criticisms assume, perhaps, that codes of ethics can do more than, in reality, they are intended to. It may well be the case that the existence of a code of ethics raises expectations about the standards of behaviour in the public service beyond that which can be reasonably expected. Thus, rather than accept all these criticisms as an indictment of codes of ethics, it is more advisable to acknowledge that no single code is going to "solve" all ethical dilemmas. What a code might do is contribute to an environment in which the highest standards of behaviour are aspired to by the organization and the individuals working therein. In this context, "While it is neither possible nor desirable to adopt rules to cover all cases, public servants must always be ready to justify their actions."[34]

Two other effective means of developing ethical behaviour in the public service are training and education, and role models.

## Training and Education

Arguments have been made that improved training is key to improved ethics in the public service. By developing the ability to identify ethical issues in day-to-day work scenarios, public servants can be stimulated to recognize ethical dilemmas and, perhaps, solve them. This allows a deepening comprehension of ethical issues and provides public servants with tools with which to engage in ethical analysis. The hope is that public servants can be socialized into the profession's highest ethical norms if their attention is drawn to exemplary ethical behaviour.[35]

The importance of training and education does not lie in the expectation that an amoral or unethical individual will, somehow, suddenly "find" morality or ethics. It is not argued that these things can be "taught" to someone whose life-long socialization has shaped him in ways that no course in ethical behaviour is going to undo. Instead, it is expected that this kind of training will promote an awareness of ethical dilemmas confronted by public servants. The point is to sensitize public servants to the issues and assist them in developing analytical skills and practical means for dealing with the issues. It is further argued that this approach is most effective for those at the early stages of their public service career.[36]

But the role of training and education needs more explicit attention. As law professor Lorne Sossin notes, "training and education are the cornerstones to the building of a new and vigorous administrative culture for the public service in which political/public service boundaries and the commitment of the public service to uphold the rule of law figure prominently."[37] But after interviewing public servants with respect to how newly hired public servants learned the boundaries between public service and political staff and ministers, Sossin reports "most of the answers indicate that this is left to 'osmosis' and 'mentorship' and 'learning by example,' but virtually no formal instruction for training of any kind specifically addressed these issues." He concludes that "this situation must change."[38]

However, the spurt of interest in ethics education in public administration schools that occurred in the 1980s may have tapered off. A 2004 survey comparing Canadian master's programs in public administration, public management, and public policy noted that only one full-time master's program in public administration has a dedicated ethics course. Several schools claim that ethical concerns permeate all of their offerings, but most schools appear to educate students only about the institutional features and mechanisms of public administration.[39] Students are well versed in the skeletal features—executive, legislative, judicial, and bureaucratic branches, and the accountability relationships between them. What seems to be lacking, however, is a systematic examination of the "guts" of those relationships—the values and ethics that animate behaviour.[40]

Part of the training of new employees in the federal public service at the supervisory level includes a program called "Orientation to the Public Service," offered by the Canada School for Public Service (CSPS). The program description states,

*Orientation programs are an important part of the human resources strategies put in place by high-performing organizations. This orientation program welcomes new employees into the public service and helps them to understand their role as public servants. Participants will be equipped with a foundational understanding of government and the concepts of the values, ethics and responsibilities that they will draw upon throughout their careers in the Public Service of Canada.[41]*

The program offers the following courses:

- Active Leadership in Values and Ethics
- Ethics for Internal Auditors
- Modern Comptrollership: Values and Ethics
- Orientation to the Public Service
- Paving the Way: Values and Ethics Foundations for Employees
- Values and Ethics in Public Sector Governance
- Values and Ethics in Public Sector Governance—Second Language Maintenance

## Role Models

Inculcating ethical standards of behaviour depends on the presence of ethical leadership. It is often suggested, for instance, that codes of conduct fail to provide the "living, breathing" consequences of ethical behaviour. Senior public servants can create a climate and set examples to be emulated by their junior colleagues, who, studies show, are significantly influenced by the tone set by their superiors.

However, the examples that exist of senior public servants effectively socializing their charges into a regime of ethical behaviour and standards tend to have happened in the past, when government was smaller and relations between public servants were more intimate. Today, government departments are so large that personal contact with the most senior administrators is rare for most public servants. As a result, it is more difficult for their influence to reach down through the organization the way it did in the past. Thus, "it is unrealistic to argue that the role model provided by bureaucratic leaders can serve as the sole means of promoting ethical behaviour in the public service. Like a code of ethics, ethical leadership is necessary but insufficient."[42] It is an open question whether the current generation of senior public servants are as committed to a focus on ethics as they could be. For instance, a poll by the Institute of Public Administration of Canada reported in 2008 that only 30% of deputy ministers and municipal chief administrative officers prioritized ethics and values in their work.[43]

In any event, contemporary demographic realities within the public service create new challenges. As the director of the Office of Values and Ethics reported,

*We are about to witness a massive change in the demographics of the federal public service. The expected turnover in the next ten years, with 60–70% of employees eligible to retire, has two major implications for government. As many have said already, we will need to attract a huge influx of new recruits—our share of the best and brightest—who will need to acquire quickly a sense of "self" as a public servant. Less often noted is the need to capture and transfer the legacy of the public service that exists now—not only the "corporate memory" but the culture, the traditions and the values that will be the solid foundation for these young people as they grapple with their own new challenges.*[44]

Moreover, the role and place of the public servant is constantly changing. It has been argued that governments are moving away from strict hierarchical accountability, which means that public servants continue to obey orders, of course, but that they do not *merely* obey orders: "Instead they take responsibility for the work they do. The stereotype of the timid, reactive and rule-bound official has become passé."[45] Discretion (discussed above) becomes ever more important.

Ultimately, some combination of a code of ethics, training and education, and role models is required to ensure that a standard of ethical behaviour prevails in the public service.[46] However, one other factor is also required: an attentive public.

## An Attentive Public

Only by being vigilant can citizens realistically expect to receive public administration of the highest ethical calibre:

*At the end of the day, ethics in public service is an issue of crucial importance. In the modern world much of life, both qualitatively and quantitatively, depends on government. Because government is now so big and deals with more than basic needs and elements of protection, the professionalism of public servants is even more important than in the past.*

*Consequently the qualities of individual public servants are also important. Public servants must be trusted to exercise judgements wisely, and they must be carefully selected for that trust. It is in their crucial work involving discretion and advice, as well as policy making, that the ethical standards of public service are evident. Nevertheless, it remains the ultimate responsibility of citizens, through their governments, to ensure that all the structures and procedures of government are best suited to their purposes, in good working order, continuously reviewed, and positively supportive to public servants when they carry out their satisfying and demanding, but also very responsible work.*[47]

Clearly, a variety of influences affect the ethical dimensions of behaviour. Research on environmental influences on ethical behaviour reveals that "generally, there is support that ethical decision making is affected by the behaviour of peers and associates, by the actions of supervisors and top management, by the existence of policies and codes of conduct, by the rewards and punishments, and by the general atmosphere or climate of the organization."[48]

## WHAT YOU HAVE LEARNED

A distinguishing feature of public administration—a rigorous regime of ethical standards—makes already complicated work even more so. But at some level, the public interest must be served, and it cannot be served by nefarious, corrupt, self-serving scoundrels abusing the public's trust (or money). Guidelines that are often absent in the private sector play a key role in shaping our expectations about public servants' behaviour. It is of the utmost importance to ensure the honesty and integrity of those dedicated to serving the public interest. While there are many ways to do this (e.g., codes of conduct, ethics commissioners, education and training, role models), it is ultimately up to the public to keep a watchful eye. Accountability of public officials is thus also a significant factor in public administration. It is to the issue of accountability that we next turn in chapter 11.

## Key Words and Concepts

ethics (339)
ethics commissioners (340)
public interest (343)
discretion (346)

partisanship (347)
public comment (348)
conflict of interest (348)
lying for the public good (349)

## Review Questions

*1. Ethical Dilemmas in the Public Service*
Some of the broad controversies surrounding the ethical standards of behaviour in the public sector were introduced in this section. Ask yourself, What does the public expect of public servants' behaviour? What dilemmas are posed for public servants in the course of their work? What is the "public interest," and how is it served? What potential ethical dilemmas can you think of that might emerge in the setting of the public sector?

*2. Codes of Conduct*
This section addressed the debate over whether written codes of conduct are useful tools in securing the highest ethical behaviour among public officials. It also suggested other ways that this might be achieved. Ask yourself, What are ethical codes of conduct, and how effective are they? What alternative measures can be taken to ensure the ethical conduct of public servants? In what way can training and education, and role models, supplement and complement codes of conduct? What role do you as a member of the "attentive public" have to play?

## Weblinks

The Institute for Global Ethics
**www.globalethics.org**

*Values and Ethics Code for the Public Service*
**www.tbs-sct.gc.ca/pubs_pol/hrpubs/TB_851/vec-cve-eng.asp**

United Nations Country Profile: *Canada: Public Administration*
**http://unpan1.un.org/intradoc/groups/public/documents/un/unpan023304.pdf**

# Further Reading

## 1. Ethical Dilemmas in the Public Service

Atkinson, Michael M., and Gerald Bierling. "Politicians, the Public and Political Ethics: Worlds Apart," *Canadian Journal of Political Science* 38, 4 (2005): 1003–28.

Cooper, Terry L., ed. *Handbook of Administrative Ethics.* 2nd ed. New York: Marcel Dekker, 2001.

Greene, Ian, and David P. Shugarman. "Commission of Inquiry into the Sponsorship Program and Advertising Activities, Phase I Report and Phase II Report." *Canadian Public Administration*, 49, 2 (2006): 220–32.

Langford, John W. "Acting on Values: An Ethical Dead End for Public Servants." *Canadian Public Administration*, 47, 4 (2004): 429–50.

Langford, John W. "Building an Ethical Public Service: Michael and Jennifer on Heintzman and Langford." *Canadian Public Administration*, 50, 4 (2007): 603–8.

Heintzman, Ralph. "Public Service Values and Ethics: Dead End or Strong Foundation?" *Canadian Public Administration*, 50, 4 (2007): 573–602.

Walzer, Michael, and David P. Shugarman. "Are 'Dirty Hands' Necessary in Politics?" in Mark Charlton and Paul Barker, eds., *Crosscurrents: Contemporary Political Issues.* Toronto: Thomson Nelson, 2006: 323–43.

## 2. Codes of Conduct

Canada. Report of the Auditor General. *Values and Ethics in the Federal Public Service.* Ottawa: Supply and Services Canada, 2000.

Canada. Task Force on Conflict of Interest. *Ethical Conduct in the Public Sector.* Ottawa: Supply and Services Canada, 1984.

Glor, Eleanor. "Codes of Conduct and Generations of Public Servants." *International Review of Administrative Sciences*, 67, 3 (2001): 525–41.

Kernaghan, Kenneth. "Encouraging 'Rightdoing' and Discouraging Wrongdoing: A Public Service Charter and Disclosure Legislation," in Commission of Inquiry into the Sponsorship Program and Advertising Activities, *Restoring Accountability: Research Studies.* Vol. 2, *The Public Service and Transparency.* Ottawa: Minister of Public Works and Government Services, 2006: 73–114.

# Endnotes

1. Warren R. Bailie and David Johnson, "Government Ethics and Ethics Agencies," *Canadian Public Administration*, 34, 1 (1991): 158. See also Desmond Morton, "Reflecting on Gomery: Political Scandals and the Canadian Memory," *Policy Options*, 26, 5 (2005): 14–21.

2. See Ian Greene, "Government Ethics Commissioners: The Way of the Future?" *Canadian Public Administration*, 34, 1 (1991): 165–70. See also Luc Juillet, "The Office of Ethics Commissioner, Accountability and Public Trust," in G. Bruce Doern, ed., *How Ottawa Spends, 2004–2005: Mandate Change in the Paul Martin Era* (Montreal: McGill-Queen's University Press, 2004): 296–316; and Denis Saint-Martin, "Should the Federal Ethics Counsellor Become an Independent Officer of Parliament?" *Canadian Public Policy*, 29, 2 (2003): 197–212.

3. See John Tait, "A Strong Foundation: The Report of the Task Force on Public Service Values and Ethics (the summary)," *Canadian Public Administration*, 40, 1 (1997). See also Canada, Treasury Board of Canada Secretariat, *Building on a Strong Foundation—The Dialogue Continues*, vol. 2, *Further Case Studies on Values and Ethics in the Public Service* (Ottawa: Canadian Centre for Management Development, 2001).

4. The recent history of the issue of values and ethics in the public service is outlined in Canada, Treasury Board of Canada Secretariat, "Creating a Value Based Public Service: Remarks by Catherine MacQuarrie, Director, Office of Values and Ethics, Treasury Board Secretariat," July 11, 2001.

5. Neil Nevitte, *The Decline of Deference: Canadian Value Change in Cross-National Perspective* (Peterborough: Broadview, 1996): 56.

6. See EKOS Research, *Rethinking Government: Trust, Ethics and Corruption*, 2002, cited in Ralph Heintzman and Brian Marson, "People, Service and Trust: Is There a Public Sector Service Value Chain?" *International Review of Administrative Sciences*, 71 (2005): 3; and EKOS Research Associates, "Rethinking Government: Exploring Changing Relationships among Individuals, Governments and Business," (Ottawa: EKOS, 2001): 10.

7. E. Pendleton Herring, *Public Administration and the Public Interest* (New York: McGraw-Hill, 1936).

8. See W.T. Stanbury, "Definitions of the Public Interest," in Douglas G. Hartle, *Public Policy Decision Making and Regulation* (Montreal: Institute for Research on Public Policy, 1979): 213–18.

9. Tait, "A Strong Foundation," 32.

10. Dennis F. Thompson, "The Possibility of Administrative Ethics," in Jay M. Shafritz and Albert C. Hyde, eds. *Classics of Public Administration*, 3rd ed. (Pacific Cove, CA: Brooks/Cole, 1992): 523.

11. Thompson, "The Possibility of Administrative Ethics," 524.

12. The Canadian Centre for Management Development (now the Canada School of Public Service) and the Treasury Board Secretariat sponsored an ongoing series of discussions and case studies of ethics in the public service. See Canada, Treasury Board of Canada Secretariat, *Building on a Strong Foundation—The Dialogue Continues*, vol. 2, *Further Case Studies on Values and Ethics in the Public Service*; and Kenneth Kernaghan, *Professional Ethics and Standards for the Evaluation Community in the Government of Canada* (Ottawa: Treasury Board Secreatariat, 2006).

13. Institute of Public Administration of Canada, "Statement of Principles Regarding the Conduct of Public Employees (1987)," **www.ipac.ca/OurPrinciples**. This statement, produced in 1987, was updated in 2005; see Institute of Public Administration of Canada, "A Public Servant's Commitments," **www.ipac.ca/PublicSectorEthics**. See also Kenneth Kernaghan and John W. Langford, *The Responsible Public Servant* (Halifax: Institute for Research on Public Policy, 1990): 205.

14. See John W. Langford, "Moonlighting and Mobility," *Canadian Public Administration*, 34, 1 (1991): 62–72.

15. Institute of Public Administration of Canada, "Statement of Principles Regarding the Conduct of Public Employees (1987)."

16. Richard A. Chapman, "Ethics in Public Service," in Richard A. Chapman, ed., *Ethics in Public Service* (Ottawa: Carleton University Press, 1993): 158–59.

17. See Sissela Bok, *Lying: Moral Choice in Public and Private Life* (New York: Pantheon, 1978).

18. Arden R. Haynes, "The Ethical Dimension in Business and Government," *Canadian Public Administration*, 34, 1 (1991): 18.

19. Frederick C. Mosher et al., *Watergate: Implications for Responsible Government*, (Washington, DC: National Academy of Public Administration, 1974), cited in Jay M. Shafritz and Albert C. Hyde, eds., *Classics of Public Administration*, 3rd ed. (1992): 416–17.

20. Kenneth Kernaghan, "East Block and Westminster: Conventions, Values and Public Service," in Christopher Dunn, ed., *Handbook of Canadian Public Administration*, 2nd ed. (Toronto: Oxford University Press, 2010): 298.

21. Elaine Todres, "The Ethical Dimension in Public Service," *Canadian Public Administration*, 34, 1 (1991): 12.

22. Kenneth Kernaghan and John W. Langford, *The Responsible Public Servant* (Halifax: Institute for Research on Public Policy, 1990): 2.

23. Michael M. Atkinson and Gerald Bierling, "Politicians, the Public and Political Ethics: Worlds Apart," *Canadian Journal of Political Science*, 38, 4 (2005): 1004.

24. John Langford and Allan Tupper, "How Ottawa Does Business: Ethics as a Government Program," in G. Bruce Doern, ed., *How Ottawa Spends, 2006–2007: In from the Cold: The Tory Rise and the Liberal Fall* (Montreal: McGill-Queen's University Press, 2006): 116–17.

25. See George Thomson, "Personal Morality in a Professional Context," *Canadian Public Administration*, 34, 1 (1991): 21–29.

26. Richard A. Chapman, "Introduction," in R. A. Chapman, ed., *Ethics in Public Service* (Ottawa: Carleton University Press, 1993): 2.

27. Warren R. Bailie and David Johnson, "Government Ethics and Ethics Agencies," *Canadian Public Administration*, 34, 1 (1991): 159.

28. See Canada, Treasury Board, *Conflict of Interest and Post-Employment Code for the Public Service* (Ottawa: Supply and Services, 1985).

29. See Tait, "A Strong Foundation: The Report of the Task Force on Public Service Values and Ethics (the summary)," 1–22. See also Peter Aucoin, "A Profession of Public Administration?: A Commentary on 'A Strong Foundation,'" *Canadian Public Administration* 40, 1 (1997): 23–39.

30. Kernaghan, "East Block and Westminster: Conventions," 301.

31. See David Good, *The Politics of Public Management: The HRDC Audit of Grants and Contributions* (Toronto: University of Toronto Press, 2003).

32. Kenneth Kernaghan, "Promoting Public Service Ethics: The Codification Option," in Richard W. Chapman, ed., *Ethics in Public Service* (Ottawa: Carleton University Press, 1993): 18.

33. The following reasons are derived from Kernaghan, "Promoting Public Service Ethics," 19.

34. J. I. Gow, "Between Ideals and Obedience: A Practical Basis for Public Service Ethics," in David Siegel and Ken Rasmussen, eds., *Professionalism and Public Service: Essays in Honour of Kenneth Kernaghan* (Toronto: University of Toronto Press and IPAC, 2008): 115–16.

35. See M.W. Jackson, "How Can Ethics be Taught?" in Richard A. Chapman, ed., *Ethics in Public Service* (Ottawa: Carleton University Press, 1993): 31–42.

36. Kernaghan, "Promoting Public Service Ethics," 25–26.

37. Lorne Sossin, "Defining Boundaries: The Constitutional Argument for Bureaucratic Independence and Its Implications for the Accountability of the Public Service," in Donald Savoie, ed., *Restoring Accountability: Research Studies*, vol. 2, *The Public Service and Transparency: Commission of Inquiry into the Sponsorship Program and Advertising Activities* (Ottawa: Minister of Public Works and Government Services, 2006): 64.

38. Sossin, "Defining Boundaries," 64.

39. James Iain Gow and Sharon L. Sutherland, "Comparison of Canadian Master's Programs in Public Administration, Public Management and Public Policy," *Canadian Public Administration*, 47, 3 (2004): 401.

40. See Gregory J. Inwood, "Teaching Accountability and Ethics to Public Servants," *Journal of Parliamentary and Political Law*, 1, 1 (2008), 379–406.

41. Canada, Canada School of Public Service, "Orientation to the Public Service," July 6, 2010, **www.csps-efpc.gc.ca/cat/det-eng. asp?courseno=E131**.

42. Kernaghan, "Promoting Public Service Ethics," 25.

43. Canada, Institute of Public Administration of Canada, *Report on 2007 Survey of Deputy Ministers and Municipal CAOs* (April 2008), **www.ipac.ca/documents/DMSurvey_Report_WithQuestions-Comparison%20wMembers.pdf**.

44. Canada, Treasury Board of Canada Secretariat, "Creating a Value Based Public Service," 3.

45. Todres, "The Ethical Dimension in Public Service," 15.

46. See Kenneth Kernaghan, "Values, Ethics and Public Service," in Jacques Bourgault, Maurice Demers, and Cynthia Williams, eds., *Public Administration and Public Management: Experiences in Canada* (Sainte-Foy, QC: Les Publications du Quebec, 1997): 100–111.

47. Chapman, "Ethics in Public Service," 170.

48. Dennis P. Wittmer, "Developing a Behavioral Model for Ethical Decision Making in Organizations: Conceptual and Empirical Research," in H. George Frederickson and Richard K. Ghere, eds., *Ethics in Public Management* (Armonk, NY: M.E. Sharpe, 2005): 63–64.

Chapter 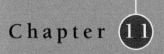 11

# Public Administration *and* Accountability

## WHAT YOU WILL LEARN

Many references have been made throughout this book to the important concept of *accountability*, which simply means being required to explain one's actions by answering to someone else. It is a central feature of public administration, which raises several interrelated issues:

■ What is accountability, and how is it related to the principle of responsible government?

■ How does the concept of accountability inform the public service decision making process?

■ Who is accountable to whom, for what, and under what circumstances?

This chapter is divided into the following sections:

### 1. Accountability and Democracy

This section reviews the central principle of responsible government, first raised in chapter 2. It then establishes the link between accountability and democracy by asking, What is the significance of the principle of responsible government? How does it work in theory and in practice in the Canadian setting in relation specifically to accountability?

### 2. Ministerial Responsibility

Responsible government depends in part on the doctrine of ministerial responsibility. This doctrine sets the parameters of ministerial action, and the guidelines that establish how government can be held to account. This section explains the pure theory of ministerial responsibility, and reveals how it has been altered by contemporary developments, by asking: What is the theory of ministerial responsibility? What is individual ministerial responsibility? What is collective ministerial responsibility? What is the doctrine of answerability? How has the traditional expectation about how responsibility is realized in the political system changed over time? What does the doctrine look like now?

### 3. Accountability and Public Servants

The traditional doctrine of ministerial authority combines with the politics–administration dichotomy to set the expectations of public servant accountability. But recent changes to the concept of accountability have left public servants on unfamiliar ground. This section addresses both the traditional and newly evolving role of public servants, and asks, How have public servants been held accountable for their actions? How has the concept of ministerial responsibility and the politics–administration dichotomy influenced the way public servants do their jobs? How have changes to these doctrines altered the role of public servants in terms of accountability?

### 4. Accountability in Action: The Role of the Office of the Auditor General

There are many links in the chain of accountability. One of the most significant is the Office of the Auditor General. Here, we review briefly the role of this important actor in terms of its contribution to the accountability process by asking, How does the government get objective, unbiased assessment of its policies? What role does the Office of the Auditor General play in this process? If the auditor general watches over government, who, in turn, watches over the auditor general?

### 5. Contemporary Issues of Accountability and Control

Recent developments have seen some of the traditional precepts of accountability change. The traditional notions of ministerial responsibility and the role of public servants have altered as new organizational systems, such as the New Public Management, come into play. This section asks, What impact has reform of public administration had on accountability? How has the New Public Management altered the relationships within government where responsibility is concerned?

## Accountability and Democracy

Central to any democracy is the ability of the people to hold their elected officials **accountable** for their actions. This point has been made several times in this book. The most general sense in which this is exercised is through the ballot box. If you do not believe your representatives have been doing a good job, or if you believe they have failed to account properly for their actions, you can "throw the rascals out." It is, after all, *power* that the citizens are vesting in their elected officials. If that power is abused or poorly exercised, the people have the right to take it back and give it to someone else. Therefore, the government ought to act in a responsible manner and be accountable to the people, or it may lose the reins of power.

While this generally describes conditions in democratic societies, it was not always thus. Imagine a time before the rise of democracy. As Weber tells us, the basis of the right to rule was often either divine intervention or the charisma of individual leaders. The masses did not question leaders or hold them accountable, for to do so would invite divine retribution and whatever punishment this might bring in the afterlife (to question the king was to question the deity that anointed the king). To question the charismatic leader was to invite scorn, ostracism, and perhaps imprisonment or death. When societies moved toward systems of government in which the people could choose (and remove) their leaders, the modern notion of accountability came into play. As one observer reports, "It took several centuries in the tortuous evolution of the modern nation state to develop a coherent, binding, respected ideology of public accountability, together with efficient means of enforcement that would permit the peaceful transfer of power and the voluntary ceding of public office."[1] It was only when the absolute rule of a single leader was replaced by the rule of representative legislative assemblies overseen by an appointed executive—which could be held collectively and individually responsible for running the state—that accountability emerged in its modern guise.

This is the basis of the principle of **responsible government** (see Box 11.1), which was achieved in Canada in the 1840s.[2] It was first adopted by Nova Scotia and the Province of Canada (now Quebec and Ontario) in 1848, Prince Edward Island in 1851, New Brunswick in 1854, and Newfoundland in 1855. Its origins can be found in the earlier development of responsible government in the British political system, the model from which the Canadian system is largely derived.[3] The British Crown had been bound by principle to seek the consent of the Lords before it could tax them; this principle was incorporated in the *Magna Carta* in the thirteenth century. In the seventeenth century, the king's obligation to consult the elected representatives of the people (which eventually meant the House of Commons) was established. At the time, the king's ministers were *not* also members of the House of Commons. As the House became more important, it gradually dawned on people that ministers ought to be Members of Parliament, and, in that way, their responsibility and accountability as representatives of the people would be more direct and could be better managed. The next step in this evolutionary process saw the rise of organized political parties in the eighteenth century, and it was largely this model that emerged in Canada.

You might ask yourself why the achievement of responsible government was a significant development in the evolution of the Canadian political system, and what bearing it has on public administration today. Consider the motivations behind vesting power in the hands of the people's representatives and making the government (that is, the Cabinet) responsible to them. You might come up with two strikingly different perspectives: one arguing that responsible government is a bulwark of democracy; the other suggesting that it is an elaborate system to actually check the power of the people and protect the privileged position of the elite.

The first argument—that responsibility is meant to democratize government by giving more power to the people (or, in the context of the 1800s, less power to

## BOX 11.1 Definitions of Responsible Government

In order to govern . . . the Prime Minister and the Cabinet require the confidence of the elected House of Commons. This constitutional principle is called responsible government. If a government loses the confidence of the House—this would be either through a defeat on an important piece of legislation (i.e., the annual budget or legislation related to government spending) or on a motion of no confidence proposed by an opposition party—it loses the right to govern.[a]

\*\*\*

The term responsible government defines the relationship of Cabinet ministers to the House, the Crown, and to each other. Collectively, the Cabinet is responsible to the House of Commons in that the government must maintain the support of a majority of MPs if it is to continue in office. If Cabinet loses the "confidence" of the House through a specific "want of confidence" or non-confidence vote, or through the defeat of a major government bill,

unwritten constitutional convention calls for the government to tender its resignation. In practice, the prime minister would usually ask the Governor General for the "dissolution" of Parliament, and would go to the people in a general election.[b]

\*\*\*

Responsible government means that the political executive is not able to act without the support of a majority in the legislature (the chamber of representatives).[c]

\*\*\*

The democratic principle is that all public officials are accountable to the people and can rule only by their consent.[d]

**Sources:** *a.* Stephen Brooks, *Canadian Democracy: An Introduction*, 6th ed. (Toronto: Oxford University Press, 2009): 140. *b.* Roger Gibbins, *Conflict and Unity: An Introduction to Canadian Political Life*, 2nd ed. (Scarborough: Nelson, 1990): 30. *c.* Larry Johnston, *Politics: An Introduction to the Modern Democratic State*, 3rd ed. (Peterborough: Broadview, 2007): 138–39. *d.* Leonard T. Hobhouse, *Liberalism* (New York: Oxford University Press, 1911), cited in James John Guy, *People, Politics and Government: A Canadian Perspective*, 6th ed. (Toronto: Pearson Prentice Hall, 2006): 76.

the Crown)—was supported by those who saw in responsible government the opportunity to transfer power from an unaccountable sovereign (as represented by the Governor General and the Governor General's appointees in Cabinet) to the people through their representatives in Parliament. We will call the people who supported these view *democrats*. The underlying assumption of the democrats was that power rightly belongs to the people and that, short of involving every citizen in the direct governance of the country (recall our discussion of direct democracy in chapter 2), it is sufficient to maximize ordinary citizens' power by giving their representatives real power.

Ironically, the opposite viewpoint also supported the concept of responsible government, but for a different set of reasons. Assuming that society was naturally divided into the *ruled* and the *rulers,* this group of people—which we will call the *conservatives*—saw in responsible government an opportunity to shelter the exercise of power from the direct interference of the "great unwashed"—that is, the people. The conservatives were inherently suspicious of democracy as we understand it today, because they saw rule by the people as destabilizing and dangerous. The mass of the citizenry was seen as too uneducated, too prone to fall under the sway of demagogues, and too likely to ignore the rights of minorities to be trusted with power.[4] By establishing institutions such as responsible government, power would be transferred not to the people but to their representatives, who tended always to come from the class of society "deserving" to rule. If certain undesirable democrats managed to get themselves elected, they could always be checked in their unsavory ambitions to further democratize government by the countervailing weight of the executive branch of government (that is, the Cabinet) and the Upper House in Parliament (the Senate), whose members are appointed by the Crown. Thus, the drive to responsible government was supported by these two groups, but for quite different reasons.[5]

Whichever perspective you find most compelling, the conventional notion has developed that accountability is enforced primarily through the ballot box. Of course, responsible government is made up of several other components through which this underlying principle is reinforced. For instance, the institutions of parliamentary government have a number of mechanisms through which the government is held to account, such as the daily question period in the House of Commons, Parliamentary committees, and opposition parties. Outside Parliament, the media and interest groups also play an important part in holding the government to account. The judiciary, also forces the government to be accountable, as when a citizen, interest group, corporation, or other government challenges a government's actions in a court of law. It is noteworthy that the emergence of modern democratic government was accompanied by the proscription that no one—not even the leaders of the government—was beyond the law. Accountability is reinforced by the judicial system through constitutional and administrative law as well: "The law would further reduce official discretion by prescribing the precise arrangements whereby public business was to be conducted, arrangements that included the structure of the machinery of government, the number and tenure of public officials, the handling of public property and monies, the code of conduct governing official behaviour, and methods for handling citizens and aliens."[6] All of these institutions are meant to support democratic governance. Ultimately, however, it is elections that allow the people to pass judgment on a government.

For public administration, this means that, at some level, everything public officials do should in some way relate to the *will of the people* as expressed through their selection of representatives in Parliament. The focus of policy formulation, implementation, and evaluation is Parliament: it receives advice from public servants, it instructs them, and it evaluates their work, all in the name of the people. In other words, Parliament is the sun around which the planets and stars in the constellation of public administration revolve. In turn, this also contributes to the uniqueness of the public service compared to the private sector:

*Public service exists to satisfy certain needs of the community. Its existence depends upon the trust, confidence and support (both financial, through taxation, and legal, through obedience to laws and regulations enforced by public servants) it derives from the public through their representatives. Unlike the private sector, it cannot (as expected) become too self-seeking and obscure. Its every action and inaction is subject to thorough scrutiny. The community expects public servants to be fair, ethical and dedicated in administering public policies and programs. And public trust and confidence is assured when public servants are found managing public programs soundly, and are found to be held accountable for their actions.[7]*

Note also that the concept of *accountability* is an empty shell unless it is connected to a system of rewards and punishments. If there is no tangible benefit from acting in an accountable manner, can people be counted on to act responsibly? Similarly, if there are no punishments or sanctions for failing to act responsibly, can people be relied upon to do so? A complex system of rewards and punishments has evolved to ensure compliance with measures designed to promote accountability and responsibility. At the most general level, failure of the government to act responsibly will result in its losing power at the next election. Moving to a more specific level, failure of a Cabinet minister or Member of Parliament to act responsibly could result in a range of sanctions—from a reprimand from the prime minister, to dismissal from Cabinet, to being passed over for plum positions, to being kicked out of the political party. For public servants, the motivation to act responsibly is tied to the system of job-related rewards (raises, promotions, status, etc.) and punishments (reprimand, suspension, dismissal, etc.). At a more extreme level, legal sanctions can be invoked against either politicians or public servants in the event of criminal abuses of power. This package of rewards and punishments serves to reinforce and remind public officials that their primary duty is not to themselves, but to the public interest. Compliance with the rules and regulations meant to support accountability will bring rewards, but any breach of trust or failure to act responsibly will be dealt with in a serious manner.

Society cannot allow public servants to simply act on their own whims and fancies; public servants must be answerable to someone. We can think of the institutions that enforce answerability as the political, legal, and administrative arrangements that seek to ensure that the power of the rulers is controlled ultimately by the ruled. The trick is to balance the requirement for some constraints with the need to be able to act. As one observer put it, "Too much independence and too few constraints have allowed too much wrongdoing. Too many controls and too little trust have stultified government and prevented rapid, flexible action."[8]

Further complicating our understanding of accountability and democracy is the idea that we can subdivide accountability by looking at both administrative responsibility and political responsibility. This will remind us of the admonition from the politics–administration dichotomy that politicians lead and public servants follow. Thus, it is conceptually useful to try to distinguish when and where purely political actions and decisions can be separated from purely administrative ones. For example, the decision to build a bridge in one riding and not another is a political decision. The decision to locate that bridge at what engineers say is the safest and most accessible point on the river, where it will serve the greatest amount of traffic in the most efficient manner possible, is an administrative decision. If the public is outraged because the bridge is built in a particular riding solely to create jobs so that the local Member of Parliament might more easily get re-elected, there may be a political price to pay. But if the bridge falls down because of poor construction or technical miscalculations about the strength of the riverbank to support the pylons, there are administrative and legal sanctions. Of course, in the real world, the neat division over responsibilities is less clear-cut. For instance, the decision to award a particular firm the contract to construct the pylons may have been influenced by that firm's financial support of the party in power, in which case the political and administrative boundaries over responsibility are blurred. It is exactly this type of scenario that makes it challenging to analyze and apply doctrines of accountability in a precise manner.

According to political scientist Paul Thomas, accountability consists of "an obligation to explain and justify how one discharges responsibilities, the origins of which may be political, constitutional, statutory, hierarchical, or contractual. Different origins give rise to several variants of accountability, which in turn differ in the degree of direct control and public disclosure involved."[9] He suggests that there are five components in any accountability relationship. First is the assignment of responsibilities related to agreed-upon goals. Second is the provision of authority, resources, and a supportive environment. Third is the obligation to answer for fulfilling those responsibilities, while fourth is the evaluation of performance to make sure that instructions have been complied with. Fifth is sanctions or penalties for nonperformance, as well as rewards for good performance.[10]

We now return to some of the features of public administration outlined earlier, to assess their usefulness in meeting the goals of accountability.

## Ministerial Responsibility

One problematic aspect of accountability is the question of who is directly and personally responsible when the government screws something up. As you now know, the theory of **ministerial responsibility** tells us that individual Cabinet ministers are ultimately responsible for all the actions of their departments, and must answer for them when a mistake is made. If the mistake is significant enough and the mistake is the result of actions that can be attributed personally and directly to the minister involved, the minister may have to resign his or her position as a sign that the minister has taken responsibility. No minister in Canada has ever resigned because of a mistake made directly by a subordinate in his or her ministry, unless the minister has been seen to be personally responsible: "If one of the minister's officials makes a mistake, the requirements of ministerial responsibility are satisfied when the minister answers to the House for the mistake and implements the necessary remedial action."[11] This is sometimes referred to as the **doctrine of answerability** and is regarded as a somewhat watered-down version of the doctrine of individual ministerial responsibility.[12] Aucoin and Jarvis suggest there are three interrelated dimensions to ministerial responsibility:

*First, the minister is the chief executive of a department, the person in charge of the offi-
cials, the one with the statutory authority to take action so that the purposes of the law
are realized. Second, the minister has been assigned the duties or obligations that are
also set forth in statutes. And, third, the minister must provide an account and may be
held to account for his or her actions, or the actions of officials, whether or not the minister had knowledge of these actions. In short, the term responsible encompasses three
dimensions of ministerial responsibility: authority, responsibility and accountability.*[13]

Another aspect of ministerial responsibility is that the Cabinet acts collectively
in every government decision, and therefore must accept **collective ministerial
responsibility** for any errors. This convention of government is tested when votes
are held in the House of Commons. When a majority supports the government
by voting in favour of its policies, the House is signalling confidence in the
government's ability to carry on. If a majority votes against the government,
the government must resign, signalling that it collectively takes responsibility for
its actions. In this way accountability is realized.

The doctrine of collective ministerial responsibility is also important in terms
of maintaining government stability and confidentiality.[14] It requires ministers to
support Cabinet decisions publicly, which promotes consensus and, as a result,
political stability. This is closely linked to the notion of Cabinet confidentiality;
even when individual ministers disagree with decisions taken at the Cabinet table,
they keep their disagreements to themselves. Confidentiality of discussions within
Cabinet promotes consensus, as it encourages open debate and a frank assessment
of all alternatives in the privacy of the Cabinet and leaves ministers secure in the
knowledge that divisions within government will not be publicly aired.

One Privy Council Office official sums up the doctrines of both individual and
collective ministerial responsibility this way:

*As a general rule, ministerial responsibility, both collective and individual, is a "guaran-
tee" that the political executive's decision making power will be exercised responsibly,
that is, in accordance with the will of the people. Collective responsibility enables the
House of Commons, and therefore the people of Canada, to hold the Cabinet accountable for its collective decisions. As for individual responsibility, it enables the House of
Commons to exercise control over the public service through the responsible ministers.*[15]

What exactly are ministers responsible for in the real world of government?[16]
There are currently more than 135 organizations that, through ministers, are
accountable to Parliament, from the Assisted Human Reproduction Agency of
Canada to Via Rail, and including departments, Crown corporations, tribunals and
quasi-judicial bodies, and service organizations of various kinds. As an illustration
of the extent of ministerial involvement, one study indicated that in one year the
Ministry of Industry, Trade, and Commerce took about 4700 decisions. While only
190 of these were kept under the minister's direct control, they accounted for well
over half of the department's expenditures.[17] Ministers are responsible for each of
these types of organizations, although the exact number and type varies by ministry.
There are diminishing levels of direct ministerial oversight as you move from
departments to service agencies to Crown corporations to tribunals and quasi-judicial

bodies. For example, departments are under direct ministerial control, and ministers can and do intervene on any departmental matters, as they wish. Service agencies, which are established by law to deliver services within an established policy and legal framework, are also closely controlled by the minister responsible. Crown corporations are less directly in the minister's purview. Generally, the minister responsible simply approves the corporation's business plans and the presentation of annual reports to Parliament. Finally, administrative tribunals and quasi-judicial bodies are subject to the least direct ministerial control. They generally require an arm's-length relationship with the minister responsible for them, to be able to do their work without fear of political interference or reprisal. Still, the minister has responsibility for them and plays an important role in allocating their financial resources. Still other organizations, such as the Office of the Auditor General, report directly to Parliament and effectively bypass direct ministerial control. In short, the levels of ministerial responsibility are many and complex, and indicate different degrees of responsibility. The ability to juggle these different degrees of responsibility successfully is a feat in itself, but must be managed if the underlying principles of responsible government are to be upheld.

Another aspect of accountability has to do with the way in which ministers delegate authority to their officials. In this case, authority to act is essentially transferred from the minister to officials who are expected to act on behalf of the minister. In general, "the minister is not involved personally and does not know precisely what actions are being taken. A minister is expected to give general direction, receive reports, ask questions, and respond to matters that require his or her personal involvement, including things that have gone wrong and require corrective action."[18] The important point to keep in mind is that the doctrine of ministerial responsibility allows ministers to delegate *authority* but not *accountability*.

Recently, there has been a trend toward a form of accountability that undermines the theory of ministerial responsibility. Public servants traditionally toil anonymously behind the scenes, allowing the elected representatives (their bosses) to take both the credit and blame for government actions. But there is now a strong movement toward holding public servants publicly accountable for the results achieved by their departments. This reflects the fact that Cabinet ministers cannot realistically be expected to be on top of every single development within their ministries, which may employ thousands of people and run hundreds of distinct programs. A case in point is the so-called Al-Mashat affair, in which Iraq's former ambassador to the United States entered Canada as a landed immigrant only a month after applying to get in to Canada. He and his family thereby jumped the immigration queue and bypassed the usual long, drawn-out process that most immigrants must go through. The Mulroney government pinned the blame for this mistake directly on the senior public servants involved, rather than having the minister accept responsibility.[19] However, the government has clarified the distinction between ministers' accountability to Parliament for the use of powers vested in them by statute, as opposed to arm's-length bodies for which their responsibility is indirect. Ministers remain accountable for the former but are answerable for the latter.[20] The government further supplemented the doctrine of answerability in 2006 with the Federal Accountability Act, which designated deputy ministers as

**accounting officers** for their organizations, a practice in place in Great Britain since the 1870s. They now have a legal obligation to appear before parliamentary committees and answer questions on their management responsibilities within the framework of ministerial responsibility and accountability. As the Privy Council Office explains this new development, "although the accounting officer is legally obliged to appear, he or she appears in support of the minister's accountability."[21]

Another difficulty with ministerial accountability relates to the politics–administration dichotomy. As we have seen, at the top of the public service sits a cadre of senior managers, who generally are career public servants specially trained in the art of public sector administration. They are extremely powerful because of their knowledge of the workings of government. Some people regard this as problematic, in that these individuals may be able to challenge their political masters (Cabinet ministers) in setting public policy by virtue of their greater knowledge of government administration. In theory, at least, the elected representatives direct government, while the appointed officials simply assist. But if the senior managers have knowledge, expertise, and experience, and the elected politicians lack these traits, it is possible that the traditional relationship between politicians and public servants may be turned on its head. Moreover, Cabinet ministers are not only responsible for running their ministries; they also perform a variety of other roles that take them away from their departments: they must attend question period in the House of Commons and perform other legislative duties; they must respond to the demands of the constituents in their ridings; they are party members with responsibilities to their political party and caucus; and so on.

However, most Cabinet ministers are not "experts" in the field over which they are given responsibility. As a result, long-serving senior public servants, such as deputy ministers, assistant deputy ministers, heads of regulatory bodies and Crown corporations, and senior managerial staff can all become major actors in the formulation, implementation, and evaluation of policy because they are the ones with greater expertise. This problem reflects a weakness in the politics–administration dichotomy, which says that ministers should be "on top," while public servants should be "on tap."[22] Ministers who must rely extensively on the expertise of their appointed aides may be at a disadvantage and become overly dependent. This implies that there is a grey area where accountability is concerned.

This reality is widely recognized within public administration, and various reforms have been implemented over the years to try to ensure that the proper relationship between politicians and senior public servants is maintained. The aforementioned central agencies (Finance Department, Privy Council Office, Prime Minister's Office, and Treasury Board Secretariat) were developed in part to give the ministers sources of information and guidance apart from their own departmental officials. Attempts to limit public servants' influence and power can also be seen in the complex Cabinet committee systems that have been developed to allow ministers in related policy fields to come together on a formal basis to exchange information and advice regarding policy. Whether these innovations have actually promoted democratic government is a matter of some contention. Some people argue that while recent reforms do provide ministers with countervailing sources of information and advice, they also immensely increase the bureaucratization of decision making and that, in any case, ministers are simply substituting one set of bureaucratic advisors for another.[23]

A relatively new twist to the accountability issue is the recent trend toward restructuring of the public service. Ministers are increasingly seeking advice from outside consultants, given the cutbacks in their own ministries, with the result that the chain of accountability is broken, since outsiders have no relationship to the traditional structures of decision making in government. Just as problematic is the trend toward calling public servants onto the carpet for the mistakes of these outside consultants, as was the case with the spate of advertising contract scandals that beleaguered the Chrétien and Martin governments in the early 2000s.[24] We explore these issues in more detail below.

Yet another factor conditioning the regime of accountability is the politicization of the public service. This is the process through which non-partisan public servants become ensnared in a more political process of assessing policy options and making decisions than theory tells us they should. Power has become increasingly concentrated in the hands of the executive—particularly the prime minister—a process under way since the 1980s, but greatly accelerated by Stephen Harper. Another development is the increasing role, power, and influence of political staff—partisan employees who give strategic political advice to ministers. Their place in the accountability regime is ambiguous. In 2006, then–leader of the Official Opposition Stephen Harper insisted Liberal political staffers appear before parliamentary committees to answer questions about the sponsorship program. In 2010, as prime minister, he forbade his own political staffers to appear before parliamentary committees to answer questions about the Afghan detainee issue, insisting that ministers appear in their stead. The controversy that resulted saw the Parliament issuing subpoenas to compel political staff to appear.

While accountability comprises a number of aspects, it ultimately comes down to the notion that in a democratic society, elected officials must accept responsibility for the actions of their public servants and the government on behalf of the people. David Stupich, a former Cabinet minister in British Columbia, who had previously been a poultry farmer, put it this way:

*Eggs have to be candled to check the interior quality as well as examining the exterior. I did not lay the eggs, but if a customer complained to me about the quality of one of those eggs that I was selling him, there was no point in me blaming the chicken, finding out which hen laid it and saying that she was to blame. I was responsible. I was the proprietor and it was my responsibility.*[25]

Where wrongdoing has occurred, the doctrine of ministerial responsibility suggests that the minister ought to resign if the offence is a serious enough one. Of course, the definition of "serious" here is open to considerable debate, and largely depends on whether you happen to sit on the government side of the House of Commons or on the opposition benches. Most would agree that no one individual minister can possibly be held personally liable for all the actions of his department. Thus, one of the ongoing struggles of governing involves trying to determine where the line can be drawn between minor breaches of responsibility and more serious ones requiring the resignation of a minister. Box 11.2 summarizes the key

## BOX 11.2 Accountable Government: A Guide for Ministers and Ministers of State, 2008

In 2007, Prime Minister Harper outlined his expectations for ministers and ministers of state (junior ministers) with regard to responsibility and accountability:

■ *Ministers and Ministers of State must act with integrity. To ensure public trust and confidence, not only in our Government but in government generally, Ministers and Ministers of State must uphold the highest standards of honesty and impartiality. Both the performance of your official duties and the arrangement of your private affairs should bear the closest public scrutiny.*

■ *Ministers are responsible for ensuring that their departments are managed soundly and with complete integrity. They must discharge their portfolio responsibilities with careful regard to the particular powers, duties and functions assigned to them by statute and convention.*

■ *Ministers are accountable to Parliament for the use of all powers vested in them. This demands constant attention to their parliamentary duties, including being present in Parliament to answer honestly and accurately about their areas of responsibility, and taking corrective action, as appropriate and within their authority, to address any problems that may arise within their portfolios. Should Ministers make any inadvertent error in answering to*

*Parliament, they must take steps to correct it at the earliest opportunity.*

■ *Ministers and Ministers of State are bound by their oath as Privy Councillors. This oath reflects parliamentary government's core convention of Cabinet solidarity, by which Ministers share collective responsibility for the actions of government and speak to Parliament and Canadians with a single voice. This requires frank discussion in Cabinet and confidentiality in Cabinet decision making. Although they are not members of the Cabinet, Ministers of State are part of the Ministry and will attend the meetings of the Cabinet committee relevant to their area of assigned responsibility. They must uphold the confidentiality of any Cabinet information to which they have access.*

■ *Ministers and Ministers of State must respect the non-partisanship of the public service of Canada and not seek to engage public servants in work that is outside their appropriate role. In this way, successive governments can have confidence that the public service will provide the support they need to fulfil their ministerial functions and mandate without regard to political partisanship.*

**Source:** *Accountable Government: A Guide for Ministers and Secretaries of State, 2007*, pp. iv–v. Reproduced with the permission of the Minister of Public Works and Government Services, 2010, and courtesy of the Privy Council Office.

principles of the doctrine of ministerial responsibility. This issue, already complex in itself, has become even more so with the latest developments in public administration associated with the New Public Management (NPM). We will turn our attention later to the set of issues this has raised.

# Accountability and Public Servants

There are five overlapping contexts within which accountability is applied to public servants:

- accountability to a superior
- accountability to elected officials
- accountability under the law
- accountability to professional norms and institutions
- accountability to the public[26]

The first context in which accountability is applied is derived from the Weberian notion of bureaucracies as hierarchical organizations defined by a chain of command. Each employee is responsible to a superior, and each office in the hierarchy is sanctioned by and established through administrative procedures and law. The organization charts of government departments in chapter 5 reflect these points. Rewards and penalties are prescribed for observing accountability and transgressing it. In some parts of the organization, accountability crosses from administrative lines (say, from a manager to a director) to political lines (from a deputy minister to his or her minister). In this way, the entire organization is held accountable to elected officials.

In addition, the strictures of accountability are derived from the public servant's responsibility to uphold the law in the course of administering programs and policies. Thus, the various acts and regulations passed by government are (hopefully) dutifully observed and upheld by responsible, conscientious public servants. This extends throughout the entire organization, from the most senior officers to the lowest clerk. But it is the senior-most officer—the deputy minister—who, under the Financial Administration Act, is given particular financial responsibilities for the department, and for personnel responsibilities under delegated authority from the Treasury Board and Public Service Commission.[27]

In addition, though, there is another context of accountability that may be less obvious than those we have identified so far. This relates to the fact that since government is such a large and complex system, it requires the services of a variety of skilled and specially trained individuals to deliver services to the public. For instance, legions of scientists, engineers, doctors, nurses, lawyers, accountants, teachers and professors, surveyors, geologists, architects, real estate agents, urban planners, and countless other professionals work either directly or indirectly for the government. In many cases, these individuals have a responsibility, not just to the government, but also to the norms and standards of their profession, which.

have their own codes of conduct, professional criteria, standards of behaviour, conflict of interest regulations, and so on. Even the right to practise in a given field may be determined by the professional body that oversees the field. Public servants who work in careers that have professional organizations overseeing them are doubly accountable: to the government, and to their professional organization.

Finally, of course, there is accountability to the public, a point we have emphasized elsewhere. Suffice it to say that accountability to the public is something of a professional ethos for public servants. While there is no firm basis in law or administration for this context of accountability, there is, nonetheless, a powerful convention derived from the subjective responsibility that public servants feel toward the public. This is reinforced by the public's expectation that public servants will behave in a responsible manner toward them.

These contexts can be expressed in a slightly different way.[28] We can think about *administrative accountability* in terms of superior–subordinate relationships; *legal accountability* in terms of the mandates of departments, reporting requirements for public servants, and contractual requirements; *constitutional accountability,* including ministerial responsibility, in terms of the approval of taxing and spending by Parliament; *professional accountability,* which refers to the need to adhere to professional standards and norms; and *political accountability,* which refers to competitive elections, and the relationship between representatives and their constituents and other societal interests. These categories roughly coincide with the five contexts above, but provide a slightly different perspective on accountability.

These five contexts and categories for accountability are not unconnected. Indeed, there is a considerable amount of overlap, conceptually and in practice, prompting one public administration practitioner to comment that "public servants sometimes feel like flies trapped in a spider's web of accountabilities."[29] In some cases, the duty to one form of accountability comes into conflict with another. For instance, a doctor's professional duty to observe the Hippocratic Oath may conflict with instructions from the minister to present scientific evidence regarding a particular health risk in a positive light.

Perhaps even more interesting is the apparent division within the public service itself over the relative importance of the various contexts of accountability. The higher the public servant is on the hierarchy ladder, the more inclined she is to feel responsible primarily to the minister and the government of the day. The lower down on the hierarchy, the more inclined public servants are to feel responsible to the public, and especially to the clients they serve directly.[30] This creates tensions within the public service, some of which manifested when exercises such as PS2000 and La Relève (see chapters 8 and 9) provoked complaints that senior public servants were out of touch with their subordinates' concerns.

Finally, the recent erosion of the pure doctrine of ministerial responsibility and the emergence of the doctrine of answerability have created a new conundrum for public servants: increasingly, as part of this process, public servants are being called on the carpet to answer for their actions. But this betrays the traditional precepts of anonymity, neutrality, and tenure of service that should characterize the public service. You will recall that public servants "are appointed on the basis of merit, they provide frank and objective advice to ministers in private, they do not express their personal views in public or engage in partisan activities, they execute policies faithfully and to the best of their abilities, and in return for their support and loyalty they are protected from being personally named for mistakes and enjoy reactive job security based upon satisfactory performance."[31]

These developments are altering the traditional concept of ministerial responsibility as well as the basis of an anonymous, neutral public service (see Box 11.3). For instance, public servants are, more and more, being required to appear before

---

**BOX 11.3 Factors Influencing Accountability and the Public Service**

According to political scientist Paul Thomas, several broad trends within the political system have altered the practices of ministerial responsibility as well as the conventions of an anonymous, neutral, and permanent public service, including:

- *the difficulty in providing objective policy advice during a period of ideological disagreement over the future role of government;*

- *changing concepts of political and bureaucratic representation reflected in programs to ensure the public service is more representative of the various publics it serves and is more open and responsive to outside influences through various consultative mechanisms;*

- *greater fragmentation of the public sector through the creation of new-style organizations (such as special operating agencies) and the growing reliance on the private sector (through contracting out and public/private partnerships) to deliver public programs;*

- *increased parliamentary surveillance of the public service through the estimates*

*process, performance reporting, and wider auditing processes;*

- *greater transparency respecting bureaucratic performance produced by access to information laws and the rise of a more adversarial media;*

- *a growing role for the courts, under the Charter of Rights and Freedoms and other statutes, to review the actions of administrative agencies to ensure that they act on the basis of public law, respect Charter principles, and dispense natural justice;*

- *the promotion of a new entrepreneurial public service culture in which such values as leadership from public servants, innovation, risk-taking, rewards for results, revenue generation, and service contracts supplement or displace traditional values such as loyalty to the minister, reticence in sharing their views publicly, prudence, process compliance, and trusteeship of the public interest.*

**Source:** "Parliament and the Public Service" by Paul Thomas in Christopher Dunn, ed., *The Handbook of Canadian Public Administration*, Second Edition, Copyright © 2010 Oxford University Press Canada. Reprinted by permission of the publisher.

parliamentary committees. These are very public forums, and this development erodes the anonymity of public servants. As Paul Thomas reports, public servants theoretically appear before these committees simply to provide background information. However, "the rules to govern the interactions between public servants and politicians in what are essentially partisan areas are unwritten or vague at best. This new procedure means that public servants must be cautious and agile in order to avoid being drawn into partisan controversies."[32] It creates situations of "mutual plausible deniability between ministers and deputy ministers, with each party referring the matter under review to the other."[33] In an episode of the British sit-com *Yes, Prime* Minister, the Cabinet secretary is called before a parliamentary committee, which questions him on certain improprieties committed by the government: "That is a political matter, and therefore only the prime minister can answer your questions," he sniffs. In the next scene, the prime minister is before the committee, suggesting that their concerns "really are administrative matters" and therefore should be answered by his Cabinet secretary.

The recent alterations to the doctrine of ministerial responsibility raise an important concern about this traditional view of the role of public servants. If ministers do not take responsibility, and public servants are not *supposed to* or are not *expected to* take responsibility, then who will? The public has both the right and the need to know who is responsible for government action (or inaction). So who will now step forward and claim responsibility? The answer seems to be that, increasingly, public servants are being exposed as the culprits when things go awry, even though, traditionally, they were not to be held responsible. If this trend is allowed to persist, it will adversely affect the work that public servants do. They may react by being overly cautious in their recommendations. They may slow down the process for fear of supplying advice that could later be used against them if a policy mistake emerges. This was the result after the 1999 Human Resources and Development Canada (HRDC) scandal broke.[34] Media and opposition party allegations suggested the department had let $1 billion dollars in contracts without properly accounting for the money or following proper procedures in awarding the contracts. In fact, after audits were done, only $85 000 was unaccounted for. Subsequently, though, HRDC staff adopted a "do-it-by-the-book" mentality, involving scrupulous attention to paperwork and risk avoidance. The result was delays of several weeks in the processing of services, as public servants sought to ensure that a complete and thorough paper trail accompanied every action.[35]

It is one of the great ironies of public administration that this new emphasis on accountability can actually promote dysfunction in government. Accountability is seen largely as being about assigning blame when things go wrong. But no one likes to accept blame, especially if it might curtail his or her career ambitions. As a result, some have observed that one of the impediments to accountability is that the emphasis on blame may lead to more "buckpassing and scapegoating by both politicians and appointed officials. In other words, because of its potential negative consequences, accountability may become something to be avoided at all costs."[36] Overall, though, the jury is still out on the erosion of the doctrine of ministerial responsibility and the emergence of the doctrine of answerability.

## Accountability in Action: The Role of the Office of the Auditor General

Much of the discussion about accountability thus far may seem abstract and disconnected from the real world. It might be useful, therefore, to briefly examine at least one mechanism through which accountability is realized. There are many links in the chain of accountability, including—besides Parliament and Cabinet—several specialized agencies and offices, such as the Information and Privacy Commission, the Commissioner of Official Languages, and the Human Rights Commission.[37] Rather than survey all these bodies, we will turn our attention to the Office of the Auditor General (OAG), which stands out for both its unique status (as an independent, arm's-length body) and its reporting function (it reports directly to Parliament, not to a minister). This body is one of the most significant institutions directly engaged in holding the government to account.[38] Indeed, the profile of the OAG is perhaps at an all-time high, with the release of its regular reports anticipated in some quarters almost as much as the Stanley Cup final game (well, maybe not quite that much) There is no doubt that the OAG has become a key institution in the efforts to promote accountability in government.

As we pointed out earlier in this chapter, the public wants and needs to know that government is managing public monies effectively and efficiently, and that this management is based on the public trust. Confidence in democracy and government are reinforced when public funds are raised carefully and spent wisely—when there is *value for money* spent. Parliament is the institution that has primary responsibility for this task and that acts on behalf of the people. The government cannot raise or spend a single penny without Parliament's authorization and must explain to Parliament the reasons for expending public money and the results of the expenditures. To maintain accountability, the government must report on its performance by submitting spending plans (estimates) for each department, as well as reports of the previous year's activities. It must produce annual financial statements showing all spending, borrowing, and taxing (these are the Public Accounts of Canada). Parliament is thus inundated with information with which to hold the government to account. But independent assessment of all that information is also needed, so that Members of Parliament can assess the government's performance on information that is unbiased and objective. This is where the auditor general comes into play. In her 2007 report, Auditor General Sheila Fraser explained:

*In the reports we present to Parliament, we provide answers to some important questions about the management of government programs and services. Are they managed with due regard to economy, efficiency, and their impact on the environment? And does the government have measures in place to determine if programs and services are effective in achieving the objectives set for them?*

*Our audit mandate covers the full range of activities of the federal government. Given the size of government and the scope of its activities, deciding what to audit is a challenging exercise. We may decide to audit an activity carried out in a single department or in several; we may select an issue that affects many departments. Choosing audit subjects well is essential to producing reports that are useful to Parliament.*

*We select areas for audit based partly on the risks they may involve. Examples of high-risk areas include those that cost taxpayers significant amounts of money or that involve public safety or national security. We may decide to audit an area that offers potential for improving government results or is of great interest to Parliament and the Canadian public. We pay particular attention to requests by parliamentary committees for audits of specific areas of concern to them, and we try to incorporate such requests into our audit planning where our resources and mandate permit.*[39]

The position and office of an independent auditor general was established in 1878. Early reports to Parliament listed every single transaction government undertook and reported on whether public money had been spent in the way Parliament intended. The contemporary OAG began to take shape in the 1950s but ran into some controversy when it began to overstep the bounds of its mandate by pronouncing on the *quality* of the government's policy choices. Later, the 1977 Auditor General Act gave the OAG a broader mandate and clarified that the office does not comment on policy choices by the government (that is, it does not pronounce this policy "bad," and that policy "good") but, rather, focuses on how those policies were implemented. In 1995, amendments to the Act established the position of commissioner of the Environment and Sustainable Development within the OAG, reflecting contemporary concerns with these issues and the role of government therein. The vision and mission of the OAG is provided in Box 11.4.

The auditor general is independent of the government of the day, and is appointed for a 10-year term to help reinforce the objectivity needed to support that independence. The Auditor General Act provided three questions to which the auditor general must address himself or herself:

- Is the government keeping proper accounts and records and presenting its financial information accurately?

- Did the government collect or spend the authorized amount of money, and for the purposes intended by Parliament?

- Were programs run economically and efficiently? And does the government have the means to measure their effectiveness?

Each question corresponds to a particular type of audit. The first question calls for *attest* auditing, which simply means that the auditor attests to or verifies the accuracy of financial statements. The second question calls for *compliance* auditing, in which the auditor general reveals whether the government has complied with Parliament's wishes. The third question calls for *value-for-money* auditing, sometimes called *performance* auditing, in which the auditor general investigates whether or not taxpayers got value for their tax dollars. In short, the accountability function of the auditor general is a thorough one, contained in a broad framework intended to allow a penetrating examination of the government's activities.

Beyond the audit functions, the OAG has added a number of other activities, including reviewing the sustainable development strategies of departments,

## BOX 11.4 Vision and Mission of the Office of the Auditor General of Canada

**Vision:** We are committed to making a difference for the Canadian people by promoting, in all our work for Parliament, answerable, honest and productive government.

**Mission:** The Office of the Auditor General of Canada conducts independent audits and examinations that provide objective information, advice and assurance to Parliament. We promote accountability and best practices in government operations.

**Elaboration of Mission:** In achieving our mission, we want to make a difference by promoting

- a fair and frank accounting of government's stewardship of financial and other resources
- efficiency and productivity in the public service
- cost effectiveness of government activities
- collection of revenues owed to the Crown.

Other effects we want to produce through our work are

- objective assurance on matters found to be satisfactory and unsatisfactory
- compliance with authority
- deterrence of fraud and dishonesty.

Source: Office of the Auditor General, *Auditing for Parliament*, (Ottawa: Minister of Public Works and Government Services Canada, 1997). Reproduced with the permission of the Minister of Public Works and Government Services Canada, 2010.

special examinations of Crown corporations, and progress reports on initiatives to reform the public service. Since 1995, the commissioner of the Environment and Sustainable Development (CESD) has reported to the House on the environment and sustainable development, departmental strategies and action plans in this realm, and petitions from Canadians relating to the environment and sustainable development.

Public awareness about government activities is a key aspect of the OAG's work. To publicize what government has and has not done, the auditor general issues several reports to the House of Commons each year. These reports contain the results of comprehensive audits of federal departments and agencies, government-wide audits, follow-up reports concerning previous audits, and audit observations, which are important matters not covered in any of the other reports. Other forms of reporting take place in regard to Crown corporations through the minister responsible or directly to the boards of directors; through the Public Accounts every autumn; and through special audits ordered by Cabinet and not part of the regular reporting process. Audits of the governments of the Yukon, Nunavut, and the Northwest Territories are reported annually to their legislative assemblies.

The 2002 and 2004 OAG reports stand out in recent history as examples of the influence of the auditor general. You will recall that, in the 2002 report, the auditor general raised the alarm that federal public servants broke "just about every rule in the book" in dealing with certain Quebec advertising agencies, and she followed that up in 2004 with a serious indictment of rampant financial abuses in the sponsorship program. These were the reports that led indirectly to the Gomery Commission of Inquiry and the downfall of the Martin Liberal government. But as Thomas suggests, the OAG must walk a fine line between attracting attention to its reports and wading into controversial partisan areas:

*To ensure parliamentary, media, and public attention for its findings, it must present reports that are controversial enough to be noticed. At the same time it must avoid drifting into policy controversies and focusing only on negative developments because such approaches will produce a backlash and lack of co-operation from ministers and departments. There is also a balance to be maintained between identifying waste and error and emphasizing constructive criticism and organizational learning.[40]*

Finally, with all this reporting going on, it is reasonable to wonder who reports on the OAG. What mechanisms exist to ensure that the government "watcher" is adequately "watched"? This is accomplished by an external auditor annually appointed by the Treasury Board. This report is presented to the Treasury Board and tabled in the House of Commons. As well, the OAG's work is the focus of 15 different parliamentary committees, and its own spending is subject to review and inspection by the Public Accounts Committee of Parliament and to the scrutiny of the Official Languages Commissioner on language issues, the Public Service Commission on staffing and classification practices, and the Privacy Commissioner through the Privacy Act.

In short, as this brief overview reveals, multiple and reinforcing sources of accountability ripple throughout the organization of government. The process is complex and convoluted, and in part explains why government business sometimes takes so long to be completed. The multiple checks within the system may seem overly bureaucratic, time-consuming, and inefficient. But the alternative may be even less palatable to citizens, who have every right to expect their tax dollars to be used wisely. Recent developments have introduced new issues and problems where accountability is concerned, resulting in the need for ongoing review of the functions and roles of bodies such as the OAG and, indeed, more broadly of government itself. We now turn our attention to some of these developments.

## Contemporary Issues of Accountability and Control

The advent of the New Public Management (NPM) and the general trend toward making government more businesslike has had important implications for accountability. The concept and practice of accountability are different in the private sector than in the public sector. So what happens when you begin to import the practices of the former into the latter? This final section addresses this issue, bearing as it does directly on the future of public administration in Canada.

One observer suggests that the accountability regime under which public servants served in the past has changed:

*Management principles like decentralization, achieving measurable results, and empowerment (key features of "managerialism") imply that public-sector managers are to be held accountable for performance results rather than for adhering to due process and to the equitable treatment of individuals. In addition, if the federal experience is any guide, individual public servants may now be held directly accountable for their own actions or those of their subordinates by parliamentary committees or their surrogates in provincial legislatures or on municipal councils (as the Al-Mashat Affair demonstrated), to say nothing of the potential for damages resulting from the increasing tendency for the public to file civil suits against particular public servants.*[41]

As we noted earlier, there is a trend toward reducing public servants' traditional anonymity. This has intensified due to NPM. As professor of public administration Donald Savoie reports, this has occurred not just at the senior levels of the public service, "but even career officials down the line have become active participants in the elaborate public consultative process and thereby abandoned their anonymity."[42] These developments imply that our traditional understanding of who should be held to account for government action or inaction should be rethought. Downsizing and privatization have also had significant impacts on accountability, as has an increasing tendency to resort to private sector management techniques focusing on efficiency and client service.[43] For example, when a government downloads to the private sector its responsibility to provide a particular service or, indeed, privatizes that service, who is accountable when things go awry? The answer to this question is not as clear-cut as you might assume.

Take the issue of responsibility for roads, for instance. Increasingly, governments in Canada are "selling" highways to private sector corporations, who would assume responsibility for their upkeep and maintenance by collecting tolls. But what if the roads fall into disrepair, and the corporations find it less and less profitable to maintain them? They could raise the tolls, but they would risk losing customers, which would translate into a loss of revenue for road repair. In the worst-case scenario, suppose a company abrogates its responsibilities altogether, perhaps by claiming that revenues cannot keep up with expenses, and that the company has no choice but to declare bankruptcy. The state is left to assume responsibility, using taxpayers' dollars, for the lack of accountability in the original arrangement.

Yet another consequence of NPM is the development of a so-called hidden or shadow bureaucracy.[44] Relatively little is known about the hidden bureaucracy since no agency or organization is charged with keeping track of it. It is composed of the thousands of former public servants who were terminated and/or seconded to or contracted out to the private sector and voluntary or not-for-profit sectors. Reasonable suspicions exist about the absence of a clear accountability framework governing the relationship of this growing sector to the traditional government public service. Speaking of the U.S. experience, Frederickson notes, "the hidden bureaucracy is exquisitely fragmented into dozens of agencies and thousands of contracts. . . . [and] is so complex and so far back in the shadows that it is unreasonable to expect the media to make it transparent."[45] Frederickson adds,

*For the new public service the central question is one of values. It is clear that the government employees are to pursue the public interest, as they see it. . . . The value*

*question is how to achieve the public interest when power is shared with organizations that have other interests and values. . . . The pursuit of public policy usually means making difficult tradeoffs between competing values such as equality and efficiency. When such policy choices are even partially delegated to or controlled by the hidden bureaucracy, we are face to face with the issue of accountability.*[46]

Consider another emerging trend. Introducing private sector management techniques into the public service often involves "letting the managers manage"—that is, decentralizing control over the actions of subordinates, giving them more flexibility in their roles, and permitting them to make more decisions regarding the provision of services to clients (i.e., citizens). These attempts to empower public servants and make them more responsive to Canadians may seem laudable; but they conflict with certain traditional values of accountability. Emphasizing efficiency and responsiveness substitutes the private sector's value system for the public sector's. This may mean that, in the pursuit of efficiency, due process will be sacrificed. As Savoie suggests, incorporating private sector management practices into the public sector "means rejecting traditional public-administration concerns with accountability and control, and giving way to the business- management emphasis on productivity, performance, and service to clients."[47] The over-riding concern is that public servants operate in a political environment involving the public trust, whereas business operates in a different environment. Savoie observes, "In business it does not much matter if you get it wrong 10 percent of the time as long as you turn a profit at the end of the year. In government, it does not much matter if you get it right 90 percent of the time because the focus will be on the 10 percent of the time you got it wrong."[48] Another view, however, is that if "managerialism enables objectives to be expressed more clearly and encourages better measurement of results, it can actually make control more meaningful and provide better information to ministers, thereby enhancing, not diminishing, their ability to account for the use they make of public funds."[49]

A variety of organizational models have recently been introduced into public administration that test the traditional doctrine of ministerial responsibility and the concept of accountability in general. Greater decentralization and more autonomy for public servants seem to be recurring themes in these models, and practices in other countries have been noted by the Canadian government. In Great Britain, for instance, the concept of *executive agencies* has been introduced. These are bodies that are delegated a certain amount of responsibility by the minister concerned. The chief executives of these agencies are accountable to the minister through certain performance contracts rather than through traditional hierarchical channels. This model leaves responsibility for overall policy making in the hands of the minister, but it transfers responsibility for operations to the chief executives. New Zealand has introduced something called the *state-owned enterprise,* in which a higher level of independence is granted to these enterprises than is traditionally the case with the older Crown corporation model. In Canada, a number of similar initiatives are underway. For instance, as a result of Program Review, the air navigation system under the auspices of Transport Canada now operates on a commercial basis. The Translation Bureau in the Department of Public Works and Government Services became a Special Operating Agency (SOA), a body that provides some operational autonomy from its department, although not as much as a Crown corporation enjoys. New agencies were developed in areas such as parks management, food inspection, revenue and securities, some of which add another layer of complication, since they cross over from federal into provincial jurisdiction. These examples and others implicitly strain the conventional understanding of accountability, leaving some observers to conclude that "the question of ministerial responsibility and the structures within which the new service delivery agencies are to be held accountable to Parliament must be seriously examined." Moreover, "to fail to do so would jeopardize the doctrine of ministerial responsibility, which could in turn undermine an important part of the Canadian democratic system."[50]

As an example of the changing nature of accountability brought on by NPM, consider the empowerment of public servants through more decentralized decision making and the encouragement of risk taking.[51] These developments potentially conflict with traditional notions of accountability. In the first place, existing structures and institutions (like central agencies) tend to constrain empowerment and risk taking, and so new structures and approaches need to be developed. In the second place, public sector managers, unlike their private sector counterparts, are typically risk-averse, fearing that mistakes will attract the attention of the media, interest groups, and opposition parties. Third, notions of neutrality and anonymity are compromised, as public servants using their increased decision-making powers come to be more and more identified with government initiatives.

Still, governments are increasingly redefining accountability, through the lens of empowerment and other precepts of the NPM, to place greater emphasis on *results* rather than *process*. As some suggest, "governments are more aware that holding public servants accountable through a variety of formal controls is a necessary but insufficient means of ensuring responsible administrative conduct." Further, "empowerment envisages increased emphasis on psychological or personal responsibility, in the sense of loyalty to, or identification with, organizational and program goals."[52] There is potential conflict between individual public servants' sense of personal responsibility and the larger framework of ministerial responsibility. Unless ministers are willing to broaden their conception of ministerial responsibility to include a defence of risk taking by public servants and of the inevitable mistakes that will be made, there seems little chance that the tensions between old and new forms of accountability will dissipate.

Political scientist Paul Thomas identifies a clear trend in relation to the erosion of the tradition of anonymity. He suggests that "under the sway of NPM ideas there is a growing insistence that public servants be personally accountable for results through, for example, the development and publication of performance indicators."[53] As political scientist J.E. Hodgetts foresaw in the early 1990s,

*if the inevitable drift of public management into the political realm of governance itself . . . is to be the path of the future, then we must be prepared to see senior managers assume the role of scapegoats for the failures of others who, in our system of responsible cabinet government, have hitherto been elected to bear that direct responsibility.*[54]

Flushing public servants out from the shadows where they traditionally reside is problematic, if for no other reason than that there is no one else, other than their own superiors within the hierarchical chain of command, to whom they are required to answer directly. The recent use of parliamentary committees (as in the Al-Mashat affair) to roast public servants on the open fires of Parliament is inappropriate, since the committees were intended as accountability mechanisms that ministers—not their public servants—answer to. In any event, only ministers can impose penalties or sanctions for errors committed by public servants; parliamentary committees do not possess that right. At the same time, however, public servants' reputations and careers can be severely damaged in the partisan arena of Parliament, leading Thomas to conclude that "placing public servants before parliamentary committees creates risks in terms of inappropriate and unfair questions by politicians, and not just from those on the opposition benches."[55]

Thomas cites some other concerns with these developments: "The NPM literature tends to denigrate existing approaches to accountability as mistaking adherence to procedures for the achievement of results, stifling creativity and initiative and adding to the costs of running government. Control is seen only in negative terms of adding to red tape."[56] Yet control through accountability measures may actually improve efficiency and effectiveness by preventing abuses that lead to waste. Thus, while the NPM is dismissive of traditional mechanisms and systems of accountability it tends to ignore the fact that the bureaucracy of accountability actually fosters the values NPM supports.

The implications of many of the contemporary developments related to accountability can be traced right back to our discussion of constitutional and administrative law in chapter 6. The Constitution, you will recall, sets out the relationship between individuals and the state, and among the different institutions of government. It does this in order to promote the rule of law, the premise of which is that no one in society—not even the most politically, economically, or socially powerful—is above the law. This includes, of course, the government itself and those who work in it. In this sense, the courts have played a prominent role in accountability, being a primary mechanism by which penalties are imposed for transgressions. The courts uphold the rule of law, and hence the Constitution, in ensuring that politicians and public servants do not overstep the bounds of accountability imposed upon them by the rules and institutions we have surveyed. However, the NPM may be changing the role and impact of the rule of law, as well as the courts, in maintaining accountability. The NPM draws for its inspiration on the literature and language of private management. Traditional public administration, in contrast, draws on the literature and language of law and political science. Clearly, the latter is more directly concerned with issues of justice and legality, the Constitution, the rule of law, and related matters. The former is more concerned with management techniques that promote efficiency, effectiveness, and economy. Yet again, we see another manifestation of the conflicting-values problem in public administration, this time related to the issue of accountability.

A large problem in accountability lies, ironically, in the premises of various recent reforms of the public service, many of which were aimed at improving accountability. First, cutting red tape and budget restrictions often focused on reducing capacity in the areas of monitoring and auditing, thereby compromising accountability.[57] Second, the new paradigm of public management disparaged traditional public service values and ethics, and the mechanisms designed to promote control and compliance. Third, the increasing tendency to politicize the public service has undermined its nonpartisan character.[58] As Aucoin and Jarvis suggest,

*In each of these three respects, the public service was confronted with major challenges that it sought to address. At the time of Program Review in the early to mid-1990s, the attitude in many quarters was that the monitoring, auditing and challenge functions were essentially "bureaucratic overhead." Scaling back on the administrative resources to carry out these functions was seen by many as a good thing to do. Second, the initial attack on traditional public administration as rule-bound bureaucracy emanated from the private sector. However, the importance of public service values and ethics has recently resurfaced as a result of several wrongdoings, in Canada and elsewhere, and then perhaps only because similar ethical lapses began to occur in the private sector. And finally, the past two decades have witnessed an increasing number of political staff who have insisted on involving themselves in public administration, and an increasing number of ministers who wish their public servants to be responsive in promoting the implementation of their agenda.[59]*

These developments reinforced concerns that institutions and standards in the federal government were defective. Prime ministers Chrétien and Martin consequently put forward an agenda of reform meant to strengthen integrity and transparency of government.[60] Prime Minister Harper then followed the trail that had been blazed ahead of his ascension to office and introduced the Federal Accountability Act (FAA) in 2006 to reinforce compliance and enforcement of rules, enhance independent oversight and review, increase transparency and disclosure, and streamline current rules to increase efficiency.[61]

The FAA represented attempts by government to move from a "culture of entitlement" to a "culture of accountability." This legislation, emerging directly in the wake of the sponsorship program scandal (see Box 11.5), sought to strengthen institutional arrangements in oversight bodies (such as the OAG and the ethics commissioner), and to make government more accountable overall. The Act was a long and complex document that amended several existing acts and introduced new ones; it was accompanied by a Federal Accountability Action Plan to aid in implementation. Among the goals of the FAA were the following:

- reforming the financing of political parties
- banning secret donations to political candidates
- strengthening the role of the ethics commissioner
- toughening the Lobbyists Registration Act
- ensuring truth in budgeting with a Parliamentary Budget Authority
- making qualified government appointments
- cleaning up the procurement of government contracts
- cleaning up government polling and advertising
- providing real protection for whistleblowers

- strengthening access to information legislation
- strengthening the power of the auditor general
- strengthening auditing and accountability within departments
- creating a director of Public Prosecutions[62]

---

**BOX 11.5 The Sponsorship Program**

After nearly losing the 1995 Quebec referendum, the federal government launched the Sponsorship Program. Its intent was simple—to raise the profile of the federal government in Quebec and promote Canadian federalism there. Prime Minister Chrétien thought spending federal money to promote cultural programs, the arts, and sporting events would help endear Canada to Québécois. From 1996 to 2003, $250 million was spent. However, it gradually emerged that at least some of the money was being misappropriated and that criminal fraud and corruption were at play.

Auditor General Sheila Fraser recommended that the RCMP investigate. She used a rather colourful turn of phrase in suggesting that federal public servants "broke every rule in the book" in their relationships with certain Quebec advertising firms with ties to the Liberal Party of Canada by funnelling contracts and money to them. In turn, some of these agencies funnelled the money both into their own pockets without delivering any substantial product, or into the coffers of the Liberal Party. In her 2004 annual report, the auditor general announced that up to $100 million had been misspent in this way, and that the senior officials running the Sponsorship Program had essentially disregarded every rule for proper financial management of the funds.

As a result of the auditor general's investigations and the subsequent pressure from the opposition parties and media, Prime Minister Martin called a public inquiry into the matter in February 2004. Justice John Gomery was directed to head it up. The televised proceedings of the inquiry and the almost daily barrage of front-page headlines about the scandal caught the attention of the public, who witnessed, among other things, the unprecedented live testimony of a former and current prime minister as part of the inquiry. The Gomery Commission issued a two-volume report, a set of recommendations for future reform, and a three-volume set of research studies. But its legacy also includes contributing to the defeat of the Martin government and its replacement by the Harper Conservatives, although with only a minority government, in January 2006. In addition, several of the key actors in the scandal were tried and convicted in criminal court.

The controversies currently swirling around the issue of accountability are unlikely to be resolved soon. It is not as though there is a single easy answer. Gradual change is called for, vis-à-vis reforms and experimentation, new initiatives, and careful consideration and analysis of existing systems of accountability. Remember that accountability is based on the underlying principle of responsible government. This fundamental democratic premise of the Canadian system should drive all attempts at coordinating the actors, institutions, ideas, and formal and informal systems and processes that animate the regime of accountability. Failure to focus on this basic point means that citizens will be ill-served, since both politicians and public servants may be less inclined to "pay attention to their respective assigned and accepted responsibilities [and] to understand that it does matter."[63]

## WHAT YOU HAVE LEARNED

The concept of *accountability* embraces several aspects of public administration; it is vital to democratic government, yet it is not always clearly understood. When modern society created democratic systems of government, the convention developed that public office was a matter of public trust, that the powers associated with public office should be used for the betterment of society (and not just the office-holder's personal gain), and that in pursuing this goal, office-holders were expected to act with integrity, honesty, and responsibility. They were to constantly account for their actions and for the exercise of power entrusted to them. This meant that they would have to report regularly on their activities in a public and visible way; that they would make themselves available to public scrutiny and be able to justify all their actions and decisions; that they would follow constitutional and administrative law in so doing; and that they would ultimately work toward improved provision of public services. Moreover, they would assume liability if they misused office. It is often suggested that public administration, in this conception, was not the administration *of* the public, but administration *for* the public. Notwithstanding the new trends in Canadian public administration, the responsibilities of the public servant are unlike those of an individual in private business, wherein the regime of accountability is less comprehensive, more limited, and different in orientation.

## Key Words and Concepts

accountable (364)
responsible government (365)
ministerial responsibility (369)
doctrine of answerability (369)

collective ministerial
  responsibility (370)
accounting officer (372)

## Review Questions

1. *Accountability and Democracy*
The central principle of responsible government, which lies at the root of the accountability issue and was first raised in chapter 2, was the focus of discussion. This principle lies at the root of the accountability issue. This section explained the link between accountability and democracy. Ask yourself, How is the principle

of responsible government significant where accountability is concerned? How does the principle work in theory and in practice in the context of Canadian public administration?

## 2. Ministerial Responsibility

Responsible government depends in part on the doctrine of ministerial responsibility, which sets the boundaries of ministerial action. It also establishes the guidelines that state how government is held to account. This section explained the pure theory of ministerial responsibility, and showed how contemporary trends and developments have affected the original theory. Ask yourself, Do I understand the theory of ministerial responsibility, including both individual and collective ministerial responsibility? How has the doctrine of answerability modified the accountability of ministers? How has the traditional approach to ministerial responsibility in the political system changed over time? What does this mean for the concept of accountability now?

## 3. Accountability and Public Servants

Where the traditional doctrine of ministerial authority meets the politics–administration dichotomy, expectations about the role and behaviour of public servants emerge. But recent changes to the concept of accountability have altered the conventional set of expectations, leaving public servants on unfamiliar ground. This section addressed both the traditional role of public servants and the newly emerging one. Ask yourself, In what ways have public servants traditionally been held accountable for their actions? How have the concepts of ministerial responsibility, the doctrine of answerability, and the politics–administration dichotomy affected the position and work of public servants in terms of accountability? What problems do public servants face in trying to live up to the accountability regime? How do public servants respond to the multiple demands of executives, legislatures, judiciary, interest groups, professional associations, regulatory boards, the media, clients, and citizens when responsibility demands conflict? Which take precedence?

## 4. Accountability in Action: The Role of the Office of the Auditor General

The Office of the Auditor General is one of the most important links in the chain of accountability. We briefly reviewed the role of this important actor in terms of how it contributes to accountability. Ask yourself, What role does the Office of the Auditor General play in the process of promoting accountability by providing the government with objective, unbiased assessments of its work?

## 5. Contemporary Issues of Accountability and Control

This section revealed that the accountability regime is in flux. Recent developments have altered the traditional understanding of who is responsible to whom for what. Traditional notions of ministerial responsibility and the role of public servants have altered due to the emergence of new organizational norms and systems such as the New Public Management. The drive to put government on a more businesslike footing is behind many of these changes. Ask yourself, How have traditional notions of accountability been altered under the influence of new developments in Canadian public administration? What impact has the New

Public Management had on the usual relationships within government, and between government and citizens? Are these developments helpful or hurtful to the accountability regime?

## Weblinks

Auditor General of Canada
**www.oag-bvg.gc.ca**

Commissioner of the Environment and Sustainable Development
**www.oag-bvg.gc.ca/internet/English/esd_fs_e_46.html**

Privy Council Office
**www.pco-bcp.gc.ca**

Federal Accountability Act
**www.faa-lfi.gc.ca**

Privacy Commissioner of Canada
**www.privcom.gc.ca**

Accountability Officers: Guidance on Roles, Responsibilities, and Appearances Before Parlimentary Committees 2007

**www.pco-bcp.gc.ca/index.asp?lang=eng&page=information&sub=publications&doc=ao-adc/2007/ao-adc-eng.htm**

Democracy Watch
**www.dwatch.ca**

## Further Reading

### 1. Accountability and Democracy

Aucoin, Peter, and Ralph Heintzman. "The Changing Nature of Political Accountability," in B. Guy Peters and Donald J. Savoie, eds., *Revitalizing the Public Service*. Montreal: McGill-Queens University Press, 2000.

Johnson, David. *Thinking Government: Public Sector Management in Canada*. 2nd ed. Peterborough: Broadview, 2006.

Mosher, Frederick C. *Democracy and the Public Service*. New York: Oxford University Press, 1968.

### 2. Ministerial Responsibility

d'Ombrain, Nicholas. "Ministerial Responsibility and the Machinery of Government." *Canadian Public Administration*, 50, 2 (2007): 195–217.

Savoie, Donald, ed. *Restoring Accountability: Research Studies*. Vols. 1–3. *Commission of Inquiry into the Sponsorship Program and Advertising Activities*. Ottawa: Public Works and Government Services, 2006.

Sutherland, S.L. "Responsible Government and Ministerial Responsibility." *Canadian Journal of Political Science*, 24, 1 (1991): 91–120.

### 3. Accountability and Public Servants

Finer, Herman. "Administrative Responsibility in Democratic Government." *Public Administration Review*, 1, 4 (1941): 335–50.

Friedrich, Carl J. "Public Policy and the Nature of Administrative Responsibility," in Carl J. Friedrich and Edward S. Mason, eds., *Public Policy.* Cambridge: Harvard University Press, 1940: 3–24.

Kernaghan, Kenneth, and John Langford. *The Responsible Public Servant.* Halifax: Institute for Research on Public Policy, 1990.

Osbaldeston, Gordon. *Keeping Deputy Ministers Accountable.* Toronto: McGraw-Hill Ryerson, 1989.

Savoie, Donald J. *Breaking the Bargain: Public Servants, Ministers and Parliament.* Toronto: University of Toronto Press, 2003.

Segal, Hugh. "The Accountability of Public Servants: Our Government Would Be Better If Senior Mandarins Were Less Secure," in Barbara Wake Carroll, David Seigel, and Mark Sproule-Jones, eds., *Classic Readings in Canadian Public Administration.* Toronto: Oxford University Press, 2005: 84–86.

Thomas, Paul C. "Parliament and the Public Service," in Christopher Dunn, ed., *The Handbook of Canadian Public Administration.* 2nd ed. Toronto: Oxford University Press, 2010: 106–30.

**4. Accountability in Action: The Role of the Auditor General's Office**

Saint-Martin, Denis. "Managerialist Advocate or 'Control Freak'? The Janus-Faced Office of the Auditor General." *Canadian Public Administration,* 47, 2 (2004): 121–40.

Sutherland, Sharon L. "The Office of the Auditor General: Government in Exile?" Kingston: Queen's University School of Policy Studies, 2002.

**5. Contemporary Issues of Accountability and Control**

Aucoin, Peter. *The New Public Management: Canada in Comparative Perspective.* Montreal: Institute for Research on Public Policy, 1995.

Aucoin, Peter, and Mark D. Jarvis, *Modernizing Government Accountability: A Framework for Reform.* Ottawa: Canada School of Public Service, 2005.

Carroll, Barbara Wake, and David I. Dewar. "Performance Management: Panacea or Fools' Gold?" in Christopher Dunn, ed., *The Handbook of Canadian Public Administration.* Toronto: Oxford Univerity Press, 2002: 413–29.

Franks, C.E.S. "The Unfortunate Experience of the Dueling Protocols: A Chapter in the Continuing Quest for Responsible Government in Canada," in O.P. Dwivedi, Tim A. Mau, and Byron Sheldrick, eds., *The Evolving Physiology of Government: Canadian Public Administration.* Ottawa: University of Ottawa Press, 2009: 118–50.

Thomas, Paul G. "The Swirling Meanings and Practices of Accountability in Canadian Government," in Ken Rasmussen and David Siegel, eds., *Professionalism and Public Service: Essays in Honour of Kenneth Kernaghan.* Toronto: University of Toronto Press, 2008.

# Endnotes

1. Gerald E. Caiden, "The Problem of Ensuring the Public Accountability of Public Officials," in Joseph G. Jabbra and O.P. Dwivedi, eds., *Public Service Accountability* (West Hartford, CT: Kumarian, 1988): 19.

2. See J.R. Mallory, *The Structure of Canadian Government* (Toronto: Gage, 1971).

3. See Canada, Privy Council Office, *Responsibility in the Constitution* (Ottawa: Minister of Supply and Services, 1993): 11–27.

4. James John Guy, *How We Are Governed: The Basics of Canadian Politics and Government* (Toronto: Harcourt Brace, 1995): 35.

5. See Keith Archer et al., *Parameters of Power: Canada's Political Institutions* (Scarborough: Nelson, 1995): 72.

6. Caiden, "The Problem of Ensuring the Public Accountability of Public Officials," 20.

7. O.P. Dwivedi, "The Issue of Accountability in the Public Service of Canada," in Joseph G. Jabbra and O.P. Dwivedi, eds., *Public Service Accountability: A Comparative Perspective* (West Hartford, CT: Kumarian, 1988): 86.

8. Caiden, "The Problem of Ensuring the Public Accountability of Public Officials," 17.

9. Paul G. Thomas, "The Changing Nature of Accountability," in B. Guy Peters and Donald J. Savoie, eds., *Taking Stock: Assessing Public Sector Reforms* (Montreal: McGill-Queen's University Press, 1998): 352.

10. Paul G. Thomas, "The Crisis of Trust in Government: Rhetoric or Reality?" paper presented at the Public Policy Forum Breakfast Series, March 29, 2007, **www.ppforum.ca/sites/default/files/Paul_Thomas_March29_07_0.pdf**.

11. Nicole Jauvin, "Government, Ministers, Macro-Organization Chart and Networks," in Jacques Bourgault, Maurice Demers, and Cynthia Williams, eds., *Public Administration and Public Management: Experiences in Canada* (St. Foy, QC: Les Publications du Quebec, 1997): 49. See also David E. Smith, "Clarifying the Doctrine of Ministerial Responsibility As It Applies to the Government and Parliament of Canada," in Donald Savoie, ed., *Restoring Accountability: Research Studies*, vol. 1, *Commission of Inquiry into the Sponsorship Program and Advertising Activities* (Ottawa: Public Works and Government Services, 2006): 106–07.

12. Thomas, "The Changing Nature of Accountability," 359. See also Peter Aucoin and Mark D. Jarvis, *Modernizing Government Accountability: A Framework for Reform* (Ottawa: Canada School of Public Service, 2005).

13. Aucoin and Jarvis, *Modernizing Government Accountability*, 14.

14. See Jauvin, "Government, Ministers, Macro-Organization Chart and Networks," 48.

15. Jauvin, "Government, Ministers, Macro-Organization Chart and Networks," 49.

16. For a list of all departments, agencies, Crown Corporations, and other government of Canada entities, see Canada, Treasury Board of Canada Secretariat, *Population Affiliation Report*, June 8, 2010, **www.tbs-sct.gc.ca/pas-srp/overview-apercu_e.asp**. The following section is derived largely from Jauvin, "Government, Ministers, Macro-Organization Chart and Networks," 55–56.

17. Ian Clark, "A 'Back to Basics' Look at the Government Decision Making Process," unpublished paper, November 4, 1983, 13, cited in Robert J. Jackson and Doreen Jackson, *Politics in Canada: Culture, Institutions, Behaviour and Public Policy*, 6th ed. (Toronto: Pearson Prentice Hall, 2006): 279.

18. Aucoin and Jarvis, *Modernizing Government Accountability*, 15.

19. See S.L. Sutherland, "The Al-Mashat Affair: Administrative Accountability in Parliamentary Institutions," *Canadian Public Administration*, 34, 4 (1991): 573–603.

20. Canada, Privy Council Office, *Accountable Government: A Guide for Ministers and Secretaries of State—2007* (Ottawa: Privy Council Office, 2007): 6. See also Mark D. Jarvis, "The Adoption of the Accounting Officer System in Canada: Changing Relationships?" *Canadian Public Administration*, 52, 4 (2009): 525–47.

21. Canada, Privy Council Office, *Accounting Officers: Guidelines on Roles, Responsibilities and Appearances Before Parliamentary Committees* (Ottawa: Privy Council Office, 2007): 1. See also C.E.S. (Ned) Franks, "The Respective Responsibilities and Accountabilities of Ministers and Public Servants: A Study of the British Accounting Officer System and Its Relevance for Canada," in Donald Savoie, ed., *Restoring Accountability: Research Studies*, vol. 3, *Commission of Inquiry into the Sponsorship Program and Advertising Activities* (Ottawa: Public Works and Government Services, 2006): 157–230; and Alan Gilmore, "The Canadian Accounting Officer: Has It Strengthened Parliament's Ability to Hold the Government to Account?" in Christopher Dunn, ed., *The Handbook of Canadian Public Administration*, 2nd ed. (Toronto: Oxford University Press, 2010): 75–84.

22. See Flora MacDonald, "Who Is on Top? The Minister or the Mandarins?" and Mitchell Sharp, "A Reply From a Former Minister and Mandarin," in Paul W. Fox and Graham White, eds., *Politics Canada*, 8th ed. (Toronto: McGraw-Hill, 1995): 448–56.

23. See Richard J. Van Loon and Michael S. Whittington, *The Canadian Political System*, 4th ed. (Toronto: McGraw-Hill Ryerson, 1987): chaps. 15, 17; and Evert A. Lindquist, "Has Federal Cabinet Decision Making Come Full Circle?" in

Paul W. Fox and Graham White, eds., *Politics Canada*, 8th ed. (Toronto: McGraw-Hill, 1995): 544–52.

24. See Graham Fraser, "Civil Service a Victim in Sponsorship Scandals," *Toronto Star* (June 16, 2002).

25. Cited in Sutherland, "The Al-Mashat Affair," 582.

26. See R.L. Gagne, "Accountability and Public Administration," *Canadian Public Administration*, 39, 2 (1996): 214.

27. Jacques Bourgault, "The Role of Deputy Ministers in Canadian Government," in Christopher Dunn, ed., *The Handbook of Canadian Public Administration*, 2nd ed. (Toronto: Oxford University Press, 2010): 504–20.

28. See Thomas, "The Changing Nature of Accountability," 356.

29. J. David Wright, "Exposing the Chameleon: Response to 'Accountability and Public Administration,'" *Canadian Public Administration*, 39, 2 (1996): 229.

30. Donald J. Savoie, *Thatcher, Reagan, Mulroney: In Search of a New Bureaucracy* (Pittsburgh: University of Pittsburgh Press, 1994): 216–17.

31. Thomas, "The Changing Nature of Accountability," 360.

32. Thomas, "The Changing Nature of Accountability," 360–61. See also Paul C. Thomas, "Parliament and the Public Service," in Christopher Dunn, ed., *The Handbook of Canadian Public Administration*, 2nd ed. (Toronto: Oxford University Press, 2010): 106–30; and Peter Aucoin and Donald J. Savoie, "The Politics–Administration Dichotomy: Democracy Versus Bureaucracy?" in O.P. Dwivedi, Tim Mau and Byron Sheldrick, eds., *The Evolving Physiology of Government: Canadian Public Administration in Transition* (Ottawa: University of Ottawa Press, 2009): 97–117.

33. See Gilmore, "The Canadian Accounting Officer," 77.

34. The definitive account of the HRDC affair is David Good, *The Politics of Public Management: The HRDC Audit of Government Grants and Contributions* (Toronto: University of Toronto Press, 2003).

35. See Good, *The Politics of Public Management*; and Graham Fraser, "Scandal Leaves Ottawa Swamped in Paperwork," *Toronto Star* (December 13, 2000): A23. The HRDC scandal is reviewed in Canada, Treasury Board of Canada Secretariat, *Building on a Strong Foundation—The Dialogue Continues*, vol. 2, *Further Case Studies on Values and Ethics in the Public Service* (Ottawa: Canadian Centre for Management Development, 2001): 41–48. See also Sharon L. Sutherland, "'Biggest Scandal in Canadian History': HRDC Audit Starts Probity War," Queen's University Working Paper 23, August 2001.

36. Thomas, "The Changing Nature of Accountability," 353.

37. See Paul G. Thomas, "The Past, Present and Future of Officers of Parliament," *Canadian Public Administration*, 46, 3 (2003): 287–314.

38. The following description of the Auditor General's role is derived from Canada, Office of the Auditor General, *Auditing for Parliament* (Ottawa: Minister of Public Works and Government Services Canada, 1997). For a critical review of the work of the Auditor General during the HRDC scandal, see Sutherland, "Biggest Scandal in Canadian History."

39. Office of the Auditor General of Canada, "A Message from the Auditor General – May 2007," *Report of the Auditor General of Canada 2007*, (Ottawa: Office of the Auditor General, 2007), www.oag-bvg.gc.ca/internet/English/parl_oag_200705_00_e_17475.html#ch0hd4a, Reproduced with the permission of the Minister of Public Works and Government Services Canada, 2010.

40. Thomas, "Parliament and the Public Service," 118.

41. Gagne, "Accountability and Public Administration," 220.

42. Donald J. Savoie, *Breaking the Bargain: Public Servants, Ministers and Parliament* (Toronto: University of Toronto Press, 2003): 247.

43. Tom Christensen and Per Lægreid, "New Public Management—Undermining Political Control?" in Tom Christensen and Per Lægreid, eds., *New Public Management: The Transformation of Ideas and Practice* (Aldershot, U.K.: Ashgate, 2001): 93–120.

44. See H. George Frederickson, "Public Ethics and the New Managerialism," in H. George

Frederickson and Richard K. Ghere, eds., *Ethics in Public Management* (Armonk, NY: M.E. Sharpe, 2005): 174.

45. Frederickson, "Public Ethics and the New Managerialism," 175.

46. Frederickson, "Public Ethics and the New Managerialism," 175.

47. Donald J. Savoie, *Thatcher, Reagan, Mulroney: In Search of a New Bureaucracy* (Pittsburgh: University of Pittsburgh Press, 1994): 283.

48. Donald J. Savoie, "What Is Wrong with the New Public Management?" *Canadian Public Administration*,38, 1 (1995): 115.

49. Wright, "Exposing the Chameleon," 232.

50. Jauvin, "Government, Ministers, Macro-Organization Chart and Networks," 58.

51. See Kenneth Kernaghan, Brian Marson, and Sandford Borins, *The New Public Organization* (Toronto: Institute of Public Administration of Canada, 2000): 175–77.

52. Kernaghan, Marson, and Borins, *The New Public Organization*, 176.

53. Thomas, "The Changing Nature of Accountability," 382.

54. J.E. Hodgetts, *Public Management: Emblem of Reform for the Canadian Public Service* (Ottawa: Canadian Centre for Management Development, 1991): 13, cited in O.P. Dwivedi and James Iain Gow, *From Bureaucracy to Public Management: The Administrative Culture of the Government of Canada* (Peterborough: Broadview, 1999): 176.

55. Thomas, "The Changing Nature of Accountability," 382.

56. Thomas, "The Changing Nature of Accountability," 383.

57. See Good, *The Politics of Public Management*.

58. Aucoin and Jarvis, *Modernizing Government Accountability*, 61.

59. Aucoin and Jarvis, *Modernizing Government Accountability*, 62. Reproduced with the permission of the Minister of Public Works and Government Services Canada, 2010.

60. See Luc Juillet, "The Office of Ethics Commissioner, Accountability and Public Trust," in G. Bruce Doern, ed., *How Ottawa Spends, 2004–2005: Mandate Change in the Paul Martin Era* (Montreal: McGill-Queen's University Press, 2004): 296–316.

61. Canada, Treasury Board Secretariat of Canada, "Canada's New Government: Federal Accountability Action Plan: Turning a New Leaf" (Ottawa: Treasury Board Secretariat of Canada, 2006): 1–2.

62. Highlights of the *Federal Accountability Act and Action Plan*, **www.faa-lfi.gc.ca/fs-fi/fs-fi_e.asp**, Treasury Board of Canada Secretariat, 2006. Reproduced with the permission of the Minister of Public Works and Government Services Canada, 2010.

63. Canada, Royal Commission on Financial Management and Accountability, *Final Report* (Ottawa: Supply and Services, 1979): 9.

# Glossary

**accountability**—a fundamental principle of democratic government that states that those who hold governmental power must be answerable and responsive to the people for the way in which that power is exercised. *See also* administrative responsibility.

**accountable**—*see* accountability.

**accounting officer**—designation assigned to deputy ministers, giving them the legal obligation to appear before parliamentary committees to answer questions on their management responsibilities within the framework of ministerial responsibility and accountability.

**accumulation**—a concept used in neo-Marxist theory referring to the need for capital to generate (accumulate) profits and for government to formulate policies that foster the conditions to make profitability possible.

**administrative evaluation**—the examination of the efficiency of delivery of government services. This evaluation is performed in order to determine if the best value for money is being realized within the framework of democracy and justice, using technical methodologies involving the compilation and analysis of data on program costs and benefits. *See also* policy evaluation.

**administrative law**—that part of the law that is concerned with the legal limitations on the actions of government officials and the remedies available to anyone affected by a transgression of these limits.

**administrative responsibility**—the requirement that public servants be answerable and accountable in fulfilling their duties as authorized by a superior.

**advisory board**—an organization composed of citizens and created by the government, but outside of the normal bureaucracy, to provide independent advice to a minister.

**affirmative action**—*see* employment equity.

**agents of Parliament**—independent statutory officers who scrutinize the activity of government and report directly to Parliament rather than to government or an individual minister

**alienation**—a concept used in Marxist analysis to describe the condition in which citizens see the bureaucracy and/or state as a distant, impersonal, and oppressive force.

**alternative service delivery (ASD)**—organizational bodies developed to deliver government services more efficiently and innovatively than traditional departments and agencies.

**amending formula**—a procedure introduced in the Constitution Act, 1982, to formally change the Constitution. Generally, the amending formula requires the agreement of Ottawa and 7 out of 10 provinces, representing at least 50 percent of the population. Some constitutional amendments, however, require the unanimous agreement of all 11 governments.

**audit**—a process of examining government accounts to see that they are correct. *See also* comprehensive audit.

**auditor general**—responsible directly to Parliament, the auditor general is the financial "watchdog" who performs an audit each year of the Public Accounts and prepares an annual report on the financial management of the government. The results of these audits are released to the public.

**authority**—the basis of state rule, in which the right to rule others and to legitimately compel obedience in the behaviour of citizens is held by state officials.

**autonomy**—freedom of action. This term is used by Marxists in connection with the freedom of state officials to formulate policies independently of the control or influence of capital.

**budget**—an annual statement of the government's revenues and expenditures.

**bureaucracy**—a form of organization characterized by hierarchy, a division of labour, a system of hiring and promotion based on merit, and management by detailed but impersonal rules.

**bureaucratic discretion**—the degree of freedom of judgment and action that bureaucrats have in implementing public policies.

**bureaucratic pathology**—a phenomenon in which the strict adherence to rigid rules and regulations supplants the real goals of a bureaucratic organization.

**bureaucratization**—the organization of human behaviour into formal organizations and structures for the purposes of efficiency and control.

**business plans**—a private sector managerial technique increasingly adopted by the public sector as part of the New Public Management movement. These are detailed plans of the multi-year objectives of line departments and their strategies for achieving the best possible service delivery at the least possible cost.

**Cabinet**—the political executive, which formulates government policies and is responsible for initiating most government legislation, the priorities of government, and the administration of policies. Cabinet generally consists of 20 to 40 Members of Parliament chosen by the prime minister to head government ministries.

**central agency**—a coordinating agency of government with the authority to intervene and direct the affairs of other government departments. Currently, there are four central agencies in the federal government: the Prime Minister's Office; the Privy Council Office; the Department of Finance; and the Treasury Board.

**charismatic legitimacy**—a form of legitimacy outlined by Max Weber in which citizens accept that an individual has the right to rule over them by virtue of his or her personal characteristics and strength of personality. *See also* legal-rational legitimacy and traditional legitimacy.

**Charter of Rights and Freedoms**—added to the Canadian Constitution in 1982, the Charter protects Canadians' fundamental freedoms, democratic rights, mobility rights, legal rights, equality rights, language rights, and Aboriginal rights.

**civil law**—law based on the French Napoleonic Code and Roman Law, in which the law is codified, unlike English-based common law. Civil law is the basis of the legal system in Quebec.

**Civil Service Acts, 1908 and 1918**—reforms to the federal civil service that eliminated patronage as the basis of hiring in the public service and set in motion the movement toward a merit-based, professional public service.

**Civil Service Commission**—*see* Public Service Commission.

**class conflict**—a central premise of Marxist theory, which argues that capitalist societies are divided into mutually antagonistic classes whose fundamental interests are ultimately irreconcilable.

**code of ethics**—a written set of regulations setting out the boundaries of acceptable and unacceptable behaviour for public servants and promoting the highest ethical conduct and standards required of public servants. Codes of ethics generally govern such matters as conflicts of interest, moonlighting, nonpartisanship, confidentiality, lying to the public, and similar issues.

**collective bargaining**—a means of determining wages, hours, and working conditions through negotiation between an employer and a union.

**collective ministerial responsibility**—the principle that members of the Cabinet (the executive branch of government) are collectively responsible for the policies and management of the government as a whole. *See also* individual ministerial responsibility.

**common law**—the rules developed by the courts and based on the principle of *stare decisis* (that is, established legal precedents guide current judgments).

**comprehensive audit**—an audit of a program focusing on its economy, efficiency, and effectiveness.

**conflict of interest**—a circumstance in which a politician or public servant has a personal interest in a policy or program such that his or her professional position and role is compromised.

**conservatism**—in Canada, traditionally an ideology that values hierarchy, order, and security above individual freedom and advocates a certain level of state intervention to restrain personal freedom for the greater good of the community.

**conservative**—*see* conservatism.

**constitution**—the supreme law of the land. Constitutions delineate the relationship between the state and citizens, between the parts of the state (executive, legislative, and judicial) and, in a federal system, between levels of government (national and provincial).

**constitutional convention**—the unwritten part of the constitution which is derived from habit, tradition, and past practices. Although not legally enforceable, constitutional conventions carry important political weight.

**constitutional law**—that part of the constitution composed of written documents and the common law, which is enforceable through the courts.

**contingency theory**—philosophy within systems theory suggesting that there are no absolutes or universal rules that apply to all organizations in all circumstances, but rather that effectiveness depends upon the relationship between an action and all other aspects of the system at that particular moment.

**contracting out**—the practice by government of employing the private sector to deliver services in order to save money.

**Crown corporation**—a corporation that the state owns wholly or in part in order to promote the national interest but that operates at arm's length from direct government control. Crown corporations are part of the arsenal of governing instruments available to the state.

**cultural analysis**—a type of policy analysis that focuses on the role culture plays in policy making. It tends to be structuralist and/or interpretive in approach. *See also* structural analysis and interpretive framework.

**debt**—the accumulation of deficits over the years.

**deficit**—the amount by which government expenditures exceed revenues during a specified period of time (usually one year).

**democratic society**—*see* direct democracy and representative democracy.

**department**—an organizational unit of government headed by a minister.

**deputy minister**—the administrative head of a government department appointed by the prime minister.

**deregulation**—the process of removing government regulations over an industry or sector of the economy, so that it may operate according to the dictates of the free market.

**direct democracy**—a form of government by the people in which citizens make all important community decisions as a whole, usually in some form of public assembly. This stands in contrast to a system of representative democracy, in which citizens choose representatives to make decisions on their behalf.

**disallowance**—section 56 of the Constitution Act, 1867 (formerly the British North America Act, 1867), which permits the federal government to disallow provincial legislation.

**discretion**—*see* bureaucratic discretion.

**division of labour**—a principle of organization in which specialization in the organization of work is imposed in order to narrow the range of tasks each person is responsible for. The goal is to improve the overall efficiency of the organization and thus boost productivity.

**division of powers**—those sections of the constitution that set out the jurisdictional responsibilities of each level of government. In general, federal powers are spelled out in section 91 and provincial powers in section 92 of the Canadian Constitution.

**doctrine of answerability**—a watered-down version of the principle of ministerial responsibility in which the minister of a department is required simply to explain the errors of her subordinates, but not actually resign as a result of those actions.

**downsizing**—the termination of employees or their reassignment to other units within government departments to effect cost savings

**elected representatives**—decision-makers in a democratic government, elected by citizens to represent their wishes.

**elite**—a small group of people who exercise considerable power in society—politically, economically, socially, and/or bureaucratically.

**employment equity**—a set of programs and policies aimed at removing systemic barriers to employment and promotion among groups historically under-represented in the public service. *See also* representativeness.

**estimates**—the government's annual request to Parliament for an appropriation of funds to support its programs.

**ethics**—rules and codes of morality guiding human behaviour.

**ethics commissioners**—officials appointed by government to oversee ethical rules and codes governing the behaviour of public servants.

**evaluation**—*see* policy evaluation.

**executive branch of government**—composed of the monarch and Governor General at the formal (or symbolic) level, and the prime minister, Cabinet, and bureaucracy at the political level, the executive is the organizational centre of power in the political system.

**executive federalism**—relations between the elected and appointed officials of the two orders of government.

**Expenditure Management System (EMS)**—the system of budgeting introduced by the Chrétien government to promote greater control over government expenditures.

**federalism**—a system of governing in which the activities of government are divided in a written constitution between a national government and regional governments, each of which is coordinate with but independent of the other in its own jurisdictional areas.

**Financial Administration Act**—the statute that governs financial accountability for federal departments, agencies, and Crown corporations, and that defines the responsibilities of the Treasury Board and the Department of Finance in the area of financial management.

**formulation**—*see* policy formulation.

**Free Trade Agreement (FTA)**—the Free Trade Agreement between Canada and the United States was passed by the Conservative government of Brian Mulroney in 1988 and took effect in 1989. It created a tariff-free border while institutionalizing the Canada–U.S. relationship to an unprecedented degree. *See also* North American Free Trade Agreement.

**garbage can model**—a theory of public policy formulation for analyzing decision making in situations of "organized anarchy," where goals are ambiguous and methods uncertain.

**governing instruments**—the array of tools available to government to realize its policy goals, ranging from the privatization of conflict to direct government intervention.

**Governor General**—the representative of the monarch in Canada, appointed by the monarch on the recommendation of the prime minister. The legal and constitutional powers of the Governor General are impressive on paper but are almost entirely symbolic in practice.

**Hawthorne experiments**—experiments conducted by industrial psychologists at the Hawthorne Works plant of Western Electric (near Chicago), beginning in 1924, to determine how physical conditions of work could be adjusted to improve productivity. The experiments are generally regarded as the origin of the human relations school of organizational theory. *See also* humanist theories.

**hierarchy**—the ordering of individuals or groups within an organization and their relationships of power and control.

**hierarchy of human needs**—a theory developed by Abraham Maslow that argues that humans are motivated by the satisfaction of a variety of needs, ranging from basic physical requirements (food, shelter, clothing) to self-actualization. As lower level needs are realized, people move on to fulfill higher level ones.

**homogeneity**—the principle that asserts that similar activities ought to be grouped together in the same unit under a single supervisor and a single plan. Thus, in public administration, things related to health care ought to be grouped in one department, those related to education in another, and so on. Moreover, within departments, there is a further division of labour, with scientists grouped in one unit, policy analysts in another, clerical staff in another, and so on, for the purposes of job function, promotion, and wages. Also referred to as *unity of direction*.

**humanist theories**—a school of thought about organizing and managing workplaces, which focuses on the inherent worth of individual workers and their needs. It originated with the Hawthorne studies on workplace organization in the 1920s and 1930s.

**ideational analysis**—a type of framework for policy analysis that focuses on the role of ideas in policy making, including how they shape the inclusion and exclusion of policy agendas, strategies, and actors. *See also* neo-institutionalism.

**implementation**—*see* policy implementation.

**Increased Ministerial Authority and Accountability**—the 1986 reform by the Mulroney government intended to allow for more flexibility in the roles and functions of ministers and their departments relative to their control by central agencies.

**incremental model**—an approach to policy making in which small, incremental changes are made to the status quo.

**individual ministerial responsibility**—the principle that states that individual ministers are responsible for the actions of their departments and accountable for their departments to Parliament and the Canadian people. *See also* collective ministerial responsibility.

**informal group**—term used to describe the phenomenon discovered by the Hawthorne experiment researchers that the dominant factor in employee productivity was workers' membership in casual associations of fellow employees, who together motivated each other to perform at certain levels by influencing values and attitudes and establishing social norms of behaviour in the workplace. *See also* Hawthorne experiments.

**institutionalism**—a framework for policy analysis that focuses on the institutions of policy making and how they shape policy debates and outcomes. *See also* neo-institutionalism and structuralism.

**interest group**—an organized association that attempts to influence the government to pursue policies favourable to its own interests.

**interpretive framework**—a type of framework for policy analysis that attempts to understand people's meanings and interpretations of reality and the contests between these interpretations as they are played out in policy making. *See also* post-positivism.

**intra vires**—a legal phrase that describes a federal or provincial statute as being within the constitutional jurisdiction of that level of government, as determined through judicial review of the Constitution Act.

**judicial branch of government**—the Supreme Court and justices and all the other courts and justices below it. The judiciary in Canada is appointed rather than elected, and is separate from and independent of the other two branches of government (the executive and legislative branches).

**Judicial Committee of the Privy Council**—the British law Lords who acted as the court of final appeal for Canadians until 1949, when the Supreme Court of Canada was made the final arbiter of Canadian legal cases.

**judicial evaluation**—concerned with the legal issues arising out of administrative actions, judicial evaluation is a facet of administrative and constitutional law that involves the judges and the courts passing judgment on the behaviour and practices of the public service. *See also* judicial review.

**judicial review**—the power of the court to determine if the actions of other branches of the government are constitutional or not.

**judiciary**—*see* judicial branch of government.

**Keynesian welfare state**—a broad term used to encompass the social welfare state constructed in the post-Second World War years on the basis of a theoretical model developed by British economist John Maynard Keynes, which promoted an activist role for government in the macro-economic management of the economy.

**La Relève**—the internal review of the public service launched by the clerk of the Privy Council in 1996 to deal with the "quiet crisis" within the federal bureaucracy. The term is an acronym for Leadership, Action, Renewal, Energy, Learning, Expertise, Values, and Excellence.

**legal-rational legitimacy**—a form of legitimacy outlined by Max Weber, in which citizens accept that an individual has the right to rule over them by virtue of the law. *See also* charismatic legitimacy and traditional legitimacy.

**legislative branch of government**—that branch of government charged with passing and amending laws. In Canada it is composed of the Parliament, which is made up of the elected House of Commons and the appointed Senate.

**legislature**—*see* legislative branch of government.

**legitimation**—a concept employed in neo-Marxist theory, referring to the need for the state to pass policies that legitimate capitalism in the eyes of those oppressed by it. Thus, social policies such as welfare and unemployment insurance are seen as policies that legitimate the system for the working class, so that they do not rise up and overthrow it.

**line-item budgeting**—a rudimentary system of budgeting, emphasizing the objects of expenditures (e.g., how many paper clips are needed, how much office space must be rented, etc.) rather than the purpose of expenditures.

**lying for the public good**—an ethical dilemma confronting public servants when they cannot disclose all the pertinent information about a policy or course of action by government

**Management by Objectives (MBO)**—a management system associated with the work of Peter Drucker and others that focuses on co-operation between managers and workers in the establishment of broad-based annual goals and objectives for the organization.

**market**—an arena in which the organization of the economy and society for the production and distribution of goods and services takes place through the mechanism of exchange predicated on the voluntary actions of individuals. The human and social costs of relying on self-regulating markets have been so great that governments have been forced over time to step in and limit or regulate certain market excesses.

**Marx, Karl**—influential German philosopher (1818–1883) and founder of the political philosophy of Communism. *See also* Marxist analysis and neo-Marxist theory.

**Marxist analysis**—a broad school of thought premised on the idea that modern capitalist societies are based on class conflict, and positing that the role of the state is to promote policies of accumulation for the capitalist class and policies of legitimation for the working class. *See also* neo-Marxist theory.

**merit principle**—the principle that all citizens should have an equal opportunity to be considered for employment in the public service based on their qualifications and skills, and should be promoted on the basis of their abilities and talents.

**minimalist state**—term used to describe the relatively minor role played by the

Canadian state in the social and economic affairs of Canadians from the Confederation period to the 1930s.

**minister**—the political head of a department of government, appointed by the prime minister.

**ministerial responsibility**—*see* collective ministerial responsibility and individual ministerial responsibility.

**Ministerial Task Force on Program Review**—task force set up in 1984 by the Mulroney government under the leadership of Deputy Prime Minister Eric Nielsen to conduct a government-wide review of programs, with the goal of cutting waste and inefficiencies.

**ministry**—*see* department.

**minority government**—occurs after an election in which no one party captures a majority of the seats in the House of Commons. Normally, the party with the greatest number of seats is given the chance to govern, but often must secure the support of other parties to do so.

**mixed-scanning**—a theoretical approach to explaining policy making, which suggests that policy-makers combine rationality and incrementalism in the process of determining what action (or inaction) to take. *See also* incremental model and rational-comprehensive theory.

**mobilization of bias**—term derived from pluralist theory to describe policy formulation as the result of interest groups acting to influence government decision-makers.

**neoconservative state**—term used to describe contemporary governments that focus on reducing the size and intrusiveness of government through policies of deregulation, privatization, reducing taxes, reducing public services and reducing spending. It is premised on an ideological world-view which favours the free market over the state.

**neo-institutionalism**—a framework for policy analysis that maintains the institutionalist analysis's focus on institutions in policy making but also looks to the role of ideas and interest groups or policy networks in policy making. *See also* institutionalism.

**neo-Marxist theory**—a broad school of thought that reconceptualizes the original theories about the capitalist state put forward by Karl Marx. *See also* Marxist analysis.

**New Public Management (NPM)**—a school of thought originating in Margaret Thatcher's Britain, advocating changes to organizational design and managerial practices consistent with neoconservative ideas. It is broadly aimed at making the state more responsive to political direction and to citizens, and at introducing more private sector practices into the public sector.

**North American Free Trade Agreement (NAFTA)**—the extension in 1994 of the Free Trade Agreement between Canada and the U.S. to include Mexico.

**Office of the Comptroller General**—created in 1978, this body has authority over administrative practices and controls in the areas of financial management and procedures for program evaluation.

**Organization Development (OD)**—a team-based approach to management decision making and problem solving.

**participatory management**—a management style that incorporates the views of workers in the decision-making process.

**partisanship**—the degree of loyalty members of a political party feel toward one another.

**party discipline**—a key pillar of responsible government, party discipline means that party members support their leaders and act in unison in the legislature. It is supported by a system of rewards and punishments.

**patronage**—the awarding of contracts and the appointment of individuals to government positions on the basis of partisan support for, or contributions to, the governing party, rather than of merit.

**pay equity**—a shorthand term for equal pay for work of equal value, in which comparisons are made between different jobs for the same employer.

**performance budgeting**—a system of budgeting in which expenditures are related to specific activities to determine the costs of providing services.

**Planning, Programming, Budgeting System (PPBS)**—a broad-based budgeting system introduced in Canada in the 1960s and 1970s in an effort to impose greater rationality over the budget process. It was premised on the view that expenditure requests should be presented in terms of the objective of spending rather than in terms of input costs and particular functions, but ultimately fell out of favour due to the layers of complexity it added to the process.

**pluralist model**—the view that power in society is widely dispersed between diverse groups that vie to influence government to produce policies favourable to their own interests.

**Policy and Expenditure Management System (PEMS)**—a system involving the use of Cabinet committees to coordinate, plan, and integrate government budgeting and policy making. It was introduced in 1979 by the Joe Clark government to improve ministerial control over financial management in the area of priority setting and to allow ministers to see the longer-range view of government policy development and financial activities.

**policy community**—comprised of actors in the policy making process with an interest in a particular policy field. These actors can be in the public sector (for example a ministry) and/or the private sector (for example a business association) and/or the "attentive public."

**policy cycle**—the theoretical construction that suggests that public policy can best be understood as a process of problem definition and agenda-setting, formulation, implementation, and evaluation. *See also* public policy; problem definition and agenda-setting, policy formulation; policy implementation; and policy evaluation.

**policy evaluation**—the part of the policy cycle involving the determination of needed policy or administrative changes through a process of in-depth analysis of institutions, programs, and policies. *See also* public policy and policy cycle.

**policy formulation**—the part of the policy cycle involving the development of public policy. *See also* public policy; policy cycle.

**policy implementation**—the part of the policy cycle involving the realization of public policy. *See also* public policy; policy cycle.

**policy network**—the interactions among members in a policy community.

**political culture**—the broad pattern of beliefs, values, and attitudes citizens hold toward politics and the political system.

political evaluation—the ongoing process by which the electorate determines the worth of government policy by supporting or opposing the governing party in elections or through the expression of views in royal commissions, task forces, parliamentary committees, or to Cabinet, central agencies, or line departments through the actions of citizens, interest groups, the media, and so on. *See also* policy evaluation.

political neutrality—the principle that public servants must not engage in partisan politics but should, rather, remain politically impartial and neutral, serving the government of the day, *not* the political party that happens to hold power.

political parties—organizations designed to secure the power of the state for their leaders.

politics–administration dichotomy—the notion that there is a distinction between the duties and responsibilities of politicians who make public policy, and their public servants, who faithfully execute it.

POSDCORB—an acronym defining the administrative process by classifying the functions of top executives in an organization as planning, organizing, staffing, directing, coordinating, reporting, and budgeting. It was devised by Luther Gulick.

postmodern approach—a type of policy analysis that rejects the simplistic, rationality-based frameworks, models, and theories. It argues that society is too complex to be understood as a science. It can only be studied on a case-by-case basis, and there are no predictable laws of political action. *See also* post-positivist analysis.

post-positivist analysis—an approach to knowledge that denies our ability to know causation or laws of social or political action. It argues that we can never really know our reality, only interpret it through our own biases and tell stories or narratives about it. *See also* interpretive framework and postmodern approach.

power—the ability to influence or coerce others to conform to one's own goals and values.

pressure group—*see* interest group.

Prime Minister's Office—a central agency of government staffed by appointees of the prime minister to provide partisan advice and monitor political developments for the prime minister.

private sector—that part of the economy not under government control.

privatization—the act of selling or turning over Crown corporations to the private sector.

Privy Council—a largely ceremonial body composed of current and former ministers of the Crown and other individuals recommended by the prime minister and appointed for life by the Governor General.

Privy Council Office—a central agency that provides policy advice and administrative support to the Cabinet and its committees. It is the main organization responsible for developing and coordinating government policy.

problem definition and agenda-setting— the part of the policy cycle involving the identification of policy problems and their placement on the government's policy agenda. *See also* public policy and policy cycle.

Productivity Improvement Program—a set of reforms introduced in the dying days of the last Trudeau government to cut red tape and procedures hampering the efficient provision of government services through initiatives undertaken by the Treasury Board.

program budgeting—a system of budgeting that seeks to measure the impact of expenditures on the goals of the organization.

Program Review—a wide-reaching initiative introduced by the Chrétien government in 1994 to review all government programs, with the goal of identifying potential cost savings. The Review was driven by the government's desire to eliminate the deficit.

province building—the process of aggressive and assertive provincial premiers and governments seeking enhanced powers and responsibilities, while also seeking to diminish the role of the federal government.

PS2000—a review of the public service meant to address the low morale and disjunction between the senior and lower levels of public servants. Launched in late 1989, it was organized around 10 task forces headed by deputy ministers charged with finding ways to simplify personnel policies, loosen central agency controls, increase the managerial freedom of department managers, and increase program efficiency.

**public administration**—the ways in which governments conduct themselves through bureaucratic processes. This includes the norms and values of government officials, the organization of the bureaucracy, the accountability of public servants, the relationship between politicians and bureaucrats, and the decision-making systems used to formulate, implement, and evaluate public policy.

**public choice model**—a theoretical approach derived from classical economics, which is premised on the notion that individuals act on the basis of a rational calculation of self-interest. Also referred to as rational choice theory.

**public comment**—an aspect of the doctrine of political neutrality, through which public servants are expected not to express publicly their personal views on government policy or administration. *See also* political neutrality.

**public interest**—the general wellbeing of society as a whole; the common good.

**public policy**—what governments choose to do or not to do.

**public sector**—the collective term used to describe the institutions and personnel of the state.

**Public Service Commission**—called the Civil Service Commission until 1967, this independent agency is responsible for recruiting employees through competitive examinations and interviews, and for staffing and promotion using the merit principle.

**Public Service Employment Act**—passed in 1967, this Act granted the Public Service Commission the exclusive authority to appoint persons to and within the public service according to the merit principle, and to administer appeals, layoffs, and dismissals. As well, it liberalized the restrictions on political activities by public servants.

**Public Service Modernization Act**—passed in 2003, this Act created a new Public Service Employment Act and a new

Public Service Labour Relations Act, as well as amending other pieces of legislation.

**Public Service Staff Relations Act**—passed in 1967, this Act sets out the responsibilities of the quasi-judicial Public Service Staff Relations Board and provides for the structure and operation of the collective bargaining process in the public service. It also oversees the resolution of disputes and grievances, and conducts research on matters relevant to contract negotiations, such as rates of pay, benefits, and working conditions.

**rational choice model**—*see* public choice theory.

**rational-comprehensive model**—a theoretical model that seeks to explain public policy decision making as the product of a reasoned and thorough consideration of all the available options and their consequences.

**rational-legal legitimacy**—*see* legal-rational legitimacy.

**recall**—the procedure by which an elected official is removed from office by a vote of the electorate.

**referendum**—a means by which a particular question is put directly to the total electorate rather than to the elected representatives of the people.

**regulatory agency**—a government body that administers economic, environmental, social, or other activities in the public interest according to guidelines and regulations established by government.

**representative democracy**—*see* representative government.

**representative government**—a political system with an elected legislature.

**representativeness**—the notion that the public service should reflect the social composition of the population it serves.

**reservation**—section 57 of the Constitution Act, 1867 (formerly the British North America Act, 1867), which permits the Lieutenant-Governor of a province to withhold assent to a piece of provincial legislation pending review by the federal Cabinet.

**responsible government**—a system of government in which the executive branch of government requires the support and confidence of the legislative branch (and through it, the people) in order to govern.

risk management—the process of measuring or assessing risk and then developing strategies to manage the risk. A systematic approach to setting the best course of action under uncertainty by identifying, assessing, understanding, acting on, and communicating risk issues.

rule of law—the principle that both the ruled and the rulers are answerable to the law.

scientific management—generally associated with the work of Frederick Winslow Taylor, scientific management is a management style that emphasized finding the "one best way" of accomplishing a task. It introduced the use of time and motion studies into the workplace with the goal of improving productivity by increasing efficiency.

social movements—informal networks of groups of citizens with shared values and identities oriented toward influencing the government on various social policies and issues through social and/or political struggle. See also interest group.

social welfare state—the term used to describe the interventionist state in postwar Western, industrialized countries, wherein governments took on an ever-expanding set of responsibilities in the areas of social welfare policy, health care, education, housing, pensions, unemployment insurance, etc.

span of control—an organizational mechanism indicating the number of subordinates reporting to a particular supervisor.

spending power—the power of the federal government to spend money on programs even if the programs are within provincial jurisdiction. This power is nowhere written in the Constitution but is nonetheless a powerful federal tool in intergovernmental relations.

state—a form of political organization encompassing governmental institutions and personnel that are capable of maintaining order and implementing rules and laws over a given population within a given territory.

statutory bodies—organizations within the government, such as departments or ministries, that are created by law passed by Parliament.

structural analysis—a type of policy analysis that focuses on how the structured elements of social organization (such as class, race, and gender) predetermine policy outcomes, predominantly through the power relations they entail.

structuralist theory—the school of organization theory that is premised on a view of workers as little more than interchangeable parts in a machine. The goal of structuralist organization theory is to devise structures within which the work of individuals could be maximized through rigid rules and regulations so as to increase the organization's efficiency. Little regard is paid to the needs or views of individual workers.

Supreme Court of Canada—composed of nine justices appointed by the prime minister, the Supreme Court is Canada's highest court for civil, criminal, and constitutional cases.

systems theory—a theory that explains organizations as open systems and methodologically studies those systems through the application of computers, statistical analysis, information systems, and quantitative measurement.

three Es—the three Es are efficiency, effectiveness, and economy. They are a set of values underlying reforms to improve the functioning of organizations within the private sector, but they have increasingly been adopted in the public sector as well, where they compete with other values such as democracy, justice, and accountability.

time and motion studies—an innovation introduced by Frederick Winslow Taylor, father of scientific management, in his effort to discover the "one best way" of routinizing workplace functions. Taylor used a stop-watch to record the time it took to complete every motion in a particular piece of work, allegedly to improve efficiency by eliminating unnecessary motions.

Total Quality Management (TQM)—a participatory management approach that developed in the 1980s and early 1990s, advocating changing an organization's culture to focus on high standards of quality throughout the organization. The guiding principle of TQM is "get it right the first time," and it was famously embraced first by Japanese car makers.

traditional legitimacy—a form of legitimacy outlined by Max Weber, in which citizens accept that an individual has the right to rule over them by virtue of divine right—that is, that the gods anointed an individual as leader. *See also* charismatic legitimacy and legal-rational legitimacy.

**Treasury Board**—a Cabinet committee composed of six Cabinet ministers (including the president of the Treasury Board and the Minister of Finance), responsible for the preparation of the expenditure budget and for administrative management of government departments.

**Treasury Board Secretariat**—a central agency that supports the Treasury Board.

**ultra vires**—a legal phrase that describes a federal or provincial statute as beyond the constitutional jurisdiction of that level of government, as determined through judicial review of the Constitution Act.

**unity of direction**—*see* homogeneity.

**user fees**—the practice by governments of charging fees to citizens for services previously provided free or for a nominal charge, to cover the cost of providing the service as a strategy for fighting deficits. User fees are a regressive form of taxation.

**Weber, Max**—German sociologist (1864–1920) generally regarded as the most influential writer on the subject of bureaucracy.

# Index

Page references ending in -*f* refer to figures; in -*t*, to tables.

# Credits

105: DILBERT: © Scott Adams/Dist. by United Feature Syndicate, Inc.

159: © Josh Beutel/Policy Options

234: Reproduced with permission, Dennis Pritchard

351: Theo Moudakis/Toronto Star